Bardadrac

World Writing in French

A Winthrop-King Institute Series

Series Editors
Charles Forsdick (University of Liverpool)
and
Martin Munro (Florida State University)

Advisory Board Members
Jennifer Boum Make (Georgetown University)
Michelle Bumatay (Florida State University)
William Cloonan (Florida State University)
Michaël Ferrier (Chuo University)
Michaela Hulstyn (Stanford Univesity)
Khalid Lyamlahy (University of Chicago)
Helen Vassallo (University of Exeter)

There is a growing interest among Anglophone readers in literature in translation, including contemporary writing in French in its richness and diversity. The aim of this new series is to publish cutting-edge contemporary French-language fiction, travel writing, essays and other prose works translated for an English-speaking audience. Works selected will reflect the diversity, dynamism, originality, and relevance of new and recent writing in French from across the archipelagoes – literal and figurative – of the French-speaking world. The series will function as a vital reference point in the area of contemporary French-language prose in English translation. It will draw on the expertise of its editors and advisory board to seek out and make available for English-language readers a broad range of exciting new work originally published in French.

Bardadrac

by Gérard Genette

Translated by Nicholas Levett

Liverpool University Press

First published 2023 by
Liverpool University Press
4 Cambridge Street
Liverpool
L69 7ZU

British Library Cataloguing-in-Publication data
A British Library CIP record is available

ISBN 978-1-80207-802-2 hardback
ISBN 978-1-80207-803-9 paperback

Typeset by Carnegie Book Production, Lancaster
Printed and bound by CPI Group (UK) Ltd, Croydon CR0 4YY

I have a vocabulary all my own.
Montaigne

There was a time when we knew what a dictionary was, even if the genre was more or less clearly divided into repertories of words and catalogues of things. It has, since then, spread itself in all directions. For this one, the implicit models are rather to be found in Voltaire (*Philosophical Dictionary*), in Flaubert (*Dictionary of Received Ideas*), in Ambrose Bierce (*The Devil's Dictionary*), in Roland Barthes (*by Roland Barthes*) or, in another disorder, in Montaigne of course, in Lichtenberg, in Mark Twain, in Stendhal's travel notes, Renard's journal, Vialatte's chronicles, Perec's remembrances, Sempé's drawings.

'This book was never made, it was harvested.' Its objects – contingent epiphanies, good or bad ideas, true and false memories, aesthetic biases, geographical reveries, secret or apocryphal quotations, maxims and characters, asides, quips and digressions – construct a puzzle that is not to be reconstructed. Of its entries, one might say, like the author of *Coaches*:[1] 'The names of my chapters do not always embrace their matter; often they denote it merely by some mark.' There remains sometimes, if you wish, to guess which one, and according to which figure.

---

[1] Michel de Montaigne, *Des Coches*, Book III, Chapter VI of *Les Essais*. All footnotes to Genette's text are provided by the translator, and will not therefore be indicated as such.

Aa. The crossword enthusiast, and by capillary action everyone else, is familiar with the name of this small coastal river that separates the *départements du Nord* and *du Pas-de-Calais*, but few know (I have just learned it myself) that it touches upon Saint-Omer to its north and Gravelines to its south, that it traverses the Audomarois nature reserve and that between Wicquinghem and Remilly-Wirquin its 'high valley' is worth the detour. The French countryside is full of resources, but 'high' is to be taken here in a purely hydrographic sense: don't look for any mountains there.

Aarhus. I'd like to have at my disposal a word other than *détournement* or *recuperation* to name the practice, probably older than is ordinarily believed and which has today become universal, that makes something new from something old by adapting the old object to a new function. I think its architectural version, clearly the most spectacular (but Picasso's minor *bricolages*, like his scale model of a car transformed into a monkey's head, are no less effective), was revealed to me, doubtless already too late, in November 1975, upon leaving the delightful doll houses of the Andersen quarter in Odense, in the Faculty of Literature building at Aarhus University, in Jutland, which has been accommodated in an old factory abandoned to the spirit of adaptation. In the room where I was endeavouring to speak, the large pipes emphasised by bright colours gave unexpected depth to a talk containing perhaps none of its own. It wasn't long before I found an equivalent, admittedly more touristic, in the old canning factory (*The Cannery*) and the old Ghirardelli chocolate factory overlooking the Fisherman's Wharf in San Francisco. This hardly forced, though often brutal-seeming, marriage of culture and industry has thus become frequent without ever becoming banal, for each of its applications bears within itself a piquancy arising from the never effaced contrast between a still perceptible old form and the always specific function imposed upon it. It's what, without looking too far afield, I would readily call the palimpsest effect,[2] and all the more readily since this name itself illustrates in its way the act of legitimate usurpation that it designates, just as every living metaphor allows at once its

---

[2] Genette is the author of *Palimpsestes: La littérature au second degré* (*Palimpsests: Literature in the Second Degree*) (1992).

figurative meaning and its literal meaning to be seen; at once, that's to say transparently, or perhaps in rapid alternation, as in Jastrow's duck-rabbit, which flickers ceaselessly between duck and rabbit – and Picasso's monkey-car, between monkey and car. I'd like to suppose that such an effect is sought, fictitiously, by the Pompidolium[3] completed in 1977, which pretends to occupy the disused premises of an old refinery. Feign at least to believe so, it will reconcile you with it, and by the same stroke with a part, and not the least, of contemporary architecture.

Ablet. 'Teasing the gudgeon'[4] was just a figure of speech. At all events, we'd hardly catch any, but more often ablets, occasionally minnows, with a little luck one or two roaches. I have no memory of pike; the real misfortune was a sodden, and inevitably odd, shoe. This would happen by the Seine, somewhere between Andrésy and Meulan, whenever my father took me along, equipped on our bikes with two archaic rods, without reels, a series of painstakingly calibrated hooks and a tin of Valda pastilles full of maggots harvested haphazardly by the spade, wriggling upon a layer of sawdust that served them both as winding sheet and funeral meal. My mother thought little of these expeditions, in which at least the preparation of a hypothetical fried meal spared her from participating. Curiously, we never fished in the Oise, though it was closer, and for me more pleasant, but no doubt reputedly less rich in fish.

Absolu Concret/Concrete Absolute. I can't recall under which nefarious philosophical influence I had branded with this oxymoron, if it is one, passionate love, about which I believed I knew a thing or two. This designation had made its way in our little group, and I can still hear one of my classmates shout one day, from one end to the other of the refectory at the Rue d'Ulm:[5] 'Concrete absolute on

---

[3] The Pompidou Centre, named after the president of France who adopted the project.

[4] 'Taquiner le goujon' would usually translate as 'to do a spot of fishing'.

[5] Site, in the 5th arrondissement of Paris, of the École Normale Supérieure (ENS), a highly selective and prestigious *grande école* founded in 1794 to provide the French nation with a body of professors in the humanities and the sciences.

the telephone!' So it was really, transparent only to the *happy few*, a metonymy, or I no longer know what's what (it's quite possible).

I should add that, in the fifties, there was still only, for the entire *École*, or at least for all its students, a single telephone box, or more precisely a wall-mounted device in a cubby-hole adjacent to the entrance hall, still called the 'aquarium'. You could, by means of I can't remember what payment, call from there whomever you wished, but being contacted externally required that someone should pass close enough by to hear it ringing, and be willing ('Don't hang up!') to take the trouble to seek the 'interested party' wherever he was supposed to be. The operation could take a few long minutes, during which time the receiver hung sadly at the end of its wire. When said interested party appeared (if I dare say) unlocatable, or less interested than one had imagined, much obligingness was required then to return to the cubby-hole and give the disappointing answer. Of course, it quite often happened that a 'third party' would naturally pass by to 'place' an external call of his own. He'd find the receiver in the state I mentioned, and to keep things short, would announce without scruple, dodging any question with potentially embarrassing consequences: 'He isn't here!' At the other end of the line, the caller (he or she) may well have noticed that the respondent's voice had changed, but it sufficed to hang up in time in order to initiate another call. It could also come about, in the more promising cases, judging by the timbre, that the third party would substitute himself for the purportedly absent other, and certain of these substitutions prompted interesting bifurcations of destiny. I had on that particular day to commend Paul Veyne for his perspicacity and to thank him for his relative discretion. The absolute in question was in fact a little less concrete than it ought to have been. But that's another story, and I'm not here to recount my life. Although.

Acacia. In my childhood garden, one of these grew, rather punily, facing the Seine. By pinching its petals between your thumb and index finger, and pulling gently, you could obtain a kind of bouquet of pale green sepals, which were perfectly transient since, as soon as you let go, they'd scatter to the winds. This exercise was not well regarded. In order to divert me from it, or punish me for it, I was taught that this acacia was in fact a black locust, or more precisely a 'black locust false acacia' (*Robinia pseudoacacia*). I've since discovered that many species of plant are some sort of counterfeit, deceptive replicas of other species. Thus, the sycamore, which is highly typical of the genre, is a 'maple false plane tree' (*Acer pseudoplatanus*). The botanical nomenclature in place since Linné could really do with a little reforming. Actually, I fear that I have never encountered a real acacia – no doubt a false black locust. On the other hand, I know like everyone else that the mimosa is well and truly an acacia. For the sake of symmetry, to our black locust had been adjoined a 'Japanese varnish tree', *alias* 'sumac', or perhaps rather 'false Japanese varnish tree', *alias* 'ailanthus'.

Accueil/Welcome. Necessarily conceived in the year of the Crisis and (so pretended my father in a rich vein of acrobatic metaphors) upon a tandem, I came into the world more comfortably, one Saturday at two in the afternoon, in a clinic on Rue Pelleport – a clinic that has today disappeared like so many other things in this neighbourhood, among which the mythical 36 Rue des Amandiers, a grandiose hovel where my father had spent his own childhood prior to the Great War, and whose memory, amplified wherever possible, would for long enliven the family legend. Rue Pelleport, and also, pretty much, Rue Orfila, where unbeknown to me we also lived for a few years, are now separated from the foliage of the Père Lachaise cemetery by a *Rue*, a *Passage* and an *Impasse* Stendhal, and even a Rue Lucien-Leuwen – a rare, perhaps unique example, and of whose date and circumstances I have no idea – of a public thoroughfare dedicated to a fictional hero; I did once know a passage Bournisien, which led onto Rue Vercingétorix, but it has since foundered in some grim 'renovation', and I doubt that its eponymous hero was Emma Bovary's maladroit confessor. The dedication to Lucien would, in my opinion, be better placed in Nancy, below parrot green louvred shutters,[6] but it was probably judged that the character would be happy to be near his creator – who yet probably never, in his lifetime, hung around in what was then a more than perfect wasteland, and who now 'rests' in person, as it were and beneath the epitaph we know,[7] in the Montmartre cemetery. For good measure, Rue Leuwen is today bounded by a 'Résidence Butte Stendhal' which somewhat

---

[6] An allusion to Mme. de Chasteller's abode in Stendhal's *Lucien Leuwen* (1894).

[7] 'ARRIGO BEYLE MILANESE SCRISSE AMO VISSE', 'HENRI BEYLE MILANESE HE WROTE HE LOVED HE LIVED'.

ridiculously exaggerates a commemorative effort as zealous as it is incongruous, even if I gather that Louis Althusser came there one day to end a fading life. With or without this belatedly novelistic patronage, I always feel myself to have descended (though too early to have any memory of the descent) from this hill, inspired in its own way, where, over the tombs, a certain spirit then wafted. It was the Ménilmontant as sung by Maurice Chevalier and Charles Trenet, and which one mustn't quite confuse with Belleville, upon which it no longer depended since their joint annexation to Paris in 1860. The townhall of the 'Twentieth arrondissement', Place Gambetta, is moreover located here, rather than there. Despite the link created by the very long Rue des Pyrénées, virtually a crest road that yet runs considerably further south as though it wished to warrant its name all the way to Spain, the difference between the two villages sharing the arrondissement was as perceptible as it was undefinable: Belleville, a little more rakish (the 'dangerous classes': La Courtille,[8] its dancehalls and its bad boys: you should watch *Casque d'Or*[9] again), Ménilmontant, which had remained more rustic and became more proletarian: the 'labouring classes'. We therefore shunned the disobliging nickname 'Ménilmuche', used only by philistines and tourists risen from the plain and the marsh.[10] This can also be illustrated by the opposition between the two 'green spaces': the Buttes-Chaumont to the north, the Père Lachaise to the south, whose Communards' Wall[11] remains the holy of holies, the Wailing Wall of revolutionary memory, which I was, many years later, to celebrate in procession on two or three successive May 28ths. Such a neighbourhood obliges you a little, without your always knowing in relation to what.

After these general considerations, as Brulard[12] would say here, I am about to be born. It was, according to the registry office, a

[8] A well-known former 'place of enjoyment' ('lieu de plaisir') situated at the top of Rue du Faubourg du Temple.
[9] *Golden Helmet*, directed by Jacques Becker (1952).
[10] A reference to le Marais, in the 4th arrondissement of Paris.
[11] *Le Mur des fédérés*, at the Père Lachaise cemetery, is where 147 combatants were shot by Versailles troops on 28 May 1871, the last day of the 'Semaine sanglante [Bloody Week]' at the end of the Paris Commune.
[12] A reference to Stendhal's *Vie de Henry Brulard* (*The Life of Henry Brulard*) (1890).

7th June, a date known since 1788, and not only in Grenoble, as the 'Day of the Tiles [journée des Tuiles]',[13] which my father never tired of recalling in a fairly constant spirit of affectionate sarcasm. The day of that particular blow [tuile[14]], then, he considered me without indulgence, and concluded from this first examination as I emerged out of limbo: 'He looks older than he is'. These words of welcome have been repeated to me so often that I feel as though I heard them myself in their original version, and that I appreciated at its true value this (for me) first manifestation of the paternal spirit. At any rate, in both its form and its substance, this statement has stuck with me.

Acoustic(s). At the beginning of the fifties, a recital by Andrés Segovia, on an instrument they didn't yet feel the need to call 'acoustic', demanded and obtained a properly religious silence: you would have heard a fly pass by, but no fly dared to pass by. Alas, for the only concert I was able to attend, at the Théâtre des Champs-Elysées, we had, Odile and I, arrived a little late, and an imprudent usherette let us enter during the first piece – to say the least, it was a Bach partita movement, transcribed by the interpreter himself, Andalousian by birth but with an entirely Castilian austerity. Reaching our seats without causing any noise would have been the stuff of miracles, and the miracle did not occur. What did occur was exactly the opposite, even if there exists no word to designate such a thing: the Master simply stopped his chaconne, stared at us, in utter silence, until the shame had transformed us, once seated, into pillars of salt, and resumed *da capo*. I'm not sure I listened to what followed in a frame of mind befitting the occasion, but, ever since that day, I have truly known what (also theatrical) *acoustic(s)* means. It's perhaps also since then that I've suffered, through self-punishment, from the illness called *hyperacusis*: living on the third floor, I can tell when my basement neighbour is eating a biscuit, and which brand. My comrade Marcel Proust, who apparently suffered, among other things, from the same pathology, lined, as we know, his bedroom with cork and imposed upon his

[13] Popular riot in Grenoble, thought by historians to be the first stirring of the revolution of 1789. In the course of the uprising, townspeople climbed onto the roofs of buildings and hurled tiles down at royal forces.
[14] A 'tuile' can also signify a 'stroke of bad luck'.

downstairs neighbour a highly insulating carpet. I'm content to offer my own little madeleines to dunk in their morning tea – with milk, if possible, which muffles the sound better. I envy doctors who need a stethoscope.

Amish. What charms the most, in the countryside of Lancaster County, in Pennsylvania, is the Amish peasants' horse-drawn carriages. Curiously, these old-style equipages seem more out of place in the bucolic decor than the tourists' modern automobiles. I think I understand the reason for this paradox: it has to do with the large surfaces of glass, apparently polished every morning with shammy leather, which turn these carriages into a kind of ambulant showcase, in truth more shimmering than transparent, like a two-way mirror. From every angle the countryside shatters upon them into glittering facets. Nothing, moreover, is less discreet than the sound of hooves on the impeccable asphalt of their roadways. And, despite the eschewal of modern technology, or perhaps because of this ostensible and as though flaunted eschewal, nothing better manifests the presence of humans upon American soil.

Amour/Love. 'In love, said Balzac, there is always someone suffering and someone getting bored' (rereading *Adolphe*,[15] he would have said rather: 'some *woman* [*une*] suffering…'). I'm not sure which naughty spirit replied: 'Perhaps you should change position.'

Amour-propre/Self-love. Alain said it was 'always unhappy'; not, presumably, for want of reciprocity, but rather for want of effective gratification. As solipsistic as we may (wish to) be, our self-esteem or self-liking only comes via the other's gaze or speech. Regarding some positive appraisal received from elsewhere, a female friend of mine sometimes said: 'It revalidates you.' She meant by that, I understood, that this third-party appraisal confirmed her own, about which she was never quite sure, and which moreover wasn't that elevated, and which she periodically adjusted by dint of what was, later, termed triangular desire. Even our relationship with ourselves is nourished by such indirect evaluations. When complimented upon one of his books, an author I know has great

[15] Benjamin Constant (1816).

difficulty in refraining from rereading it entirely in light of this praise, which he hopes to confirm by this simulacrum of mimetic reading. Doubtless by virtue of a happy nature, negative reviews never suggest to him the excessively mortifying converse test.

Angèle. A 'literature' stand (read: for printed propaganda) at the Fête de *L'Huma*,[16] under the dual reign of Maurice and Jeannette.[17] A militant is doing the sales spiel: 'Buy the *Communist Manifesto*, by Karl Marx, and Angèle,[18] his wife!' Another nudges him, to indicate his blunder. Thinking he'd understood, he hastily corrected himself: '... by Karl Marx, and Angèle, *his companion!*' Another comrade – or perhaps the same – believed our emblem was (as it really ought to have been) 'the anvil and the hammer', and learned Russian in order to read Marx in the original. Another, charitably, wished to release him from his error. But he, nobody's fool: *'Capital*, in German, you're kidding? And *Mein Kampf* is in yiddish, perhaps?'

Antisèche/Crib Sheet. In those days, respectable young girls didn't wear faded jeans, but rather, in the spring, light dresses or skirts and of a reasonable length: neither too much nor too little. On the day of the baccalaureate, one of them had scrawled on her thighs a cheat sheet in view of some test or other – a written test, I mean, for in an oral test, before an examiner who was in principle potentially suspicious or liable to abuse his position, this gambit might have gone awry – a crib sheet that she showed us, blushing a little, after she'd used it and was on her way out. Reading upside down the partially erased scrawl took us a little while, but the audacity of the procedure imposed respect.

Après-guerre/Post-war. Euphemism for *pre-war*.

---

[16] The 'Fête de *L'Humanité*' is an annual funding event for the newspaper *L'Humanité*, formerly an organ of the French Communist Party (PCF).

[17] Maurice Thorez, secretary-general of the PCF from 1930 to 1964; Jeannette Vermeersch (1910–2001), Maurice Thorez's companion then wife, PCF Politburo member.

[18] The French pronunciation of this name is the same as a 'naive' French pronunciation of 'Engels'.

Arrogance. Infuriating flaw that consists in resenting other people's.

Assemblo. I'm certain of never having had, nor even asked for, at Christmas time, the intelligent game that was Meccano. As I saw it working in my little friends' homes, I found it, with its pulleys and gears, to be too technical, or too industrial. To it I preferred another, doubtless since vanished, and which was called Assemblo. It was a simple construction game, like Lego today, or rather like the most basic versions of Lego. It consisted of plates of metal fitted with cylindrical edges, which you assembled by inserting rigid shafts able to pass through their alternating cylinders, a bit like a pivot pin in a hinge. In fact, the only movement allowed by this construction was one of a door turning on its horizontal or vertical axis. Some of these plates were triangular, which enabled you to finish off a tower with a four-sided apex. Even when enriched over the years by complimentary parts, and placed upon axles that could accommodate wheels, the ensemble remained necessarily static, more akin to Calder's stabiles than to his mobiles, or to Tinguely's machines, and that is perhaps what, obscurely, endeared it to me – with the supreme merit that I encountered it at no one else's, and that no one, coming to mine, displayed the slightest desire to take it up, as though it had been invented for my use alone. It was truly quite the contrary of a parlour game.

Atlas. I can indeed see that Chicago is on the left bank of Lake Michigan, which is consequently situated to the east of the Windy City. But I have great difficulty accepting it, and that, in order to return to New York, you must not move away from said lake but rather cross it, be it by swimming – not to mention that, for a European, to see the sun *rising* over the sea, or over a kind of sea, is always rather troubling, hence a certain malaise on the east coast of the New Continent. I must also accept that on the town plan, on the map, and even, presumably, on *every* town plan, on *every* map, and even what's more on every globe, the west is found to the left and the east to the right. Chicago, then, to the left of the lake. OK. But that is, or rather here is where something goes wrong (for me). I know, for instance, that the town of Mâcon is situated on the west bank, thus, on my map, to the left of the Saône, just as Valence is situated on the east bank of the Rhône, on the right on my map. But when I 'descend' towards the South on the N 6 or the A 6, I find, on the actual territory, Mâcon (which yet hasn't changed banks) to the *right* of the Saône, and Valence (ditto) to the *left* of the Rhône (go and have a look for yourselves, if you don't want to believe me). So what's going on? Let's think a little. When I 'ascend' from the South by the same route (either way), I do indeed find Valence to the *right* of the Rhône, and Mâcon to the *left* of the Saône, *as they are on my map*. It would seem that my map was designed for people returning from the South, and not for those heading there. Legitimate compensation at the end of one's holidays? Of course not, and the inhabitant of New Orleans returning home, on a paddle steamer, from a vacation at Yellowstone, finds indeed on his right, though it lies to the west of the Mississippi, the city of Saint Louis which, in accordance with the cartographic direction, he'd seen to his left when heading the other way. So holidays have got nothing to do with it: the truth (presumably) is that all the maps in the world are designed from the point of view of an observer, and for the usage of travellers, who are looking northwards (from the south to the north), and for whom the north is above (in front) and the south below (or behind their backs), whichever meridian they may be straddling. There must be for this bias a reason unknown to me, and which I do not propose to oppose: a convention of course had to be chosen, and adhered to, save for a world, or even a universal, revolution. With or without a map, when an explorer finds themself lost in the backwoods, they are advised to turn northwards, by courtesy of their compass, if they haven't lost it, or to the Pole star, if they can see it, or to the tree moss, if there is any, and, thus 'orientated', they will have the east to their right, the west to their left, and the south behind them: that's the way it is, and not otherwise. But I've allowed you to put your finger (tip), I hope, on the real-life, though not always perceived, inconveniences of this exorbitant northern-centric tropism. If you'd like to correct it occasionally for your private use, thankfully, nothing could be simpler: when leaving Paris, or Lille, or Stockholm, or Rovaniemi, Lapland, or Point Hope, Alaska, in the direction of (I'm not saying bound for) the South pole, take your Michelin map, and *consult it upside down*, vertically if possible, the south at the top, the north at the bottom. You'll have a little difficulty reading the names of cities, provinces, States, mountains, rivers, seas, deserts, but at least you'll find on the right what is actually (through the car door) to your right, on the left what is *in reality* to your left. For ease of reference, since in fact only the verbal markers really obey this unfortunate North-mania, have yourself printed, if it doesn't exist already, a whole series of maps with inverted letters, head facing south, feet facing north: an *ad hoc* software programme will easily provide this. You will thus have a dual set of maps alternatively in keeping with your orientation on their territory, and you'll cease reading upside down, half the time, a world you always see the right way up.

I also struggle a little, across the Atlantic, with the topographic use of the terms *up* and *down*. I can of course see that in New York, city (at least Manhattan) and State, *up* means north (*uptown*, *upstate*) and *down*, south: *downtown*, and (less often) *downstate*. Again, this way of speaking accords with the configuration of a map held vertically, and perhaps it derives from it. It so happens that this orientation also coincides with the course of the river Hudson, which flows, as it should, north–south. Yet I'm not sure that the *downtown*, which everywhere signifies 'city centre', is everywhere to be found to the south on a map. I see on the contrary that the southern quarters of Boston and Chicago are reserved rather for black and/or poor ghettos, and that the civic and commercial *downtowns* of Boston and San Francisco are squeezed into a north-eastern corner. To make everything simpler, in New Orleans, the centre, touristically at least (*French Quarter*), which is also to the north-east, occupies, as everyone has recently become only too aware, the highest, or the least low, and the least poor, part of the city: to go from *uptown*, the black city, to *downtown*, the white and 'creole' city, Buddy Holden had to cross Canal Street, and climb a bit (but not too much).

Auschwitz. We do wrong to history and to reason by so often refusing to explain this monstrosity on the grounds that explaining is already excusing – just as offence is taken at a film showing Hitler 'like a human being'. For once, the old distinction between *explanation* and *understanding* would suffice to cut this knot: we must not understand (from within, by *Einfühlung*) Nazism, or any other historical horror, but we must seek to explain it by its causes, alas multiple, among which, precisely, the monstrosity of certain human beings, which it is most naive to deem inhuman. This explanation is the historian's task, which implies no empathy: there is no place here for any 'Stockholm syndrome'. As for Adorno's phrase that, such as it is glossed, purports to forbid or condemn any artistic creation in the wake of (and in the name of) this event, I note that it is cited, like so many others, more often than it is applied. One does well not to apply it, but I doubt that one does well to cite it so much.

Auscultator. My childhood 'family' doctor's only function, as far as I was concerned, seemed to be that of placing his head on a towel, itself placed on my chest, and of listening to my breathing: this was called 'auscultating'. So for quite some time I thought I should call him the 'auscultator'. He prescribed me for all practical purposes a kind of granule, with a strong taste of lemon, which I never had the patience to let melt, chewing them instead with a guilty greed: anyone who has never chewed calcium glycerophosphate hasn't experienced the sweetness of life in the 1930s.

Autopsy. I can't recall from which other doctor, cynical on account of professional conscience, I picked up this expression, appropriate for any suspension of prognosis, indeed of diagnosis, not only as regards illness, but on any occasion of provisional uncertainty – and these occasions are not wanting: 'we shall see at the autopsy'.

Autoréférence/Self-Reference. We are perhaps familiar with 'Last Sign Before The Motorway', extrapolated from the old 'Last Petrol Station Before The Motorway', which could be seen at the time when motorways were not (or hardly) endowed with such facilities; I think I've seen elsewhere: 'Sign For Sale', but it seems to me that 'sign' doesn't have exactly the same meaning in the two cases: the first is functional, the second merely material, awaiting a function, and thus doesn't pose the same logical difficulty. In the same order of ideas perhaps (but the precise relation eludes me), Rosanette, at Fontainebleau, which she was visiting for the first time, said: 'It reminds me of memories!', evidently without knowing which ones, and Louise, gazing upon a weir on the Seine at Nogent, ventured to say: 'It's like the Niagara!', where she had never been. If I'm not making this up, or even if I am, Bouvard and Pécuchet[19] found a 'good likeness' in portraits whose models they did not know. 'A

---

[19] The protagonists in Gustave Flaubert's *Bouvard et Pécuchet* (1881).

good likeness to whom?', Valéry asked an admirer of Frans Hals' *Descartes*: 'It's the only portrait we have of him!' Shame it isn't true: there exists at least one other, by Weenix, not to mention those that are anonymous and apocryphal; besides, Hals' *Descartes* and Weenex do not resemble each other, which rules out any suspicion of copying. So we do not know which, or even if either of them, is a 'good likeness'. And why should Descartes look like himself?

Autrefois/Once. A rich American farmer visits his cousin who'd remained in Europe, where he cultivates a modest plot of land. 'Me, he boasts, when I drive off from my farm in the morning, come evening I still haven't left my ranch. – I see, replies the cousin, I had a car like that once too.' The principle of this joke is obvious, but, for some reason, I find the adverb *once* particularly juicy here.

B. I regret the recent disappearance of the generic–axiological concept (but which is neither entirely generic nor entirely axiological) designated by this letter, in at least two domains: the recording industry and that of cinema. In the Hollywood studio tradition, 'B series' described a clearly determined category of low-budget movies, with a more modest duration (1hr 10 versus 1hr 30 for the A series) and ambition, but with a very well-defined commercial niche. The B series comprised in fact all the classic genres (western, detective, comedy, melodrama, etc.), but targeted at low cost what used to be called a 'Saturday night' audience, and which it reached with near certainty, thus guaranteeing its economic profitability. It was almost exclusively practised by certain directors, like Don Siegel, or certain actors, like Ronald Reagan, who perfectly mastered its norms. These accredited specialists, of whom I have just not by chance (since the others remain unknown to me) cited two atypically renowned specimens, had greater difficulty leaving this discredited field than did celebrated directors or actors like Howard Hawks or James Stewart in moving from one canonical genre to another: the border between artisans of the B series and of (what was scarcely called) the A series was apparently as impermeable as the one separating actors specialising in secondary roles and those topping the bill: you no more easily became a canonical director by succeeding in popular direction than you became a star by shining as a second fiddle. There was here, you might say, (two times) two distinct professions, and doubtless two separate professions, a separation that pretty much excluded the very idea of a 'promotion' from one to the other: the quasi-axiological congealed into the pseudo-generic constituted a scale of values without intermediary rungs, meaning in sum an absence of scale.

I don't believe that French cinema, among others, ever knew so clear-cut a situation, which doubtless depended upon economic criteria peculiar to the activity of the great Hollywood studios. (An equivalent – sometimes named 'paraliterature', a comparable way of accepting while relegating it – could more easily be found in the literature of the XIXth century, where the popular novel had a fruitful career away from 'great' literature, without its authors, Paul de Kock, Eugène Sue or Ponson du Terrail, ever dreaming of rising a level.) I guess the relative effacement of this distinction depended on that, no less relative, of these studios themselves, and on the many other upheavals cinema in general has undergone since the advent of television, then of the DVD, but I'll refrain from further examining this historical hypothesis: I assume others have already done so. Of course, in the name of free individual or collective judgement, nothing has ever forbidden enlightened amateurs of the seventh art, Hollywoodian or not, from discovering in certain products of the B series, or in the category as a whole, aesthetic merits elevating them to the pantheon of unappreciated masterpieces, or even of 'cult films', which are often turkeys for the uncultivated, adopted by generational whim. These are the sophisticated pleasures of the second degree and of the deliberate countercurrent, and it is typically (and, to my mind, legitimately) the case for Siegel's *The Killers*, a remake of a Siodmak film from 1946, shot (in 1964) originally for television but transferred to the big screen due to its excessive violence (!), featuring the above-named future president but also, no less, Lee Marvin, John Cassavetes and the exquisite Angie Dickinson. Ultimately, this exception is perhaps no such thing, but rather a hybrid produced in a laboratory as if to show what might issue from one or two marriages against nature, and to illustrate the well-known reversibility of any binary pair: since certain B series movies are better than certain canonical movies, a good 'B series' is doubly superior to a would-be masterpiece laboriously 'nominated' for an Oscar.

In the phonographic industry (for popular music), they used – meaning in the days of two-sided wax, then vinyl records – to call the 'B side' the track not anticipated to be the biggest hit, and for which they thus didn't go to any great promotional expense. It featured clearly *on the rear* of the other, as though not to waste the material medium to the point of pressing just *one side* – which must nonetheless have been done here or there in the name of *de luxe* ostentation. I specified 'for popular music', but classical music wasn't entirely ignorant of this binary hierarchy, and it is said that Glenn Gould, upon sending one of his records to a friend, made him promise never to listen to the B side. Of course, the relation between the terms A and B was here of quite another kind than in the cinema, since there existed no specific market or separate circuit for the B sides, whose downgraded status remained moreover tacit. It could therefore happen, given the hazardous nature of this type of forecast, that a B side would ultimately eclipse its A side, according to the already invoked principle of reversibility: to prefer a B side is a doubly gratifying choice, for the promoted side and for the one who displays by promoting it their aesthetic freedom of choice. The historians of these things are doubtless aware of some dazzling examples thereof, but not the mere amateur I barely am, since these reversals of fortune lead quite swiftly to adjustments of strategy, and a redistribution of sides on subsequent compilations. Today, the one-sided compact disc has (provisionally?) effaced the concept by abolishing the thing, whose traces may now only be found by rummaging through dusty period collections, *oldies but goodies*.

I appear to be confusing (if not conflating) two distinct facts in the name of a vague designatory kinship. This is indeed the case: what interests me in these two facts is the derogatory role assigned to the letter B, as opposed to the letter A, or rather to an implicit letter A, and all in all to an absence of a letter A which isn't, however, the absence of just any letter: B is opposed to a virtual A which isn't just any non-B: whoever says B thinks (of) A. This ghostly A (one scarcely speaks of an 'A side') is a degree zero of designation, or, to extend a dubious reference to the linguistic model, an *unmarked* term, whose absence of mark tacitly manifests its dominance – like that of the masculine in French, where one used to say quite simply '*le sexe*' to refer gallantly to the *other* sex. But since this implicit term is not exportable, the exemplarity of this relation can only be transferred through that of its marked term. I'm happy to advocate for this transfer, with even less scruple given that its original use is about to sink into oblivion, and that the A/B relation, dethroned in the meantime by the rather more formidable relation 0/1, can pretty much only survive in metaphors, such as 'So and so is beginning to show his flip side [face B]', or 'Contrary to the pessimistic – or optimistic – predictions, so and so wasn't exactly a B series president.' These two assertions are moreover by no means incompatible. Sixtus V, faking imminent death throes, was elected as a B series pope.

In strategies of all kinds, one often calls a 'plan B' a substitute arrangement implicitly held to be inferior in quality (in effectiveness) to a first-choice plan that is seldom named a 'plan A', and which thus again remains generally unqualified. There's the plan tout court, then, in case of failure, there's the plan B, less brilliant but more accessible. Yet the failure of plan A clearly shows that its supposed superiority was illusory. It happens too, from an excess of optimism, that no plan B is foreseen. Pretend then that it's been mislaid, and lambast the guilty party.

Barbe/Barbara. When he found the remonstrances and recommendations of his wife a little too ear bending, my father used to quote, half in jest, half in earnest, this phrase from *At the Sign of the Reine Pédauque*:[20] 'Barbe, you are a saintly and worthy woman.' Having become proverbial, this quotation generally sufficed to pacify any conflict by relativising the scale of moral values. The mere statement 'Yes, Barbe' ended up serving this purpose. My mother, though protestant, would have gladly become a saint,[21] but that one weighed a little heavily upon her. I've never known what earned the patron saint of artillerymen and firemen the supplementary patronage of the importunate,[22] which she has incurred, presumably, by a purely chance homonymy. The very connection between *la barbe* [beard] and ennui isn't the clearest, even if '*barber*' can (I'm not sure about this) signify 'to shave', and thus appeal to the synonym '*raser*',[23] which defers the enigma without resolving it. Anyway, Saint Barbara is no more the patron saint of barbers than Saint Ignatius – as they claimed in the playgrounds of my childhood – is that of hairdressers.

---

[20] By Anatole France (1893); Barbe Ménétrier is a character in this novel.
[21] 'Sainte Barbe' is French for Saint Barbara.
[22] In French, 'barbe', 'beard', can also refer to something boring, a nuisance, a 'drag', as in the expression 'Quelle barbe!', 'What a bore!'.
[23] As well 'to shave', 'raser' can also signify 'to bore to death' or 'to bore stiff'.

Bardadrac. With this term of her own making,[24] Jacqueline designated a bag as vast as it was shapeless, which she dragged everywhere with her, inside and outside alike, and which contained too many things for her ever to be able to find a single one of them. But the deceptive certainty that it was there reassured her, and the word was applied by metonymy to its improbable contents, by metaphor to any kind of disorder, and by extension to the whole universe, the area surrounding it included. It rippled outwards, in extension, in comprehension, in use and in mention. It was to remain in the family idiom, and even somewhat in that of the village. I wish for it to spread further.

At Launay, save for an extreme heatwave, she used often to wear, over a light thin-strapped dress, a faded grey cardigan that she'd forget to fasten, whose sleeves she then turned inside out, like a glove, in order to remove it, whereby it was worn the wrong way round every other time, unlabelled side on odd days, labelled side on lucky days, or the converse, without doing any great harm to the floppiest of attires. Abandoned on a table, you might have mistaken it for a kitten, or for a furniture cloth, if it weren't that instead of an odour of wax, it emitted by capillary action a perfume identified as 'Mitsouko', for me a source of half-erotic half-affective value its memory has retained. Late in the afternoon, on the immense dining room table, or, Rue du Quinconce, in the window-less linen room still enveloped in shadow by a no less immense walnut wardrobe, she would occasionally herself iron a few personal fineries that she'd have entrusted to no mercenary hand. I'd never have grown tired of these moments of redoubled intimacy, whose odour of fresh iron-dried linen and surreptitiously incestuous flavour I relished. The frequency and length of my stays occasioned chatter among the country neighbours and within good city society. Even a few months after my entry at the Rue d'Ulm, a rather dry grand dame who was apparently a stickler for age differences affected to ask, in order to highlight the, let's say, Julien at Vergy[25] aspect of the situation: 'But when is he going to the *lycée?*'

[24] In French, 'le barda' is an informal term for 'stuff', 'gear', 'kit', 'things', 'clobber'; the neologism also clearly evokes *bric-à-brac*.
[25] An allusion to Julien Sorel's sojourn at the summer home of Mme. de Rênal in Stendhal's *Le Rouge et le noir* (*The Red and the Black*) (1830).

To the *lycée*, in fact, it wouldn't be long before I returned in order, as Queneau says, to multiply the error of learning by that of teaching: but, in many ways, I was still occupied with the former. I was then leading in part a double life: in Paris, the obligation of studies, militant discipline, the torments of the concrete absolute; on the banks of the Loire, the more relativistic pleasures of a rootless existence. In those days, adolescents weren't yet 'youths', and this age was not yet an autonomous category, but a formative phase, which was spent in the company of and, in every respect, in contact with adults: coming-of-age years, elective affinities, sentimental education, the light brushing of generations, murmurings of the heart, love on a gentle slope.

Aggressively in jest and out of ideological prejudice, as though she belonged to what Drieu[26] had called the 'dreamy bourgeoisie', I described her as a heroine of the personal diary. But she didn't keep one, as far as I'm aware, and I later realised, reading Michelet's,[27] that the heroine of a diary isn't necessarily the one who keeps it. I ought perhaps to have devoted myself thereto, but this role didn't fall within my remit, and it's a bit late to think of doing so more than I am here. To greet an involuntary memory induced by the 'miracle of an analogy', she never spoke of a *little madeleine*,[28] but would say: '*Ça me fait un charme* [It charms me]', and this saying too became part of our language. Consequently, the notion of 'charm' was never applied to a person, but always to those occasions of reminiscence, or sometimes, and by way of exception, of objectless reverie, such as before the dilapidated graves of the country cemetery where she'd sometimes take me, without any other explanation, so to speak, than this: 'It's odd: it doesn't remind me of anything, and yet it charms me.' It was perhaps a reminiscence resistant to identification, as for Marcel before the trees of Hudimesnil,[29] but I suppose that

---

[26] Pierre Drieu La Rochelle (1893–1945), French novelist, short-story writer and essayist.

[27] Jules Michelet (1798–1874), French historian, author of a monumental *Histoire de France* (*History of France*) completed in 1867.

[28] In the first section of the first volume of Marcel Proust's *À la Recherche du temps perdu* (*In Search of Lost Time*) – *Du côté de chez Swann* (*The Way by Swann*) (1913) – the narrator famously experiences involuntary memories of his childhood upon tasting a 'little madeleine' dipped in a cup of tea.

[29] An allusion to an episode in the second volume – *À l'ombre des jeunes filles*

she would have rejected this overly literary reference for an entirely personal state of mind; besides, anything that concerned her was absolutely peculiar to her, without possible sharing or comparison, and without pertinent definition: she was what she was and refused any qualifying term as unduly reductive.

One did her no justice by saying that she was the soul of Launay, for she meant to be the soul of everything: this was the Oriane side of her Guermantes side.[30] As for 'charm' in the commonplace sense of the term, she herself, who was not wanting in that respect, feigned to scorn this futile advantage in favour of qualities of soul deeper or more elevated, which remained carefully unspecified, but which were, however, evidenced by a few writings, left in the main in the form of drafts without hope of publication. It was perhaps for a reason of the same order that she'd profess great detachment with regard to what was for her merely a somewhat overly vast holiday home. Her 'real life' was supposedly elsewhere, at her music stand in the orchestra of so-called 'popular' Concerts, and on every floor of a 'private' hotel called, owing to its strange *bow-window* and its Belle Époque style, 'Villa 1900', where she'd receive the finest intellectual flowers of the neighbouring *lycée* (this was her Verdurin[31] side), and sometimes gathered a string quartet.

She used in fact always to take her violin along to the country, but it would most often remain in its case, for want of time and, perhaps, of fondness for solitary exercises, except occasionally, for my instruction, Kreisler's cadenza for Beethoven's concerto or the above-mentioned chaconne by Bach, which she also played on the piano, in Busoni's transcription, but more often Beethoven's sonatas, claiming to find there everything one might wish for in music. As one who'd still get tangled up in the least key of F, I

en fleurs (*In the Shadow of Young Girls in Flower*) (1918) – of Marcel Proust's *In Search of Lost Time*.

[30] 'le côté Oriane de son côté Guermantes': the Guermantes are a prominent aristocratic family in *In Search ...*; the charismatic Oriane, Duchess de Guermantes, long fascinates the Proustian narrator, who is eventually admitted to her salon. Genette's phrase inevitably evokes the titles of Proust's *Du côté de chez Swann* (*The Way by Swann*) and *Le côté de Guermantes* (*The Guermantes Way*) (1920).

[31] Madame Verdurin, a prominent bourgeois character in *In Search of Lost Time*.

naively admired her for knowing how to 'read the notes' so well with her left hand, and she wouldn't fail to retort, with a touch of commiseration, that music isn't in the notes, but *between* the notes – a lesson in structuralism before its time and coinage. Like almost all those who 'practise' music, she rather looked down upon those who were content just to listen to it, especially on record: pancake music [musique en galettes]. Her favourite pianist was, then not well-known, Vlado Perlemuter, an inspired choice which still forces my respect. However, the distended strings and the moth-eaten hammers of the upright piano housed in the 'billiard room' often betraying her intentions, she preferred to take beneath the cedar a score to be read in silence, seated upon a wicker chaise longue in order to extend a bare leg always threatened by some improbable phlebitis [phlébite], which a euphemism borrowed from the repertoire of kitchen malapropisms would cause to be ritually pronounced '*faiblite*'.[32] Of this leg on borrowed time, right or left depending on the day's inspiration, she'd lightly brush the flawless curves with a dreamy hand, adorned, if I remember aright and if such a things exists, with a kind of signet ring with a flat bezel-set mauve, or purple, or periwinkle agate, before a tray upon which cooled the tarnished tin of what she called, a period pun, her '*théière de jardin* [garden teapot/garden teahouse]'. The dreaded complication was ominously called 'cavernous sinus thrombosis'. Her medical knowledge impressed me without worrying me. Like Jesus, but more often than him, she was wont to announce: 'You will not have me for long.' None of us took seriously a prognosis that belonged to goodness only knew which game. Its fulfilment, many years later and along another route, applied the finishing touch to this game.

She would readily sing nursery rhymes that she'd improvised, lyrics and music, a few years previously for her very young children. 'Lyrics' is quite a grand word for some of them, which she called 'organic songs', and whose libretto consisted rather in labial gurgling supposed to express a purported maternal tenderness. But her true affective register was humour, and its most developed tenor that of a not always benevolent comedy (still Oriane), with which said children, and a few adults, made do as best they could. A

[32] Derived from 'faiblesse', 'weakness'.

distant cousin endowed with remarkable ears inspired in her this sort of rondel:

Quand Ernest
S'en va-t-à Brest
Sur la rade
Le vent vient de l'est.
Dans ses oreilles s'engouffre l'air
Et v'là mon Ernest en Angleterre.
Pas besoin
D'prend'le bateau
Car il est
Rendu plus tôt:
Ses oreilles faisant voiles
Il irait jusqu'aux étoiles,
Quand Ernest
S'en va-t-à Brest.

[*When Ernest/Goes off to Brest/On the harbour/The wind comes from the east./Into his ears rushes the wind/And there's my Ernest in England./ No need/To take the boat/For he is/There before it:/With his ears become sails/He'd go right to the stars,/When Ernest/Goes off to Brest.*]

Such were the lyrics. As for the melody, you'll find the score on my website if ever I think of opening one. In the meantime, here is its primitive note–name summary (patented method), assuming it to be, let's keep things simple, in C major: *so do mi, do so mi re, so ti re, ti so re do, do ti la do, do si la do si la do, ti, fa, fa mi re fa mi re fa, mi, so, so do mi, do so mi re, so ti re, do # re re # mi, re mi fa mi fa so la, so fa mi re mi fa so, so fa mi, re so mi do.* Each comma marks a silence.

Beau. Its meaning is always enigmatic, especially in the expression *avoir beau*: 'No matter what I say [On a beau dire] … ' 'No matter what I do [J'ai beau faire], everything interests me' (Valéry); 'No matter how well-preserved you are [On a beau être bien conservé], you're still only ever a preserve' (René Dorin); 'No matter how much I listen to him [J'ai beau en écouter], I still can't get to like Wagner. – It doesn't matter, Madame' (Debussy?). Chamfort goes a step further in these two fairly perverse quotations: 'A man at the table said: "No matter how much I eat [J'ai beau manger], I'm no longer hungry"', and: 'A very rich man [perhaps the same] said while speaking of the poor: "No matter how often you give them nothing [On a beau ne leur rien donner], these funny folk keep on asking." This remark has remained topical, so much does ingratitude nurture obstinacy. And again, irrefutably, I can't remember where in Giono: 'No matter how they kept an eye on each other [Ils avaient beau se surveiller], they eyed each other too much [ils se surveillaient trop].'

Beaubourg. In the 1950s, it was, bearing the very old name 'plateau', an immense wasteland surrounded by fences as mysterious as Couperin's barricades,[33] he who had once been an organist not far from there. In fact, everything here was mysterious and, at night-time, imbued with a frankly disquieting poetry. It was used primarily as what is elsewhere called a *parking lot*, a provisionally empty space between two buildings, and of which we hardly have any equivalent today, where our 'car parks' are instead underground, or scattered along pavements controlled by paid 'parking meters'. I assumed it was reserved for lorries servicing Les Halles, but I've never known through where they could enter or leave, and I only saw them, between two loose slats, immobile and silent, abandoned, as through stricken by some sinister embargo, of which what lay ahead confirmed indeed the ill-boding.[34] A little further west, below Rue Saint-Martin, then a convivial place and which smelled strongly of vegetables and love, a lady of the night, between two trips up a staircase that kept her in shape ('I rest on me feet, I do'), sang untiringly and in a beautifully resonant voice the period repertoire of Charles Aznavour: *Just yesterday, when I was young* ... .

Beffroy. Taller than it was wide, bolting upon sloping ground that already rose too high above street level, and built, as you were expected to know, not from vulgar millstone but – named after a nearby Vexin quarry – from 'Vigny stone', the house in Conflans wasn't very spacious, for it was afflicted, through the fault of an architect appointed by the state in accordance with the Loucheur

[33] François Couperin (1668–1733), *Les Barricades mystérieuses* (*The Mysterious Barricades*), harpsichord piece composed in 1717.
[34] An allusion to the development of the Pompidou Centre on the site of the *Plateau Beaubourg* in the 1970s.

law, with an internal three-section staircase, lighted from the west by two narrow parallel windows, and which used about half of its volume to service an itself oversized landing, which no furniture humanised. Life thus evaporated for the most part in this vertical space, which conveyed to it a little of its sonorous inanity.[35] In order to find ourselves, we had to withdraw into one of the undersized rooms it was willing to grant us: two bedrooms upstairs, on the ground floor a dining room also used, as best we could and so to speak never, as a lounge, and a kitchen where the main things occurred, including daily meals, and where, when I took up too much room, my sweet mother would unceremoniously push me out of the way, but not without bidding me, as though to excuse herself: 'Don't move.' My parents didn't particularly feel the discomfort of this awkward layout, quite happy as they were to have a roof, albeit one that was exaggeratedly pointed.

Besides the two bedrooms, the house comprised upstairs two small attics in the roof space, one to the north, the other to the south, which we always called 'storerooms'. In the one facing south, there took pride of place a 'dummy' proportioned to my mother's (modest) size and covered in whitish cloth, which only came out on grand dressmaking occasions; tobacco leaves, none too licit, were also dried there, hung upon a line like bats. The one facing north, adjacent to my bedroom, didn't store much at all. When I was about 14, pleading that my bedroom wasn't wide enough to contain a desk worthy of my labours, I managed to instal in this loft a work table lit by a rack and pinion skylight, which we unduly called 'vasistas', a book shelf to its left, and on its right a sofa where I spread out my cogitations, like Descartes in his stove, but without a stove: the winter cold contributed to the health of the spirit. I realise that I have often sought, subsequently, to reconstitute elsewhere this original arrangement in my various ventures in spatial planning, without always being able to respect the principle of hygiene dear to my parents, a popular superstition whose origin or justification I have never known: to sleep, if possible, with your head to the north.

---

[35] 'son inanité sonore': an allusion to the sixth line ('aboli bibelot d'inanité sonore', 'abolished bauble of sonorous inanity') of Stéphane Mallarmé's 'Sonnet en X' (1887).

To the south, the façade was adorned with fairly large front steps where on fine days we would have dinner, then the slope continued, sharply down, with a second stairway, between two low walls flanked by two rows of privets or spindle trees, then, more gently, across the front garden – devoted by my mother to dahlias and tulips, by my father to vegetables of all kinds and to strawberry trees ('The earth is low'), and by myself to white and red currants – then, steeply once again, with a third stairway, more hemmed in, which fell abruptly upon a front door, whose most obvious function, but one often dashed, was to bear a letter box on its rear side. The street was itself still just a brief artificial landing beyond which the slope became yet more acute, plunging almost vertically, a few houses clinging to its sides as in the favelas of Rio, until it reached the level of the Seine, whose right bank here hardly exceeds the width of two streets, houses and small gardens included. In order to reach this final level, you had to descend, a few metres further on the right, a fourth stairway with iron handrails, of which I shall perhaps speak later. From all of this resulted the most vaunted [vanté], and also the most windswept [venté], merit of our site, which was a very clear 'view' of the river, the industrial plants occupying the opposing bank and the vegetable fields that stretched out there, between Maisons-Laffitte, Achères and Poissy, interesting to behold only when flooded in times of spate. This limitless and restless prospect put me forever at odds with dominant positions.

The only more or less flat and really habitable part of the garden could thus be found to the north, behind the house, a cramped space with a view, through transparent wire mesh fences, of the neighbouring gardens, sheltered from the overly external world by the mass of the house. There lay the veritable haven of privacy, especially since the kitchen led there directly via another stairway, far shorter, more prosaic and amiable. This *backyard* was home, in the middle of a kind of arbour embalming the honeysuckle, to a linden tree planted a few years before my birth, which had apparently grown faster than me, and where I'd spend as much time as possible, by dint of ladders and various constructions *à la* Swiss Family Robinson. The same side also bore a Royal Ann cherry tree [un cerisier de bigarreaux Napoléon], the earliest fruiting and most flavoursome kind, and a square of rhubarbs with which my mother made compote. And a large disused flowerpot where there would ever be 'soaking', in vinegared water, awaiting a fricassee, the snails harvested from the rest of the garden on days following rainfall. It was again onto this side that opened the door of the 'basement', an annex where the essentials of our home industry were gathered: laundry, ironing, odd jobs carried out on a workbench; we reserved the name 'cellar' for a more sombre cubbyhole, though it was on the same level, where a tall cast iron boiler reigned over a few piles of coal of various kinds and with carefully graded usages: lumps, briquettes, 'brownray knapweed', anthracite. Finally, we'd obtained from an obliging neighbour a passage through his garden allowing us to emerge onto the next street, in the direction of the station, the gendarmerie and the area's only grocery. Like Combray's,[36] our locality thus had two sides, and two doors, one of which by agreement with our neighbour. Since the street on the northern side was called 'Avenue du Château' and that on the southern side 'Avenue du Beffroy' (with a y), these two sides were named 'castle way' and 'belfry way'. Said château could indeed be found at the end of its street, but the 'belfry', for its part, remained unfindable, and perhaps it was simply a person's name ('Avenue Beffroy [Beffroy Avenue]', moreover, and not 'Avenue du Beffroi [Belfry Avenue]'). But then which person might actually have been called Beffroy? I have never found the key to this other mystery.

Along this avenue there'd come, besides the postman, a few street vendors, including a daily milkman in a horse-drawn carriage with a black leather hood, whose brakes he applied by turning a handle on an upright axis, as he would have stirred a spoon in a pot, and a foul-mouthed butcher [un boucher mal embouché] who seldom failed to propose 'a nice piece in his breeches' to his female customers. Private cars, as they were still called, passed scarcely more than once or twice per day, that's to say far less frequently than barges upon the Seine.

Belle-soeur/Sister-in-law. We had at Launay a fairly vulgar-natured lodger whom between us we called 'My sister-in-law', because each of her observations on the human race – and there was no shortage of them for her to pour forth – was always reinforced by a reference to this relative by marriage, an apparently bottomless

---

[36] The imagined village in Proust's *In Search of Lost Time*, inspired by his childhood village Illiers (now called Illiers-Combray), in north central France.

reservoir of memorable cases. The invocation invariably began with this fairly common clause ('You see ... ' for 'Take for instance'), but it acquired all its might from being applied always to this unique model. We unfortunately never had the opportunity to meet for ourselves a person about whom we yet ended up getting to know every facet, physical ('You see, my sister-in-law, she catches every illness') and moral: 'You see, my sister-in-law, she hates rhubarb compote' – how can you?

In principle, I believed at the time, one may 'see' in this way all kinds of people, close or less close, and not only sisters-in-law. But then last week, in the bakery of Saint-Sauveur-en-Puisaye, hotbed of village conviviality, complaints bureau where one tells one another all about the highs and especially the lows of destiny in general and the neighbourhood in particular, in the bakery, then, how delighted was I to hear, from the mouth of a customer awaiting her change and overflowing with philosophy, a 'You see, my sister-in-law ... ' that took me back a good half century: that's what I call a charm. It obviously wasn't *our* sister-in-law, no doubt snatched away long ago from her own and everyone else, but you have to think that the humankind capable of supplying examples evocable at will effectively consists exclusively of sisters-in-law. A structural anthropology worthy of its name could probably explain this fact, for which I think I can find, in the meantime, the beginnings of a plausible reason in the mixture of proximity, reciprocity (a son-in-law's relations with a father or mother-in-law, as you are doubtless aware, are *not* reciprocal) and (in principle) absence of natural kinship that characterises this type of relationship. A sister-in-law to 'see' will always, I fear, have been missing from my own experience and understanding of life.

Beltway. This English, or rather American, word is more graceful than its (French) counterpart *périphérique*. Greek, I came to know something about this, often encumbers us with prickly and ungainly words we'd sometimes be spared by a simple metaphor, like the charming *'petite ceinture* [little belt]', which passed away shortly after the thing to which it referred. I am aware that *beltway* is used elsewhere than in Washington, but it has become its (*capital beltway*) conventional designation, thus by metonymy. This ring road, which can only be crossed via one of the numerous bridges projecting over it, is perhaps the most significant of all the internal frontiers in the United States: more so than the Mason-Dixon line, between North and South, more so than the course of the Mississippi, between East and West – and I'm not counting here the double ideological frontier, far more impermeable, isolating heavy continental America from its two narrow ocean façades, on the East (in fact, above all north-east, from Boston to Baltimore, for its southern continuation scarcely has any ports) and on the West (from Seattle to San Diego). Beyond the *beltway*, then, lies what some would call the real country; within, lies the legal (or virtual?) region, the famous District's quadrangle drawn with great precision upon Maryland and Virginia, with its Mall, its Capitol, its White House, its Executive Office, its ministries, its Pentagon, its Blair House, its FBI, its CIA, its charming residential quarter in Georgetown, its mournful Arlington suburb beyond the Potomac – in short, federal politics and its convoy, since, contrary to many others, this city was founded only by and for it, tempered more recently by a few scientific and artistic institutions. In truth, I think that this antithesis, with its verbal emblem, is a rhetorical artefact, become obsolete since politics itself has striven to reduce its divisiveness to the advantage of neo-populist mass thinking: heralded demise of the symbol, and of the heroic enterprise of the Founding Fathers that it subsequently represented. Meanwhile, for the ordinary visitors who venture there on four wheels (if possible, all of them motorised), the *beltway* is a *parkway* like any other, and which was designed with enough breadth still to let one drift through one of the most beautiful landscapes of a continent not lacking therein. I shan't say as much about our '*périphérique*', decidedly as tiresome to travel along as it is to pronounce.

Bestiary. The elephant lets itself be stroked, the louse, no (Lautréamont). *La pervenche*, the periwinkle, isn't a bird: you're confusing it with *la mésange*, the tit. The girolle isn't a fish: again you're confusing it with *la girelle*, the wrasse. *Le chevreau*, the kid, isn't the son of *le chevreuil*, the roe deer. *Le porcelet*, the piglet, isn't the husband of *la porcelaine*, porcelaine. *La chouette*, the owl, isn't the female of *le hibou*, the tufted owl. *La fourmilière*, the anthill, isn't the female of *le fourmilier*, the anteater, but anyone can make a mistake, as the hedgehog said while climbing down, in frustration, from the hairbrush. The lark, which in the past just dropped into your lap,[37] is pretty much only now known for the recipe of its pâté, half-lark half-horse, that's to say one lark, one horse, etc.[38] *La grenouille*, the frog, moreover, isn't the female of *le crapaud*, the toad; it isn't the former that wishes to be as big as the ox,[39] but the latter, and again it that inhales without being able to exhale all the air it's given by means of a tube or a cigarette, which can only make it pop off [crever[40]]; never do this to it, if you do not wish to have it done unto you; the frog, for its part, aspires only to have a king, which it will live to regret;[41] the biologist passes, the frog remains (Rostand), but it's no longer the same one; it lives in the font,[42] the bug in the vestry,[43] the cockroach in the confessional,[44] the ravens in the church tower:[45] each to their own trade. In all of fruit fly memory, no genetician has ever been seen to die.[46] The cow has four legs that reach down to the ground, which makes the cowherd's task easier: in order to number his herd, he counts the legs and divides the sum by four (Vialatte). The carp and the rabbit don't spend their honeymoon

[37] Allusion to the French proverb 'Attendre que les alouettes tombent toutes rôties dans le bec', 'to wait till the larks fall already roasted into your mouth', 'to expect everything just to drop into one's lap'.

[38] In French, 'un pâté d'alouette' (lark pâté) can refer figuratively to any arguably fraudulent proposition, for instance in advertising or political discourse, where a minor named element is foregrounded in order to veil the effectively main, often less attractive, element, the deceptive recipe for this pâté being 'half lark, half horse, one of each'.

[39] An allusion to La Fontaine's fable: 'The Frog that Wished to be as Big as the Ox'.

[40] 'to burst' and 'to die'.

[41] An allusion to Aesop's fable: 'The Frogs Who Wished for a King'.

[42] A 'grenouille de bénitier', a 'font frog', refers to a 'churchy person'.

[43] A 'punaise de sacristie', a 'vestry bug', refers to a Christian zealot, typically female.

[44] 'Cafard' is also a slang term for a police informant (a 'narc' or 'snitch').

[45] 'les corbeaux dans le clocher': an allusion to the species known in French as 'le choucas des tours' ('tower jackdaw', western jackdaw) or 'la corneille des clochers' ('belfry crow').

[46] Adapted from 'De mémoire de rose, on n'a jamais vu mourir un jardinier', 'in all of rose memory, no gardener has ever been seen to die', Bernard le Bovier de Fontenelle (1657–1757).

together.[47] The duck and the rabbit play hide-and-seek. Mares aren't impregnated by the wind: Virgil, who propagated it, wasn't fooled by this legend. The viper is lecherous,[48] the rat is slimy,[49] the hyena is a typist.[50] The mouse can do nothing without its chip. If a mouse gives birth to a mountain, it's a casting error.[51] *La chauve-souris*, the bat, is neither *chauve*, bald, nor a *souris*, a mouse. Can a scapegoat be a cash cow? – Yes, and it even helps its executioners. *L'Œuf de Colomb*, Columbus's egg, isn't an *oeuf de colombe*, a dove's egg. A *musaraigne*, a shrew, as its name indicates, is born from the crossing of a (male) mouse and a (female) *araignée*, spider, or conversely. The *orfraie*, the sea eagle, only screams blue murder when it's taken for an *effraie*, a barn-owl.[52] The hummingbird, hybrid of fly and bird, is geostationary, like the lark. The platypus is unclassifiable [inclassable]. The slug is unbreakable [incassable]. The stork asks nothing of the ant.[53] The tortoise smashes the heads of tragic poets with its shell.[54] The wild ass has less and less skin.[55] The *congre*, the conger, isn't *malingre*, sickly, nonger [nongre]. The perch isn't always easy to grab hold of.[56] The falcon is born in a mass grave (Heredia), where it dies isn't known. The peacock isn't always giant. The snail moves slowly, but it never goes backwards (Vialatte). The

[47] 'Le mariage de la carpe et du lapin' is an expression signifying the combination of incompatible elements, 'like chalk and cheese'.
[48] An allusion to Stalin's alleged description of Marshal Tito.
[49] An allusion to a political insult that gained notoriety in the Moscow Trials of 1936–1938.
[50] In 1948, Alexander Fadeyev, Soviet writer and co-founder of the Union of Soviet Writers, described Jean-Paul Sartre as a 'typewriting hyena' and a 'jackal armed with a fountain pen'.
[51] Inversion of the French expression (via Aesop, Horace and La Fontaine) 'c'est la montagne qui accouche d'une souris', 'it's the mountain giving birth to a mouse', signifying a great deal of effort with very little result.
[52] Genette is here playing on the expression 'pousser des cris comme une orfraie', 'to scream blue murder', as well as on the homonymy 'effraie-barn owl' and 'effraie-frightens'.
[53] An allusion to La Fontaine's fable 'The Grasshopper and the Ant'.
[54] Aeschylus is thought to have died when a tortoise dropped by an eagle landed on his head.
[55] An allusion to Balzac's *La Peau de chagrin* (*The Wild Ass's Skin*) (1831).
[56] Play on the homonymy 'perche', perch, and 'perche', pole, in the expression 'tendre la perche à quelqu'un', 'to throw somebody a line'.

zebra never takes its pyjamas off. Moray eels love slaves.[57] The horns
of a gazelle are edible. The fox likes grapes,[58] but prefers cheese; my
mother's, adorned with false glass eyes that fascinated me, only left
its wardrobe on grand occasions. The eel never goes green: you need
a Fleming [Flamand] for that.[59] The flamingo [flamant], for its part,
sleeps upon one leg, like the fakir. The chaffinch isn't always happy.[60]
The doe has soft eyes and hard feet. Never let a butterfly flap its
wings over the bay of Sydney: it would bring about a cyclone in
Jamaica; the converse (that a Jamaican cyclone should cause an
Australian butterfly to flap its wings) hasn't been confirmed. *La
coccinelle*, the ladybird, hasn't always been a car in love [un amour
de voiture]:[61] in my childhood, we didn't even suspect that one day
it would be, we called it a *bête à bon dieu*, an 'insect of the good
Lord', without knowing why, but the fact is that we never crushed
one; we avenged ourselves upon another species, also red with black
dots, whose individual members, a little longer, moved in single file,
hitched onto each other like carriages, and of which I've never known
the name; not scolopendra in any case: the scolopendra, for its part,
is sometimes animal (millipede), sometimes vegetal (hart's-tongue
fern), and it's the only case known to me of this (purely verbal) dual
belonging, since coral is just an animal turned into stone. *La salicorne*,
glasswort, is always vegetal, and it is neither a close nor a distant
relative of the unicorn, which isn't related to anyone. The mole is
always old. 'The chimpanzee has genius, it lacks talent' (Vialatte).
The Capitoline geese are close to those of the Tarpeian Rock;[62] those

---

[57] An allusion to the Roman equestrian Vedius Pollio (died 15 BC), friend
of Emperor Augustus, who reputedly fed slaves condemned to death to his
eels.

[58] An allusion to La Fontaine, 'The Fox and the Grapes'.

[59] An allusion to the traditional Flemish dish 'eel in green sauce' (Paling
in't groen).

[60] An allusion to the French expression 'gai comme un pinson' ('happy as a
lark').

[61] The Volkswagen Beetle is known in France as the Coccinelle; *Un Amour
de coccinelle* (*Ladybird in Love*) is the French title of the film *The Love Bug*
(1968), featuring this car.

[62] Genette is here alluding to Livy's account of the Gauls' attempt to scale
the Capitoline Hill in Rome (390 BC): honking geese are said to have alerted
the Romans to the attack, saving the capitol; he is also referencing the Latin

of the Pont de l'Alma are just a bad play on words.[63] The nightingale never sings a duet with the lark. The dromedary is the vessel of the desert, but the camel overtakes it on the bumps [le double sur les bosses[64]]. The crocodile doesn't share its marshland, so the alligator has taken refuge in the New York plumbing network, and the caiman on the Montagne Sainte-Geneviève.[65] Mosquitoes only marry cousins.[66] *Le cafard* (in English *cockroach*) can only be seen at the rate of one in 50; its Spanish name, *cucaracha*, is nicer. But what has happened to the May bugs of my childhood? At dusk or *entre chien et loup* ['between dog and wolf'], you can't always tell the difference, but if the wolf is sometimes a dog for man, it is always a wolf for the lamb.[67] If the American Indians were afraid of the conquistadors' horses, it's because they hadn't known the time when the horse, which wasn't yet called horse, or even *cheval*, lived exclusively in America, before, driven away by the winter, heading over to Asia via the future Bering strait, which didn't yet bear this name, not yet being a strait. The hinny is the son of a horse and a she-ass, the mule is the son of an ass and a mare, *la mule*, the female mule, isn't the wife of the *mulet*, the male mule, but its sister, and the sister of the *bardot*, the hinny, doesn't have a name, nor even, whatever people may say, a first name. It is the herring that makes the North Sea salty (Allais). The pearl is an illness of the oyster, the oyster is a sore point [plaie] for the pleaders [plaideurs].[68] Malebranche's dog doesn't feel. Schrödinger's cat is both dead and alive. During the siege of Paris, and even much later, in certain quarters of Paris, they'd eat

expression 'Arx tarpeia Capitoli proxima', 'The Tarpeian Rock is close to the Capitol', meaning that one's fall from grace can come quickly – the 80ft high Tarpeian Rock, on the south side of the Capitoline Hill, was used as a site of execution.

[63] An allusion to the statue of the *Zouave* (originally an Algerian light infantry soldier) on the Pont de l'Alma in Paris; there is a partial homophony in French between 'les oies' (geese) and 'le Zouave'.

[64] Meaning both 'overtakes it on a bumpy surface' and 'has double the number of humps'.

[65] A *caïman* is the informal name given to a supervisor or teacher at the École Normale Supérieure, situated close to the Montagne Sainte-Geneviève in the 5th arrondissement of Paris.

[66] 'Un cousin' in French can also signify 'crane fly', or 'mosquito hawk'.

[67] An allusion to La Fontaine's fable 'The Wolf and the Lamb'.

[68] An allusion to La Fontaine's fable 'The Oyster and the Pleaders'.

'gutter rabbit' and 'mutton-flavoured rat'. The ass, like the Duke of Guise,[69] is more of a burden dead than alive,[70] but, alive is better than a dead lion.[71] The lion, even when alive, was very nearly called Leon, which would have made it less wild. If the hare cannot catch the tortoise, it's not by dint of grazing on wild thyme, nor of listening for which way the wind is blowing, nor of daydreaming in its shelter, but on account of a famous sophism: it's Zeno's fault. It was once thought that a handsome man (as they used to say) was the synthesis of three animals: jack in the morning, boa at midday, raven in the evening. I find that we don't speak well enough of the mandrill, the African cynocephalus in danger of extinction which I discovered a little belatedly in the zoological gardens at Asheboro, NC: with its so finely drawn features and ever pensive air, I find it to be more anthropomorphic than many of my fellows, myself included. I know a squirrel, if at least it's the same one every year, and if knowing a squirrel consists in furtively catching sight of its russet cloud from my window, near the end of summer, undulating upon the lawn and spiralling up a wild plum tree it uses merely to tease me, for I very much doubt that it feeds on plums. Maybe it hides its hazelnuts there. 'Catch sight of' is, besides, a rather grand way of putting it, for, even if I freeze into a pillar of salt, it seems to sense my gaze through the window, and to be sufficiently alarmed by it to disappear at once into its branches. So that'll be for another day, with a little luck. Much to the contrary, the grey squirrels of the New World are of an almost bothersome size and familiarity, and not only in Central Park. On a wooden table at the Point Lobos reserve, south of Monterey, it suffices to leave a few peanuts lying around to find oneself overrun, not without risk of bites. I struggle to believe that it's the same species, but if this is so, it provides yet another refutation of the excellent Buffon, who averred that all the animals, on this continent, are smaller than their equivalents in Europe, Africa and Asia. I knew personally a fennec, or 'desert fox', which lived in such

---

[69] An allusion to the fatal consequences for (the French) King Henry III of Henry I's assassination in 1588.
[70] An allusion to the French expression 'peser un âne mort' (originating in La Fontaine's fable 'The Two Dogs and the Dead Ass'), 'to weigh a dead donkey', 'to weigh a ton'.
[71] An allusion to Ecclesiastes 9.4: 'For to him that is joined to all the living there is hope: for a living dog is better than a dead lion'.

proximity to its female owner that it too smelled of 'Miss Dior'. The genet [genette], for its part, is dappled, carnivorous and nocturnal; when my eldest daughter was three years old, she was shown one at the Tertre Rouge zoo, with all due insistence on the perfect homonymy; a few days later, she proudly proclaimed to her grandmother: 'I saw a beautiful little Christine asleep in its cage.'

Bibliothèques/Libraries. Roland Barthes would often say: 'I became a structuralist in order no longer to have to go to libraries, but then structuralism has itself become a vast library.' That was well observed, but what he perhaps didn't foresee was that he would one day himself become a library, soon an institution. At any rate, I'm not far from sharing this slight phobia, compounded for me by a strong allergy to dust and paper: it once took me more than a year to find the entrance to the library at Rue d'Ulm, and many years to find the exit of the Sorbonne's, more labyrinthine than is reasonable. Since then, I have sometimes dreamt that I'm walking along a street in Paris whose Haussmannian façades gradually turn into shelves of books stacked and aligned to infinity, each floor becoming a shelf, each window the spine of a book. I'm seeking an address, and find only a reference number – one that, empty, belongs to a book absent from its place, and I awake with a start before its 'phantom'. This nightmare is unfair, for the pleasure peculiar to libraries consists precisely in finding what you weren't seeking there, and *vice versa*.

That of my parents included no books by Jane Austen, but, whatever Mark Twain may say, this lack did not suffice to make it perfect, even if it didn't contain a great deal else. I'm exaggerating: it featured in fact – today 'dispersed' – about a hundred titles, eclectic and dated, with a predominance, if memory serves me, of Loti, Farrère, Bourget, Bordeaux, Marcel Prévost, Édouard Rod (*The Shadow Spreads over the Mountain*), Chardonne (*Loving One's Neighbour*), Georges Duhamel (*Pleasures and Games*, where his two sons appear, nicknamed 'le Cuib' and 'le Tioup', who were indirectly a part of our own folklore, where I was at once le Cuib and le Tioup), Maxence van der Meersch (*Bodies and Souls*), Alexis Carrel (*Man, The Unknown*), Axel Munthe (*The Story of San Michele*) – I don't know why these three last books, whose content I have forgotten, still form a trilogy in my memory – Boylesve (*The Fragrance of the Borromeo Islands*), Colette (only for

Sido and *Claudine's House*), Giono, lots of Giono, inevitably from his first period: *Second Harvest* (whose beginning I have always remembered: 'When the postman from Banon arrives at Vachères, it's always around midday. No matter if you leave Manosque later on the days when habits while away the hours, when you arrive at Vachères, it's always midday. Regular as clockwork'), *Hill*, *Lovers Are Never Losers*, *To the Slaughterhouse*, *True Riches*, *Joy of Man's Desiring*, d'Annunzio (*The Child of Pleasure*, slightly hidden, probably because of its overly evocative title), Rostand (*Cyrano* and *The Eaglet*, of which we knew a few soliloquies by heart), Emily Brontë (*Wuthering Heights*), Margaret Mitchell (*Gone with the Wind*), a pacifist trilogy consisting of Barbusse (*Under Fire*), Dorgelès (*Wooden Crosses*), Remarque (*All Quiet on the Western Front*), Mauriac (*Thérèse Desqueyroux*), Maurois, for a novel I shall return to, and for a few biographies with cleverly chosen titles, by metaphor or metonymy: *Ariel* for Shelley's life, *Don Juan* for Byron, *René* for Chateaubriand, not to mention a life of Lyautey, which nurtured, for a few weeks, a colonial vocation, and another, of Disraeli, whose presence still remains enigmatic to me. I suspect that my mother liked the genre for its own sake, irrespective of its objects: she had certainly read nothing by Shelley or Byron, but it was their lives that impassioned her: her novelistic penchant was rather more readily invested, I can understand her, in supposedly lived reality than in the artificial plots of novels. The same may be said for the musicians (Liszt, Chopin, Berlioz, Wagner) recounted by Guy de Pourtalès. And furthermore Louis Hémon (*Maria Chapdelaine*) and Marguerite Audoux (*Marie-Claire* – I also somewhat confuse those two), Romain Rolland (*Jean-Christophe* and *Colas Breugnon*), Édouard Schuré, *The Great Initiates*, and even, by Lamartine and in verse, *Jocelyn* and (you'd think you were dreaming) *The Fall of an Angel*. Again in verse, *Gringoire* by Théodore de Banville (which I must be the last living person to have read) and, perhaps for the sake of contrast and doubtless a paternal contribution: by Jehan Rictus, *The Soliloquies of the Poor*. Some of these books, and no doubt a few others I've forgotten, featured there in really kitsch editions, illustrated with horrid 'woodcuts', published by Ferenczi or Arthème Fayard, because in those days Fayard was still Arthème.

My mother's favourite novel was, then, *Climates*, by André Maurois, of which I have only retained this psychological outline:

in the first part, the hero suffers from an unhappy passion for a young rather reluctant *femme fatale*, a 'being of flight [être de fuite]' whom he married regardless, and who will leave him before committing suicide. In the second part, he inflicts upon his second wife behaviour akin to that from which the departed made him suffer, as though to punish the one for the faults of the other. The whole thing eventually turns in favour of kind feelings and conjugal love, but I wondered how it would be, following another plot line, if, the first – and, in this version, only – wife having survived and returned, with remorse, into the hero's life, the roles were reversed within the same couple, the man becoming in his turn a sort of 'blithely handsome one [bel indifférent]' – a period notion. I don't know whence came to my mother her fondness for this 'psychological' novel [roman 'd'analyse'], as they used to say, nor why I can still remember it.

My father summarised it in his fashion with this rather hackneyed jibe: 'This guy has utterly screwed up his married life: his first wife left, and the second one stayed.' More generally, he feigned in relation to this slight excess of literary baggage a no less slight disdain, which he took pleasure in exaggerating, occasionally humming this somewhat macho parody of I can't recall which old song: 'I've two blue stockings in my stable ... ' (I was apparently one of the pair). Despite this principled reservation, in all things meticulous, he was anxious to cover some of these books, and the good idea occurred to him of using scraps of wallpaper whose un-scrapped remainder covered our bedroom walls, and the space called the 'dining room'. In this room, a table and six chairs and a dresser 'in the *genre hideux* [hideous style]' (as I later learned one could say) occupied the entire area, with my mother's sewing machine (for working on 'patterns' supplied by *Modes et travaux*[72]), a strange chair whose back could be tilted at various angles thanks to a kind of adjustable cogwheel, and finally the small piece of furniture of undefined style that contained said library, plus a few easily discoverable family secrets. The wallpaper, I'm getting back to it, fortunately plain-coloured, was less fortunately embossed (a period luxury), and unyieldingly stiff. The fragile original covers thus doubled over failed not to curl up in these shells, and their

[72] A haberdashery in Paris (*Fashions and Works*).

binding didn't survive for long. My first 'school' books and exercise pads benefited from the same protection, to the great hilarity of my little classmates, whose parents found in shops book covers fashioned in a less artisanal manner. In the name of Republican standardisation, I was eventually given dark blue paper which was more academic-looking, but not much more graceful.

Some of these books gave rise to readings aloud [à haute voix]: the voice [voix] was always my father's, to which my mother listened respectfully, all the while 'pressing on' with some Penelopean knitting, and which was sometimes accompanied by the dry hiss of the paper cutter between two pages. This useless instrument (I soon learned that a mere kitchen knife was more efficient) consisted of an unsharpened blade whose handle was finished off with a kind of metal bird's claw holding a translucent agate marble; the temptation was great to unclench the claw so as to free the marble, but I have no memory of having yielded to it, nor of having successfully completed this operation; the memory, in that case, would doubtless have remained stinging. I seem here to be pastiching a page from *If It Die* … ,[73] but I'm doing no such thing, even if, in fact, this book also featured in our family library. I can't quite recall at what age I was admitted to these sessions, nor at which other I decided to excuse myself from them – all of it contained in a necessarily brief lapse of time. But I do remember a reading from Louis Bromfield's *The Rains Came* that stopped somewhat abruptly in the middle of a scene whose beginning seemed promising to me. I had, the following day, no great difficulty finding the contentious page, but the censured continuation was rather disappointing. The threshold of tolerance was then, at least with us, fairly low.

To this repertoire of printed matter my mother added for her personal use a few poems that she had, I know neither when nor whence, copied out by hand in a notebook that has now disappeared, like so many other relics of forgetfulness. Hugo, Lamartine, Musset, Desbordes-Valmore, Samain, Sully Prudhomme ('The vase where this verbena is dying … '), 'the' Arvers sonnet, Banville, Verlaine, Miguel Zamacoïs made up the collection, in a typically romantic and post-romantic key. Prior to my birth, my parents had had a first son, who died at his own. This precedent, which

---

[73] *Si le grain ne meurt*, by André Gide (1924).

wasn't hidden from me, inevitably convinced me, like Henri Beyle before me, that I was merely some kind of consolation prize. To put everything right, my mother, very early on, made me read and reread, from her notebook, the poem from the *Contemplations*, 'The Revenant', where a youngest child in the same circumstances one day whispered to his mother: 'It is I, do not tell.' Under the influence of a somewhat theosophical neighbour, my mother added to her primary Christianity a vague, and not very compatible, belief in reincarnation. The interpretation of this verse thus wasn't too arduous, and I have always known that for my mother, without, moreover, any depreciative nuance nor deficit of affection, I was (also) another's revenant, and that I had to live for two. I've applied myself to this as to the rest, not without occasionally wondering, like Mark Twain and Borges, whether I weren't the one who died before my birth, and he the one writing this sentence. Thanks to which – and perhaps to my star sign – I never feel quite alone. Which, paradoxically or not, feeds a certain tendency towards solipsism, while also protecting me against any egocentrism: 'Ego? Which one?'

Bien/Good. Enemy of the best.[74]

Bière/Beer. We aren't reminded often enough that Proust's favourite drink, even at the bar of the Ritz, was beer – iced, preferably. We overlook it because this fondness doesn't square too well with his oh so refined image. My father used and abused a saying whose origin eludes me, but whose meaning is clear: 'If you don't like it, we'll bring up some beer for you.' When I say that its meaning is clear, this is to neglect the fact that the remark, contradictorily, could comment just as much upon a manifest satisfaction (but in this case, it was preceded by an amusingly admirative exclamation: 'Well I never, if you don't like it … ') as upon a poorly concealed repugnance, and which it was appropriate to sanction; to neglect too, today, the uncertainty that then overcame me at the sight of the froth expanding in the glass, to the extent that 'bringing up [faire monter] the beer' primarily evoked in me that kind of rising

---

[74] Inversion of the French proverb 'Le mieux est l'ennemi du bien', 'The best is the enemy of the good'.

[montée], which already intrigued the hero of a hilarious joke reported or invented by Immanuel Kant.[75] I would have preferred: 'We'll froth up some beer for you', but the result was really the same: the beer arose from the cellar, then continued to rise in the glass, and besides for a long time I was only allowed it in its so-called 'mixed' state (with lemonade). Another popular expression, with a more specific application, and which had been turned into a song,[76] went: 'If you don't like it, don't put the others off.'

Big Band. With the exception of Duke Ellington, then of Count Basie, I've always had a culpably moderate liking for large-scale jazz formations. This reservation dates back to the end of the 1940s, where our rather old-fashioned, backward-looking [passéiste] and even Panassiéiste[77] preference for the New Orleans style (in fact, for small ensembles in the style of Armstrong's Hot Five or Hot Seven, or of Bechet's Feetwarmers) led us to describe as 'symphonic jazz' (to be understood as: 'industrial and commercial') anything exceeding seven or eight instruments. I came to understand much later that listening to records doesn't do justice to the big bands, whose orchestral expanse and visual display call for a live audience in a position to appreciate the spectacle of the aligned music stands, the gleam of the instruments, the soloists rising to take their chorus, each in turn between two riffs. However, it seems to me that a large venue, like that, in France, of the Olympia (which saw a few of them pass through), and however good the quality of its acoustics, diminishes by placing it at a distance the essential virtue of this type of performance, which pertains to the balance of its sonic depth. So for me the right scale is a medium-sized formation: 15 or so musicians performing in the restricted space – and not on a 'stage', but on the more confined podium – of a club.

[75] In his *Critique of Judgment* (1790), Kant recounts a joke about an Indian man at the table of an Englishman in Surat: astonished upon seeing a bottle of ale opened and the beer turn into froth and overflow, he explained his surprise thus: 'I am not at all astonished that it should flow out, but I do wonder how you ever got it in.'

[76] 'Si vous n'aimez pas ça (n'en dégoûtez pas les autres)' (1923), by Maurice Chevalier.

[77] Refers to Hugues Panassié (1912–1974), influential French jazz critic, record producer and impresario, enthusiastic promoter of traditional Dixieland jazz.

There, as long as you avoid the first two or three rows, you can enjoy a proper dose of spectacle and sonic volume: *what you hear is what you see*. The ideal formula may therefore be found between the smoke-black walls of the Village Vanguard, whose Monday evenings were presided over for 20 years (1966–1986) by the group belonging to the trumpet player Thad Jones and the drummer Mel Lewis, a small big band that was still for a few years, after the death of the first, led by the surviving second, and which never recorded much in the studio, which may account for my bias. Nowadays deprived of its two founding members, the orchestra keeps going as best it can, and ought to last as long as the site of memory [lieu de mémoire] where it performs. The privilege of the big bands (as of their counterparts in classical music) is that their formula can survive its elements indefinitely, like the ship *Argo*. It's certainly less often the case with small groups, more exposed to the vagaries of career and health, but all the same, since 1953, with or without Art Blakey, the Jazz Messengers quintet (trumpet, saxophone, rhythm section) has quite often changed its hull, its sails and its crew, not to mention the belated, and rather welcome, addition of a trombone. Always more welcome than you think, the trombone.

The fact is that on a Sunday evening in May, 1986, Blakey was giving one of his last concerts at the Apollo Theater, I can't recall with which group – perhaps still one of the final, but further expanded, avatars of the Messengers. It was above all an opportunity, become rare, to go and hear this music at that venue on 125th Street, between Seventh and Eighth Avenue – rather large as it happens, but once as famed in jazz terms as its neighbour the Cotton Club. The audience, nearly exclusively black, bore no resemblance to that of the Village clubs, intimate and elitist in their own way, and just barely mixed. Its 'response' was loud and unruly, in truth somewhat more audible for us than that to which it was responding, and which was for it little more than a pretext to express the joy of a vigorous *Mitsein*. This session was well worth the trip, but on the final clash of the cymbals we had to leave, and attempt the return home. The local crowd dispersed *pedibus*, but the small number of whites, as politically correct as it doubtless was, wasn't keen on risking a walk in ragged order to the next metro station, through what is the heart of the heart of the black neighbourhood. We thus remained prudently clumped together in front of the now darkened façade, awaiting the passage of taxis cruising for customers, quite rare at this advanced hour and in a place nowadays far less popular with tourists than in times past. The group dwindled slowly, and our final square considered itself more or less doomed to a grim mugging [un sinistre *mugging*]. A most exaggerated and passably ridiculous fear, I thought bravely once aboard an old yellow banger which lurched at full speed towards Bleecker Street, across the potholes and geysers of urban heating, a journey undoubtedly more dangerous than what it spared us. There were apparently no noteworthy assaults in Harlem that night: after all, it was already Monday.

Big Bang. Clearly, Austin didn't exhaust the combinatory potential of his famous formula: *How to do things with words.*[78] *How to do words with things*, it's classic literature; *How to do words without things*, it's modern literature; *How to do things without words*, it's speechless action (the true kind); *How to do things with things*, it's D.I.Y.; *How to do words with words*, it's a portmanteau word; *How to do words without words*, it's the art of mime; *How to do things without things*, it's the Big Bang. 'God, said Valéry, made everything out of nothing. But the nothingness shows through.'

Big One. In their comprehensible obsession with the next one, the residents around the San Andreas Fault hardly appreciate those all too frequent little premonitory tremors they don't call *small ones*. For the visitor, on the contrary, always a bit of a gawker, a stay without any telluric allusion would be insipid. Fortunately, it's really quite rare that a month should pass by without satisfying, however slightly, this perverse curiosity. As you learn quickly upon these shores, the mini-earthquake can appear in two distinct ways: the least enjoyable is the tremor properly so called, where the ground rises and falls quite sharply, enough for instance for the plates to make a dreadful rattle in their dresser. It's the time to stand under a doorway, or even to sit beneath a supposedly robust table, while praying to the Heavens, which physically have nothing to do with it, soon to have the opportunity to recount the incident, amplifying it just enough to make the story worthwhile. The other

---

[78] Austin's phrase and Genette's variations are all in English in the original.

variety presents as a more or less slight undulation more evocative of the movement of a small boat at sea. The latter clearly has my preference, and I admit to deriving from it a pleasure that I wouldn't say is unalloyed, because what's about to come is never certain, but where the immediate physical rapture offsets any anxiety about the future. When I stupidly mention it, I'm accused of having an unhealthy fondness for 'powerful sensations', but for me, on the contrary, it's a matter of a gentle sensation, whose erotic nature is too evident for it also to require any great commentary. I moreover ceased fairly quickly to mention it, following a conversation where my table companion discreetly confided to me that one of his relatives had perhaps experienced enjoyment of this sort just before paying for it with a heart attack.

In either case, the French term *tremblement de terre* and the English *earthquake* do not seem to me quite appropriate: the earth undulates, or shakes, or opens with a bang, but to remain faithful to my impressions I wouldn't say that it quakes. The spectacle of a quaking building is sometimes shown on television, but if you think about it, it isn't so much the building that is quaking: it's the camera, and/or doubtless the cameraman. When the earth moves, it is man who quakes.

Big Sur. We're told everything about the distant origins of this name (*El País Grande del Sur*), which is also that of a tiny village by its stream, the only one on the whole of this most sublime (it's now or never for this word) fraction of the Californian coast, but nothing really explains the highly evocative blend of an English adjective and a Spanish noun, even if this state's toponymic heritage (and of two or three others neighbouring it) is typically bilingual – multilingual if you include names borrowed from a few indigenous languages. This one implies that the place was discovered and named from the north: it was the *terra incognita*, then pretty much impenetrable by land for want of a road and inaccessible by sea for want of a port, south of Carmel. It is therefore from the north that one ought to approach it, by following, there's no choice, the State Highway 1, which now descends, a fabulous setting for a *road movie* in Cinemascope and Technicolor, from Fort Bragg to Los Angeles, and which is here almost constantly a cliff road carved directly above the Pacific. Yet it was coming up from the south, on my way back from a lecture at the UCLA, that I first discovered it in the spring of 1976, spending a night at the Fernwood Inn, which I seem to recall is hidden in one of the rare inhabitable clearings. I returned there more appropriately four years later, coming from San Francisco, in order to sleep at the Big Sur Lodge, following a drink on the vertiginous terrace of the Nepenthe, formerly the very second home of Rita Hayworth, and dinner at the restaurant of the Hotel Ventana. Fourteen spring times later, I took Babette, this time for a night at the same hotel – to my (poor) knowledge the most idyllic on the New Continent. This all sounds horribly touristy, but we must admit that Big Sur, whatever extent you grant it (for me, barely 100 kilometres between Carmel and Lucia: the rest is different in kind, and destined to a different type of tourism, with, in San Simeon, the Hearst Castle paraphrased by Orson Welles in *Citizen Kane*), is nothing but a narrow and sinuous road, squeezed between the ocean and the Santa Lucia coastal mountain range, with virtually no way of heading inland, three or four guest-houses, and a few uncomfortable houses at the shaded foot of the mountains, haunted by old hippies and older beatniks, the antique Harley-Davidson at the ready on its kick-stand, Epicurean hermits as was for 18 years here, a devil in Paradise, Henry Miller. Buried in their ravines, the few remaining redwood forests nearly escape one's view; what strikes me the most each time, plunging into a Mediterranean-blue ocean where the whales blow, are the rather nordic apple-green meadows of the foothills: *hills like green elephants*.[79] Thank God, no shadow of any palm tree.

Blindfold. When I was teaching, among other things, 'French' in secondary school, I quite often submitted for commentary, typed and mimeographed by myself, pages that I'd hand out to my pupils, marked with brown ink but detached from any context and with the author's name removed. I was certainly neither the first nor the last (I was unaware that the English philosopher I.A. Richards had done so in the 1920s) to propose this kind of 'blind' reading, as is more aptly said apropos of listening to records, and more specifically, under the term *blindfold test*, to jazz records. It's my

---

[79] Genette is here alluding to Ernest Hemingway's short story 'Hills Like White Elephants' (1927).

understanding that Richards' aim differed slightly from my own, as is shown by his account of this series of experiments in *Practical Criticism*, but I do know that my intention wasn't primarily to have my pupils *guess* the author's identity. I just wanted to free their reading from this knowledge, and from the preconceived stereotypes this knowledge was in danger of imposing. The riddle concerning the 'source' was a merely subsidiary question, which I'd invite them to consider as such, and to which moreover few among them would have been capable of responding, but this casual *épochè*, by depriving them of any extratextual data, forced them to pay keener attention to the historical (from the state of the language), stylistic, thematic and other characteristics of the proposed page: its reading became something like the deciphering of a succession of clues, in the manner of a criminal investigation – generally without (the discovery of a) guilty party. Incidentally, the exercise would become a kind of game, to which each would eventually lend themself without any ill humour, a non-negligible bonus of pleasure. Since my own ignorance wasn't so very remote from theirs, it was only a little later that I saw the relation between this perversely pedagogical experiment, an in principle wholly transitory *de-authorialisation* therapy, and the attacks of Péguy, Proust or Valéry on biographical determinism in general, and what would soon be called 'new criticism', 'formalism', 'structuralism' – with everything that would ensue for better and for worse. I'm only sorry, occasionally, that the *blindfold* condition of the thing should be so hard to respect in our practice of reading, but it's a little late to enclose critics, as Condillac did with his child guinea pig, in a salutary bubble of ignorance, and to impose upon them by this iron rule the criterion – for once, the word is compulsory – of *immanence*. This experiment was my first and final contribution to the progress of pedagogical practices.

Bonheur/Happiness. Flaubert (among others) has been credited with this three-point recipe: be stupid, selfish, and in good health. That helps, obviously, but in truth happiness isn't a state, just a feeling. Hence the fact that you are always, by definition, precisely as happy (or unhappy) as you believe yourself to be: *all sentiment is right.*[80]

---

[80] The quotation is from David Hume, *Of the Standard of Taste* (1757).

Bon sens/Common Sense. Descartes, as we know, saw in it the most widely shared thing in the world; Valéry commented: 'Nothing to brag about.'

Boomerang. During the summer of 1955, I killed time in what were then called picture houses, and I read with bewilderment a few editions of the *Cahiers du cinéma*, where the future heroes of the New Wave would practise their critical ingenuity. It was their so-called 'Hitchcock–Hawksian' period, an association I still find highly improbable. Even if hermeneutic agility can be applied to anything, the preferred object of their unfettered interpretations was in fact the work of Alfred Hitchcock, appointed as a moralist, a metaphysician and even somewhat as a theologian. I saw in him nothing of the sort (neither did he, I suppose, but he took unreserved advantage of the windfall), and perhaps to tell the truth not much else either. A reader's letter published a few weeks previously pushed my disagreement to the hilt, and I went to town on a kind of aggravated pastiche of what I took to be their extravagant flights of fancy, which I sent as a joke to the 'Readers' letters' page of the *Cahiers*, then edited and 'responded to' by François Truffaut. But mystification is a type of jesting to be exercised with circumspection, for it isn't always acknowledged as such. Despite its really very heavy dose of caricature, my letter was published in another edition of the *Cahiers*, and this misunderstanding today appears to me to be, in hindsight, premonitory of a few others: when you express yourself *cum grano salis*, contrary to all the laws of physics, nothing evaporates more quickly than that particular salt, and your intention may come back to you ballasted with one or two tons of serious-mindedness; this is called being punished for sins you believed not to have committed. Forty-five years later, the same text was reprinted in a catalogue for an exhibition devoted to said Alfred, and I had to reveal its initial intention to the organisers of this volume, who had no more detected it than had apparently Truffaut in his time. This reprint was in sum for me a chance belatedly to set the record straight, and I'm grateful to its unwitting instigators. But I said 'apparently' apropos of Truffaut's reaction, because in fact nothing proves that he was duped by the mystification: the very wording of his presentation ('Since we've been asked for it, a little metaphysics to finish off with') leaves room for doubt. If this doubt is founded, and the publication was merely a way of mystifying me in turn, I will have fallen into my own trap, an editorial remake of a cinematographic theme long predating Hitchcock, that of the biter being bit [l'arroseur arrosé[81]]. It's what you might call the boomerang-prank.

Boston. On Copley Square, the reflection of the neo-Romanesque Trinity Church on the façade, or rather on one of the sides of the prism of the very modern John Hancock Tower, is a marvellous summary of a century of western architecture. At night, Beacon Hill, a serene highly residential enclave in the heart of the city, for a moment makes me feel that this socially inaccessible neighbourhood would be the most enviable place to stay in the United States. It seems to me, moreover, that, if one leaves aside New York, which is much more, and Los Angeles, which is much less than a city, Boston might be, all in all, the most pleasant of all the (real) American cities: Chicago is by far the most beautiful (and in the world) for its architecture, but hardly bearable in all seasons, San Francisco is in many respects the most likeable, but it isn't quite a city: with the exception of a few streets in North Bay and the surroundings of Union Square, there are too many open spaces, too much air that's too crisp, too much sky that's too blue, too many hills that are too Russian [trop de montagnes trop russes],[82] too many horizons open on all sides for my slightly agoraphobic idea of urbanity. At any rate, it's a little late to delve deeper into these cavalier comparisons, and nothing is more futile than the memory of a fantasy.

At the door of the Gardner Museum, a young black man, handsome as Miles Davis at the same age, was reading a commemorative plaque very attentively. Visibly perplexed, he asked me, in English, the meaning of the word *tradition*. Before attempting to answer him in his language, I worried in my own about a definition of the thing and realised that it eludes any such attempt. I used my linguistic handicap as an excuse, exaggerating it if possible. His disappointment saddened me in the extreme, but the situation was now beyond remedy, and the place, apart from him and me, was perfectly deserted: this museum is, it must be said, consigned

---

[81] 'the sprinkler sprinkled'.
[82] 'Une montagne russe' is the French name for a rollercoaster; Russian Hill is a residential neighbourhood in San Francisco, named after its eponymous location.

to some distance from the city. I tried for a moment to guide this young man towards the interior, where someone ought to have been able to clarify this point for him, but he refused to follow me, perhaps believing that I wished to inflict a visit on him, while his curiosity bore merely upon a word, which he might just as well have encountered elsewhere.

Boulot/Job. An inadvertent candidate, in 1980, for a then prestigious chair, I had like everyone else to write the little booklet of self-satisfied self-presentation traditionally entitled *Titres et travaux* [*Titles and Works*]. Chore completed, I had then only to find someone to print it. The first in my suburb to whom I spoke, used to more literal announcements of death, had me explain the whys and the wherefores of the thing; then, referring me to a provincial colleague, he made by way of encouragement this disabused remark: 'What don't you have to do, these days, to get a job!' Once printed, I had to send the accursed booklet to the members of a kind of panel, then – with time for them to pretend to have skimmed through it – begin a series of ritual 'visits' that reserved its share of good and bad encounters. Among the most favourably disposed, a few cordially spared me a superfluous visit. The most hostile, as though in compensation, entertain you more readily: one of them even invited me for dinner in order to confide in me, over dessert, his preference for another candidate, and to assure me that I'd stand more chance upon my next attempt – from which however I was to refrain. The chattiest of my opponents kept me for an hour on the telephone, in order to explain to me in minute detail, in confidence, the reasons behind his contrary choice. Out of tokens (for I was calling him from a public phone box), I ended up agreeing with him, given that in a sense I thought he was right, and that after all I already had one, a job that is.

Boursier/Bursary Student. It was, I believe, my master Albert Thibaudet who first opposed the category of *bursary students* to that of the *inheritors*. Statistics notwithstanding, I can hardly entertain any doubt about my own place in this field. In sport, they call it having come 'through the qualifiers' ['issu des qualifications'], when it's not 'from an immigrant background' ['de l'immigration']. I occasionally recapitulate, with a pleasure tempered by a vaguely bad conscience, everything I owe to the much-vaunted republican meritocracy, apparently from having one day, in my first year of secondary school, successfully taken the *'Concours des bourses* [Bursary Competition]', if indeed it was so named, and even though one didn't yet speak, figuratively, of the 'social elevator [ascenseur social]', no doubt because of elevators, as of the rest, one speaks only when they are broken. A bursary student, then, up until the baccalaureate; a bursary student in *khâgne*,[83] for three years; supported by some equivalent of Social Security, for a few months of sanitorium, then for a year of convalescent care; again a bursary student, then a student–civil servant at Rue d'Ulm, and finally a civil servant tout court. A bursary student for life in short, I might have paid for it all with a long pedagogical ordeal, if I'd disliked the profession as much as I had in advance imagined. But I discovered very swiftly that teaching is pleasanter to give than to receive. And more profitable: the little I learned was initially, as a student, by deserting pointless classes in order to read in secret more instructive books, but above all and later, as a teacher, by preparing lessons that, a just return of things, were only so, I mean instructive, for me. A bursary student for life, but ever the autodidact.

Bovary. That Flaubert said or wrote 'Madame Bovary is me' is only too well known, enough at least for this identification to be made fit for every occasion. What is less well known is *to whom* he said, or wrote it, and for good reason: for what isn't at all known is that maybe he *never* said or wrote it. I would of course have great difficulty proving this, but I've been waiting for ages for someone to prove to me the contrary. Jean d'Ormesson, who like everyone else peddles the apocryphal phrase, parodies it nicely with 'Jean d'Ormesson is me'. I don't know whether Flaubert would have said as much. I occasionally say 'Frédéric is me', yet, despite appearances, this has got nothing to do with Flaubert.

Brahms. The pertinent question is not 'Do you like Brahms?', but 'Do you like, by Brahms (or by anyone else), such and such singular work?' To say 'I like X' or 'I hate Y' is based on a metonymic

---

[83] 'Khâgne' is a jargon term for the 'classes préparatoires littéraires', a post-baccalaureate academic programme undertaken by students of literature and the humanities seeking to access the École Normale Supérieure, Rue d'Ulm.

slippage from certain works to their author: no works (understood as the complete catalogue of an artist's productions) can be 'liked' or 'hated' in their entirety. Of course, I can, like everyone else, reservation internally made with respect to this necessary correction, continue to say (for instance) 'I like Stendhal' or 'Bruckner (Anton) is a drag', and I've no intention of not doing so, but I always find rather more meaningful the liking or aversion I feel for a given singular work, in breach of the liking, aversion or indifference the rest of the author's work inspires in me. I can clearly also see that this character of exception only really presents any interest (and, of course, pleasure) in the *positive* sense of a singular liking against a background of habitual aversion or constant boredom: the inverse case (if occasionally I do not like a given page by Beyle) can most often be reduced to a banal explanation implicating the author's loss of form: *quandoque dormitat* ... .[84] The wisdom of nations indeed states that we must judge people at their heights, and not in their potholes, and Lenin, presumably quoting some Russian proverb: 'An eagle can fly as low as a hen.' But to like what in all 'logic', or generic coherence, one ought not to like, as Swann loves Odette against his type, is a pleasure multiplied by its, let's say, paradoxical character. This powerful (and perhaps unreasoned) bonus of pleasure through the charm of the exception is expressed by Barthes when he concedes: 'By Stieglitz, I'm enamoured only (but madly so) of his best known photo, *The Terminal*.' It seems to me that the same, by Chopin, was enamoured only of the *Mazurkas*, the reason for which I think I can discern. I don't wish to linger here on a subject evoked elsewhere, nor to launch on my own account into a futile list of miraculous exceptions, but I can say – for instance and by preterition – that, by Melville, I'm enamoured only (but madly so) of *Bartleby*, which moreover turns out to have become his best known work, but also of *Benito Cereno* and of the impalpable story *The Piazza*. And by Conrad, only of *Youth*. And by Faulkner, only of *A Rose for Emily*. And by Lowry, only of the more or less autobiographical narrative *The Forest Path to the Spring*. But I wouldn't say in relation to them that a hen can fly as high as an eagle. The hidden part of the proverb is obviously that it admits

---

[84] 'quandoque bonus dormitat Homerus' (Horace), 'sometimes even good old Homer nods off'.

of no reciprocity: whoever can fly as high as an eagle *is* an eagle. I therefore still regard as such a Saint-Évremond[85] by whom I'm enamoured only of the *Conversation of Marshal d'Hocquincourt with Father Canaye*, for me an absolute masterpiece of classical prose.

Brooklyn Heights. You had to take, late in the afternoon, the metro line 2 or 3, which descends *schuss* from Harlem and the North Bronx following more or less, after 'Columbus Circle', the course of Seventh Avenue until 'Chambers Street', before, leaving line 1 to head due south towards 'South Ferry', branching off to the east. After 'Wall Street', there came a rickety dive beneath the East River. You'd catch your breath at 'Clark Street', whose lift leads straight to the lobby – and, perhaps, to the swimming pool – of the venerable Saint George Hotel. Meanwhile, night had almost fallen (it falls pretty quickly in New York, which lies, they never fail to remind you of it, upon the same latitude as Naples) and, even if you had expressly contrived your timing, you'd be surprised by the sudden dusk. At the end of Clark Street, you discovered at once the terraced promenade overlooking the East River, which afforded, back-lit and over the Expressway, the docks, the warehouses and manoeuvring cargo boats of the port of Brooklyn, the most beautiful side view of Manhattan's glistening tip. I speak of this today from memory, several years after my last visit. I know, like everyone else, what is henceforth missing from this spectacle, without being able to imagine very clearly what will come to fill the gap in an indefinite future. To tell the truth, I don't anticipate anything particularly good from the projects underway, burdened with symbolic intentions, and anyway I don't think I shall ever see their outcome, if outcome there be. Mark Twain said of New York: 'It will certainly be a beautiful city, when it's finished.' This doesn't seem likely.

Since the promenade looks towards the south-west, you saw from this angle, from left to right, the modern buildings that, rather welcomely, occupy the terrain between Walter Street and the estuary, towering above New York Plaza and a Jeannette Park whose eponymous heroine remains a mystery to me; then the two

---

[85] Charles de Saint-Évremond (1614–1703), soldier, hedonist, essayist and literary critic.

or three old-school skyscrapers, virtually the last to bespeak here the eclectic style of the beginning of the XXth century, behind and above which would thus rise the long regrettable and now lamented [regrettées] Twin Towers, those stock-still donjons all of whose charm consisted in the coupled effect uniting them in a play of shadow and light, like, in the approach to Combray, the bell towers of Martinville; then the still white and elegant Chase Manhattan Bank; then the now ageless gothic spire of the Woolworth, and, in response, the distinctive profile of Brooklyn Bridge. On the far right, beyond the low plains of Chinatown, SoHo, the Village and Chelsea, the Empire State Building receded, almost effaced by the distance. The real modern centre, *Midtown*, with the Rockefeller Centre, the Chrysler, the Pan Am, the UN headquarters and the rationalist glass cages between Park and Seventh, was completely lost to the eye. It was all as though the promenade had been deliberately orientated, at the time, to make visible what was, before the First World War, still tightly squeezed into its narrow and variously oblique streets to the south of Canal Street, the only part of Manhattan then really to have emerged.

The private houses lining the promenade and continuously enjoying this view are inevitably luxurious, obviously beyond the financial reach of mere mortals, and are moreover somewhat too ostentatious for a neighbourhood – a little draughtsboard of ten or so streets built from reddish brown sandstone (*brownstone*) at the turn, I imagine, of the century – that cultivates provincial sobriety and the shaded streets of an elitist haven, scorning these follies for the *nouveaux riches*, and leaving the glittering spectacle to the tourists. If you've come to live at Brooklyn Heights, it obviously isn't to gaze at Manhattan, where one goes only when necessary, as seldom as possible, and when invited by one's publisher.

Bruits/Sound. My favourite, since you've asked, is that of water running in the gutter above my window during nocturnal summer rain, when the storm is over Moutiers.

Campus. In the United States and Canada, I must have got to know around 30 of them, which is no record, as resident professor or speaker for an evening, and visited a good ten as an anonymous tourist. Raised as I was in *khâgne*[86] (and, what's more, Péguy's *khâgne*) with a definite disdain for the Sorbonne, I have never been particularly keen on university practices, even American ones, but 'the' campus can be, in itself, a memorable place. For me the charm of these places, when charm there is, pertains to the fact that their scattered buildings have grown one after the other on their English-style lawns, without any premeditated design, without symmetry, according to the vagaries of their functions, on a scale in keeping with the spaces available, and preferably in disorder. I have in truth no particularly sharp memory of Toronto's, of McGill's in Montreal, of Case Western Reserve's in Cleveland, of Penn's in Philadelphia nor of Buffalo's, and a rather unpleasant impression of Columbia's, really too mineral. I struggle a bit to describe as a *campus* the assembly of buildings that New York University has dispersed around and near Washington Square, right in the centre of Greenwich Village, and broadly, I imagine, by dint of successive annexations, including a Bobst Library where I have spent, ultimately, more hours than in any other library in the world. On Harvard's, which has some fine remains and a few fine additions, you may contemplate from every angle – as it were, for nothing could be less angular – a very heavy and very light bronze (or brass?) sculpture with vaguely foetal forms: *Large Four Piece Reclining Figure* (1972–1973) by Henry Moore. Yale's must indeed have originally had some provincial flavour, around a *green* typical of New England, with its three churches of three faiths and in three different styles (Gothic, Georgian and Federal), even though from the same period, but it has inevitably, over the centuries, expanded with often crude buildings, like those, devoted to the biggest sciences, which overwhelm a hill to the north of an original site (*Old Campus*) thankfully redeemed by the neo-Gothic Harkness Tower, Eero Saarinen's skating rink and the two Italianate creations that are its twin colleges, Morse and Ezra Stiles.

The most endearing are those that have preserved their rustic landscape and original style, neo-Gothic or Georgian, as in Baltimore (Johns Hopkins), Williamsburg (William & Mary) in Virginia, Princeton in New Jersey or, better still, Bryn Mawr in Pennsylvania, for me the most seductive of all. Cornell, to the far

[86] See note 84.

north of the State of New York, isn't a campus in the middle of the countryside, it is a vast countryside – hills, dells, rivers, lakes of all kinds – turned campus, and moreover largely 'dedicated', among other things, to agricultural research: it certainly doesn't want for hectares. The university of Virginia, like its own Monticello house and the Declaration of Independence, is a characteristic work of Thomas Jefferson, and thus of our neoclassical Enlightenment, but the small teachers' houses, along the large grass pathway, have a more easy-going appeal. That of Wisconsin in Madison, monumental on the shores of Lake Mendota, has the merit of proximity to a few masterpieces by Frank Lloyd Wright. To Rice (Houston), I went a year too early for the opening of the Menil Collection, but not for the Rothko Chapel, as lugubrious as one could wish. Berkeley upon its hill, around the little stream called Strawberry Creek, and even Stanford on its plain, are Northern Californian, which says everything, and UCLA Southern Californian, and with a real whiff of Sunset Boulevard – and for good reason. Midway between them, upon a lawn of the Santa Barbara campus, at the edge of a lagoon a stone's throw away from the ocean, I read this sign which, I hope, may still be found there: *Please do not disturb plants, animals, or other people.*

But the most pleasant thing about these universities is often the name they bear. This name is owed far more rarely than in Europe to the city or town in which they are found, like New York, Pittsburgh or Chicago, or Princeton, Swarthmore, Bryn Mawr, Wellesley. The names of States often designate universities, public or private, for which any reference to the city or town is incidental: Michigan (in Ann Arbour), Wisconsin (in Madison), Pennsylvania in Philadelphia or Penn State at University Park, Virginia (in Charlottesville), Colorado (in Boulder), Massachusetts (in Northampton), Texas (in Austin), North Carolina (in Chapel Hill); some of them, like Wisconsin or Colorado, possess moreover more than one campus, in more than one city; this is eminently the case of the University of California, whose flagship, Berkeley, bears the name of its city only as a convenient abbreviation: its real title is 'University of California, Berkeley', also shortened to UCB, just as the Los Angeles campus is known as UCLA. But my favourite names owe nothing to their location, and everything to their founder, benefactor or other kind of godparent: for example Harvard, Yale, Brown, Cornell, Rice, Emory, Brandeis, Johns

Hopkins, Smith, Vassar, Stanford, William & Mary – an homage to the royal couple. To tell the truth, I'm not quite sure about these various sponsors' respective roles. I believe at least to have seen at Duke the statue of the nicotine magnate, who is supposed according to legend to greet with a nod every student still a virgin, and who for this reason – that's to say for the contrary reason – is often himself greeted with a prudent detour.

The tintinnabulating practice of the carillon is very present on the campuses of New England, on Yale's at least, where it in no way upsets the local colour. It sounds more bizarre beneath the Californian sunshine, but the pseudo-Venetian campanile of Sather Tower, at Berkeley, houses an altogether charming one at its apex. I was there *in vivo* for an impromptu concert given by a musician student – enough to feel certain that this instrument, with its cords and its pedals of every kind, doesn't have too much reason to envy, in means and in difficulties, our church organ keyboards. Since then, I've found it rather difficult to bear – among other things – its absence in French universities. They really should think about addressing this shortcoming, once they've addressed all the others.

Cancale. In the 1940s, a certain family home in Éragny represented for me, Little Good-For-Nothing[87] in pursuit of Grand Meaulnes,[88] the very height of bourgeois comfort, with, on the ground floor, its flag-stoned living room, furnished with French windows and a baby grand piano oddly painted white and blue, like a Delftware tile. A vast lawn overlooked from a fair height the course of the Oise; I'd never imagined that one might devote so extensive an area to the luxury of a plant as little edible as grass. That this family should be 'large' (three boys of whom one was my classmate at Pontoise, and two girls for whom I had an equitably silent soft spot) also expressed a kind of class superiority: judging by my own, it had never occurred to me that even poor families could be numerous, and to see that each of the five children had their own bedroom and, especially, to hear

---

[87] Allusion to *Le Petit Chose* (*Little Good-For-Nothing*) (1868), by Alphonse Daudet.
[88] Allusion to *Le Grand Meaulnes* (*The Lost Estate*) (1913), by Alain Fournier.

them address their parents as *'vous'* [vouvoyer[89]] confirmed for me my sociological analysis.

Some years later, coinciding stays in treatment and aftercare led me to encounter this family again through another of its sons, whom I undertook to recruit into we shall soon know what, no doubt to efface via politics the erstwhile social differences. He resisted for a few months, but would, paradoxically or not, ultimately remain there longer than I did, and perhaps always bore me a grudge for having got out. Their holiday home, in Cancale, in fact the permanent residence of a delightful grandmother, accommodated a few young boarders in a vast attic converted into a dormitory. The few rare evenings too rainy to allow an outing *chez* Titane, the welcoming and loud-mouthed owner of a bistrot-crêperie on the ramparts of Saint-Malo, we spent in a small country lounge hung with toile de Jouy, listening 'as a family' to songs by Brassens, and I discovered that the respectful use of personal pronouns [le vouvoiement respectueux[90]] didn't preclude a certain form of free speech: I can still hear one of the boys say to his mother, in a conversational tone, and incurring neither refutation nor rebuke: 'But Mother, everyone knows that you are frigid [que vous êtes frigide] ... .'

Cancale's location afforded us, at any time and whatever the state of the tide, an accessible beach or cove. It sufficed to consult the timetables, and to decide between Port-Mer and Port-Briac, to the east of le Grouin, to the west le Verger, la Guimorais, le Guesclin with its small inhabited fort a few strokes from the shore, some more favourable at high tide, others at low tide, not to mention le Grouin itself, whence one could go, by kayak, all around the Île des Landes, a haven for seabirds. One could also, at high tide, dive straight from the tip of le Hocq and swim, beneath the cries of the seagulls, all the way to the famous Rock. I recall that one day, while one of us, a less than hardy swimmer, thought he was about to sink bang in the middle of the oyster farms, we believed to be encouraging him to survive by yelling out: 'Think of Stalin!' This exhortation was somewhat lacking in relevance, for nothing in

---

[89] In French, the use in the singular of the second-person 'vous' pronoun (*vouvoiement* as opposed to *tutoiement*) denotes formality, politeness or respect.

[90] See note 89.

our golden legend attested to the excellence in swimming of 'the man we loved the most'. An invocation to the other Helmsman, hero of the Yang-tsé, would have made more sense, and perhaps been more effective, but Mao's thought wasn't yet at its zenith. In short, we had to resort to the less politically correct assistance of an oyster vessel, passing by just a boat hook away.

In the distance, and much too low on the horizon for us really to be able to see it, the Chausey archipelago, to which access for tourists, still restricted, depended rather on the ports of Saint-Malo or Granville, was at Cancale the business of fishermen alone, who'd occasionally embark on their motor boats, and for a fee, a few additional passengers. One July day, seeking an unexplored beach, we treated ourselves to a day trip to the largest of these islands. The day was without the shadow of any cloud, and I hadn't deigned to take a hat. On the way back, at first I felt my head erupting, then nothing at all for two or three days, which I spent in the attic, it really must be said, between life and death. Upon waking, I was apprised, on the fisherman's behalf, of these words of intended consolation: 'Just as well it was a nice day!'

Canopy. I can still see the shoes fitted with lateral spurs on their inner side extended into a semicircle (the English, ever practical, just says *climbing spurs*) thanks to which workers responsible for the maintenance of electrical and telegraph lines scaled their poles, then made of wood; and the strap, a little but not too slack, which held them against the pole, and which they had to make slide, or jump, with each vertical step towards the top or, task completed, towards the bottom. I've since learned in my favourite magazine that the botanists of the North Californian coast, in order to climb to the summits of their redwoods (in French, *Sequoia sempervirens*, not to be confused with the *Sequoiadendron giganteum* of the Sierra Nevada: the first is on average the highest of trees, around 100 metres, the second is merely the oldest: two to three thousand years give or take [et des broquilles]), do not make use of said spurs, which might damage their bark, but rather of a complex system of ropes, carabiners, saddles and harnesses adopted from mountain climbing, which I've never really understood a great deal about. And that the bushy canopy of these giant trees, whose crowns, however, avoid touching each other (they call this the 'shyness of trees'), form a second floor of nourishing earth at something like

36 floors above the first (our own), and where grow in mid-air, but amid the soil brought by the wind, all manner of shrubs, among which certain blueberry, or huckleberry trees, whose fruit is it seems succulent, and whose name, you see, serves as a first name for one of Mark Twain's heroes. They still have to be picked though.

Since the word *canopée* (canopy in English) doesn't feature in my Petit Robert dictionary (no more for that matter than does *broquille*,[91] which came to me from way back), lovers of etymological strolls as poorly equipped as I am will find its principal stages under *canapé* [couch]. It's quite eloquent; I shall summarise while pruning: originally, the Greek *konops* (found in Aeschylus, Herodotus and Aristotle), which means 'mosquito', hence *konopeion*, in Latin *conopium* or *conopeum* (present in Horace), which means 'mosquito net' and, by extension, 'bed-curtain'; since a bed-curtain can only hold up when hung from something, the word comes, at I don't really know which stage of its evolution from ancient Greek to the modern languages, to mean (metonymically) 'four-poster bed'. Californian or Amazonian, the forest canopy is fairly clearly (metaphorically) a four-poster bed produced by nature. From an *o* to an *a* (or even from two *o*s to two *a*s in *canapé*, whose relation to all of this bears no mystery), the vocalic shift is commonplace, vowels being what they are, that's to say capricious, indeed superfluous. I hope the vegetal canopy provides a home to, among other insects, a few mosquitoes, which would bring us full circle, but I haven't had the opportunity to verify it for myself: *doctus cum libro*.

Carte/Map. I don't know what brings to mind this faintly sexist and two-pronged riddle: 'Dear friend [Chère amie], do you know what a woman's second best quality is? – Tell me the first one, to start with – It's never asking idle questions.' The second, obviously you'll have guessed it, is knowing how to read a map. In the spring of 1980, the (Northern) California climate was once again deserving of its reputation: light, crisp, radiant, and the overlong poppy-red Chevrolet I'd hired for want of anything better ventured upon all the roads of the coast and the interior.

---

[91] A small piece of wood, also a worthless piece of jewellery, by extension something of very little value or an insignificant amount of something: 'et des broquilles', as above in this passage.

My regional road map, like all its counterparts, took its qualifier literally, reducing the territory to a schematic grid of fine broken lines, numbered with insignia varying according to the roads' administrative status (*state*, *interstate*, etc.). Used to the analogical, almost picturesque, portrayals of French maps, I had, as ever, some difficulty in mastering this type of representation simplified to the point of abstraction. Charlotte, on the other hand, found her way around marvellously and was unerring in her role as navigator, all the while distancing herself from what was in her eyes my excessively touristy curiosity. As a good American, she could identify at any moment the four cardinal points, not only within the urban grid but also in the depths of the countryside. I shared this ability, but I'd never thought of having to share it with a person of her gender. There was nothing like this country for confounding one's prejudices.

The Californian countryside is moreover never deep, and is often as bucolic as the Vexin of my childhood, only enriched with vineyards, giant sequoia and silvery mountain streams. I'm in no danger of forgetting, among others, a certain coastal road journey, to the north of the Golden Gate, overlooking the bay between Sausalito and Tiburon, nor a longer trip into the *Gold Country*, zigzagging through the western foothills of the Sierra Nevada approached from the south at Sonora and continuing north all the way to Coloma, there where everything began on the 24th January 1848 (*Gold in the American River!*), then up to Auburn, and a night-time return via Sacramento, the sleepy capital. This region may well have been at the root of the state's fortunes, nothing could be more different from the familiar image of California. Its small roads, and even the well-named (in memory, I suppose, of the boom year) State Highway 49, which crosses its full length from north to south, cares little about the rectilinear route suggested by the maps, and meanders nonchalantly between hills sometimes furrowed for more than a century by the brutal technique of hydraulic drilling. Here and there, a multicoloured and mismatched row of tunnel-shaped letterboxes, exposed to just anyone but respected by everyone under the threat of federal punishment, betrays the invisible presence of isolated houses whose inhabitants scarcely meet save under this postal banner: *Howdy neighbour!* Certain ghost villages have been resuscitated for the benefits of tourism, thanks to the rustic inns, commemorative monuments (one of which, at

Angels Camp, is devoted to the acrobatic frogs celebrated by Mark Twain), old style *general stores* like those in westerns, and 'souvenir' or (there's a slight difference) *antique* stores. The difference matters, for I still have in a corridor, found in a second-hand shop in Sutter Creek, a kind of window box in crude blue opaline glass whose weight, if not fragility, troubled my travelling companion as she estimated the excess baggage of my return flight.

The lightest thing was not to be taken back. *A road is a woman: soft shoulders, dangerous curves ... :* B.B. King it was who thus lauded, paraphrasing public safety warnings, the analogies between the shape of the road and the sinuous geography of the female body, and this metaphor was insistent during the days of a doubly sunlit sentimental *road movie* – until dusk, when the horizon of clouds burgeoning far over the Pacific too often conceals from you the green ray of the final dip.

Castelet. Our way to the station ran alongside the grounds of a dwelling with a neo-Gothic turret, no doubt of recent construction and somewhat ridiculous-looking, which we would always call, perhaps because an enamel plaque decreed this appellation, 'Le Castelet'. In fact, there was in our semi-rustic vicinity, to the east the 'Château' way (a far nobler edifice, thus more discreet, and even, from this angle, half-concealed by the trees in its park) and to the west the 'Castelet' way, and I didn't doubt that the latter name was also a generic term: 'a' castelet was quite clearly a little castle. I've just noticed that the word doesn't feature in the Littré dictionary of the French language, and I infer from this that 'Castelet' pertained to a toponymic fancy certainly more pretentious but just as arbitrary as the neighbouring 'Sam Suffy'[92] or 'Do-mi-si-la-do-ré'.[93] So if the grand château was hidden behind a stone wall crowned with miserable bits of glass, the little castelet blew its trumpet upon the hillside looking down on the Fin-d'Oise quarter. It was also distinguished by a kind of old-fashioned wind turbine, such as one sees in certain Westerns, a squeaky and gangling but rather pleasant insect, whose rear

[92] Phonetically equivalent, in French, to 'ça me suffit', 'it's good enough for me'.
[93] Phonetically equivalent, in French, to 'domicile adoré, 'beloved home'.

side weather vane confirmed for me the diagnosis of a moistened finger concerning the wind's direction. I assume that it wasn't on the other hand used to produce any electric 'current', but more simply to raise water from a well reserved for the usage of the little-lords-of-the-manor; I assume this today in the absence of any guaranteed memory, but back then I must have known it through hear-say. It was also, for us, a kind of symbol of seigneurial affectation, like the dovecotes of the Ancien Régime. The castelet's domain spread, in effect, quite far, since it spanned our street, over the part of it leading down to the other station (Conflans-Fin-d'Oise), by means of a kind of private bridge whose even more feudal privilege I found especially impressive.

Cauchemars préférés/Favourite Nightmares. I borrow from Borges this amiable oxymoron, in order to designate dreams whose affective colouring is somewhat undecided, but whose recurrence suggests that I find in them some unconscious and perverse pleasure:

I'm again taking an exam, with the certainty, moreover well founded, that I shall now fail it, and the feeble consolation of having already successfully passed it.

I'm again teaching in a provincial secondary school, having God knows why requested, and God knows how obtained for this purpose a year's secondment; anguished by the timetable, I find myself skipping most of my classes; I haven't given any assignments for months, nor marked the only one that I did give.

I have to give a conference, I can't find the text, I improvise, and I understand nothing of what comes out of my mouth.

I'm contemplating a superb, ever radiant landscape, and I notice, with annoyance, that I have yet again forgotten my camera.

I park my car in town, and I can *never* find it again.

I wish to turn on the light, and all the bulbs emit one that is *almost* useless.

I'm descending a long stairway, not one step at a time, nor even several at a time, but by sliding upright along their edges, as though the soles of my shoes were a skateboard (I'm not, for that matter, certain that a skateboard would allow such a manoeuvre). This one is in fact quite simply enjoyable.

I find myself before a nonetheless familiar piece of equipment, a computer, television or hi-fi system, unable to turn it on, lost in an incomprehensible and ineffectual screen, dashboard or manual.

I wish to make a telephone call, but I can't manage to dial the number on an old-fashioned device whose rotary mechanism foils my every attempt – this one doubtless dates back to my first real telephonic experience, which was however quite late.

I'm attempting to finish packing suitcases for a trip, or boxes for a house move, but there's always one final object needing to be packed, which renders my departure forever asymptotic.

Another, of a type that might be called metaleptic, occurs when, awoken too early and having turned on the radio, I again fall half asleep, and dream that I turn off the radio, and that it refuses – and with reason – to fall silent. Sometimes, in this remainder of somnolence, I hear a talking programme (music doesn't suit these occasions): I thus dream that I'm in the studio, and that I take part, mutely, in the programme (I never dream that I'm invited to speak). After years of this oneiric participation, the 'thing itself' actually happened to me: one day, in the middle of a literary programme on Radio-France, a short news bulletin intervened, during which I didn't have the presence of mind to leave the studio. I thus remained in my seat, and three or four journalists, without taking offence at my indiscreet presence, settled down around me, and went in turns about their business. It was one of the occasions when, rather than dreaming a moment of my life, I lived a moment from my dreams.

Occasionally, too, I dream that I'm pinching myself and, of course, this wakes me up. Besides, in general, as soon as a nightmare becomes truly unbearable, I channel-hop.

Cave. I read somewhere that Aristotle would have loved the cinema. There's nothing audacious about this conjecture: the late seventh art was by very far the most 'mimetic' of all. What the author should have added is that at any rate Plato would certainly have loathed, or rather condemned, and banished from the City, this particular art form – along with a good many others. Let's reread the VIIth book of *The Republic*: the prisoners in the cave, backs to the light, and who can see only the shadows projected onto the far wall-screen, are evidently our cinema audiences. I'd be most surprised to be the first to hazard this comparison.

Cavistes/Wine Merchants. In the seventies, Jean-Baptiste Chaudet worked on Rue Geoffroy-Saint-Hilaire, and was thought to be the best wine merchant [caviste] in Paris. He was definitely the most distinguished, the most talkative, and also the best stocked in white and red wines from Savoie, his province of origin. Another Jean-Baptiste, but Besse, and from Corrèze, worked a little further up, somewhere on the Montagne Sainte-Geneviève. His stock was a *cave* [cellar] in the literal sense, or rather a vertical series of *caves*, a gloomy well into which, with each customer, he'd disappear for long minutes on a ladder as narrow as it was steep, and which appeared to descend at least to the level of the Seine. He'd emerge therefrom with a grunt, equipped with one or two bottles which he'd dust off with a wave of the beret he removed on no other occasion. The choice of these bottles was rather his than yours, but you could trust him, for his taste was as sure as his foot, and his recommendation was unanswerable: 'If you don't like it, bring it back to me, I'll finish it without you.'

Champs/Fields. During a radio debate, in the sixties, and thus well before the 'Sokal affair', with two already famous philosophers (I'm not sure which producer had the idea of gathering so lopsided a trio), one of them pointed out to me that I borrowed imprudently from the vocabulary of the physical sciences. Rather taken aback, I asked him which specific borrowing he was referring to: 'Well, he replied, you've just spoken of the literary *field*.' Increasingly taken aback, but somewhat disappointed (so that's all it was), I found the strength to ask him how the word *field* could *initially* be a term proper to the physical sciences. I have forgotten his answer, which perhaps isn't, on my part, a sign of particularly good will.

Chevet. At the end of the fifties, then the only secondary boys' school in Le Mans was found roughly on the left flank of the Saint-Julien cathedral – the right flank, therefore, for whoever approached it from the rear, Place des Jacobins, as we did upon each arrival from Paris, climbing up from the station via the avenue du Général-Leclerc, Place Aristide-Briand and what wasn't yet Rue

François-Mitterrand. An ever striking approach, past the grandiose Gothic chevet that dominates the whole square, and particularly the part devoted, on certain days of the week, to a cattle market. You had to cross this market, squeezed between two cows' bellies, in order to reach the little door on Rue Robert-Trigier, climb a stairway narrow and steep like the one from my childhood, and find yourself in one of the school courtyards. There began the pedagogical area, where the dual vicinity of church and cattle could still be felt. The church side of things was prolonged at least, in the very courtyard of what had once been an Oratorian college, by a former chapel that housed for one or two years our little class, and where I celebrated, among others, Stendhal, Baudelaire and Proust. The cattle side of things subsisted in truth only in the bad jokes of patronising or disgruntled teachers, who thought it necessary to allude to it so as to oppress their students, or their colleagues. The *hypokhâgne*[94] was the only mixed class. It wasn't a barracks. One of the female students, of Laotian origin, was not without reason nicknamed '*Patte de velours* [Velvet Glove]',[95] and the others to match.

The old Le Mans, perched on the hillside overlooking the Sarthe, between the cathedral and the Saint-Benoît church, hadn't yet been subjected to the work of 'rehabilitation' that has since made it a stylish tourist area. It was a large sleepy village, where the grass grew in carelessly paved streets. Before the façade of Saint-Julien, the semi-circular forecourt was somewhat disreputable: it was said that the diocese had long been the proprietor there, and thus indirectly the beneficiary, of one or two now disused brothels. On the short lane leading from the school to this deserted forecourt, an unassuming café served as a glorified canteen for two or three Parisian teachers in transit. An old radio set, though poorly tuned, broadcast punctually, at lunch-time, the political editorial by Jean Grandmougin, chanted in amplitude modulation, on Radio-Luxembourg, like a muezzin's call.

I'd meet there, on and off, my colleague Pascal Fieschi, who spent, like me, one or two nights a week in Le Mans, he in a room

---

[94] 'Hypokhâgne' is the first year of preparatory classes (khâgne) for students seeking to enter the École Normale Supérieure.
[95] The French expression 'faire patte de velours' means 'to turn on the charm'.

rented above the café. My own, a 'homestay', was a little further to the north, opposite the girls' secondary school also known as 'Bellevue'. The host was a family of the most right-thinking kind, which seemed rather aggrieved to be accommodating, however spartanly, a member of the overly lay *Éducation Nationale*, a member who was supposedly disbelieving, which was well judged, or even subversive, which was no longer really the case, if ever it had been other than in intention.

A Corsican with flat hair, olive skin and an intense gaze, possessed of a demeanour eliciting from himself a comparison with Falstaff, Fieschi was doubtless the most unlikely philosopher you could encounter prior to the invention of a '1968 philosophy [pensée soixante-huit]' which he probably wouldn't have valued very highly. His pedagogical method dumbfounded his students, galled our principal and a few inspectors, and earned him on behalf of our colleagues a contempt founded upon occasionally inaccurate rumours. His lessons were but distantly related to a discipline whose mysteries he kept carefully to himself. Instead, he'd tell of pitiful puns and approximate spoonerisms (which he'd write neatly on the board for the edification of his students, and my own perplexity when I went in after him), daily life, the passing of time, the weather [du temps qui passe, du temps qu'il fait], the 'Fantasy' poets of the turn of the century (Raoul Ponchon, Paul-Jean Toulet, Tristan Derème), the *Centuries* by Nostradamus, and the superiority of Italian cuisine: 'The only country, he averred, where bread is made from flour, and wine from grapes.' But his love of this country never took him further than San Remo: it sufficed for his happiness to have placed the border between himself and the French Administration – especially its fiscal branch.

Ever late with a few tax instalments and even with a few declarations of income, thereby perpetually incurring garnishments from his pay, his main expenses known to me, meaning associated with the two or three days of his weekly presence in Le Mans, consisted of taxi rides, and of semi-lavish meals from which his waistcoat profited as much as did his stomach, and to which he occasionally invited some young person whose turn of phrase and firmness of calf he esteemed, moreover fully satisfied with this modest form of intimacy. For my benefit, the more sober lunches at said canteen, or the extra rillettes and cheese which he'd invariably greet as 'joy on a platter', all of it toasted with a dry white come from the slopes of the Loir, on a little square at the foot of the old town, were enlivened instead with long quotations from Saint-Simon, whom he knew almost by heart, or by Hugolian tirades: with reference to my supposed acquaintance with the Basque country, he'd recite for me in one breath 'El Cid in Exile'[96]: *Being sons of Basque blood, they have this advantage … .*

There followed about 40 stanzas, of which I can only recall a few snippets, and I'd feel bad if I needlessly cheated on this point by resorting to the printed text. He'd occasionally also recite, still for my benefit, but in their original language, poems by Leopardi, by Carducci, by Pascoli, the best part of which would elude me, and which I always confused. Himself a poet, he'd published in 1943 a collection entitled *Air Bubbles*, a copy of which I still own, and in 1945 another entitled *Fun Fair*, from which I copied a few pieces by hand, in the absence of a print run. They had a muted, almost hushed, lyricism, somewhere, if one has to place him, between Marceline Desbordes-Valmore, the Supervielle of *Forgetful Memory* and the Aragon of *Heartbreak*. There or elsewhere, he really wasn't fond of being placed, and he didn't take too well a kind of pastiche after his manner that I was imprudent enough to offer him by way of tribute, sincere nevertheless.

From his years – belated and recent, following a long stint in more humble pedagogical positions – of studying for the *agrégation*[97] there'd remained a friendship with Gilles Deleuze, about whom I then knew nothing else. He was eager to introduce us and organised a dinner in a small Parisian restaurant situated just a short walk away from the main door of the (now vanished) Vaugirard abattoirs. I have forgotten, if ever I knew, the reason for this choice, but I do remember the contrast between our intellectual assortment, already bizarre in itself, and the entirely professional clientele bustling around us. Deleuze's speech was seductive anyhow, but it was all the more charming as it wove its way, *mezza voce*, through this noisy concert of horse-dealers and butchers. I have never quite been able to detach from this first meeting my reading, much later, of *Difference and Repetition*. Quite at the beginning of my civil and

---

[96] By Victor Hugo: 'Le Cid exilé' features in *La Légende des siècles* (*The Legend of the Ages*) (1877).
[97] The 'agrégation' is the highest level competitive examination for service in the French education system.

professional life, I was for my own part, save for a brief political itch in the spring of 1957, deep in a period of writing latency, and I could see neither a reason nor a way to exit this phase. Fieschi was convinced to the contrary, and every week, sipping his second green Chartreuse, the back of his left hand held flat beneath his chin in an attempt not to waste a single drop thereof, he'd assure me: 'I know that you'll write. If I were as certain of waking up alive tomorrow morning, I'd sleep easy.' At the start of the school year in 1959, I don't know by what administrative miracle, he was appointed to a secondary school in Paris, which deprived him of the contemplation of a few young provincial calves, but spared him some travel and lodging expenses. A few years thereafter, one morning, alive or dead, he quite simply forgot to wake up.

Chèvrefeuille/Honeysuckle. Avens [La benoîte] delighted Jacqueline, but only by virtue of its name,[98] just as Queneau marvelled at finding, on restaurant menus, the mention of: 'quenelles'. Her favourite plant was in fact, and for a thousand reasons, the honeysuckle. Of this word, the etymology seems to me to be as mysterious as it is obvious. I doubt that its leaf attracts goats [chèvres] more than any other, as 'catnip' (valerian) is supposed to attract cats – which it doesn't always do, I've been able to verify this a hundred times. Its leaf isn't goat-shaped either, nor is its flower, except in its horns. Do you want to evoke the capricious appearance of its branches? That would be well observed, but it so happens that *caprice* comes from the Italian *capriccio*, whose origin has nothing to do with the Latin *capra*, 'goat', but with the Italian *capo*, derived from the Latin *caput*, 'head' (*caporiccio*: 'bristly-haired [tête hérissée]', whence perhaps 'which makes the hairs of one head stand up [qui hérisse les cheveux sur la tête]'), as does *capiteux* [*heady*], which suits quite well, not the appearance, but the scent of this flower. Unfortunately, this adjective (I'm cutting through a fibrous history) initially meant 'pig-headed' (obstinate), before arriving, in sum, at 'heady' (intoxicating). And, on the other hand, the (Low) Latin *caprifolium* also designates the privet, a shrub which has nothing capricious in its

---

[98] As we later learn (see 'Manor'), 'Benoît' is Jacqueline's family name.

appearance or intoxicating in its scent. Let us pity once again the lovers of botany and etymology.

Chiens/Dogs. The other day, on the bus. An old lady with her dog, a tiny mongrel. As often, the 29 is brought to a standstill on Rue Michel-le-Comte by a van in a more or less advanced state of delivery. The traffic jam drags on. Madame is losing patience. The dog keeps quiet. Too quiet for her, she's exasperated, and really must take it out on someone. She shakes the dog and says: 'Of course, you, it makes you laugh, but mummy isn't laughing at all.' Another (or the same), later, walking along Rue de Turenne. Her dog (the same?) apparently isn't obeying as it ought. She, severe but pedagogical: 'What have I just said?' It charms me by surprise: this was the question that, beneath the cedar, Jacqueline would ask at every turn to assure herself of her audience's attention; the right answer was not, as I initially thought, to repeat the question. A few paces away, an Afghan hound we called Zino, whose stupidity, it seems, was in keeping with its breed, strove without success to catch butterflies. We'd sometimes throw for him a ball or a stick, which he'd watch land with no reaction beyond an expression of intense indifference. At this game manifestly bereft of meaning for him, he'd nonetheless never take offence, and was never the first to weary of it. Following which his sleep would be troubled by dreams whose tenor forever eluded us.

For two weeks, holding a seminar in Madison, Wisconsin, there was in my classroom, on the first row, a dog, permitted there because he was accompanying a non-seeing female student. It was a magnificent Labrador, which followed my speech with stupefying attentiveness. I must confess that I spoke primarily for him, feeling a compulsion to satisfy a curiosity that was for me so unusual. When the perilous moment of the 'discussion' came, he never turned to look towards the speaker, but kept his eyes fixed upon me, manifestly wondering what indeed I would come up with in response. I ought perhaps to have asked him: 'What have I just said?'

Chosier/Container of Things. I find it unjust that a word so necessary should, in the French language, be a sort of *hapax*: 'Used only, affirms Littré, in the proverbial expression: *Come, come, when you are grown up, you will see that there are many things [choses] in a container of things [chosier]*.' And, furthermore, I'd never encountered elsewhere this 'proverbial expression', which Vialatte attributes more precisely to Rabelais, nor consequently this term that refers, however, to the vastest of objects, since the entire universe is nothing but an immense *chosier.* Or maybe, if we wish to split ontological hairs, a *chosier* of *chosiers.*

Chute. In order to designate what we name thus, English uses *fall* (one says *Niagara Falls*), and even Adam's, from which we have all fallen, is still or already a *fall.* Doubtless adopted from Latin by way of the Normans' French, the English *chute* has a more modest and technical use: it represents our *toboggan* (which derives, for its part, but not directly, from the Algonquian – a false friend, of course: the English *toboggan* signifies 'luge'), and any means fit to spare us a pointless or dangerous vertical journey: in the United States, *garbage chute* denotes for instance our *vide-ordures*, and *mail chute* a device of which I know no equivalent in France, and which in every fairly modern and slightly elevated building guides your letters directly towards the outbound mail basket, which awaits them in the restricted access service area on the ground floor or in the basement – very restricted access: it's at the least a federal crime to enter there when the *mail man* is distributing into the individual pigeon holes the post arrived in its grey canvas bags. On the 11th floor of Washington Square Village, beside the elevator, that's to say in the middle of a corridor a good 100 metres long, I therefore had at my disposal a well-polished copper-mouthed *mail chute*, which I never used without fearing some unfortunate thrombosis. This was sworn to be impossible, but I remained suspicious, if not uneasy: outgoing or incoming, the *US Postal Service* was for me a bottomless pit of anxiety.

Cimetières/Cemeteries. Although born just above the most popular among them, I haven't always been able to appreciate the charm of some, which preserve in the heart of the city, in the shade, a haven of serenity. But I say *some*: in Paris, I can't bear to see, even in painting, that of Montparnasse, so mineral, so exposed, so pitilessly urban, almost industrial. I applaud Stendhal for having preferred that, far more rural, of Montmartre, over which you stride quite happily as you climb up Rue Caulaincourt, which leads moreover to the very rustic Saint-Vincent, on the right (meaning north) side of the Butte. I've somewhat frequented that of Saint-Geneviève-des-Bois, undeniably Russian before its blue onion-domed church, with its silver birches and its tombs with Orthodox crosses: a cross of Lorraine underscored halfway up by a third bar prettily placed, I don't know for what reason (did Jesus have one leg shorter than the other?), at an angle. But the most unforgettable is the old Jewish cemetery of Josefov, in Prague, with, beneath its great trees and amid the wild grass, its headstones heaped lopsidedly one against the other like the oblique teeth of a badly set jaw. As soon as you enter there, you are, in the spring, besieged by the cries of thousands of birds: all those from the city, you'd say, have adopted it as a natural aviary. I know that no one has been buried there for more than two centuries, but I wouldn't like to call 'disused' a place so welcoming, the least mortuary there is, since you'd swear it was without tombs, and thus without any dead. I fear that on no account may I lay claim to it.

Circuit. Those associated with motor racing are all 'mythical', but that of the Twenty Four Hours, on the south-eastern edge of Le Mans, was, besides, accessible the rest of the time to ordinary motorists, who could appreciate, at a more prudent speed, the respective difficulties of the grandstand straight, the Mulsanne Straight (which didn't yet comprise any speed-limiting chicane), the Mulsanne Corner and the Arnage Bends. During the fateful week in June, the city no longer breathed anything but the castor oil fumes and exhaust gases of the racing cars come there to be admired by the connoisseurs – but in Le Mans, land of Bollée father and sons,[99] everyone knew a thing or two about 'prototypes', as in Dax about bulls.

I'd landed there two years after the memorable catastrophe of 1955, which was still spoken of with an ever-growing number of horrific details. The glorious weekend was often wet, and the strategic points of the spectacle swiftly transformed into a quagmire, except for the stands reserved for those who'd had strings pulled by the Rotary and the Automobile-Club de l'Ouest – ACO for the initiates of initials. The dry years brought some

---

[99] Amédée-Ernest Bollée (1844–1917), French engineer, bellfounder and inventor, specialising in steam cars; his sons, Amédée-Ernest-Marie Bollée (1867–1926) and Léon Bollée (1870–1913), both followed their father into the motor-manufacturing business.

unforgettable nights, although interspersed with the howling of overheated engines. It was the period when the Belgian Olivier Gendebien and, if I'm not mistaken, the American Phil Hill were together dominant – I mean by replacing each other at the wheel during pit stops – both of them specialists of endurance rather than of Formula 1, a sport they feigned to scorn between Huisine and Sarthe. The alleged reason was that, contrary to the single seater competitions, a business for overpaid professionals, the Twenty Four hours were, and were to remain, like rugby at the time, a sport for *gentlemen*, almost for amateurs. So the name of the English driver held responsible for the aforementioned catastrophe was only uttered with abhorrence. It shan't be given here.

Civilian Life. From his years of barracks and trenches, he had, like many others, retained an expression that may perhaps be heard in *The Grand Illusion*,[100] and which he readily used outside of any military context: 'What does he do in civilian life [dans le civil]?' was his usual way of obtaining information about other people's circumstances, without moreover excluding the reply, in fact quite rare: 'colonel'. I am myself campaigning for an extension of the domain of this expression, which adds a little sparkle to the rather limp notion of 'civil society'. It may be used to refer to any activity foreign to the closed doors of the present situation, and exercised in the vast external world, still called the 'real world'. I used to ask it myself, *in petto*, during university encounters, in order to ponder where taught, and what, the 'colleague' I had opposite me, and whose badge, on his lapel, omitted this decisive indication. I can also imagine, in the candle-lit half-light of the Sistine Chapel, a cardinal thus receiving a tip-off from someone about a third party's extra-conclave role, before thinking of voting for him. In the same spirit and the same half-light, I fantasise yet further about a somewhat curious lady of the night asking her fleeting brothel mate: 'So what about you, what do you do, in civilian life?'

Clou/Nail. In a tale, perhaps by Andersen, any trace of which I cannot find, and which I'm doubtless going to ruin somewhat, three artisan ironworkers are facing off in a competition for the most

---

[100] *La Grande Illusion*, by Jean Renoir (1937).

handsome nail, a test supreme in its simplicity like, in cooking, that of the soft-boiled egg. The first places an iron bar in the fire, pounds it once red hot for a few minutes on his anvil, and presents to the judges a fine and handsome nail. The second works similarly, and produces a nail so much more handsome that none can imagine that it might be surpassed. The third competitor scorns the forge, and begins hammering his bar cold. Those present can't see what he's up to, and envisage for an instant disqualifying him for neglect of the most elementary formulae of ironwork. Without losing heart, he hammers his iron until his repeated blows have brought it to the necessary degree of heat; he then shapes the bar, and eventually reveals a nail every bit as handsome as the second competitor's. No more so, since that was impossible, but the way he accomplished it makes all the difference, and he wins the prize unanimously. A debatable moral: in art, it's all in the manner.

Cogito. In my childhood, when I appeared to be miles away, I was invariably asked whether I was thinking 'of the death of Louis XVI'. I've never known if this joke was then in common use, but I assume so. The fact is that on those occasions, the certainty I'd be asked that question led me no less invariably to 'think' – if thought it were, for I didn't know a great deal about it – of this unfortunate event, so much so that I could respond very sincerely 'Yes', and spare myself any further account. There's nothing like clichés to simplify one's existence – in the event, my own and my parents', since their question was fairly broadly rhetorical. It's not that they weren't interested in my thoughts, but rather that they posed this false question just to make me aware that I presently had my mouth open and looked a bit stupid. May those nostalgic for the monarchy forgive me, but all things considered, 'thinking of the death of Louis XVI', save perhaps on the 21st January, meant simply: thinking of nothing. I can't recall what test, perhaps imaginary, of more or less cognitive psychology, simply enjoins the benevolent guinea pig *not to think*, for a minute, of a certain object. Assuming it's possible to monitor this, they observe every time that the instruction inevitably entails its transgression: how can you think of not thinking of it other than by thinking of it? 'I don't want to think, says Roquentin[101]

---

[101] The protagonist in Jean-Paul Sartre's *La Nausée* (*Nausea*) (1938).

feverishly, I think that I don't want to think. I mustn't think that I don't want to think. Because that is still a thought.'

'Thought, said Jean Paulhan, has its dark side, like the moon: it is the business of words to illuminate it and I can see no observation on language, however paltry it may be, that might not serve to answer the old question: what are we thinking when we are thinking of nothing?' Husserl thinks that each thought is a thought about something, Raymond Queneau, that thinking of nothing is better than not thinking at all, Descartes thought that it suffices to think in order to be (or to prove to yourself that you are), and Roquentin, again, confirms: 'My thought is *me.*' Valéry thought on the contrary that you can't do both at once ('At times I think, at times I am'; and elsewhere: 'The more I think, the more I think', and not: '... the more I am'). Ambrose Bierce improves in turn upon the Cartesian performance with: 'I think I am thinking, therefore I think I am', but it would perhaps be humbler to amend: 'I say I am thinking, therefore I think I am.' And Lacan (oral tradition): 'I think where I am not, therefore I am where I do not think.' As for me, I have never been there where I was thinking, and things really aren't getting any better.

Colloquia. Ordered succession of soliloquies, in French bizarrely named 'communications', in principle related to a common subject, limp pretext for all manner of digressions. In July 1967 I was 'communicating', then, in the stifling heat of a room at the Collège de France,[102] at the annual colloquium of the International Association of French Studies, devoted to the 'Theme of Light in French Literature'. The session was chaired by Jean Rousset, seated to my left on the podium, bizarrely wearing leather strap sandals then known as *nu-pieds*[103] over white ankle socks. My talk was written on a few pages that, for a reason still unknown to me, I'd placed on a much thicker pile of sheets which were blank, or perhaps devoted to something else entirely, in anticipation of another paper. Time was of course limited, and at some point the chairman, whose function was to ensure respect for the schedule, noticed the apparent

---

[102] Founded in 1530 by François I and originally known as the Collège Royal, the Collège de France is a prestigious higher education and research institution situated near the Sorbonne in the 5th arrondissement of Paris.
[103] 'bare-feet'.

extent (and thickness) of what I had left to say. His disquiet, which courtesy prevented him from expressing too openly, was betrayed by various indirect and almost involuntary signs, throat clearings and fingers drummed on the desk, which couldn't but impart it to an equally impatient audience, since the principle of any colloquium is everybody's impatience with everybody else's talk. I sensed the situation pretty quickly and, while continuing to discourse upon the day and the night, I strove to reassure my neighbour with signs that were equally indirect, but apparently too indirect, to which he replied with some objurgation written on a slip of paper, which I greeted with a smile that was intended to be reassuring. The tension was at its height when I suddenly reached, as a professional timed to the minute, the final line of my final page. This unexpected conclusion was for everyone a cause of such relief that it met with a success evidently without relation to its merit. The president's customary thanks were undoubtedly sincere: I had taken the time to be brief.

I fear that I may have somewhat shocked the same Jean Rousset, the following year, when I showed up, in Montauban, at the hotel where the participants for a colloquium on 'The Baroque' were staying: I had, with one breakdown after another, come down from Paris in a period car on period roads, and I was still slightly abuzz from the drive, not to mention the smell of oil and the grease stains. At the bottom of a staircase, I met Rousset and his teacher Marcel Raymond, and gratified them in all innocence with a cordial 'Hi!', which quite poorly became the academic dignity of the latter, and the esteem the former held him in (as indeed did I). I can still see the stupor on Rousset's face, which made me realise what had just come out of my mouth: one is aware of having said such things rather than of actually saying them. This nonchalance was doubtless credited to an already rather cooled 'spirit of May', whose communicative warmth, in fact, had scarcely possessed me.

I have as it happens the ambiguous memory of another intellectual jamboree, organised one or two months previously by the University of Urbino under the sign, then very prominent, of Greimasian semiotics. It was held, then, just after the French 'May', but still during the Italian '68', which stretched out a bit longer, in the sunshine of the Marches, in a carnivalesque rear-guard leftism. The conference room was, on at least one occasion, invaded by a gang of students who deemed the holding of this colloquium to be prejudicial to the Cause of the Movement and semiotics in general to be an inherently reactionary discipline, and who expressed this twofold conviction with means closer to physical intimidation than to intellectual controversy. The two co-chairs of this session, whom I do not wish to denounce here, evinced amid this turmoil an equanimity that appeared to me to verge on indulgence, and I fear I may have allowed this rather to be seen in an intervention against the grain, where I more or less compared the methods of the demonstrators to those of fascist hit squads. I still bore the marks of some rather worrying Parisian memories, among which a session, precisely, of Greimas's seminar, where he'd had to confront a kind of popular tribunal, with some of his closest 'disciples' in the role of Red Guards, and I could see in Urbino a bad farcical repetition of this frankly odious scene. My protestation was greeted with perfect indifference, perhaps because of the language barrier, but doubtless also by virtue of the principle, always pertinent in this type of situation, that the most frontal opposition is less poorly received than the most minute disagreements: the only real enemies are warring brothers, the others pass unnoticed.

The sideshows were more pleasant, with Umberto Eco in the role of the inexhaustible story teller. I particularly recall the presence, on a day of calm, alone on the front row during an interval, of Italo Calvino, thin, sombre and silent, who seemed to be intensely pondering the sum of 'scientific' information he thought he'd received during the session. This vision in itself made up for the prevailing shambles.

In February 1968, Paul de Man had organised in Zurich an international meeting supposed to prolong on this continent the one that, more memorably, had taken place two years earlier in Baltimore. Of the participants from the first edition, he had invited back Jacques Derrida and Jean-Pierre Vernant, to whom he had added Jean-Pierre Richard and Jean Starobinski. From Derrida and myself, whom he then readily associated with each other, in the attention he paid to what he still loosely perceived as the 'young critical generation', he expected no formal communication, but merely a diffuse participation continually improvised on the fly. As far as I was concerned, this expectation was really quite utopian, but Derrida, for his part, impressed the colloquium with an already irresistible charisma, to the point of overawing one of the participants, who felt compelled to alter at the very last minute, in order to make it more correctly subversive (I can't recall through which indiscretion we discovered this), the final sentence of his future paper.

De Man had lodged his group in a charming hotel in the old town, but for want of space he squeezed us, Jacques and me, into the same twin bedroom. So far, nothing alarming; it was when the lights were about to go out that my roommate for one night realised that he'd forgotten his pyjamas – but not, fortunately, his portable typewriter. The latter making up for the former, he asked whether the noise from his work was liable to bother me. Upon my necessarily conciliatory answer, he occupied a good part of his night, and of my own (since I have, and not in a good way, perfect pitch) with typing, presumably for a future colloquium, a paper of which, if I'd had an even more perfect and above all better-trained ear, I would have been able to infer the content from the acoustically differentiated tones of the keys on his keyboard. And I shall say nothing of the delicate bell of his typewriter carriage, a period detail that no longer evokes much for the digital generations who don't know what they have, musically speaking, lost out on. The following morning, De Man, struck by my rather haggard look, asked me if all was well. Thinking to put him at ease, I replied valiantly: 'Well, one just has to make the best of things'. This was apparently not entirely reassuring, for he replied, in rather tight-lipped English: '*You are not very helpful!*'. I believed, however, that I had been so to the extent required by the situation, but one is never, for sure, helpful enough.

We are often punished, albeit indirectly, in the very places where we have sinned. Thirty-one years later, I thus found myself once again in the same city, almost in the same hotel, for a kind of informal seminar [*séminaire à bâtons rompus*] with Lucien Dällenbach's students at the Polytechnicum. *À bâtons rompus*[104] isn't actually a very fortunate expression. On the morning of this performance, and without apparent cause, my sweet other half fell on a hip – one of her own, I mean. On a splint stretcher that didn't fit into the little lift and which we had to shimmy down three flights of a hardly less pokey staircase, we took her to the university hospital fortunately very close by. After an hour or two, we had confirmation that it was indeed a fractured hip bone,

---

[104] 'with broken sticks'.

and that it (the fracture) would be 'reduced' at six o'clock in the evening. That was precisely the time of my seminar, and, since my presence there would ultimately be of more use than in front of the closed door of the operating room, we decided to continue with the session, which didn't go worse than any other, though for my part very much on autopilot. After an hour and a half, Lucien and I crossed the boulevard separating the two buildings, and found Babette perfectly awake, just a little anxious about my own state. I reassured her, she fell back asleep, and the rest of the week was spent awaiting the removal of the bolt by comparing the Rösti recipes of the little restaurants in the old town, by visiting, in its secluded villa, the Bührle Collection, which is to Zurich what the Barnes Foundation is to the chic suburbs of Philadelphia, and by pursuing the ghost of Dada in places so unconducive to its evocation. The return to Paris by car, advised against by the Faculty, was painful, but led us safely home, and the rest was a matter of a humdrum, but still arduous, rehabilitation. As happens sometimes, the punishment had mistaken its target.

Coma. During the years of Occupation, a kind of camp bed had been set up for me in the ground-floor dining room, the only room more or less heated in the winter, no doubt through the wall separating it from the kitchen. It was there that I learned, my parents having been unable to shield me from the noise of the comings and goings in the entrance hall, of the sudden death of my little neighbour and playmate, whose first name was Micheline. *Almost* sudden: the word I heard, no doubt for the first time, was *coma*: 'Micheline is in a coma', and this strange sentence sounded like the certain herald of an impending death, which it effectively was: at that time, meningitis was even less forgiving than it is today.

After the Liberation, an upright piano took the place of this little bed, which suggests that my learning how to play was as belated as it was laborious, and of which only the negative effects can still be felt. Having come through the *Méthode rose*, Clementi's sonatinas and Hanon's scales, my teacher, who gave her lessons in town, at the back of her school stationery store, thought to rouse me with a futile transcription of *The Blue Danube*. A tuner came two or three times, and, to illustrate the efficacy of his work, knew no other concert piece than a dance hall version of the song *Le P'tit Cœur de Ninon* [*Ninon's Little Heart*]. None of this was, musically speaking, particularly thrilling, especially since the site of my piano still bore the scar of that gloomy winter night. I'd never set myself there without associating with it the word *coma*, which I'd confuse moreover with that, just as mysterious, of *comma*, which marks the difference of a ninth of a tone, for instance between a D sharp and an E flat, fortunately unknown to the keyboard. Coma or comma, it's an imperceptible interval.

Communion. Throughout the *Belle Époque*, water was thought to be a dangerous liquid, because a drop of it sufficed to cloud a bottle of absinthe. My father, in his childhood, one day learned this the hard way, for having decanted, from a flask whose hiding place he'd spotted in a dresser, a good thimbleful, which he replaced with an equal quantity of *aqua simplex*. The bad taste of the beverage consumed 'neat', then the bad memory of his punishment, and finally the rejection of a lineage somewhat marked by the abuse of the 'green fairy' led him shortly thereafter to campaign in a temperance society called, no doubt by chromatic succession, 'The Blue Cross'. By another uncertain but plausible chain of events, he met my future mother in a kind of Protestant youth club [patronage parpaillot[105]] in Ménilmontant, or perhaps in Belleville, for young people from a modest background, believers or not, seeking moral salvation and supposed social advancement, called for its part 'The Good Home'. Myself baptised, a little later, with clear water and at the temple known as 'The Soul's Home' (still present today, Rue Pasteur-Wagner, after the name of its founder, a great figure of Protestant liberalism), I still somewhat confuse these different charitable institutions, to which, in sum, I owe my existence, and even a part of my essence. For example, I have never been able to forget the date of St Bartholomew's Day, nor take the notion of reform to be defamatory, nor the title of liberal.

Raised then, as they say, 'in' the reformed religion by a mother loyal to her family tradition, under the benevolent neutrality of an officially 'freethinking' father (more officiously a 'non-practising atheist' – the depressing euphemism 'agnostic' was yet to be used), but one holding, like Renan, Jesus-Christ to be a great man, and

[105] A 'parpaillot' is a generally pejorative term designating a French Protestant; originally used in the sixteenth century to refer to the Huguenots.

like others to be 'the first of the socialists', and all things considered with Huguenot affiliations, at least for the sake of a peaceful marriage, I disengaged fairly swiftly from it in the following circumstances.

Young Protestants [parpaillots], as everyone ought to know, 'receive' their first Communion later than Catholics: at around 14 or 15, an age of reason when you're meant to know what you're doing, and why. The 'religious instruction' supposed to prepare for this considered act was provided, at the Pontoise secondary school, by a pastor who exercised his ministry in a spirit that wasn't exactly that of the Soul's Home. In his lessons, he strove however to place Scripture within the reach of his inevitably restricted audience, which could well in the event be restricted to my simple self. Unfortunately, he'd poorly estimated my reach, and the ravages already exerted upon it, among other things, by reading authors notoriously capable of throwing you to the ground, your nose in the gutter.[106] With fine theological fervour, he thus used one day, concerning I can't recall which decisive episode in the Old Testament, this regrettable prosopopoeia: 'And then, God said unto himself: 'Since that's the way it is, *je vais changer mon fusil d'épaule* [I'm going to switch my gun to the other shoulder, 'I'm going to change tack'].'

The metaphor finally convinced me of the absurdity of this whole business of Creation, Original Sin, Predestination, Redemption, efficacious or sufficient Grace, Crucifixion, Paschal Resurrection, Ascension, Pentecost and Last Judgement. For some vaguely political reason, I was already rather hard put to admit that the faithful of a religion in principle so refractory to authority should call their God, or his supposed son, 'Lord': when you think you have God not above but (each of us) in one's depths, this feudal title has something at the very least incongruous about it. For a more aesthetic reason, 'fusil d'épaule [gun to the other shoulder]' sent me home dechristianised down to the bone. I there declared myself to be frankly atheist, at best 'deist' (since I'd read Voltaire

---

[106] An allusion to Voltaire and Jean-Jacques Rousseau, via Victor Hugo's 'La Chanson de Gavroche', in *Les Misérables*: 'Je suis tombé par terre, c'est la faute à Voltaire/Le nez dans le ruisseau, c'est la faute à Rousseau [I fell to the ground, it's the fault of Voltaire/My nose in the gutter, it's the fault of Rousseau]'.

and Rousseau), and I swore on my own life that I'd never receive said first Communion, nor consequently any of those to follow. There was a family drama with many twists and turns, but my poor mother had to bow down, dismayed but convinced that a more 'liberal' pastor would have gone about it better. But these domestic controversies left me already indifferent: farewell Luther, farewell Calvin, I had no more shoulders for that particular rifle. Nevertheless, considering from here the few years that remained for her to live, I now regret having caused my mother so much pain for an unfortunate figure of speech.

I know that in a sense my anti-religious rebellion had also been a continuation of the spirit of the Reform by other means. Of the Protestant spirit [l'esprit parpaillot], has abided with me at least some aversion to papist play-acting, a recourse, too facile perhaps, to the kind of detachment that André Gide expressed on every occasion with his famous 'I couldn't care less, I'm a Protestant', a well-anchored vocation for the minority state – Ghibelline with the Guelphs, Guelph with the Ghibellines – and a certain fondness for the Huguenot cross (a Maltese cross overlapping a circle) which my mother wore constantly around her neck, underscored by a dove symbolising the Holy Spirit, a secondary pendant that ought to prevent it from being mistaken for the Occitan cross, whatever the Reform owes (or not) to Catharism. It was in sum her sole piece of jewellery, which I wasn't able to keep with me – perhaps because she took it with her to the next world.

Adhesions of language are, furthermore, often more tenacious than spiritual adherences. In the spring of 1979, returning, from a brief stay in Middle Egypt, to my friend Guy Borelli, who was then teaching in Cairo, I told him at which hotel in Luxor, a rather pleasant row of bungalows aligned on the banks of the Nile, I had spent two or three nights. 'I see, he says, it's just south of the temple. – That's possible, I answer, but I didn't see the temple.' Since I'd gone there, of course, in order to visit those of Karnak and Luxor (and, alas, on the back of a donkey, the funerary valleys opposite), this reply left him somewhat astounded, and this astonishment revealed to me my blunder: in a flash, the word *temple* had taken me back about 40 years, to the time when it designated for me the site of the Protestant cult, even if, in my childhood, its Sunday practice was held, opposite the town hall in Conflans, in a kind of disused shed with minimalist decor. The breath-taking monuments

I'd just left behind hadn't managed, in these unsuspected depths, to supplant the meaning ever since associated with this word. All of this, if I'm retracing the sequence of causes aright, for a drop of water in a bottle of absinthe.

Compartment. The 'Amiens train' didn't take you to Amiens, but headed directly farther north. So you had to leave it at Longueau for a short line shuttle that eventually led us to this city forgotten by the 'main-line', though not by the war, and whose dead-end station, reconstructed by Auguste Perret, faces the tower by the same author, a strict allusion to the belfries of the Nord region. After a few hundred steps along Rue de Noyon, the way to the girls' secondary school, in the heart of the city, separated from the one leading to the 'School Campus', recently pitched at its southern extremity, far away from the miraculously surviving cathedral and on the edge of the immense beet plains. This parting put a provisional end to a near daily journey that somewhat eased the start of my professional life. I'm not sure by which favour, a virtually private compartment gathered, on the way there and back, a small group of teachers from both establishments. It wasn't quite what was then called a 'ladies only compartment', but the fairer sex was sufficiently prevalent to make each journey feel like a stay in a mobile gynaecium, where there blossomed a quasi Proustian bouquet of young women in flower whose morning fragrances got along pretty well. There was nothing intellectual or political about the conversation: they'd leaf four-handed through the latest *Elle*, I was forgetting my post-Stalinian troubles, May '68 lay upon the very distant horizon, it was still almost the old regime and its sweetness of life. I wasn't really tended to, I wasn't particularly forgotten, I was there like Céladon in his sheep pen,[107] like Chérubin between Suzanne and his dear Countess.[108] The journey went too quickly. These railway niceties lasted for the few months of my first year of 'teaching'.

Concept. Jean-Toussaint Desanti taught at the *Lycée Lakanal*, in a

---

[107] An allusion to the male protagonist in *L'Astrée* (1607–1628), by Honoré d'Urfé.
[108] An allusion to *Le Mariage de Figaro* (*The Marriage of Figaro*) (1778) by Pierre-Augustin Caron de Beaumarchais, and/or Mozart's eponymous opera.

class that, alas, wasn't my own – but we'd occasionally desert our lessons discreetly to follow his. At the beginning of the year 1948 and as part of a ritual session of 'membership card renewals', the Sceaux communist cell, under which fell the teachers and students at our school, had charged him with a kind of recruitment conference addressed to the 'sympathisers', docile fellow travellers by definition considered to be potential members. The bulk of these neophytes consisted of *khâgne*[109] students, and our silent philosopher[110] spoke to us a bit about Marx and a lot about Hegel and Spinoza. Returning *in fine* to the purpose of the session, he concluded fairly abruptly by saying that upon entering the Party we'd be sure to find ourselves 'on the side of the Concept'. There's no resisting such a capital letter, even when spoken, and I found myself, for a few years and by automatic renewal, equipped with said card, and embroiled in a practice whose conceptual definition would soon become for me increasingly obscure. In any event, none among us had then thought for an instant to ask: 'Which concept?' It was obviously a question of the Concept in general, which seemed to us to be, quite rightly, the most glorious of commitments: the 'concept', though already a very effective fool's gold, didn't yet refer either to marketing practices or to those of so-called contemporary art – and it hadn't yet been decreed that it 'belongs to philosophy and belongs to it alone'. I don't know whether Desanti would have approved of that particular stranglehold, which came later, and would be well worth his own. I don't really blame him: his Hegelian shot in the arm was just one among many others capable of having the same effect, and we know that he found himself, a few years later, as distressed as I was for having believed the moon was made of such cheese.

The fact remains that I was, for two or three years, a member of this cell, and one of the leaders of the sub-group, by far the most active, formed by the '*khâgne*' students. Given our status as, for the most part, boarders detached from the world and shielded by the authorities, our main 'activity' consisted in internal agit-prop, a brainwashing machine whose efficacy was gauged by the number of conversions carried out among our fellow students, even if some

---

[109] See note 84.

[110] Desanti is the author of *La Philosophie silencieuse, ou critique des philosophies de la science* (*The Silent Philosophy, or a Critique of the Philosophies of Science*) (1975).

of them proceeded from a more autonomous labour of maturation, if I can put it that way. I recall in particular one start of the school year, probably in October 1948, when Emmanuel Le Roy Ladurie, whom we'd hitherto taken to be the most incorrigible reactionary (he claimed, besides, to have chosen Lakanal in order to be closer to the prison at Fresnes, where his father was atoning for his Vichy years), announced to me that some holiday reading had made him decide to join the party of the working class. Before slaughtering in thought the fatted Calf thus presenting itself, I asked him *what* reading had produced this miracle: it was, no more no less, *The Phenomenology of Spirit*. I knew already that the ways of the Concept are impenetrable, but that one I found staggering, and I must confess to never having sought to use it for any other attempts at recruitment – never having for my part succeeded in following all the stages of this odyssey of consciousness, the reading of which, in Jean Hyppolite's gruelling translation, contributed only to dispelling my final vague hopes of any philosophical vocation. The essential merit of this 'system' derived for us from the fact that Marx had been able, in one fell swoop, to 'put it right side up'. Besides, I seem to remember that Emmanuel described his road to Damascus in the following terms: 'Previously, I was a vulgar materialist, and thanks to Hegel, I have risen to the level of dialectical materialism.' Others had reached the same stage by the converse detour: thus Marx, from Hegel to himself passing through Feuerbach. At least that's what we were told.

I described our little cohort of communist 'khâgne' students as a 'sub-group', and in fact the Party statutes gave us permission for nothing more: the entity one day known as the 'Union of Communist Students' was yet to be born, and what was to follow proved that its absence at that time betokened, on the part of the leading authorities, great wisdom. I remember only having once written, at the head of one of my dissertations, as pompous as it was misleading, 'For the Philosophy Section of the Group for Marxist Studies of the Lycée Lakanal'. Our official philosophy teacher, who called himself an 'impenitent liberal' (which he must indeed have been to withstand our provocations, such as the one that consisted, every time he uttered the word: 'Man', in shrieking in unison: 'Which man?'), was no more offended by this than he was by many other rodomontades; at most he ventured one day to chide me for an abuse of the expression (highly typical, indeed) 'in the final analysis', and to advise me, without success, to make rather more use of the *first* analyses'. He was moreover convinced, as was his French colleague, that I was destined to a professional political career, preferably in parliament.

This forecast intrigued more than it encouraged me: like most of my comrades, I viewed my militant engagement as nothing but a benevolent activity on the margins of my future profession; a communist student, I planned thereafter to become a future communist teacher, with no prospect of any career in the apparatus. Our adhesion to the Party, which comprised a good dose of naivety, bigotry, sectarianism and a few other equally criticisable traits, comprised none of personal ambition. We were simply good little soldiers, with no expectation of any advancement in what we didn't perceive as a hierarchy, let alone as a *nomenklatura*. Furthermore, the only communist among our official teachers, Jean Bruhat, didn't think otherwise after decades of devotion to militancy, and I can still hear him say, about I can't recall which of our brilliant journalists for whom I professed a certain admiration: 'All the same, he's just a failed teacher.' This harsh tribute well expressed his conviction, very 'old school', that, even for a communist, nothing should rise above one's intellectual vocation and professional excellence. Besides, officially and via the irrefutable voice of 'Maurice', the Party required of us to be the 'best' in our respective disciplines and I remember having, three or four years later and from the height of I can't recall what podium, exhorted the communist students of Paris, above all, to take their exams. This rather fawning declamation was rigorously in step with the line: it hadn't been so long ago that Thorez had called upon the working class itself to 'roll up its sleeves' so that 'things might get better'. Basically, and contrary to what would happen, at the end of the sixties, with our distant successors, 'the' Revolution was by no means our fundamental 'concept'. We wielded it only with caution, subject to the specification: '*Which revolution?*' In fact, we didn't think of ourselves as 'revolutionaries', no more than, inanely, as 'of the left', still less, of course, as leftists [gauchistes] (this word was for us merely that of an 'infantile malady' diagnosed by Lenin and treated with the means we know), but more prosaically as 'progressives'. As François Furet was to reassure us many years later, Marxism (let's call it that) had been for us a 'good investment of labour'.

Labour: that was it, our Concept, and I believe that for some time I had pinned above my table the phrase by Marx which came to me, I can't recall via what channel and in which precise form, from the famous *1844 Manuscripts*: 'Hegel grasps labour as the essence of man, as man's essence in gestation.' That made two fathers for a single thought (assuming that Marx agreed with what he attributes to Hegel, and that his attribution was correct), but, all questions of paternity set aside, I'm not certain to have since found a better definition of the human species – which doesn't oblige one to abuse it.

Concessions. Louis Jouvet[111] was, long ago, Jacques Copeau's[112] assistant. The latter, rehearsing a play, adopted a very-pared down stage direction, with a spartan set design: no furniture. After a while, under the influence of some practical necessity, he nonetheless sent Jouvet to fetch a stool. Jouvet did so, muttering away in his syncopated diction: 'There we go, the concessions have begun.'

Conférences/Lectures. Most onerous way of travelling for free. Its practice isn't always so gratifying for the speaker's ego, unless it be ample enough to take everything in 'good part', or, on the contrary, naturally inclined to savour the humiliating comedy of certain situations. At some Maison Française,[113] a nonchalant young director introduced me more or less in the following terms: 'Gérard Genette, specialist in ... in ... (feigning to abandon a fruitless search), in short, certainly a specialist in something.' Terms that are thoroughly disobliging but involuntarily incorrect, for if ever there was anything of which I may not be accused, it is in fact of being a specialist in anything at all: it thus wasn't without reason that he hadn't found what he wasn't even seeking. At the same place, a slightly less young and visibly overwhelmed director called me 'Jean Genet'. In another no less French Maison, I was sometimes the author of *Mythologics*, sometimes of *Mythologies*

---

[111] French actor, theatre director and filmmaker (1887–1951).
[112] French theatre director, producer, literary critic and dramatist (1879–1849).
[113] 'La Maison Française' is a network of foreign-based French research institutes in the humanities and social sciences.

(the connoisseurs will rectify[114]), sometimes, more gratuitously, of *Theories of the Symbol* – moreover, on another campus, they gave the floor to 'me', 'Tzvetan Todorov' (in those days, we were reputedly interchangeable). Elsewhere, I was shown with great pomp around the library (ever a highlight, the visit to the library) and taken up to a shelf where a few editions of *Littérature* were gathering dust: 'You see, we've got the whole collection' (the initiated will judge[115]). The only absolutely distressing moments (I mean too distressing for the comedy to offset the unpleasantness) related occasionally to the material conditions of the welcome: I can still picture myself, when I was starting out (April 1969) in this career, in a 'hotel' near Columbia where I'd been dumped around midnight, and where enormous cockroaches, plus a few rats, made me decamp a few minutes later, without awaiting the arrival of the alligators. I had great trouble, in that neighbourhood and at that hour, finding somewhere scarcely better, and much fortune to survive this nocturnal quest.

In the course of a conference in Edinburgh, in March 1967, I had quoted Pascal, I can't recall in relation to which topic – that's to say rather off-topic, as is usually the case. When it came to the questions at the end of the session, a student more Scottish than Sean Connery stood up and simply declared: *I do not agree with Pascal*; I attempted to make him clarify the bearing of his disagreement; he absolutely refused to do so, and repeated, with the obstinacy of a Bartleby: *I do not agree with Pascal*. However much I mightn't, personally, endorse on every point the thought of the *Pensées* [la pensée des *Pensées*], I felt myself thereby indirectly concerned, contested and finally consternated, all the while admiring the laconic firmness of the statement. I've since been assured that this negative attitude was a hallmark of the local character, but I haven't had the chance to verify it by way of statistics.

Towards the end of a long series that occupied, in a room at the CNAM,[116] Rue Saint-Martin, and under the direction of the

---

[114] *Mythologiques* (1964–1971), by Claude Lévi-Strauss (translated as *Introduction to a Science of Mythology*); *Mythologies* (1957), by Roland Barthes. Genette is the author of *Mimologiques: Voyages en Cratylie* (1976) (*Mimologics*).
[115] The journal *Littérature* was founded in 1971 by Jean Levaillant; *Poétique* was founded in 1971 by Genette, Hélène Cixous and Tzvetan Todorov.
[116] Conservatoire national des arts et des métiers (National Conservatory of

philosopher Yves Michaud, every evening of the (leap) year 2000, there came my turn, on the 26th December, to disappoint an audience thirsting for knowledge of every kind. For this reason or another, Michel Deguy was in the room. Wishing to return him the courtesy, and besides always delighted to hear his deep voice and energetic diction, I made arrangements to attend his conference, which was due to close the session, on the evening of the 31st, so as to touch upon the final minute of the millennium. These arrangements consisted of averting any untoward lateness, which brought me to the venue a ridiculous 15 minutes in advance, which I spent circling around the glacial Square Émile-Chautemps, insofar as one can circle around a square so rectangular, shedding with every lap a rapidly frozen tear upon the nowadays meaningless façade of what was, in more carefree times, Offenbach's final theatre. This respectful timeout having elapsed, I presented at the entrance of said Conservatory, to find there a discreet little poster indicating that Michel Deguy's conference had been postponed, let's say, until late morning the following day – that is, to a time when I could no longer make myself available. To inform him of this misadventure would have been to redouble the blunder. I got but little, and irremediably so, for my efforts at reciprocity. He'll appreciate my compunction, if he reads these lines.

A few months later, I was due to officiate at the Villa Gillet, a laudable cultural institution located at 25 Rue Chazière, a remote, and, after six o'clock in the evening, rather deserted place on the Croix-Rousse hill.[117] Around seven o'clock, a taxi left us, Babette and me, in the park surrounding this Villa, and vanished into the night. We approached the door, and read on a poster, as you've already guessed: 'Gérard Genette's conference has been moved to such and such a room, at number such and such on Rue de la Chazière.' This number was apparently a few hundred metres away from the villa. Protesting that I really could have been given notice of this transfer, we hurried, in the rain, towards the new room. At the door, we were asked whether we had booked our seats, and I had to reveal, quite piteously, that I was none other than the advertised speaker. Excuses, embarrassment, we were

Arts and Crafts).
[117] In Lyon.

taken to the edge of the platform while being informed that the organisers were still awaiting us inside the Villa – that is, beyond the dissuasive poster – in order to welcome us and lead us where we'd regrettably arrived all alone. I actually thought I'd be asked to return there, so that reality might be reconciled with the virtual protocol, but the miracle called 'the mobile phone' put paid to this misunderstanding. The rest was more mundane, but, all the while deciphering as best I could the still damp text (nothing soaks more, I've always known this, than the rain in Lyon: hence the Traboules[118]) of a talk premonitorily entitled 'Irony, Humour, *Nonsense* and Company', I attempted for an hour, *in petto*, to count the number of times I'd been honoured with this type of mishap, or mis-placement, often officially justified by an unexpected (why?) influx of audience members, but the real reason for which is always a mistaken room, a closed door, a lost key, a recalcitrant lock, a deaf caretaker, a dumb usher, a blind corridor.[119]

Confluence. In those days, as Alphonse Allais had already observed, the environs of Paris were still the most beautiful environs in the world, and the meeting of the Seine and the Oise the most beautiful confluence imaginable (I knew of no other). For want of resources in Conflans-Sainte-Honorine, the children of Conflans of both sexes destined, as a deserving elite, to secondary studies would generally attend one of the schools [collèges] in Pontoise, eight kilometres to the north. There were four schools there: two state, or 'lay' (and municipal: the distinction between *collège* and *lycée* pertained at the time to this purely administrative difference), one for each sex, and two 'free', meaning private and denominational: Saint-Martin for boys and, for girls, Notre-Dame-de-la-Compassion, but we, from the lay school, had added to the latter title an extra syllable allowing the spirit of this rigid institution to be designated more aptly. The class struggle was active within our local petite-bourgeoisie, between *upper* and *lower middle*, a struggle that didn't preclude various exchanges. Besides, good families who were judiciously broad-minded 'put' (one said

---

[118] Covered passageways characteristic of Lyon's old town.
[119] 'un couloir aveugle', 'a windowless corridor'.

'put') their girls in Notre-Dame and their boys in the municipal school.

But to return to the eight kilometres. The journey was made in two ways, according to the season, plus a third, virtually out of season. I'll explain. In winter, there was an antiquated local train, sometimes pulled, sometimes pushed (pulled on the way out, pushed on the way back) by a steam locomotive nicknamed 'Titine', or more precisely 'la Titine'. Its coaches were entirely divided into compartments without connecting corridors between them, save for a risky passage via the external running board. The risk wasn't huge, given the overall speed, and didn't prevent the unexpected visits of an acrobatic inspector tasked with recording our dodged fares.

One of la Titine's terminuses was thus Pontoise station, or rather one of its dead-end 'sidings'. Around five o'clock in the afternoon, la Titine 'entered the station', that's to say ended its asthmatic journey on a buffer stop, pending the time of its departure, in reverse, towards its other buffer, situated in Conflans, which shows that the very young SNCF[120] (it was still called the 'Compagnie des chemins de fer de l'État [State Railway Company]') had at the time no qualms about running a 'line' for an eight-kilometre journey for the almost exclusive usage of a few schoolkids. A game, not much more stupid than any other, consisted, in the event of a prolonged wait, in placing upon the rails of this track, at the appropriate distance from the end of the line, a few coins – those greyish coins of the French state which presented, I believe, on one of their sides, the inevitable francisque or perhaps the handsome benevolent face of the Victor of Verdun.[121] I've forgotten the metallic composition of these coins, but the fact is that they could hardly resist the passage of the locomotive and three or four coaches. Each coin would therefore end up in the shape of a thin elongated plate, where the monetary and other figures had more or less disappeared in the compression. The interest of the operation, into which vanished a share of our pocket money, consisted in comparing these effects, the details of which

[120] Société nationale des chemins de fer français (French National Railway Company).
[121] The 'francisque' was the personal symbol of Marshal Philippe Pétain, head of the French State, 1940–1944; it became the emblem of the Vichy regime. Pétain was also known as the 'Victor of Verdun'.

were always unpredictable. The risk was nil for the equilibrium of la Titine, and apparently low for the operators: the railway men found this game, at worst, gratuitous (for them), and the law enforcement agencies were dealing with more serious forms of resistance.

Another way of reaching Pontoise, by bike, was enjoyed in the summer months. Each would leave home alone but, with swift support [par un prompt renfort[122]], barring punctures or various temptations, the final peloton formed after Saint-Ouen-l'Aumône, only to break up in the final 500 metres, along Boulevard Jean-Jaurès, a category two slope: at the top, the municipal school towered supreme over the Oise valley. A more idyllic variant, departing from Éragny, followed the towpath and took interest in one or two locks. But the third mode, even more summery in its enjoyment, was of a purely aquatic nature, and its description calls for a few technical considerations, which may be savoured a little further on.

Congères/Snowdrifts. My stays in the United States have often been marked by the type of weather there called *blizzards*. In January 1969, barely dropped from the Paris plane, then from the Connecticut Limousine that brought me, somewhat groggy, from New York to New Haven, after a nightmarish time in a campus dormitory where I'd been helpfully thrown, I rented in haste, without seeking any further, the first flat I could find, one left languishing on the list made available to necessitous students. It was as miserable as it was poorly located, on Orange Street, quite far, northwards, from the campus, and nearly as far from any kind of food store. I deferred until later any concern for my subsistence, but in the morning I saw that the snow had begun to fall hard, as it knows how to in New England. The blizzard lasted one or two days, following which the road-clearing services opened for me a long trench between two snowdrifts, as far as the French Department building, where I had to initiate into the mysteries of Proustian narrative a handful of graduate students as benumbed as I was by the contrast between the cold outside and the excessive

---

[122] This phrase appears to cite Pierre Corneille, *Le Cid* (1636), Act IV, Scene III: 'Nous partîmes cinq cents; mais par un prompt renfort/Nous nous vîmes trois mille en arrivant au port [We were five hundred, but with swift support/ Grew to three thousand as we reached the port]'.

heating indoors. I ventured at the outset a few sincere reservations about my competence relative to this subject, or to any other. This exordium was evidently taken to the letter and, following the class, a few students went to see a Department head in order to complain about it. The head, caring little to disparage for his own part a service that the university sold for a higher price than it paid for it, explained, without really convincing them, the continental oddity called, not 'modesty', but 'self-denigration [autodépréciation]' – not to be confused with the local self-derision (*self-deprecation*), a coded variant of the *opening joke*, always uttered and received as such. The snowdrifts remained in place for one or two weeks – just long enough to develop a taste for them before the muddy thaw.

In November 1978, I was stuck for one or two days in a friend's house in Boulder, Colorado, the time it took to clear the airport runways. But the snowfall overnight had been as brief as it was abundant, and the following morning, to the west, the first slopes of the Rockies glistened in the sun. The morning walk was biting but superb.

In December 1981, or 1983, the captain of the plane due to take me from New York back to Paris informed us at the last moment that the wings were too laden with snow for it to be reasonable to attempt a take-off. The fact, moreover, could be registered fairly well through the window, but by I know not what procedure they then removed the snow from the aeroplane wings, and what happened next that evening merges in my memory with images from *Airport*, a film I seem to remember, quite implausibly, being shown that night, once we were over the Atlantic, that's to say as soon as we'd taken off. So I shan't venture to recount this sequel, lest I should spoil both scenarios.

Conseil de classe/Class Council. In the days when I took part in this type of activity, I'd lie in eager wait, in order to relieve my boredom, for manifestations of what I secretly called the 'psychology of the class council'. Its constant principle, a paradox for all purposes, was that, with the pupils, the appearance *always* concealed a contrary reality: 'He's insolent, but out of shyness', 'He's arrogant, but out of modesty', 'He's attentive in class, but basically he's a slacker', 'People think he's lazy, but he hides away to work', etc. As Proust more or less says, *buts* are often unacknowledged *therefores*. On another level, when the Council came to consider the case of a *female* pupil, it was better if one didn't say 'She's rather cute', not for what such a remark contained of sexism (this disparaging notion wasn't yet prevalent), but because a, and most often *female*, colleague wouldn't fail to follow up with a somewhat tart: '... and she knows it!' They did, in fact, always know it.

Contaminations. The Latin comic playwrights had no qualms about 'contaminating', that's to say fusing together, two or three Greek comedies, in order to offer their public a more complex plot. In the seventies, and probably on account of a colloquium (perhaps a 'Décade de Cerisy'[123]) dedicated, conjointly and under the title 'Artaud-Bataille', to these two icons of the period avant-garde, an American student came to see me one day about a dissertation she was planning to devote to what Borges, I think, would describe – as he does for the single author of the *Tao Te Ching* and the *One Thousand and One Nights*, or of *The Imitation of Christ* and *Journey to the End of the Night* – as an 'interesting man of letters', an Artaud-Bataille whose composite name bothered her no more than that, let's say, of Sainte-Beuve or *Michel-Ange* [Michelangelo], or than had bothered me, in my childhood, the author I believed to be called Erckmann-Chatrian.[124] I withdrew behind an undeniable lack of competence, but not without dreaming a bit about the variant of the famous 'technique of erroneous attribution' that is the pure and simple contamination of authors. Since the whole is always worth more than the sum of its parts, the work of Artaud-Bataille is undoubtedly a considerable monument, as would be that of Rousseau-Voltaire, of Hugo-Lamartine, of Stendhal-Flaubert, of Poussin-Picasso, of Mozart-Stravinsky or (to illustrate somewhat better the fusion of geniuses) of the famous Tolstoyevsky. I believed in the existence of the latter for too long, at an age when I also (con)fused Haydn and Handel into Hayndel, to wish to oppress the enthusiasm of the creators of artistic chimeras – who, besides, have no reason to stop at two terms: what can be done with two

---

[123] The Château de Cerisy-la-Salle in Normandy hosts the 'International Cultural Centre of Cerisy-la-salle', a venue for intellectual encounters; the 'Cerisy colloques' last for ten days, hence 'décades de Cerisy'.

[124] Émile Erckmann (1822–1899) wrote novels and plays jointly with Alexandre Chatrian (1826–1890).

can at least be done with three. After all, Borges, again, has indeed suggested – ten times rather than once – that all works are the work of only one timeless and anonymous author, and, though hardly anonymous, the chimerical-work of X-Y deserves in effect as much attention as the indefatigable parallel of X and Y, or the sempiternal influence of X upon Y. If I haven't mentioned Corneille-Molière, nor Bacon-Shakespeare, nor obviously Menard-Cervantes, it's because their respective identities are today virtually established. A French jazz musician became known under the composite name Erroll Parker, as a (misleading) promise of the 'two for the price of one' type.

Conversely (or not), it's said that Stéphane Grappelli, upon hearing a record by Art Tatum, as ever mind-boggling with gratuitous virtuosity, and thinking it was a question of, at least, a piano duet, asked who was playing, and thought for a while, bolstered by this illusion, that he'd heard '*Art et Tum* [Art and Tum]'. I long refused to believe that the duet 'Yehudi-Menuhin', virtual virtuosi in the evergreen *Chaconne in d minor*, could be one and the same violinist, recorded aged 20, and without the assistance, nowadays commonplace, of any *rerecording*. The invention of creators by scissiparity (can you say *anti-contamination?*) isn't less capable than its contrary of 'peopling with adventures' the peaceful course of the history of arts and letters. There'd be nothing extravagant about crediting another author (not Molière, of course) with Corneille's comedies, or Voltaire's tragedies, Marivaux's novels, the semiotic treatises of the novelist Umberto Eco, Picasso's blue paintings, Shostakovich's quartets, Verdi's *Requiem*, Rossini's *Stabat Mater*, and about giving a different name to each of these clearly characterised artists, as Pessoa did for each of his countless heteronyms. The real superiority of contamination over these daring disassociations would relate to the principle of economy we owe to William of Occam: don't multiply entities beyond the necessary. Borges, once again, condemned, in the name of an analogous principle, mirrors and copulation, which 'multiply the number of men', and thus, among other things, authors. It would be better therefore to reduce this number by way of synthesis than to increase it by way of analysis. But this advantage might well be illusory, since the bicephalous unit 'Artaud-Bataille', which proceeds moreover from a kind of laborious coupling (more laborious, at least, than the 'Blanchot-Bataille' that rose to prominence of its own accord a little later), increases more than it reduces, adding in its way a complex author to two authors who couldn't be simpler, which makes *three* for the price (but what price?) of two.

Contemporary. This adjective once had only a factually temporal meaning, 'absolute' if you will, by implicit relation to the moment of the utterance (contemporary tout court, understood as: with the speaker) or relative (contemporary with Louis XI, with Napoleon, with Félix Faure); it tends nowadays to assume that of an aesthetic predicate. This is what had already occurred for *modern*, except that one can still say 'contemporary with ... ' (the grammatical relative still operates), and that one will surely never be able to say 'modern with ... ': here, the grammatical absolute still prevails, even if our modernity is no longer that of Baudelaire. Thus are distinguished more or less clearly, today, and at least for the visual arts, two stylistic periods: modern art (English prefers to say 'modernist', which attenuates the ambiguity somewhat) and contemporary art. I say 'stylistic periods' in the sense that these two periods (very roughly, the first and second half of the twentieth century) each present a coherent ensemble of styles: on the one side, what one perceives (or believes one perceives) to be shared by Picasso, Stravinsky, Mies Van der Rohe; on the other, by Warhol, Cage, Gehry. Ensembles as coherent (no more) than those indexed beneath the terms 'baroque', 'classical', 'romantic', with the play between the temporal definition and the stylistic definition allowing one for instance to consider as 'baroque' a work that, without belonging historically to the baroque period, presents some of its characteristic stylistic features: Lucan, Claudel, Cecil B. DeMille in this sense and each in their own way. The historico-stylistic distinction of the modern and the contemporary is nowadays sufficiently well accepted to justify, for example, the existence of separate museums or of separate sections in the same museum, and one knows more or less what to expect – with the exception of a few transitions, or passing chords, for instance Rauschenberg or Jasper Johns, still 'modern' by virtue of a technique that owes so much to abstract expressionism, and already 'contemporary' by the way in which they inaugurate pop art (Rauschenberg), minimalism or conceptual art (Johns). All's well with *contemporary*, then, which seems to have supplanted, for the same object, *postmodern*, which moreover

presented pretty much the same ambiguity (period? style? both?).
I can see nonetheless a difficulty in moving this predicate around
past history as freely as we do with the others: supposing I find,
let's say at random in Arcimboldo, traits liable to establish a parallel
with Oldenburg, I'll be somewhat harder put to describe him quite
simply as 'contemporary' than to declare as 'modern' – pertinently
or not – Vermeer or Caravaggio. Another difficulty will doubtless
stem from naming future stylistic ensembles. *Post-contemporary*
might do the trick for the next one, but then? Must we align the
coaches to infinity, if infinity there be? Fortunately, this will no
longer be our business.

I restricted a moment ago the legitimate use of the predicate
'contemporary' to the so-called visual arts (of which are more or
less exclusively thinking those who uphold the label 'contemporary
art', for whom, instinctively, there is no art but the visual), for a
stylistic concept is so to speak never placed beneath the term, in fact
uncommon, 'contemporary literature' – and 'contemporary music' has
primarily served to name, after the Second World War, a filiation,
or reaffiliation, to the Viennese atonal school, which is in no way
posterior to Stravinsky's 'modernism', quite the contrary. In all of
his characteristic traits, even during his neoclassical phase ('return
to ... ') and with the exception of his late serial demonstrations,
Stravinsky belongs typically, like and with Cocteau and Picasso, to
the 'modernist' art of the first half of the twentieth century, and this
co-belonging even constitutes, in history, one of the rare examples
of a pronounced trans-artistic symbiosis. Yet, from this 'modern'
music, the abovementioned and subsequent 'contemporary music' is
by no means distinguished in a manner analogous to that separating
so-called 'contemporary' visual artists (moreover nowadays more
'conceptual' than 'visual') from their modernist predecessors: Boulez
or Nono are in no way to Stravinsky what pop art was to Picasso or
Rothko, and it seems to me that with the expression 'contemporary
music' the composers of the following generations designate a highly
respectable stylistic tendency, but one they more or less abandoned
to the benefit sometimes of a 'return to' named in all simplicity
'neo-tonal'. In short, nowhere is periodisation an easy thing, and the
famous 'correspondence of the arts' is here, as almost everywhere
else, found wanting.

Almost: the only manifest counterpart, in so-called 'serious'
music, of 'contemporary' visual art – in the version of it presented

by Duchamp, then by conceptual art – can doubtless be found with John Cage, but one may find for it a kind of approximate equivalent in the period of the history of jazz characterised by the passage from *bop* to *free*. Coincidence or not, the dates tally perfectly: Ornette Coleman's *Free Jazz* appeared in 1960, the inaugural year of Warhol's adventure and everything that ensued. Jazz historians generally consider the era of *bop* and *hard-bop* (1940–1960) to be the age of 'modern' jazz, opposed to the 'classical' age of the thirties (*swing*) and the 'antique' age (*New Orleans*) of the twenties. This era coincided quite well with that, in painting, of abstract expressionism, which is held not without reason to be the most typical culmination of modernist painting. There are consonances, more obviously perceived than they are easy to define, on the one hand between the innovations of modernist painting (at least since cubism) and those of *be-bop*, on the other hand between the enterprises of 'de-definition' in *free jazz* (abandonment of harmonic progressions) and in contemporary visual art (abandonment of the non-figurative point of honour), not to mention the ideological connotations shared by these two movements, especially in the United States of the 1960s: *free jazz* is in many respects, and besides was intended to be, a *pop* jazz (moreover often grafted onto a *New Orleans* revival), by way of reaction against the elitism of *bop*, which was, beneath Gillespie's antics, a rather learned music. But the historical parallel stops here, for, since the sixties, 'contemporary art' hasn't ceased to flourish, whereas the vogue of *free*, for its part, appears to have declined in one or two decades, for reasons unknown to me, in favour of a return to a neo-*bop* become classical in its turn – a *revival* in its own way, 'post-contemporary' in Danto's sense, of which painting and sculpture offer no such clearly marked equivalents. As for contemporary architecture (in a purely chronological sense), it seems to me to be illustrated by the peaceful coexistence of a sustained post-Bauhaus modernism (for instance, Tanigushi at the MoMA, Pei almost everywhere, Foster in Hong Kong and at the Hearst Tower in Manhattan) and a postmodernism, at last freed from neo-eclecticism *à la* Philip Johnson, which culminates in a controlled extravagance: see Gehry at the Cinémathèque française or at the Guggenheim in Bilbao, Liebeskind at the Jewish Museum Berlin, Calatrava in Malmo, Koolhaas at the Television Headquarters in Peking, and already Saarinen in Yale and at the TWA, and Utzon at the Sydney Opera House – proposed in 1956, completed without him, and even against him, at least for the interior, in 1973, and today in the process of being more or less restored by him according to its original plans: it will only have been a half century in the making.

I've just learned what will supersede the *post-contemporary*. I should have guessed: it is, deliciously retro in advance, the *neo-contemporary*. Meanwhile, *contemporary* operates quite simply, pretty much everywhere, as a trendy synonym for *modern*: 'This new restaurant is friendly and very contemporary.' Recently heard, from the mouth of a profound jazz critic (they're all profound, these days): 'Coleman Hawkins has always been contemporary.'

Cordonnier/Cobbler. Among other manual talents, my father was something of a textile worker, in the sense that he would weave bedside rugs on a kind of loom whose equivalent I've never since seen. He was also, and much more so, an amateur cobbler. That is, he had, in the 'basement' of the house – not far from a bottle rack whose artistic merit we did not suspect – a workbench for all purposes, and, upon this workbench, a sort of anvil he called an 'iron foot [pied de fer]',[125] all kinds of awls, punches, skiving knives, splicing spikes, waxed or tarred threads, tins full of nails and tacks, various peculiar hammers and a stock of pieces of leather and rubber out of which he'd cut soles and heels for all our worn-down shoes. The iron foot, it goes without saying, in fact comprised several foot shapes and sizes for the fitting of the sole, and another more narrow one for that of the heels, the whole thing shaped like a triangle in three dimensions. It was for me, and still is, a pretty fascinating object: Chillida[126] isn't far away.

For the rare operations of a trickier nature, there was a professional cobbler very close by, whose shop was at the bottom of a very steep stairway that descended from our hill until you were level with the river. I'd enjoy conversing with him because, like any self-respecting shoe repairer, his mouth was always full of nails, which added zest, and even suspense, to his speech: I was forever awaiting an accident that never came.

---

[125] A 'cobbler's last'.
[126] Eduardo Chillida (1924–2002), Spanish abstract sculptor.

It was down the same iron-railed stairway that I would race to the Fin-d'Oise neighbourhood's small primary school, at least for the first two years (reception class, then second-year class, since I'd escaped 'nursery school' thanks to the patience of my mother, who taught me to read with a textbook named *Syllabaire Regimbeau* [*Regimbeau Syllabary*]) of an interminable education, since it hasn't yet ended, and which began, incidentally, better than it was to continue: the presence in class of my young first-year 'mistress' was for me overwhelming. Without contesting her pedagogical merits, my mother wouldn't refrain from saying at every opportunity, in an ever so slightly pinched tone: 'I don't know what he sees in her.' For my part, I think I still can see it.

Couples. I wonder if feminism has sufficiently 'denounced' (to whom?) or condemned (to what?) the male chauvinism presiding over the order in which famous couples, in fiction or elsewhere, are referred to: Adam and Eve, Orpheus and Eurydice, Theagenes and Chariclea, Calisto and Malibea, Chaereas and Callirhoe, Daphnis and Chloe, Philomena and Baucis, Perseus and Andromeda, Acis and Galatea, Ulysses and Penelope, Hector and Andromache, Paris and Helen, Tristan and Iseult, Paolo and Francesca, Dante and Beatrice, Tancred and Clorinda, Renaud and Armide, Paul and Virginia, Faust and Marguerite, Hermann and Dorothea, Ruslan and Ludmilla, Antoine and Antoinette, Edward and Caroline, Samson and Delilah, David and Bathsheba, Solomon and the Queen of Sheba, Pierre and Marie Curie, Anthony and Cleopatra, César and Rosalie, Troilus and Cressida, Hippolytus and Aricia, Pelléas and Mélisande, Porgy and Bess, and even, in groups, Sodom and Gomorrah. Commendable exceptions, variously explicable: Thetis and Peleus, Dido and Aeneas, Ruth and Boaz, Beatrice and Benedict, Héloïse and Abélard, Bonnie and Clyde, Ginger and Fred – I also have *She and He*, but it doesn't count: the author is a woman, although named George,[127] and Alfred's surviving brother[128] replied at once with a more compliant *He and She*.

---

[127] George Sand (1804–1876).
[128] Paul de Musset (1804–1880), brother of Alfred de Musset (1810–1857).

Bardadrac

Courage. 'Few people have enough to be cowardly in public' (Gautier).

Courrier/Mail. For several months, I had a copious correspondence with a geographically distant friend, apropos of a book that was constantly calling for some final tweaks. Perfected at last, the book was published. Satisfied, the friend wrote to me: 'At last, I shall be able to write to you about something else!' From that day onwards, not a single line.

Crampon/Clingy. The municipal library in Pontoise was housed in a semi-rotonda shaped outbuilding of the town hall, where none would think of behaving badly. The very fact of entering was actually in itself, on our part, a sign of misconduct, since it generally meant that we were there to skip class. But it was apparently for a good cause, and with the complicity of the master of the house, who appreciated this token of preference. I consulted there, for the first time, a Pléiade[129] volume, which was brought to us like the Holy Sacrament, wrapped in tissue-paper – not without reason: it was a Baudelaire, one of the first volumes published, in 1931 if I'm not mistaken, in the collection. Unaware of this fact, and of the very concept of a collection, I long believed that this work was the only one to benefit from so miraculous a presentation. The miracle evidently had to do with the 'bible' paper, of which I was aware of no use other than for the one belonging to my mother. It must have been Crampon's[130] translation – hence the ritual joke, when one of us became too pestering: '*Il n'y a pas que la bible de crampon* ['There isn't just Crampon's bible'/'The bible isn't alone in being clingy'].'

Crapaud/Toad. As ugly as its cousin the frog is (almost) graceful, it is actually it (the latter, as is well known, croaks in a shrill and frankly unpleasant way) that emits a minimalist and persistent song, at regular intervals, in a single note that Maupassant calls 'metallic and short' ('metallic' is needlessly unkind: it sounds, if anything, like a recorder [flûte à bec], but without the beak

---

[129] The *Bibliothèque de la Pléiade* (Gallimard) is an editorial collection publishing the complete works of classic authors in a reduced format.
[130] Augustin Crampon (1826–1894), Catholic theologian and Bible translator.

[sans bec]). Balzac, before him, frequented the countryside around Tours, between Saché and Montbazon, often enough to know the difference. But the noble style he inflicts upon his hero in *The Lily of the Valley* forbids him any mention of this animal's name. So on four occasions he resorts to disingenuous periphrases, worthy of the Abbé Delille:[131] '... the clear song, the single note cast incessantly in even time by the tree frog whose scientific name is unknown to me, but which ever since this solemn day I cannot hear without infinite delight' (I admit that neither do I know the *scientific* name of this species, but we weren't asking for so much); 'The roulades of the bard of amorous nights and the single note of the nightingale of the waters'; '... what the bard of the marshlands repeats when intoning its plaintive note'; '... voice of the waters, the plaintive cry of the tree frog'. The 'bard of amorous nights' is obviously the nightingale, the nightingale of the waters, bard of the marshlands, is our anonymous amphibian: so many periphrases to get around a toad!

Cravate/Tie. In the hierarchy of school classifications and awards, the prize of 'honour' came just after the prize of 'excellence'. Since there were, in my secondary school class, two rival and alternating 'brainy types' (one more scientific, the other, alas, more literary), sometimes I missed out on the latter, and had to be content with the former, until the favour could be returned. My father didn't fail, in his oblique way, to sanction this temporary demotion, feigning to inquire: 'So what do they call the *first* prize, again?' I knew, besides, that one or two notches beneath that and it would seriously be a question of my being 'apprenticed'. Someone recently told of how once, as he was returning from school with his teacher's congratulations for coming fourth, his father administered a vigorous slap with the commentary: 'Your teacher is very nice, but me, I don't work round the clock for you to come fourth!' Shift work aside, I think I can recognise my own in a gesture I was always spared by my presence upon the podium.

Hailing, as I've said, from the most illustrious hovel in Ménilmontant, and having become I'm not sure how, after the Great War, as it was still called, a tailor in a small workshop in the

---

[131] Jacques Delille (1738–1813), poet and translator of Virgil's *Georgics*.

Sentier neighbourhood,[132] we now lived on his 'pay' alone – since my mother had left her job when I was born – in what was no longer hardship, nor certainly comfort, but somewhere in-between which we especially didn't call 'poverty', a word reserved for the hardships of the penniless ex-bourgeois: it was simply the honest mediocrity of skilled manual labour. He thus viewed my scholarly performance with a rather wary satisfaction, detecting a promise of all manner of complications. Liberal but economical, he took a dim view of the costs and risks inherent in a hypothetical social promotion whose nature he sensed poorly, and the benefits none too clearly.

And yet: to be concerned with the state of the zodiac (I couldn't ignore for long, let alone dodge the slightly schizophrenic tendency ruled by the sign of Gemini) or mutually to 'have one's cards read', according to combinations such as 'great game [grand jeu]' or 'dog of spades [chien de pique]' – with each noteworthy trick, one had to 'cover' the litigious card with another supposed to confirm, clarify, belie or attenuate its forecast – was one of the weaknesses of the 'weaker' sex in my family. We went, on Sundays, as far as 'having our palms read', as though their patterns might alter from one week to the next. A more onerous superstition, we occasionally consulted professional 'clairvoyants' – the fees were professional, at least. So a clairvoyant, then, had predicted, in my very earliest infancy, that I would later be a 'great intellectual'. This imprudent forecast, perhaps exaggerated by my mother and by the adjective, had for her assumed the weight of a certainty, and she drew from it the conclusion that I should 'continue my studies', meaning sit the entrance exams for secondary school. For the reasons mentioned above, my father resisted as much as he could, objecting with something like 'Great or small, being an intellectual isn't a profession.' This remark proved incidentally that he didn't entirely contest the fatal oracle, as though Laius (I wonder where this comparison comes from) had merely objected to Jocasta that it served no purpose, on the contrary, to send the little one away. Ignoring this stingily professional detail, my mother rectified with gentle firmness: 'Mademoiselle Hubert said: *great*.' I think she took that to mean above all *a writer*, disregarding without

---

[132] In the 2nd arrondissement of Paris.

giving it too much thought the fact that a scientist, a doctor or an engineer, among others, is also an intellectual. Neither was anyone astonished by this ontological peculiarity, namely that there is no such thing as a *minor* intellectual: read the obituaries in your favourite newspaper. In short, the decision was made, doubtless in the middle of the 'phoney war', since I entered the Pontoise secondary school in October '40. My father had been mobilised in September '39, but I struggle to believe that my mother took advantage of this circumstance, for she was all the more loath to force his hand in that she had no need to do so in order to achieve her aims. By the grace of a leave of absence, perhaps? For there was at least one of these during this latency period: I can still picture him, returning one evening to kiss me unexpectedly as I'd just fallen asleep, terrifying for me in his khaki greatcoat – like, for Astyanax, Hector beneath his glancing helm – and dismayed by my terror. So there I was embarked upon an 'intellectual' destiny, as grandiose as it was undefined.

A destiny and not a career, for I shared the paternal opinion on that point. Still today, after a few decades of dubious practice, I couldn't say that this category appears to me well founded, in light of the use to which it has been put for more than a century. Less and less do I think that one human activity is essentially more intellectual than any other. Man, as is well known, is intelligent because he has a hand, of which the brain is just an extension, there is no so-called 'manual' profession that doesn't demand some mental participation, and I'm not sure that those who use their hands the least are necessarily those who make the best use of what at home we called the 'grey matter' – above all in the typical expression 'wearying the grey matter', where the wearying redeemed everything. When he was asked what manual profession he'd like to have, Proust replied quite simply: 'writer', which, *a contrario*, puts things pretty well in their place – even if, through the fault of the computer, this profession has ceased being manual to become merely *digital*,[133] and if one may no longer say, like my holy mother, that these people earn their living from the sweat of their wrists. It is therefore true that being an intellectual is not a profession, and I would add: nor a magisterium, and especially

---

[133] I.e. involving one's fingers, but also exercised by way of digital technology.

not the one nowadays assigned to 'intellectuals' considered to be an enlightened caste and endowed with a privilege of competence expressed by manifestoes, petitions, opinion columns, participation in debates and other commission headquarters. I can see no responsibility linked to the exercise of thought that isn't shared by the whole of (right or wrong) thinking humanity, that's to say by humanity tout court.

For this reason or another, my supposedly intellectual destiny was then for me quite distinct from the choice of a profession: I would be an intellectual just as others are asthmatic or diabetic, and I wondered merely at what age it would happen to me, because undoubtedly this state, though prescribed by my birth chart and the lines of my palms, lay essentially in the future. As for professions, things had a more empirical aspect, though they weren't always realistic. As a child, I wanted to be a naval officer, since I'd read Pierre Loti and Claude Farrère, then an architect, then a film-maker, or maybe a sound engineer, like the hero of *Days of Hope*[134] in his civilian life; of all that, my only – but inconsolable – current regret certainly concerns architecture, which nothing has ever dissuaded me from regarding, like the author of *Eupalinos*,[135] as the art *par excellence*. Each of these successive, and purely virtual, choices arose from a renunciation for economic reasons. As for schools able to guide me towards a profession, there remained the 'Normale Sup',[136] we shall see why.

I was happy to become the intellectual I was supposed to have to be one day or another, but the profession of teacher, which appeared to be more and more bound to this alleged vocation, had never figured on my list of wishes, doubtless for want of sufficiently prestigious models. The compromise between the desirable and the possible consisted in 'doing' the École Normale Supérieure, then branching off, upon leaving, onto a path that was in my eyes more glorious, such as, I fear, that of journalism (we had never heard, thank God, of the École Nationale d'Administration[137]).

---

[134] By André Malraux (1937).
[135] Paul Valéry.
[136] The École Normale Supérieure, Rue d'Ulm.
[137] Another *Grande École*, the 'National School of Administration', was founded in 1945 in view of democratising access to the Senior Civil Service; originally in Paris, since 2005 fully relocated to Strasbourg.

In my mother's eyes, there was nothing blameworthy in this change of direction: a journalist was perhaps closer than a teacher to intellectual glory, and the prospect of Rue d'Ulm was for her illuminated by the examples of Romain Rolland,[138] Jaurès,[139] Léon Blum[140] and Édouard Herriot,[141] the latter what's more the mayor of her hometown: as can be seen by the orientation of this honours list, my parents thought and voted to the left, and I had myself, perched atop the paternal shoulders, shouted (but without raising my fist, lest I should fall) 'Long live Blum!' in a few demonstrations for the Popular Front, whose rapid collapse went initially unnoticed by us in the euphoria of the 40-hour week and paid holidays.

But we didn't know much about how to negotiate this necessary passage. Luckily, I had at Pontoise a good history teacher, whom we called 'Bodeste' in tribute to the denasalised pronunciation imposed upon him by a perpetually congested organ. His sudden and fleeting furies and his liberal use of the expression 'bloody little cretin' had often stimulated my schooling. Between two bouts of wrath, he had a soft spot for me, and discreetly encouraged me to embrace his discipline. Already less inclined to find my way in time than in space, I would more gladly have become a geographer: since I'd done well at it in primary school, my father had, inevitably, dubbed me 'top of the atlas [premier de l'atlas[142]]'. He claimed, moreover, that I had distinguished east from west well before knowing my left from my right (that, too, has remained with me). Even so I had, and still do, some trouble situating those archipelagos nowadays more or less threatened with submersion like the Comoros, the Celebes, the Seychelles, the Maldives and the Maluku Islands, or, on the other side of the globe, Madeira, the Canaries, the Azores and Bermuda. Things would deteriorate more seriously in secondary school, with geology, which was treacherously called 'physical geography': I lost my way in the Lias, the Trias, the Jurassic and the Cretaceous. I have never found my

---

[138] Dramatist, novelist, essayist and art historian, Nobel prize winner in 1915 (1866–1944).
[139] Jean Jaurès, French socialist leader (1859–1914).
[140] French socialist politician and three-time prime minister (1872–1950).
[141] French Radical politician and three-time prime minister (1899–1957).
[142] Adapted from 'premier de la classe', 'top of the class'.

way back there, and I'm often infuriated by not being able, like Julien Gracq, to understand and decipher the landscapes I love.

We knew from hearsay, as it happens, that Bodeste had once sat, without success, the competitive examination for the Rue d'Ulm. Of course, we weren't aware that the important thing, in this matter, is not to pass the examination, but to have prepared for it for two or three years, following which the years at the École represent hardly more than just another (open) boarding school, and we retained above all the fact of this 'failure'. But anyway our historian nonetheless enjoyed a kind of intellectual authority, and I went to consult him about this dubious prospect. The official pretext was to thank him for what my own success at the baccalaureate owed to his competence, and to reward him, in this regard, with one of the ties that owed everything to my father's (competence), and which had already, in other analogous circumstances, symbolised the tribute of the hand to the spirit. In my family, as with the *Légion d'honneur*, whoever said reward said tie, but I don't know to what extent, let's assume it was legal, the *Maison Hamberger*,[143] which we shall find later in its place on Rue de la Jussienne, contributed thus to our various demonstrations of civility. Bodeste appeared more touched than embarrassed by this mark of gratitude, till the moment when, informed by him of the mysteries of the 'khâgne', the *licence* and the *agrégation*,[144] I asked him in all stupidity whether, at the end of this journey, one was really 'obliged to teach'. This man who, otherwise obliged, had taught all his life without having, and for very good reason, ever 'left' the École or been endowed with the *agrégation*, didn't take my question too kindly, and, furiously crumpling up the paternal offering, which he nevertheless refrained from throwing back in my face, he replied in a legitimately outraged tone: 'Bloody little cretin, try to get in there first!'

Unable though I still was really to understand why, I took this final quarrel as a kind of rite of passage: seven years of on the whole joyous education despite the rigours of the times were crystallised in that sentence before sinking into a long forgetfulness, while seven others, more austere, were thereby foreshadowed. I thanked

[143] The tailor's shop where Genette's father worked, in the 2nd arrondissement of Paris: see the entry 'Jussienne', below.
[144] For 'khâgne', see note 83. The 'licence' is equivalent to a 'bachelor's degree' in the UK; for the 'agrégation', see note 97.

him for his advice without taking offence at its form, and we left each other almost good friends, he equipped with his tie, and I with my viaticum, since one didn't yet say 'road map'.

Credibility. Manifest or proven ability to execute one's threats; curiously isn't applied to promises.

Crédulité/Gullibility. Naive tendency to believe that others believe everything you tell them.

Crévoux. Hard to imagine a more rudimentary ski resort than that one, as it looked in December 1952: just one piste, no chairlift, not a single ski tow. The slope, opposite the gite, could only be climbed by lining your skis with sealskins, which it was better to remove for the descent, even if, in the direction of the nap, they didn't completely refuse to slide. Yet, in this remote village in the Hautes-Alpes, somewhere between Embrun and le Col des Vars, the light was dazzling and the air exhilarating. A year later, at Les Houches, there was already the grand luxury of the 'ski lifts', but the sunshine was too wanting on the southern side of the Vallée de l'Arve, since, contrary to all verbal logic, all southern slopes look north, and my heart was no longer in it.

Criticism. Just in case I haven't already written it elsewhere (and even if I have), I've often wondered why they described as 'new' the variety that caused such a stir, and for some so much scandal, at the beginning of the sixties. New, it doubtless was in relation to the diet of literary history on which lived the 'old Sorbonne' (which had been in Péguy's day the 'modern Sorbonne'), but nothing essential, in my view, distinguishes it from the extra-university criticism of the interwar period [de l'entre-deux-guerres], itself the heir, at the turn between-the-centuries [de l'entre-deux-siècles], of the revolt of a Proust against Sainte-Beuve or of a Péguy against Lanson. As with all such labels, this one had a certain media-friendly virtue: in the sixties, this practice was recognised as a literary genre in its own right, and the least collection of critical essays was entitled to its place 'downstairs' in *Le Monde*. But I find it in the present case to be rather inappropriate; *needlessly* inappropriate, moreover, for novelty is never in itself a merit. The 'pathways' of literary criticism have been without any notable interruption for a good century, and

I think justice ought more often to have been done to the masters that were, each according to his own detour, Valéry, Charles du Bos, Albert Thibaudet or Jean Prévost. Moreover, Georges Poulet, Jean-Pierre Richard or Jean Starobinski neglected not to do so, but it was in journalistic criticism that this memory was lacking, hence the inappropriate qualifier. I can also remember reading, at the end of the forties, Thierry Maulnier's *Racine*, Schlumberger's *Pleasure with Corneille*, Groethuysen's *Rousseau*, Giraudoux's *The Five Temptations of La Fontaine*, Bénichou's *Moralities of the Great Century*, and above all perhaps a collection of short and very free essays published by Gallimard under the title *Tableau of French Literature from Corneille to Chénier* – where I discovered, with a few highs and lows, what criticism practised as one of the fine arts could be.

But to say that the 'new' in fact dates back to the beginning of the XXth century is perhaps still not to cast the net sufficiently far. Poulet would declare to us, at Cerisy, that Proust had founded 'thematic criticism'; I'm not sure that we oughtn't to look earlier for the first fruits of modern criticism: in France, at least, we can in truth go back to Baudelaire, to the ensemble of studies that were collected after his death under the titles *Romantic Art* and *Aesthetic Curiosities*. I don't wish to develop this superfluous reminder, but merely to emphasise a detail, which really isn't one: Baudelaire's critical work bears not only upon literature (Hugo, Balzac), but also and especially upon painting (Delacroix, Constantin Guys and others) and upon music (Wagner's). That particular novelty hasn't aged, quite the contrary.

Crosson. At a summer camp in Sully-sur-Loire, it was obviously forbidden to swim in the river, reputedly as perilous here as elsewhere. By way of compensation, and on their own initiative, our supervisors let us splash around in a watercress bed that extended, at the foot of the château, over the bottom of a riverlet called la Sange. The acidulous taste of the aquatic plant nibbled in passing added to the pleasure of the bathing and reminded me of the family roast chicken, always accompanied by this obligatory garnish, and of the fact that my mother, maybe from a vestige of her Lyon dialect, would always ask: 'Who wants some *crosson* ['cresson'/watercress]?' Hugo, as is known, loved 'Chelles and its watercress beds [cressonnières]' and, in 'El Cid in Exile', he sends the young Basque girls to 'wash in the watercress beds', which probably no more improves the flavour of this salad than did our semi-clandestine plashing. But with him, the word and the thing are perhaps brought forth by the rhyme.

Croyances/Beliefs. One of my teachers, fanatically 'secular', when anyone was careless enough to say 'I believe that … ', invariably interrupted with: 'You aren't here to *believe*, but to *learn* and to *know*.' From which has abided with me – belief or knowledge – the idea that one cannot at once believe and know the same thing. Obviously, as John Searle writes somewhere, *to believe* consists in *believing to be true*, meaning in sum *to believe that one knows*: I believe, that's to say I believe that I know, that the Earth moves around the Sun; yet, just as obviously, what one believes to be true is neither necessarily true nor necessarily false. Simply, the ways of belief and of knowledge are independent, but not incompatible, when the belief happens to be a right opinion (a true belief), which grants some legitimacy to the bizarre-seeming utterance: 'I believed that *p*, but it was true.' The bizarreness is due to the *but*, but this *but* is correct: subjectively, I believed that I believed it, but objectively I knew it.

I broke with my mother's religion a little too early to recall what faith represented for me before I 'lost' it; everything happened in fact as though I'd lost it at birth, or at least on the day of my baptism. Another word would perhaps be required in order to name the particular (though very common) kind of belief to which Paul Veyne referred when asking whether the Greeks believed in their myths, and when replying, appropriately enough, 'yes and no', or 'it depends': which Greeks, moreover, and on which days? The same historian, bolstered by a personal and shared experience of this coexistence of heterogeneous and contradictory 'programmes of truth', elsewhere detects an ambiguity, if not of the same order, at least of the same power, in the belief of Western Stalinian militants in the excellence of the communist regime. That belief, like most religious certainties, consists not in *believing that one knows*, but in *wanting to believe*, without seeking too much to know, or rather in seeking not to know too much, and sometimes even in knowing quite well, but in the mode of 'I know it very well, but even so', or of the paradoxical 'Even more reason' (*Credo quia absurdum*), since certain people, myself included, had masochistically 'joined' (absolute verb) after reading *Darkness at Noon*,[145] and no doubt others, later, *after* reading Khrushchev's secret speech or *The Gulag Archipelago*.[146] These twists and turns are unfathomable, and even my pious mother 'believed' rather more on Sunday mornings than on other days. On Sunday afternoons, as I've already mentioned, she almost believed more in cards and palms.

Cuir/Malapropism. Littré accounts for this word through the fact of 'flaying' a word, just as one flays an animal in order to remove its skin.[147] The thing proceeds most often from the resemblance, hence a contagion, between two expressions; those, collected by Proust, from Françoise or the manager of the hotel in Balbec are of this order. Encouraged by this precedent (of collecting), I have myself pinpointed a few, unintended or deliberate, most of which more or less form part of my family inheritance, and of which none is entirely devoid of meaning: *Vieux comme mes robes*, As old as my dresses [from 'vieux comme Hérode', 'as old as the hills'], *Hernie fiscale*, Fiscal hernia [from 'hernie discale', 'slipped disc'], *Canal de Suède*, Swedish Canal [from 'Canal de Suez', 'Suez Canal'], *Vieilles noiseries*, Old hazelnut orchards [from 'viennoiserie'], *Acheter une maison en vieil âgé*, Buy a house in old age [from 'acheter une maison en viager', 'buy a house in life annuity'], *Jeter l'eau propre*, Throw out the clean water [from 'jeter l'opprobre', 'cast scorn'], *Fier comme un petit banc*, As proud as a little bench [from 'fier comme Artaban', 'as proud as a peacock'], *Nouvelles hybrides*, New hybrids [from 'Nouvelles-Hébrides', 'New Hebrides'], *À contre-gouttes*, Against the drops [from 'au compte-gouttes', 'by the dropper', 'sparingly'], *À pied, asphalte et en voiture*, On foot, asphalt and by car [from 'à pied, à cheval et en voiture', 'on foot, on horseback and by car'], *Éparpiller ses yeux*, To scatter one's eyes [from 'écarquiller les yeux', 'to stare wide-eyed'], *Avoir pognon sur rue*, To have cash on the road [from 'avoir pignon sur rue', 'to have one's gable above the road', 'to be well established'], *Éclairage génital*, Genital lighting [from 'éclairage général', 'ceiling lighting'], *Être comme un coq en pâtre*, To be like a rooster dressed

---

[145] By Arthur Koestler (1940).
[146] By Aleksandr Solzhenitsyn (1973).
[147] The French 'cuir' also signifies 'leather'.

as a shepherd [from 'être comme un coq en pâte', 'to be like a rabbit in clover'], *Séparer le bon grain de l'ivresse*, To separate the wheat from the drunkenness [from 'séparer le bon grain de l'ivraie', 'to separate the wheat from the chaff'], *Bouc hémisphère*, Hemisphere goat [from 'bouc émissaire', 'scapegoat'], *Spectre royal*, Royal spectre, *Dessus du palmier*, Top of the palm tree [from 'dessus du panier', 'the top of the basket', 'the pick of the bunch'], *Bassin de gras-double*, Bowl of ox tripe [from 'bassin de radoub', 'dry dock'], Deus ex quinquina [from 'deus ex machina'], *Alice au pays des merguez*, Alice in Merguezland [from 'Alice au pays des merveilles', 'Alice in Wonderland'], *Immaculée contraception*, Immaculate contraception, *Immatriculée conception*, Registered Conception, *L'épée de Madame Oclès*, The sword of Madame Oclès [from 'l'épée de Damoclès', 'the sword of Damocles'], *Touchez pas au grizzly*, Don't touch the grizzly [from 'Touchez pas au grisbi', 'Hands Off the Loot'], *Ménagère approvisionnée*, Well-stocked housewife [from 'La Mégère apprivoisée', 'The Taming of the Shrew'], *Chapelle Strychnine*, Strychnine Chapel (allusion to the Borgias), *Horloge gastronomique*, Gastronomical clock (the stomach is calling), *Impératif parégorique*, Paregorical imperative (the intestine is protesting), *Semelle sainte*, Holy sole (suitable for pilgrimages) [from 'semaine sainte', 'Holy Week'], *Simulateur cardiaque*, Cardiac simulator (it's a start), *L'Amour et l'accident*, Love and the Accident (see Félix Faure[148]) [from *L'Amour et l'occident*, *Love in the Western World*[149]], *Qui trop embrasse manque le train*, Whoever embraces too much misses the train (railway proverb) [from 'qui trop embrasse mal étreint', 'whoever embraces too much hugs poorly', 'grasp all, lose all'], *L'occasion fait le lardon*, Opportunity makes the kid (demographic saying) [from 'l'occasion fait le larron', 'opportunity makes the thief'], *On ne peut pas naître et avoir tété*, You can't be born and suckle (*idem.*) [from 'on ne peut pas être et avoir été', 'you cannot be and have been', 'you can't have your cake and eat it too'], *L'amour mesclun*, Mesclun love (orgy) [from *L'Amour médecin*, *Dr. Cupid*[150]], *L'amour mesquin*, Mean love (jealousy), *Le mesquin malgré lui*, The mean one in spite of himself

---

[148] Former president of France (1841–1899): died at the age of 58 from apoplexy while engaged in a sexual act with 30-year-old Margeurite Steinheil.
[149] By Denis de Rougement (1939).
[150] Play by Molière (1665).

(Harpagon,[151] presumably) [from *Le Médecin malgré lui*, *The Doctor in Spite of Himself*[152]], *Jugement de Salomé*, Judgement of Salome ('Each condemned person shall have his head cut off'), *Hurler dans les brancards*, To howl in the stretchers (there's often cause to) [from 'ruer dans les brancards', 'to lash out in the stretchers', 'to kick up a fuss'], *Presque station de service*, Nearly a petrol station (I know one like that) [from 'prestation de service', 'service provision'], *Congelé payé*, Frozen goods paid for (sperm bank donor) [from 'congés payé', 'paid holidays'], *La preuve par l'œuf*, Proof by the egg (Columbus) [from 'la preuve par neuf', 'the proof by nine', 'irrefutable proof'], *Never moins le quart*, a quarter to never (bilingual agony) [from 'neuf heures moins le quart', 'a quarter to nine'], *Ad Vietnam aeternam*: this one, obviously more recent, is owed to the *Canard enchaîné*,[153] which applied it judiciously to the second war in Iraq. I also really like (probably less intentional): 'On essaie de nous refiler le bébé avec l'eau du bain', 'They're trying to pass us the baby with the bathwater' [from 'refiler le bébé', 'to pass the buck' and 'jeter le bébé avec l'eau du bain', 'to throw the baby out with the bathwater'], and 'On veut me faire passer pour un bouc émissaire, mais je ne me laisserai pas faire', 'They want to make me look like a scapegoat, but I shan't be pushed around' [from 'une bonne à tout faire', 'a maid-of-all-work', 'a skivvy'].

I also like faux-malapropisms: by this I mean expressions, to my knowledge perfectly correct, that some people feel the need to amend, denouncing therein a folk etymology. Thus, 'cor anglais' would be a malapropism for *cor anglé* ['bevelled horn'], 'homard à l'américaine' ['American-style lobster'] another for *homard à l'armoricaine* ['Armorican-style lobster'], 'bouchée à la reine' ['queen's morsel', 'chicken vol-au-vent'] another for *bouchée à la lorraine* ['Lorraine morsel'], 'prendre la vie par le bon bout' ['look on the bright side of life'] a fourth for the overly exotic *la vie par le bambou* ['life by the bamboo'], 'connu comme le loup blanc' ['known like the white wolf', 'known to one and all'] for *comme le houblon* ['like hops'], 'un nègre en chemise' ['a negro in shirt sleeves', 'chocolate mousse with whipped cream'] for *un aigle en*

[151] Protagonist in Molière's *L'Avare* (*The Miser*) (1668).
[152] Play by Molière (1666).
[153] 'The Chained-Up Duck' or 'The Chained-Up Paper', French satirical weekly newspaper.

chemise ['an eagle in shirt sleeves'], and 'Harris Tweed' for *Irish Tweed* (in fact, this tweed, as I've never been able to ignore, isn't Irish at all, but is of course woven on the Scottish Isle of Harris; the real Irish challenge to Scotland is Irish whiskey, older than Scotch, triple distilled, and guzzled without moderation on St Patrick's Day); I shall explain later, a paternal bequest, *s'ennuyer comme un bras mort* ['to be as bored as an oxbow lake', from 's'ennuyer comme un rat mort', 'to be as bored as a dead rat', 'to be bored to death']. I admit that these few apocryphal examples don't make for a particularly handsome set, but I'm working on it, and besides I have never known, between 'de pommes de terre en robe des champs' ['potatoes in field-dress', 'jacket potato') and '... en robe de chambre' ['... in a dressing gown'], which one is the malapropism.

Cumul[154]**/Cumulation.** 'The baccalaureate for all, said Vialatte, is a good thing. But it's still not enough. One ought to reserve this diploma for people who cannot obtain it. For otherwise some have it all, knowledge and the diploma, and the others nothing. Where's the justice? Those with knowledge would cope perfectly well; the others likewise with their diploma. We'd put an end to the scandal of cumulation.' It is certainly true that the world isn't fair: things only benefit those who don't need them. Folk version: 'It always rains on the drenched.'

Cuti. At Launay during the Easter holidays of 1950, I was suspected of having the rather benign form of primary tuberculosis (then still known as 'tuberculin conversion') that is pleurisy. Moved fairly swiftly to Angers, in a bedroom on the second floor of 'Villa 1900', I have especially retained, among others, three unequally pleasant memories. The first is the sweet scent (jasmin? violet? iris?) used by the doctor, by all accounts a distinguished phtisiologist, who very quickly 'made' the diagnosis by means of a simple manual auscultation: the index and middle finger of the left hand placed on the patient's chest and struck with two fingers, the same ones,

---

[154] In French, the term 'cumul' is commonly used in contexts referring to a person's concurrent, and often deemed unfairly advantageous, holding of several official titles or posts.

of the right hand). The dull sound elicited by a pleural cavity congested with 'serofibrinous' liquid left no room for any doubt; this sound was designated by a Latin expression invented (like the stethoscope) by the great Laennec: *sicut percussi femoris*, that's to say as though one were tapping similarly upon a thigh – why a thigh? Perhaps with reference to Diderot, who thus tormented those of Catherine II. This expression is my second memory; the third is more involved. I had to be rid of said liquid, by means of a drain between the walls of my left pleural cavity; the good doctor had invented an ingenious instrument consisting of a trocar to be introduced, between two ribs, into the litigious area, and (here was the piece of practical genius) a kind of food mill pump, which seemed to me to be fashioned from the music mill of my childhood, whose handle he carefully turned, and which produced, without any music, the necessary suction. At the end of the operation (a little over two litres, all the same), he asked whether I'd experienced any pain, in a gentle tone of voice strongly suggestive of the answer. I thus politely assured him of the contrary; actually, and apart from the slight pain resulting from the introduction of the trocar between two ribs, the internal sensation of *vacuum cleaning* had been rather pleasant. Having also cleaned and packed away his equipment, the doctor advised, still sweet-smelling, a few months' stay in a sanatorium to allow me to regain strength. I then noticed, belatedly, that he had in his brown hair an elegant strand of white that I must have gazed upon throughout the entire operation, then it dawned on me that the end of my school year and consequently my presentation for the entrance exam at the Rue d'Ulm had just been cancelled on prescription. 'Meanwhile, he added, by way of a temporary diet, give him fruit.' I wanted not for it, nor for anything else, during the few weeks of this sojourn betwixt and between: bread, love and the chemist. My benevolent home nurse enlivened her role, among other ways, by quoting – I can't find the source – either Hamlet, or Laforgue,[155] or Laforgue's Hamlet, or goodness knows which other ungrateful valetudinarian: 'They're all nurses!'

Daltonism. Among other marked peculiarities, he was (and declared himself to be, in order to avoid misunderstandings) *daltonic*. Within

[155] Jules Laforgue, Franco-Uruguayan poet (1860–1887).

the family context, I thought for ages that it concerned a mysterious religious or political sect. The mystery was inevitably transferred onto the person of this eponymous leader, a Dalton whose exploits were yet to be sung by the newspapers and cartoon strips. When the truth of the matter was explained to me, I remained perplexed, failing to understand how you could, not confuse green and red, but take the one for the other and contrariwise without a simple lexical permutation being called upon to put everything right: when you see red, say it's green, and *vice versa*, it's merely a question of words. For that matter, I still can't understand it.

Décade/Ten Days. Sub-genre of the genre *colloquium*, once peculiar to the encounters at Pontigny, and long ago transferred to Cerisy-la-Salle, deep in the Aurevillian[156] bocage. I participated in two of them, of which only the first was actually held for ten (11?) days, from the 2nd to the 12th September, 1966. Organised by Georges Poulet and entitled 'The Current Pathways of Criticism', and despite the double absence of Roland Barthes and Jean Starobinski, it was the opportunity for a kind of – in effect very limited – 'clarification' [une sorte de 'point' – très ponctuel en effet] of what had for two or three years been called the *'Nouvelle Critique'*. The practice so designated was not, as I've said, quite as radically innovative as the newspapers believed it to be, nor as homogeneous as its detractors feigned to imagine it. In fact, two tendencies were fairly clearly distinguishable there: on the one hand, a so-called 'thematic' criticism, with a more psychologising (Poulet, Richard, Starobinski) or sociologising (Lukács and Lucien Goldmann) orientation, on the other hand a so-called 'formalist' or 'structuralist' criticism, which I was supposed to represent there by default, or perhaps in an acting capacity. Between these two tendencies, the opposition didn't go as far as confrontation, owing to the amicable relations between their various adherents, and because their division of the field of studies rendered them more complementary than antagonistic. The sole polemical note was introduced by a participant then of Sartrean affiliation, and who, like his mentor, took structuralism to be a bourgeois ideology, and

---

[156] Jules-Amédée Barbey d'Aurevilly (1808–1889), novelist and short-story writer, born in Lower Normandy.

more precisely to be the expression of a neo-capitalism bordering on the totalitarian; I even think that he let slip a comparison with Nazism on this subject, in respect of which Georges Poulet, concerned with the intellectual standing of his *décade*, demanded of him a solemn retraction, and which doesn't therefore feature in the minutes – it's rather a shame, but nothing, as you can see, is ever entirely lost. The best memory I've kept from the whole of this meeting is that a series of withdrawals and misunderstandings led us, Babette and me, to an immense and luminous bedroom, which was still called the André Gide room. Such an inheritance justified all the rest.

My second 'décade', organised as it happens by Serge Doubrovsky and Tzvetan Todorov, and devoted to 'The Teaching of Literature', lasted only five days, from the 23rd to the 27th July, 1969: it was a half-décade (Michel Deguy said more delicately: *pentade*), as there are elsewhere, more heroically, half-brigades. The André Gide room had been otherwise assigned, and I was quartered at an inn 20 kilometres away, which didn't incite me to attend regularly. The whole thing wavered between a rehash of 68 and an anticipation of Woodstock, at least as regards the nocturnal consumption of products supposed, mistakenly, to improve all kinds of performance. The quarrel of the *Nouvelle Critique* had meanwhile lost its theoretical significance, and the question was reduced to its lowest pedagogical denominator. Of the founding fathers, the only one to have made it this time, doubtless by way of compensation, was Roland Barthes, for a brief paper that afforded him the opportunity to ratify said reduction in the following abrupt terms: 'Literature is what is taught, and that's that.' It was just, as he'd candidly announced, 'a few improvised observations, simple and even simplistic, which were suggested to me by reading or rereading a manual of the history of French literature'. This rather virtual manual wasn't named, and I don't recall its identity being revealed in the course of the discussion: Lagarde and Castex, perhaps. I do on the other hand recall, thinking I was 'informing the debate', having proposed between the different levels of teaching a distinction that RB, no doubt interpreting this proposition as an indirect objection, greeted with a glum 'Perhaps you are right' which doesn't appear in the published acts either, and where I recognised the typical expression of an affectionately flat refusal.

The other highlight was the contribution of Michael Riffaterre, who then had a reputation for arriving at each colloquium, at the precise time of his turn to speak, in a taxi supposed to await him until the end of the associated discussion, no more no less. It was even claimed that, to underscore the insolence of the slight, he'd ask the driver to keep the engine running. I can't recall whether he confirmed on that day this alleged habit, which would serve to illustrate fairly well the Gatsby side of his personality – even were this side purely legendary: as they say out West, *'Print the legend!'* Job done.

I had a few obscure personal reasons to decline, some years later, the proposal for another *décade*, which was in danger of embalming me ahead of my time. But perhaps it never is the right time, and I believe I had already sensed, between my person and the genre colloquium (and its various species), a certain incompatibility of intellectual mood and psychic habitus, or the other way round. Seldom at ease in exchanges exceeding the one-to-one, I tack laboriously, in these circumstances, between the desire to impress and the wish for the earth to swallow me up. These competitive occasions are always unwholesome for one who doesn't live on very good terms with his ego – nor any better, it must be admitted, with that of others.

Dédicace/Signing. 'One day, said William Golding bitterly, someone will discover an *unsigned* copy of one of my novels, and it will be worth a fortune.' This valuation might stem from a cause other than scarcity: signing [dédicacer] a book (in fact, one of its copies: *dedicating* [*dédier*] the book itself is another matter, no better, but easier to avoid: you're never obliged to dedicate a book) doesn't go without an at least implicit and inevitably oblique reference to this book, and thus to its author, and this return upon the self, albeit one tinged with self-derision, in an act in principle turned towards the other, doesn't occur without a share of narcissism that is disagreeable to everyone, save no doubt to truly narcissistic authors, since they do exist. True discretion would therefore consist in merely inscribing the dedicatee's name, with no trace of any other commentary: 'Copy belonging to … ' It would not, I fear, always be very well taken. The best would obviously be to have nothing to sign. But one must live after all, even poorly.

I therefore send, suitably signed, a copy of a such and such a book to a friend, not to give him any highly doubtful pleasure, but to avoid causing offence by appearing to have forgotten him; the many services involved being what they are, he will perhaps moreover not receive it, and will think that I've effectively forgotten him; as for me, I'll think that, having received it, he doesn't care to thank me for it: more offence; but if I ask him about this, I'll appear to be reproaching him for his silence, and to be displaying a little authorial vanity. This little drama is a dead-end (it's the definition of tragedy).

I really value the slightly perverse attention of this other person, who, for years now, each time I send him something, fails not, with a supporting commentary as pertinent as it is retrospective, to thank me for the one preceding it. This perpetual lag in reading, which I admire for the organisation it supposes, reassures me in the feeling, perhaps illusory, of persevering in my being.

Depression. Bout of lucidity.

Destiny. When the gods wish to punish us, it is well known, they fulfil our desires and, should we survive, we harbour a just rancour against them for so doing. But we ought, no less justly, to be grateful to them for all the satisfactions they have refused us, thereby sparing us the worst setbacks, sometimes the worst catastrophes, since there are opportune failures, and gratifying disappointments. I can count for my part about ten of them, of various kinds, which I run through now and again with almost unalloyed pleasure. 'Fate, said Hugo, opens one door only by closing another'; but of these two gestures, the most salutary isn't always the one we think.

Devises/Mottoes. For a long time I, *in petto*, borrowed from Mies Van der Rohe (who himself, I suppose …) the motto *Less is more*. Disheartened by the circular reciprocity implied by the copula *is*, I subsequently abandoned it in favour of *Moderato ma non troppo*, eventually forgotten in its turn, in favour of a rather more minimalist, and less onerous, absence of motto. Not quite, as you can see.

Diagnosis. Nothing could be easier, say the shrinks: if the patient arrives late, they are an aggressive type; if they arrive early, they are an anxious type. But if they arrive on time? They are an obsessive.

I think I know into which slot of this irrefutable classification I may be squeezed, but I don't wish to overdo the self-portrait here. In the seventies, the following perhaps apocryphal anecdote went the rounds: during some unhappy love affair, thinking he'd pull through it with a quick therapy, a great Parisian intellectual booked a meeting, without specifying the reason, with a reputedly expeditious psychoanalyst. Convinced – a misunderstanding typical of the time – that the intellectual was there to present him with an inevitably subversive petition, the Illustrious one received him in his, if I dare say, civilian office. The intellectual, abashed, set him straight. Relieved, the analyst then guided him towards his professional consulting room, equipped with the requisite accoutrements. The intellectual began the story of his woes; the analyst interrupted him very swiftly, for one doesn't trifle with the rules of art: 'Sorry, I don't treat heartaches.' Disappointed, the intellectual was set to bid farewell. The analyst stopped him even more swiftly: 'That'll be 300 francs.' This was, it seems, the price of a consultation, and, after all, our intellectual, relieved in turn and otherwise, had been given one, and even a diagnosis he perhaps would not have been able to 'make' himself.

Dissimulation. It's easy to dissimulate; the hard thing is to dissimulate the dissimulation: nothing can be seen more easily.

Divination. A likeable film by Nancy Myers, *What Women Want* (2000, with Mel Gibson and Helen Hunt), rests upon this straightforward, but not excessively banal, postulate: following I can't recall what traumatism, the protagonist is able to 'hear' what is being thought silently in his presence, indeed *about* him, by all the women he meets. *Hear* is clearly an expedient variant, in a cinematographic context, of simply *divining* (word for word), and the restriction of the phenomenon to the divination of women's thoughts a convention necessary for the romantic comedy genre, with the consequences and unforeseen developments you can imagine all the way to the de rigueur *happy ending*, with the welcome loss of an aptitude that had become troublesome. I'm amazed that such a premise, potentially extended to every encounter irrespective of gender, hasn't been utilised more by novelistic, dramatic or more generally cinematic fiction. It clearly pertains to the supernatural or the fantastic, like that of the woman without a shadow, the invisible man or the time machine. A host of skilful storytellers would certainly derive from this divinatory capacity innumerable effects each juicier than the last. The conditional is doubtless merely due to my ignorance of the genre, but I admit that I'd prefer to this immense virtual corpus a brief and stunning rendering akin to the one Borges provides, in a few pages, for the hypermnesia of *Funes el memorioso* – which is primarily a hyperaesthesia: in order to retain everything, one must initially perceive everything, and to perceive the other's invisible thoughts is no more miraculous than to perceive the infinite detail of the sensory world. Its ending would be just as tragic, for analogous reasons: save for a feelgood convention or a timely cure, it is more perilous than beneficial to know *all* of the other's thoughts. The interpretation would moreover be roughly of the same ilk: the story of Funes, as we know, is a 'metaphor for insomnia'; that of our hero, or heroine, might be, just as modestly, a metaphor, let's say, for a migraine. This baleful gift was once called, in easy-going narratology, *omniscience*.

Dogwood. For a reason unknown to me, this is the name given, in anglophone countries, to what we call *cornouiller*. But I've never seen in France a splendour to match the blossoming of those thousands of absolutely pure white flowers (in fact, it seems, the bracts surrounding them), which after a few days appear to turn gradually green, with the opening of the leafy buds, in anticipation of the fruits, similar to elongated cherries, which are here called, logically enough, *des cornouilles* – but I can't really see what name for a fruit might derive from the English *dogwood*.[157] In the south-west corner of the garden separating the two buildings of Washington Square Village, they've planted two or three that, at the beginning of May, explode so to speak overnight. It is the Rite of Spring.

Donner Pass. In April 1976, during a stay at Berkeley, some friends spending a few days in a house on the shores of Lake Tahoe invited me to join them. The Californian sky was as radiant as it can be in this season. In my hire car, I followed, in the early morning, but in the opposite direction, the wretched migrants' route in the winter of 1847, now the *Interstate 80* highway, the one running

---

[157] Dogwood berry.

virtually straight between San Francisco and New York, via Salt Lake City and Chicago. At Sacramento, the sky grew overcast above the foothills of the Sierra Nevada, which certainly lives up to its name. A few miles from the Donner Pass (so named in homage to the pioneers frozen on the spot during the cruel winter of 1846–1847), the police informed me that the pass was already too snow-covered to be approached without chains or special tyres. I had nothing of the sort, and I was urged to return whence I had come, since apparently I had come from somewhere. Sorely disappointed, I headed back down to the ocean, where I found the purest sky and, as the English say, the most *exhilarating* air. I thus decided to devote these couple of days to following the sublime coastal road no. 1 northwards all the way to Mendocino, then returning inland up the Russian River to the vineyards of Napa Valley. I had no cause for regret, but the fact remains that, I know not what superstition having dissuaded me from again confronting the sinister pass, I've never seen Lake Tahoe, save for in a few sequences of *Godfather II*. At least I learned on that day never to take literally the old wisecrack: 'Why is it never freezing in California?' – 'Because it's never cold enough there.' You'd need, to lend it credence, never to have taken your eyes off the coast. I'm more inclined to believe Mark Twain when he declared: 'The worst winter I ever spent was a summer in San Francisco.' The summer is often more trying than the winter in the vicinity of the Golden Gate, on account of the fog come from the Pacific. But actually, the phenomenon can easily occur in all seasons, and some have bought, hired or built a house on the crest of the Berkeley or Oakland hills just to be able to enjoy, in the late afternoon, the virtually daily spectacle of this phantasmagorical invasion.

Double bind. Read on an American car this helpful *bumper-sticker*: *If you can read this, you are too close.* Must I specify that I am, mercifully, referring to a rear bumper? Incidentally, I wonder why this usage of bumpers as a platform for various (in particular, electoral) messages has yet to cross the Atlantic. A law, probably, opposes it by virtue of the precautionary principle.

Doutre. In Angers, this word refers to the district situated *beyond-the-Maine* [*outre-Maine*], on the right bank of this river, the Maine – which actually isn't quite one: it's simply the name given to the resultant of the Mayenne, the Sarthe and the Loir, which converge a little to the north of the city. According to good toponymic logic, this shared trunk ought to bear the name of the largest of the three, of which the other two are mere tributaries, and I'm unaware of the reason for this bizarre exception – to which Anjou in turn owes the departmental name given it by the Constituent,[158] 'Maine-et-Loire'. The whole thing is, in fact, somewhat muddled: if one were to adopt length as the criterion (as between the Seine and the Yonne), it's the Loir that would be flowing through Angers, having absorbed the Sarthe, then the Mayenne; the *département* would then be called Loir-et-Loire. It's generally reckoned that it's the Sarthe that receives the Loir, then the Mayenne, perhaps owing to its greater rate of flow. But that criterion is no doubt more fragile (by nature more fluctuating) than the other; it's apparently the reason why it is the Seine, and not the Yonne, which is yet generally more extensive, that flows beneath the Pont-Neuf. It is thus officially the Sarthe, once enlarged by the Mayenne, that assumes the name (here, feminine) of the Maine, a name it retains for a few kilometres, the time it takes to cross Angers, then to rejoin the Loire in the place called, judiciously, Bouchemaine [Mainemouth]. They also say that if the estuary shared by the Garonne and the Dordogne, downstream of Ambès, is called the Gironde, it's because neither of these waterways wished to acknowledge that it was the other's tributary.

But I shall return to my Doutre, which is for that matter the first district in Angers where I lived, however briefly, in the forties: my aunt Marthe and my cousin Annie inhabited in this suburb a small, low and still rustic house, Rue La Révellière. I'm not sure whether the name Doutre, very well-formed and perfectly transparent, is used for other places, but I think one really ought to generalise it for all the cases where a city is unevenly split between two sides, of which one hosts merely a kind of somewhat subsidiary or disadvantaged suburb in relation to a 'city centre' which flourishes on the other. It's very typically the case in Angers, despite the two or three respectable monuments boasted by its Doutre, including the former Saint-Jean hospital. It's again that of Rouen, of Nantes, of Toulouse, of Orléans, of London, of Florence, of Pisa, of Antwerp, of Rotterdam, of Cairo,

---

[158] The French *Assemblée nationale constituante* (National Constituent Assembly), 1789–1791.

of Lisbon, of Zaragoza, of Prague, of Hamburg (left banks), of Basel, of Turin, of Rome, of Tours, of Bordeaux, of Auxerre, of Budapest, of Shanghai, of New Orleans (right banks), and so forth, not to mention cities built upon a confluence, like Pittsburgh – or Lyon, whose centre, Presqu'île and Croix-Rousse, is squeezed between a right bank and a left bank, leaving Fourvière and Brotteaux to spread out on each of the remaining sides. The inequality in urban status may be offset by an inverse inequality in geographical level, when the centre is situated at the foot of a suburb beyond the river that dominates it from its height, as does Buda opposite Pest or the Hradcany facing Prague's Old Town, but it can also be exacerbated thereby, as in Basel, Auxerre, Le Mans, Angoulême – or precisely in Angers, where it's the 'historic', administrative and cultural centre that gazes down like an acropolis upon the suburban lower part of town. I thus propose, as you'll have understood, to call 'doutres' all such districts separated from the heart of the city by a waterway, and which – even in Paris, which is however nowadays almost equitably distributed – lead in isolation a humbler and more provincial way of life. What best approximates this judicious denomination may be found in Italy, where they know how to express things, here by declining the term according to the name of the median river: Rome's *doutre* is the *Trastevere*, that of Florence the *Oltrarno* and that of Turin, I believe, the *Oltrepô*. I don't know on the other hand why the one in New Orleans is called *Algiers*. As for the Asian side of Istanbul, beyond the Bosphorus, it is indeed a *doutre*, but since the Bosphorus isn't a river and thus doesn't 'flow' in any direction, neither a right nor a left bank can be distinguished there, no more than one can for the Grand Canal, which places, however, the *Accademia* upon its *doutre*.

Throughout this irritating investigation, I've been able to gauge the difficulty a Parisian may have in accepting that a right bank should be to the south, as in London, meaning, in sum, that a river should flow from west to east (which is all the same, no less, the case with the Amazon); or that the centre of a city should lie upon a side that's both to the left and to the west, as in Bordeaux, almost entirely located beyond the Garonne, which here flows from south to north, its eastern *doutre* being called la Bastide. The *doutre* in Angers is on the contrary to the west, since the Maine flows obediently north–south, like the Mississippi in Saint Louis. I have besides just as much difficulty incorporating into my worldview the fact that Saint Louis lies on its west bank – with a *doutre* on the east bank, and in the neighbouring state of Illinois, just as Kansas City, but without any fluvial reason, straddles the two states of Missouri and Kansas – and above all that Chicago should be on the left side of Lake Michigan: I always think they've drawn the map the wrong way round (but I've already evoked this crucial point). And, furthermore, the fact that south of the equator the sun shines in the north, yet without rising in the west. I suppose our cerebral hemispheres are themselves also orientated, thus quickly disorientated, bereft of bearing, or with cross-bearings, and subject to various Cariolis effects. I note finally, with pleasure, the fairly limited number of rivers flowing stupidly from south to north, descending from the bottom to the top: the Rhine, the Elbe, the Oder, the Vistula, the Ob and the Yenisei, the Xingu, which meets the Amazon at its estuary, the São Francisco, which meanders through the red earth of the sertão before veering towards the Atlantic without having irrigated the Nordeste (but it's periodically a question of sorting that) – and I was about to forget, a trifling matter, the Nile, it too born beneath the Southern Cross. But I'm not alone in suffering the perverse effects of cartographic orientation: I read in a commemorative hagiography that François Mitterrand once undertook to 'travel down the Nile from Luxor to Aswan'. If you'd like to repeat this presidential oxymoron, there's only one way: pin a map to the wall, and follow the felucca from north to south – for Upper Egypt is right at the bottom.

Be that as it may, I once knew a very long-term student at the École Normale who, returning to Paris after several years of teaching in the provinces, prided himself on never having crossed the Seine. He only knew the right bank by hearsay, and I don't think he has ever, since then, deigned to visit, even as a tourist, what remained for him a distant and negligible *doutre*.

Écoles/Schools of Thought. Swift recounts the controversy between Big-endians and Little-endians, apropos of the way one should remove the end of a boiled egg. With or without quarrel, other alternatives of cultural habitus, though more modestly invested in, divide the human race into equally irreconcilable camps. One then says, politely: 'There are two schools of thought.' For instance, between those who hang, on their rails, clothes hangers the right way round or back to front (I know what I mean); those who respect the expression 'between the pear and the cheese [entre la poire et le fromage[159]]' and those who contradict it; those who place their fork to the left and those who place it to the right, along with the knife; those who read the newspaper from the beginning or from the end; those who count their ideas on their fingers (seeming always to count the fingers of their left hand with the tip of their right index finger, or perhaps the opposite if they're left-handed) starting with the thumb or, as often with Americans or like Raymond Aron, starting with their little finger – the one and the other side most often contriving things so that the number of ideas they utter reaches and doesn't exceed five, which goes to confirm the famous observation: 'Man is intelligent because he has a hand', and grants it the meaning 'Man cannot be more intelligent than his hand'; those who put their shoes on starting with the right foot or with the left foot, their sweaters with the sleeves or with the neck; their sleeves with one arm or with the other; those who tuck their T-shirt into their trousers and those who wear it over the belt; those who place their shirt collars above or below the sweater, folded into the jacket's neckline or broadly open over the collar thereof; those who turn off their bedside lamp prior to falling asleep or only after their 'first sleep'; those who underline their books and those who mark the margins; those who note the important pages on an index card to be lost or on the final page; those who prefer the aisle or the window; the upper deck of double-decker trains or the lower; the direction of travel or I don't mind (I don't know anyone who *prefers* the opposite direction, but perhaps there are some who do, preferring the reassuring vision of a landscape in flight to that, more threatening, of a landscape bearing down upon you); leg or thigh; pot-au-feu starting with cold water or with boiling water; black pudding with apples [pommes-fruits] or with mashed potato [purée de pommes de terre]; flat or hollow oysters; goose or duck foie gras; cheese or dessert; tea or coffee; lobster or crayfish; scotch or bourbon; with or without water; bicycle or bike; sedan or coupé; manual or automatic gearbox; belt or braces; underpants or boxer shorts; Plato or Aristotle; Luther or Calvin; Descartes or Pascal; Locke or Leibniz; Taine or Renan;

---

[159] Expresses the traditional order of dishes at the end of a meal; the saying now more generally refers to a situation where a relaxed or casual conversation may take place.

Sartre or Camus; Sartre or Aron; Corneille as he ought to be or Racine as he is;[160] Balzac or Stendhal; Mozart or Wagner; Schubert or Schumann; Verlaine or Rimbaud; Coltrane or Rollins; Matisse or Picasso; ring or knock; hyphens or brackets; shower or bath; 'ordinary' or 'typographic' quotation marks;[161] Mac or PC; Europe 1 or RTL;[162] Oxford or Cambridge; Stanford or Berkeley; parting to the right or to the left; evenings or mornings; stockings or tights; short sleeves or rolled-up sleeves; sleeves rolled up below or above the elbow; matching or mismatching pocket handkerchief; cap the right way round or back to front. I'll spare you here the enumeration of my own preferences, which would only interest people who already know them. Some of these alternatives, try to spot which ones, connote what Brecht, if memory serves, called a *social signum*.

Education. Concerning the quarrel between partisans of the old designation, 'Instruction publique [Public Instruction]', and of the (no longer very) new, 'Éducation nationale [National Education]', I know of no better commentary than these two ripostes by Michel Audiard (in two different films and from the mouth, presumably, of two different characters): 'I don't speak to idiots, it teaches them', and: 'Education can't be learnt.' Comparing these two strong statements leads you to think about the difference between two concepts that are often somewhat blurred by pedagogical practice. The first is certainly arrogant, but optimistic: if one fears to teach idiots, all misgivings are permitted for the others. The second bespeaks a radical pessimism, and is thus comforting: if education 'can't be learnt', seeking to teach it is pointless (Taoist principle: 'The things that can be taught are not worthy of being learnt'), but it isn't out of the question that it might be acquired, in mysterious ways peculiar to it, and of another order. I haven't said either which is my preferred designation, but this should go without saying, and I'll add that, of the two adjectives, 'public' seems to me far more

---

[160] An allusion to the philosopher and moralist Jean de La Bruyère (1645–1696): 'Corneille portrays men such as they ought to be; Racine portrays them such as they are'.
[161] Or so-called 'English' and 'French' quotation marks.
[162] Radio stations; RTL was formerly Radio Luxembourg, now a radio network owned by RTL (Radio Télévision Luxembourg).

congenial than 'national'. 'National Instruction' would be almost worrying, and 'Public Education' wouldn't be far from being an oxymoron: education, in the way I understand it with Audiard and Montaigne, is an entirely private affair, where the nation has nothing to do. Besides, it does indeed do nothing there.

Ellipses. To reduce dead time, you would have to be able to perform ellipses in lived experience, as there are in narratives, in plays or in films. The closest thing is doubtless general anaesthesia, but we're advised against overindulging therein. The best thing would anyway rather be an effect of rapid acceleration, as when a novelist summarises several years in one page, even in a couple of lines ('He travelled ... '[163]): a ten-hour chore would take ten seconds, and you'd see the hands of your watch turning at full speed. The best thing, because instead of waking after a syncopation, you'd *experience* the acceleration. You could offset this time bonus (?) with an opposite effect, for moments that are too short-lived, but since they are distinctly less numerous, I fear a negative balance sheet, and thus a hastened end.

I was thinking that these manipulations of duration belonged to the fantasy genre, but then I happened upon Jules Renard's acerbic observation: 'There are people who make you lose a day in five minutes.' In truth, I don't really know how one should account, credit or debit, for this type of feat, whose existence is at least beyond doubt.

Embusqué/Shirker. Thus was called (or 'planqué', 'cushy number]'), ever since the Great War, he who had obtained through special favours ('string-pulling') a risk-free posting – most often in the office of a Parisian ministry. Hence 'à l'embusqué', 'shirker-style', which named a haircut: 'far from the front,[164] all at the back'.

Enclume/Anvil. During the summer of 1942, or 1943, for dietary reasons, my parents sent me off to a farm in the Puy-de-Dôme, near Estandeuil, that's to say, for whoever knows the region a

---

[163] A reference to Gustave Flaubert, *Éducation sentimentale* (*Sentimental Education*) (1869), Part 3, Chapter 6.
[164] 'loin du front': as well as a military 'front', 'front' also means, in French, 'forehead' or 'brow'.

bit, not far from Saint-Dié d'Auvergne – half-way, then, between Billom and Cunhat, so the deepest Auvergne that could then be dreamt of. My stay was, as it were, that of an au pair, meaning that I was fed and housed in a barn so as to be able to help out with work on the farm and in the fields. In the main, my task consisted in going each morning to fetch huge round loaves from the county town bakery, then of keeping together, all afternoon, in a rather cramped private preserve [pré carré], a cow, a goat, a sheep and a pig who, without having read Dante, instinctively knew that happiness is always to be found in the *other* meadow [pré], where the grass is, as is also known, always greener. So the only thing on their minds was to scatter themselves into the four neighbouring plots, each of which offered a pasture (clover, lucerne, dandelions, what do I know) more enticing and more unwholesome for each of these four species. So that I might in vain exhaust myself catching them in turns and so forth, I had the assistance, so to speak, of a poorly trained dog, except when it came to attacking the bad shepherd, and who would sometimes succeed in reaching a fifth adjacent field – in defiance of all instructions and all geometry. One day, I was spared this labour of Sisyphus to go and fetch, a few kilometres from there, an anvil from some farrier or blacksmith. Like all anvils, this one was as good as its weight, no more no less, but it wasn't the heaviest thing: on my way back, a violent storm was looming, or rather broke without looming, and I found myself on the grass, half lightning-struck, without anvil and virtually without consciousness. After a while, the farmer, basically a decent fellow, grew concerned for his anvil, which he eventually found, intact, a few steps away from its discomfited bearer. Since I was there, he took me back to my barn as well, and that evening I was soothed with a generous portion of cherry, or maybe apricot, *millard*. This word, which I hope I'm not distorting, designated locally what is elsewhere, and maybe in the surrounding area, saddled with the ugly name *clafoutis*. I've never eaten any, ever since then, without again seeing in thought that accursed anvil, an instrument I'd recommend no one to use as a lightning rod.

Enfants sages/Well-behaved Children. I entered my usual chemist's. Two children, manifestly sister (about four) and brother (two), both blonde with blue eyes, stood side by side (but quite apart[165]) in the middle of the dispensary, while their mother, at the counter, settled the apparently complex details of her prescription, her *carte Vitale*[166] and/or her 'medical claim form'. The two children were frozen in absolute silence and an almost perfect bodily immobility, as though stunned by respect for the place, or by a fairy tale spell. Only their gazes escaped this apparent catalepsy as they followed, intensely, what was going on around them, but hardly anything was going on, the negotiation at the counter was itself fairly hushed, and as I awaited my turn, I was gradually benumbed in a state of contemplation that, any reason for impatience vanished, I'd gladly have prolonged interminably. Then, very slowly, the boy crouched down to touch the ground with his fingertips, as though the floor tiles were a precious and delicate material. His sister reacted not at all to this change of position. After a lapse of time it was impossible to measure, the mother took her leave, and roused her children with a liberatory 'okay you two, let's be off!' They at once regained the vivaciousness befitting their age, and the boy even muttered a few enthusiastic syllables. It all happened as though these two children had taken quite literally the cliché *sages comme des images* ['as good as pictures', 'as good as gold']. Performed by adults – for instance, old people warming themselves in the sun upon a bench – such a scene wouldn't have had the same power of fascination, perhaps because children are ordinarily more restless, and there was something unusual about their reverence, but also because their attitude evoked that of pets, like the cat Rilke speaks of, which further enhances the silence by sliding along rows of books 'as though it were effacing the title from their spines'. The visual image is accurate – whoever has had a cat in their library may attest to this – but the most perceptive thing here is undoubtedly the observation that the presence of a cat, or of a well-behaved child, 'further enhances the silence'.

Entends/Hear. In the French oral exam for the baccalaureate, I had 'drawn' a Baudelaire sonnet that discourages commentary,

---

[165] ' ... se tiennent (sans se tenir)': literally ' ... stood (without holding on to each other)'.

[166] Health insurance card.

but it wasn't the moment to let myself be discouraged. I glided without a hitch over the first 13 lines, and to end with a flourish saw fit to venture for the 14th a somewhat mimological hypothesis, which I argued with a particularly emphatic reading – *Entends, ma chère, entends la douce Nuit qui marche*, '*Hear, O my dear one, hear the soft Night coming*' – with very strong stress on the two *tends* and on the final *marche*. 'You can indeed hear it coming', such was more or less my triumphant conclusion. My examiner, who'd hitherto followed me with indulgence, baldly interrupted me, and asked me how a night so soft could come with so martial a step. 'You might at least have understood that if one has to say *hear* twice, it's precisely because it can barely be heard!' A little disconcerted, I wondered for a split second whether I mightn't suppose the 'dear one' to be slightly hard of hearing, but I feared to exacerbate my case. I had just understood that the famous 'agreement of sound and meaning' was a cliché for mediocre poets and critics short on inspiration. Some years later, I found in Valéry this severe and definitive confirmation: 'The power of verse arises from an *undefinable* harmony between what it *says* and what it *is*. *Undefinable* enters into the definition. This harmony must not be definable. When it is, it's an *imitative* harmony, and that is not good.'

Épinards/Spinach. We owe this very green vegetable a paralogism that is hard to refute: 'I'm really glad not to like spinach, for if I did, I would eat it often; and since I don't like it, I'd be really miserable.' The most common objection is that this reasoning could be applied just as well to other vegetables, other foodstuffs, to all sorts of things and people. Objection sustained, but I find all the same that it applies *better* to spinach. This wasn't Stendhal's opinion.

Escalier/Stairway. Her relationship with her native country wasn't always as idyllic as a reading of *Sido* or of *Claudine's House* might incline one to believe, nor as might the 'Colette country' signposts indicating the borough of Saint-Sauveur-en-Puisaye to culture-starved tourists. Her memorable childhood home, with its wobbly front steps, on Rue de l'Hospice aptly become 'Rue Colette' (they haven't dared rename 'Rue Sido' Rue des Vignes, on the far side of the double garden), has remained a property deprived of any indiscreet visits [propriété privée de toute visite indiscrète[167]]. By way of compensation, the château with the once creaky doorway has for a few years now hosted a 'Colette museum', which doesn't have a great deal more to show than, doubtless repatriated from her room at the Palais-Royal, a fine collection of glass paperweights: much blue paper to press. Yet, in this custodial museum [musée pour la conservation du titre], you can see something perhaps nowhere else to be seen: on the inner stairway leading to the upper floor, each stair riser bears – a brainwave – the title of a book by the author of *Green Wheat*. I wasn't able to verify whether this spiralling Pleiad comprised enough steps to exhaust the list of the complete works, nor have I retained in which order, alphabetical, chronological or thematic, the titles are thus itemised, a fine illustration of what she would perhaps have called, with a chortle, stairway wit [l'esprit de l'escalier].

Esprits/Spirits. Without laying claim to either, I admire equally the spirit of finesse and that of geometry;[168] to that of the stairway I have, indeed, resigned myself; with that of teams, parties and clans, I believe I have finished forever; that of seriousness I flee as fast as my legs can carry me whenever I encounter it, meaning at every turn, yet it does occasionally catch up with me; I apologise for this in advance – perhaps already too late.

Étoile/Star. The yellow star was enforced, in the occupied zone, on the 7th June, 1942. Some of our classmates had therefore to wear it, subject to a punishment whose nature we were yet to suspect. At Pontoise as elsewhere, a few of us wore it too for a day, in solidarity and defiance. Our teachers deterred us as much as they could from further tempting fate. In the evening, I was assured that it hadn't been a very intelligent way of celebrating my twelfth birthday – an opinion accompanied by a mention, customary on such occasions, of the famous 'Day of the Tiles'.[169] But as for strokes

---

[167] Genette is here playing on the two senses of 'propriété privée (de)': both a 'private property' and a 'property deprived (of) …'.

[168] 'l'esprit de finesse et celui de la géométrie': the two *esprits* made famous by Blaise Pascal (1623–1662), sometimes translated as 'intuitive mind' and 'mathematical mind'.

[169] For the historical significance of the 'Journée des Tuiles', see note 14.

of bad luck [tuile], that one so far surpassed all the others that the witticism stood no chance of being apropos, albeit under the guise of black humour.

Etorki. Between 1954 and 1956, years of transition, I was a bit of a Basque singer and dancer. A very little bit, if truth be told, and rather a singer in the wings than a dancer on stage, for want of being able to tell the difference except in theory between a leap and a grand jeté. I participated as a privileged observer in the activities of a group named Oldarra, which owing to serious disagreements (in the 'Country', everything is serious) became fairly swiftly Etorki – what 'remained' of Oldarra becoming for its part a rival group, and one justly reviled. The connection was my aftercare companion Agustin Alberro, whose brother-in-law led the group; the whole family, among whom a delightful little girl named Ochoa, in fact pretty much belonged to the troupe; me too, then, by way of a presumptive Sigognac of I can't recall (I know very well) which Isabelle[170] in espadrilles. In my rather disordered memory, these activities occurred in three very distinct places. One of them was Launay, where we'd managed to accommodate as paying guests these 20 odd beanpoles of both sexes, one summer month, for final rehearsal sessions for the spectacle *in progress*. As well as the lady of the manor's family and more habitual lodgers, that amounted to no mean number of young people to house meanly, and this joyous logistical nightmare was no doubt the only occasion that saw every nook and cranny of the château occupied, including the open-air ruins, in a state of comfort and hygiene for which the adjective 'spartan' would be a euphemism. The 'lawn' of weeds was used for rehearsals that were more enthusiastic than rigorous. Etorki was, then, at once a choir and a dance group, and the word 'folklore' had to be avoided: Basque music and dance are artforms in their own right, I shan't be the one to contest this, even if I consider folklore in itself to be a more than estimable artform. This wasn't quite the opinion of the mistress of the house, who, insensitive to the distinction between the Northern and Southern provinces, considered the whole troup to hail from beyond-the-Bidassoa,

[170] Sigognac and Isabelle are characters in Théophile Gautier's *Le Capitaine Fracasse* (*Captain Fracasse*) (1860).

mistook in the same disdain the fandango for the flamenco, and hummed by way of satire smatterings of *L'Heure espagnole*[171] ('And these people call themselves Spanish!'). Without quite (a little even so) identifying herself with Ravel and Franc-Nohain's heroine, she didn't despise hearing herself described in the following terms: 'Now that's what I call a charming woman.' Each contributed in turn, with various accents.

The second place was the (French) Basque country itself, where the troup went to get its show into shape before an audience of connoisseurs. The base was at Anglet, and we toured around from there by coach, from one pelota court to the next, via Labourd, Soule and Basse-Navarre. The Spanish provinces were forbidden us for political reasons, the majority of our 'Southern Basques' being exiles, moreover far more due to anti-Francoism than to Basque nationalism: as far as I can recall, the latter theme still wasn't particularly present, and the group's dominant ideology was instead internationalist.

The third place was the Théâtre des Champs-Élysées, where Etorki appeared in the autumn, the brief apotheosis of a sympathy-born success [succès de sympathie]. I spent several days and evenings there, more in the wings than ever, but it was already in itself a pleasure to walk through the performers' entrance, a small door facing the alley to the right of the building, a little beyond the public entrance to the Studio and the Comédie of the same Champs. The Bar des Théâtres, just opposite, was already a site of memory, but the troup's meals were most often had, on the corner of Rues Marbeuf and du Boccador, in a 'self-service' restaurant, then the first of its kind in Paris, and where this peculiarity allowed one to forget the already too conformist cuisine. My actual contribution, I was about to forget, consisted mainly in the vocal depiction, with two or three others, of a Basque crowd, that's to say in shouting at the right moment and, thank God, still from the wings: '*Hou ha, Hou ha, Hou ha.*' It's Basque, apparently, but I don't know what it means.

Exodus. At the end of May 1940, my father still mobilised, and 'retreated [replié]' with his company into goodness knows which fold

---

[171] 'Spanish Hour' or 'Spanish Time', a one-act opera (1911) with music by Maurice Ravel and a libretto by Franc-Nohain.

[pli], my mother remaining valiantly behind to 'guard the house' like Scarlett at Tara, I was dispatched to my dear aunt Marthe's, who ran in Angers, Rue des Lices, a textile store, with the plain and simple name *The Duchess of Anjou*. More affable by dint of its commercial orientation than the Parisian workshop on Rue de la Jussienne, which we shall find, I repeat, in its proper place, this store seemed to me the height of luxury. It's true that, at the time, the ladies of the provincial bourgeoisie were wont to buy, for their personal dressmakers, 'yardages' drawn from the lengths of silk, wool, cotton or rayon awaiting them there, carefully rolled up in their mural lockers. Raised with respect for all textile materials, I spent many an unwearied hour in the dry odour of this store where presided, along with my aunt, a shop assistant, a strong personality whom we called the 'first' though there was no other and who, in civilian life, was called Mme. Alex. This matron owned a black cat, with matching weight, which never accompanied her to Rue des Lices, and which I should never have met. But Guderian's[172] tanks were progressing more rapidly and further than Gamelin and Weygand[173] had foreseen, and Angers was soon to become an endangered refuge, to be abandoned without delay. So there we were walking the roads, my aunt, Mme. Alex, her cat and myself. This phase was painful for me, because Mme. Alex's cat, in its crate wire-meshed like a salad spinner, was under my care [à ma charge] and, at the end of my arm, its convulsive starts at the very least doubled this burden [cette charge] by virtue of I know not which of Newton's laws. I have a recollection, as precise as it is suspect, that we crossed the river at the memorable Ponts-de-Cé, for a fresh strategic withdrawal at Denée, somewhere between the Loire and the Layon, on a vineyard-rich and supposedly unassailable left bank. What happened next is fuzzier, except that we found ourselves one day, I'm not sure how, in a little port south of the estuary – Pornic, I suppose. Meanwhile, moreover, the defences on the river had yielded in their turn, and Guderian's tanks had forgotten us in their rush to Bordeaux. The fact remains that on the 17th June, at Denée or Pornic, passing by an open window, I heard the Marshal's[174] capitulatory speech,

---

[172] Heinz Guderian, German general (1888–1954).
[173] Maurice Gamelin, French general (1872–1958); Maxime Weygand, French military commander (1867–1965).
[174] Marshal Pétain, then prime minister.

which I greeted, not with a 'Long live de Gaulle!' which would have miraculously anticipated the march of History by a day,[175] but with a 'Long live Blum!' pertaining less to any protest than to a conditioned reflex: as I saw it, for the last four years at least, whoever said politics said 'Long live Blum!' I was reminded to be prudent and, a few days later, with Guderian's tanks drinking on Hendaye beach, there remained for me only to return, perhaps by train, to Angers, Paris, then Conflans, no more nor less occupied than our dubious Atlantic refuge.

It was obviously on this occasion that I learned the meaning of the word *exodus*. I've always had a little trouble, as a result, in admitting that thus is called the book in the Bible recounting the *return* of the Jews to Canaan, which had allegedly been their land at the time of the Patriarchs. It's true that their sojourn in Egypt had lasted longer than my own in Piriac, and that we've known at least since Freud that Moses and his people were quite simply Egyptian dissidents – monotheists, perhaps. I had, however, become familiar, in a single month and like thousands of others, with exodus in both senses of the word.

Fadaises. 'Nobody, says Montaigne, is exempt from saying *fadaises*.' I know something about this, but this word is generally derived from *fade* [bland, insipid], and is interpreted accordingly.[176] The situation is quite different, or at the least it is more complex: the etymology is (it seems) doubtful, and can just as well refer us back to *fat* [vainglorious], or further to the Pagnolesque *fada* [foolery], and other nonsense [fariboles]: a *fadaise*, in old language, is more a folly, for instance that of Don Quixote, than a commonplace *à la* Sancho. Montaigne's Gascon (if such it be) might then be warning us here less against the universal risk of banality than of inanity. For each to beware of the side they believe themselves most prone to fall, or to follow their predilection – notwithstanding mixed forms, since platitude doesn't rule out absurdity, which it occasionally aggravates.

Fayot/Boot-licker. Apart from the bike ride that led there along the shady avenues of the plateau, I have so to speak no memory

---

[175] Charles de Gaulle became the Leader of Free France on 18 June 1940.
[176] 'Dire des fadaises' is, in this sense, to 'talk twaddle' or 'piffle'.

relative to the drab years of my schooling at the 'big' primary school (more officially 'groupe Jules-Ferry') in Conflans, which sat proudly between the 'big' station and the wire works factory known as LTT (Lignes télégraphiques et téléphoniques [Telegraph and Telephone Lines]), except that one day, during the 'phoney war', one of our teachers, obviously under governmental orders and by way of a contribution to the war effort, enjoined us to draft a kind of appeal in favour, I believe, of the 'recovery of non-ferrous metals'. I can still see myself fine-tuning with conviction the following sentence: 'We already have, of course, non-ferrous metals, thanks to the foresight of our ministers, but we are in continual need of more … .' The shame of this patriotic toadying overwhelms me every time there occurs in conversation, not the word 'recovery [récupération]', which has seen other days, but indeed the expression 'non-ferrous metals'. Fortunately, it barely ever does occur, and, for some reason, the very notion of it appears to have deserted our military–industrial horizon; indeed, it pretty much survives only in me, as an insuperable emblem of what is nowadays called, too leniently, the language not of metal but of wood.[177]

Fenêtre/Window. During my first year of teaching, I happened one day, upon God knows which sudden inspiration, to throw a piece of chalk out of the open window. Shortly afterwards, in an essay on the shamefully narcissistic subject, 'Portray your teacher', I read, from one pupil, a tad Lolita moreover, the following sentence: 'Whatever pops into his head, he lobs out of the window.' I have always striven, since then, to justify this description, which is worthy of becoming a precept, and which has thus far spared me any analytic assistance.

Festival. At the beginning of the Cold War, the World Festival of Youth, a grand occasion for rallying and mutual warming, took place in the summer, at more or less regular intervals, in a 'popular democratic' city, such as Berlin already or Wrocław. In August, 1953, it was held in Bucharest, which, yet to be ravaged by the

---

[177] 'la langue, non de métal, mais de bois': in French, 'la langue de bois', 'wooden language', designates the vague, abstract, pompous or rigidly repetitive language typically associated with political discourse.

efforts of the Ceauşescu, remained pretty much the peaceful provincial city Paul Morand[178] had known. Stalin had been torn from our affections for a few months, and a certain quite provisional climate of 'thawing' could be felt even upon these steps to the buffer zone. The local leader of the moment had just eliminated, guilty of a Titoist deviation, the veteran Cominternist Ana Pauker, and would soon be opposed to a Khrushchev deemed too liberal. One could neither ignore nor forget his name, for the city, bristling with loudspeakers, reverberated at every instant with the heavily chanted slogan, *Georgiu-Dej, forte lucator, pentru pace si popor* – I hope not to deform in writing this vernacular utterance. The rest of the time was spent on international but ideologically correct displays of folklore, and which had no room for jazz, even in the old style. The Peking Opera, however, was not lacking in charm, with much recourse to dragons, flags and multicoloured snakes. I can no longer recall how or with what we were fed. We slept in dormitories permanently disinfected by means of a product whose chemical formula is unknown to me, but whose efficacy was certain, judging by the acrid odour it left behind, and which still today I could recognise without risk of error, a charmless 'little madeleine' of a socialism that could not have been more real.

On a branch of what was no longer quite the Orient Express, the train journey was in both directions of an unforgettable diurnal and nocturnal length. The iron curtain, at the Austro-Hungarian border, raised a few bureaucratic issues, which we again encountered at the Hungaro-Romanian border, less explicable for whoever remained unaware of the delicate relations between these two satellites of distinct orbits. During these lengthy halts, one could gaze upon a Danubian countryside in the same state as the preceding century, villages with white thatched cottages with for only traffic, upon the dusty roadways, horse-drawn carts with strangely silent rubber wheels. Between Cluj and Bucharest, the rugged countryside of the Transylvanian alps afforded some chillier stopping places. On the way back, the Viennese stage lasted a good day, enough time to visit – a tricky

---

[178] French writer (1888–1976) best known for his short stories and novellas; was a French ambassador in Romania under the Vichy regime (1940–1944).

choice to bring such a heavily ideological pilgrimage to a close – the Albertina's Dürer, then, more inanely, to seek the Danube, which we initially thought we recognised in a modest canal, and which we had a little trouble actually reaching, by tram, in a then distant suburb, asking perplexed passers-by something like '*Danube, bitte*'. In spite of this ridiculous barbarism, we eventually found ourselves beside a yellowish water more redolent of punishment than of reward.

Feutres/Felt-Tip Pens. He[179] made much use of felt-tip pens, of a quality he claimed to find only in a certain store in Tangiers, as others buy their ink only in Venice. Whenever it was a question of this very special purchase, his mother, believing herself not to be fooled, or wishing to make believe that she was only half so, would comment in a whisper: 'Ah, those Moroccan ladies … he's so fond of them!'

Fictions. As it is practised today, the 'genre' of autofiction responds almost faithfully, if not worthily, to the broad, and deliberately disconcerting definition given it by Serge Doubrovsky, inventor of the term and proponent of the thing such at least as it was defined by him ('a fiction, based on strictly real events and facts; if you like, *autofiction* … '). Definitions are free and usage is king, but it still seems to me that this broad, now received, definition is too vague not to be applicable just as well to any autobiography, a narrative of the self always more or less tinged, even nourished, wittingly or not, by self-fiction: everyone acknowledges this, and how could it be otherwise? This is, besides, more or less the opinion of Doubrovsky himself: 'All autobiography is a form of autofiction and all autofiction is a variety of autobiography. There is no absolute separation.' Yet, thus defined, the term loses much of its necessity, save to refer, no longer to a genre, but simply (simply?) to the part of fiction inevitably implied by any autobiography, be it the most 'sincere'. The more narrow definition that I defended for a while, thinking I was doing the right thing, was aimed at something entirely different: a narrative, contradictorily, with a *declared* autobiographical status (according to Philippe Lejeune's

---

[179] Roland Barthes.

criteria: by a homonymy between the author, the narrator and the character) but whose content is *manifestly* fictional (for instance: fantastical or supernatural), like that of Dante's *Divine Comedy* or Borges's *Aleph*. I maintain my generic definition, but I must abandon the idea of retaining for it a term that I'd today gladly call hackneyed, if I weren't conscious of having myself previously improperly borrowed it from its inventor to designate a genre of which he was not thinking. In any case, the corpus to which I applied it is quantitatively tiny, compared to that of autofiction in the sense henceforth current, even overflowing, as is said of a flood, or an oil slick. But as a result, that corpus (my own) no longer has a name. I fleetingly envisaged the equally contradictory concept of *unauthorised autobiography*, but I'm not sure it's appropriate, and I'd rather save it for another occasion.

I have also (too) long toyed with the idea of another study of literary genre, a genre that would be to heterobiography (that is, biography tout court) what autofiction would be to autobiography, in the now obsolete sense that was mine. In what I would have wished (badly) to call *heterofiction*, or (just as badly) *allofiction*, one finds a kind of narrative, of an equally but otherwise contradictory character, which has for its hero a historically attested figure, and ascribes to her or him such and such a manifestly fictive adventure: a fictive biography, then, albeit partially so, of a real person distinct from the author. Of course, no 'serious' biography (and *a fortiori* no 'romanced' biography) can absolutely forbid itself at least hypothetical incursions into the personal or private life of its object, but I'm thinking here rather of narratives (or dramatic presentations, such as the 'historical' plays of Shakespeare, Musset or Brecht) that adopt a share of fictionality manifestly contrary to the historically attested experiences of their characters. The historical novel, at least since Walter Scott, hasn't failed to resort to this procedure, but it generally does so in a marginal and complementary way, in narratives whose central character (Ivanhoe, Cinq-Mars, Prince Andrei) is, to my knowledge, entirely fictional (this isn't, granted, the case with d'Artagnan or of Cyrano, but no one is supposed to realise this). The narratives I still have in mind, just for memory and forgoing any further discussion, fictionalise overtly and centrally a real historical character – who most often happens to be an artist, preferably a writer: see, for example, Thomas de Quincey's *The Last Days of Immanuel Kant*, Mörike's *Mozart's*

Journey to Prague, Lucien Daudet's *Shakespeare's Journey*, some of Marcel Schwob's *Imaginary Lives*, Hermann Broch's *The Death of Virgil* (there's obviously nothing fictive about the fact of this death, but the amplitude of the narrative and of the interior monologue the author affords it does indeed turn it into a fictional event, and one may say the same, variously, of Michel Schneider's *Imaginary Deaths*), Thomas Mann's *Lotte in Weimar*, or Giono's *Melville: A Novel*, for me the pinnacle of the genre, some of Pierre Michon's narratives, Frédéric Ferney's *The Last Love of Monsieur M.* (for Matisse), or Jean Echenoz' *Ravel*. It's also a type of *Künstlerroman*, but whose hero, contrary, for instance, to the Adrian Leverkühn of *Doktor Faustus*, is an artist whose existence is historically attested. I would append here, however, D.H. Lawrence's narrative *The Man Who Died*, whose hero, as is known, is none other than Jesus resurrected, an artist in his own fashion. This genre's 'specific pleasure', as Aristotle would say, no doubt relates to the relation one seeks, and that one does in fact eventually find, between the fictive adventure the narrative grants them and the climate of their actual work. Plato's Socratic dialogues, precisely, and one or two of Xenophon's texts, already flirted with this fairly modern mini-genre, except that their hero left behind nothing else, adept as he was of the wise precept: 'Never write.'

Figurines. I wasn't too fond of tin soldiers in my childhood, doubtless for want of a battlefield setting able to give life and proportion to the models, but I did like the name 'figurine', which didn't really suit these excessively martial statuettes, their scale notwithstanding. If I'd lived further south, I doubtless would have dreamed a little more before the nativity scene figures in the manger. Long afterwards, in order to celebrate I'm not sure what occasion, Benjamin Jordane,[180] who'd always view me in my seminar as in his classroom a schoolmaster in a black frock coat from the Jules Ferry era, gave me a little open box, a naive evocation of the village school, with its blackboard, its map of France on the wall, its display cabinet topped with a globe, its black-piped stove and its windows overlooking a village square *à la* Grand Meaulnes.[181] With his stick,

[180] Pseudonym of French novelist and essayist Jean-Benoît Puech (1947–).
[181] See note 89.

the master is pointing out a sentence calligraphed on the blackboard to three good pupils sitting at their wooden tables equipped with earthenware inkwells full of violet ink, of whom one is raising his hand to answer the question, and the inevitable 'dunce' with his cap is standing, facing the wall, by the stove. To avert any breakage or untimely movement, I glued the tables, the master and the dunce to the cardboard floor and the good students to their bench, and placed the whole thing upon a shelf in my country library. I often gaze at this model classroom, which in sum I once more or less knew 'in reality', at the Fin-d'Oise municipal school. A big difference: instead of the master in his black coat, I'd see a mistress in a flowery blouse and a long skirt. I wonder in what era the 'black hussars'[182] began to make way for these more graceful figurines.

Flagellation. On the occasion of a colloquium at the University of Urbino, I visited the Ducal Palace with a colleague far more of a connoisseur than I am. Halt before Piero della Francesca's *Flagellation*, and a brief dispute, whose terms I have forgotten; in the end I uttered an overly sincere, and above all overly generic: 'Oh, you know, me and Italian painting … '. Dismayed by my stupidity, my companion said not a single word during the rest of the visit. Overly generic, obviously: I very much like some Italian painters, including occasionally Piero himself, and the best thing would doubtless be not to burden oneself with so crude, and so irrelevant, a category. After all, Masaccio, Gozzoli, Carpaccio, Caravaggio, Canaletto, Tiepolo are among my favourite painters. But it seems to me that my sally was obscurely baulking at the tendency, so common among 'art' historians, to reduce, first of all, art to the plastic arts, then the plastic arts to painting, and finally painting to that of the Italian Renaissance – when it doesn't reduce the latter to the question, for me truly flagellant, of perspective.

Flèche/Arrow. Throughout my driving lessons, in February 1953, the driving school instructor would yell at every opportunity, I mean at every turn: 'The arrow, monsieur, the arrow!' The car we were using was, however, already equipped with indicators,

---

[182] 'Hussard noir' was a nickname given in the early twentieth century to the schoolmasters of the French Third Republic.

but he'd retained this term from the time when most merely had small luminous arms built into the coachwork, which, save for any malfunction, would rise to a horizontal position in order to signal a change of direction. I suppose 'arrow' was easier for him to holler than 'indicator', hence this metonymy by anachronism, or remanence. Yet this order reminded me of something quite different, which I could hardly convey to him. In the thirties, my father, whose only regular reading matter was *Rustica*, the amateur gardener's weekly bible, occasionally bought *La Flèche* [*The Arrow*], a newspaper run by the ex-Radical Gaston Bergery, who'd founded as early as 1933 a 'Common Front against Fascism'; the emblem of this movement was a thick upwards-pointing arrow, whereas the SFIO[183] logo consisted of three diagonal arrows. Bergery, who was later to espouse Vichyism, and thus to some extent fascism, was then associated with the Popular Front, and *La Flèche* was a 'left-wing, but intelligent' newspaper, as would be, after the war, Albert Camus' *Combat*, and as is nowadays still, but elsewhere, the *New Yorker*. Its commercial slogan was: 'Don't forget to forget *La Flèche*'. The aim, of course, was for it to be left lying around, for instance on the train or on the metro, once it had been bought and read. I still wonder whether this practice increased or diminished its circulation, but I can see that the aim was, in any case, to increase the number of readers. Regardless, 'forgetting the arrow' was an error that came to me from quite far back.

Fois/Time. At the head of his *The Eighteenth Brumaire of Louis Bonaparte*, Marx applauds Hegel for having observed that great historical events and characters occur twice, but chides him for not having added: the first time as tragedy, the second as farce. This famous addition seems to me almost pointless, for the specification goes without saying, and I cannot believe that Hegel didn't imply it: any imitation, any repetition is by nature comical. Besides, History doesn't always await recurrence in order to reveal itself as a farce. '*Twice: once too often*', said Bierce, pretty optimistically as it happens: the first time is often itself too many. It would often

---

[183] *Section française de l'Internationale Ouvrière* (French Section of the Workers' International) (1905–1969).

be wise to begin with the second time [la deuxième], or rather the second-and-final-time [la seconde], and leave it there.

Folie/Madness. I see in a reasonably reliable biography (and besides confirmed by Paul Veyne) that Michel Foucault, not entirely unhappy to be leaving the Vincennes philosophy department, declared: 'I'd had enough of being surrounded by people who were half-mad.' I don't care to suppose that the author of the *History of Madness* was reproaching his colleagues and students for only having been semi-afflicted. Let's rather read in this sentence one of those refreshing moments when theoretical vigilance steps aside in favour of the most common sense. I can still hear, although it was silent, the dismay of a narratologically correct person to whom I was speaking, in the course of a very casual conversation, of Combray apropos of Illiers and of Proust apropos of Marcel: I was truly the last person from whom she would have expected such irresponsible slippages, from the author to the narrator, and from fiction to reality. But it seems to me that principles of method (and others) must be reserved for their specific field of application, and overlooked there where they have nothing to do. Galileo, presumably, was present like everyone else at the rising and setting of the sun, and yet ... . The worst confusion is the confusion of registers: Pascal wasn't wrong to mock the half-educated who can never forget the little they have learned – and who conflate everything of which they are ignorant.

Frappe/Strike. It was to bolster the Normandy landings, just before or shortly after, that allied aircraft undertook to destroy in Conflans the four bridges (two road, two railway) over the Oise and the Seine. I can't recall to what extent nor how long it took before they were hit – precision targeting, as is known, was already neither the forte nor the concern of this type of operation – but, at the first failed attempt, several houses in our area were razed to the ground, collateral damage, as it wasn't yet called at a time when already, however, civilian victims weren't taken into consideration. When I returned home from school, the lacerated body of our closest neighbour lay beneath the line where I would no longer see her, stood on tiptoe, her apron pocket [poche de tablier] laden with wooden pegs, hanging up her washing a stone's throw away from my linden tree. Our own house was merely, but seriously, dented, and my mother owed the salvation of her body to having been in the 'basement' at the instant of a strike that wasn't yet called 'surgical', but which was, however, already so, in its own way. Stricken, then, we were evacuated to another part of town, at a greater distance from the supposed objectives, meaning further upstream the Seine, beyond the Parc du Prieuré. It was a fairly low little house, without any pretension to the 'villa' style and rather pleasant to reside in, whose uncultivated garden sloped down to the Seine and gazed upon the poplars on the opposing bank, a far more rustic landscape than that, already industrialised, of our confluence. This respectful distance allowed me to witness without danger a few other raids, truly spectacular ones because performed, this time, by dive-bombers. There remained fortunately but few people to kill on the spot, and but little to demolish, except precisely the famous bridges, which indeed eventually rendered their roadways [tabliers] one by one. For one or two years the crossing of the Oise between Conflans and Maurecourt, much needed by reason of 'food supplies', was the business of a rather artisanal ferryboat, which came and went between two cables, and which was towed without excessive ardour by a town hall employee whom after the Liberation passengers used to call a lazybones, because he was known to be a communist, and who ended his career as a town councillor, no doubt for the same reason.

The reconstruction of our own house had itself to wait several months, and it was in our provisional quarter that I encountered, in August, my first American soldier, who must have been rather lost, for he appeared to have come straight from the east, meaning in sum from Paris. But, after all, since Paris had, as we know, been liberated 'by itself' and by the Leclerc division, there remained only for General Patton to dispatch one or two of his men to liberate what remained of its suburbs, great and small. Actually, my GI was busy seeking the way to the town hall, which, intact like the church, was already in the hands of presumed members of the Resistance. I accompanied him there in exchange for a stick of chewing gum, and thus it was that Conflans made its entry into the free world, and vice versa.

Frenchy. During the 1971–1972 season, I can't recall since when, nor for how long afterwards, Pierre Boulez conducted the New York Philharmonic. On the 4th October, he directed *The Legend of St*

Elizabeth.[184] This rather unusual choice was presumably of the kind that nurtured the slight irritation of a New York public enamoured of opera and of symphonic music, one of the most conservative in the world, and, to make matters worse, still nostalgic for the 'flamboyant' Bernstein years – but to spurn Gustav Mahler, at the beginning of the same century, it hadn't had the same excuse. Flamboyant, Boulez was too in his own way, which one had to discern, and which had nothing in common with the all-consuming seductiveness of his predecessor: his conception of his role was rather militant and pedagogical; what he sought was to enlarge the repertoire and to educate the public. He was thus seen as a giver of lessons, a grievance to which his *Frenchy* quality inevitably added a shade of supposed 'arrogance'. I'll confess to not having retained a particularly vivid impression of this romantic oratorio for special occasions, but I can still see the little Frenchman, impatient and concentrated, bursting into the auditorium of the Philharmonic Hall, from one of the doors at the rear, to reach the raised podium. Yet this isn't the route by which the conductor is supposed to take his place before this orchestra; perhaps he hadn't had the time to go by way of the artists' entrance; perhaps too it didn't displease him thus to defy his audience; perhaps even my memory of this performance is, as happens sometimes, as false as it is precise.

Gabardine. This word, nowadays rather departed, like the thing, from common usage, literally referred to a wool and cotton twill, from which one could cut all kinds of clothing, trousers in particular, but also, by metonymy, certain rainproof coats (most often a dull grey colour like that of librarians' smocks), and by extension any type of raincoat. When it was threatening to rain, my father would 'take his gabardine', but, somewhat insensitive to the cold, as long as the rain remained in a state of threat he almost always used to carry it, neatly folded, draped over his left forearm. This way of holding a coat without donning it has now completely gone out of fashion: by dint of its respectful inconvenience, it connoted (as did the concern to button one's shirt collar even without a tie) a type of very petit-bourgeois dignity that no longer corresponds to very much in the current state of society; nowadays, we (men, I mean: it's

[184] By Franz Liszt (1873).

clearly a secondary sexual characteristic) prefer to hold this type of clothing, and more often still a jacket, thrown behind the shoulder hooked by an index finger to a little internal tab sewn beneath the collar. At the time, it was moreover an item of clothing for adults, so much so that, the tide having meanwhile turned, I have, for my own part, never worn any gabardine, neither upon my back, nor upon my arm. I regret this not at all.

Gag. I'll confess to my insatiable preference for one that's truly basic, whose origin I cannot trace: someone drops something into an aquarium; to recover it, he rolls up the right sleeve of his suit, and immerses his left arm, wrist watch and all. It's a metaphor for all our pointless precautions.

Gandilleux. The language of Anjou is considered, in the textbooks, to be the purest in France, I'm not really sure why. It isn't for want of an accent, at least in the countryside: I can still hear the peasant from the environs of Saumur describing the preceding year's flood: 'D'ici ch'quà Longué, c'était qu'eun'Louère! [D'ici jusqu'à Longué, ce n'était qu'une Loire!/From here all the way to Longué, there was nothing but Loire!]' I've retained two other typical words, used for that matter also in the city: *ramasse-bourrier* ['remnant-gatherer'], which denotes, if I understand aright, a silent butler; and *gandilleux*, which denotes a synthesis of 'difficile [difficult]' and 'périlleux [perilous]'.

Gares/Train Stations. My first Parisian train station was of course Saint-Lazare, whose concourse served as a rallying point, beneath the clock, for the whole of our north-eastern suburb, and whose shopping arcade, at street level, was home to a record store where I bought my first *be-bop* record – a fairly temperate one, incidentally: it was *Bird's Nest* and *Cool Blues*, by Charlie Parker and Erroll Garner (the latter being the tempering influence, in his nonchalant way; I shall return to this). For a long while Paris was for me confined to this quarter: to the west, Cour de Rome, Rue de la Pépinière and Rue de la Borde, which lead, each at its own rhythm, to the wedding cake dome of Saint-Augustin; to the east, Cour du Havre, Rue du Havre, Passage du Havre, Rue Caumartin, with the charming rear façade of the *lycée* Condorcet, opposite Rues Joubert, de Provence, de Budapest, all three then 'ill-famed [mal famées]' – which we understood, as it happened quite rightly, as 'mal femmées', that's to say populated by bad (not so bad) women.

Few others (train stations) deserve my recollection, other than, very much later, that of Le Mans, at the foot of its city, with, as in Pontoise, a long pedestrian climb before you get to the thick of things, and that of Angers, rather forsaken upon its square adorned with the statue of goodness knows which hennin-clad gentlewoman, but which one couldn't miss, heralded as it was, coming from Paris, by a first station, Saint-Serge, where one was careful not to alight, which left intact all its mystery as a supernumerary, and for us otherwise pointless, station. But there's always something charming about these successive stations in the same city, as also in New York, at least long ago, between Grand Central (coming from Boston) and Pennsylvania Station (going to Washington), which gives the *Metroliner* the air of a small local train able to lead you, not only from one city to another, but from a district of one to a district in the other. And the fact that those two stations are now profoundly subterranean reinforces the feeling of a vast interurban network: at Penn Station, you step down to take the Amtrak from its raised platform averting any misstep, just as you take from platform level the metro for the Lincoln Center. Paris missed this trick from the outset by forgetting to connect its six or seven stations: it would have been pleasant though, coming from Marseille, to choose between alighting at the gare de Lyon, d'Orsay, d'Austerlitz, Montparnasse, Saint-Lazare, du Nord, de l'Est, de la Bastille. The only hint, in my childhood, of this aborted round: the Pont-Cardinet station, which lay ahead of the Saint-Lazare terminus, and the late sequence Austerlitz-Orsay, which afforded a little freedom of choice upon your return from the South-West. It appears that they're thinking of sorting all of this, for the coming century.

I'm not forgetting the bifid station in Lausanne, which opens from its two sides onto two opposing squares, making it hazardous to arrange meetings there, nor Santa Lucia in Venice, which throws you without transition onto the Grand Canal. But one of the most fascinating, for me, is Saint-Paul, in Lyon, on the square and roughly opposite the church of the same name, nestled against the foot of the Montée Saint-Barthélemy (it's crazy how much train stations love saints, and vice versa), virtually without anything to indicate its status, pretty much secret: you really have to know that it's there, and what it's for, and enter it to notice that it comprises, like the real thing, two or three more or less active platforms, and that its rickety trains stop at a few rather suburban destinations, like Charbonnières-les-Bains, which no longer has anything to warrant its name.[185] One fears for its future. Presumably this was somewhat the case with the former Bastille station in Paris, which I never used as such, and whose highly improbable function hasn't obviously survived its organ, as though the suburbs in question had, as a result, ceased wishing to join the capital. I wonder if one mightn't have housed the Opera of the same name there, without altering its appearance, just as the Musée d'Orsay was crammed into its former station. For train stations die too, or steal away: Montparnasse has moved 500 metres backwards on the surface, I don't know how many in depth, such that no locomotive can dive out from it, as you might have seen in October 1895, then hurtle down Rue de Rennes as far as the forecourt of Saint-Germain-des-Prés; Orsay, erstwhile railhead, is thus now merely a nineteenth-century museum, the Bastille an Opera that continues to shed its scales beneath its fishless nets,[186] and Perrache, garrotted by the Part-Dieu, a forlorn survivor. The idea, apparently inspired by Alphonse Allais, is that one should, as has already been done in Amiens (real station at Longueau, between two rows of beetroots), in Auxerres (Migennes), in Tours (Saint-Pierre-des-Corps), in Orléans (Les Aubrais), declutter cities by placing their stations in the countryside, midway between so to speak: you'd get there snugly by coach, or by a connecting shuttle. Yet the same Alphonse told the station master at Puget-Théniers:[187] 'If you had one of those in Paris, you'd make a killing!'

But the height of this luxury was the three stations at Conflans, two of which were on the same line, Mantes-Paris-via-Conflans (another, Mantes-Paris-via-Poissy, follows the left bank of the Seine, greeting in passing the late Émile [Zola]'s garden at Médan), which follows, for its part, the right bank, beneath l'Hautil which it skirts between Meulan and Maurecourt. After Maurecourt, it crosses the Oise from a fair height along the pont Eiffel (built by

---

[185] The toponym 'les-Bains' indicates the (at least former) presence of thermal baths.

[186] An allusion both to the architectural style of the Opéra Bastille and to its frequent state of disrepair.

[187] A *commune* in south-eastern France.

Gustave, destroyed as I've said in 1944, and since rebuilt in a more modern style). From our station (Conflans-Pont-Eiffel, then), you could see in the distance, and obliquely, the train coming from Mantes arrive at Andrésy, take a breather at Maurecourt, then, head-on, and causing the bridge to sway a little, bear down upon you as though in a silent film, greeted by the flag, the whistle and a broad movement of his acetylene torch by a becapped station master named 'M. Gral', or perhaps even 'Graal'. The next station in the direction of Paris was the 'large' station of Conflans-Sainte-Honorine, where I'd 'change' to 'take' la Titine from Pontoise, as already celebrated. As for the third station (the closest to where I lived), Conflans-Fin-d'Oise, it lay on a third, very discreet, line, which connected Achères to Pontoise, running alongside the left bank of the Oise from Conflans, after having passed *underneath* the other line (under the pont Eiffel, then). For whoever would like to follow me, I can only advise against the current Michelin 101 map, called 'Banlieue de Paris [Paris Suburbs]', on a scale of 1/53,000 (1cm = 530m, no more no less), which, on account of town planning, no longer corresponds much to any of this. For example, the last-mentioned line is nowadays assigned to an RER[188] that no longer serves Pontoise, but the appalling 'new town' fraudulently called (I wonder about the meaning of the hyphen) 'Cergy-Pontoise'. At the time only one or two passenger trains passed along it each day, which for us robbed it of any usefulness, for the recourse of jumping onto a moving freight car was then curiously foreign to us, doubtless owing to our not having watched enough Westerns, or of having read enough by a Kerouac who was yet to start writing. This line thus barely served us beyond certain days (of breakdowns, strikes or snowstorms) without trains, where the shortest route was, seemingly, to follow it, obviously on foot, from Pontoise to Fin-d'Oise.

I have, if truth be told, but a single memory in this regard, but a rather painful one. It was an instance of 'snowstorm', 50 centimetres at least, falling without warning in the course of the day, and the idea of avoiding the road and returning more directly along the railway line proved unfortunate. At the end of the

---

[188] The RER (Réseau Express Régional [Regional Express Network]) is the commuter rail system in Paris.

Bardadrac

journey only two of us remained (the others hadn't dropped dead as in the retreat from Russia, but made it home earlier, somewhere between Éragny and Neuville), and as far as I was concerned the consequences were indeed distressing, for in such circumstances my parents made preventative use not only of boiling milk bizarrely flavoured with tincture of iodine but also of a homemade poultice, a textile sandwich with mustard seed, named not without reason a 'wrap', and occasionally replaced by a less artisanal but no less grievous 'rigolot' (this antiphrastic term[189] was doubtless nothing more than the name of the father of this fine invention). But the fact remains that, courtesy of mustard and tincture of iodine, I survived this signalling error.

Garner. Boris Vian once dubbed him 'the greatest jazz pianist since Chopin'. One could doubtless go back a little further in the history of the instrument, and even into its prehistory – for example, as far as Domenico Scarlatti, whose preface to his only anthumous collection ends on these two simple words: 'Live happily'. Every even slightly informed jazz-lover knows in which traits – staccato or legato chords played in any which time with his left hand, the fractional lateness of his right hand, the ascending figures floating out of tempo, the sudden drops in dynamic intensity, and the high notes that also honour his tuner – consists the acutely singular style of this autodidact who placed a telephone directory, not upon his stool like Glenn Gould (I'm simplifying), but upon his music stand in order to make people believe that he could read music, a style at once subtle and direct, without the least affectation, wholly upfront: 'Garnerisms', as Alain Gerber calls them, are not mannerisms. He isn't, moreover, the only pianist one can identify from the outset: Ellington, Tatum, Monk, certainly, are as rapidly identifiable, and for completely different reasons, on an instrument which, however, doesn't offer the same diversity of timbres as, let's say, the tenor saxophone. Of course, singularity isn't the sole artistic merit, nor perhaps the most important (one may like as much, or even prefer, Bill Evans, Hank Jones or Kenny Barron without always being able immediately to distinguish them from one another), and Garner's doesn't prevent him from finding himself, in his own special way,

[189] In French, 'rigolo' is an informal term for 'funny'.

at the centre of a historic web so many of whose threads pass through him – a very un-missing link between Fats Waller and Keith Jarrett – without any of these connections rendering him in the least reducible. But for me the most pleasurable thing is the feeling of space, of lightness, of joyful airiness communicated by his playing. I do mean *airiness*: Garner certainly isn't the most feather-light [aérien] of jazz pianists, yet he is the airiest [le plus aéré]: a sea breeze traverses each bar. I'm probably allowing myself to be influenced by the title and sleeve of a memorable record, *Concert by the Sea* (which was actually recorded, at a concert in Carmel, in a neo-Gothic church, yet, *dixit* the sleeve, after descending by car from San Francisco along the famous coast road), for I always hear him as though he were playing outdoors: on a beach, on a pier, on a terrace, or in a large room with open windows whose curtains raised by the breeze ripple and billow like sails, as in *Death in Venice* (the film), but fresher, crisper: Californian, of course, but Northern. If this stupidly pejorative term might be turned into a compliment, Garner was the greatest 'lounge (brasserie, open-air café, dance hall, brothel, casino ...) pianist' since – I don't know – Schubert, maybe? He remains at any rate the only one to have had a girlfriend called, you couldn't make it up, Rosalyn Noisette.[190]

Genius. 'I feel infinite admiration for your genius. – Why the restriction?' This dialogue, whose source I've forgotten, illustrates fairly well the irrepressible character of artistic sensitivity. When you compliment an author upon his work, avoid mentioning any specific element, aspect or merit: they'll judge forthwith, sometimes not without reason, that you scorn all the others. Another famous reply, which can be heard for example from the mouth of Vittorio Gassman, in I can't recall which Italian comedy where he plays the part of a ham actor: 'But that's enough about me, let's talk a bit about you: how did you like my last film?' I say 'artistic sensitivity', in general, but the fact is, it seems to me, quite peculiarly literary. One speaks, almost pleonastically, of an 'author's vanity' – such as illustrated, for example, by a particular scene in *The Learned Ladies*.[191]

---

[190] 'Noisette' signifies 'hazelnut' in French, and also refers to an espresso coffee with milk.
[191] By Molière (1672).

This peculiarity doubtless derives from the fundamental precariousness of literary talent, whose 'criteria' are ungraspable; but also
from the especially solitary nature of its exercise, and to that, all in
all abstract, of its public reception: no public or private concerts, no
visits to the studio, no private viewings, no grand openings, nothing
but the bleak giddiness of the blank page, the appalling ceremony
of the 'signings' and that, no less paltry, of its media 'promotion',
the dry statement of its print runs, its unsold copies, its pulpings,
the humiliation of awards obtained or missed out on – everything
Friedrich Schlegel already called 'the ridiculousness of being a
writer'. The encounter of two authors thus almost always resembles,
in terms less forward, the dialogue between Vadius and Trissotin.[192]
More wholesome, however, and in truly American style: when they
met – it was, as though by chance, on a Hollywood film set – what
did Faulkner and Hemingway talk about? Their respective royalties.

Genres. Pretexts for confusion. One might designate with the
acronym *GNIO* all kinds of generically non-identified objects,
or those with a complex generic identity, or with a deliberately
contradictory status, like autofiction *stricto sensu*. In the theatre,
Ionesco's inventions (*The Lesson*, comic drama, *The Chairs*, tragic
farce, *Victims of Duty*, pseudo-drama) are no doubt too attached to
his singular achievements to become generic labels. Cinema, or at
least critical discourse upon the cinema, explores these possibilities
more boldly, perhaps precisely because its generic awareness is
more alert. In the 1950s Hitchcock was already credited with the
metaphysical cliff-hanger, and, since then, we have witnessed the
flowering (if they are indeed flowers) of retro futuristic science
fiction, the mystical detective story, the ethical thriller and many
others. We still await the Gothic Western, the transcendental
vaudeville and the ontological burlesque.

Yves Michaud, philosopher of All Knowledge,[193] considers the
category of *best-sellers*, in principle purely commercial, to be a
'literary genre'. This flippant, and even somewhat cynical, ascription

---

[192] Characters in *The Learned Ladies*: the dialogue referred to occurs in
Act III, scene iii.
[193] Genette is here alluding to 'L'Université de tous les savoirs [University
of All Knowledge]' (2000), a French government initiative headed by Yves
Michaud.

is more pertinent than it may at first seem. Everyone – beginning with the publishers – knows that success, in this domain, doesn't stem from recipes that might be applied in advance, nor even inferred after the fact, like the codified rules of a classical genre: Umberto Eco, though a fertile theorist, has never claimed to 'explain' that of *The Name of the Rose* with any particular reason, let alone by way of a generic law. In my view, the meaning of the categorial annexation performed, perhaps in passing, by Yves Michaud, is that in literature as elsewhere the 'genres' are often constituted, and thus defined, more sociologically than artistically. For the 'general public' in question here, *best-sellers do indeed share a generic trait, which is neither formal nor thematic, but which consists quite simply in their success.* This trait is obviously retrospective, and gloriously uncertain, like a sports performance, but it isn't completely random, since it suffices for the publisher (or for its press officers) to 'make known' as swiftly as possible (but not *too* swiftly) that thousands, even millions of readers (viewers, listeners …) have loved this book (this film, this record …), which already features on 'all the best-sellers lists'. The 'new' readers thus solicited then know perfectly well what they're purchasing: success itself, in itself and for itself. It's a price that is never paid too highly.

Germes/Seeds. In a sort of summer camp situated in Magny-en-Vexin, where I was moping around for my own good during the summer of 1939, just prior to being rushed away from there by the decree of a new 'mobilisation-not-the-war', we'd been force-fed on wheatgerm, excellent for growth or some such thing. I can still feel its bland odour in my nostrils, and in my mouth its faintly bitter flavour, but above all I can still see, upon a window sill, those damp-bottomed plates where little piles of softened seeds endeavoured to sprout in the sunlight. I didn't really understand why this phenomenon, which was feared for tubers (we'd spend hours in the cellar removing from our potatoes their off-white tumours unfit for consumption), was welcomed for cereals. Either way, this mobilisation was well and truly the war, the sprouted wheat on its plate was forgotten, and it would be five years before we saw any again. But in the meanwhile its dietary fashion had passed.

Gestation. 'It's not, said Mao Tse Tung, because you have nine wives that you can have a child within a month.' This is for once well observed, and with most salutary figurative applications, but in this company and by tending to your *timing*, you can have one child per month – which, I grant, isn't at all the same thing. Nevertheless, demographically, the outcome is the same.

Ghost-writer. In 1962 I was trying to convince Roland Barthes to collect his then dispersed articles, prefaces and other essays, which I assured him were already circulating by *samizdat*, like Prévert's poems prior to the publication of the volume of *Paroles*. For obscure reasons, but into which may have entered this probably unwelcome comparison, he resisted a suggestion that I was, however, I assume, not alone in making. I thought I'd be able to overcome this resistance with the following, in my view decisive, argument: 'If you were dead, someone would indeed have to do it on your behalf.' By his grimace, I understood that he didn't share my opinion concerning the quality of my argument, but he added straight away: 'If you don't mind, I'd rather take care of this myself.' I had apparently managed to convince him by shocking him. He then claimed to be unable to trace these texts, and proposed that I make a contribution, which amounted in sum to feigning between us the fatal hypothesis he'd just rejected. Stung into action, I handed him, one or two weeks later, a highly lacunary list of which he pretended to approve by calling me a 'wonderful bibliographer'. When the definitive table had been established through his care, I could gauge just how indulgent and/or ironic (with him, nothing was excluded by anything else) this appraisal had been, and to what extent his personal bibliography was in fact perfectly up to date. In the meantime, the whole collection had been split into two books, his studies on Racine appearing under this name in May 1963 in the 'Pierres vives' collection, the others to appear, in March 1964, in the 'Tel Quel' collection. We had at the same time concocted a laborious interview by correspondence that appeared in the February edition of the journal, and which serves as a conclusion to the *Critical Essays*. But my participation in this enterprise knew yet another episode, for at the last moment he wrote to me saying that he now felt himself incapable of writing the text, to be printed on the back cover, which at the *Éditions du Seuil* was called, tactfully, a 'lining': 'Since it's a matter of a *retrospective*, it bothers me to speak about myself and to find a meaning there [*et de me trouver un sens*[194]] ... .' Flattered by this new mission, I executed it as well as I could. Ever benevolent, he declared my lining to be 'perfect', and and in effect corrected just two details, replacing a most mistaken *décade* [ten days] with the requisite *décennie* [decade], and suppressing a clause containing the word *path* [*parcours*], or perhaps *itinerary*, 'a notion, he explained to me, that is quite foreign to me'. I'd have liked to have him say more on this point, but I sensed that his patience had its limits, and that I'd just touched one of them. On the other hand, the expression 'empire of signs', borrowed from Sartre ('The empire of signs is prose'), struck a chord, and it wouldn't be long before he afforded it the echo we know.

In the March of the same 1964, an evening newspaper published an article by Raymond Picard against *On Racine*. Very upset by this attack, but little tempted by polemics, Barthes asked me to write, for whatever purpose it might serve, a rough copy of a reply. Ever more flattered, I produced with more enthusiasm than pertinence some kind of initial outline. He began by making a few amendments to this sketch, which he eventually wisely dropped: Picard's article had in the meantime become the pamphlet entitled *New Criticism, New Imposture*, which impelled him to provide for his own part a thoroughgoing response (*Criticism and Truth*) that owed nothing to my supposed draft. My role as *ghost-writer* thus ended there, to everyone's utmost benefit.

Girl. 'A 48-year-old Israeli businessman who utilised the services of a call-girl in a hotel in Eilat, on the Red Sea, suffered a heart failure on discovering that the prostitute was his daughter. When he had recovered, the businessman curtailed his visit to Eilat, returned to his home in the north of the country and recounted his misadventure to his wife. Upon hearing her husband's story, she burst into tears, decided to set her daughter back on the right path, but requested the divorce of her adulterous husband.' One could be blamed for pretending to improve upon such a scenario (signed AFP[195]), but one might at least rid it of its incidental geopolitical circumstances, and perhaps of its anticlimactic epilogue. The wife's

[194] 'and find a meaning in myself'.
[195] 'Agence France-Presse', French news agency.

reaction seems to me to be a mite conventional, and the husband's (cardiac) failure dodges far too quickly the developments offered by the obligingness of chance – of chance? So here's the situation reduced to its essential elements: a travelling businessman utilises the services of a call-girl; when she meets him in his hotel bedroom, he discovers that this girl is none other than his daughter.[196] For each now to embroider the rest according to the inclination, tragic or vaudevillesque, of one's dramatic genius; there is here, to say the very least, 'a scene to be made'.

Golf. I learn from an article by Mark Singer in the *New Yorker* from the 11th August, 2003 that the inhabitants of the very rustic and very elegant little *wasp* town of Norfolk, Connecticut, in the Berkshires (1,700 inhabitants in winter, twice as many in the summer, but all of them – locals, summertime dwellers or weekend commuters – residents for a respectable number of generations; in Yankee territory, money very swiftly founded its aristocracy), rose up against a plan seeking to build on their land, in the hamlet known as *Yale Farm*, a high-class golf club, obviously accompanied by all the 'amenities' such an activity brings with it, and that 'money can buy'. The 'citizens'' protest movement pertained precisely to what they call over there a *Nimby* campaign, the standard acronym for *Not in My Back Yard* – in French: 'Pas de ça chez moi [Not at mine]' or, more informally: 'Allez faire ça plus loin [Go do it further away]', but this time it was a matter neither of a nuclear power station nor of an open landfill site. The reason for the revolt was that a golf club, especially one of high class, would attract a vulgar clientele of *nouveaux riches*, perhaps even, *horribile dictu*, given the dubious acquaintances of its promoter, a few hooligans from the White House. The affair occurred in 2002 (and I'm unaware of the outcome), but the date matters little: the American political class (among others) has seldom shone through its hereditary elegance, and besides, at the Guermantes', one would never have consented to receive a character as 'ordinary' as a president of the Republic, whosoever he might have been. This is snobbery as I like it, that's

---

[196] 'cette fille n'est autre que la sienne', more literally 'this girl is none other than his own': in French, 'fille' can signify both 'girl' and 'daughter'.

to say against the grain of the official social scale: 'A golf course! and why not a tennis court, whilst you're about it?'

Gould. His life is (among other things) a tissue of anecdotes each more colourful and fabricated than the last. Here's my favourite, which isn't the most apocryphal: in his final years, he'd decided to take up orchestra direction. But his gestures were rather muddled, and he happened one day to beat in four-four time an undeniably ternary piece. The musicians delegated the first violinist to tell him how much this *contretemps* was unsettling them. Gould, conciliatory: 'You don't have to watch me!'

Goût/Taste. What they dogmatically call 'good taste' is obviously nothing but the taste that is shared and objectified, just as 'poor taste' is merely that which is censured. So the important thing isn't to have 'good' taste – which simply has no meaning – but to have one that is *genuine*, that's to say, as far as possible, autonomous, independent of 'influences', fashions, the intimidations of surrounding tastes, or quite simply of 'other people's tastes'. The difficult thing isn't to have a 'sure' aesthetic judgement – like the diagnosis of an expert in attribution – but to be sure of one's judgement, that's to say to judge for oneself. Many people don't really *know* what they like: without being aware of it, they always ask others (for example, the diktat of media role models) to tell them what they *must* love. Stendhal rightly castigated this heteronomy, which he calls 'affectation' or, more bizarrely, *priggishness* [*bégueulisme*], and which consists in 'enjoying with tastes that one doesn't feel'; it's hard to push the statement of contradiction any further. He simply rather forgot to admit that none, not even he himself, escapes this as much as they would like. Thus I believed myself, for a while, to (have to) love a few laborious masterpieces – which mentioning here would suffice to send me to sleep.

Grain. Roland Barthes did much to promote the 'grain of the voice', in an article from 1972 where it was primarily a question of extolling the art of his master Charles Panzéra at the expense – the word is weak – of that of Dieter Fischer-Dieskau, whom he more or less describes as having a voice 'without grain'. The use he makes of this notion concerns a fairly subtle relation between voice and language, and its subsequent success owes nothing to this subtlety: everyone simply sees there a chic synonym for the more common notion of *timbre*, which besides isn't only applied to the human voice: every even remotely practised jazz lover can distinguish from the first bar, even from the first note, John Coltrane's tone from that of Sonny Rollins, Dexter Gordon, Stan Getz or Joe Henderson, to cite only tenor saxophonists from the same period, and irrespective of their stylistic differences. The difference here derives from many factors, among which that, purely technical, of the choice of make of instrument or type of reed – hence the fact that an instrumentalist's timbre may more easily be imitated than can a singer's, which owes far more to natural character-istics. The peculiarity of the *vocal* timbre – which the word 'grain' evokes fairly well, by a quasi-physiological metaphor and beyond any Barthesian nuance – is that it relies upon no external element (one can't call external an alteration of the phonic apparatus by an ailment of the larynx, a sex change, ageing, smoking, etc., and the external modifications brought about by modern techniques of broadcasting and/or recording affect only the reception, not the voice itself, which one will find intact *in praesentia*). With a reasonably good ear, you can recognise it just as well in spoken utterances as in sung performances: an actor, an orator, an average speaker possesses a timbre unique to her or himself, just as personal as a singer's, and again notwithstanding the other features of their utterance: strength, speed, accent, etc. The timbre is a natural given which a professional of speech or song can 'cultivate [travailler]' (in height, volume, in the art of 'placing' one's voice), but which is just as singular in a raw state and for each and everyone as it is for the cultured [travaillé] timbre of the professional. Probably the most sincere thing Barthes expressed (orally) concerning Fischer-Dieskau was 'I *don't like* [n'*aime pas*] his voice' – qualifying one day for our information: 'By that I don't mean that I don't *like* [n'*aime* pas] his voice, but simply that I don't love [n'aime pas] his voice, that I'm not *in love* with his voice.' His displeasure (or rather, then, his absence of pleasure) wasn't here of a stylistic order (as it was, incidentally, in relation to his other musical *bête noire*, Gérard Souzay, even if Panzéra was an equal antithesis to both of these singers), but indeed of a physical order – and, in the commonplace meaning that wasn't his own, of the order of the vocal grain. He was able to describe with a word the peculiarity of a timbre, calling for instance, quite amusingly, but accurately, 'tubular' that of Maria Callas. One *loves* or one doesn't *love* the timbre (also called, and even more metaphorically, the 'colour') of voice of a singer or a cantatrice, and it can even happen that one simply does *not* like it, and I think that in fact, despite his cautious language, Barthes frankly loathed Fischer-Dieskau, hence this recrimination: 'If you like Schubert and if you don't like FD, Schubert is nowadays *forbidden* to you.' A manifest exaggeration, such as a bad mood could inspire in him, for between Hans Hotter in *Winter Journey* and *Swan Song*, and Fritz Wunderlich (tenor) in *The Miller's Daughter*, not to mention women's voices, there were still a few ways of escaping the accursed 'FD'.

Since we're on the subject of baritones, I wish here to note my preference, in general, for those tenors with a somewhat sombre timbre, heroic tenors (opposed to 'lyrical' tenors, Mozartian *par excellence*, like Dermota, Simoneau, Gedda, Alva or Schreier). These *Heldentenor* (Lorenz, Björling, Windgassen, Haefliger, Vickers, King, Thomas ...) often give (as once did, they say, Caruso himself) the impression of being converted baritones, who have conserved the vocal depth of their original tessitura, when age or fatigue, at the end of their career, doesn't add to it its shade of wounding. This was, as is known, literally the case with Lauritz Melchior. Wagner isn't their exclusive repertoire – listen to Vickers as Florestan, as Othello, as Don José – but there they reign supreme. I ought no doubt to justify this preference, but I shall be content with its affirmation, since its example has come from the top. I can see, moreover, that my preferences are rather old, sometimes going back to the thirties and forties, and I do wonder if the spring hasn't dried up. I find some of the flavour of this vocal in-between with certain repertory crossovers apparently cast against their type: Domingo in Wagner, or Fischer-Dieskau – once again – in an opera or an oratorio (the Count or Don Giovanni with Böhm, Hans Sachs with Jochum, Amfortas with Solti, the Wotan of *The Rhinegold* with Karajan, Falstaff with Bernstein, the Jesus of *St John* with Forster and that of *St Matthew* with Klemperer or Karajan, the Simon of *The Seasons* with Marriner). In effect, this is where I prefer him, more at liberty and with a better adapted vocal sweep than in the delicate nuances of the *Lied*, and more balanced by the orchestra than by the piano, albeit that, moreover famously discreet, of Gerald Moore. In what is for me the difficult genre of the piano-accompanied melody, I only find him to be completely at ease (meaning at my own) in Brahms's *Four Serious Songs*, which are thus a twofold exception.

Guerre/War. Nothing like it to revise one's geography: in the sixties, I learned everything about that of the ex-Belgian Congo, future Zaire and future Congo ex-Zaire. Prior to 2003, who could remember that the Euphrates [l'Euphrate] flows to the *west* of the Tigris, and not the other way round? In my first form, at least, we were taught by way of mnemonic that it was impossible to make good mayonnaise in Mesopotamia. 'Why? Because the housekeeper sees *le Tigre* [the Tigris/the tiger], and *l'Euphrate* [l'œuf rate[197]/the egg is ruined].'

Guide. Romanesque grandeur may perhaps be best experienced at Jumièges, in its openness on all sides to the sky and the Normandy forests. The state of ruin there purifies the forms against the emptiness they throw into relief. In a rather offhand manner, the official guide expounded upon the misdeeds of the *Bande noire*[198] and the meritorious efforts to redress them by one whom he affected to call Prosmer Périmé, a gratuitous spoonerism,[199] perhaps unintentional and moreover unsuccessful, most of the tourists only listening with half an ear, the others believing themselves enlightened and correcting *in petto* apparently erroneous memories from their school days. Between two sentences, he whistled the chorale 'Joy of Man's Desiring', marking with a firm step the supposedly ternary metre: sol la *ti* re do *do* mi re *re* sol fa *sol* re ti *sol* la ti *do* re mi *ri* … . I've never been able, since then, to hear this chorale without again seeing the sublime jagged silhouette of the abbey church rising over its freshly mown lawns.

Guirlande/Garland. The avenues of Manhattan, theoretically 12 in number (in fact, I'll get there, 14), are numbered from east to west (from the East River to the Hudson), that's to say run counter

---

[197] In French, 'l'Euphrate' and 'l'œuf rate' are phonetically equivalent.
[198] The 'black band' were speculators who purchased abbeys and castles in the aftermath of the French Revolution, only then to demolish them and sell their contents and materials.
[199] For Prosper Mérimée (1803–1870).

to the direction of our reading (from left to right) on a map. They were built (and their buildings are numbered, in blocks) from south to north. The symbolically central avenue is obviously the Fifth, from which are counted, eastwards and westwards, the buildings of the streets perpendicular to it. Park Avenue, which was for a long time called Fourth, is so arithmetically, but since Lexington is interposed between three and four and Madison between four and five, said 'Fifth' is actually the seventh, to the west of which come the supposed 'Sixth' ('Avenue of the Americas'), 'Seventh', 'Eighth', etc. As far as I can remember, most of them are one-way (for traffic), alternatively north–south and south–north, with the exception perhaps of Park, which is divided along its whole length by an imperturbable flowerbed. I can't recall much about Broadway, which doesn't count as an avenue, and which traverses all of this obliquely from Battery Park till well beyond the limits of Manhattan, and even of the Bronx; one really ought to extend it, and number its buildings, at least as far as Albany, the state capital. I believe in any case that Lexington 'descends' (north–south), that Madison 'rises' (south–north), I'm sure the Fifth descends, that the Sixth rises, that the Seventh descends, and that the Eighth rises, and is called, between 59th and 110th Street, 'Central Park West', for the candid reason that it skirts the western side of Central Park.

This rise was the point I was getting to. During the autumn of 1974 I shared with Tzvetan Todorov an apartment at 302 West 12th Street, that's to say on the corner of this street and of Eighth Avenue. I can't recall on which floor the apartment was situated, but what I do remember is that the lift, then a service staircase bizarrely always open for whoever would like to throw themselves from as high up as possible, led to an asphalt terrace bearing the inevitable water reservoir, and which gave onto the immense rectilinear prospect of the avenue, covered, on five or six lanes, with cars attempting to head north, and whose rear lights, in the evening, formed a fascinating spectacle. This glowing garland represented for us the very essence of the city 'that never sleeps'.

For a few weeks, on a tiny black and white television set that rendered respectably well Walter Cronkite's journal on CBS Evening News ('*That's the way it is*'), but more mediocrely Westerns in Cinemascope, some of our evenings were occupied with the hearings, before a Senate committee, of Nelson Rockefeller, whom Gerald Ford, unelected vice-president (but in the meantime appointed by

Richard Nixon to replace an overly compromising Spiro Agnew) become president by default for the reason we know, had himself chosen as presumptive heir in the event of fate's further persecution of the Oval Office and its occupants of good or bad faith. If I can reconstitute aright a tortuous process that awaits its Saint-Simon, this new appointment without popular vote required, as its supposed final phase, a kind of retroactive ratification, doubtless by Congress, which demanded in turn an examination by said committee of the applicant's merits and demerits. This elegant billionaire, incidentally a former governor of the State of New York, wasn't just any old applicant. His patrician charisma, his intellectual calibre, his status as the leader of the liberal wing (today vanished) of the Republican Party, almost made you forget the unwelcome pedigree connecting him to the most famous of the *robber barons*. For us, these hearings illustrated, at its institutional summit, the functioning of what one could still with a straight face call American democracy. We very nearly believed ourselves to be back in 1787, present at the deliberations of the Philadelphia convention. But this Rockefeller wasn't a new Jefferson, and his political career didn't take him any higher than this mortifying folding seat, the chain of successive failures stopping there for want of a new Watergate.

Hautil. This region's Romanesque churches are often distinguishable, like I can't recall which one in Proust, by their squat bell towers clad with fine stone scales. The one in Conflans perhaps isn't the most remarkable, but its position on the hillside overlooking the Seine, facing the Achères plain and the forest of Saint-Germain, makes it the most visible. I've never known why a village devoted to the relics of Saint Honorine named its church Saint-Maclou, but this accumulation of saints of both genders wasn't our business. It could be seen in the distance from the bridge downstream, with a white clock face on each side of its heavy grey-stoned steeple, the village's oldest houses plunging from its midst all the way down to the river, whose right bank itself here becomes, upriver, more rustic, at least as far as la Frette, then a kind of literary resort owing to the presence of the novelist Jacques Chardonne. But our universe wasn't angled in that direction: starting from the famous confluence, we used, *go west*, to descend the Seine towards Meulan, Mantes, Vernon, Les Andelys, Rouen, Honfleur, or walk back along the Oise towards

Pontoise, Auvers, L'Isle-Adam – never any further, I'm not sure why. This centre of the fluvial world thus radiated primarily, for us, westwards and northwards, a double heading circumscribed at sunset by the back-lit profile of the hill at l'Hautil.

The most charming of these churches may be found, precisely, at the foot of l'Hautil, on the right bank of the Oise: it's the one in Jouy-le-Moutier, of which the sprawling disaster named Cergy-Pontoise hasn't yet, today, come to ravage the immediate vicinity with its misshapen housing developments and its ring road interchange loops. In fact, its only Romanesque feature is its bell tower, directly above its transept, but this bell tower, with on each side its split-level double openwork bays and its external clock hung upon its south-west angle like a craftsman's shop sign, would give style to the most humdrum of naves, and the whole thing, overhanging the road slightly, possesses a rustic elegance whose equivalent I have found only at the Cunault abbey church, on the left bank of the Loire, between Saumur and Gennes.

But to say 'at the foot of l'Hautil' is faintly hyperbolic, since from its height this hill really dominates only the Seine, on its southern flank, between Chanteloup and Vaux. From the east, having crossed the Oise, coming thus from Jouy, but as well from Maurecourt, from Glatigny, from Vincourt or from Vauréal, the long uphill bike ride was performed in three stages: a short steep climb up from the valley led to a kind of gently sloped cereal-growing plateau, tiresome to cross and hard going like all false flats, but which gave all its merit to this approach march, ever initiatory despite the frequency of its repetition, then another steep climb, very wooded, leading to the crest at whose centre lies the place actually called Hautil. Now, as I said, ruined, the northern part of this crest, which merges into the plateau of the Vexin français, then consisted of three other villages named, truly in the old manner, Boisemont, Courdimanche and Menucourt. Each of them had its own very special character. Courdimanche, atop a fairly pronounced hillock, was typically rural, surrounded by cultivated fields, bereft of shade and often stiflingly hot. Menucourt, ringed with woods, had (still has) a ceramic church in a neo-kitsch oddball style, which afforded it an exotic and scarcely credible backdrop; in effect, it was already a different territory: you couldn't go beyond it without toppling, via Evecquemont, into a kind of Far West, with its view over the course of an already Norman river. Boisemont, on the contrary, looks eastwards, right over the bend of the Oise: you arrived there to turn round and behold the distance travelled from the river; this somewhat residential village had a discreet chapel beneath the trees, dedicated, I know not why (I'm not aware of her having made this ascent), to Mary Magdalene, which has lost nothing of its mystery. This place remains in my memory the symbolic endpoint of the 'climb to l'Hautil', the door of paradise – a paradise that, it must be said, was more or less confined, like all the others, to its door. On the same side, but a little further south, you could see the remains of a Gallo-Roman farm, and, yet a little further on, a castle-farm run by fervent Huguenots, a kind of Île-de-France version of the Mas Soubeyran[200] which for a while housed I'm not really sure what replicas of the Assemblies in the Desert.[201] Upon this unobstructed slope whence you can see, to the east, as far as the steeple of Saint-Germain-l'Auxerrois, we could commemorate every year the massacre of the 24th August 1572. Our protestant memory [mémoire parpaillote] (we didn't yet say 'duty of') bathed in a very specific temporality: between Jesus and Lucifer there lay centuries of Papist usurpation that we wished to forget, then the history of Christianity resumed its course in the new martyrology of the Wars of Religion, of St Bartholomew's Day, of the revocation of the Edict of Nantes, of the dragonnades in Languedoc, of the Calas and Sirven affairs,[202] persecutions that for a time I believed myself, through my maternal lineage, to have miraculously survived.

The hamlet of l'Hautil, which belongs to the *commune* of Triel, amounted to a few houses, and one or two inns on either side of the ridge, as though its only purpose were to give the hill its

---

[200] A hamlet in the Cévennes region in south-central France, a major site of Protestant resistance in the seventeenth and eighteenth centuries.

[201] Clandestine meetings held by persecuted French protestants between the revocation of the Edict of Nantes in 1685 and the Edict of Toleration in 1787.

[202] Jean Calas, a Protestant merchant, was sentenced to death in Toulouse in 1762, having been convicted for the murder of a son who converted to Catholicism; Pierre-Paul Sirven, a Protestant archivist and notary, was sentenced to death in Toulouse in 1764, accused of murdering his mentally handicapped daughter; both cases were defended by Voltaire: Calas was posthumously rehabilitated, Sirven's sentence was overturned in 1771.

name, unless it's the other way round. The rest in fact constitutes a pretty handsome forest, with, in a clearing, a tiny and perhaps artificial because perfectly circular pond, whose precise name is 'Mare de l'Hautil'. I recall having bivouacked, meaning spent a night in a sleeping bag and without the protection of a tent, by the side of this pond. Bivouacking so close to home certainly didn't appertain to any grand excursion, but to the understandable lure of the thing known as 'sleeping under the stars', which owes, like so many others, all of its charm to its name. Meteorological science was then, also, in its infancy, and the stars were extinguished in the early morning downpour.

The southern side, then, falls quite sheer upon the Seine via Triel, and via Chanteloup upon a vast prosaically cultivated bend, which we avoided by heading left towards Andrésy, with its market beneath the linden trees, its weir, and its mysteriously inaccessible islands. In Triel, then a smart village, like all of those bordered by the Seine, but tightly constricted between the bank and the abrupt slope, the principal attraction was Saint-Martin's church, motley in style, but under which runs a street. Well, I say *under*, but I gather that the choir was quite simply built, in its day, over the street that begins the steepest rise towards the *summit*. Again, I say summit: 165 metres and a few twigs.

Hésiter/Being in Two Minds. Is it *still* to be deciding, or *already* to have decided? I'm in two minds.

Heureusement/Fortunately. I love this 'amusing' story, a fine lesson in optimism: a test pilot is flying over a wheat field; unfortunately, his engine breaks down; fortunately, he has a parachute; unfortunately, his parachute doesn't open; fortunately, he's right above a fine bale of straw; unfortunately, the bale has a pitchfork sticking vertically out of it; fortunately, he manages to fall beside the bale. The theoretical formula for this type of chain of events is found in Alfred Capus:[203] 'In life, everything works out, but badly.'

History. Contrary to Stephen Dedalus, it's a nightmare I rediscover upon each waking.

---

[203] French journalist and playwright (1858–1922).

Homme/Humankind. The definition 'featherless biped' was swiftly discredited for being equally applicable to a chicken flayed alive; 'political animal' overlooks ant-hills and other hives, and suffers in addition (from) a few exceptions, including me; 'endowed with reason' doesn't bear examination; more observantly, Jules Renard proposed: 'the only animal to have money troubles', which is primarily valid by dint of its adjective *only*: if *certain* humans do not have such troubles, *no* animal experiences them, as far as I am aware. It was discovered more recently that human beings are also, thanks to a certain lobe in their brain, the only animals to believe in God. I wonder if the latter compensates for the former.

Horizon. Funereal.

Hublot/Window. In December, 1964, in the gardens of the Alcázar, there lay warming in the sun a family of ginger cats, which we rediscovered intact two, then three or four generations later – always in December – before wandering through the exquisite Santa Cruz quarter, in hopeless quest of a restaurant open before ten o'clock at night, since Andalusian time is an aggravated version of Spanish time. What I was never again to see was the very old-style hotel where I'd been accommodated, perhaps indeed on *Reyes Católicos* street (I like this unisex manner, whose historical reason is very clear, of crowning Ferdinand and Isabelle simply 'kings', and not 'king and queen'). The English consul, a jovial scale model of Winston Churchill, lived for his part in one of the houses bordering the Alameda de Hércules, the long square with a mysterious name, almost deserted, silent and then unknown to tourists, in the outlying district of the Macarena, where we had laboriously bilingual conversations, interspersed with bad Castilian. Even the miniscule chapel of San José, a quintessence of the baroque, which can scarcely be seen from the very bustling Sierpes, appeared abandoned, like the arch-Classical Casa de Pilatos, where you could lose yourself for a few hours.

Three days later, a small passenger plane apparently dating from the *Frente Popular* took me back to Madrid over the plateaus of a New Castile still spared by the snow. Through the window, I strove in vain to catch sight of Toledo, the yellow curve of the Tagus and the silhouette of the other Alcázar, which perhaps wasn't quite beneath our trajectory. I reminded myself of the peasant taken

aboard by Magnin,[204] in one of those crates whence bombs were
dropped through the hole in the toilet, so that they might find the
little wood where the Francoist planes are hiding, near the road
to Zaragoza, and who is unable even, from this for him baffling
angle, to recognise his village in Teruel. The scene is even more
poignant in the film, where the face of the disorientated peasant
[paysan dépaysé] expresses unfathomable distress. This anachronic
comparison gave me the illusion of discerning, in its timeless
identity, what Unamuno had called the essence of Spain.

The following day, Lucile and Jean-Pierre took me along to taste
a first-rate suckling pig at an inn in Segovia's old town, somewhere
between the cathedral and the Roman aqueduct admired in his day
by Saint-Simon: it was no doubt once again the essence of Spain.
On the way back, in the late afternoon, I had to change a burst
tyre on the DS, a few kilometres away from the airport where the
plane to Paris had no reason to wait for me. I don't recall having
ever turned the handle of a jack so energetically.

Huma.[205] The rue d'Ulm was reckoned, by right-wing politicians, to
be the Communist bastion that it wasn't quite, despite our efforts,
which some resisted, not without merit. Here's the reason for this
mistake: one of us, freshly recruited and volunteered to attend a
trade-union delegation at the Assemblée [Nationale], to whom a
'Gaullist' deputy asked elegantly: 'How many 'cocos'[206] are there in
this *École*?', and who wasn't familiar with the political meaning of
this word (which we obviously didn't use among ourselves), took it
to be a colloquial synonym for 'students', and replied in all candour
something like: 'Roughly 250.' In those days of Cold War at every
level, this exorbitant proportion (clearly 100 per cent) occasioned a
sudden rise in the budget for the Parisian police, at least in the Vth
arrondissement. For eventual verification, there was indeed General
Enquiries, but their information was generally no less fantastical.

One of the 'militant tasks' of the (less numerous) communist
students consisted in pinning every day a few fine pages of our 'class
paper' upon a wooden or cork board on a corridor at the *École*, near

---

[204] In *L'Espoir* (*Days of Hope*), by André Malraux (1937).

[205] *L'Humanité*, see note 16.

[206] 'Commies', 'reds'; also 'coconuts'.

the refectory, and in posting at least the 'headline' on a wall of the Rue d'Ulm, perhaps right over the Republican inscription (which one hardly sees nowadays) *Stick No Bills, law of the 29th July 1881.* In this case, *posting* meant 'pasting', and I can't recall where we stored the bucket of glue and the brush indispensable for this daily operation (since even Sunday had its *Huma*), apparently protected by the respect owed to their militant function. You quickly learned at which degree of thickness the previous days' pages should be torn off, and how to place a new layer of glue upon the current day's to ensure its adhesion. The deed was obviously in itself illegal, and during periods of great political tension the billposter had to be accompanied by a lookout alert to police manoeuvres. This precaution didn't always spare the first, nor even the second, from a courtesy visit to the Vth arrondissement police station, located as though by chance at the other end of the street, on the corner of Place du Panthéon. The master of the place, I don't know why, was called Joseph – or maybe 'Joseph' was merely the nickname a whole generation of students had attached to his person, or more broadly to his function. The visit occasionally lasted long enough to require an 'action', which consisted in an appeal to the School director, who would in turn intervene with the Joseph of the moment in order to obtain the 'liberation' of the militant considered to be a victim of police violence. On the day it was my turn to be a martyr, I was, after two or three hours of custody, returned to that of Jean Hyppolite, whom an apparently superficial reading of Hegel hadn't prepared for this type of accident of History. By way of reprimand, this excellent man attempted for a good further quarter of an hour to have me explain the purpose of this 'experiment'. My answer must have lacked persuasive force, to the point that I felt my own conviction gradually melt away. To be quite sincere, I should add that the paper founded long ago by Jaurès had become, over the years, pleasanter to paste than to read and, I assume, than to write.

Hypallage. She liked this word for itself. She gathered it was that of a 'figure', but didn't care to specify which one. I respected this reserve for a time, all the while finding that by refusing to go beyond the word she was depriving herself of a pleasure, the most delicate of all those analysed by a then mysterious discipline, improperly called 'rhetoric'. In the end, I let drop before her, in a brazen pastiche of Proust, that the sound of the bell calling us to dinner was rusty. She looked at me askance and replied: 'I assume that you have just served me a hypallage [*un* hypallage].' She assumed correctly, as often, but continued utterly to refuse that this word was feminine. I left her alone with this half an error.

Ideas. I can't recall who more or less said about I can't recall which other (who wasn't M. Teste): 'His mind was so pure that it was never sullied by anything so vulgar as an idea.' Vulgar or not, the fact remains that most are bad (which doesn't prevent them, quite the contrary, from being ideas), but they can be spotted fairly swiftly. The most dangerous are the *false good ones* (meaning good in principle but bad in practice because dangerous, inapplicable or finally pointless), such as: the plastic shield on the bonnet to deflect insects from the windscreen, the anti-static rubber hanging in the rear to avoid car sickness (those two only knew one or two seasons), cruise control, the four-colour ballpoint pen, Seltzer water, the Leyden jar, the pulsating shower, the jacuzzi tub, pizza home-delivery, fruit yoghurt, meat-and-bone meal, the eight o'clock News, the prose poem, the verse novel, the psychological novel, psychology in all its guises and whatever its reason, warm beer, the quarrel of the Ancients and the Moderns, the French Academy, theme parks, country clubs, the symphonic poem, sauerkraut without mustard, mustard with cassoulet (I do add it though), the chastity belt, the security fence, revisionism in history, divisionism in painting (and elsewhere), surrealism in painting, free jazz, new figuration, the return to Bach, the return to Ingres, the Eternal Return, the Return in general, the H bomb, the disposable phone, the mobile phone, the backpedal brake, 3 D cinema, Kinopanorama, the Crusades, the Hundred Years' War, *jardins à la française*, direct democracy, Appeals to the People, the General Strike, the Big Night, a Brighter Future [les lendemains qui chantent[207]], the Ems Dispatch, the Big Bang, the Tobin tax, the assassination of the duke of Guise,[208] whose stature

---

[207] 'the singing tomorrows'; the expression derives from Paul Vaillant-Couturier's poem 'Jeunesse [Youth]' (1937). Vaillant-Couturier participated in the founding of the French Communist Party in 1920.
[208] Henry I (1550–1588), founder of the Catholic League in 1576, assassinated by King Henry III's bodyguards.

it enhanced, Martini dry, olives in non-dry Martini, savoury cakes for aperitif, the aperitif in general and especially the fact of calling it 'apero', the teaspoon in the neck of the bottle to prevent the bubbles from leaving the champagne, the electric coffee grinder, which chars the beans, the Sacré-Cœur of Montmartre, the *Très Grande Bibliothèque*,[209] the Pompidou Centre, the *Opéra-Bastille*, the Maginot Line, the Siegfried Line, the Berlin Wall, the second war in Iraq, the ISF,[210] the 35-hour week, the CAC 40,[211] the *Bison Futé*,[212] the Great Criss-Crossing of July and August holidaymakers [des Juilletistes et des Aoûtiens], the cigarette-holder, the cigarette case, the categorical imperative, instant coffee, powdered milk, low-fat butter, freeze-dried water (patented), the *Front de Seine*,[213] pure duration [la durée pure], hard purée [la purée dure], the words to say it, the rule of three, the proof by nine,[214] the *Unigenitus* bull, the answering machine, 'fancy' ringtones for mobile phones, the fax, emails, the Internet, all the different kinds of skateboard and roller skate, the CPE[215] (next employment contract), the pivoting head electric razor, the Legion of Honour, literary quotations, the reusable toothpick, the electric toothbrush, fake wood painted over real wood, orange flower water in pancake batter, the cigarette lighter on the dashboard, the baccalaureate, globalisation with a

---

[209] The *Bibliothèque nationale de France* (French National Library) in the 13th arrondissement of Paris.

[210] 'Impôt de solidarité sur la fortune', 'solidarity tax on wealth': introduced by the Parti Socialiste in 1981 as a wealth tax applicable to those with assets in excess of 1,300,000 euros; abolished in 2017.

[211] A French stock market index ('Cotation Assistée Continue', 'Continuous Assisted Quotation').

[212] The 'smart bison', a French TV and radio traffic monitoring service.

[213] A modern highrise commercial and residential development in the Beaugrenelle district in Paris, south of the Eiffel Tower.

[214] 'La preuve par neuf': in French, this originally mathematical expression referring to a method for checking multiplication and division ('the proof by nine' or 'casting out nines') is also commonly used to signify the 'irrefutable proof' of something.

[215] 'Contrat première embauche', 'First Employment Contract': promoted in 2006 by Prime Minister Dominique de Villepin, the contract applied to workers under 26, aiming to encourage the additional hiring of staff by making it easier for employers to dismiss employees; repealed later that year following massive protests.

human face, cinema criticism, bridge, card games, parlour games in general, cotton oversleeves, the magic knife holder, which sharpens the blade each time it's inserted, the piezoelectric gas lighter, bottled gas, the cherry on the cake, the cake beneath the cherry, strawberry with rhubarb, truffles in omelettes, port on melon, 'bonuses' on DVD, pliers with one jaw, music in Hitchcock's films, film music in general, intercoms with drop-down menus, the neighbour's digicode, the cardboard digipak for CDs, out of order cashpoints, rechargeable batteries, Father Christmas, pebble beaches, beaches without pebbles, pebbles without beaches, plastic sandals for swimming, the electronic foot-warmer (patented), car seats with programmable back massages, the unisex headrest (patented), Business Class, the secateur for the left-handed, the mug for the left-handed (handle on the left, patented), the lunchbox with three compartments, square plates, glass plates, square glass plates, the roof rack over the front wheels, colour photography, digital photography, terrestrial digital television, the pedal bin, the electric gas stove, the submarine with sails, the helicopter with an ejector seat, the three-wheel drive car (patented), the silk-ribboned bookmarks of the volumes of the Pléiade, the removal of their expressive covers, street theatre, slimming diets, sun cream, Columbus's Egg (another one gone to waste!), attempts to straighten the tower of Pisa (farewell Galileo!), new ideas in theatre and especially in Opera stage direction, seeking a needle in a glass of water,[216] putting all your eggs in the same clog,[217] throwing away the handle with the bathwater,[218] putting the baby before the plough and the sponge before the axe,[219] remaining with

---

[216] A hybrid of 'chercher une aiguille dans une botte de foin', 'to look for a needle in a haystack' and 'se noyer dans un verre d'eau', 'to drown in a glass of water', meaning 'to make a mountain out of a molehill'.

[217] A hybrid of 'mettre tous ses oeufs dans le même panier', 'to put all your eggs in the same basket', and 'avoir les deux pieds dans le même sabot', 'to have both feet in the same clog', meaning 'to be lacking initiative/in get up and go'.

[218] A hybrid of 'jeter le manche après la cognée', 'to throw away the handle after the axe', meaning 'to give up/throw in the towel' and 'jeter le bébé avec l'eau du bain', 'to throw the baby out with the bathwater'.

[219] A hybrid of four expressions: 1) 'jeter le bébé avec l'eau du bain'; 2) 'mettre la charrue avant les boeufs', 'to put the plough before the cattle', meaning 'to

your backside between two shirts,[220] biting the hand you're sitting on,[221] taking stories for lanterns,[222] calling a liner *Titanic*, and I'm perforce overlooking some. Winston Churchill, who explained his own longevity by the fact of absolutely never having practised any kind of sport, saw in golf 'the surest way of spoiling a fine walk'. I'm not sure that walking isn't already the surest way of spoiling a fine countryside, but one could doubtless lengthen the list of the surest ways of spoiling things, which form a sub-species of the false good ideas.

So as to drive no one to despair, here are a few examples of (rare) *actual* good ideas: old-style black and white film, the device that lets you disengage the automatism of the automatic exposure camera, the one that suspends the automatic blanking of the computer screen, the one (*source direct*) that disables the regulation of the amplifier's treble, bass and 'balance', the one that suspends the functioning of the cruise control, the one that locks into a fixed position the pivoting head of the electric razor, the one that lets you transform a pulsating shower into an ordinary shower or a jacuzzi into a traditional bathtub, the one that unplugs the electric toothbrush and turns it into a pre-war toothbrush – and more generally all the inventions fit to neutralise, once their noxiousness has been registered, the false and occasionally the actual good ideas. The latest is the *free* option for a brand of car where *everything else* is a paying option: the 'non-smoker's pack', which consists in having the cigarette lighter removed – perhaps even, for a modest additional cost, the ashtray.

put the cart before the horse'; 3) 'jeter l'éponge', 'to throw in the sponge/the towel' and 4) 'jeter le manche après la cognée'.

[220] A hybrid of 'rester le cul entre deux chaises', 'to remain with one's backside between two chairs', meaning 'to be caught between two stools' and 'comme cul et chemise', 'like backside and shirt', meaning 'as thick as thieves', 'like a house on fire'.

[221] A hybrid of 'mordre la main qui te nourrit', 'to bite the hand that feeds you', and 'scier la branche sur laquelle on est assis', 'to saw off the branch you are sitting on', meaning 'to cut off your nose to spite your face'.

[222] 'prendre les récits pour des lanternes', derived from the saying 'prendre des vessies pour des lanternes', 'to take bladders for lanterns', meaning 'to think the moon is made of green cheese', or 'to have the wool pulled over one's eyes'.

There are, finally, *false bad ideas*. These are evidently the best, but also the rarest; they might fall prey to the objection, famous in all scientific laboratories: 'Your thing perhaps works in practice, but in theory?' Yet this isn't quite the case with my favourite: the boat made of granite, which ought to sink, given its weight, but which floats by virtue of Archimedes, and which, contrary to the boat made of wood, *never* rots. But others may be found in the compendium of inventions, alas purely virtual: Carelman's[223] *Catalogue of Unfindable Objects*, which was my breviary of everyday aesthetics long before the *Languages of Art*. One there finds, as an epigraph (captioned beneath a necessarily empty frame), Lichtenberg's famous minimalist, and even conceptual, implement: the knife without a blade which is just missing its handle, really convenient when you don't have any pockets. I'll add Magritte's non-pipe, for the exclusive use of non-smokers.

Impôt/Tax. The fairest, if not the most democratic, is the one that in my family was called the tax on stupidity. It's one of the rare examples of an actual good idea. Its definition speaks for itself, its basis is broad, its rate fortunately progressive, its collection automatic and without limitation period, and it's perhaps the only one not restricted by the well-known principle: 'Too much tax kills tax'; nothing, not even itself, can kill this one, and we're all subjected to it. Examples of it abound; beyond some of those previously cited, here are a few, more institutional and more intentional: the Lotto, Trifecta Bets [Le Tiercé], one-armed bandits (etc.), Macdonald's, Las Vegas, Planet Hollywood (alas discontinued), Valentine's Day, Father's Day (I'd be loath to mock that of mothers), televised phone-in game shows, contemporary art, the Stock Exchange – and occasionally, let's say it, Life. My father, an amateur liberal economist, said in his own way: 'As long as there are fools to buy it, there'll be tricksters to sell it, and conversely'; I didn't really understand where the converse was to be applied, but I trusted him. I later became acquainted with an eccentric, somewhat mad but most resourceful, who'd founded an overtly profit-making association named Company for the Exploitation of Human Stupidity (CEHS), a Company that operated thus: as soon

---

[223] Jacques Carelman (1969).

as a gullible individual appeared interested in this vast programme and was curious about its operational mode, he'd ask him first and foremost to pay a modest subscription. Once relieved, the new member saw himself dubbed with the words: 'There, you've been exploited.'

Incarnation. Mary: 'But what have I done to the good Lord to deserve such a child?'

Incendie/Fire. Displayed in a hotel bedroom in Uzerche: 'In the event of a fire in your room, stay calm, do not shout 'Fire!' If you cannot control the fire, leave your room, taking good care to close the door behind you. Inform the chambermaid or management. In the event of hearing the alarm bell, leave your room without further delay, close your door behind you and, taking the staircase [en empruntant l'escalier], head without panic towards the exit.' I don't really understand, first of all, why we call 'borrowing [emprunt]' this usage often without return, then I think of all the roads I've borrowed without ever giving them back.

Index. In July 1951 we spent a few hours, Odile and I, in a mezzanine room with a very low ceiling, arranging in alphabetical order, for the index of a soon to be famous *General History of Cinema*,[224] the list of Chaplin's short films whose titles began (in French) with *Charlot* … . The operation, which the most rustic of computers would nowadays expedite in a few seconds, was long and fortunately fumbling. The spoiled pages and unusable carbon paper were strewn across the floor tiles, and the author in person, emerging from his office, feigned impatience with an almost silent guffaw. But the fact is that we'd hardly placed at the top a *Charlot à la banque* [*The Bank*] when we had to start again and demote it in favour of a *Charlot aime la patronne* [*The Star Boarder*], which deserved it in every respect; I've never seen this promising sketch in a form other than that of an underscored entry – thus were italics then prescribed. Time passed quickly, and the few hours lasted a few days, or maybe it's my memory dilating them, for a reason that doesn't quite escape me.

---

[224] *Histoire générale du cinéma* (1959) by Georges Sadoul.

Ingratitude. Pettiness of kings. Of the feelings of Louis-Philippe[225] with regard to the banker Laffitte, to whom he owed (among other things) his throne, Dumas wrote: 'There are services so great that they can be repaid only through ingratitude.'

Intervals. In Oudin and Rosset's peerless translation of *Quixote* we read that don Lorenzo describes the hero as a '*fou bigarré et plein d'intervalles lucides*', 'a variegated madman replete with lucid intervals'. I could easily refer to the Castilian original, but I'm wary of so doing, for fear of disappointment: I find in the two or three (tiny) semantic anomalies, 'variegated' (taken in a moral sense) and 'lucid intervals' (you or I would have written at best: 'intervals of *lucidity*', or perhaps, more blandly still, '*bouts* of lucidity'), a truly, how can I put this, untranslatable appeal. Then, since impertinent curiosity is always strongest, I turn to it nevertheless, and find: '*un entreverado loco, lleno de lucidos intervalos*'. It's just about literal, yet, seen from here, the anteposition of the two adjectives weakens them sufficiently to render, in accordance with the old Borgesian paradox (which befalls many other cases, often more extensive), the original inferior to – let's not say 'unworthy of' – its translation. The effect common to the two versions remains the discreet oxymoron: 'replete with intervals'; since the interval is an emptiness, how might one be replete with them? I suppose, furthermore, that *intervals* connotes a 'variegation' with alternating streaks (one dark, one clear – one mad, one 'lucid'), like that of the zebra, or rather of the tiger: Borges is decidedly never very far away.

Jargon. There is often some enjoyment to be had in seeing yourself described as a pedant by a prig. Roland Barthes had long since, in speech and by example, stopped me feeling guilty about the use of neologistic 'jargon'. 'Jargon, he'd say, is better than obscurantism, and besides, the dogs bark, the caravan passes' (but this consoling proverb entails an overlooked converse: the caravan passes, but the dogs remain, and they continue to bark). Of this use, he sensed and shared the ludic and sometimes even 'greedy' aspect, linked to the half-intellectual, half-gustatory pleasure of defining, of

---

[225] Louis Philippe I, king of France from 1830 to 1848.

distinguishing, of classifying, of naming afresh. I remember that Marie-Jeanne Durry, who had done much to allow me to defend at the Sorbonne, in 1972, what was called a *'thèse sur travaux* [a thesis based on works]' (it was in fact a matter, a false bad idea and an undeniable 'benefit from May [acquis de Mai]',[226] of a thesis defence *without a thesis*), gently chided me, during this ceremony, for a pointless recourse to a 'technical jargon' that was passably 'barbaric' (in fact, generally derived from the Greek, just like the adjectives 'technical' and 'barbaric', which she'd just used without qualm). 'You could, she insisted, write it in ordinary French, and it would mean [voudrait dire] the same thing.' I thought at once, *in petto*, that it would perhaps *mean* [*voudrait* peut-être dire] the same thing, but that it wouldn't *say* it [ne le *dirait* pas] (since a word always connotes as much as, even more than, it denotes, and a new concept necessarily calls, lest there be confusion, for a new term). Half a second later, I realised that my *in petto* had expressed itself more loudly than I had believed, and that this inadvertent response might be deemed insolent. But it was a day of indulgence, and the rest was entirely amiable.

After the session, my generous protectress asked me behind the scenes for what reason I engaged in a practice in her view so against nature, and I replied to her quite frankly: 'Because I enjoy it. – My poor friend, she declared, I do fear that you should have to enjoy yourself all alone.' This time, I scrupulously refrained from thinking out loud: 'Well it's still better than being bored in a group.' Whereby I think so still, and even ever more so, and in other terms.

Far more recently, perplexed by the impenetrable instructions of a 'user's manual' translated literally from Korean into a techno-commercial pidgin by an inspired polyglot, I appealed to the assistance of the French distributor's *hotline*. After a few bars of looped Vivaldi, an employee, prior to any exchange, took note of my 'contact details': name, first name (here, a brief silence at the end of the line), address, telephone, invoice number. I eventually presented my 'problem'. Half-frostily, my saviour interrupted me: 'Dear Sir, when one has written *Figures III*, one really ought to be able to decode the user's manual for a DVD player.'

---

[226] I.e. related to the institutional reforms that followed the French 'May '68'.

Jeton/Token. Through oral tradition, I long thought that 'faux-jeton [phoney]' was written *faucheton*, then I discovered that you can also say 'faux comme un jeton [as phoney as a token]', which logically implies that all tokens are phoney, and therefore that *faux-jeton* is a pleonasm. I'm not sure to whom was originally applied the sentence: 'You're allowed to be two-faced, but not to appear so to that extent.' One day I undertook to count the public figures to whom it might be applicable, but I gave up on account of the abundance (I have, even so, someone in particular in mind, and you do too, I think). It is, in truth, far more extensively applicable, for hypocrisy, owing to the effort it requires – at least before becoming a second nature – marks your features far more than does sincerity. 'You can't at once, said Gide, be sincere and seem it.' As a matter of fact, I wonder whether you can at once be and seem to be anything at all.

Joconde/Gioconda. I can't remember which character, real or fictional, said something like: 'My father managed a bar, I was an activist for ten years in a political party, so go figure how much bullshit I've heard!' Although endowed with a different curriculum, the poor Mona Lisa – who a costly software programme recently taught us was '83% happy' – could probably say the same, and if one were to place behind her a machine able to record the commentaries she inspires, you could derive from it a quite Flaubertian collection, even censoring questions about her price. I must at least mention this one, heard with my own ears, and which incidentally taught me about the word order in the language of Mark Twain: '*I like Grand Canyon better*' (and not, as I would naturally have said, in the French way: '*I like better Grand Canyon*'). Of course, I too like the Grand Canyon better, and even far more modest landscapes, which feature in no sightseeing directory, but the idea of this comparison had never occurred to me. I suppose, furthermore, that Immanuel Kant, who preferred the 'beauty of nature' over that of works of art, and sometimes the 'sublime' over beauty in general, would have gladly countersigned it, if he'd been acquainted with either of these two spectacles.

Journal. The index of Gide's *Journal*, in its old Pléiade edition, curiously included an entry *Gide (André)*. Disappointment: it referred there only to the pages where the author mentions his own works – among which the *Journal* itself: a referral, in sum, to the pages where the *Journal* mentions itself. New disappointment: this sub-entry is incomplete. Probable excuse: where, in a Journal, do reflexivity and self-reference begin and end? Is there anything more omnipresent in a Journal than the awareness of keeping one? But I should perhaps consult the *new* Pléiade, in two volumes.

Jussienne. My father officiated, on the edge of the Sentier district, on Rue de la Jussienne. This name was utterly opaque to me. No dictionary at the time told me what a Jussienne was, and none will tell you today, for the *jussienne* does not exist, or, to say this more correctly, nothing exists that is a jussienne. I learned much later that 'la Jussienne' is simply a popular deformation of 'l'Égyptienne', from the name of St Mary the Egyptian, to whom had once been devoted a chapel on the corner of this street and Rue Montmartre. A stained-glass window there showed her, 'in accordance with Jacques de Voraigne's *Golden Legend*' (*dixit* Hillairet), hitching her clothes up to the knee before a boatman, not to avoid soaking the bottom of her dress but to pay for her passage of the Jordan, in a manner confirmed by this quite explicit inscription: 'How the saint offered the boatman her body for her passage.' The same Hillairet goes on to tell us that 'the vicar of Saint-Germain-l'Auxerrois had this stained-glass window removed in 1660', and that 'young girls who feared to become mothers came, in secret, to pray for the intervention of St Mary the Egyptian' – the relation between the latter and the former remaining implicit. If I'd known about it, this legend would have truly intrigued me, not knowing whether you must really climb aboard a boat to cross the tiny stream that is the Jordan, if showing your knees is the beginning or the entirety of what is called 'offering one's body', no more than how such an action might deserve the honours of the calendar, let alone by what miracle of immaculate conception its memory or its representation could dispel a risk of pregnancy. That would have involved tracing one enigma back to a few others, and I remained at the first.

Destroyed under the Revolution, said chapel was replaced, I'm unaware after how long, by the outfitter's that employed my father, and whose owner, in the thirties, was a M. Hamberger, in association with a M. Blum; I've never known how their duties were divided, but he held them in the same esteem, with a shade of particular affection for the second, perhaps in homage to the other Blum. Rue de la Jussienne, one of the shortest in Paris, connects obliquely and in a few steps Rue Montmartre and Rue Étienne-Marcel, and the Maison Hamburger opened onto 43 Rue Montmartre (official address) from its shopfront, and onto 11 Rue de la Jussienne via its hidden staircase leading directly to the first-floor workshop. A cutter [ouvrier coupeur] (he used to add: 'like Gary') recently promoted to – or rather no doubt renamed, by a purely verbal promotion – 'head cutter', he had under him only two or three male or female apprentices to whom he 'showed' the profession, as they said in the days when a profession was taught by being shown, and was learned by watching. Before or after this promotion, it was ever a matter of cutting while following a paper or cardboard pattern and by means, sometimes of heavy scissors, sometimes of a kind of paper trimmer with a circular blade and an electric motor, a bundle of fabric a few centimetres thick. The pattern might have been that of a shirt or of pyjamas, but I have no such recollection: the noble items of the house were *par excellence* scarves, cravats, 'headsquares' and especially ties, always cut from one piece. Noble by dint of their purpose, but also of their material, invariably silk: I only later realised that woollen ties exist too, and my father was always supposedly working 'in the silk trade', a more gratifying expression than 'in textile'; one didn't yet speak of 'ready-to-wear', and I imagine moreover that few people in Paris (but maybe in London) order ties made-to-measure. The ensuing operations eluded my curiosity, for he always cut and never sewed. I don't really know, either, on what occasions I was allowed into the workshop, but I suppose that it wouldn't have irked him to acquaint his son with a real profession. Meanwhile and just in case, he taught me to distinguish wool, silk, cotton, linen, hessian, twill, serge, combed cotton, carded cotton, taffeta, satin, faille, crêpe-de-chine, crêpe Georgette (and not Suzette), crêpe tout court, duffle, flannel, piqué, ratine, cachemire, watered mohair, tulle, muslin, brocade, percale, denim, drill, chintz, reps, poplin, tussore, shantung, jersey, gabardine, pinstripe, velvet, corduroy, needlecord, tartan, herringbone, tweed, harris tweed (there's a subtle difference, but I've already explained this), pied-de-poule, houndstooth, prince-of-wales check, to name but a few, which I was careful not to confuse. Rayon ('artificial silk') was spoken of only with contempt, and the other 'synthetics' remained to be discovered, at the Liberation, as did chewing gum, pocket books, Coca-Cola, blond-tobacco cigarettes and Nylon stockings. His competence extended to 'suits', or 'complets' (two- or three-piece), and I believe he never wore what he called 'fantasy jackets', meaning mismatched with a pair of trousers cut from a different fabric: that would have been 'frowned upon' on Rue de la Jussienne. The collar and cuffs of his shirts, obviously in cotton poplin, were, for grand occasions, stiffened by my mother's care, according to a procedure that escapes me, using little packets of powdered starch that waited by a folding ironing table equipped with the indispensable 'sleeve board [jeannette]'. Nowadays, starch has negative overtones, and you can scarcely still see, other than in old films, the cuffs with fancy links known as 'musketeer cuffs'.

A non-*kosher* employee of Jewish employers, he'd often claim to be, with quaint hyperbole, 'a *shabes goy* with the *schmattès*'. The Ashkenazi survivors of the Sentier district will decipher without difficulty this more or less Yiddish expression, which I'm perhaps distorting along the way (I suppose moreover that the original form is *shabbat goy*: it's the goy tasked by proxy, on the day of the *shabbat*, with forbidden household tasks, such as pressing on an electrical switch), and which revealed on his part no hint of anti-semitism: in this quarter, it was self-evident that the majority of workshops and stores belonged to Jewish owners, whom their workers, very often *goys*, asked only to be good bosses. This was apparently the case with MM. Blum & Hamberger, and, except for the chronic insufficiency of his 'pay', I never heard my father reproach them for anything save for having advised him one day to treat his sinusitis, no less chronic, at Luchon, a thermal resort they described as being 'within the reach of everybody's purse'. The alleged reach of this purse somewhat ruffled what remained of his class consciousness, and the free prescription remained without effect.

Under the Occupation, the Maison Hamberger had been 'Aryanised', meaning expropriated to the benefit of unscrupulous competitors, by definition 'good Aryans', as one didn't refrain from whispering in a veiled reference to their mediocre competence. At the Liberation, these usurpers were banished in their turn and, I hope, duly judged. The legitimate owners had escaped the Shoah thanks to what were already called the Just, and, after a few months of temporary lay-off, my father resumed on Rue de la

Jussienne his role as head cutter and was happy to be so until the end of his days, far closer than anyone could have imagined. The old 'Maison' survived him, and it appears to have remained with its original family, at least according to its sign, which is still to be found at the same address, on the first-floor fascia, 'P. Hamberger, ties'. However, the address on Minitel indicates only: 'Shawls, scarves, cravats', as though *ties* were a generic term encompassing these three species. This company name thus remains a mystery, which discretion, or shyness, prevents me from elucidating with the legitimate heirs. I shall go no further than my astonishment that *jussienne*, a word as graceful as it was erroneously forged, has come, in hindsight, to name nothing but a little street and its distant memory.

Justice. During the frequently empty hours (emptied by ourselves) at school, we often used to sit, as idle neighbours, at the equally empty hearings of the Art Deco style courthouse that has since somewhat burned down, and where I saw the sentencing, in lots and without any needless sermonising, of a few minor delinquents, generally for 'vagrancy', in some cases aggravated by insulting behaviour towards officers, of the 'Down with the pigs!' type, an expression that has itself today also gone out of fashion. In those days, persons with no fixed abode were supposedly 'vagrants', meaning aimless wanderers, without currently valid papers and without the hundred-*sous* coin that then defined the threshold of local respectability. In the absence of any more glorious offences, these hearings gave a fairly dreary idea of the exercise of judicial power.

A little later, I had the opportunity to frequent a few law students, and even to have them recite a few pages from the Dalloz[227] as their examinations drew near. I've retained from these rehearsals the opinion that law (in particular its intellectual pinnacle, private international law) isn't merely a question of memory but also of logic, almost of intelligence. And here's a little *vademecum* for the use of potential litigants: a crime isn't an offence; a testimony isn't proof; neither is a confession, yet, since many are unaware

---

[227] Dalloz is a French publisher specialising in legal matters; it produces the standard encyclopaedic reference works for French students of law.

of this, it's better never to confess; you may always retract after having confessed (wouldn't it be simpler to retract straight away?); a false testimony is an offence; a closing speech isn't a verdict; a verdict isn't a sentence; a discharge isn't a dismissal; a dismissal isn't an acquittal; doubt isn't a mitigating circumstance; an alibi isn't an excuse; a criminal investigation [la mise en examen] isn't a diploma; the Bar isn't at the sitting[228] nor is the sitting in the public prosecutor's office;[229] you can't plead on the courthouse steps, except in the presence of a microphone and/or a camera, and to affirm that the 'dossier is empty' and list all the offences of which the client is not guilty (this crook didn't kill anyone, this misappropriator of company assets made no personal gain, this rapist didn't kill his victim, this murderer didn't rape his ...); a lawyer may be court-appointed, not his client; complicity in the concealment of the incitement to vindicate tax evasion is neither an offence nor a crime, but don't broadcast this, you'd attract the attention of what Claudel called the constabulary's thoughtful eye [l'œil pensif de la maréchaussée]; 'military justice' is an oxymoron; the criminal police isn't a pleonasm; the accused is presumed innocent until proven otherwise, but you're responsible for proving your innocence even so; someone charged with rape can't invoke legitimate defence; an assistant public prosecutor [avocat général] isn't a lawyer [avocat]; a prosecutor of the Republic [un procureur de la République] isn't a chief prosecutor [procureur général];[230] a chief prosecutor isn't a prosecuting chief [général procureur]; an examining magistrate [juge d'instruction] can examine in all ignorance; a denial of justice [déni de justice] isn't an offence of justice [délit de justice]; stupidity is never an alibi, but occasionally a motive, and often a mitigating circumstance; intelligence isn't always a crime: it depends with whom. There is talk these days of reforming all of this, but in what way isn't known. In the meantime, cross the street.

[228] 'le barreau n'est pas au siège': this phrase could also be taken to signify 'the bar isn't on the chair'.
[229] 'ni le siège au parquet': this phrase could also be taken to signify 'nor is the chair on the parquet floor'.
[230] In France, a *procureur général* is superior to the *prosécuteurs de la République*, superintending cases at the higher level courts of appeal (*cours d'appel*) and Court of Cassation (*Cour de Cassation*) – the highest court of criminal and civil appeal.

Kitsch. In San Francisco as virtually everywhere else in the United States, but a little more than elsewhere because the whole city or pretty much is a crooked suburban draughtsboard, the lower-middle-class residential districts are devoted to over-elaborate Victorian kitsch: hyperbolic stairways, columned porches, recessed wings, corbelled bow-windows, decorative mouldings. But Californian fancy saves the day through systematic recourse to the most amusing colours, candy pink, pistachio green, canary yellow, pomegranate red and others, which you never know whether to credit to an excess, forever possible, of 'bad taste', or to a burst, never to be excluded, of retrospective irony. Usually, these garish daubs are purely ornamental and non-figurative. But at least one of them, added to a façade doubtless deemed too discreet, represented an entire emphatically Alpine landscape, with its forests, its snowy slopes, its foaming torrents, its green pastures. One or two inevitable windows punctuated it. I hope it has, since then, been listed as it deserves.

Labyrinth. Under Stalin (or Brezhnev?), they told this supposedly funny story, to the glory of totalitarian organisation. After several years of exhausting administrative steps in view of acquiring a voucher for shoes, an honest citizen finally receives the voucher, along with a summons to the Vice-Ministry of Capital Goods, section Clothes, sub-section, Shoes. Equipped with his provisional birchbark slippers, he heads to this imposing edifice, presents his summons at a counter, crosses almost without hindrance one or two security vestibules, reaches a new counter where he presents his voucher, and where they direct him towards a corridor with two doors; on the first, a sign indicates: 'Men's shoes'; on the second: 'Women's shoes'. He knocks at the first, waits for a few minutes; the door opens, and he finds himself in a new corridor with two doors; on the first, a sign indicates: 'City shoes'; on the second: 'Sports shoes'. He knocks at the first door, waits for a few minutes; the door opens, and he finds himself in a new corridor with two doors; on the first, a sign indicates: 'Black shoes'; on the second: 'Brown shoes'. He knocks at the first door, waits for a few minutes; the door opens, and he finds himself in a new corridor with two doors; on the first, a sign indicates: 'Shoes with a buckle'; on the second: 'Shoes with laces'. For a change, he knocks at the second, waits for a few minutes; the door opens, and he finds himself in a new corridor with two doors; on the first, a sign indicates: 'Straight laces'; on the second: 'Crossed laces'. For a change, he knocks at the first, waits for a few minutes; the door opens, and (I abridge the series of binary choices) he finds himself in a new corridor, a longer one, with several doors, each of which proposes an indication of size. Sensing that he's finally nearing his goal, he heads towards the door indicating: 'Size 42', knocks, waits for a few minutes; the door opens, and he finds himself back in the street. It's the inverted labyrinth, the most benign, which forces you to leave it. The worst is the one whose entrance you find in the belief you're making for the exit.

Lacs/Lakes. A lake is in sum nothing but a momentarily broadened river, without a very discernible current, and whose opposing shore is, more or less, at the foot of a mountain. A valley lake is a contradiction in terms, a tourist boast in fact denoting a large pond or a muddy reservoir. In this sense (my own), Lake Geneva is only a lake on its Vaud side, somewhere between Rolle and Montreux, with the steep and mysterious slopes of the Chablais Alps on the horizon: if you like one shore, live on the other. Lake Lucerne is one especially on its eastern and southern side, the 'wildest', beyond the strait that narrows it between Ober Nas and Unter Nas, and which takes you from 'Lake Vitznau' to 'Lake Gersau' and, more to the south, to 'Lake Uri', moving upstream along the Reuss towards its source at Gotthard Pass, since the whole thing, from Altdorf to Lucerne, is but the capricious flourishing of this river come from the south, and which will end, via the Aar and the Rhine, amid the docks of Rotterdam. Balzac lovers are familiar with those pages, Stendhalian for once, attributed to Albert Savarus with the title 'Ambition for Love's Sake', a novel-within-a-novel which begins in Gersau with love at first sight for the face of a woman at her window and the landscape surrounding her; as for Wagner lovers, they will forever envy him having lived for six years in his park at Tribschen, a little to the south of Lucerne – albeit in the company of the mortifying Cosima. Lake Como, for its part, is to be beheld, preferably, from its truly Stendhalian shore ('Grianta'), between Tremezzo and Dongo, with its Alpine view to the north-west, ablaze at sunset. Beyond these hills, whose summits reveal hermitages all of which one should like to inhabit, your astounded eye perceives the peaks of the Alps, ever covered in snow, and their stern austerity recalls to it of life's misfortunes just enough to enhance one's present sense of delight. It isn't me, of course, who is using such exalted language, but la Gina, who was at the time merely the Countess Pietranera.[231] After that, the other Italian lakes will no longer recall to you very much at all.

In France, the lacustrine spectacle par excellence – virtually the only one – is that enjoyed from the Baie de Talloires looking south-west: the little port of Duingt, so simple and so welcoming, and its château, half-Viollet-le-Duc half-Walt Disney, on a tiny peninsula, the terraced flanks of Le Taillefer and Entrevernes, whence winks at you, in the morning from the reflection of the rising sun upon its windows, in the evening from the light shining behind it, an isolated farmhouse we'd always promised to go and see from closer to; and, more directly to the south, the rugged summits of the Bauges: Charbon, Trélod, Arcalod, if memory serves. Between Talloires and Duingt, a strait bounded by the shallows of le Roselet, the remains of an erstwhile lacustrine town (still called 'Bird of Sand', owing to its shape seen from the sky, or from the viewpoints of la Tournette), separates two parts of the lake: the Great, to the north, from the Small, to the south. It's the smaller one that touches the mountains, Annecy, at the downstream outlet, representing, all things being equal, the Lucerne of a lake occupying – presumably – just one *canton*.[232] Acting as its Rhône, or its Reuss, is the Combe d'Iré torrent, which tumbles down fairly briskly between Charbon and Arcalod before spreading out in the grass at Doussard, and whose ascent on foot is most refreshing. The shore of Talloires, at the foot of the village, is but a tiny harbour, with its wooden pier for the passengers of the tourist cruise boats. The hotel and restaurant of the Père Bise are perhaps beyond your means, but you can always splash out on a late afternoon drink under the linden trees, on the terrace at the water's edge. Beyond may be found, not too visibly, the municipal wading pool, then the sloping meadow of the Hôtel Beau Site – the only one in sum to possess its own beach, not sandy, grassy rather, beneath a row of trees, once again linden trees if I'm not

---

[231] The Contessa Gina Pietranera – subsequently the Duchessa Sanseverina – in Stendhal's *La Chartreuse de Parme* (*The Charterhouse of Parma*) (1839).
[232] In French, Lake Lucerne is known as the 'lac des Quatre-Cantons', the 'lake of the Four-Cantons'.

mistaken. For a few years it was the starting point for swims over to the port of Duingt, an initiation rite with accompanying boat should anyone falter. Immediately on the left, two or three 'manor' houses, of which the closest is adorned with elephant frescoes, occupy the bank, each with a small private port at its disposal, really handy for doing your shopping in town without the hassles of the road. We could but dream of such things, but I seemed to recall that one of them features in the film *Claire's Knee*.[233] It was therefore, rightly or wrongly, 'Claire's house', and you could gain easy access to it only by water, at the oar or by swimming, all the way to the entrance to its discreet jetty.

Laideur/Ugliness. 'The advantage of ugliness is that it lasts' (Gainsbourg). The irony here obviously resides in the estimation of an *advantage*, for the durability of ugliness is in itself a highly probable hypothesis. This irony pertains to consolatory humour, since it invites you to rejoice in a feature ordinarily held to be regrettable, as though its definitive character at least provided a guarantee of longevity. But *advantage* doesn't express an absolute judgement of value, as though one were to say, simply: 'The good thing about ugliness ... '; it's a judgement of relative superiority – evidently over the implicitly evoked contrary feature, beauty, which everyone knows does not last. The underlying commonplace is therefore the (also) perennial 'When you are very old ... ',[234] subsequently rejuvenated as 'If you figure ... '.[235] But the *advantage* of Gainsbourg's version is that it spares the wait: the superiority of ugliness lies in this immediate guarantee of a (as they say in Greek) *ktèma es aei*: a benefit for ever – or almost. Yet Mauriac, in his way, took issue with this, as though beyond a certain age aesthetic appreciation lost all relevance: contemplating a very old lady, he murmured, admiringly, in his toneless voice: 'She must have been really ugly!' Thus she was so no longer.

Language. As is only too well known, Roland Barthes taught us, during his inaugural lesson at the Collège de France, that

---

[233] *Le Genou de Claire* (1970), by Eric Rohmer.
[234] 'Quand vous serez bien vieille', a poem by Pierre de Ronsard (1578).
[235] 'Su tu t'imagines', poem by Raymond Queneau (1948), with reference to Ronsard; also sung by Juliette Gréco.

language is 'quite simply fascist' (around the same time, Sartre discovered that 'silence is reactionary', which leaves you in a bit of a fix). I don't know whether Michel Foucault appreciated as he should have an effort of intellectual radicalism that was manifestly dedicated to him, but this rather Parisian episode reminded me at once of earlier conversations, from the time when Barthes was drafting the postface of *Mythologies* – this nowadays overly forgotten manifesto of nascent semiology – where I chided him for yielding to what Pierre Hervé had recently called 'ideological extremism'. Barthes listened to me patiently, without exercising his right to reply; his response, all the same, may be found, if you look, at the end of said postface. A suitably ambiguous response ('The mechanic, the engineer, the user her or himself [of the DS] *speak* the object; the mythologist, for his part, is condemned to metalanguage. This exclusion already has a name: it is what they call ideologism'), but not without a polemical edge, since the objection found itself immediately referred – a period commonplace – to Zhdanovism, supposedly appealing to 'the reserve of a real inaccessible to ideology, like language [le langage] according to Stalin'. As perhaps hasn't been forgotten, what Stalin (or his scribe) defended against Marr was, more moderately, that *language* [la *langue*] (not le *langage*, an obviously vaster notion) isn't a *superstructure*. I don't know whether Barthes, in 1956, would have literally maintained the contrary, but one sees that he got there in 1977, all subtlety momentarily left behind in the professors' cloakroom. I might, on one or another occasion, have reminded him of his own analyses in *Degree Zero*, which made language (opposed, in this, on the one hand to *style* and on the other to *writing*) a quasi-natural horizon 'on this side of literature', but I'd fairly swiftly given up placing him in contradiction with himself. The most unfortunate thing in the present case was perhaps the recourse to the fearsome adverb, which should always be avoided wherever possible: 'quite simply'; the social status of language is anything but simple, and Barthes knew this better than anyone. Besides, languages [les langues], as Mallarmé rightly said, are 'several', which should also make us prudent in our use of the absolute singular 'language [la langue]'. Lenin (indeed …) said, as I've already recalled, that an eagle can fly as low as a hen. But why seek so far afield: it was Barthes himself who wrote: 'The blunders of intelligent people are fascinating.'

Lariboisière. I can still see, transported to this Parisian hospital following a stroke (we were told it was a 'hemiplegia', I'm not sure why, for her paralysis was from the outset complete) during the heatwave of the summer of 1948, on a large ward such as they would no longer dare have, my mother, frozen, aphasic, her last vestiges of life seeking refuge in an intense and hopeless stare; I can see her white, parched lips already as though retracted over her gums, which were ceaselessly moistened with a damp cloth. This mute agony lasted several days.

Lavoir/Wash-house. I'm not sure of which other, evidently older, I'm always reminded by the sight of the one, fairly well-preserved or restored, at Saint-Sauveur: as far as I know, I saw no such thing in my childhood, and besides, my mother, content with her nozzle-pipe washpot that simmered away on the gas in the basement, would have had no use for it. My first encounter with this object is therefore as impossible to situate as it is to forget. Proust somewhere evokes the type of semi-aborted, perhaps deceptive, reminiscence (it's the ambiguous, occasionally irritating 'charm' of paramnesia, or imaginary 'déjà vu') which leaves you in suspense, a paw of one's memory in the air, like a dog pointing. The same Proust recounts his hero's disappointment upon discovering that the source of the Vivonne was 'just a sort of square wash-house where bubbles rose'. But there is, I find, nothing here to disappoint: it's quite something, a square wash-house where bubbles rise. Where indeed can they be emerging from, these bubbles? From what hidden soap, from what submerged magnum?

I quite often see in my dreams a not particularly broad river, rather a prairie stream on level ground, whose cold water flows very rapidly, but with an absolutely smooth surface, perfectly silent, without ripple, or eddies, or seam of any kind. From afar, its surface appears as stock-still as a mirror's, and yet a few almost imperceptible clues, like the passage of a drifting leaf or of an aquaplaning dragonfly, betoken the speed of its slopeless current. Perhaps I've seen my original wash-house too, but also in a dream [en rêve]. Bachelard indeed speaks of the paradoxical 'precession' of life by dreams [le songe]: a landscape, an object, a person perhaps, recalls, authentically as it happens, not another landscape, another object, another real person, but a dream vision forgotten as such, and yet still active: most truthful false memories, which remind you not of lived events but of dreamed episodes.

Legion of Honour. Butt of innumerable jokes, of which the most scathing have doubtless been proffered by rejected candidates: 'It's not enough not to have it, you still have not to deserve it'; 'So and so refuses it, but all his work begs for it', etc. I quite like Jacques Doucet saying: 'I've got it, but my secretary wears it' (a bit like the characters in *Axël*,[236] who had their servants 'live' in their stead). And Coco Chanel: 'There's nothing like it to screw things up for a tailor.' Churchill, more sagely, and concerning honours in general: 'Never demand any, never refuse any, never wear any.' I can't remember where I heard the story about Léon-Paul Fargue,[237] who, dissatisfied with his mere ribbon, one day sported an unearned rosette, and found himself at the station (the anecdote has a punchline, which I've forgotten). In those days, you didn't joke around with such illegal bearing, and the police had its eyes on serious matters.

Lenny. One Sunday afternoon in October 1971, Christa Ludwig, accompanied on the piano by Leonard Bernstein, was performing a recital at Carnegie Hall advertised as *All Brahms*. We had, Michel Deguy and I, hesitated before what we took to be the threat of his complete works, before understanding that this formula merely announced that nothing but Brahms' melodies would be sung. It was a magical moment for me, thanks to the warm complicity of the two performers. I also remember a concert given, I can't recall at which Parisian venue, by the same Lenny. He was conducting the Orchestre de Paris in Mahler's *Third Symphony*, and, deep in a Dionysian trance, he jumped and danced upon his podium as though on a trampoline. Anyone else would have broken his neck, but he was in perfect control of his choreography. M. Croche, I imagine, would have found him to have, like Nikisch, 'the attitude and the lock of hair',[238] but he had much more: it is called charm, and all of his music exerts it.

[236] A play by Auguste Villiers de l'Isle-Adam (1890).
[237] French poet and essayist (1876–1947).
[238] Claude Debussy wrote music criticism under the pseudonym 'Monsieur Croche'; Arthur Nikisch was a Hungarian conductor.

Librairies/Book Stores. That of the *Maison des Amis des Livres*, 7 Rue de l'Odéon, recently 'liberated', after the Ritz, by Hemingway, and where Maurice Saillet presided at the time, was in my eyes, for two or three years, the only one worthy of being respectfully frequented – I mean the only one where I deemed it necessary to pay for all the books, thereby few in number, that I took from it. Perhaps too the layout of the place rendered exemption more perilous; they say, incidentally, that Genet himself, as though to shame Simone de Beauvoir, never sought to steal anything from this store. One day, having resigned myself to the ruinous purchase of the first edition of *Paroles*,[239] which owed to Brassaï its graffiti-styled cover, I was in two minds about the equally deterrent price of the bound GLM[240] edition of Lautréamont. With a knowing smile, Saillet made off to the back room to find for me the paperback version, apparently reserved for deadbeats, to the great fury of some sort of tramp wearing a battered titfer, armed with a shopping bag from which protruded a few manuscripts and one or two leeks, unknown to me but unforgettable in his look and fulminating eloquence, who I was subsequently told was called Paul Léautaud,[241] and who accused in by no means veiled terms Adrienne[242] and her kind of corrupting youth. Youth, for the moment, was me. The paperback version was scarcely more within my means than the other, but I couldn't decline such a favour. So I paid for the whole lot, was skint for a few months, and, since honesty is never rewarded, some time thereafter lost both of these incunabula.

On the other hand, I do still possess a few copies of Malraux, Sartre and Camus, other glories of the era, definitively borrowed from a certain suburban book store where shoplifting was *almost* discouragingly easy. You'd enter with a disinterested air, saying: 'I've come to steal some books from you', and, one shelf concealing another, you'd do as you'd said (like the hero of a certain cartoon: '*I'm just looting*'). I've never known if this insolent formula served

239 By Jacques Prévert.
240 Éditions Guy Lévis Mano.
241 French writer and theatre critic (1872–1956).
242 Adrienne Monnier (1892–1955), French bookseller, writer and publisher; she opened the *La Maison des Amis des Livres*, a bookshop and lending library, in 1915.

to divert suspicions, but the fact is that no untoward incident ever thwarted our culpable activity. Now, having converted in the meanwhile, for some too obvious reason, to a more legalistic conception of book store commerce, I'd gladly return the extant bodies, but to whom? Besides, their condition is truly deplorable: the paper from this period wasn't worth the stealing.

Loin/Far Away. Fabrice Luchini, brimming with enthusiasm, extolled a lousy sitcom in these terms: 'Rohmer isn't far away!' I like this way of hoisting a supposedly minor work to the level of one supposedly major, without it really being possible to discern if the real movement isn't the other way round: *Pauline at the Beach*[243] isn't, in effect, so far away from *Hélène et les garçons*.[244] The Russian formalists more or less canonised the phenomenon, and there'd be a whole history of art, with or without names, to revise in this way. It is well known, besides, that art is never very far away from that which isn't, and vice versa. Reality TV having in the meantime dethroned the sitcom, someone has nicely observed the relation one may establish, for the use of sixth-form students, between *Loft Story*[245] and Marivaux's *The Dispute*.

Lois/Laws. I don't know (I know very well) why the majority of 'laws' accounting for the functioning of things in society bear the stamp of pessimism. Examples? *Gresham's Law*: 'Bad money drives out good.' The *Matthews Effect* as described by Merton: 'The rich get richer and the poor get poorer.' *Murphy's Law*: 'Anything that can go wrong, will go wrong' – or perhaps, a more everyday version: 'Any dropped slice of bread will always hit the floor jam-side down.' *Peter's Principle*: 'Barring any external intervention, everyone tends to reach, then surpass, their level of incompetence' (in literature, the application of this principle is called 'the book too far' – which isn't necessarily the final one). *Parkinson's Law*: 'Every manager tends to recruit a deputy to perform his own work, and so forth.' I doubt that this Parkinson also discovered, or invented, the illness bearing his name; I also doubt that he (but then who?) is the author

---

[243] *Pauline à la plage* (1983), by Eric Rohmer.
[244] 'Hélène and the Boys' is a French sitcom.
[245] The French version of the UK's 'Big Brother'.

of this no less profound maxim: 'Beyond the noble art of having things done by others, there is that, nobler still, of awaiting that they be done by themselves.' We shall find in its place what I call *Caillon's Law*.

Longitudes. Japanese proverb: 'Any further east, it's the West.'

Louisiana Story. I'd always associated the word *bayou* with a kind of backwater, of stagnant marigot, covered with water hyacinths, infested with mosquitoes and alligators. I thus had a pleasant surprise the day when, in the spring of 1986, on the occasion of a seminar at Tulane University in New Orleans, I was taken to dinner at a colleague's who – beyond Lake Pontchartrain, which we crossed on a gruelling freeway overpass – lived near a kind of river with free-flowing, thin, clear, transparent water, the like of which I hadn't gazed upon since my summers by the Loire. The trees surrounding it, some of which grew from the riverbed itself, bore foliage of a still tender green, and the Spanish moss that hung here and there made for so many weeping willows. There was almost nothing exotic about any of it: I imagined myself to be somewhere in Sologne. The evening was idyllic, beneath the blossoming magnolias. You could hear the good times roll.

Over the years, the city of Satchmo, of Sidney Bechet, of Jelly Roll Morton had assumed a somewhat artificial cheerfulness, a Saturday night fever laid on for the tourists, with its politely kitsch French Quarter, its cast iron columns and wrought iron balconies, its double doors with mosquito nets, its reheated cajun cuisine and music, like the old-style Dixieland whereby the onlookers thought they were capturing living jazz at its source. The red-light district at Storyville had been out of action since the decree of 1917 and the subsequent diaspora of its brothel pianists. I know not what menace seemed to me to weigh upon these false collective high spirits, but, like everyone else, I had a striking intuition thereof upon seeing pass by, on the other side of the enormous levee, a boat the height of whose hull surprised me. I climbed one of the stairways leading to the top of the levee, and I understood (I really should have known before) that the height intriguing me wasn't the ship's, but indeed that of the river, whose surface, or even bed, looms over the urban basin by several metres, as does the accursed lake on the other side, a reservoir of disaster viewed from low angle.

As San Francisco had earlier, the *Big Easy*, without paying it too much attention, awaited in *big band* style its own *big one*. For the local and federal politicians, the good times were still rolling. As ever, reinforcing the dykes represented no emergency: 'Nobody could have imagined that the levees would break', George Bush would say in September 2005 (they had already done so, among other times, during the floods of 1927 and with hurricane Betsy in 1965). Perhaps it will all be rebuilt, but I don't think I shall see this new *revival*, which risks lasting no longer than the others.

Lundi/Monday. Every Sunday evening, he'd say, resignedly: '*Demain, c'est fête à bras*',[246] 'Back to the grindstone tomorrow'; and he'd add, without suspecting the future philosophical bearing of this clause:[247] 'It's crazy how it's *always already* Monday.' Yet he didn't live long enough to notice, like me, that it's *always ever more already* Monday, Tuesday, Wednesday, etc. I've assumed for some time that this universal, and always already ever more striking fact must be related to that other effect of ageing consisting in the loss, always already ever more rapid, of short-term memory, to the benefit (if one may say) of long-term memory, remaining intact, although perhaps inventive. If it's ever more already Monday, it's because you forget ever more the (short) week that has just elapsed as though in a few hours, while you remember the time when the weeks lasted, go on, let's call it seven days.

Lune/Moon. It is said that everyone remembers the circumstances in which they learned of John Kennedy's death. I can indeed still picture very clearly the room in the small suburban flat where the radio brought us this news, on the 22nd November 1963. I can also still picture that July night in 1969 where, in the courtyard of a small hotel in Saint-Félix, on the border of the two Savoies, we listened on our car radio, for want of a set in our room, to the report [reportage[248]], so to speak, of the first steps, small but giant, of man on the moon. We could also see,

---

[246] 'a feast [a festival, a party] for one's arms'.
[247] Associated in particular with the thought of Jacques Derrida.
[248] 'Reportage' refers in French to a televisual report.

live and with our naked eyes, said satellite, more serene than ever, and where, evidently, nothing unusual had deigned to occur.

Magic. In my childhood, I scarcely believed in it, I never had any 'magician's' paraphernalia, and I only found magical things that were in fact quite commonplace, but whose appearance or behaviour were incomprehensible to me. I shall recite in disorderly fashion and without concern for exhaustivity. The magical object *par excellence*, I've no need to explain why, was a magnet. I say *a*: we only had one of them at home, which was used especially to gather pins and needles fallen to the floor, which were drawn to it in spiky clusters. It had the typical 'horseshoe' shape, or rather that of an extended arc with parallel tips, one of which was red, and, in my ignorance of the magnetic phenomenon, I credited its power to this shape and contrast of colours. I attempted to bend and paint a large rod of iron according to this model, and was disappointed with the result. The relationship between the magnet and the compass [boussole] somewhat eluded me, and equally the reason for which a mariner's compass is called *un compas* (the ability of the most commonplace of terrestrial compasses [compas] – my own – to trace impeccable circumferences also filled me with wonder). Marble: I couldn't understand (I still can't) why this stone is always so cold, whatever the external temperature; but I assumed that it owed to this peculiarity its mortuary usage, or vice versa. Alum: I've pilfered from a rival dictionary that it consists of a hydrated double sulphate of potassium and aluminium, which half reassures me. But in my childhood, I knew it in the form called 'alum stone', a rather soft stone, like Brazilian soapstone, somewhat translucent and waxen, which the barber would use to heal the cuts sometimes occasioned by his straight razor. Its effect was all the more mysterious in that one saw it employed nowhere else. This philosopher's stone wasn't, for that matter, this shop's only marvel: it lay side by side with a fairly thick leather strap used to sharpen the dangerous razor. I deemed it, naively, always to be plenty sharp enough, and I also wondered why the blade wasn't sharpened directly upon the alum – as would my father, for kitchen knives and his cobbler's cutters, on a slate stone, apparently buffed since Cro-Magnon times. Ether: not having read Einstein, I attributed its omnipresence in the universe to the staggering speed [vitesse sidérante[249]] of its evaporation, which you had to thwart by recapping its flask as quickly as possible. Putty: I admired this extremely malleable substance, which took so long to harden once applied to the joint of a window pane sometimes broken on purpose, just to see. I was told that it was due to the linseed oil [huile de lin] that it contained, which only served to displace the question, by adding this other one: how can you extract an oil from a fabric? Because for me, *le lin* [linen] (like hemp) could only be a fabric. I have subsequently made much use (applied to wood for shelves) of linseed oil, and I learned very quickly, nearly the hard way, that it's better to add to it a few parts of siccative if you don't wish to ruin your library by replacing it too soon. The bubble (or 'spirit') level, perpendicular antithesis of the plumb line, both indispensable for any even remotely 'well-aligned' construction, and concerning which I understood poorly how the bubble could *know* that the surface in question was finally horizontal – and no better how the plumb line could *know* where lay the centre of the Earth, and the compass needle (and the North Star) where was the north. Mercury, the liquid capable of rolling into marbles on the floor: my parents used to hide the thermometers to protect them from my experiments; besides, the mystery of mercury began with the first attempt to measure its expansion, for the glass column could only be seen from a certain angle, and neither did I understand why a few shakes at arm's length sufficed to return it to its starting point. (Since heard on the radio: 'The mercury is rising in the thermometer, which is causing a heatwave'; and again, less contrary to the laws of physics, but more stylistically refined: 'This week, mercury will prove to be in season'.) The kaleidoscope, which needs no description. Or minium: this strangely named substance, short for *minimum*, which no one had taught me to identify as plain and simple lead oxide, had the property, to me miraculous, of preventing rust from attacking iron. But it presented the disadvantage of making you wait for it to have dried before applying the first coat of 'real' paint. I tended to skip or shorten this intermediary stage, which earned me a few tellings-off. I purported to salvage the situation by applying a layer of minium *over* the offending coat. The outcome would soon disappoint. I

---

[249] The French word derives from the Latin 'siderari', from 'sidus', 'star'.

should also have liked quite simply to use the minium, with its fine orangey-red colour, as the definitive paint, but I was never allowed to: minium is *not* paint – but I gather that this distinction is nowadays obsolete. I also admired, without really understanding it, the ability of asbestos to temper the effect of fire, in the then widespread guise of a round plate that you'd insert, like a dry bain-marie, between the stove and the base of the saucepan, and which yet seemed to me to consist of common-or-garden blotting paper; I used to scratch a little off with my fingernail to taste its mystery. I shudder to think of this in hindsight, but we were all at that stage of fatal ignorance.

Maillon/Link. Always weak. The notion of a 'strong link' is, moreover, physically absurd; as all manufacturers know (and as is concealed by almost all vendors), what used to be called, for instance, a 'hi-fi' system [chaîne] only ever has the strength, or the quality, of its weakest link: if you have a poor amplifier, don't buy good speakers, they won't rectify anything – perhaps they'll even accentuate the shortcoming for which you wish to compensate. I call this principle *Caillon's law*, after the name of the artisan in electronic equipment who taught me it at an age when I ought to have known it for some time, having already suffered its effects in various situations having nothing to do with high or low fidelity. It applies indeed to every 'chain' of command or of cooperation, to all kinds of physical, intellectual, amorous, familial, social, professional, political, military or other relations. Generalised Caillon's law: *A system is only ever as good as the most mediocre of its elements.* The inhabitants of the quarters beneath the levees in New Orleans know a thing or two about this.

Mains/Hands. Adam Smith's is invisible; Pascal's, on the contrary, is for Valéry too visible; Kant's are pure, but for the wretched reason we know; Marxism had dirty hands, and now it's its turn to have no hands at all. Jesus's right one doesn't know what his left one is doing. Of Glenn Gould, Roland Barthes used to say that he was the only pianist to have two right hands (or perhaps, more cruelly for the others, to have a left hand). Hearing how he makes the middle parts stand out, I sometimes feel that he has a third one between the two others.

Mairies/Town Halls. Despite its modest size, the one in Conflans was (still is, spared as it was by the successive bombardments) stylistically exemplary, I mean typical of the Neo-Renaissance canon that became for a few decades, at the end of the nineteenth century, a kind of unwritten article of the Third Republic's Constitution (itself barely written). The Hôtel de Ville in Paris, which was perhaps their model (followed by the capital's *arrondissement* town halls and those of its inner suburbs: see at least the one in Levallois), was for its part authentically Renaissance from Boccador's plans, and it is courtesy of the Commune that it became its own pastiche while quadrupling its volume like the frog in the fable. For those that had to be built, or sometimes rebuilt, after the war, this canon seems to have broadened to include other forms, not to mention the redeployment of buildings initially devoted to other uses. I'm thus unaware of what is, stylistically, the share of this style in the overall architecture of our communal buildings, but for me, and for the reason I've given, only a building in conformity with it is really a Town Hall, just as the church in Combray, recognisable in all those that more or less recall it, is, for the narrator of *In Search* ... , 'the Church!' If I'd had the time and the competence, I'd have liked to write a book about this occasionally ridiculous, but often touching, heritage. Moreover, this book really must exist somewhere, but no inventory could depose the town hall at Conflans from being for me, *par excellence*, The Town Hall!

Malentendus/Misunderstandings. I can see that I am credited with an unhealthy attachment to Aristotle's *Poetics* – the author Roland Barthes had, for a while, glorified as 'the first structuralist'. This confirms that I had explained myself poorly; just a few words in an attempt to dispel – and thus, no doubt, to nurture – this misunderstanding.

Certainly, the oldest of the poetics remains an exemplary text through the rigour and fecundity of its intentions, even if this example was seldom followed, over the centuries, by those most officially claiming to adhere to it. But its intellectual merit mustn't obscure this crucial fact: that the definition it gives (itself) of *poièsis* is much too narrow to be applied to everything we nowadays call 'literature', and even already to everything we've for much longer called 'poetry', including the type of poetry of which Aristotle was by no means unaware, and which we have subsequently called, well or badly, 'lyric' poetry, and which he excludes from the field of his treatise, deliberately and legitimately: everyone chooses their field [chacun choisit son champ[250]], it only behoves you to declare it, and Aristotle certainly does so. His *Poetics* doesn't pretend to bear upon (what we call) poetry in general, let alone upon (what we call) literature more broadly, but only upon 'mimetic' (representative) poetry, narrative or dramatic. He can't be blamed for the exclusions that ensue from this choice of object, that one in particular among others, including clearly that of all prose works, such as those of orators, historians or ... philosophers. Aristotle thus bestowed upon himself a limited object, he treated it as he saw fit, and the error of most subsequent poetics up until the end of the eighteenth century was to believe that this intention might legitimately apply to objects that didn't fall within its scope. This long error consisted not in betraying Aristotle but, more seriously, in betraying the 'genres' of which he hadn't spoken, believing or feigning to believe that one could speak of them in the terms of a discourse that did not concern them. These 'classical' poeticians, in my view, were thereby only *too* Aristotelian, by excessive extrapolation, and we all know why: Aristotle had become, for other reasons, *the* universal philosopher, everything had to be treated in his work, and covered by his doctrine; and you can see, therefore, to which contortions yields a Corneille, and occasionally a Racine, in order to profess in their discourse an orthodoxy that their work did not refrain from transgressing.

Much time, as is known, will have been needed in order to shake so weighty a tutelage. Too much time for my liking, and demonstrating this does not amount, I think, to holding Aristotle to be 'the oracle', let alone to constructing an edifice upon this overly narrow basis. In advocating for an *open* poetics, then aesthetics, I don't think I have pledged allegiance to a text in which I see the very epitome of a *closed* poetics. Yet it remains that his approach and his categories were sufficiently fertile to anticipate practices he couldn't have known, since they didn't yet exist. This feat in no way proceeds, moreover, from superhuman genius, but from a proper use of the capacities of combinatory intelligence. As they say in the laboratories, 'nothing is more practical than a good theory'.

---

[250] Derived from the expression 'choisir son camp', 'to choose one's side'.

To free ourselves from this closure, it wasn't enough to recognise, as gradually happened, the existence and importance of so-called 'lyric' poetry. One had still to recognise that of the *other* literary practices forgotten by (or unknown to) the *Poetics*. This is what most of modern poetics has done, by reprising and broadening Jakobson's question: 'What makes a verbal message a work of art?' I once attempted to contribute to it by adding cavalierly to the Aristotelian criterion of fiction (*mimèsis*) that, evidently non-Aristotelian (at least in its function as a criterion of literariness), of *diction*, and by adding to constitutive literariness a *conditional* literariness allowing us to recognise as works, or at least as aesthetic objects, all kinds of prose texts, written or oral, without generic condition and in the name of a free aesthetic appreciation. But 'adding' doesn't here denote a subordinate inclusion. If this were an opportunity to express a personal preference, I would gladly say (I sense that I am going to say it) that my own, quite to the contrary of and diametrically opposed to Aristotle's implicit choice, goes to 'conditional' aestheticities [ésthéticités], which stem more from an attention than from an intention. If I had one day to choose between works of fiction [par fiction] and works of diction [par diction], I know where my choice would go. But little matter: the interest of this couple, as of every other, is precisely to make a couple, with everything that usually follows.

Leopardi admired Galileo's prose for its precision and elegance. In his wake, Calvino once declared to Carlo Cassola that he believed Galileo to be the greatest Italian writer. Cassola pounced: 'What, I thought it was Dante! – Thanks for the discovery!', Calvino commented ironically, before clarifying – since it seems that clarification is always necessary – that he was speaking of prose writers, and conceding that one might in this respect be unable to decide between Galileo and Machiavelli, but that he found, despite being himself a novelist, more nourishment in Galileo 'for the precision of the language, the poetic–scientific imagination, the construction of conjectures'. Cassola persisted: 'Galileo was a scientist, not a writer!' – we are familiar with these antitheses. Calvino continued (for us, abandoning Cassola to his certainties) that Dante was himself also, in his way and in his culture, a kind of scientist, or of encyclopedist. I find this exchange, if it is one, quite revelatory of the normative power of received categories, and of the effort we must exert in order (doubtless to fail) to resist them.

This concern with openness, when by chance it has been discerned, has elicited the charge of cultural laxism and 'piecemeal relativism'. It would be too easy to dismiss back to back two accusations as contradictory as those of Aristotelian rigorism and unbridled relativism. I thought I'd replied in advance to the latter criticism that my 'relativism' bears only upon aesthetic appreciation, but one cannot ask a media host to know the entire body of writing he is censuring. I note, however, that the latter saw in this relativism 'the logical culmination of structuralism'. There lies perhaps a grain of truth in this cavalier shortcut. Because it focuses more on the relations themselves than on the terms they relate (for me this is its only definition), the structural method, to which a large part of modern poetics has effectively claimed to adhere, does indeed depose the *absolute* meaning of each element in favour of the overall structure: it isn't red that means 'Stop!' but red *as opposed* to a green meaning 'Go!', and vice versa. Lévi-Strauss indeed says that this relation, in itself arbitrary, might without inconvenience be inverted, even if it meant symbolically motivating this inversion by a new relationship of analogy. Aesthetic relativism is doubtless linked to cultural relativism, since the latter notes the diversity of tastes according to cultures, but its relation to semiotic structuralism has to do, more profoundly, with the idea of the conventional character of meaning – in other words, with the fact that each particular meaning is contingent upon the ensemble of its relations.

It is therefore at least paradoxical to portray structuralism as the 'gravedigger' of culture: what structuralism refuses isn't the notion of value, but the idea of the *absolute* character of value. Saussure maintained that in a system such as language there are only differences, thus only *values*, the two terms here being quasi-synonymous: there is only value through difference and a position within a system, and each value is by definition relative. As Lévi-Strauss said again apropos of totemism, 'it isn't the resemblances, but the differences which resemble each other'. I think that in its own field the *Poetics* implemented a typology that is emblematically structural and, if not relativist, then at least, if I dare use this chimera-form neologism [néologisme en forme de chimère], *relationalist*. One might alternatively call it, more pertinently, *proportionalist*: regarding metaphor, Aristotle defines analogy through a system of crossed and reciprocal equivalences

('By relationship of analogy I mean all the cases where the second term is to the first as the fourth is to the third'), and it is evidently this proportional relation that grounds his implicit definitional system for the 'mimetic' genres: supposed 'parody' is to comedy what the epic is to tragedy, but also to the epic what comedy is to tragedy, and this entirely relative definition can be applied in advance to any term that might eventually respond to it. Of the others, he says nothing, but our fathers have changed all of that.

In the end, I'm not certain (to each his own paranoia) that these two apparently contradictory accusations of long-term Aristotelianism and piecemeal relativism do not proceed from a common source, which I shall refrain from naming, and which has no doubt a few reasons to detect within me a preference for 'calculating thought' over 'meditative thought', meaning, if I translate this into plain language [en français direct], a dreadful deficit of spirituality. I am indeed lacking, and, I fear, for good, a sense of the sacred, of the sublime, and perhaps even of seriousness. This entry ought therefore to be an exception: let's pretend I've said nothing.

Mandarin. Then a professor at the Collège de France and director of studies at the EHESS,[251] Raymond Aron devoted half a day each week to receiving his students. His assistant, presumably, prepared a list in order of appearance, from which he would progressively cross off the names. One of the benamed, attentive or indiscreet, noticed one day that Aron struck him out (like, he supposed, all the others), not after, but just *before* the meeting. He felt himself to be at once – as Gide was fond of saying, if not of being – *eliminated*. Yet such was not his intention, I'm sure, for this supposedly model 'mandarin' – as he described himself through severity or complaisance, he who had, however, before 68, laid siege to a few mandarinal bastions – was far more generous of spirit than people think, as was proven by the way he supported and promoted, providing he saw in them some talent, people who

---

[251] The École des hautes études en sciences sociales (School for Advanced Studies in the Social Sciences), founded in 1868 originally as a department of the École pratique des hautes études (Practical School for Advanced Studies), is a prestigious graduate-only research institution, situated on Boulevard Raspail in the 6th arrondissement of Paris.

were by no means in his camp, insofar as he really had a 'camp'. I remember moreover everything that, from the end of the fifties, the neo-Marxist attempts to describe the 'industrial society' owed to Aron's open lectures at the Sorbonne, which became in 1962 the famous *Eighteen Lectures.*

Neither was he, quite the contrary, as 'icy' as he was alleged to be; I even felt him to be rather warm, if you can capture this type of warmth, which owes nothing to exuberance. But he happened to have been, for several decades, the observer of a 'Cold War' he endeavoured to analyse as coldly as was necessary in order not to succumb to it. As for his practice of pre-emptive strikethroughs, I suppose that this always busy man (under his presidency, the commissions didn't dawdle) liked, as we said at home, to 'press on [s'avancer]' with his work. Alas, he didn't manage to do so enough to make known to us – nor even to allow us to guess – what he would have thought of the two events he hadn't foreseen (but who else had?), and which marked the end of that war and the beginning of another: the fall of the Berlin Wall and of the empire it had long protected, then that of the Twin Towers, which nothing apparently was able to protect. Press on as one might, there always comes a time when History leaves you behind.

Manor. Since the final remnants of his modest erstwhile fortune sustained [soutenaient] a way of life you might describe, like Lampedusa to nobler effect, as one of 'shabby grandeur', his daughter and, by contagion, the whole household used to call him 'the Procurer [Le Souteneur]'. Only a former student friend, even more decrepit-looking and passably hard of hearing, called him by his first name, in sentences always beginning with the booming address: 'You see, Paul … ' – a clumsy address, moreover, for 'Paul', afflicted with bad glaucoma, failed not to mention it at every turn by proclaiming: 'I can't see a thing! [J'n'y vois pus rin!]' It was better all the same not to take this profession of blindness too literally.

The irreverence of the title didn't seem overly to shock this very dignified elderly gentleman with small and prodigiously constricted features between his blotchy cheeks, who virtually only ever spoke, at the dining table, in order to attempt vainly ('Ahem') to clear his throat. He also sustained [soutenait], from his other pocket, the small Huguenot community in Angers, where, with his white goatee à la Sully,[252] lacking only the ruff, he represented fairly well the last survivor of St Bartholomew's Day. I can still see a Christmas 'service' in the temple situated, unless I'm mistaken, on a little square a stone's throw away from the overbearing fortress. This performance no longer had for me anything but ethnographic significance, but wasn't devoid of flavour, with its Communion under both kinds, with real dry bread and Cabernet rouge, as though one sought to celebrate rather Ceres and Bacchus than the Son of God; we sang, seasonably, *O Christmas Tree, How lovely are thy branches* ... . On the other hand, I have no memory associated with Saumur's well-known Huguenot past. The fact is that the summer months were also, apparently for the whole household, like vacations away from religion. As Edgar Morin (only the rich get credit) has since said, *la vacance des grandes valeurs fait la valeur des grandes vacances* – 'the vacancy of grand values makes for the value of the summer vacation'.

Regarding his former businesses, which he'd pretty much liquidated in order to buy Launay, allusions were still made to two activities whose synergy has always escaped me: a gloomy and very odorous plant oil mill, half-shop half-factory, located in Angers in the Doutre suburb, and elsewhere a small lead shot factory. With the latter industry, the principle then consisted of melting lead, and of letting it fall drop by drop from a height sufficient for each drop to reach the ground (perhaps in a water-filled basin) cooled into a shot. The requisite height could be that of a bell tower or a disused dungeon, providing that room were made for a vertical chimney, or that advantage be taken of an external overhang, like Galileo in Pisa for a different experiment. I don't recall ever having visited his 'lead tower', but I do remember having believed, for a while, that it might have involved the Saint-Aubin tower, which may still be seen at the corner of Rue des Lices, somewhere between the prefecture and the Logis Barrault.

At Launay, the Procurer remained almost constantly aloof, in what was for me a most mysterious corner bedroom, where only the children would enter, among whom I wasn't really included. It was virtually only at meal times that he'd leave this bedroom,

[252] Maximilien de Béthune, duke of Sully (1560–1641), statesman, soldier, nobleman and counsellor of King Henry IV of France.

where he listened ritualistically, on goodness knows what radio, to the stock exchange prices – which listening was in itself most often depressing, judging by his mood at the dining table afterwards. In his moments of dejection faced with ever unforeseen maintenance fees, he'd threaten no less ritualistically: 'I'm not paying a penny', and (an unanswerable consequence) 'Let's sell Launay!' Nobody (including himself) took this threat seriously, and the household went on its merry way, also sustained, but more poorly, by the meagre revenues it drew from its farm and from its summertime function as a guesthouse. 'Let's sell Launay' had become between us an expression with a more general application, fit to express any kind of lassitude, or perhaps simply of detachment: 'Let's say no more about it.' But it was always mentioned, and 'by dint of saying terrible things',[253] towards the end of the sixties, that's to say perhaps after the death of its only backer [soutien], Launay was effectively sold, then restored by its new owners – I hope within the limits imposed by the administration of national heritage sites. Doubtless owing to affective superstition, I have never attempted to visit it in its more or less modernised state, but I do quite often picture it, manor of my dreams,[254] in the Chekhovian splendour of its former dereliction.

Its oldest part, built in the fifteenth century 'by' King René, formed a rectangle around a closed courtyard overrun by nettles. This ruined manor was uninhabitable, save sometimes, in its most remote wing, for secret occupants whose contact we avoided. The most noble room, superb with its monumental fireplaces, its embrasures with stone benches and its mullioned windows, bore no name. You gained access to it along a long gallery named, for its part, the 'guardroom', and of which it was occasionally said, without further action, that it would make a fine library. Beneath this room were disused stables and a washroom converted into a 'bathroom', which amounted to a rusty bathtub we'd heat up once a week using wood, as though under Louis XI, for a pretence of hygiene.

---

[253] From a well-known line in Marcel Carné's film *Drôle de drame* (*Bizarre, Bizarre*) (1937): 'À force d'écrire des choses horribles, les choses horribles finissent par arriver' – 'By dint of writing horrible things, horrible things end up happening'.

[254] An allusion to the Django Reinhardt song 'Manoir de mes rêves' (1943).

The inhabited part comprised, opposite the guardroom, across what was known as the courtyard 'of honour', but entered from the other side, a wing in turn primarily reserved for a couple of caretakers and other service staff, although I'm sure that I spent the first night of my first stay, on Palm Sunday in 1949, in an attic room I barely ever saw afterwards. There it was that, from a telegram brought by a cyclist, I learned of the death in Paris – it too mysterious, from an illness without prior warning nor commentary – of my father, who had thus only survived the woman of his life by a few months. I returned to Paris to see him one last time, laid upon a bed that was not his own, in an abode of which I knew nothing. He therefore never came to Launay, but it had been with him that, the previous winter, in my aunt Martha's little flat in Anjou, we had, at dinner, come to know Jacqueline and Jean Benoît. He'd thus accompanied, without knowing it, my transplantation from one family to another, from one age to another, from one world to another, by the transverse link of the reformed religion that wasn't really his, no longer at all mine, and very perfunctorily theirs.

Beyond the service wing and a shadowy space where a ping-pong table flaked away, a tower detached from the main edifice, which also dated from King René – it especially, since you could see there the remnants of frescoes attributed to the author of *Cuer d'amour espris* [*The Love-Smitten Heart*[255]] – was now home to the variously poetic activities of Jean Benoît. He haunted rather than inhabited Launay, called upon all day, and a part of the night, by mysterious ambulatory tasks from which he'd occasionally emerge, as ghostly as the old gentleman of Combourg,[256] but more cordial and less inquisitorial. He wouldn't ask 'What were you talking about?', but would in his own manner carry on the conversation underway, which he'd then abandon just as swiftly, or else, immobilised on the threshold and brandishing some part of a machine dismembered through his efforts, declaim by way of reparation a few lines by Nerval, Mallarmé, Valéry, Rilke – or occasionally, with the same humorous insistence, by himself. His work *in progress* supplied the whole household in snippets

[255] *Le Livre du Cœur d'amour épris* (*The Book of the Love-Smitten Heart*) (1457) is an allegorical romance written by King René of Anjou (1409–1480).
[256] An allusion to a character in François-René de Chateaubriand's *Mémoires d'Outre-Tombe* (*Memoirs from Beyond the Grave*), Book I (1849).

and through oral tradition with a repertoire of codewords and sidereal apostrophes. At the end of the forties, a few of us thus knew it by heart before it was published, or even quite written. He strove to disguise his Idumean nights in domestic wanderings. It would then be said, with a deliberately ambiguous verb: *'Jean vaque'*, 'Jean is attending to things.' He was doubtless attending to his business, poetic or handyman, and often also astronomic (a kind of telescope occupied a room in the tower unfortunately bereft, I believe, of any opening onto the infinite other than a slender arrow hole); but in fact he *vaquait*, was on vacation, and in the absolute sense, vacant to the world and to all things.

The main building looked to the east onto the courtyard of honour, to the west onto the 'park', meaning a vast fallow grassy area shaded by an immense cedar and prolonged by a small wood we virtually only ever frequented so as to hide there, for one reason or another. We'd thus arrive, on foot, by bicycle or by car, either through the park, after having passed through an arthritic gate, or through the courtyard leading to the buildings of the adjacent farm. This farm belonged to the estate, as bespoke a van adorned with the inscription *Benoît exploitant, Benoît farmer*, which was a motive for various dissenting jokes, even if nobody knew whom nor what 'Benoît' could actually be exploiting. In the summer months, the fields all around were invaded by sinister-looking day labourers come from who knows where, and whose day and night time presence sent a shiver through the cottages, and even the châteaux. The doors were closed as best one could with chains and padlocks, and at each meal we'd chew green beans stitched together with yellow thread. In the uneasy silence of the summer nights, you'd hear the passage, along the railway line running between the park and the levee road, of an express train always referred to as 'the Lyon–Nantes'. Never 'the Nantes–Lyon': I suppose we were respecting, from up to downstream, the course of the river that this line follows at least from Tours.

This 'modern' wing had been built or modified at the beginning of the nineteenth century, as could be seen, on the park side, from a sober façade where, around the windows of the upper floors, lighter marks, which you might have said were shaped like flames, from a wild vine that had died of old age and recently been torn down, evoked the vestiges of a fire. To the right of the entrance door there rose a branch of intensely sky-blue trumpet-shaped morning glories

– if a blue sky can be intense. Hollyhocks surrounded it all along the façade, with colours varying bizarrely according to the years' whims.

On the ground floor, the most official area was an immense oak-panelled dining room. To the rear, a narrow corridor prevented it from receiving daylight from the east, so much so that it was only lit at dinner time, by the setting sun. A few stone steps descended to a basement kitchen, nearly as vast, even more shadowy but brightened by an enormous highly functional fireplace. Hung above the door on the park side, a forever husky bell roused the lodgers for each meal. On the vast oval table, the 'little Cabernet' grown on the opposing bank passed from bulbous carafes to carefully mismatched crystal glasses. The mistress of the house would endeavour for a moment to 'make conversation', but it wasn't long before the talk reverted to very private allusions which the uninitiated greeted with a knowing air, having fairly swiftly forsaken obtaining any explanation that would not pose a fresh enigma. In the embrasure of the window overlooking the park, a little table was reserved for the children, among whom was my cousin Annie, who learned to understand us, without really knowing in reference to what.

Beyond the transverse entrance hall there opened a room whose double exposure, between the courtyard and the garden, rendered it brighter and more welcoming, but which you virtually only ever passed through, hence it was referred to as the '*salon de passe*': it led to the 'billiard room'. Thus was named a fairly large room occupying the north-western corner of this wing, and which no longer contained any table *ad hoc*. In the gloomiest corner there was an old upright piano which sounded as well as it could, and a record player that was fuelled, so to speak, by a small collection of breathless 78rpm records comprising all in all the final chorus of the *St Matthew Passion* in Willem Mengelberg's romantic interpretation, which didn't let you guess that one day Bach would become a baroque composer, the overture to *Tannhaüser* by I'm not sure whom, Beethoven's *Seventh Symphony* conducted by Bruno Walter, the first act of *The Valkyrie* by Lotte Lehmann and Lauritz Melchior, conducted by the same Walter, by Prokofiev the *Classical Symphony* and a suite derived from *The Love for Three Oranges*. I can no longer ever hear these works without finding myself back in this place. The opposite corner was lighted by a large window overlooking the park to the west, to the north by a small French window opening onto bushy greenery. On the mantelpiece lay yellowing amid others, traces of glorious recent visits, some inscriptions by Chardonne and Aragon. The cheerfulness of this room was due above all to a large number of wing chairs, sofas and shabby chaises longues, but hung with shiny chintz patterned with large white foliage against a red background. It was the actual living room, bizarrely forbidden to the children, who feigned to respect this taboo and fantasised about its reasons.

The entrance hall also led onto the already-encountered narrow corridor, at whose end the main staircase took you to the 'noble' floor, onto which opened four or five bedrooms with windows overlooking the park, one of which, hung with Toile de Jouy, forever reeked of Mitsouko. The most handsome occupied the north-western corner, above the billiard room, and since it benefited from a kind of bathroom, it was reserved for distinguished guests. But the most cheerful, through an insignificant-looking little door, led to the aforementioned guardroom, of which it was in sum the antechamber. Its walls had been whitewashed, and its doors and windows, and even a large country wardrobe devoid of any pretensions to style had been painted navy blue. From this strategically positioned bedroom, you could also descend directly to the courtyard of honour by way of a tiny spiral staircase. Taking the same staircase, you could climb as well to the second floor, where along its loose-tiled corridor there languished a series of bedrooms abandoned to the bats, and which was called, for some reason, 'Golden Misery'. Climbing further and looking carefully, you found a miniscule room, whose matching window looked from a fair height over the nettled courtyard. Its almost secret location had pretty quickly seduced me, and in the end I awarded it to myself, somehow installing a kind of bed, a wobbly chair and a semblance of a table where I thought to be devising, I shall return to this in a moment, the 'new formula' for *Clarté*. The mistress of the place in no way objected to this annexation, maybe because no paying guest would have known what to do with so frugal a cell. I spent many summer days and nights in this monastic comfort tempered by Angevin sweetness.

Among other vestiges from its feudal past, the estate was surrounded by a moat long reduced to a mere semicircle, which stagnated in the undergrowth within a general disregard. Saddened by this state of affairs, one day I found a way to buy, in great secrecy, an old flat-bottomed fisherman's boat, till this day used on the Thouet, the tributary come from the south that rejoins the river between Saumur and Saint-Hilaire-Saint-Florent. I'm not quite sure how I managed to bring it to one of the ends of the semi-moat, whence I proceeded, still in secret, to launch it. I'd bought a few paper lanterns to boot, and, when the evening came, I invited a *happy few*[257] to a nocturnal sculled crossing. Its success was short-lived, especially since Jacqueline didn't really know where to put this cumbersome present, once the summer months had passed. Nobody did, the ephemeral gondola was forgotten in its sludge, and the following year we found in the same place a rotting wreck, invaded by frogs and covered in duckweed.

Marbre/Surface Plate. Most irregularly periodical, the communist students' newspaper – or rather the communist newspaper aimed at students, which was read only by communist students – was still, in 1952 and 1953, printed, somewhat as a surplus run of *La Terre* [*The Earth*], a Party organ with, for its part, an agricultural target, somewhere between Saint-Eustache and a Rue de la Jussienne of longer-standing renown, on a shop floor on Rue Jean-Jacques-Rousseau, a 'catering trade [métiers de bouche]' quarter (food, kitchen equipment, dental surgeons). A somewhat anarcho-syndicalist spirit reigned there. The wholly artisanal techniques and its officiants' very colourful slang resurrected for me my maternal grandfather, whose language, however, connoted a different origin. I think our typesetters, who by profession only read backwards, on their old-style forms, prior to inking the final proof with brushes, wisely attached no importance to the 'content' of our publication.

Throughout those years of lead, a modest low-level apparatchik catapulted for a year into the position of 'editor-in-chief' by who knows which higher body, for me the lightest lead was still that one, literal in every sense, and the days on the surface plate were by far the most gratifying, with the hopeless intention of making, a vast programme, an intelligent newspaper on the basis of an idiotic politics – whose idiocy in truth still largely eluded me. Such a pretension, nurtured, then, fitfully during a summer at Launay, would have been very badly received had it come to the attention of those concerned, but the weight of the 'line' fortunately stifled any manifestation thereof. The reorientation could only come to

[257] Genette is here alluding the close of Stendhal's *The Charterhouse of Parma*.

bear on questions of form – perhaps only of format (I'd proposed a reduction of the latter, which was declined as being inspired by the example of I can't remember which 'bourgeois', albeit 'left-wing', magazine). For the death of Stalin, I unearthed a photo of the hero as an almost young man, still quite a good-looking guy, leaning, pipe in mouth, over a table where the photographer had 'caught' him in the act of writing. My intention was obviously to adapt the character to the newspaper's readership by illustrating the 'intellectual' side of the author (or at least signatory) of the *Principles of Leninism*. The photo was accepted, but not without reservations: a little too intellectual, precisely. It was mercifully corrected by a more orthodox-style headline: *May We Everywhere Ensure the Triumph of the Living Force of Stalinism*.

A few months earlier, in order to evoke the Rosenberg affair, we'd obtained an article from Pierre Hervé (already suspected of 'reformist' deviation, as had shown at the time the scuttling of *Action*, the only communist newspaper capable, and thus culpable, of an entirely relative open-mindedness) and a drawing by Louis Mitelberg – not yet Tim – depicting two children in front of a highly premonitory double electric chair. For the front page, the following headline was firmly suggested to us: *Let's Save Two Innocents from the Electric Chair!* Its grandiloquence bothered me a little, and perhaps even more so the overly conspicuous blank verse: I'd been taught in my childhood, like the Autodidact in Sartre's *Nausea*, to 'hunt down the alexandrine'. After hours of fierce discussion, I managed to obtain, from a certain level in the hierarchy, *The Latest Cold War Weapon*, which was heavily criticised, subsequently, at a higher level: not 'mobilising' enough, too allusive (despite the very explicit drawing beneath it), and above all deplorably bereft of any exclamation mark. And then, this 'cold war', it was all very neutral: there was on one side American imperialism, on the other peoples in struggle, the fatherland of socialism, the side of peace. I might at least have headlined it: *The Latest Weapon of Imperialism*, or, better: *The Latest Weapon of Imperialism!* This blasted imperialism, in fact, always posed a thorny problem: we either said 'imperialism' full stop, which risked not being clear enough in its condemnation, or we said 'American imperialism', but the specification was pleonastic, lest one should think, a detestable supposition, that there might be other kinds. In the end, the expression 'American-imperialism' was passed (on and on [et repassait]), as long as it was taken to be indivisible, as signifying 'imperialism, American-by-definition'. Analogous cases must occur in other theological domains.

The fact remains that the printing house on Rue Jean-Jacques-Rousseau and its odorous environs were the sole consolation of an editor-in-chief [rédacteur en chef] here (and elsewhere, presumably) branded a 'reducer-in-chief [réducteur en chef]', because the crux of his work on site consisted in making a 50-line article fit a 30-line column. Once completed, the exercise was greeted with a typical expression of the professional idiom: 'It'll make it to Rue Michel.' The context, and the presence in the area of a Rue Michel-le-Comte, provided the key to the riddle, but it seems to me that the expression has since made its way, if it hadn't already, beyond the limits of the shop floor and the quarter.

I've never known why this already gratifying title of 'editor-in-chief' had, subsequently, changed its application in the press in general, now designating different kinds of specialised heads of department, as numerous hither and yon as colonels in the Mexican army, and making way, to describe the person with overall responsibility, for the even more high-flown 'editorial director'. Such wording would not have been conceivable at *Clarté*, whose official 'director' was then a Corsican MP, Arthur Giovoni, the person responsible, before the senior levels, for the communist students' militant activity, and who so to speak never showed himself to his faithful. In those days, there existed no (even minimally) autonomous organisation for said students, and it was appropriate that control over this vaguely suspect category be vested in a 'politician' of a certain standing, and, as a former teacher, one hardly an outsider in this milieu. I said *Arthur* Giovoni because I think I can remember his first name, but only his surname featured, curtly but in capitals, on the front page, to the left of the title: 'Director: Giovoni member of the National Assembly. Editorial Directors 120 rue Lafayette PARIS (Xth).' The '120' was the headquarters of the Paris Federation of the Party, a way of binding the running of the newspaper to this local authority, which must, presumably, have shouldered the budget for printing, and, as it were, for distribution – for the most part unpaid. The official mention, beneath the title, was 'Edited by Communist Students'; 'edited' doubtless meant 'written by', but the articles were usually anonymous or pseudonymous – a fact still to be welcomed by a few of us today: one of us, a future genetician, shrewdly signed 'Germain Sauma' an all-out criticism of genetics, a reactionary pseudo-science founded by 'the monk Mendel', and another, future herald of the *Annales* school, greeted the publication of Fernand Braudel's *The Mediterranean* with an unsigned but devastating review entitled 'The Drunken Boat'.[258] The only student name mentioned in black and white was that of the 'director of publication', my comrade Pierre Averbuch, who assisted me with my tasks on the surface plate, and whom I occasionally took along to share a plate of oysters opposite the Pavillon Baltard, in order to forget our other *coquilles*.[259] According to the law, it was he who, quite unjustly, would have been held responsible for our press offences, but I'm pretty sure that there weren't any in our time, save for stupidity, which doesn't count.

Despite the infantilism of its political investments, this first journalistic experience was for me the most instructive. I should actually say that it was the only one, since it was the first and last time I knew the thing from the inside. As I was much later to understand, to write *in* a newspaper when you are not *of* this newspaper amounts to little more nor less than writing *to* this newspaper: 'Dear Sir: loyal reader and long-time subscriber … '. In I can't recall which tale, Alphonse Allais describes an average Joe's advancing paranoia: 'Then, he started writing to the newspapers.' From which none is totally immune. Luckily, journalism is a trade, and above all a profession. A 'professional' therefore I was, albeit unpaid and on official duty, throughout that year. A year too many, certainly, but all lessons are good, providing you learn from them.

Marcel. Nothing to do with I know not what other narrator.[260] One of my father's sisters, who was called Marcelle, had married a Marcel. Marcel and Marcelle, it was already Lelouch,[261] but nobody could have foreseen it. With their son Roger, thus my cousin, they lived in a tiny attic flat on Rue Philippe-de-Girard, within touching (and, at daybreak, hearing) distance of the overground metro station *La Chapelle*, but on the 'right', meaning the southern, side: Xth arrondissement. North of the boulevard, it was the 'bad'

[258] After Arthur Rimbaud's poem 'Le Bateau ivre' (1871).
[259] A 'coquille' is in French both a 'shell' and a 'misprint'.
[260] 'Marcel' is the narrator in Proust's *In Search of Lost Time*.
[261] Claude Lelouch (1937–), French film director.

XVIIIth, nearly the Goutte-d'Or – of which one didn't yet speak ill, nor well for that matter. Marcel was a craftsman goldsmith and engraver, and I admired his masterwork atop a dresser, a small bronze depicting something like a knife-grinder at work, whose mill and pedal were movable. Marcel and Marcelle had equipped a cupboard with a kind of kitchen whose sink also served as a washbasin for summary ablutions, but the real luxury was a shower subsequently installed, with special authorisation from the landlord, on the landing, above a Turkish toilet. I can't remember whether the water of this country shower in an urban milieu was hot or cold, but it was definitely running, and it was better not to slip on the oblique tiles of the Turquerie.

On both sides of the boulevard, the entire Chapelle quarter has been eviscerated by the cuttings of the railway lines of the Nord and the Est,[262] which you cross along bridges whence the view is grandiose and desperate. Upon one of these bridges – the most frequented on our Sunday walks – lies Rue Louis-Blanc, and on the same street, I believe, could be found a café where 'uncle Marcel' used to take us to (watch him) play on a contraption, the anticipated missing link between table football and the pinball machine, of which I have never encountered an example anywhere else, and whose name I've forgotten, if ever I did know it. It was, beneath some sort of transparent globe akin to those of cheese covers or fin-de-siècle clocks, a kind of miniature crane you had to manoeuvre from the outside with levers and pushbuttons, so as to make it grab and remove from their cage small trinkets placed at its feet, and which were sometimes edible. A certain dexterity was required, one my uncle possessed from his trade, manual in the noblest sense.

Marriage. 'Yet another bachelor's idea' (Vialatte). Henri Michaux advised, from the wedding night onwards, having one's wife soak all night in a well: 'My oh my, she says, so that's what marriage is. This is why they kept its exercise so secret. I've been taken in by this business.' I can't recall which husband, happy or unhappy, asserted quite logically: 'If there'd only been me, I never would have married.' Yet another, an Egyptian, irascible and vindictive,

---

[262] The 'Gare du Nord' and the 'Gare de l'Est', in Paris.

'who had, after 15 days of marriage, thrown his wife out of the window, then denounced her for abandoning the marital home' (*Le Monde*, 4th November, 1997). After the 'maxims' that Arnolphe made Agnès[263] read, with the outcome we know, and the ten commandments imposed upon his young wife by Albert Einstein, the Nobel prize for the most serenely chauvinist attitude goes to Gustav Mahler for declaring to Alma, until then herself a composer and who, as was later seen, wasn't just anyone: 'Your job will henceforth be to make me happy', or perhaps to Sigmund Freud: 'With my wife, I've resolved the problem of marriage: she's faithful and in good health.' But here, as elsewhere, and as Borges said, the word 'problem' is no doubt a petition of principle. By way of catharsis, here again is a compendium of sexist remarks: 'A woman who writes is like a dog walking upon its hind legs: it isn't that it's beautiful, but it is always surprising' (Samuel Johnson[264]). 'We mustn't say that women cannot do anything: it's as though we were to say that a whetstone can't cut meat' (Jules Janin). An(other) uncle of mine, without being strictly speaking misogynist, but owing to plain linguistic incompetence, persisted in calling women: 'the opposed sex'.

Marmite/Cooking Pot. Under the Occupation, he'd made with his own hands a 'Norwegian cooking pot', a wooden crate stuffed with sawdust, which cluttered up a corner of the kitchen, and which allowed you to save gas by finally braising, for example, a beef and carrot stew, without any further expense of energy, and unfortunately without any beef.

Maroc/Morocco. The white or purple vats, with their suffocating odour, of the tanners' quarter in Fez, and the swifts' strident cries as they skim, in the evening, the cornices of the ramparts. The Andalusian gardens in Rabat, at the foot of the Kasbah of the Udayas, lemon trees, oleanders, bougainvilleas, mint tea on the terrace of the Café Maure, overlooking the mouth of the Bou Regreg and the white Sale Medina at sunset. Before the Hassan

---

[263] In Molière's *L'École des femmes* (*The School for Wives*) (1662).
[264] Boswell's quotation actually reads: 'Sir, a woman's preaching is like a dog's walking on his hind legs. It is not done well; but you're surprised to find it done at all.'

Tower, a truncated minaret, the immense esplanade planted with uneven white columns, such as will perhaps be in a few centuries the courtyard of honour of the Palais Royal. A tinkling water merchant, waving his cups beneath a gleaming one-man band hat bedecked with medals and bells. The palm grove of Marrakech, for the field of wheat, or barley, at the base of their trunks, enjoying their dry shade, and wasting no crumb of soil. The climb to the snows of the High Atlas through the cool Ourika Valley, as far as the Setti-Fatma pass, where the road abandons its pursuit and yields to a mule track.

Mars. They're starting to say that there is water on Mars, and I'm suitably delighted about it, but I wonder all the same if this water is drinkable. For me, in fact, the right question is: 'Is there any *earth* on Mars?' One could at least take a little along, like the bacteria deposited by the kind robot responsible for discovering it. This planet will soon be the potluck dinner of the solar system, the practical illustration of the principle according to which one cannot observe without altering that which is being observed.

Marseilles. One of the manifestations of French ill-will with regard to the languages we call 'foreign' is the way we gallicise the world's geography: Londres, Prague, Lisbonne, Venise, Turin, Anvers [Antwerp], Varsovie [Warsaw], Vienne, Florence, Danube, Toscane [Tuscany], and so forth and I shan't mention Russian, Chinese, etc. place-names, necessarily transliterated, which we do with exceptional incompetence. An anglophone must make a great effort to guess what we might possibly be referring to with Pékin [Peking], Le Cap [Cap-Haitien], La Havane [Havana] or Le Caire [Cairo]. The converse is far rarer, but I quite like the Italian *Parigi*, and above all, a virtually imperceptible modification, the English *Marseilles*. For the latter, I could doubtless find the explanation somewhere, but I prefer to remain with this strange plural, which makes one dream. Apropos of transliteration, I recently discovered, in a Spanish book, that the author of *The Cherry Orchard* is there written *Chejov*; whereby the Castilian speaker pronounces this name rather more correctly than do you (unless you are one) or I.

Marthe and Marie. For some reason, I've retained a fairly vivid memory of the successive abodes of my aunt Marthe, whom I've the feeling of having closely followed throughout her life – but not, alas, my own. In my childhood, she worked in an establishment selling fabric in the Sentier area, Rue de Cléry, but lived with her husband in a small flat on Rue des Pyrénées, in Ménilmontant, meaning not far from the place of my own birth. I don't really know what this street then looked like, but it was for my parents the backbone of their youth, and visits to Marthe and André were like a pilgrimage to their origins. This flat owed much to André's talent as a professional decorator, and I experienced there a foretaste of aesthetic pleasure. But, after the birth of their little daughter, the couple split up, and Marthe went to live for one or two years on Rue des Cloys, at the northern foot of the Montmartre hill. It was another popular quarter, with a very lively market on Rue du Poteau, where you felt yourself to be very far from the heart of Paris. I believe I spent a few days there at the outset of the 'phoney war', quite happy to discover alone, in the daytime, an unfamiliar quarter. Then her boss sent her to Angers to run the fabric store I've already spoken about. She lived there with said little girl, my cousin Annie, in a small house in La Doutre where I spent a few days, and which we left in 1940 for the famous exodus. Then, unsurprisingly, my tracks blur somewhat, but what's certain is that in the winter of 1948/9 she'd left La Doutre for a flat situated on Rue Lenepveu, more pleasant and closer to the (central) Place du Ralliement and her shop on Rue des Lices. She lived there a few more years, which corresponded to my stays at Launay, where we'd often meet. I'm not sure in which year she returned to live in Paris, but it was in September 1954 that she was found dead [sans vie] in the little lodging she inhabited in Levallois. She had been my second mother [seconde mère], or rather, until the age of 18, I'd had two mothers who were, not sisters-in-law, like those of Fabrice at Grianta,[265] but actually two sisters, of whom the youngest thus survived the eldest by only six years. In their Huguenot piety, my maternal grand-parents had named their first daughter Marie, and the second Marthe – you can see in reference to what, and according to what order of precedence. If family legend is again to be believed, the youngest often contrived, under variable pretexts, to leave the household tasks to her elder sister: laying the table, wiping the dishes, etc. The usual remark

[265] In Stendhal's *The Charterhouse of Parma*.

was: 'They're giving the lie to the Gospel.' The learned pleasure procured by this Biblical allusion allowed everything to be forgiven, which wasn't overly to the liking of my future mother, uncertain of having 'chosen the better part', and who eventually withdrew into her middle name, as though to escape this allocation; but the two sisters had meanwhile each in turn married, and the question of the distribution of tasks was no longer posed. From my point of view, both of the two parts were the best, and my filial affections were almost equally divided. But I should perhaps rather describe her as my second mother *and counting* [ma *deuxième* mère], since I'd yet have a kind of third, whose role is somewhat more complex to define. But, as Oedipus says (wrongly) in *The Infernal Machine*,[266] 'the main thing is that she is not'.

Martroy. In Pontoise, the Church of Saint-Maclou (which has only been a cathedral since 1966) has nothing Romanesque about it; its style is rather late, somewhat misbegotten, Gothic, and its most remarkable feature, visible from all sides, is a peculiar lantern-turreted Renaissance bell tower rising far above the lower town. But this lower town is itself spread around a street that descends *schuss* from the church to the station, and affords an 'unobstructed' view, but one devoid of any charm, especially since the bombardments of 1944. Saint-Maclou thus presents from this side only a right flank without a portal, and only in fact opens onto the two Places du Martroy – since there are in effect two triangular squares there, named (perhaps in homage to two unequally important martyrs' sepulchres) 'Grand' and 'Petit' Martroy, not quite separated by a row of gable roof houses, and which are joined by their shared apex, in front of a book and stationery store that I'd frequent for, let's say, romantic [romanesque] reasons. At their base, then, the church, with a western porch looking towards Petit Martroy, and a small, almost hidden eastern door, to the left of the choir, facing Grand Martroy, which lends this church, too, an air of romance [une allure, elle aussi, romanesque]. I know there are many other churches with secondary exits, but most of them open more broadly onto the arm of a transept. This one, by dint of its unobtrusiveness, suggests all kinds of vaguely Stendhalian intrigues: you were seen

[266] Play by Jean Cocteau (1932).

entering, you weren't seen leaving; at least two policemen would be required, or two Swiss Guards.

Roughly opposite the large porch, on Petit Martroy, then, a kind of quite civilian carriage door seems to lead to a private courtyard; in fact it opens, at the end of an alley a few metres long, onto the public gardens, whose presence is unsuspected, at least from this side (its main, more monumental door is situated elsewhere, upon another little square most aptly named 'Place du Souvenir [Memory Square]'). This secret entrance is quite in harmony with the two exits of the church lying opposite, and grants this park a mystery I'm not alone in feeling: 'Pontoise and its church high above the town and those mysterious public gardens where I could cast but an enthralled glance', Julien Green would write some ten years later.

For a few years, I cast much more there, and more often. This setting fit for a *fête galante* comprised at least two other charms: one was a graceful bandstand, which I have moreover never seen in use (perhaps only on Sundays), the other a kind of split-level belvedere, it too overlooking, from its hillside, the lower town and the river, and which was well seen by Pissarro. I mean to say: Pissarro saw well that what had to be painted was, not blandly the panorama taken in from the belvedere, but the belvedere itself, a small circular balcony, seen from behind, meaning from the garden, leaving you only to guess at its plunging site, and outlining upon this vacant space the silhouettes of some fine *promeneuses* in crinoline. This balcony made for an unmissable meeting place, for once most indiscreet, but meetings don't always require discretion: one had sometimes to avoid misunderstandings by publishing there the anticipated, often illusory, and ever ephemeral banns.

The same age as Juliette, Madeleine had a sombre and luminous beauty, evocative of her native South, and had everything to stir my emotions. Tinged for me with the hint of incest (another one) once evoked by Apollinaire, by Musil (by Wagner), our still almost childish love consisted mainly, after a day of lessons impatiently followed or skipped, in hesitant walks for which I'd meet her on the ridge path that led from one school to the other, and, as summer approached, in shivery dips in the arm of the Oise that stretches from the foot of the Hermitage to a desert island whose name I've forgotten, if ever it had one. We'd exchange postcard-format reproductions, borrowed from the shop at the Louvre, of Monet, of Cézanne, of Van Gogh and, of course, of Pissarro, who had in advance painted, between Auvers and Giverny, our most familiar places – not to mention the living Matisse or Gauguin I saw by my side, in a pleated skirt. We'd recite verses by Verlaine such as heard, on one side of a raspy record, in the even raspier voice of Charles Dullin:

> *Dansons la gigue!*
> *Elle avait des façons vraiment*
> *De désoler un pauvre amant,*
> *Que c'en était vraiment charmant!*
> *Dansons la gigue!*
> *Mais je trouve encore meilleur*
> *Le baiser de sa bouche en fleur*
> *Depuis qu'elle est morte à mon cœur...*

[Let's dance the Jig!/She truly had ways/To ravage a poor lover,/How truly charming it was!/Let's dance the jig!/But I find still better/The kiss from her mouth in flower/Since she's been dead to my heart...]

Said jig was sung in three-four notes: *do, mi, mi, re*. In a bright bedroom overlooking the square, we'd sometimes listen, with the window open, on her record player, to music from a limited repertoire, where floods of Wagner lay cheek by jowl with Django Reinhardt (*Nuages*, I believe), Duke Ellington (*Caravan*, I fear), and, towards the end no doubt, an ill-boding *Feuilles mortes* [*Dead Leaves*], which was yet to be called *Autumn Leaves*.

Memories and regrets too:[267] as it says in a novel I hadn't yet read, 'passions wilt when they are transplanted',[268] and, for this reason perhaps, this *blushing romance* hardly withstood the abandonment of its site. For private use, I recorded this heartbreak in a painstakingly nonchalant song I entitled *Viaticum*:

> *Je te remets au temps qui passe,*
> *À la pierre qui roule,*
> *À la mousse qui pourrit,*
> *À la fortune, à l'avarie,*

---

[267] This appears to be an allusion to the actress Catherine Allégret's autobiographical *Les Souvenirs et les regrets aussi* (1994).
[268] From Gustave Flaubert's *L'Éducation sentimentale* (*Sentimental Education*) (1869): 'Les passions s'étiolent quand on les dépayse.'

Je te remets au ciel qui tremble,
À la terre qui s'évapore,
À l'orage qui se rassemble,
À la jachère, à l'insomnie,
Je te remets au battant de la cloche,
Aux ailes du moulin,
À l'essieu de la charrette,
Au sillage du navire,
Au vertige, à l'intempérie.
Je te confie au vent et à la pluie,
À l'impatience et à l'oubli.

[*I return you to passing time,/To the rolling stone,/To the rotting moss,/To fortune, to taintedness,/I return you to the trembling sky/ To the evaporating earth,/To the gathering storm,/To fallow land, to insomnia./I return you to the bell clapper,/To the windmill's blades,/ To the cart's axle,/To the ship's wake,/To giddiness, to inclemency./I entrust you to the wind and the rain,/To impatience and forgetfulness.*]

But you can no more control forgetfulness than the wind or the rain. A few centuries later, in the days when certain learned commissions still sat, overlooking the Seine, in a richly kitsch building on Quai Anatole France, professional happenstance placed us at the same canteen table. Recognising her, in a fraction of a second, I experienced a dazzling return journey through time. The place and the crowd left no place for retrospective, even less for retroactive, outpourings. A few days thereafter we had a less public meeting, which she feared would disappoint, and which for me was merely – what else? – melancholic. A quatrain came back to me from just as long ago, out of the blue:

Toutes les passions s'éloignent avec l'âge,
L'une emportant son masque et l'autre son couteau,
Comme un essaim chantant d'histrions en voyage
Dont le groupe décroît derrière le coteau.[269]

[*All the passions depart with age,/One taking its mask and the other its knife,/Like a singing swarm of roaming minstrels/Whose group dwindles behind the hill.*]

---

[269] From Victor Hugo, 'Tristesse d'Olympio' ('Olympio's Sadness') (1837).

None of this is quite 'dead to my heart'. The passions depart with age, wilt in the distance, return and again turn back, behind a hill that alone has not moved, in the green paradise of opportunities lost, and which shall return no more.

Maryland. In the period comfort *Metroliner* that takes you there, coming from Penn Station at the speed of a slowly trotting horse, the inspector announces to you with the appropriate accent: *Bol'moâ.* It's now the South – not yet Faulkner's 'deep South', just the Old South, of which, on the map, the first state you encounter clings, like a Hindi word to its own, to the Mason–Dixon line, drawn perfectly straight between Pennsylvania and Maryland. A local joke, equally applicable to a few other cities here and elsewhere, describes Baltimore as a *'nice place to be from'*. To this may be compared W.C. Field's epitaph, doubtless somewhere near Los Angeles: 'Anyway, you're better off here than in Philadelphia', the remark by Harold Arlen (the insufficiently celebrated composer of *Over the Rainbow*): 'Committing suicide in Buffalo [where he was born] is really a pleonasm', the inevitable Mark Twain: 'Pittsburgh, a good place to die: you won't even see the difference', and the saying, obviously from New York: *Outside Broadway, everything is Bridgeport* – you have to be acquainted with Bridgeport, Connecticut, to appreciate it fully, but its sense can probably be guessed from the context. 'There are, said Calvino once again, places where I couldn't live, even if I were dead.'

To return to Baltimore even so, I owe it to the truth to protest that in 1970 I spent a perfectly pleasant autumn there. The port, the ill-famed 'Block' and the official *downtown* district hadn't yet been renovated such as I was to see them 22 years later, but the blue crab at O'Bricky's was still *the best crabmeat in the world*, and the Johns Hopkins campus was idyllic, like the parks surrounding it and the semi-countryside that extends northwards. The very residential and very discreet Guilford district, between Johns Hopkins and Loyola College, is one of those that make you want to teach thereabouts. We were lodged a stone's throw away, precisely opposite the campus, on Charles Street, in a heavy turn-of-the-century building, no doubt a university property, but the flat I occupied upon these heights had, they said, housed in his day Scott Fitzgerald, and his presence still made itself felt, at least once you knew this. The sad thing, here, was rather the 'Edgar Poe House', further south, in an area that had at the time gone thoroughly to seed. It was his final dwelling, and it wasn't far from there that fell the basalt (not granite) block for which Mallarmé wrote the *Tomb*[270] we know. I don't know in what water of death (a vulgar gutter, or a torrential stream, of which there was no shortage in this still rustic area) he was found, after a drinking binge, 'in the pale darkness of daybreak',[271] one morning in 1849. It wasn't the best way to leave the city, where, for that matter, he hadn't deigned to be born.

I had also to search downtown, during my first few days there, for the Maryland State Capitol, until I was reminded that Baltimore was by no means its political capital. Annapolis, then, is a small colonial-style port town, on Chesapeake Bay, and what you might take to be its Capitol, with a dome imitating that of the Invalides, is in reality the monumental chapel of the US Naval Academy, which, on the banks of the Severn, is to the navy a more cheerful version of what West Point, to the north of New York and towering over the Hudson, is to the land army. Looking harder, I eventually discovered the real Maryland *State House*, an exquisite little edifice with a small pointed bell tower, built in 1779 bang in the centre of a round square, and which was originally in 1784 the headquarters of the federal government then in its infancy. Nothing in common with the heavy wedding cakes you behold in Washington, in Providence, in San Francisco (City Hall) and elsewhere – I'll make exceptions for the one in Wisconsin, adroitly differentiated from Wren's St Paul's, and the one in Minnesota, derived, for its part, from Michelangelo's St Peter's by the excellent Cass Gilbert. Of the streets descending towards Port Annapolis, the most agreeable are lined with former slave houses, low and humble, but nowadays spruce with their neatly repainted *shingles*. A very old-style hotel, and which I assume to be more or less contemporary with the State House, is called *The Maryland Inn*, and one cannot forget the night spent there.

Massinissa. In *khâgne*, at the Lycée Lakanal, the most popular

---

[270] Genette is here alluding to the oft-quoted line from Stéphane Mallarmé's sonnet 'Le Tombeau d'Edgar Poe' ('The Tomb of Edgar Poe') (1876), 'Calme bloc ici-bas chu d'un désastre obscur', 'Calm block here fallen from some obscure disaster'; Mallarmé refers to 'ce granit' in the following line.

[271] 'dans les pâles ténèbres du petit jour', from Charles Baudelaire's preface to his translation of Poe's tales, *Histoires extraordinaires* (1856).

teacher, in every respect, was the already lauded Jean Bruhat, a Marxist historian born in Brioude, who was second to none when it came to churning out for you a three-part plan for any subject whatsoever. I long owed him a few successes in the exercise still called the 'dissertation', and which, a veritable rhetorical door opener, then decided the outcome of a few competitive exams [concours]. Indifferent to the purely formal nature of this gift, he deemed me capable of shining in the three 'subjects' (literature, history, philosophy) based upon the mastery of this exercise, and gratified me with the unmerited label of 'multifaceted genius'; unmerited in various ways, for I felt myself to have rather more facets than genius. I realise somewhat belatedly what my destiny owes to two historians, one of whom encouraged me to attempt, and the other of whom equipped me with the means to achieve what without them I might perhaps have shunned, for better or for worse.

Besides his innate talent for tripartite arrangements, and a more savoury dash of the Auvergne accent, Bruhat peppered his lessons with already outmoded narrative clichés, along the lines of *battre en brèche*, 'beat into retreat', *rompre en visière*, 'break a lance', *avoir maille à partir*, 'have a bone to pick', *aller à Canossa*, 'go to Canossa', which we'd greet ritualistically with an admiring hiss (we called it 'phushing [pchuter]'). One of us, no less Auvergnat, once composed with this rhetorical material a fairly charming double quatrain whose recollection, buried for years, came back to me very recently, in a single stroke that I hope is faithful, a memory bubble almost as disquieting as the river of forgetfulness whose surface it breaks:

> *Nous n'irons pas nous battre en brèche,*
> *Nous n'irons pas à Canossa,*
> *Nous irons cueillir des fleurs sèches*
> *Aux jardins de Massinissa.*
> *Nous n'irons pas rompre en visière,*
> *Nous n'aurons pas maille à partir,*
> *Mais nous partirons en croisière*
> *Sur l'océan de nos désirs.*

[We shall not beat ourselves into retreat,/We shall not go to Canossa,/ We shall go and pick dry flowers/In the gardens of Massinissa./We shall not go breaking lances,/We shall not have bones to pick,/But we shall set out to cruise/Upon the ocean of our desires.]

Maxim's. 'Vaudable Academy' was, I believe, the title boasted by a kind of private class for foreign, preferably American, auditors, founded in the sixties by the wife of the manager of this then very Parisian gastronomic shrine. During the winter of 1969/70, I was recruited there for the umpteenth rehash of a lesson on Proust that I'd already hauled from Yale to Reid Hall, Rue de Chevreuse, an almost rustic venue where they'd gather a few Cornell and Johns Hopkins students residing in Paris. The audience of the Vaudable Academy, meanwhile, met, then, on Rue Royale, in a first-floor room and well away from meal times. This performance formed part, like the aforementioned, of a transatlantic university network whose 'éminence grise' was Paul de Man. It had the advantage that, at the close of the session, Mme Vaudable, on the same floor, honoured its occasional professors with a house dinner. I have never known the reasons for this strange association: doubtless it was about making the most profitable use of a room spurned by its clientele, deemed too discreet for it to be any question of being seen there. I assume at all events that the author of *In Search* … would have appreciated the choice of this establishment for a discussion of his work. The Ritz, another place of memory, would in truth have been even more appropriate, but perhaps it had no rooms available for this didactic usage.

Médialecte/Medialect (abbrev. *Med.*). Dialect peculiar to the media in a broad sense (written press, radio, television, Internet presumably, pending something better), recent avatar of French, whose occasionally unfortunate evolution it accelerates and reflects. A cliché, an infelicity, an impropriety, a lapsus may be pleasing, savoury, even delectable when it springs spontaneously from ignorance or from popular inventiveness, from those whom Malherbe[272] called the 'dock-hands of the Port au Foin',[273] more rarely so when it proceeds from a pretension to elegance, and the desire to distinguish oneself by substituting for an ordinary word or turn of phrase another word, another turn of phrase whose vague homonymy thus makes for a supposedly *trendier* synonymy,

---

[272] François de Malherbe (1555–1628), French poet, critic and translator.
[273] The 'Port au Foin' ('Hay Port') is an old Parisian port, formerly on the Île de la Cité.

sometimes by the addition of a superfluous prefix ('rajouter' for *ajouter* [to add], 'démultiplier' for *multiplier* [increase]), often by 'franglicism': 'supporter' for *soutenir*. This abuse of the valorising solecism is the linguistic version of the aforementioned Gresham's law, a variant Proust would have called the law of Françoise,[274] or of Cottard,[275] or maybe of Norpois:[276] bad language drives out good. Medialect might merely be a specific professional jargon, a 'trade idiom' among others, but the media trades are not limited to media professionals, entertainers or journalists, notwithstanding the hybrid forms – unless you include within this profession politicians, men of letters, the old new philosophers or the inevitable 'hotshot lawyers', sitting or prosecuting, who by dint of passing through it wind up partaking in it. Irrespective of its source, the media, by their very role, broadcast medialect along with everything else, and often without anything else. Mirror and model of our dominant subculture, it is gradually becoming everyone's doublespeak [langue de bois], and the media are nowadays our Port au Foin (without hay [foin], except in the colloquial sense of the word[277]), to which one may, with the dose of false ill humour and real bad faith proper to any satire, attribute all the verbal turpitudes of the modern world. Here are a few specimens, picked according to the vagaries of an inevitably floating attention, hence this modest proposal, a short catalogue of instructions for beginners, umpteenth dictionary (within a dictionary) of received ideas and chic malapropisms, survival kit for anyone who would like to pursue a career therein. The alleged examples are not all apocryphal; quotations are occasionally without quotation marks, and in compensation certain quotation marks are without quotations.[278]

Abnegation. Med. for (presumably) *resignation*: 'As the strike drags on, the combativeness of the first days makes way for a certain

---

[274] The narrator's loyal family maid in *In Search of Lost Time*.

[275] Doctor Cottard, member of the 'Verdurin clan' in *In Search* ... .

[276] The Marquis de Norpois, diplomat and friend of the narrator's father in *In Search* ... .

[277] 'Un foin' can also signify 'a fuss', 'a din' or 'a racket'.

[278] Genette's 'medialectal' examples being, by definition, derived from French language use, I have included in my translation as much French as is necessary to permit their understanding. I have, on the other hand, generally omitted the relatively few instances where an entry's intralinguistic play would have little resonance for the Anglophone reader.

abnegation', or on the contrary for *courage*: 'With much abnegation, the Auxerre team eventually levelled the score, then won 3–2.' A word whose meaning you no longer know may signify anything you wish.

Acquis/Nurture. Always on the Left (see *Inné/Nature*).

Acronym. Med. for *initials*. If CFDT[279] is an 'acronym', what will you call UNESCO, duly pronounced UNESCO?

Activist. A frowned-upon militant.

Activity. Always bustling (this type, which we shall find again, of set expression has had its credentials ever since *The Iliad*, under the name of *Homeric epithet, natural epithet* or *oral-formulaic style*).

Ad nominem. Med. for *ad hominem*.

Adulate. Med. for *admire*.

Aficionados. Med. for *aficionado*; the principle is simple: a Spanish word, even in the singular, must always end in -os. Another example: 'a *desperados*', or better, 'a *desesperados*'. According to the same principle, say 'a *paparazzi*', 'a *tifosi*', 'a *missi dominici*', 'a *pizzicati*' (but I heard, on a reputedly musical radio station, a more fortifying *pizzacato*).

Agglomérer/Cluster. Med. for *agglutiner*, 'pack together': 'Some 35,000 *ravers* clustered on the Larzac plateau'.

Agitation/Unrest. Always futile.

Aisance/Ease. See *Facilité*.

Albion. Always perfidious (arch.).

Alchemy. Always strange.

Alciabiade/Alcibiades. First of the demagogic men of means, first of the media darlings, inventor of 'modern communication': seeing himself one day forgotten, or ignored, by public opinion, he had his dog's tail docked; consequently, Athens could now think of nothing but this sacrificed tail, thus of the dog whose tail it was,

---

[279] *Confédération française démocratique du travail* (French Democratic Confederation of Labour), a national trade union federation.

and thus of the master of the dog whose tail it was, without any consideration relative to his political villainies. This type of trait or prop, of preferably insignificant, deliberate or unintended biographeme, can nowadays still, and this has long been the case, guarantee you the sympathetic attentions of the media, and thus perhaps of posterity: after all, we still talk (proof thereof) about the tail of Alcibiades' dog. See among others and in disorder: Captain Cousteau's hat, Jankélévitch's strand of hair, Pierre Rosenberg's red scarf, José Bové's moustache and pipe, B[ernard-]H[enry]L[évi]'s white shirt, Marc Veyrat's hat, Michel Houellebecq's cigarette held between his middle and ring fingers, Diogenes' barrel and that of Sartre, Balzac's cafetiere, Newton's apple, Einstein's tongue, the finch on Darwin's rifle, Proust's cork-lined bedroom, his madeleine, and 'his' questionnaire (I once moreover heard someone refer to 'the questionnaire concerning Proust's madeleine'; not only does whoever say madeleine say Proust, but increasingly whoever says Proust says madeleine), Butor's overalls and those of Coluche, Larry King's braces, Karajan's jets, Michelangeli's engines, Hélène Grimaud's wolves, Spinoza's lenses, Kant's daily walk at the end of his dogmatic siesta, the sugar melting in Bergson's cup, Flaubert's *gueuloir*, Céline's little music, Foucault's pate, Deleuze's nails, Van Gogh's ear, those of Beethoven, Goya, Ronsard, Homer's white cane, Rimbaud's silence, Verlaine's absinthe, Molière's armchair, Saint-Ex[upéry]'s chain bracelet, Descartes' stove and that of Zola, Francis Ponge's soap, Michelangelo's ladder, Monet's water lilies, Picasso's women, Pollock's pierced can, Ravel's bolero, Josephine Baker's bananas, Maurice Chevalier's boater, Gilbert Bécaud's hand over his ear and that of the Corsican polyphonists, Corot's three thousand paintings, of which four thousand are in the United States, Churchill's cigar, that of Brecht, that of Castro, Aragon's mask, Elsa's eyes, Irene's cunt, Mérimée's dictation, Hugo's desk and that of Hemingway, Nabokov's butterfly net, Cézanne's apples, Cleopatra's nose, Cromwell's bladder and that of Rousseau, Duchamp's urinal, Marat's bathtub, Chamberlain's umbrella, Clemenceau's forage hat, Nehru's rose, Mitterrand's black hat, Stalin's pipe, Mossadegh's pyjamas, Arafat's keffiyeh, and I'm certainly forgetting some. To my knowledge the only one of all these 'emblematic' gimmicks to have wound up on a national flag is Gandhi's spinning wheel, which well deserved it.

Altéralisme/Differentism. I can find only this word to designate the way we nowadays disguise any type of refusal as an *unspecified* alternative proposition: 'I'm not against Europe, I am against *this particular* Europe, I am [here, assume a deep and complicated air] in favour of a *different kind* of Europe'; 'I'm not against reforms, I'm in favour of a *different kind* of reform'; 'I'm not against globalisation, I'm in favour of a *different kind* of globalisation'; 'We're going to govern in a *different kind* of way' (etc.).

Amateur. Always enlightened.

Amnesty. Always broad.

Anecdotes. Med. for *anicroche*, '*hitch*': 'He had a few anecdotes with the law'.

Anecdotique/Anecdotal. Med. for *anachronic.*

Anonymes/Ordinary folk. 'Amid the crowd of ordinary folk, a few important people may be recognised.' In fact, the ordinary folk can also be easily recognised, by the infallible sign that you do not recognise them.

Antan/Yesteryear. Med. for *autrefois*, '*in former days*': 'At 95, M. Martin no longer has the legs he had yesteryear.'

A priori. 1st Med. for *apparently*. No longer say 'When we entered, the place was apparently empty', but 'When we entered, the place was *a priori* empty'. 2nd Med. for *prejudice*. No longer say 'Initially, he encountered a few prejudices', but 'Initially, he encountered a few *a priori*'.

Arbre/Tree. Always hides the forest. When there is no longer a single tree to hide it, maybe we shall finally see the forest.

Archetype. No longer say 'So and so is the very epitome of the opportunistic politician', but 'So and so is the archetypally opportunistic politician'. It's more chic.

Arrêter/Stop. Prohibition in the form of a positive injunction. No longer say 'You mustn't count your chickens', but 'You must stop counting your chickens'. In short, you must stop saying 'You mustn't … ', and start saying 'You must stop … '.

Aseptic. Clean-cut and vaguely sterile.

Associer/Associate. Med. for *assimiler*, '*assimilate*': 'Jehovah's Witnesses are sometimes associated with a sect'.

Asymptotic. Med. for *exponential*: 'The growth of greenhouse gas emissions is asymptotic'; you will never know in relation to what, you'll be dead before then.

Atmosphere. Always pronounced with Arletty's[280] accent, and always evoked apropos of the Canal Saint-Martin, or of the 'mythical' *Hôtel du Nord*. The film's best line, however, isn't that one, but this one, from Jouvet and in regard to a comb: 'Look, a fish bone!' You still need to know a bit about fish, enough at least to be able to tell the difference between a mackerel [*maquereau*[281]] and a whiting.

Audience/Listeners. Med. for *public*, '*audience*'.

Aune/Yardstick. No longer say '*À l'aube*, 'at the dawn' of this new millennium … ', but '*À l'aune*, "by the yardstick" of this new millennium'. It's more elegant.

Aussi/As. In the medialect, it's recommended to use *as* (or *as much*, or *like*) countersensically; for instance: 'During this heatwave, it's almost as warm in the daytime as it is at night-time.'

Autoroute/Motorway. Med. masculine noun for *autoroute*, feminine noun. No longer say 'The minister unveiled the first stretch of *une nouvelle autoroute*, "a new motorway"', but 'The minister unveiled the first stretch *d'un nouvel autoroute*'. Said minister, nevertheless responsible for the thing, often leads by example. It's peculiar, as Proust says more or less, how people make a point of honour of using words whose meaning, or gender, they do not know.

Autre/Other. There has been developing for some time, in the medialect, a use one might qualify, kindly, as expletive: 'The

---

[280] Léonie Marie Julie Bathiat (1898–1992), known as 'Arletty', French actress, singer and model. In Marcel Carné's *Hôtel du nord* (1938) Arletty's prostitute character famously exclaims to her protector (played by Louis Jouvet), who has just referred to her somewhat disparagingly as his 'atmosphere': 'Atmosphère! Atmosphère! Est-ce que j'ai une gueule d'atmosphère!', 'Atmosphere! Atmosphere! Do I look like an atmosphere?'
[281] Also signifies colloquially a 'pimp'.

police arrested the gangster and his other accomplices'; 'The United States and its other allies'. I must, however, acknowledge that a perfectly classical turn of phrase, though logically just as strange, says, for instance: 'beetles, millipedes, and other scorpions'. In the same vein, and with the amicable participation of Jean de La Fontaine, I propose: *The Hare and the Other Frogs*, *The Fox and the Other Grapes*, *The Labouring Man and his Other Children*, and additionally, for that matter: *The Grasshopper and the Other Ant*, *The Fox and the Other Crow*, *The Wolf and the Other Lamb*, *The Oak and the Other Reed*.

Avancée/Progress. Always significant.

Avare/Miserly. Med. for *avide*, '*eager*': 'Long scorned, you sense they are miserly for public recognition.'

Axis. Everything is now organised along two, three or even more axes; hang the expense, but I recall that our good old planet has but one. And yet it works, and turns [Et pourtant, elle tourne] (and so does the axis, or at least it oscillates). Similarly, there is wrangling between partisans of a *unipolar* or a *multipolar* world. It's the confrontation of two planetary howlers. In all matters serious, I mean physical (among others: electrical), the poles always come in pairs, no more, no less. The Earth is by definition bipolar, and even somewhat pleonastically. And that's why it has a northern hemisphere, a southern hemisphere, no eastern hemisphere, no western hemisphere, and that's how it works, and turns [et c'est comme ça qu'elle tourne].

Baisse/Drop. Med. for *rise*, and vice versa: 'The Cac 40[282] has today dropped by +0.5 a point' (or: 'has risen by -0.5 a point'). This inversion doesn't even spare the specialists, who nevertheless correct themselves almost immediately, one time out of ten. The others never do, and I suspect them of holding these two words to be quite simply synonymous. Any symmetry engenders giddiness, every binary choice is a source of confusion: *east* for *west*, *north* for *south*, *upstream* for *downstream*, *left* for *right*, *yes* for *no* and vice versa, *right* for *duty* and vice versa, *cause* for *consequence* and vice versa: 'This poor harvest had as consequence

[282] See note 211.

the hard frosts of last spring'; 'The attacks in London [in July 2005] are the cause of the English participation [since 2003] in the Iraq war' [I wonder if this type of blunder doesn't stem from a purely formal mistaking of 'being because of' for 'being the cause of'; language sometimes falls prey to its own traps), *unemployment* for *employment* and vice versa: 'Mass unemployment is far from being a European affliction. With regard to the rate of unemployment, out of the 21 countries of the Union, France occupies the 21st place!' (if this reasoning seems strange to you, read it again replacing 'the rate of unemployment' with 'the rate of employment'). The vagaries of the euro/dollar parity are also responsible for this type of error: 'The dollar is at 1.30 euros'. Don't object that it's the other way round, they'd reply at once that one can't see the difference.

Balade/Walk. Med. for *ballade*, '*ballad*'.

Ballade/Ballad. Med. for *balade*, '*walk*'.

Banality. Always depressing.

Banditisme/Crime. Always organised.

Barreau/Bar. You'd seek in vain for a baritone there. Besides, the habit is spreading of calling anyone who expresses themself in a courtroom a 'hotshot lawyer', even the public prosecutor.

Besogneux/Plodding. Med. for *laborieux*, '*laborious*': 'This novel's style is a bit plodding.'

Bien/Really. It's recommended to place this adverb in the conditional subordinate proposition. No longer say 'If a reform is necessary, it really is that one', but 'If a reform really is necessary, it's that one'. It really is better.

Bijou/Gem. Always little.

Bilan/Assessment. Always, alas, provisional.

Biography. Med. for *life*, and *in relation to a life*: 'In his *In Search …*, Proust remained silent about certain details of his biography', or 'certain biographical details'. It's best to forget that a biography is merely the, in principle written, *narrative* of a life. Roland Barthes, who very helpfully coined the word *biographeme*, clearly intended it to mean an element in the *narrative* of a life, and not just a lived episode.

Bon/Well. A certain somewhat (not too) media-friendly philosopher literally punctuates his discourse with a highly recurrent 'well': it's his comma.

Bonheur/Happiness. To be used preferably in the cliché *'Que du bonheur!'*, 'What happiness!'

Bordel/Mess. See *Shambles [Capharnaüm]*.

Bouger/Get moving. Media description for any kind of political action, inevitably positive because it *'fait bouger les choses'*, 'get things moving'; one knows neither in which direction nor for that matter which ones.

Boulot/Job. Always little.

Bras/Arm. Occasionally strong, often secular, always right, never left.

Brebis/Sheep. Sometimes lost, sometimes black, occasionally both.

Briscard/Pro. Always old.

Brochette/Array. Always fine.

Buveur/Drinker. Always inveterate.

Ça. The interrogative form is often awkward for an interviewer, especially if it must affect a somewhat long sentence (more than three words). So some of them prefer to formulate their questions in the guise of an affirmation, followed by the properly interrogative, and moreover almost expletive, clause: *'C'est ça?'*, 'Is that right?' Don't ask: 'Is the economic situation in danger of deteriorating in the coming months?', nor even: 'Do you think that the economic situation is in danger of deteriorating in the coming months?' Say simply: 'The situation is in danger of deteriorating in the coming months, *c'est ça?*, is that right?' The conjecture is generally sufficiently low-risk to impose the answer: 'That is indeed right', possibly followed by an explanatory and supererogatory development on the part of the consulted 'expert', which can always be edited out later: if only we listened to them … . In sports journalism, the custom is moreover to eschew any interrogative mark or intonation. Grab the breathless victor and declare to them: 'Duchemol, this is the finest phase of your career.' If he's well trained (the respect due to the media forms part of his professional consciousness, and even of his contract), Duchemol will acquiesce, and improvise a pointlessly confirmatory commentary.

Cadences/Rates. Always diabolical.[283]

Cadre/Executive. Always young, dynamic and overworked.

Camaraderie. Always genuine.

Candour. Always naive.

Capharnaüm/Shambles. See *Désordre/Mess*.

Capitalism. See *Liberalism*.

Caracoler/Skip. Always ahead.

Carambolesque. Med. for *rocambolesque*.[284]

Career. Always say 'I don't like that word', and assure that: 'I don't have a career plan.' Actually have several, just in case.

Cartesian. Med. for *logical*. The French are always excessively so. Rail against it.

Catastrophe. Always natural; to speak of a *cultural* catastrophe, for instance in relation to a summer festival, is politically incorrect.

Cause. Always just.

Cave. Always Ali Baba's; the entry to Plato's has been lost.

Ceci/This. Med. for *cela*, '*that*'.

Cela/That. Med. for *ceci*, '*this*'.

Célibataire/Bachelor. Always confirmed.

---

[283] As in the slogan 'À bas les cadences infernales!', 'Down with diabolical production rates!', featuring on posters designed by the Atelier Populaire ('People's Workshop') during the French May 1968.
[284] 'Rocambole' was the hero of adventure novels written by Ponson du Terrail (1829–1871), the derived adjective entering the language to mean 'far-fetched' or 'fantastic'.

Ce sont/They are. Med. for *c'est*, '*it is*', when a plural is lurking in the vicinity: '*Ce sont dans les vieux pots qu'on fait les meilleures soupes*', 'It's in old pots that the best soups are made, aren't they?'

Chaînon/Link. Always missing.

Chaleur/Warmth. Always infectious.

Champollion. He read hieroglyphics, but didn't speak them.

Champs-Élysées. Finest avenue in the world.

Chance. Med. for *risk*: 'This week, the chances of a new earthquake are very high.'

Chantier/Construction site. Always mammoth.

Chaos. Always indescribable: that's its only description.

Chaotique/Chaotic. Med. for *cahoteux*, '*bumpy*': 'The roads in this country are often chaotic.'

Charge. Always heroic.

Charismatique/Charismatic. Med. for *photogenic*.

Charm. Always discreet.

Chaudron/Cooking Pot. Sequence of contradictory, or at the least incompatible, arguments. This form of sophism owes its name to the story of the woman who returns a borrowed cooking pot with a hole in it and maintains successively that she's returning it without a hole, that it already had a hole when it was lent to her, and that it functions better with the hole. Everyone can create their own to infinity, but I have a preference for this one, used for a while by the defenders of Saddam Hussein: 'Not only did he not possess any weapons of mass destruction, but furthermore they'd been supplied to him by the United States.' I also admire the fact that the extermination may at once be approved of and denied.

Cher/Dear. The expression 'dear to X ...' is a media delicacy for *of which spoke X*, or even: *which has some kind of relation to X*. For example, 'the human comedy, dear to Balzac', 'time regained, dear to Proust', 'pure reason, dear to Kant', 'the grain of the voice, dear to Roland Barthes', 'war and peace, dear to Tolstoy', 'the grasshopper and the ant, dear to La Fontaine'.

Cheval de bataille/Hobbyhorse. Med. for *bête noire*: 'The 35 hours are the hobbyhorse of French employers.'

Chevauchée/Horse ride. Always fantastic.[285]

Chez soi/Home. 'Philosophers speak to us a great deal about the *en-soi*, the *in-itself* and the *pour-soi*, the *for-itself.* They never speak to us about being *chez soi, at home*' (Bachelard). Jacques Chirac, leaving the Val-de-Grâce following a week of medical examinations, said that he was 'happy to be returning home [chez moi]'. He means, obviously, to the Élysée. I'm not aware of anyone having noticed this truly telling sentence: I do know that every tenant is 'at home' in the apartment they rent (by paying), but I struggle to imagine de Gaulle or Mitterrand speaking of this national palace as their 'home'. De Gaulle was at home at La Boissière, Pompidou on the Quai d'Orléans, Giscard in Passy, Mitterrand on Rue de Bièvre, at Latche or on Quai Branly, Chirac is only at home on Rue du Faubourg-Saint-Honoré. This way of treating an official residence somewhat resembles squatting. At the (eventual) end of his term of office, I suppose he'll feel not that he is being replaced by a successor, but that he's being *evicted*, and thenceforth has *no fixed abode.*

Chiffres/Figures. Always eloquent, but always tedious: 'I'll spare you the figures.' Besides, when they're unfavourable to you, they're only ever just figures.

Choc culturel. Med. for *clash of cultures* (or *of civilisations*). We ought, however, to retain for this expression its originally, I assume, English or American (*cultural shock*) meaning: what happens when you find yourself suddenly transported from one sociocultural milieu to another. For example, the Parisian in Marseille, who saw there 'the only Oriental city not to have a European quarter'.

Choses/Things. They require 'straightening out' from time to time, but if possible 'in depth'. That must be quite painful.

---

[285] *La Chevauchée fantastique* is the French title for the film *Stagecoach* (1939).

Chrétien/Christian. Med. for *Catholic*, and vice versa; one doesn't actually deny that Protestants are Christians, one simply forgets that they exist; in a way, this suits them: they've known worse.

Chronicle. Always of something foretold.

Circumlocution. Med. for *circumvolution*: 'This snake is describing worrying circumlocutions.'

Circumvolution. Med. for *circumlocution*: 'Enough of these circumvolutions, let's call a spade a spade.'

Cœur/Heart. Always this big (roughly).

Cohue/Crowd. Always indescribable. Good thing.

Colis/Package. Always suspect. Bad thing.

Colle/Awkward one. Question to which the questioned party doesn't know the answer. In the past, when asked about a point beyond their competence or their sphere of knowledge, the average citizen would simply admit their ignorance. Now that there are no average citizens anywhere, but everywhere specialists of every kind, hyper-informed and omni-competent, the answer is: 'Now, that's an awkward one!' [Là, vous me posez une colle!]', which expresses legitimate irritation and before which it is advisable to offer a plain apology ('I didn't mean to ask you an awkward question!'), or else face a severe penalty. 'I don't know' has entirely exited discourse, and soon, I think, language and 'thought'. Whereby nobody informs anybody of anything anymore, for 'That's an awkward one' has become the universal and automatic non-response to any question, rejected as a 'trick question' as soon as asked, and if possible a little beforehand. A more affable version of this flat refusal, but one just as categorical for those who can hear it, is: 'Good question!' Don't insist.

Combien?/How much? It is often the only pertinent question, but it's always 'an awkward one'.

Commis/Civil servant. Those of the State are always top.

Communication. They have nothing to say, and they can't even manage that.

Compression. On one of the latest models of mobile phone you can 'store' the sound and video recording of the Bayreuth production by Boulez and Chéreau of Wagner's *Tetralogy*. Amazing for long tube journeys.

Compter/Count. 'C'était sans compter sur ...', 'That was without counting on ...': med. for *c'était compter sans ...*, '*that was without taking into account ...*' I even read a 'c'était sans compter avec l'opposition', 'that was without counting with the opposition', a crazed hybrid of French and medialect, which should be able to count on a fine future.

Concertation/Dialogue. Always broad.

Concorde. Finest square in the world.

Condemn. Péguy said: 'I don't judge, I condemn.' Reprehensible actions are no longer blamed, they are condemned; we're never told what to.

Confisquer/Confiscate. Med. for *consigner*, '*consign*': 'He confiscates all his ideas in a little notebook which never leaves his side.' As long as they're his own ... .

Confrère/Colleague. Always excellent.

Conjugation. Med. for *conjunction*: 'It's the conjugation of these two factors that has led us where we are.' *But, or, and, so, yet, nor, for* will soon be 'coordinating conjugations', which won't make the teaching of grammar any easier.

Connoisseur. Always fine.

Conscience. We were familiar with the *crise de conscience*, the 'crisis of conscience' and the *prise de conscience*, 'consciousness-raising', which were starting to be confused; then the *crise de confiance*, the 'confidence crisis' conveniently came along, which can be lumped together with them; inevitably, the *prise de confiance*, 'confidence-raising', is nowadays making an appearance, the meaning of which really can't be discerned, and which will be made to fit, for that very reason, every occasion.

Consensus. Always weak. Rail against.

Consumerism. Med. for *compulsive consumption*, in other words 'binge-shopping [fièvre acheteuse]'. In that case, Ralph Nader must be a fashion victim. As a result, we're lacking a simple word to designate the organised defence of consumers.

Convalescence. 'After a month, he duly returned home; he is still very well for his age: he hasn't lost a wrinkle, and proudly bears the remains of his baldness.'

Conviction. Always intimate.

Conviviality. See *Proximity.*

Cornelian. Said of a distressing choice between two equally painful decisions; canonical example: *To be or not to be.*

Côté/Side. Nowadays everyone proclaims their *this side,* their *that side,* and ultimately boasts of being a myriagon; but I find this truly unassessable [incotable] utterance more peculiar: 'It's my Janus side.'

Cousin (female). Always little.

Cow-boy. Med. for *sheriff*: 'The Americans increasingly take themselves to be the world's cow-boys.' It appears that one no longer watches (one no longer makes) enough Westerns.

Crash. Med. for [the French] *krach*: *'La bourse n'est pas à l'abri d'un nouveau crash.',* 'The stock market isn't immune to a new crash.' It is equally recommended to confuse it with *clash.* All onomato-poeias tend to coalesce, even in English. But I see that, here, we're beginning to say *scratch,* which sounds more vigorous. This one is an imaginary Anglicism, for the English word it believes itself to be importing is *scratch,* which has many uses, including *from scratch,* which means (starting) 'from nought'. When there is an air disaster, there's no dearth of witnesses stating: 'I could clearly see that it was going to *se scratcher'*, which makes for an unintended litotes, since *to scratch* means [in French] rather 'érafler'.

Crime. Med. for *murder*: 'He eventually confessed to his mother-in-law's crime.'

Criminalité/Crime. Always serious.

Crossing. Always criss.

Debate. Ever broader.

Débit/Delivery. Always high-speed. I'm not so much thinking of the technical transmission capacity of data-processing 'channels' as of the way in which media speakers are accelerating their own vocal delivery, as though they were increasingly short of time and had to 'compress' their messages accordingly. We know roughly by how much the average size (height) of human beings has increased since Cro-Magnon, and doubtless too their average waist size (girth), but I know of no investigation concerning the fact, for me obvious, that the average rapidity of their speech is ever-increasing, for instance among radio and television 'news' presenters, as though they were obliged to compensate for the poverty of the information by the speed of its transmission. Said compression is accomplished moreover less by agility of articulation than by the omission of a syllable here and there. That *inéligibilité*, '*ineligibility*' should have become, almost universally, *inégibilité*, '*inegibility*', or *Le président de la République*, '*The President of the Republic*', *Le présent de la Réplique*, '*The Present of the Replic*', is merely a commonplace, and quite comprehensible, case of what the phoneticians call a haplology (in the strict sense: the suppression of one of two identical syllables, as one would say *haplogy*). But some are capable of far superior performances, such as rolling *President of the Republic* into a single syllable (*Pric*; I'm not pretending that this title always deserves better). Perhaps we should also blame the scrolling speed of a poorly adjusted teleprompter that they must catch up with at any cost. It is also, no doubt, to the accursed prompter, now lagging behind, that should be credited the lowerings of voice that seem to place a full stop in mid-sentence, for instance: 'This morning, at the close of the Cabinet meeting.' The prompter had frozen on this line, and the presenter, non-contrarian, judged that the sentence stopped there. But the faulty machine starts up again, and we hear this 'new' sentence: 'The government's spokesperson made no declaration.' (Voice lowered anew, syntactically justified this time.). It also often happens that the initially poorly prompted presenter, I mean one deceived by the prompter, feels an untimely mistrust, and avoids lowering their voice at the actual end of the following sentence. The 'hazards of live broadcasting' are then invoked. The double full stop, if one may so call it, has moreover become, all prompting left aside, somehow indicative of the finale (Over to you, studio): 'After the long holidays by the sea, today it's the start (full stop; silence). Of the school year.'

Debrief. Med. for *brief*: 'Prior to the operation, the participants were thoroughly debriefed.'

Décade/Ten days. Med. for *décennie*, '*decade*': 'This elderly man is beginning his ninth *décade*.' That makes him barely three months old.

Déception/Disappointment. When a sportsman or woman screws up, it's a failure. When a *French* sportsman or woman fails, it's a disappointment.

Decimate. Med. for *massacre*: 'The inhabitants of this village were all decimated to the last man.'

Décolleté/Neckline. Always plunging.

Decorum. Med. for *decor*: 'Hard discount stores display a very sober decorum.'

Dédicacer/Sign. Med. for *dédier*, '*dedicate*': 'Beethoven had envisaged signing his *Third Symphony* for Bonaparte.'

Dedicate. No longer say 'I devote …', but 'I dedicate all my efforts to this noble task'.

Défaillance/Failure. Always technical.

Defeat. Always stinging.

Deficit. Always yawning.

Défunt/Deceased. Always say: 'We're missing him already'; besides, we are missing him already.

Delinquency. Always minor.

Delusion. Always logical.

Denial. Always sharp. Remember though that two denials are worth a confirmation, and conversely; but the converse isn't that a confirmation is worth two denials, but that two confirmations are worth a denial.

Dénoter/Denote. Med. for *détonner*, '*jar*': 'This initiative denotes a bit in the current circumstances.' The vogue for this malapropism is perhaps related to the success of a discipline (logic or semiology) from which one will have retained nothing else.

Départements. I find somewhat ridiculous the obsession with renaming certain *départements* on the pretext that there was something derogatory about their original name. I thus continue to say *Seine-Inférieure, Loire-Inférieure, Basses [Lower]-Alpes, Basses [Lower]-Pyrénées, Côtes-du-Nord*, and I admire the *Bas [Lower]-Rhin* for not having minded remaining low, and the *Nord* for remaining *North*. Corsica's case is caricatural: when they felt obliged to split in two this *département* turned 'région', *Haute [Upper]-Corse* would have logically entailed *Basse [Lower]-Corse*, which would have caused local pride to suffer; so let's go for *Corse-du-Sud [Corsica-of-the-South]*, but there could be no question of opposing to it a *Corse-du-Nord [Corsica-of-the-North]*; hence the odd couple: *Haute-Corse – Corse-du-Sud*. Yet I don't believe that Upper Corsica is higher than Southern Corsica, except upon a map hung on the wall, which renders the retention of the opposition *Haut-Rhin – Bas-Rhin* obscure to school children.

Derivations. A Minister of the Interior still at large was once determined to 'terrorise the terrorists'. I quite like these etymologically derived slogans. I propose further to nationalise the nationalists, naturalise the naturalists, pacify the pacifists, *bouder* [shun] the Buddhists, *fâcher* [anger] the Fascists, integrate the integrists, essay the essayists, intern the internauts, *licencier* [fire] the licentious, insult the insulars, *emballer* [wrap] the handball players [les handballeuses], harangue the *harangères* [fishwives], *papoter* [natter with] the papacy, *entarter* [throw a pie at] the Antarctic, *faire ami-ami* [make friends] in Miami, *labelliser* [label] the *belle* Ysé,[286] put the kulaks in the Gulag (it's been done), and ensure, as soon as possible, *l'égal accès aux galaxies* [equal access to the galaxies].

Dernier/Last. When a great man 'disappears', we feel a need to crown him forthwith the 'last' of his species, as though this proclaimed ultimacy inspired, far more than his intrinsic merits, a necrological fervour to which the penultimate or the antepenultimate were apparently not entitled. In fact, they were indeed

---

[286] An allusion to the character in Paul Claudel's *Partage de Midi* (*Break of Noon*) (1906).

entitled to it, each in their turn already crowned 'the last'; only, once the presumed last has departed, the next to leave will be the next last – electively: of the dinosaurs, of the Mohicans, of the 'godfathers', or in more gratifying terms, of the 'giants'. Fortunately for the supplicants, nothing is more arbitrary than the determination of species. Just as you are always, in your lifetime, the 'best' of your generation within your speciality (you just have to define the latter, if not the former, sufficiently restrictively), you're always certain to be, upon leaving, the last to turn out the lights before closing its door. And since the last of one can be seen more easily than the first of another, the forest of glory always has more trees falling than growing, which gives me a rather depressing idea of it. A sound management of numbers ought therefore to oblige us always to accompany the homage to the last of yesterday's giants with a greeting of the first of tomorrow's, taking inspiration from the visionary town hall employee to whom General Hugo had just declared the birth of his son. 'Name? – Hugo. First name? – Victor. – Victor Hugo? *(he rises:)* Ah, my General, congratulations!'

Désordre/Mess. Always unholy.

Désormais/Henceforth. (Outdated) newspaper 'headline': 'There are henceforth six billion of us'; this slight impropriety calls to mind that of another injudicious fellow who'd ask at every turn: 'What's the time henceforth?' But would to Heaven that there were *henceforth* six billion of 'us', with a guarantee never to surpass this already overwhelming figure. In fairness to the headline editor, to whom we owe many others, it must be admitted that, the day when there are seven billion of 'us' (without me) – which *henceforth* shouldn't take long (unless …) – there'll still (also) be six billion of us: whoever can do more can do less. It's this venerable principle that allows any elderly person to be, *a fortiori*, 25 years old, any giant to be, incidentally, one metre 50 centimetres tall, Falstaff to weigh, for example, 60 kilos, and each and every one still to say, at any age whatsoever, '*Depuis que je suis tout petit* … [Ever since I was very little[287]]'.

---

[287] A literal translation of the French would be the agrammatical but temporally apposite 'Ever since I am very little'.

Despotism. Always enlightened (initially).

Detail. Always juicy.

Determination. Always unwavering.

Determined. Med. for *resolute*; one never knows in relation to what; generally paired with *serene*: 'I am serene and determined.'

Detriment. Crasis of *detritus* and, presumably, *excrement*: 'The streets were strewn with detriments.'

Diagnostic. Med. for *pronostic*, '*prognosis*': 'Her condition is stable, but the doctors are reserving their diagnosis.' I assume that this substitution stems from the idea that the common use of *pronostic* is reserved for horseracing and pre-electoral opinion polls, and that medicine requires a nobler term, consequently entrusted with indiscriminately naming both acts, supposed to have gradually become just one (I do realise that this is sometimes the case).

Dilemna. Med. for *dilemma*. Always cruel.

Diplôme/Certificate. Always precious.

Discuss. Med. for *talk*: 'Prior to making love [or even afterwards], it is seemly to discuss things a little.' Not too much. In civilian life (I mean: all feelings left aside), beyond a certain hour and a certain amount of alcohol in the bloodstream, say rather 'set the world to rights'.

Dissipate. Med. for *disperse*: The one doesn't always exclude the other: 'The procession eventually dissipated on Place de la Bastille.'

Distinguo. Always subtle.

Docufiction. Broadcast nightmare.

Donc/So. This coordinating conjunction ('*Mais où est donc* ...[288] [*So where is* ...]') has become a catch-all expletive term, awaiting a continuation that generally doesn't arrive, for the relation of cause and effect doesn't always function as one would wish. The sentence thus often ends with a purposeless '*donc*', often

---

[288] The beginning of the mnemonic for the teaching of the French coordinating conjunctions (*mais où e[s]t donc ornicar*, 'but where and so yet nor for').

prolonged as a *donque* ... . If you care about the logical conduct of your discourse, you'll conclude peremptorily: '*Donc, voilà*', 'So, there we are.'

Doublet. Fact of joining two synonymous words whose stammer, ever since Cicero, is supposed mutually to enhance their meaning; the most active in the media nowadays are *morality and ethics, science and knowledge, mondialisation and globalisation.* Nobody can really see where the semantic nuance lies, and for a very good reason (there is very often merely a dual linguistic origin: Latin and Greek, Latin and English), but the precautionary principle forbids you to sunder that which media-language has united, lest you should miss out an entirely imaginary difference, and deprive yourself of some always welcome padding when improvising, in speech or in writing. Yet a courageous politician braved this prohibition by risking the antithesis: 'My position isn't moral, but ethical.' The stunned listener took it as read and refrained from requesting any explanation. The explanation came on another day, in the following form: 'It's a question of morality in the noble sense of the term, that's to say of ethics.' We can see here the dawning of a wholly ideological distinction: morality isn't good (it's *bourgeois*); ethics is better: it's noble, vaguely scientific and almost 'deontological'.

Drastic. Med. for *draconian*: 'The minister proposed a drastic savings plan.'

Eau du bain/Bathwater. We're always advised against throwing the baby out with it, but we're never told with what else.

Échec/Failure. Always resounding.

Écorché/Flayed. Always alive.

Écouter/Listen to. Opposed to *entendre*, '*hear*': 'We were listened to, but we weren't heard.'

Écoutez/Listen. Med. for *open quotation marks*: 'He said: listen, it's already five o'clock' means simply: 'He said to me: "It's already five o'clock."' Nothing has yet been found [in French] to mark the end of reported speech. 'Stop listening' would be somewhat clumsy, and without any citational plausibility. The English pair *quote* ... *unquote* is perfect, but it's English, and I've given up advocating for its literal translation in these circumstances: *citation ... fin de citation*. As for the gesture of forming finger quotation marks on either side of your head, it's reserved for learned, or at least formal, usage, preferably to express a distancing from what is being said, like italics in Stendhal.

Écrits/Writings. Always minor (see *Oral*).

Effect. Always perverse.

Efficiency. Always formidable.

Effort. Always superhuman.

Égayer/Liven up. Med. for *égailler*, '*scatter*'. The one doesn't always exclude the other: 'The procession eventually livened up on Place de la Bastille.'

Égérie/Muse. An influential woman within a masculine group: Mme. Roland[289] was the Girondins' muse. A supercharged muse is a *pasionaria*.

Elections. Med. for *election*. No longer say 'The next presidential election ...', but 'The next presidential elections will take place in two years' time', as though several presidents were being elected – which would simplify the situation. One can even call 'elections' a mere referendum.

Electron. Always free.

Elucidate. Med. for *elude*: 'The minister elucidated all of the MP's questions' (there is occasionally some merit in this).

Éminence. Always *grise*, especially in publishing. Never mention Jean Paulhan without describing him as the '*éminence grise* of French literature', that's to say of the *NRF*,[290] at the time when those two notions were interchangeable. It's true that one wouldn't really know what else to say about him.

Emotion. Always intact. It's the supreme value, and the real fuel of the media engine: 'Stade 2: 30 years of emotion'; 'TSF: All

[289] Marie-Jeanne 'Manon' Roland de la Patière (1754–1793), French revolutionary and writer.
[290] *La Nouvelle Revue Française* (*The New French Review*), a literary journal directed by Jean Paulhan from 1925 to 1940.

Bardadrac

the jazz, all the emotions'; 'AOL: Your emotions first.'[291] Induce it, if necessary, with an 'I can really feel your emotion'. Nobody will dare reply 'Well I can't'.

Encalaminé/Sooted up. Med. for *encalminé*, '*becalmed*': 'The single-handed yachtsman's sailing boat has been sooted up for several days.'

Entartrer/Cover in tartar. Med. for *entarter*, '*throw a custard pie at*'. But the one doesn't exclude the other.

Entendement/Comprehension. Soon surpassed.

Entendre/Hear. Opposed to *listen to*: 'We were heard, but we weren't listened to.' 'We were listened to, but we weren't heard.' Public communication is based upon what in physics is called an uncertainty relation: you can never be at once listened to and heard (but you may very well be neither the one nor the other).

Entente/Agreement. Sometimes unlawful, but always cordial.

Entériner/Endorse. Med. for *enterrer*, '*bury*'. 'The government has created a commission charged, in fact, with endorsing this embarrassing project.'

Enthusiasm. Always infectious.

Environment. Don't say 'As a child, he suffered greatly from the harshness of his family circle', but '… of his environment'. The one, moreover, does not exclude the other.

Eponym. Med. for *homonym*: 'Carmen, the heroine of the eponymous opera' (it is evidently Carmen, the title role, who is the eponymous heroine of this opera, to which she *gives* her name). This counter-usage is to this day one of the finest jewels of medialectal elegance. You have to see the cheerful expression of the presenter who has just thereby distinguished himself: he can't get over being so learned.

Épopée/Epic. Med. for *odyssée*, '*odyssey*': 'The epic journey of the liner whose engine failed fortunately ended without any victims.' I understood on that day that not only is *The Odyssey*

---

[291] Stade 2 is a French television programme; TSF and AOL are French radio stations.

an epic (which very many critics, and even readers, may doubt) among others, but that it was the epic *par excellence*, hence the synonymy. This drift perhaps owes something to *A Space Odyssey* [*L'Odyssée de l'espace*], a perfectly correct title, but which through a play on words (tempting, I admit) gave rise to *A Species Odyssey* [*Odyssée de l'espèce*] which, in turn, accredits the idea that the history of the human species is a long navigation. What flies out of the window, in all of this, is *The Iliad*, that's to say the veritable epic.

Époque/Era. Always great; just one was *belle*, but we no longer know which.

Épouse/Wife. Always perfect.

Épreuve/Test. Always severe.

Équilibre/Balance. Always precarious.

Équipe/Team. Always tight-knit.

Erotomania. Med. for *sexual obsession*. Whereby one no longer knows how to name the other affection, so well illustrated by the 'fantasies' of Bélise,[292] and which my excellent colleague Petit Robert defines correctly as the 'delusion of being loved'.

Error. Always human.

Érudition/Learning. Med. for *culture*. 'He doesn't look it, but he is learned: he's read Proust.'

Escarpé/Craggy. Med. for (presumably) *étroit*, *'narrow'*: 'The craggy streets of the Medina of Marrakesh' (as flat as a pavement).

Espérance de vie/Life expectancy. Tends to increase with the average age, if it isn't the other way round.

Étalonner/Calibrate. Med. for *étaler*, *'stagger'*: 'Parents' associations have spoken in favour of the calibration of the school holidays.'

Étape/Stage. Always mythical.

---

[292] A character in Molière's *Les Femmes savantes* (*The Learned Ladies*) (1672).

Été/Summer. Always deadly.[293]

Étiquettes/Labels. It is said that, in France, people are fond of 'labelling, of putting people into ready-made categories'. It seems to me above all that in France people are fond of saying that in France, etc.

Et/ou/And/Or. The logical value of this expression (which is also expressed as an *inclusive or*) is quite subtle, but never mind: *and/or* is simply in the process of becoming a chic medialectism for *or* quite simply, and sometimes for *and*. No longer say either 'Cheese or dessert', or 'Cheese and dessert', but, more elegantly, 'Cheese and/or dessert'. The waiter will interpret in the best interests of the establishment.

Euphemism. Med. for *litotes*: 'I'm not too keen on salsify, and that's a euphemism.'

Évident/Obvious. In a negative sentence, med. for *easy*: 'Carrying a menhir on one's back isn't obvious', or *pleasant*: 'Living at your place of work isn't always obvious.'

Expletives. There'd be no end to enumerating these rhetorical padding techniques, something like toothing-stones [pierres d'attente] used to begin or continue speaking while you figure out what you have to say, which tirelessly saturate spoken discourse (to spare the written form here), of the type 'let's say', 'so to speak', 'we'll say', 'how might I put this?', 'sort of', 'in a way', 'to some extent', etc., among which the most sincere is quite simply: 'Hang on!' I'm also really fond of the following, which I assume to be infinitely extensible, and which I shall designate with the formula 'This *x* is an *x* that is an *xy*' – so, for instance in political discourse, in order to say 'This law is bad', amplify it into: 'This law is a law that is a bad law.' But the expletive may also serve, while you feign to seek the right word, to underline and emphasise what's to come, and whose great importance the speaker can gauge in advance: 'This book is, how might I put this, a challenge to one-track thinking.' The ultimate consists in stopping as though to reflect, then continuing with a self-acquiescent 'yes': 'This book is … *yes*, a challenge, etc.'

[293] Due to heatwaves.

Explicate. Med. for *explain*: 'The defendant attempted to explicate his behaviour.'

Exuberance. Always irrational.

Face/Side. Always hidden.

Facilité/Ease. Always disconcerting.

Factor. Always human.

Faible/Weak. Med. for *strong*: 'There is a sense of dismay in the victim's village – and the word isn't too weak' (deft synthesis of 'is weak' and 'isn't too strong').

Famous. Med. for *that which has just been referred to*: 'This morning, I saw a yellow dog. This evening, on my way home, I again saw this famous yellow dog.'

Fatalism. I can only guess at the meaning of this recently heard utterance: 'Wishing to be fatalistic, he says at every turn: "Ah well, we'll pull through!"' Fatalism would thus be a form of optimism, just as being 'philosophical' is a form of resignation.

Faux/Forgery. Always crude.

Favours. Med. for *favour*: 'Through his deeds in the ministry, M. X has gained the President's favours.'

Feminine. Endangered grammatical gender: 'L'initiative qu'a pris le gouvernement[294] [The initiative that the government took].' Decline begins with declension. The only word whose feminine gender is scrupulously observed is inevitably the masculine *Mémoires*: 'Les *Mémoires* qu'il a publiées l'année dernière [The *Memoirs* that he published last year].'

Fictitious. Said of a salary received for a fictitious job.

Figure. Always emblematic.

Finalise. Med. for *conclude*.

Flegme/Phlegm. Always British.

---

[294] The grammatically correct version would be 'L'initiative qu'a pris*e* le gouvernement', the *e* reflecting the feminine gender of *une initiative*.

For/Heart. Always of hearts [Toujours intérieur[295]].

Formalities. Always cold. Rail against.

Form. Med. for *content*, or for *by way of*: 'The negotiations resulted in a communiqué in the form of a compromise'; read: *The negotiations resulted in a compromise in the form of a communiqué.* 'He gave him the finger in the form of a thank you', read: *He gave him the finger by way of a thank you.*

Fouet/Whip/Force. Always full, when striking therewith.[296] And how else might you use it?

France. Always deep.

Franglais. It is perhaps time to recall that we owe to Étiemble (at least the popularisation of) this chimera-word, designating the misuse of English words (first-degree Anglicisms), and especially (second-degree Anglicisms, or *franglicisms*) of French words used with the meaning of their English false friends – which often happens to have been that of the French, or Norman word formerly imported into the English language: to say *librairie* [bookshop] for *bibliothèque* [library] would, will perhaps one day be, if the programmed demise of the book doesn't come to oppose it, at once a Franglicism and an archaism: it's Montaigne's word. My *franglicism* (or *frangleme*), which clearly derives from it, names an occurrence of *franglais*.

Fry. Always small.

Future. Clemenceau said unkindly (but not entirely inaccurately) of Jaurès that in his speeches all the verbs were in the future tense. It's the definition of utopia. I'm more amused by the use of the future (generally of the 'immediate future' constructed with the auxiliary *to go*, as in 'I'm going to die') in the oral summary of a narrative work, as occurs in relaxed conversations, or in 'literary criticism' such as it flourishes nowadays in the media. For instance, this *digest*

---

[295] The French 'for' (from the Latin *forum*) is uniquely found in the expression 'Dans/en son for intérieur', 'In one's heart of hearts/innermost self'.
[296] 'Toujours plein, quand on en frappe': 'frapper de plein fouet' means 'to hit hard' ('to strike with a full whip').

of a novel you'll recognise:[297] 'It takes place in Verrières, a small town in the Franche-Comté; a young carpenter's son with a talent for studies *is going* to be employed as a private tutor at the home of M. de Renâl; he *is going* to fall more or in less love with Mme. Renâl, whom he *is going* to seduce by taking her hand, one evening, under the chestnut trees; he *is going* to be sent to the Besançon seminary, etc.' Or this other, purely virtual one: 'She's a Marquessa, she *is going* to leave at five o'clock.'[298] I was once reproached for this overly lapidary résumé: 'Marcel becomes a writer', which I thought subsequently to amend as 'Marcel eventually becomes a writer'. The correct, firm and definitive formula, which I'm surprised to have overlooked for so long, is thus obviously: 'Marcel *is going* to become a writer.'

Gadget. Med. for *gag*: 'When I was told that, I thought it was a gadget, but no: it was the truth.'

Galvauder/Tarnish. Med. for *galvanise*: 'With a few sentences he managed to tarnish the room.'

Gascon. Med. for *Norman*: 'I'm going to give you a *réponse de Gascon*,[299] a "Gascon answer": *p'têt'ben qu'oui, p'têt'ben qu'non*, "pr'aps yes, pr'aps no".'

Geometry. Always variable.

Gérer/Manage. Always add: 'I don't like this word.'

Gesture. Always powerful.

Global. Med. for *planetary*. This galloping Franglicism allows for some amiable euphemisms: 'réchauffement global' (*global warming*) is less disturbing than the molten planet they're concocting for us. This is because our *global* had something reassuring about it through its vague hint of approximation,

---

[297] Stendhal's *The Red and the Black* (1830).
[298] 'La marquise sortit à cinq heures, 'The Marquessa left at five o'clock', is a phrase attributed by André Breton (in the *Surrealist Manifesto*) to Paul Valéry: it exemplifies the type of traditional narrative convention shunned by both writers.
[299] In French, a *réponse de Normand* (a 'Norman answer') is a noncommittal reply.

as is still attested by the adverb *globalement*, 'on the whole': 'a report that's *globalement* positive' means something like 'a report one may consider to be basically positive, provided that one not look too closely at it'. So, as long as the warming is only *global*, there's no cause for concern: it isn't as though it were warming the entire planet, or even my village.

Golden Boy. Med. for *wonder boy*: 'Aged 20, Orson Welles was already Hollywood's golden boy.'

Gothic. As its name indicates, this style was born in Germany.

Grossièreté/Crudeness. The only way, nowadays, of escaping vulgarity.

Guillemets/Inverted commas. Med. for *brackets*. 'He fell on the floor, and, in inverted commas, it served him right.'

Habileté/Skill. Always consummate.

Hasard/Chance. 'The Constitutional Council left nothing to chance: it went as far as drawing lots for the candidates' order of appearance.'

Heil. 'Between Stalinism and Nazism, there's a difference all the same: in the URSS, they never said *Heil Stalin*.'

Himalaya. Roof of the world. A little uncomfortable with this nevertheless inevitable cliché, a journalist moderates: 'It's *somewhat* the roof of the world.'

Hommage/Homage. Always vibrant, preferably posthumous.

Homme-orchestre/One-man band. Med. for *chef d'orchestre*, '*conductor*' (generally *secret*); e.g.: 'In the wings, so and so is the one-man band of this whole affair.'

Honte/Shame. 'I'm a believer, and I'm not ashamed to hide it from myself.'

Horizon. Always unsurpassable.

Huîtres/Oysters. With the 'holidays' looming, a doctor warns of the danger posed by the opening of oysters. Advice for beginners? 'Yes: it's always better to open them *from the outside*.'

Humanitarian. Med. for *human*: 'This operation resulted in a humanitarian catastrophe.'

Humour. Always caustic.

Icon. Med. for *idol*. 'For 40 years, Johnny [Hallyday] has been an icon for young people.'

Ignorance. Always crass; it is even, nowadays, the only thing that can grammatically be so.

Image. Always branded.

Imparti/Allotted. Med. for *pressing*: 'Unfortunately, time is allotted'; or for *elapsed*: 'Your speaking time has been allotted, ask your question!'

Implosion. Med. for *explosion*: 'Following a gas leak, this decrepit building literally imploded.'

Impondérable/Imponderable. Med. for *imprévisible*, '*unforeseeable*': 'Governmental action necessarily comes up against two imponderable factors: the heat in the summer and the cold in the winter.'

Impromptu. Med. for *incongru*, '*incongruous*': 'Please excuse this perhaps impromptu detail.'

Impunément/With impunity. Med. for *inopinément*, '*inadvertently*': 'I presume that you didn't make this choice with impunity: no doubt you'd thought about it at length.'

Inanity. Med. for *inanition*: 'I wouldn't like to die of inanity'; many people, however, expose themselves to this sanction, harsh but fair.

Inaugurer/Inaugurate. Med. for *augurer*, '*augur*': 'This first encounter inaugurates badly for what's to come.'

Incontournable/Inescapable. Med. for *encombrant*, '*inconvenient*'.

Index. 'Il est montré à l'index', 'He was shown on the index': a contamination, presumably, of 'montrer du doigt', 'point the finger at' and 'mettre à l'Index', 'place on the Index'; a double punishment, in sum. After Coluche, everyone knows that the pope *met le préservatif à l'index*, 'puts condoms on [with] the index [finger]'.

Individual. Always suspect.

Industry. Always guilty.

Inexpugnable/Impregnable. Med. for *inexpiable*: 'An impregnable hatred.'

In fine. Med. for *finally*, *ultimately*. If you hear *in faïne*, understand that your interlocutor has taken this expression to be a chic Anglicism, like the man who pronounced *sine die* as *saïne daïne*. 'Adolescents' are fond of peppering their speech with French words pronounced in the English way: *no souçaï* [*pas de souci/ no worries*].

Inné/Nature. Always on the Right.

Instar/Like. Med. for *inverse*, *'unlike'*: 'Like Proust, I never went to bed early.' Proust did three things in his life: replied to a questionnaire, ate little madeleines, went to bed early in a cork-lined room.

Insuffisance/Inadequacy. Always notorious.

Insults. It is, as is well known, forbidden to insult the future. In the meantime, I propose that one cease to insult the past.

Interview (littéraire)/(Literary) Interview. Each of them refers to one preceding it ('You once said …'), so much so that you wonder what questions might actually have been asked in the first, which perhaps, as Giraudoux said of the first literary work, never occurred. Once the cliché has been established, it slips seamlessly, not only from one interview (and from one review) to another, but from one book to another. Journalists (homage paid, therefore, to the exceptions) doubtless have entirely collegial reasons to read each other more than they read the books about which they talk, but it seems to me that this incestuous practice ought to serve them not to cultivate, but on the contrary to *avoid* repetition and copy/pasting: 'Everyone is saying *p*, perhaps I shall try, for a change, to say *q*.' My proposal doubtless disregards what in my childhood was called the 'law of the least effort', and the irresistible charm of the standardised orthodoxy. When the subject of an interview is a novel, under no circumstances must one fail to ask these two questions: 'What is the part of autobiography here?' and 'Your writing is already very cinematographic: are you thinking of deriving a screenplay from it?' To the first, the right answer is: 'One is bound to put a little of oneself into each of one's characters', and to the second: 'I haven't thought about it at all, but I await a reply from Spielberg.'

Inventaire/Inventory. Always 'in the manner of Prévert'.[300]

Inventorier/To inventory. A wild crasis, I imagine, of *invent* and *innovate*: 'Picasso inventoried everything in modern painting.'

Invest. In the military medialect, apropos of a city, sometimes means *surround*, *besiege*, sometimes *take possession of*. For those affected, the difference isn't slight, but those affected [les intéressés] are seldom interesting, and in any event one seldom fails, these days, to invest oneself – one never really knows what in.

Isolation. Always splendid.

Jardin/Garden. Always secret.

Je ne sais quel .../Goodness knows what ... Expression of denial used to reject something embarrassingly obvious. E.g.: 'There's no question of exerting goodness knows what pressure ...', for 'I know perfectly well what pressure I wish to exert, but I do not want it to be said.'

Jeunes/Young people. There are two kinds: the young properly so-called, and the not so young, who were formerly old.

Kafkaesque. Med. for *Ubuesque*.[301]

Label. Always prestigious.

Laïus/Boring speech. Father of Oedipus, and vice versa.

Lapidaire/Terse. Med. for *laconic*: 'Asked about this point, the government's spokesperson remained terse.'

---

[300] See Jacques Prévert's poem 'Inventaire', in *Paroles* (1946).
[301] From the grotesque protagonist in Alfred Jarry's *Ubu roi* (*Ubu the King*) (1896).

Lapsus. Always revealing; to be emphasised all the more strongly when you do not know what it reveals.

Légèreté/Lightness. Always unbearable.

Lequel, laquelle …/Which … Med. for *qui*, '*who*'. '*Auquel*' for *à qui*, 'to whom': 'The Prime Minister met the President, to which he handed in his resignation.' I await the emergence of *dont auquel*, '*whom to which*', which we once mocked as an imaginary solecism.

Liberalism. Always unbridled, always ultra. Rail against, or try to sweeten it with soft drugs such as: *fair trade, sustainable development, solidarity economy, cooperative banking, renewable energies,* or again *ethical funds.*

Libertine. Thwarted virgin.

Lieder. Med. for lied: '*The Erlking* is Schubert's most beautiful lieder.'

Liesse/Jubilation. Always popular.

Limier/Sleuth. Always super.

Lingouiste.[302] Med. for *linguiste*, '*linguist*'. I'm assured that this pronunciation comes from Belgium, but for some reason I find that Belgium is a convenient scapegoat.

Livrer/Deliver. Med. for *give*, or *express*: 'The minister did not wish to deliver his opinion upon this matter.'

-logy. This suffix was originally meant to name a science, or more modestly a study, or more modestly still (and more often) a discourse, whose object is designated by the preceding radical: *theology* is the study of religious questions, *teratology* is that of anomalies and monstrous formations (a linguistic anomaly, in passing: *philology* unfortunately isn't the science of love – I'd have noticed – but simply the love and, through a shift in meaning, the study of language, as *philosophy* is the love and, through a shift in meaning, the study of wisdom, and not the wisdom of studying, and even less the wisdom of love). As a result of the prevailing pretentiousness, it finds itself nowadays at the service

---

[302] Evokes 'langouste', 'crayfish'.

of the most otiose derivations, like a sort of expletive appendix with connotations of learnedness. We have long been familiar with the passage from '*psychology*: science of the psyche' to '*psychology*: psyche', from '*sociology*: science of society' to '*sociology*: social composition', or from '*technology*: science of techniques' to '*technology*: techniques'. At the same time, *demography* has come to designate the evolution of a population (a 'galloping demography' isn't a science-of-the-population that is progressing rapidly), and *geography* the physical state of a region (a 'difficult geography' is merely a terrain unconducive to military operations, like the mountains in Afghanistan). *Methodology* for 'method' has made a good start, and shall not be halted (a minister even announced his intention to proceed 'in a methodological manner'), and I heard recently that the removal of a few level crossings would reduce the *accidentology* of a given main road.

Loi/Law. Always wicked.

Louvre. Greatest museum in the world.

Machiavellian. Med. for *masochistic*, presumably: 'All the same, company directors aren't Machiavellian enough to lay off, just for the pleasure of it, an employee with whom they're completely satisfied.'

Machin/Thing. Always old.

Madeleine. Always little.

Madrigal/Gallant remark. A television presenter co-presenting with an attractive colleague believes he owes it to his own public image to offer her from time to time a more or less emphatic gallant remark. The colleague, modestly lowering her eyes upon her pretty low-cut neckline, tolerates this slightly protective come-on, a one-way flourish [marivaudage[303]] performed for the gallery.

Maguenat. Med. for *magnat*, '*magnate*', no doubt by contamination with the earth's *magma*; but I've also heard Robert Maxwell described as a newspaper *maniac*. It's true that a magnate is often a maniac: see Howard Hughes.

---

[303] Mannered, precious speech, supposedly in the style of playwright and novelist Pierre de Marivaux (1688–1763).

Main/Hand. A young actress, speaking of an old producer: 'He was the first to let me get my hand in the door.'

Majority. Seldom qualified.

Maladresse/Clumsiness. Always signal.

Mangrove. Obligatory appearance on the programme *Thalassa*, 'magazine of the sea' and its environs. The typical tree of these marine marshlands, the mangrove [palétuvier], owes its glory to a song by Albert Willemetz[304] which, from metathesis to metathesis, resulted in the irresistible invitation: 'Let's love each other under the sink [sous l'évier].'

Marais/Marsh. Type of *marécage*, 'swamp'.

Marécage/Swamp. Type of *marais*, 'marsh'.

Margin. Always narrow.

Marketing. Med. for *commercial practice in general*. This abusive synecdoche, a perverted Anglicism, doesn't thrill the specialists of the thing, who can see their specific activity being conflated with a few too many others. One reads, among other things, that 'literature has become a veritable *marketing*'. If we remember that *marketing* is in the literal sense the study of the market, and an ensemble of efforts to adjust one's offer to this market's acknowledged demand, it can perhaps be seen that what we purport to condemn under this term almost never responds to its definition: only the industrially formatted collections and series of the Harlequin or SAS[305] type are adjusted to a market by respecting the rules of a generic formula called a 'bible'. Everything else meant by the word *marketing* is of a different order, although one no less vulgar: a book appears, or is about to appear, and the editorial and media hullabaloo endeavours after the event, or just before the event, to 'sell' it by dint of polemics, scandals, 'revelations', and what have you. Yet, most of the time, neither the 'launch' campaign, nor even less the writing of the book itself, have been preceded by a genuine study of the

---

[304] 'Sous les palétuviers', 'Under the Mangroves' (1934).

[305] Harlequin is a romance and 'women's fiction' publisher, founded in Winnipeg, Canada, in 1949; SAS is the protagonist of a series of 200 spy novels (1965–2013) authored, among others, by Gérard de Villiers (1929–2013).

market, among other things because the public isn't a market: in literature as more generally in art, it is the work that *creates* a public which it therefore hasn't been able to 'study'. The snowball effect of 'word to mouth' often operates more effectively, and ever unpredictably, outside of any editorial effort. The professionals know this, and express it in simpler terms: publishing is not an exact science. The only preliminary datum is that success – immediate or deferred, and, at the outset, often fortuitous – will certainly entail success, hence the irrefutable advertising slogan: 'Buy this book: it already features on all the best-sellers lists.' But advertising, even when dishonest, isn't marketing, and this herd effect [effet Panurge] isn't a formula: it tells you neither when nor how to throw the first sheep.[306]

Mat/Dull. Med. for *dark*; consequently, we no longer know how to name the opposite of *shiny*.

Match. This one was hard-fought: a minute after the kick-off, the score was already 0–0.

Media. The most unfortunate thing about this 'service' industry is perhaps the shadow it casts upon philosophically necessary notions like *mediation* or *mediatise*, irreparably relieved of their meaning, and which we don't know how to replace. We shall soon come to think that there is no mediation other than that of the 'media', and this will as a result be true.

Mélanger/Mix. Med. for *confuse*: 'One mustn't mix speed with haste.' The trouble with this substitution is that it conceals behind a generally benign error (mixture) the considerably graver error of confusion. There's no great harm (although …) in mixing wine and water, but it may be dangerous to confuse them.

Melting-pot. Med. for *méli-mélo*, '*mish-mash*', *horrible mélange*, '*horrible mixture*', occasionally too for *medley*, or *compilation*. It's the chic version of my grandmother's *pot-pourri*.

Méritoire/Praiseworthy. Med. for *mérité*, '*deserved*'. 'The President paid his predecessor a praiseworthy homage.' The one

---

[306] The 'Paunurge effect' – 'herd or bandwagon effect' – derives its name from an episode in François Rabelais' *Gargantua* (1534): Panurge acquires a sheep and throws it into the water, and the other sheep blindly follow it there.

doesn't exclude the other, for it is often praiseworthy to pay an homage, especially one that is deserved.

Merveille/Wonder. Always little, or maybe the eighth of the world. One generally forgets what the seven others are, like the names of Snow White's seven dwarves.

Message. Always powerful.

Mesure/Extent. 'Dans la mesure où …', 'To the extent that …', med. for *because, since, for, indeed* … : 'I shan't be able to come tomorrow, to the extent that I've broken my leg.' A well-known trade-unionist, virtuoso of the social monologue and sometime stylist, once made it even worse by substituting it for *dans la limite*, 'within the limits': 'I don't approve of this action, within the limits that I deem it counterproductive.'

Migouel. Med. for *Miguel*.

Militant. Approved-of activist.

Minimiser/Understate. Med. for *minorer*, *'reduce'*: 'I drive more slowly in order to understate my fuel consumption.' For greater safety, it is recommended to 'understate' anything undesirable 'to the max'.

Minorer/Reduce. Med. for *minimiser*, *'understate'*: 'In his speech, the boss reduced the number of lay-offs entailed by the sale of his factory.'

Minority. Always active. Rail against.

Miss. I still await the election of a Miss Vatican. At the end of a laborious conclave, white smoke would emerge from the famous stove-pipe, and an exhausted cardinal would come to proclaim, in official Latin: *Habemus missam* – or perhaps simply: *Ite, missa est.*

Mode/Fad. Always passing.

Mohican. Always last.

Moment. Always privileged.

Monstre/Star. Always super.

Morbid. Med. for *sordid*: 'The boss demonstrates morbid greed.'

Morosité/Gloom. Always with doom.

Mozart. A journalist to a musician: 'How can you tell a good Mozart from a bad one?' The musician remained speechless. The right answer was: how can you tell that a question is idiotic?

Nader (Ralph). Med. for *Adair (Red)*: 'I won't be the Ralph Nader who extinguishes that fire.'

Narratology. Pernicious pseudo-science, its jargon put a whole generation of illiterates off literature. Dissects merely the 'corpses of narratives' (just as well).

Nationalise. Med. for *naturalise*: 'He was born Mexican, but was nationalised in 1964.' I don't know if it's now a question of privatising him.

Necessity. Always imperious.

Nécro/Obit. Being unable to read one's obituary in the newspaper is one of the advantages of being dead, or unknown – or better, both. Fortunately, said Rameau's nephew, 'the dead hear not the bells ring.'

Neophyte. Med. for *beginner* or *apprentice* ('After her fiftieth hold-up, Julot the Sardine was no longer a neophyte'), or for *ignoramus, novice, rookie, uninitiated, uninformed about the subject*: 'Excuse this neophyte's question …', that's to say in short: for *layman*.

Nominalism. Med. to designate the belief in the reality of that to which words refer (namely, the exact opposite of what it denotes philosophically): 'Let's not push nominalism to the point of believing that it suffices to speak of growth for it to be real.'

Norman. Med. for *Gascon*: 'I don't wish to make you a Norman promise.'[307]

Norme (hors)/Unusual. Med. for *hors pair*, *'peerless'*: 'You've got an unusual assistant there.' I can, however, picture one case where this use might be pertinent: in *Monkey Business* by Howard

---

[307] In French, a *promesse de Gascon*, a 'Gascon promise', signifies a vain or idle promise (in the XVIth century, Gascon soldiers are said to have boasted of their military prowess).

Bardadrac

Hawks, an old libidinous boss (Charles Coburn), fondly contemplating the swaying rump of his assistant (Marilyn Monroe), explains to his guest (Cary Grant): 'Anybody can type.'

Nostalgia. Guilty feeling. Always forbid it yourself.

Notoire/Notorious. Med. for *notable*: 'Her state of health didn't exhibit any notorious improvement.'

Noyau/Core. Always hard.

Nuage/Cloud. Always small, when you're above; always large, when you're beneath.

Obligation. Always urgent.

Obsolète/Obsolete. Med. for *désuet*, *'outdated'*: 'This man's elegance is somewhat obsolete.'

Œuvrette/Minor work. When you excel therein, why pose as a missionary?

Ogive. Gothic arch.

Ombilical/Umbilical. Med. for *sanitaire*: 'The government is attempting to surround this affair with a *cordon ombilique*, "an umbilical cord".'

Opportunist. Med. (sport) for *quick-thinking*.

Opposition/Confrontation. Always sterile.

Oral. Always final.[308]

Pamphlet. Always vitriolic.

Pan/Section. Always whole, especially when it collapses.

Panacea. Nobody knows what it is, but it's known no longer to be universal, and that moreover *nothing* is one; '200 euros per month is no panacea': *no fortune*, presumably, and in truth it's neither the one nor the other. In fact, the only treatment that is *almost* a panacea is no doubt the placebo.

Pandora. Certain politicians less cultivated than others (there are some) seem to believe that Pandora was *in* her box: 'If you open a Pandora's box, don't be surprised to see Pandora emerge

[308] 'Toujours grand': 'un grand oral' is a 'final oral exam'; it can also signify a 'parliamentary hearing'.

from it.' It would surprise me all the less, personally, since the expression 'Pandora's box' referred, in my childhood, to the *gendarmerie* located on Rue du Château, along the way that led to the train station, and those Pandoras just couldn't wait to emerge therefrom.

Panorama/Overview. Always comprehensive.

Papyrus. On paper: 'It's a papyric victory.'

Paradis/Heaven. Always a slice of.

Parallel. Med. for *symmetrical*: 'The parallel attacks from the left and the right converge upon the government's plan.'

Pardon. Med. for *act of asking to be pardoned*: 'The pope's pardon to the victims of the Inquisition.' That's really nice of him. Said victims are unfortunately no longer in a fit state to grant that particular pardon.

Parenthèses/Brackets. Med. for *inverted commas*: 'This lawyer is what you'd call, in brackets, a hotshot.'

Pari/Bet. Always risky.

Paris. Most beautiful city in the world.

Parler/Talk. Always straight.

Parleur/Talker. Always smooth.

Parodie/Parody. Med. for *pastiche*: 'Proust wrote a marvellous parody of Balzac.'

Participle. Is tending [in French] progressively to oust the relative proposition: no longer say *'l'homme qui rit,* "the man who is laughing"', but *'l'homme riant,* "the laughing man"'. One may in this way replace any final subordinate proposition (previously introduced with *pour, afin de, en sorte de …'in order to, so as to, so that …'*) with a participial (?) phrase introduced by the elegant clause *l'idée étant que, 'the idea being that'*, where *idée* means, by Franglicism, *intention ('That's the idea')*: 'The *carte Vitale*[309] will be filled out upon each medical visit or intervention, the idea being to gather all the useful information.' But true media chic consists

[309] Health insurance card.

in establishing the participial as a pseudo-independent clause, by placing before it a full stop: 'The *carte Vitale* will be filled out upon each medical visit or intervention. The idea being, etc.'

Pastiche. Med. for *parody*: '*La Belle Hélène* is an amiable pastiche of *The Iliad.*' Too amiable, perhaps, for a pastiche.

Pavaner/Swagger. Med. for *pavoiser*, '*show off*': 'There's really nothing to swagger about.'

Pays/Country. Politically, a 'country' is something like a nation: France is a 'country', China too. But our administration has recently given this name to a new territorial subdivision, which is obviously to be confused neither with the *région*, nor with the *département*, nor with the *arrondissement*, nor with the *canton*, nor with the *commune*, nor with the community of *communes*, nor with the flabby 'conglomeration'. The Basque country, presumably, is a very old example of this (but, out of misplaced pride, it now aspires to the dubious dignity of a '*département* in its own right'), and La Puisaye, which moreover straddles two *départements*, would deserve this title – if it doesn't already have it (I really ought to know). But this uncertain innovation might equally pass away of its own accord; there would remain at least the refreshing appellation 'vin de pays', which is hardly binding.

The derisive expression '*ce pays*' as a way of referring to France dates back, I think, to the beginning of the sixties. The distinction between the 'legal country' and the 'real country' is evidently older: I think I've seen it attributed to the 'Doctrinaire' Royer-Collard,[310] herald of the 'censitary monarchy'. I'm not sure what value he granted it, but its resurrection by Charles Maurras[311] at the beginning of the twentieth century was clearly that of a rejection of representative democracy: the 'real' country is the one they wish to seduce in order to set it against the 'legal' country. The use of this opposition is the very sure sign of a right- or left-wing demagogy, for a while called an 'appeal to the people'. Another marker with the same meaning is the pejorative use of

[310] Pierre Paul Royer-Collard (1763–1845), French statesman and philosopher.
[311] French author, politician, poet and critic (1868–1952), principal philosopher of *Action Française*, a monarchist, anti-parliamentarian, counter-revolutionary political movement.

the word 'elite' – preferably in the plural: the elite can be more or less respectable, but *the elites* are always wrong.

Pensée/Thinking. That of others is always one-track.

Pérenne/Enduring. Med. for *sustainable*. But since one isn't quite sure about it, a minister proposed a measure that is 'sustainably enduring': two guarantees are worth more than one.

Performatif/Performative. Med. for *de pure forme*, '*perfunctory*': 'This speech is all the more performative for being irrelevant.' Besides the narcissistic pleasure the commentator feels in the mistaken usage of this really *classy* adjective, I suppose we must incriminate the proximity of *performance*, which suggests that a performative utterance is a kind of oratorical feat.

Perpetrate. Med. for *perpetuate*: 'We must perpetrate tradition.'

Perpetuate. Med. for *perpetrate*: 'It was here that he perpetuated his crime' (moreover a correct usage with regard to Landru's[312] stove, which saw a few such occurrences passing through it).

Perplexed. Med. for *sceptical*: 'He swore that it wasn't him, but I remain perplexed.'

Perte/Loss. Always cruel.

Peste/Plague. Correlate of cholera.

Petition. Med. for *position*: 'I shan't be swayed, for me it's a petition of principle.' I'm just waiting for a politician to *stick to his petition*.

Pharaonique/Pharaonic. Presumably by contagion with *pharamineux*, '*gigantic*', this adjective is applied to anything whatsoever, with the meaning of *enormous*: 'I received a Pharaonic bill from my plumber', 'I left the waiter a Pharaonic tip'.

Philo. Certain abbreviations, like *radio*, *bike* or *cinema*, have become so commonplace that they're no longer perceived as such. Others are (for me) still irksome, like *apero* [*aperitif*], or even more so *ado* [*adolescent*], or *intello* [*intellectual*], which congeal

---

[312] Henri Désiré Landru (1869–1922), notorious French serial killer; he allegedly used his oven to burn the remains of his victims.

into supposed social categories transitory states or very unspecific activities, which unfortunately eventually identify themselves with them. The least bearable for me is *philo* [*philosophy*], this erstwhile schoolboy but now media-friendly expression, which unfailingly reminds me of the tiny room on the first floor of the school at Pontoise, where we'd stave off the boredom of an, it must be said, insipid lesson by looking out for opportunities for revengeful puns, along the lines of: *'Je trouve Kant aride* [I find Kant arid/*Je trouve con ta ride*/I find your wrinkle stupid], *'Nietzsche est veau* [Nietzsche is a calf/*Nitchevo*/No matter], *'Que Bergson ne sorte!* [Let Bergson not leave!/*Que personne ne sorte!* Nobody leave!], *'Occupe-toi de ce Kierkegaard!* [Look after this Kierkegaard!/*Occupe-toi de ce qui te regarde!* Mind your own business!], *'Va te faire Fichte!* [*Va te faire fiche!*/You can get lost!], *'À poêle Descartes!* [Descartes to his stove!/*À poil Descartes!*/Descartes in the buff!], *'Qu'est-ce qu'Ilissus?* [What is Ilisos?/*Qu'est-ce qu'il y suce?* What is he sucking there?], or, at our favourite bookstore: *'Avez-vous des bouquins d'Hegel?* [Do you have any books by Hegel?/*Avez-vous des bouquins dégel?*/Do you have any books that are thawing?]. Thanks to the all-too-famous 'massification', this activity of the mind (I'm speaking about philosophy) has become a mere subject for dissertations, the stuff of exams, final-year tests, a pretext for grades. The baccalaureate season is conducive to this joyful exercise: from the very evening of the (as is said of a sport) 'national' examination, they ask an authorised philosopher, if possible one purporting to be anti-establishment and preferably the author of a recent book whose promotion renders his contribution gratis, how he would have 'dealt with' one or another of the 'published' subjects, and there he is improvising, a reflex acquired during his *agrégation* years, a nice little three-part spiel, thesis, antithesis, synthesis, summoning (Here, I'd quote ... There, I'd recall ...) in one Plato, in the other Kant or Leibniz, in the third, depending on the fluctuations of the market, Nietzsche, Freud, Benjamin, Wittgenstein, Deleuze or Foucault, since to philosophise is to learn how to manipulate the thought of other philosophers. It suffices to listen to these programmes *ad hoc*, with an evenly poised attention, to hear turn beneath the well-oiled discourse, like the chord pattern of a jazz standard beneath the improvised chorus, the dialectical machine with its programmed reversals on their way to a triumphant, and if possible interrogative, coda – that's to say opening, you never know, onto the next subject. I sometimes wonder what the great minds thus summarily recycled would have thought of this mediatised cramming. We have seen 'philo cafés' functioning in this mode, and on-stage improvisations at I know not what festival. From being a media star, the philosopher is thereby becoming a kind of casual worker in the seasonal spectacle. But let's be fair: Plato's dialogues, already, sometimes show us Socrates in such a role, and his whipping boys the sophists made it their stock-in-trade, and not for peanuts.

Picaresque. Med. for *picturesque*: 'Decked out as he is, this character is rather picaresque.'

Pilori/Pillory. Med. for *pilon*, '*pestle*': 'Since this book wasn't selling at all, its publisher very quickly pilloried it [le mit très vite au pilori[313]].' Pulping is indeed a kind of pillory, but it's more discreet.

Place/Room. 'Make room for': med. for 'succeeds', 'takes the place of': 'As the unfavourable polls are announced, concern makes room for hope.'

Plagiarism. Med. for *parody*, for *pastiche*, and occasionally even for *plagiarism*.

Planifier/Plan. Med. for *aplanir*, '*to iron out*': 'The two ministers endeavoured to plan their differences of opinion.'

Pleonasms. I quite like 'seismic quake', 'universal panacea', 'selective sorting', 'angry hunters', 'Brazilian samba', 'Girondins de Bordeaux',[314] 'cognitive sciences', and 'Islamic jihad'. I'd associate this with the supremely redundant gesture that makes one, for example, describe the Coliseum as 'colossal', the Pyramids as 'Pharaonic', *The Iliad* as 'Homeric', *Father Goriot* as 'Balzacian', *The Divine Comedy* as 'Dantesque', and *In Search of Lost Time* as 'Proustian'.

Plethora. Med. for *many*, with no pejorative nuance: 'There is fortunately, nowadays, a plethora of kind souls.'

---

[313] 'le mit très vite au *pilon*' would mean 'very quickly pulped it'.
[314] Football Club des Girondins de Bordeaux.

Point-virgule/Semicolon. The height of priggishness; rail against.

Political. It is advisable nowadays to distinguish between *politics* [*la* politique] and *the political* [*le* politique], or rather to assume, between these two concepts, a difference that one avoids defining, but which marks a difference in value: politics is sometimes good sometimes bad, but the political is always good. If you wish to express the importance of the thing, pronounce the word with a closed *o*: 'Everything is p*eau*litical.'

Portion/Share. Always meanest.

Posture. Once pejorative term, indicating an artificial position or attitude, assumed for the gallery. Now that everything is a gallery, this word has lost its pejorative connotation; one may simply ask, without danger of causing offence, on the contrary: 'Which posture are you looking to adopt at your next party conference?'

Power. Always abusive. Rail against. Seize it as soon as possible.

Pragmatic. Med. for *opportunist.*

Précision/Clarification. When a radio or television journalist commits a manifest factual error, 99 times out of 100 by no means do they correct themself: this would be anti-union and counterproductive. In the exceptional remaining case where you notice your mistake and, more exceptionally still, where you believe you ought to take the trouble to rectify it, do so in the elegant form of an additional 'clarification [précision]'. Example: 'So and so has stepped down [brief message received in the earpiece] … or, more precisely, he remains in his post.'

Prémices/First sign. Med. for *prémisse*, *'premise'.*

Prémisse/Premise. Med. for *prémices*, *'first sign'.*

Pressuriser/Pressurise. Med. for *pressurer*, *'squeeze'*: 'The government must stop pressurising small businesses.'

Prestigious. Adjective applied to certain intellectual institutions by those who see in intellectual activity merely an eventual source of media prestige; is always placed, as an epithet, before the name of the institute concerned; are prestigious, for instance, the Collège de France, the Nobel Prize, the 'Pléiade', the 'Collection blanche',[315] the 'Série noire',[316] some American (no French) universities like Stanford, Columbia, Berkeley, Harvard, Yale, the New School, the Juilliard School, a few journals (*Critique*, *Commentaire, Le Débat*, formerly the *NRF*). An intellectual or an artist, in themselves, are never prestigious: prestige only attaches to institutions, and to awards.

Prêt/Ready. Med. for *près*, '*close to*': 'That's my position, and I'm not ready to change it.'

Prêt/Loan. Med. for *borrowing*, too humiliating. One no longer borrows money, one 'takes out a loan'.

Princess. Always far-away.

Principles. Always grand.

Prisme/Prism. Always distorting.

Privilege. Med. for *prestige*: 'Land of human rights, France enjoys great privilege in the world.'

Problematic. Med. for *problem*: 'Fortunately, we have resolved this problematic.'

Problem. Med. for *difficulty*.

Profoundly. Med. for *sincerely*, or *obstinately*: 'I profoundly think that there are no just wars.' Don't be afraid of thinking too profoundly. Do you want to say that it's raining? Don't say 'It's raining', say 'I think that it is raining', or better 'I profoundly think that it is raining', or better 'I am among those who profoundly think that it is raining', or better still 'I belong to those who profoundly think that it is raining'.

Progress in art. 'The profession of precursor, said Debussy, dates back to the earliest Antiquity.' The value of an artist is apparently that of always heralding another, whose value is to herald a third, etc. I await with impatience the last, who'll have none at all (value).

---

[315] Literature collection published by the Éditions Gallimard.
[316] Crime fiction collection, also published by the Éditions Gallimard.

Prolific. Med. for *prolix*: 'So and so is no longer invited: he's a good customer, but on stage he's sometimes a little too prolific. You have to cut him short.'

Prolix. Med. for *prolific*: 'So and so is a prolix writer: he's written 54 novels.'

Prolongation. Med. for *prolongement*, *'extension'*: 'Rue de Rivoli is a prolongation of Rue Saint-Antoine.'

Prolongement/Extension. Med. for *prolongation*: 'The Quai d'Orsay is seeking an extension of the negotiations.'

Promiscuity. Med. for *proximity*: 'The government has decided to increase the manpower devoted to promiscuity policing.'

Prôner/Extol. Med. for *préconiser*, *'advocate for'*: 'The Quai d'Orsay is extolling a resumption of negotiations in view of furthering the peace process.'

Prophet. Always of doom (it's more reliable).

Provocation. Passes nowadays for a feat. In the olden days, one was not so indulgent: a provocateur was necessarily an *agent* provocateur, that's to say, to keep things brief, a 'cop'.

Proximity. Remedy to all the ills of life in society: the more madmen and women there are, the more we bunch together.

Psychosis. Med. for *collective anxiety*.

Public. Med. for *private*, and vice versa. Besides the general tendency to confuse antagonistic terms, already encountered here, which Freud made one of the features of 'dream thought', and which one could easily make one of the features of all woolly thinking, I presume here a more specific reason: in various domains, among which at least those of teaching and the audio-visual media, the 'public' (remit of the State, and other eventual official collective bodies) can appear to be a relatively restricted domain within the vaster field of activities shared by the whole of 'civil society': in a liberal society, private activity has a broader scope than public activity, the 'private' sector is in this respect more public than the 'public' sector, and this paradoxical relationship may explain – and even justify – the misunderstanding.

Pur et dur/Hardcore. Med. for *pur et simple*, *'pure and simple'*: 'It's a hardcore miscarriage of justice.'

Quatres. Med. (oral) for *quatre*, *'four'*: 'This series comprises *quatre-z-épisodes*, "four episodes".' This dangerous liaison applies moreover to *cinq* [*five*], to *sept* [*seven*], to *huit* [*eight*], to *neuf* [*nine*]. I can't recall which grammarian predicts, with some plausibility, that the mark of the plural in French will soon be a z at the head of every word beginning with a vowel; but what will we do for those beginning with a consonant?

Quelque part/Somewhere. I miss this adverbial expression, nowadays somewhat forsaken, and which at least reminded me of Pierre Dac's[317] sound reply: 'I think I've seen you somewhere. – That's quite possible, I sometimes go there.'

Question. Med. for *reason*: 'He excused himself for health questions.'

Quolibet/Gibe. Med. for *sobriquet*, *'nickname'*: 'He'd been saddled with a gibe.'

Rabat-joie/Killjoy. 'I don't want to be a killjoy, but really, there are more important things than Lady Diana's death.'

Raccourci/Turn of phrase. Always pithy.

Rajouter/Add more. Med. for *ajouter*, *'add'*: 'After his written address, the minister was keen to add a few more words.'

Rancœur/Rancour. Med. for *rancune*, *'grudge'*: 'He holds a tenacious rancour.'

Rastaquouère/Flashy foreigner. A political columnist is indignant about being accused of describing a female candidate for the presidential election as a 'flashy foreigner'. It would be a bit much, in effect, but the truth is probably – as usual, one word replaces another – that his censor said 'rastaquouère' instead of *outsider*.[318]

---

[317] French humourist (1893–1975).

[318] A French pronunciation of this term would at least evoke *rastaquouère*.

Rattraper/Catch up. We always pity the people whose 'past catches up with them'; never those, more numerous however, whose future finally catches up with them.

Rebondir/Pick up on. Med. for *reply, react, follow on from*. Don't say 'I'd like to contradict you', but 'I'd like to pick up on what you've said.'

Reciprocal. Med. for *respective*: 'Each returned to their reciprocal occupations.'

Recueil/Collection. *Bête noire* of publishers, critics and literary interviewers. Hence the ritual question: 'Is this book really a book, or merely a collection?' It is asked, however, only apropos of essays, since short stories and poems are hardly presented otherwise than in the form of a collection, and one imagines it ill-posed regarding the *Flowers of Evil* or *Open All Night*.[319] If you're in this rotten situation, insist aplenty upon the profound unity of the *bardadrac*, and/or upon the fact that all of these 'texts' (carefully avoid 'articles') have been 'reprised' (euphemism for 'rehashed') from this highly coherent perspective, and that they aren't there in the chronological order of their writing, and that even, if you look closely, certain among them are unpublished. You won't fool anyone, but the denial will help you to save face.

Redeployment. Med. for *withdrawal, retreat*, or even *defeat in the middle of nowhere*.

Refute. Med. for *contest, deny*: 'The minister refuted the information given by the press' (don't believe that he showed its inaccuracy: he merely batted it away, without any other form of argument), or *refuse*: 'The strikers refuted the owner's proposals (they kindly sent him packing – until the favour could be returned). As a result, we no longer know how to name the act of demonstrating the falseness of an assertion or the absurdity of a reasoning; it's true that the very idea of such an act no longer occurs to anyone: *demonstrate*, what's the point? It's enough to refute. The height of (logical) impertinence may be seen in its first-person usage, where *refute* pretends to behave like a

---

[319] Short-story collection by Paul Morand (*Ouvert la nuit*) (1922).

performative (how to do things with words): '*I refute* any idea of a dysfunction in the machinery of State.'

Region. Med. for *the provinces*: 'In Paris or in the regions.' This sad euphemism is supposed to attenuate the 'inferiority complex' of the provincials, who once learned, from a minister's mouth, that the word *province* was 'hideous', which hardly did much honour to the thing. For me, the most hideous thing is the euphemism itself, imposed upon a reality that had no need for it. A good connoisseur of the two poles – Balzac, unless I'm mistaken – wrote: 'Everything happens [arrive] in Paris, but everything takes place [se passe] in the provinces.' In the wake of this fine technocratic invention, we no longer know what to do with the 'Parisian region', which was already striving in vain against the larger Parisian Basin and is now enmired in its administrative region *Île-de-France*, which remains too close to the capital to be 'in the regions'. A weather forecaster, no longer daring to use 'region' in the fortunately vague sense it used to have, was forced to resurrect *contrée*, '*land*', which in point of fact doesn't, for once, sound bad.

Rentrer/Return. Med. for *entrer*, '*enter into*': 'After a stormy youth, Rancé returned to religion.'

Renumerate. Med. for *remunerate*.

Repercussion. Med. for *consequence*: 'In this job, the least carelessness can have grave repercussions.'

Répercuter/Echo. Med. for *repeat*, *report*: 'It's what I was told, and I'm only echoing it.'

Réprimer/Repress. Med. for *réprouver*, '*condemn*': 'The union leaders repress these excesses' (if truth be told I'm not sure that they condemn them either).

Republican. Without wishing to enter into the fusty quarrel between 'democrats' and 'republicans', I notice that the latter adjective often covers with its euphemism some strange wares: in my adolescence, the branch of the Communist Party dedicated to the recruitment of young people was called 'Union of the *Republican* Youth of France.' They also used to call (and still occasionally do) '*republican* discipline' (never 'democratic') the automatic withdrawal, in the second round, of 'left-wing' candidates. In October 2005, 'angry' employees sequestered their boss; the practice is commonplace, although debatable; but here's the cherry on the cake: the kidnappers declared to the press that they'd placed their boss in *'republican* custody.'

République bananière/Banana Republic. Med. for *tax haven*, or *flag of convenience*. It's true that these different statuses are not incompatible, quite the contrary.

Resilience. They've rather bored us to death with it lately, but the fact remains that it is better to be resilient than resiliated.

Respectable. Med. for *respectful*. No longer say 'He maintained a respectful distance', but '... a respectable distance'.

Réticence/Reluctance. Med. for *reservations*: 'The president expressed some reluctance, which set a few tongues wagging.'

Retombée/Fallout. Med. for *consequences*: 'This downfall won't be without fallout.'

Return. Alway grand.

Réussite/Success. Always unexpected.

Revenge. Always magnificent.

Révision/Reconsideration. Always radical.

Rien de moins que/Nothing less than. Med. for *riens moins que* ... , 'anything but ... '.

Rien moins que/Anything but. Med. for *rien de moins que*, 'nothing less than ... '.

Risque zéro/Zero risk. The less it exists, the more it is spoken about.

Riverain/Residents. Med. for *voisin*, *'neighbour'*. 'Fifty little corpses were found in the paedophile's cellar. The residents claim never to have noticed anything.'

Roboratif/Invigorating. Med. for *rébarbatif*, *'forbidding'*: 'The text of the European Constitution is austere, nay even somewhat invigorating.'

Rossignol/Nightingale/Shelf-warmer. I regret the progressive disappearance of this word in the commercial sense, still very active in my childhood, of 'unsold item'. The mystery of this metaphor fascinated me. I learned a little later that supposedly unsellable objects are relegated to the very top of the shelves, just as the nocturnal virtuoso perches on the highest branch, and I remained astonished before a certain *ad hoc* drawer, which was without qualm called the 'nightingale's drawer'. It mostly contained outdated-looking ties, for which one awaited, without really expecting it, a hypothetical return to fashion. Conditioned by his profession, my father applied this term to all manner of objects that had become useless, but which we couldn't decide to throw away. It must indeed be admitted, our attics, our cellars, our wardrobes, and especially our libraries are nightingales' nests. But the most fertile nest is that of the media: the seasonal 'current affairs' that recur every year are well suited to the return of old already-spent 'subjects', since nothing more resembles, let's say, yesterday's traffic jam than the traffic jam from last year. Nightingale lover, seek them then in the branches of the seasonal article [du marronnier/of the chestnut tree[320]]. They aren't lacking, the Lille Braderie,[321] the Grand Criss-Crossing of the Holidays, the New Words in 'the' dictionary, the First Names in fashion this year, but my favourite is still the Return to School, which nowadays lasts, thanks to its staggering, a good fortnight: seasonal article of seasonal articles [chestnut tree of chestnut trees], the season lends and devotes itself entirely thereto. The most paradoxical chestnut tree is evidently the sales, since they[322] serve to offload the nightingales.

Rubicond/Rubicund. Med. for *Rubicon*. The former sometimes crosses the latter.

Rhythm. Med. for *tempo*: 'As election day approaches, the rhythm of reforms is slowing down.'

Saborder/Scuttle. Med. for *saboter*, '*sabotage*': 'The president

---

[320] In French, a 'marronnier', 'chestnut tree', can also signify a 'seasonal article'.

[321] An annual flea market held on the weekend of the first Sunday of September in Lille.

[322] '... les soldes, puisqu'ils (dites plutôt 'elles', si vous voulez qu'on vous comprenne) ... ': 'since they [masculine] (say rather 'they [feminine]', if you wish to be understood) ... '.

secretly [en sous-main] scuttles all of his minister's initiatives.' An editor-in-chief winces at this strange sentence, and corrects what he believes to be a misprint by replacing *sous-main* with *sous-marin*, '[in a] submarine'. It's at once more coherent, and more interesting: almost a *scoop*.

Saga. Med. for *long story with multiple episodes*. Far more chic than *serial*.

Scene. Always primal.

Sceptic. Media euphemism for *hostile*. One thus calls 'Eurosceptic' a fierce adversary of European integration. This usage is somewhat archaic; it is making way for the method, thought to be more positive, that I have proposed to call *alteralism*: we no longer find Eurosceptics, but only *alterEuropeans*, always partisans of an*other* Europe (than Europe).

Scoria. Med. for (presumably) *consequence*: 'The closure of the Statue of Liberty is a scoria of the 11th September 2001.'

Second/Runner-Up. Always brilliant.

Seducer. Once always vile, nowadays always great.

Seing/Signature. Often white [blanc-seing, 'free rein'], occasionally private [sous seing privé, 'private agreement']; I read somewhere, apropos of film censorship: '*blanc-seeing*'; the editor-in-chief doubtless believed he was dealing with a misspelt English word, and hastened to correct it.

Selection. Always ruthless.

Semantic. Med. for *lexical*, or more simply *concerning vocabulary*: 'Pension funds, employee savings schemes, let's not fall into a semantic quarrel: it means the same thing.'

Sensibility. Med. for *political tendency*. Politicians are apparently all highly sensitive types.

Seringue/Syringe. On television, obligatory synecdoche for any 'subject' of a medical nature.

Siège/Seat. Always ejector.

Signal. Always strong.

Silence. Always deafening.

Simplicity. Always stunning.

Sinon/Otherwise. I regret the apparent extinction of an adversative expression that was once commonplace [familière], at least in my own family: not only did we disregard the use of *en revanche*, 'however', in favour of *par contre*, 'on the other hand' (of which our teachers would expend great effort attempting to rid us), but we went as far as replacing it with 'for example': 'He ate nothing yesterday, but for example he did drink a glass of milk, which is better than nothing.' I long took this usage to be a feature of the Lyon dialect, like *passé un temps*, '*past a time*' for 'long ago', or *ni trop ni peu*, '*neither too much nor little*' for 'a lot', but Ferdinand Brunot[323] mentions it without this regional attribution, which I have perhaps dreamed up. Its most recent substitute is apparently *sinon*, 'otherwise', which, among others and without trace of a conditional, is flourishing in weather reports: 'It will rain all day north of the Loire; *otherwise*, the sun will shine in the southern half.'

Slogans. The defenders of the French language take offence at the proliferation of advertising slogans in English (*Think different*, *Volvo for life* …). But when you see the way the admen use French, you begin to regret rather that they don't *always* express themselves in English.

Solidarity. 'There are ever more old people, they are getting ever older, they cost us ever more: we ought to drown them all at birth.'

Solution. Med. for *hypothesis*: 'Either so and so is an idiot, or they're making fun of us; but I think it's the second solution.' Where's the problem?

Sordid. Med. crasis of *sinister* and *morbid*: 'A sordid detail: his aggressors tore out his eyes before slitting his throat with a jagged knife.'

Sortir/Bring out. 'So and so has brought out a book [bouquin]':

---

[323] Linguist and philologist (1860–1938), editor of a *History of the French Language from its Origins to 1900*.

med. for 'So and so has published a book [livre]'. One brings out [sort] a book as one lets out [sort] one's dog, sometimes with the same effect.

Souffle/Sweep. Always epic.

Sourire/Smile. Always devastating.

Soutien/Support. Always unwavering.

Status-enhancing. Said of certain objects, cars in particular, which were once called 'external signs of wealth'. Being rich is no longer an advantage, but a status. It's true that a status often expresses a privilege that is not to be abolished.

Stigmatise. Med. for *point an accusing finger at*: 'The Minister for Employment stigmatises the unemployed.' Do not stigmatise anyone, if you do not wish to be stigmatised yourself.

Strapontin/Folding seat. Med. for *tremplin*, '*springboard*', or more modestly *marchepied*, '*stepping stone*': 'This election will serve as a folding seat for his presidential candidacy.'

Stress. I learn that this word appeared in Franglais in 1953. I thus spent my first 23 years, and a few others, without experiencing the thing, nor even knowing that I ought to have. For some time still, this Anglicism was used to refer to a specific disorder, which one might equally have continued to call *shock*, or *traumatism*. Nowadays, it's a chic synonym for *anxiety, discontentment with life, depression, sudden feeling of exhaustion, a bad patch*, and everyone gets their fill, with no regard for the drought stress of a poorly watered fig tree. I also learn that 'in order to manage your stress, you must focus on your unconscious'. I'd like to know how.

Structuralism. Rigid and sterile doctrine, far from historical reality. Rail against.

Sulfureux/Scandalous. Very effective term for converting a dubious reputation into a media profit.

Surreal. Med. for *just a bit bizarre.*

Suspense. Always unbearable.

Symbol. I hate symbols, they've done us so much harm, but I notice with pleasure that the adjective has become perfectly ambivalent; a sentence like 'This decision is symbolic' may mean: 'This decision is very important on account of its symbolic value', or, on the contrary: 'This decision is devoid of any practical effect.' If you wish to be understood, add an adverb capable of specifying the force, positive or negative, of this symbolicity: for instance 'This decision is *highly symbolic*' (meaningful), or 'This decision is *purely* symbolic' (*peanuts*).

Symmetrical. Med. for *parallel*: 'On this point, France and Germany are in symmetrical lock step.' Beware the collision.

Syndrome. Med. crasis of *symptom* and *prodrome*: 'This fall in the stock market is a first syndrome of the anticipated economic crisis.' May also refer to a kind of fear, as persistent as it is irrational, which was once, and already poorly, called a 'psychosis', or a 'complex': the OM's footballers hope nowadays to induce in their opponents the 'Vélodrome[324] syndrome'. Certain members of Oulipo have the palindrome syndrome.

Tache/Stain. Med. for *tâche*, '*task*': 'This stain is infinite.'

Tâche/Task. Med. for *tache*, '*stain*': 'This task is indelible.'

Talkie-walkie. Frangl. for *walkie-talkie*.

Tangent. Med. for *tangible*: 'We are starting to see the first tangent signs of an improvement.' The fact is that an improvement is more often tangent (and even asymptotic) than tangible at the end of the month.

Technologies. Always new.

Television. Always say: 'I prefer the radio'; besides, I do prefer the radio, which spares us the image, even if the television, when you turn the sound down, can possess a charm that a silent radio absolutely lacks. Regarding the miraculous recovery of a public figure, I'm not sure which of his friends said: 'He's starting to watch the television; in a few days perhaps we'll be able to turn it on.' This joke obviously relies on the double meaning of the word *television*, which refers at once

---

[324] The 'Stade Vélodrome' is the stadium home to the 'Olympique de Marseille' (OM).

(or rather alternately) to a 'receiving device' and to a television 'programme'; the first meaning, apparently but deceptively more immediate, in fact derives from the second: television devices exist only by virtue of the technical invention and the media (cultural) practice that is 'the television'; the first meaning is thus metonymic: the instrument for the function. But here's where things get complicated: the joke made possible by the double meaning of the word *television* is also condensed in the verb *watch*, which has here just one physical meaning, but two functional meanings: watching a television screen and watching a television programme are (almost) the same physical act, but are two intentional activities, since in the second case I'm watching a programme 'in', or 'on' (through?) a screen – which I'm no longer seeing or watching. However, one doesn't strictly speaking watch 'programmes', but what these programmes show us, or at least enable us to see. We often say (for example when replying to a nuisance on the phone): 'I'm *watching* the television now', but rather 'Last night, I *saw* so and so on the television', which follows fairly logically from said intentional relation; hence this frequent dialogue, towards the end of the last century: 'I watched Pivot[325] last night. – Did you see so and so then?' One watched (the programme by) Pivot and, quite often, saw so and so (there). Today, Pivot has gone, but so and so has remained.

Tempo. Med. for *rhythm*: 'In Vienna, they danced to a waltz tempo.'

Temporise. Med. for *temper*, or perhaps for *relativise*: 'In the face of the outcry caused by his declarations, the minister had to temporise his remarks.'

Temps/Time. Ever more real.

Tendency. Always strong.

Tenderness. Always infinite.

Tension. Always palpable.

---

[325] Bernard Pivot is a journalist, interviewer and host of cultural television programmes, including *Bouillon de culture* (*Culture Broth*) (1991–2001).

Tergiverser/Procrastinate. Med. for *wait, hesitate, temporise, delay*, even *dawdle*: 'At 200 metres from the finishing line, there's no time to procrastinate.'

Tête/Head. *Se prendre la tête* [to take one's own head] used to mean simply 'to complicate one's existence', and *avoir la grosse tête* [to be big headed], 'to believe oneself to be more important than one is'. But we've recently witnessed a semantic contagion between these two expressions: *Il ne se prend pas la tête* may now mean either that he isn't wearying his grey matter, or that he doesn't take himself to be Einstein. Let's suppose, to make matters worse, that Einstein *ne se prenait la tête* in either sense, he who finally declared that: 'If I'd known, I'd have been a plumber.' But known what? The story goes that, since in his own way he played the violin and was stumbling over[326] the quarter and eighth notes, Yascha Heifetz[327] gently chided him: 'My poor Albert, you really cannot count.'

Theme. Always recurring.

Theory. Always abstract. Distracts from practice. Rail against.

Tollé/Outcry. Always general.

Tout de suite/Right away. Med. for *following a commercial break*.

Toute une série/A whole series. Med. for *three or four*.

Tragic. Always Greek.

Tranchant/Edge. Always double.

Travail/Task. Optionally, Titanic, Herculean or painstaking.

Travestissement/Fancy dress. 'To execute their hold-up, the real gangsters were disguised as fake policemen.'

Trésor/Chest. Always war.

Tribut/Toll. Always heavy.

---

[326] '... et se prenait, cette fois, les pieds dans ... ', '... and was taking, this time, his feet in ...'.
[327] Russian–American violinist (1901–1987).

Trop/Too. Is being more and more readily used, in a childish manner of speaking that could spread, with the sense of a commendatory superlative: 'Nana, your jam is too good!'

Turpitude. Med. for *turbulence*; the one doesn't exclude the other: 'The world economy is entering a zone of turpitudes.'

Ubuesque. Med. for *Courtelinesque*.[328]

Urgence/Something urgent. *Ne plus ultra* of any artistic achievement. Nobody knows what it is, yet they can be seen everywhere.

Vegetation. Always lush.

Veine/Roll. Med. for *[en] peine [de]*, '*at a loss for*', or *[en] manque [de]*, '*lacking*', or *[en] panne [de]*, '*out of*': 'Auxerre's manager, never on a roll with metaphors, declared: "We're still in the prologue, there remain another 30 stages before the finale."'

Versailles. Most beautiful palace in the world.

Vétuste/Decrepit. Med. for *désuet, old-fashioned*: 'This man possesses a rather decrepit charm' (they're often the best: Swann, or someone close to him, told me: 'I don't buy my clothes, I keep them').

Veuf/Widower. Always inconsolable.

Veuve/Widow. Always tearful (nuance).

Vide/Vacuum. Always cosmic.

Vieillard/Old man. Always very.

Vies/Lives. We're told that 1,510 lives have been saved this year on the roads of France, but we aren't told which ones.

Vieux/Old person. Always little.

Viking. Med. for *Scandinavian*, itself med. for *Nordic*: a Finnish racing driver is readily called a Viking.

Vindicte/Condemnation. Always public.

Visibility. Med. for *renown*.

Vœu/Wish. Always pious.

---

[328] Georges Courteline (1858–1929), satirical dramatist and novelist.

Voici/This is. Med. for *voilà*, *'that is'*: 'I'm a candidate for the next presidential election, this is my decision.'

Voilà/That is. Med. for *voici*, *'this is'*: 'That is my decision: I'm a candidate, etc.'

Voire/Even. Med. for *or at least*: 'This serial killer murdered 15 people, even perhaps 14.'

Volant/Steering wheel. Med. for *volet*, *'section'*: 'This manifesto comprises three steering wheels'; not easy to drive, or lead with,[329] presumably. But who's talking about leading?

Zigue/Fella. Always good.

Mediocrity. 'Not just anyone can be mediocre', said Renan. I long found this quip paradoxical, but I realise that for many (from whom I do not except myself) mediocrity would constitute significant progress, as for the Sun King whose talent Saint-Simon placed immediately 'beneath the mediocre', or for the man of letters of whom Beaumarchais says somewhere (I'm exaggerating a bit) that he's lacking just a little talent to attain the level of triteness. However, the paradox remains, for in fact nobody aspires to mediocrity, but indeed to excellence, and nobody is conscious of being mediocre: we alternate between depressive phases, where we imagine ourselves to be naught, and those of elation, where we believe ourselves sublime. We struggle to come to terms with being average, somewhere in the middle of the class, and nothing is harder than getting the, necessarily relative, measure of oneself. This inability affects not only individuals but also groups, particularly nations, and even more particularly our own: in sport and elsewhere, French chauvinism constantly oscillates between self-exaltation and the self-denigration that is its inseparable flip side.

Mégalauque. Let's call him that. He'd written a copious study on a contemporary author; at the front of this book there appears a full-page photo not of the studied author but of the critic in person. He was coming, he said, to consult me about a professional matter, and embarked upon a speech so egocentric that I very swiftly sank

---

[329] 'pas facile à conduire': in French, 'conduire' can mean 'drive', 'steer' and 'lead'.

into absolute muteness, just nodding my head here and there to prove that I wasn't asleep yet. My silence, which he could scarcely perceive through eddies of his sentences [ronds de phrases], didn't bother him in the slightest, since his monologue visibly gratified him more than any kind of exchange. The inventory of his merits, his successes, his titles, of the tokens of esteem he garnered from all quarters (with the exception of a few envious colleagues) and of the proofs of his inexhaustible modesty went on for a fatal hour. Suddenly, a glance at his watch reminded him that another conversation awaited him in another place. He arose, I finally opened my mouth to thank him for his visit. But he had still one more sentence to utter, which amply rewarded me: 'Now that I've got to know you, I better understand what you write.'

Memory. The less it works, the more it wearies. It has its dull parts and its shiny parts, for, as Hugo would say, in *mémoire* there is *moire*. With its dead spots, blind spots and black holes, it is evidently a filter: the crux of its functioning consists of sorting, excluding, choosing, keeping and jettisoning, transforming, interpolating, extrapolating. Borges speaks somewhere of 'the indefatigable labyrinth of dreams'; the labyrinth of memory [souvenir] is doubtless more fragile, but no less misleading. 'Memory [Le souvenir], said Valéry, is just debris and is clarified only by those that are false.' The false are often clearer than the true: after half a century of latency, just one feature of *Rashomon* had remained with me, but it was indelible: the vividness of its colours. Of course, a false memory [un faux souvenir] is, if you insist, a memory that is false [un souvenir faux], but it's no less a memory, since finally, whatever its relation to reality may be, it is experienced (received) as such. Even today, moreover, I remember far better the *Rashomon* in colour I thought I'd seen in 1950 than the one, in black and white, that I 'saw again' four or five years ago.

I wonder if anyone has ever studied the particular kind I propose to call *reflex-memory*. I instinctively distinguish it from the kindred type that allows us for instance (when all is well) to associate a name with a familiar face (which is called 'putting a name' to a face). In the latter case, the association relies upon consciously memorised knowledge, and when it fails us, we know very well that we have in reserve (in memory) the name that is provisionally missing, which we will eventually find on a list, or by seeking it through various approximations (as when you have a name 'on the tip of your tongue', which generally means that you have some idea of what it is, and that a similar name is 'screening' it), or sometimes – most often – when we are seeking it the least. Of the reflex-memory, the best example I can give is the following: I'm listening on the radio to the first movement of a sonata, a quartet or a symphony that I perhaps know well enough to identify, but not enough to be able, upon suspending my listening at this point, to say what the following movement will consist of: being able to do so would pertain to conscious knowledge, constitutive of what is called 'musical culture'; my own would doubtless allow me, for example, to indicate in advance, because I *know* it (to 'predict', therefore, by drawing from my conscious memory), the theme of the following movement, let's say of the *Pastoral Symphony* or of *The Tempest* sonata, whose succession I know sufficiently well, just as I can 'predict' the second line of the *Invitation to a Voyage* upon hearing the first, because I know this poem 'by heart'. In the (type of) case I wish to speak about, for lack of a conscious knowledge of its structure, I am unable to *predict* the second movement of my sonata, my quartet or my symphony. However, here's the thing: at the final note of the first, I can already hear the first bar of the next sounding all alone 'in my head'. Quite clearly, this recollection is triggered by the memory I have conserved, though unconsciously, of the sequence linking the attack of the second movement to the final note of the first. This sequence is indeed purely one of memory, if at least no thematic logic, as can elsewhere be the case, is here at work. A minute beforehand I would have been incapable of predicting this succession, for want of having at my disposal an adequate conscious knowledge of the work, but it is sufficiently etched into my unconscious memory to impose itself upon me, virtually available at the very moment when it is actually about to occur. Its appearance in my head, a few seconds prior to its sounding to my ear, appears to me to pertain quite faithfully to what was once called a 'conditioned reflex', with the (slight) difference that the reflex link doesn't determine, as in Pavlov's experiments, a physical act, but the actualisation of a buried memory, and one that, in the absence of the current sequence, a conscious investigation ('How does the second movement of *Jupiter* begin?') wouldn't succeed in bringing to the light of consciousness. I'm not sure whether the 'involuntary memory' experienced and described by Proust involves the same mechanism, but perhaps this is so: the common sensation (taste of the madeleine, uneven paving stones …) indeed triggers a memory that nothing had announced prior to its appearance, and which is linked to it by a reflex coordination established many years before. I have qualms about thus associating the Proustian narrator and Pavlov's dog, but maybe others have already proposed this sacrilegious comparison.

Menottes/Little Hands/Handcuffs. 'I love the smell of *menottes* in the morning.' There's no question here, as you might think, of the little 'ladies' hands' sung by Félix Mayo,[330] but rather of the device called more coldly, in English, *handcuffs*. We owe this phrase to a sheriff from North Carolina, who apparently isn't lacking in flair – nor in culture, for this phrase parodies another, even more *hardcore* [*hard*], from Lieutenant Colonel Kilgore, in *Apocalypse Now*: 'I love the smell of napalm in the morning.'

Mépris/Contempt. Be sparing with your contempt: few people are worthy of it.

Méprise/Misunderstanding. Basis, as is known, of most human relations. But one must, furthermore, admit the following: when someone is mistaken about you, it's probably because you were mistaken about them. Not every feeling is reciprocal, but every misunderstanding is double.

Merguez. I owe to Jacques Derrida, who himself owes them to his childhood in El-Biar, two humorous stories whose philosophical bearing seems to me pretty clear.

A *pied-noir*[331] about to settle in the 'homeland' seeks out a former classmate turned king of the merguez on the Paris marketplace, in view of borrowing from him a fairly large sum of money; the friend listens to him in silence, then leads him towards the window and shows him, on the other side of the street, the sign of a branch of

---

[330] French singer (1872–1941); the song alluded to here is 'Les Mains de femme', 'Ladies' Hands' (1906).
[331] People of French or European origin born in Algeria during the period of French rule (1830–1962), most of whom departed for France or Corsica when Algeria gained independence.

the *Crédit Lyonnais*: 'Can you see that bank? Well, I've cut a deal with them: they don't sell merguez, and I don't lend money.'

Another merguez salesman, who traded in Bab el-Oued before the 'events', places on his shop window the sign: 'The best merguez in town.' The first retorts with 'The best merguez in Algeria'. The competitor thinks he's emerged definitively victorious with 'The best merguez in the world'. It's hard for the first to outbid him in extension, but there remains for him the card of true modesty: 'The best merguez in the street.'

Messe/Mass. In the minutes following the announcement of Pope Jean-Paul II's death, the television showed a few live images of a mass proceeding as though nothing had happened. A journalist was astonished by this fact. A duty ecclesiastic in the studio, without any satirical intention, on the contrary, explained: 'What do you expect, as they say, *The show must go on*.' As they say, that says it all.

Metalepsis. I think I may have recently forgotten to mention[332] one of its most perverse species, the one playing upon the border between the word and the thing: Hugo spoke, as everyone knows without knowing where, of the 'women farmers [cultivatrices] bent over their furrows, and whose first syllable[333] could be glimpsed'. And this other, perhaps a little sexist, which subverts the autonomy of dreams: a woman dreams that she's walking along a badly lit street; a man approaches her and appears to block her path. 'Ah, sir, leave me alone or I'll call out!' And the man replies: 'Madame, let me point out to you that it is you who are dreaming!' I also like this drawing, whose author I've forgotten and whose principle is based upon the ambiguity of a pronoun: someone is consulting the map of an area, such as may be found at the exit of certain metro stations. On the map, an arrow indicates the precise place where the map has been displayed, with the mention 'You are here'. The person, visibly surprised and mildly troubled: 'News travels fast!'

---

[332] Genette is the author of *Métalepse. De la figure à la fiction* (*Metalepsis. From Figure to Fiction*) (2004).
[333] 'cul' signifies 'arse'.

Métissage/Intermixing. I struggle to understand how one can sing the praises *at once* of intermixing or (in art, and especially in music) 'fusion', and of diversity. It seems to me that the peculiarity of intermixing is progressively to annul diversity, and to engender through homogenisation something like an entropy, physical or cultural. These two benefits are irreconcilable. One ought, if not to choose between them (each has its merits), then at least not conflate them.

Metros. The *BART* (*Bay Area Rapid Transit*) had the clean and cool elegance of a computer-generated product. The two lines then in service formed a large X intersecting at the centre of Oakland. The highlight for me was the system of automated inspection: you could invest, in 1980, up to 20 dollars in a ticket the size of a credit card, from which the automatic entrance and exit gates calculated and subtracted the cost of each journey. At the final exit, if your reckoning was good, the machine retained your card; if it was in deficit, it barred your passage and sent you off to seek a complimentary fare. I suppose this method has become commonplace, but I frankly admired its intelligence and efficiency. I must acknowledge however that, inversely, the 'Big Apple' metro doesn't lack a certain brutal charm. Thanks to the decrepitude of its infrastructures and its equipment, the speed, at least on its direct lines, manifests itself in jolts, trepidations and ear-splitting screeches to great tonic effect, even seated upon those grey-metal lengthwise benches, daily polished and repolished by thousands of backsides of all ages, sexes and colours. Adroitly to leave, at a 'transfer' station, a *local* for an *express* and to manage the converse manoeuvre at the other end of the journey brings you an intense feeling of mastery over space and time. Studying the map, an enigma to dishearten mere tourists, eventually rewards somewhat perseverant lovers of puzzles.

Between these two extreme achievements, one may find, I imagine, all kinds of intermediary cases of which I have no experience, nor even knowledge. The good old Parisian metro – for which my paternal grandfather, if I'm to believe the family grapevine, contributed with his pickaxe to dig the *Télégraphe* station, perhaps the deepest, despite its aerial name – is simply old and Parisian, good enough, but no more, to take or leave, which I can do with my eyes closed. One of its stations is occasionally renovated, but seldom its trains. Céline evoked their gaseous characteristics in terms too vigorous for me to be able to relate them here, but in I know not which very French film you could once see exiles nostalgically sniffing a punched ticket, piously retained in memory of Paname.[334] Nowadays, of course, no one punches their tickets anymore, no one gets stuck in an automatic turnstile, and no one, between two stations, any longer reads *Dubo-Dubon-Dubonnet*. There remains for us to contemplate, on the lines' nomenclature above the doors, the mystery of the odd couples teamed up by the late TCRP, now RATP:[335] male couples, like Lamarck and Caulaincourt, Richelieu and Drouot, Faidherbe and Chaligny, Bréguet and (saint) Sabin, (saint) Sébastien and Froissart, Michel-Ange and Molitor, Barbès and Rochechouart (at last a man and a woman – what am I saying, a nun: Marguerite de Rochechouart, abbess of Montmartre; Barbès and the abbess, a whole programme); couples of places, like Strasbourg and Saint-Denis, Sèvres and Babylone; couples of places and men, like Réaumur and Sébastopol, Le Havre and Caumartin, Sèvres and Lecourbe; not to mention the monadic false couples, like Ledru and Rollin, Denfert and Rochereau, Mouton and Duvernet, La Tour and Maubourg, La Motte and Piquet.

You can never dream enough in the metro, but I happen also to dream *of* the metro: I mistakenly take a line of which I discover to my great surprise the destination and stations, which correspond for me to nothing familiar, or even conceivable, a wholly strange and perforce disquieting Paris. Still enjoying a certain dream-control, I hasten to channel-hop away from this nightmare.

Mews. Of all the institutions unofficially designated by the terms 'Maison Française',[336] I've retained a fond memory of the one at New York University. It is situated at the entrance, on University Place, of Washington Mews, that's to say of the most exquisite little street in Greenwich Village, lined on either side, all the way to its other extremity at the very beginning of Fifth Avenue, with

[334] Nickname colloquially given to Paris and its suburbs.
[335] STCRP: *Société des Transports en Commun de la Région Parisienne* (*Public Transport Company for the Parisian Region*); RATP: *Régie Autonome des Transports Parisiens* (*Independent Public Company for Parisian Transport*).
[336] See note 113.

low houses that are, as the name *Mews* indicates, former stables and other kinds of outbuildings belonging to the noble neoclassical houses (once patrician, as in James, and nowadays largely converted into administrative offices belonging to the same university) on Washington Square's northern row. These maisonettes are generally built from solid brick, variously whitewashed, but the Maison Française (doubtless more recent) has conserved, or retrieved, its original hue. The ground floor opens almost immediately onto a conference room whose platform bears, behind the podium destined for the day's speaker, a baby grand piano opened on rarer occasions. This little room with its hushed acoustics for me epitomises the spirit of NYU, as unpedantic as a university can be, at least with regard to French studies. This institution's critics readily brand it as one just for fashionable 'society', and it's true that its transatlantic cultural activities are chiefly aimed at an urban, gently ageing audience, always glad to hear French being spoken, at least during the first half an hour. On the first floor lies the small director's office where the lecturer patiently awaits the passage of the 'academic quarter', the only subsisting trace of academia within these walls. It was in this office that I recall having been invited, following a conference in November 1970, to come and teach the following year, then a few others. Next door may be found a little room for the post-conference dinners, delivered by a Chinese caterer. It was all intimate, warm and rather cheerful; since one was in polite company, one hardly ever spoke of what one had, more or less, just heard.

Milonga. In January 1983 Borges came to speak publicly about one thing or another in a jam-packed room at the Collège de France, after having received, from the presidential hand, some insignia awarded, a fact of which he'd often complain and to which he had always to resign himself, to his intimate rival *'José* Luis Borges'. It was our first physical encounter, if one may thus abuse this adjective; my first encounter with his being of paper, I must have recounted this elsewhere, dates back to the spring of 1959; this shock had triggered my own *libido scribendi*, and I have never forgotten this chain of events, nor of course dared to evoke it before him. Yves Bonnefoy, who had organised the appearance, guided me in turn towards the author of Pierre Ménard, who, awaiting the time of the advertised conference, stoically welcomed the procession of his admirers in an adjacent room. He obviously didn't know me, but courteously pretended to recognise me. Paralysed by what he himself would have called a generous mistake, I asked him, rather foolishly, if he preferred the blues or the tango. 'Rather the milonga, *non?*' he replied, as I should have expected, with the characteristic clausula he used to present every affirmation, albeit the most resolute, in the form of a question, as though he were consulting you about his own sentiment. It is only, of course, the Hispanic equivalent of the French *'n'est-ce pas?'*, but he always placed in it a touch of bemused bashfulness that was with him, also (or perhaps only), a form of politeness.

It was probably in the autumn of the same year that I caught a glimpse of him, one evening, on the illuminated terrace of *The Cookery*, on University Place, awaiting, or so I assumed, the first set of his virtual contemporary Alberta Hunter, a blues singer from the twenties, thirties, forties, fifties, recently returned for a miraculous retroactive anachronism – in French: a *comeback.* I refrained from once again spoiling for him the ambiguous pleasure of patience. Eighteen months later, on the 9th March, 1985, during a stay in Montevideo, Lisa and Isaac Behar took me along to his house, 994 Maipu Street if I'm not mistaken, for a four-way conversation – in fact rather an induced monologue, an amoebaean mixture of French, for the visitor, and Spanish for the invisible internal text, which continued during dinner at the restaurant over the way. If I'm to judge by the few books of 'interviews with Borges' that I've happened to read, this genre is a little more abundant than varied, and our colloquy, on that day, hardly contravened any of its laws: a preferably nondescript question is asked, and the master unwinds the skein of his hesitant memories and indefatigable paradoxes, where the regular can welcome in passing a few old acquaintances. He managed to surprise us though by asking me, since the subject of conversation had by chance fallen upon the name of Umberto Eco: 'How did he die, by the way?' Fearing to embarrass him with too brutal a contradiction, I replied that I had no idea – which, in strict logic, wasn't really false. I only hope that, in spite of his visibly compulsive curiosity, he asked no one else after me about this delicate point of world literary history.

Enlarging upon this funereal theme, he then urged us to visit his own tomb at the Recoleta, an honourably populated cemetery in the northern Quarter, where he thought he'd end his days, or rather begin his night. It was a strange invitation, but we neglected not to pay it a visit the very next day. The 'tomb' in question was the emphatic vault of the Borges-Acevedo family, a 'rhetoric of shadow and marble', he'd written many years previously: 'I thought of these things at the Recoleta, at the site of my ashes.' The site of his ashes, as he was not then to know, would not be at the Recoleta, but very far from there, in Geneva, where he'd betake himself, a little over a year later, to honour the Plainpalais Cemetery with his definitively silent presence. Thus befell him in turn what he had written, in the same collection, about the dictator Rosas: 'The sea is today a long distance between his ashes and his homeland.'

By a stroke of luck, this conversation does not remain my very final image of him: a few hours later, I saw him advancing, escorted by María Kodama, on Florida Street, a fragile Homer in a sable suit, very upright on his walking stick, arm in arm with his Antigone (I know) in the shimmering *porteño* night. A double silhouette of grace and elegance, greeted by the murmur of a respectful crowd – the scene was then, we were told, almost quotidian, and various photographs have perpetuated it in various places. But there was really no question, that night, of approaching this apparition, as impalpable as a hologram image, more inaccessible than the virtual ghosts of *Morel's Invention*.[337]

Minuit/Midnight. I always wonder, for example, what is meant exactly by the 'night of the 4th August', or by the 'winter of '45': the night from the 4th to the 5th, or from the 3rd to the 4th August? The winter beginning on the 21st December 1944, or on the 21st December 1945? Of course, the historians know what's what, and can get us out of trouble: the abolition of the privileges[338] took place during the night that began on the evening of the 4th August, and it's not only well known but self evident that the German counteroffensive in the Ardennes took place during the winter of 1944/5; by the following winter, the time for this had truly passed. But in our private life we don't always have this kind of historical marker at our disposal: if I've stupidly noted that a given event occurred during the night of the 23rd September, I then risk an error of 24 hours, which, in a court testimony, could have a fatal consequence. We ought rather, and more precisely, to register the hours and the

---

[337] *La Invención de Morel* (1940), a novel by Adolfo Bioy Casares.
[338] I.e. the abolition of the feudal system by the French National Constituent Assembly in 1789.

months: 'the 5th August from 3am to 4am', 'February–March '45', etc. Ancient calendars, which had the year begin in the spring, were more reliable than our own, avoiding the awkward straddling season [saison à cheval] that is winter, but for the straddling nights [les nuits à cheval] I know of no such solution. It might well be decreed that the night commences at zero hours, or, as for the centuries, at one o'clock in the morning, but we'd have to forsake our (in any event most misleading) *midnight*, which obliges the scrupulous (I know such people) to sleep precisely, forever astraddle [à cheval[339]], from eight o'clock in the evening till four o'clock in the morning.

Minute. In my pedagogical beginnings at the lycée in Amiens, in a blessed era when the quasi-juridical notion of 'parents' associations' was yet to be born, a pupil's somewhat rustic father approached me one day and asked, very respectfully: 'Do you have every minute [chaque minute]?' The question, unexpected, required reflection. I envisioned an alas negative answer, but my interlocutor appeared not to be in so metaphysical a mood. The situation was becoming awkward, when I suddenly understood that the 'chaque' that was perplexing me owed everything to his Picardy accent, and meant simply 'cinq [five]'. Relieved, I granted him more than that, and gladly, but I've forgotten what (else) he had to ask me.

Miron (François). This Parisian magistrate, who died in 1609, owed to his defence of private incomes [rentes] the nickname 'Father of the People' – a people of independent means [rentiers], apparently. Perhaps also thereby leaving his name for one of the capital's most endearing streets. It begins at an angle beneath the façade of Saint-Gervais, and meets up with Rue Saint-Antoine a stone's throw away from Saint-Paul, another entirely Roman façade, disfigured only, on grand ritual occasions, by the lurid banners suspended by its churchwarden, as discreet as a driving school window display: 'Jesus is coming, be ready to welcome him!' (or something like that); meanwhile, you can see, with its undulating baroque style, that of the Hôtel de Beauvais, and, as long as you can dodge the watchdogs, you enter the prettiest oval

---

[339] 'Être à cheval (sur quelque chose) ... ' can also mean 'to be a stickler (for something) ... '.

courtyard, incestuous daughter of Bernini and Borromini; as a bonus, there's the Izraël grocery store, where one goes regularly to check that it's resisting the ambient threats, and from which one returns ever richer in taste.

Misanthropy. 'They say I'm a misanthrope, but I'm not at all, quite the contrary. I just contrive to make them believe so: nothing like it for keeping people at a distance.' Julien Sorel, in prison, complains of one thing only: being unable to close his door. This applies to hospitals too, and also, I fear, to any sort of tomb. Even the funeral urn isn't safe: prefer scattering in the open air.

Monde/World. The world is small, but the *demi-monde* is big, the Third World even more so, and the Fourth World is everywhere.

Monotheism. One God is a bit *cheap*. Luckily, monotheistic religions are several; the latter compensates for the former.

Montre/Watch. 'The white man always has a watch, but he never has the time'; this Iroquois proverb is mistaken about the conjunction: it isn't *but*, it is *therefore*. We don't have the time, it is time that has us.

Montsoreau. It fortunately isn't the most popular with tourists among the châteaux of the Loire, nor besides the most necessarily admirable, but for me it is the most unforgettable. Not for the memory of the Lady whose husband had her lover killed and who, as a result, discovered enough merit in the first to, they say, remain faithful to him for the next 40 years, but because its harsh fifteenth-century façade, facing north, falls virtually sheer upon the fast-flowing water. The *almost* refers to the road that has since been threaded along its base, extending just far enough over the riverbed. After a dip in the nearby (and safer) Vienne which brings its sandbanks a little to drink, and a pause beneath the pillars of the porch and the (very Angevin and somewhat warped) vault of Saint-Martin de Candes, guardian of the confluence, it is in the very late afternoon that you must linger at the foot of this false cliff, when against the current the oblique light of the setting sun turns the wavelets into iridescent scales, beneath the cries of the swifts ricocheting playfully off them.

Morals–Sociology. Around the middle of the twentieth century, I can't recall which peculiarity of the university curriculum encouraged *khâgne*[340] students to pick up, along the way, a few *licence*[341] certificates at the Arts Faculty, in case the hazards of the competitive examination should prove unfavourable to them. For the 'pure literature students' (by default, that's to say neither historians nor philosophers), the certificates for French, Latin and Greek generally didn't present too much difficulty, but the '*licence* in Education' for classics comprised yet a fourth, somewhat more technical, exam in 'grammar–philology', for which the years of *khâgne* by no means prepared them, and which had to be postponed for better days. Luckily, said curriculum allowed for something called a 'free *licence*', consisting of four potentially disparate certificates, and which guaranteed the same benefit, whose nature I have forgotten. You would therefore take any old final certificate, provided that it was less demanding of specialised knowledge than 'grammar–philology'. The most accessible to our highly generalist culture was entitled 'morals–sociology': at that time and at this level, sociology functioned as a modest appendix to morals, this couple falling in principle, with psychology, logic and God knows what else, under the *licence* in philosophy. In the course, no doubt, of 1949, I thus took this exam, and, rendered eligible after a three-part dissertation on some vague point of ethics, I went to the Sorbonne to undergo an oral consisting of a test in morals and another in sociology, this twofold test finally justifying the double-barrelled title. I was obliged to appear first of all, for morals, before the philosopher Le Senne, whom I knew neither in speech nor writing. Noticing in a corner of the *ad hoc* room, behind a little table, an equally unfamiliar examiner who appeared to be awaiting a candidate, I ventured a rapid mental heads or tails, moved towards him, and, like Stanley encountering Livingstone in the heart of Africa: 'Monsieur Professor Le Senne, I presume?' Whereupon the examiner, with a start that spoke volumes about the relations between the two disciplines, and with an accent I'll forgo transliterating here: 'You presume wrongly, young man: I am Professor Gurvitch, and I apologise to you for

---

[340] See note 84.
[341] See note 144.

that!' Bad move, as one didn't yet say: Professor Le Senne awaited me behind another little table, in another corner of the same room. What followed was a little awkward, but without further occasion for misunderstanding, and, in regard to what had brought me to these suroundings, with a finally positive outcome: except among themselves, the 'mandarins' were nice fellows. I emerged from the room free and graduated [licencié[342]].

Motive. There are things one does merely to avoid abstaining therefrom.

Mots-chimères/Chimera-words. The generally received term is [in French] now '*mot-valise*', which dates back (in English, *portmanteau words*) to Lewis Carroll, but it so happens that this awkward and scarcely transparent word serves ever more, and in a way that is on the whole far better justified, to designate something completely different, to wit: a word, like nowadays *stress*, *culture* or *liberalism*, used indiscriminately without its meaning being known, and granted instead the meaning one wishes: suitcase indeed, but used as a *bardadrac* or a potluck dinner [auberge espagnole[343]]. So there is a pressing need to rename (as I am doing here, or quite differently if one finds better) the thing I wish to say a few words about, and which is thus itself also a word, or rather a class of words. It isn't unknown to everyday language, since *foultitude* [*foule/crowd* + *multitude*] has existed, apparently, since the middle of the nineteenth century. Instances of it may notoriously be found in Heine, who spoke of the *famillionnaire* ways of Salomon de Rothschild, in Sainte-Beuve, who rightly viewed *Salammbô* as a *Carthaginoiserie*, in the Goncourts, who contrived the graceful *mélancolieusement*, '*melancoliously*'. Recent current events have supplied us with *gangster-rorism*, promised a bright future, as word and thing. Nor do I ever tire of the *volupté*, '*voluptuousness*' whose author I cannot trace, nor of the *palimpsestueux*, '*palimpsestuous*' coined by Philippe Lejeune. Joyce's *Finnegan's Wake* overflows with them, preferably ones that are more complicated, if possible multilingual and consequently

---

[342] A 'licencié' is a graduate, but also someone who has been 'dismissed' or 'laid off'.
[343] 'a Spanish inn'.

barely translatable. We also know that Freud's essay on the *Witz* begins with an analysis of these kinds of learned punning neologism formed by the linking or mixing of words, verbal hybrids whose every element contributes, more or less effectively, to the synthetic meaning of the whole. Hence my proposal in the form of a message in a bottle: *chimera-word*, since a chimera is a monster produced by grafting – a lion's head upon a goat's body, etc. One might just as well, or no more badly, call them *mots écrasés*, 'squashed words', but let's not take too many pointless risks. I'd gladly append to them, incidentally, pseudo-derivations such as those words or brand names ending in *-rama* improperly taken, at least ever since the student jokes at the Vauquer boarding house,[344] from *panorama* or from *diorama* (in fact, words ending in *-orama*), or like the English *talkathon*, or the French *téléthon*, which pretend to take the *-thon* from *marathon* as a suffix signifying the length or the duration of an ordeal; or *Irangate*, then *Monicagate*, *Plamegate* (etc.?) derived from *Watergate* to refer to any type of slip-up – in speech or writing – at the White House; or our *autobus*, derived in 1906 from *omnibus*, making *-bus* a pseudo-suffix applicable to any kind of public transport (not to mention, alongside this, the semantic passage from 'transport for all' to 'transport making every stop', as opposed to '*express* transport'), hence later on *trolleybus*, *Airbus*, and quite simply, in French as in English, *bus* – or in Marseille (or elsewhere) the *traminot*, 'tram driver', which diverts the *-minot* from *cheminot*, 'railway worker', evidently derived from *chemin*, 'way or path', by a simple *-ot* suffix: folk etymologies, in sum, but semi-learned and deliberate. The list of chimera-words grows every day, virtually inexhaustibly. Here are just a few, original or not:[345]

Abbécédaire/Abbocedarium. Ecclesiastical tutor.

Adonaissant/Adonascent. Pre-adolescent.

Adulescent. Post-adolescent.

Alambigu/Alembiguous. Over-elaborate to the point of ambiguity.

---

[344] 'La Pension Vauquer' features in Honoré de Balzac's *Le Père Goriot* (*Father Goriot*) (1835).

[345] In what follows, I have omitted only those relatively few entries allowing no even proximate rendering in English.

Alibicyclette/Alibicycle. An excuse invoked for an offence committed on a bike. Know, however, that the police can very well punish you, e.g. for having ridden on the pavement, with the removal of your ... driving licence.

Altermoiement/Altemporise. Adjournment under the pretext of dithering over two choices.

Amnéricain/Amnerican. Citizen of the United States lacking memory.

Analphabétisation/Analphabeastisation. Ongoing regression to the oral stage of culture.

Anarchévêque/Anarchbishop. Libertarian prelate.

Anarchitecte/Anarchitect. Disorderly builder, supposedly post-modern.

Anarchiviste/Anarchivist. Shambolic librarian.

Anarcisse/Anarcisst. Egocentric libertarian.

Arborigène/Arborigene. Eucalyptus.

Aristotechnocrate/Aristechnocrat. Graduate of the École Nationale d'Administration[346] with a nobiliary particle, genuine, or, more often, apocryphal.

Artriste. Melancholic aesthete.

Asphasie/Asphasia. Silent hetaera.

Assassignat.[347] Hard, and sometimes cold, revolutionary cash.

Aubergyne. Southern family boarding house stuffed with single women.

Autobiodafé/Auto-bio-da-fé. Pyre for narcissistic vanities, now out of use.

Autofiction, of course.

Automnomie/Autumnomy. Old age without dependency.

---

[346] See note 137.

[347] 'Assignats' were paper money issued by the Constituent Assembly in France from 1789 to 1796.

Autopsy[348]/Autopsy. Narcissistic analyst.

Autosujétion/Self-Subgestion. Voluntary servitude.

Banjonéon/Banjoneon. Stringed and gusseted instrument, used in Cajun tango clubs.

Biografiction. Romanced life.

Burlesconi. Italian politician.

Cantactrice/Cantactress. Opera singer capable of playing her role; there are fortunately ever more of them, since Maria Callas, but one should definitely cite Cathy Berbérian, for whom, if I'm not mistaken, this chimera-word was invented.

Caricanicule. Ridiculously exaggerated heatwave.

Caricatouriste/Caricatourist. Traveller inclined to malicious clichés of the type: 'All Italians are womanisers, all English women are redheads, all French people are witty'.

Castronome. Cuban gourmet.

Catastrofiction. Literary genre in vogue, but dire.

Catastrophysique/Catastrophysics. Science of planetary disasters, also in full swing.

Célébriété/Celebriety. Sunlamp intoxication.

Chiraclette. Parisian *moto-crotte*,[349] popularised by an aedile from that time.

Cinédiégétique/Cinediegetics. Hunt for good film scripts.

Cléricatural/Clericatural. Priest who overdoes it.

Coalisation. Civilising mission exercised jointly by several colonial powers.

Cogitôt/Cogitoo (early). Morning insomnia, hence vesperal siesta: *cogitôt ergo somme* [*snooze*].

---

[348] Derived from the French 'autopsie'.
[349] The 'moto-crotte' or 'caninette', informally 'chiraclette' (Jacques Chirac was then mayor of Paris), was a motorised vehicle designed to vacuum up dog faeces in Paris and other French cities.

Comparaison/Compareason. Neither compass nor reason.

Copernicieux/Copernicious. Said of a system liable to harm its predecessors, or occasionally its promoters.

Crucifiction. No comment.

Cyberstructure. Final *high-tech* stage of social organisation.

Cyclopathe/Cyclopath. Bike maniac.

Décidérata/Deciderata. Clearly affirmed desires.

Diarrhiste/Diarrhist. Incontinent with the personal diary.

Diplodomate/Diplodomat. Very old ambassador.

Dodécalcomanie/Dodecalcomania. Servile pastiche of Schönberg.

Duplicodocus. Dinosaur clone.

Éclecteur/Eclector. Fickle citizen.

Éclectrique/Eclectric. Fickle and plugged-in citizen.

Éphéministe/Epheminist. Inconstant suffragette.

Épiscolaire/Epischoolary. Novel told through the medium of letters for use in junior classes.

Épizoode/Epizoode. Transitory malady affecting an animal species.

Erradiquer/Erradicate. Expurgate a fault.

Errotisme/Erroticism. Sexual vagabondage.

Errudit/Errudite. Scholar gone astray.

Évanaissance/Evanaissance. Transplanted effect of Adam's rib.

Explosition. Attack in a museum.

Faitichisme/Factishism (Bruno Latour).[350] Positivist superstition.

Fascicule/Fascicle. Young Mussolinian.

---

[350] Bruno Latour (1947–2022) was a French philosopher, anthropologist and sociologist, author of *Sur le culte moderne des dieux faitiches* (*On the Modern Cult of the Factish Gods*) (2009).

Fêtichisme/Festishism. Cult of the party.

Freuduleux/Freudulent. Said of the illegal practice of analysis.

Gallimatias. Gibberish sometimes heard on Rue Sébastien-Bottin.[351]

Glagolithique/Glagolithic. Cyrillic character engraved upon stone.

Hallurissant/Hallustunnatory. Said of a fact one cannot believe.

Hamsterdame. Batavian female of the guinea pig.

Happyculteur/Happyculturist. Contented beekeeper.

Hardu/Harduous. Very arduous.

Hassidu/Hassiduous. Very practising orthodox Jew.

Hebdromadaire/Hebdromadary. Desert magazine.

Hérédisiaque/Heredisiac. Said of a genetic capacity for enjoyment or bliss.

Hiérogifle/Hieroclipic. In my childhood, we mocked the Catholic ritual of 'confirmation', which consisted, apparently, in the bishop giving a little tap on the already baptised boy or girl's cheek.

Himaladresse/Himaladroitness. Monumental gaffe.

Homicidre/Homicider. Murder in the apple press.

Hommophobe/Humophobe. Misanthrope.

Horroscope. Very bad omen.

Hymalady. Giddiness upon the summits.

Hypersonnalité/Hypersonality. Public figure with an oversized ego.

Hystrion. Excited exhibitionist ham.

Infractuosité/Infractuosity. Any gap inviting a transgression.

---

[351] Home of French publishing house the Éditions Gallimard, in the 7th arrondissement of Paris.

Inisciatique/Inisciatory. Rite of passage leaving one with a painful thigh.

Jargonaute/Jargonaut. Virtuoso of technical vocabulary.

Jocastre/Jocastrates. Very abusive mother.

Justifiction. Mendacious apology.

Léninifiant/Leninifying. Said of a revolutionary sentiment without any practical bearing, fit only to soothe the masses. Vladimir moreover himself said 'One has to dream'.

Lithurgie/Lithurgy. Art of cathedral stonemasons.

Maîtronome. Conductor exclusively respectful of the tempo.

Majesticulation. Hysterical pretension to royal grandeur.

Malthusalem. Prophet of modern times: have fewer children and live longer.

Manichiavélisme/Manichiavellianism. Cynical and simplistic morals.

Marx Weber. Famous German economist and sociologist.

Mécontemporain/Miscontemporary. *Laudator temporis acti.*

Médiocratie/Mediocracy. This chimera-word dates from Balzac, with the well-known and right-wing connoted meaning of 'government by the mediocre'. But by splitting it otherwise, as one does with *medio-logy*, it can also denote the supposed power of the media. The two etymologies are by no means incompatible, on the contrary.

Médiocritique/Mediocriticism. Level of critique honoured in the media.

Mélancomique/Melancomic. Black humour.

Mélodisque/Melodisc. Recorded song.

Méphistopotamie/Mephistopotamia. Iraqi hell.

Mozartiste/Mozartist (Lanner).[352] Performer of Wolfgang.

---

[352] Josef Lanner (1801–1843) was an Austrian dance music composer and

Narcommunisme/Narcommunism. Highest stage of Marxism–Leninism in its tropical version, illegitimate child of Escobar and Guevara.

Néfastidieux/Nefastidious. Dreadfully boring.

Néfastudieux/Nefastudious. Prone to be dreadfully bored.

Négromancie/Negromancy. African spiritism.

Nostalgérie/Nostalgeria. Regret shared by immigrants and the repatriated.

Nostradivarius. Prophetic luthier.

Octobiographie/Octobiography. Life story in eight volumes.

Officionado. Keen on public sector jobs.

Omnibulé/Obusessed. Passionate about public transport.

Ovnibulé/UF-Obsessed. Preoccupied with extraterrestrials.

Parallélipomène/Parallelipomena. Everything one leaves aside and carefully avoids interfering with.

Paranorama. Suspicious overview.

Passifisme/Passivism. Spirit of Munich.

Pénombrilisme/Penombrilism. Crepuscular egocentrism.

Phallacieux/Phallacious. Said of a sexist sophism.

Phatidique/Phateful. Said of a prophecy with a purely verbal effect.

Phrygide/Phrygid. Disappointing Oriental.

Pipolarisation.[353] Magnetic divergence of French politics: image against image.

Proustituée/Proustitute. Courtesan in search of lost time.

Pseudopole/Pseudopolis. Imaginary city on the fringes of the real one.

---

conductor; arranged Mozart melodies into waltzes in *Die Mozartisten* (1842).
[353] In French, 'un pipole', derived from the English 'people', is equivalent to 'a celeb', hence 'la pipolisation', 'celebrification'.

Psyttacisme/Psyttacism. Freudian logorrhoea.

Réciproquo[354]/Reciproquo. Double misunderstanding.

Rédactionnaire/Redactionary. Far-right journalist.

Réminiscience/Reminiscience. Platonic definition of knowledge.

Rétrocrastination/Retrocrastination. To say that this is the opposite of the *procrastination* for which Baudelaire reproached himself, and which Saint-Loup ascribed to Marcel, perhaps isn't illuminating for everyone. One might define it somewhat more positively as the unfortunate habit of always putting everything back to the day before, but this definition will perhaps seem rather glib, even though you could describe in these terms the obsession with always 'getting ahead', and that – characteristic of anxious types according to my psychoanalyst – with arriving too early for all of one's meetings. But I take this chimera-word in oxymoronic form (*cras*, in Latin, means 'tomorrow') to signify a more serious, and frankly paralysing, infirmity, which consists in never considering one's work, whatever it may be, to be finished. I knew an author who spent more time on his final sentence than on the 300 pages preceding it, and from whom you had *literally* (I've done it) to tear his manuscript, not without a cold sweat at the prospect of correcting the proofs. The more commonplace word *perfectionism* has been suggested to me, but I'm not sure it's quite the same thing: the retrocrastinator only ever stumbles [bute], asymptotically, when two steps, one step, half a step, etc. away from the goal [but], like Zeno's Achilles. Sportspeople speak of the 'fear of winning': my object, you understand, is the *fear of finishing*.

Révolupté/Revoluptuousness. Enjoyment experienced upon each rotation, or change of régime.

Salamandragore/Salamandrake. Mythical creature, hybrid of vegetal and animal, which is born beneath the gallows and lives in pyres.

Sarcaustique/Sarcaustic. Doubly satirical.

---

[354] In French, 'un quiproquo' is a mistake or a mix-up.

Sarkome/Sarkoma.[355] Tumour on the right.

Sexuagénaire/Sexuagenarian. Ageing Don Juan.

Spectaculation. Thought as risky as it is ostentatious. Twentieth-century philosophy wasn't sparing therewith.

Starchitecte/Starchitect. Celebrity builder.

Starilisation. Negative effect of glory.

Stimulacre/Stimulacrum. Erotic sham.

Syphilisation (Freyre).[356] Genocide by venereal contamination: combines the useful with the enjoyable.

Unaniversel/Unaniversal. Said of a planetary consensus.

Viragauchiste. Anarcho-Trotskyist tricoteuse.

I have evoked elsewhere the unforgettable *Dictionary of Words Regained.*[357] I've realised that its fanciful definitions often consist in analysing an existing word as though it were a closet chimera-word, just as Charles Nodier feigned to analyse certain equally ordinary words as onomatopoeia: for instance, *catacomb* as 'the resounding of the coffin rolling step by step upon the acutely angled stones, and coming to rest all of a sudden amid the tombs' (closer still, some of Leiris's 'glosses' – '**Cratère [Crater]:** *il crache la terre*, 'it spits the earth', '**Labyrinthe:** *la Crétique hait Thésée, mais l'Ariane aide, et suis fil*,[358] 'the Cretic hates Theseus, but Ariadne helps, and follow the thread' – that one is apocryphal). In the *Words Regained*, one finds for instance '**Estragon [Tarragon]:** province of Spain (obvious pseudo-chimera of *Estrémadure [Extremadura] and Aragon*), or '**Aspirine [Aspirin]:** wife of an *aspirant de marine* [a

---

[355] Refers to Nicolas Sarkozy, president of France from 2007 to 2012.
[356] Gilberto de Mello Freyre (1900–1987), Brazilian sociologist, anthropologist, painter and writer.
[357] *Dictionnaire des mots retrouvés*, published collectively by the French literary magazine the *Nouvelle revue française* (*NRF*) in 1938.
[358] *Labyrinthe* was a literary and artistic journal (1944–1946) founded by Albert Skira, to which Michel Leiris himself contributed. The sentence itself is contrived to echo the French expression 'La critique est aisée, mais l'art est difficile', 'Criticism is easy, but art is difficult'.

midshipman]; generally very elegant, she gives fashion a particular cachet' (pseudo-chimera of *aspirant* [*aspirant*] and of *marine* [*navy*], embellished with an ambiguity regarding *cachet*). Since its publication by the *NRF* (1938), on two or three occasions they've had the good idea of republishing it, and the perhaps not so good idea of expanding it, or of imitating it. I would myself have liked to add, among others:[359]

Aréopage [Learned Assembly]. Fiasco.

Biscornu [Quirky]. Deceived twice [bis = second/cornu = horned].

Courtisane [Courtesan]. Rapid infusion [court = short/tisane = herbal tea]: 'M. de *** could only fall asleep after enjoying two or three *courtisanes*' (Tallemant).

Crépuscule [Crepuscule]. Little crêpe late in the day.

Diverticule [Path]. Sodomitical pastime [divertir = entertain/ cul = arse].

Égoïne [Handsaw]. Small saw for strictly personal use.

Équitable [Equitable]. Said of a horse providing a well-balanced *assiette* [une assiette = a seat (on a horse), also a plate].

Félibrige.[360] Provençal antipyretic [*febris* = fever].

Groupuscule. Twilight of the group.

Introït [Introit]. Entrance of the celebrant [*intrare* = enter/coït = coitus]: 'Mme. was in the habit of dozing off from the moment of the *introït.*'

Libellule [Dragonfly]. Tiny book [*liber* = book]

Matricule [Serial Number]. Tiny mother [*mater* = mother]

---

[359] In what follows, one finds first, and where necessary, a 'straightforward' translation of the original term in bold within square brackets, then Genette's 'pseudo-chimerical' definition, then, again in square brackets and wherever necessary, translations of the semantic elements to which this definition appeals and which it alleges to find in the original term.

[360] The *Félibrige* was a cultural association founded in 1854 in order to protect and promote the Occitan language; the name derives from the Provençal *félibre*, meaning pupil or follower.

Minuscule. Tiny mine.

Moleskine [Moleskin]. Fake skin, soft and mean [molle = soft/mesquin = mean].

Nycthémère [Nycthemeron]. Double incest committed in 24 hours ['Nique ta mère!' = 'Screw your mother!'].

Palliatif [Palliative]. Wisp of straw remaining in one's hair after a siesta in the barn [paille = straw/aperitif].

Récipiendaire [Recipient]. Grantee with an inflated sense of their own importance [récipient d'air = air container].

Sédentaire [Sedentary]. Local anaesthetic used in city odontology [aire = area].

Toxine [Toxin]. Female of the tocsin.

Joyce, once again, more elegantly allows the definition to be guessed, being content to rewrite, for instance, *grasshopper* as *gracehoper*.

Motus/Mum's the Word. 'I'm a man of very few words,[361] said he, and even then, not every day', and he congratulates himself (rather more, all the same, than would be required to illustrate it) on what he calls his *motus vivendi*. Regarding Thelonius Monk, a more celebrated and consistent silent type, a New York joke from the fifties went: 'If nobody called, it can only be him.' A witless journalist once asked him, in an airport waiting lounge, whether he liked country music; he glared at him, and answered nothing; the journalist, raising his voice a little, repeated his question: 'I asked you if you like *country music*'; Monk's silence intensified; a third attempt; Monk shrugged his shoulders and moved away, muttering: 'This guy is really hard of hearing.'

Mourants/Dying People. During a plague epidemic in Marseilles, under the *Régence*[362] and if I'm to believe Michelet, a galley slave

---

[361] 'Je n'ai qu'une parole', 'I have only one word', usually means 'I'm true to my word' or 'My word is my bond'.
[362] The period (1715–1723) during which the prince regent Philippe d'Orléans, nephew of Louis XIV, governed France.

instructed to gather corpses happened upon dying people who yet still had the strength to protest. 'Well, he said, if you listened to them there wouldn't be a single one dead!'

Museums. The most endearing are perhaps those devoted to a single artist, as you can see (almost) only Memling at the old Saint John's Hospital in Bruges, Frans Hals at the Haarlem Almshouse, Carpaccio in San Giorgio, Tintoret in San Rocco, Greco in Toledo, David d'Angers at the Toussaint Abbey, Rodin at Rue de Varenne or at Meudon, Gustave Moreau at Rue La Rochefoucauld, Picasso at the Salé Hotel, at the Aguilar Palace in Barcelona, at the Château Grimaldi in Antibes, Torres-Garcia in Montevideo, Boudin in Honfleur, Rothko in his octagonal chapel in Houston, and I'm forgetting some (including, not without reason, Matisse's chapel in Vence and Cocteau's in Milly-la-Forêt). I regret that they have, for a reason unknown to me, transferred to the Prado the Black Paintings with which Goya had adorned (so to speak) the walls of the Quinta del Sordo. Certain perhaps less transportable ensembles pretty much fulfil the same function, like Piero's frescoes at San Francesco in Arezzo, Masaccio's at the Brancacci chapel in Florence, Giotto's at the Scrovegni in Padua, Gozzoli's at the Medici-Riccardi Palace in Florence. These monographic groupings clearly combine, as in music, the charm of variation with that of unity of tone, without lapsing into the pedagogical demonstrations of *ad hoc* temporary exhibitions. In the days when the Jeu de Paume was reserved for impressionism (the rooms at the Orsay, more dispersed and steeper of access, don't lend themselves so well to it), this pleasure could be spread over the whole of so homogeneous a group, and you could there refine a Goodmanian sense of 'discernment' through contact with slight differences. Beyond this, we fall quite swiftly into the random displays of the large generalist museums – unless you limit your visit to a single felicitously arranged room, like the one for Poussin's *Seasons* at the Louvre. Below it, one might (one must) pay due regard to those rare places selective enough to invite you to view just a single work: *The Mystic Lamb* at St Bavo's in Ghent, Queen Mathilde's 'tapestry' in Bayeux, Nicolas Bataille's *Apocalypse* at the Château d'Angers, or, in the same city – but, as I've said, in the Doutre – Lurçat's *Song of the World* in another old Saint John's Hospital. The bonus of pleasure also derives, of course, from the *in situ* character thereby afforded the works of painting or sculpture, a character and supplementary *aura* they consequently share with those of architecture. One can understand all of this upon discovering, after the tremendous shambles of Cairo, the charming little Luxor Museum, where each well-chosen object finds its place and its light. But perhaps it suffices, leaving behind a day at the Metropolitan and if you still have the strength, to cross Fifth Avenue in order to rest for a few moments in the intimate shadows of the Frick Collection.

Naivety. Its most optimistic form consists in believing yourself to be suspicious.

Nappe/Tablecloth. I can still picture the tourist-abandoned trattoria on the Piazza della Signoria where I dined virtually alone, out of season, in March 1976, on a *bistecca* roasted Florentine style, a truly bitter rocket salad, Parmesan cheese and a small carafe of Chianti, on a perfectly white and slightly starchy tablecloth, such as may only be found in Italy, even upon the most modest of tables. I'd return to the room offered by the French Institute, Piazza Ognissanti, always passing scrupulously through an already deserted Oltrarno (Ponte Vecchio, Via San Spirito, Borgo San Frediano), as silent as a Masaccio fresco.

Nationale 23.[363] Before the construction of the A 11 *autoroute*, the journey from Paris to Angers was made along this road that branched off from the *nationale* 10 – Paris–Bordeaux, of course – at Chartres. The Paris–Saumur alternative branched off from it in turn at La Flèche, heading due south via Baugé and Longué. I don't know how many times I've made this double road trip, in both directions, by car from 1952 onwards, and perhaps, prior to this date, once by bike, if my memory isn't here erring on the side of boastfulness. Then fairly rural for a *nationale*, this road obviously traverses Eure-et-Loir, Sarthe and Maine-et-Loire, but also, for ten kilometres or so, somewhere between Nogent-le-Rotrou and La Ferté-Bernard, an advanced pocket of the Orne *département*, which was announced by a sign indicating, via a smaller road that

[363] In France, a *route nationale* is equivalent to an A road in the UK or a highway in the US.

bears right (coming from Paris): 'Le Theil, 2km.' I had very often to curb, at this point, the desire to see for myself this village whose name was for me so mysterious, and which, not content with belonging to a *département* so incongruous on this journey, even disdained to allow itself to be crossed by the main road. I eventually granted myself this detour, which immediately afforded me the inevitable disappointment: so that's all it was! However, the Orne *départment*, an undecided Percheron stepping stone between Maine and Normandy, has retained for me a certain no less undefinable appeal, and when, later, I lived in Le Mans, I always struggled a little to differentiate, between Sarthe and Orne, towns such as Bonnétable, Mamers, Bellême and Mortagne-au-Perche.

This uncertainty was not dispelled, quite the contrary, by an episode in local political life. At the beginning of the sixties, Louis Mermaz, who with one hand taught history at secondary school in Le Mans, and with the other campaigned under François Mitterrand for the Convention of Republican Institutions,[364] stood at the legislative elections in a ward one respectfully recalled had once been (give or take a few *cantons*, perhaps) that of Joseph Caillaux.[365] Now, history has retained that the father of income tax, who was born in Le Mans and died in Mamers, had been an MP, then a senator, for Sarthe. It was, however, I do believe, in Mortagne, and thus (finally) in Orne that, during this campaign, a meeting was held where we went, Babette and I, along with a few deserving pupils, to support our local hero. Mitterrand himself was due to come to endorse his party's candidate. He did indeed come, after the obligatory hour's delay, which the candidate had to try his best to fill. The senator from Nièvre was as brilliant as he was belated, in the polemical vein justified, in our eyes, by the Gaullian dictatorship, before an audience already half-exhausted, and more impassioned by local questions than by this searing denunciation of the permanent coup d'État. After the meeting, there was a kind of dinner at the Hôtel du Palais (of justice, presumably), where Mermaz sat us next to the great man, who was supposed to devote

---

[364] The *Convention des institutions républicaines*, founded in 1964, was a socialist and Republican party, led by François Mitterrand; it became the Socialist Party in 1971.
[365] Joseph-Marie-Auguste Cailloux (1863–1944), French politician during the Third Republic, Radical Party leader.

himself more closely to his presumed electors. Apparently satisfied to evade for his part this type of obligation, the future president of the Gentle Strength [Force tranquille[366]] made amiable, even amicable conversation with us, which bore primarily upon the appeals and amenities of his summer house in Hossegor – he hadn't yet acquired the sheepfold at Latche.[367] But two or three peasants, twisting their caps with emotion, came up and attempted to set forth their economic and administrative difficulties. Far enough away from his own stronghold to do as he pleased, he ushered them away quite unceremoniously, advising them to form together something like a syndicate of *communes*, and promptly resumed, to our astonishment, the description of the system, novel for the period and not yet called 'home automation', which allowed him to 'set everything in motion' in his house, with a single turn of a dial, upon each of his arrivals on the Landes coast. This somewhat overly marked distance was perhaps one of the causes of our friend's provisional failure, he who would doubtless have done better to forego such condescending support, and who would find himself a few years later MP for Isère and mayor of Vienne – the site (thanks to him?) of a famous jazz festival.

But I shall return to my *nationale* 23, which I thus had many an occasion to take, at least between 1952 and 1963. I say simply 'take [emprunter]', but I've just remembered that it was some way along it, at La Ferté-Bernard, that one day, having had a breakdown and awaiting repairs, I could read, on the fence of a building site, the inscription: 'Please *empreinter* [*footprint*] the other pavement.' In damp weather and on muddy terrain, this accidental neologism wasn't so unwarranted. North of Le Mans, between Connerré and Saint-Mars-la-Brière, a tiny townlet is called, I don't know why, *La Belle Inutile*, '*The Pointless Beauty*'. I assume it belongs to a neighbouring *commune*, no doubt Montfort-le-Gesnois, whose hill, to the north-west, can be seen from there, adorned with a rustic belltower and a classical or neoclassical château. Without this probable administrative connection, how should one call the fortunate inhabitants of this pointless Beauty? And how too those

---

[366] François Mitterrand's presidential campaign slogan in 1981.
[367] The converted 'bergerie' formed part of Mitterrand's summer residence in Les Landes in the south-west of France from 1965.

of another townlet, somewhere between Le Mans and La Flèche: *La Belle Entreprise*? Now that beauty is even harder to interpret, for I don't know whether it concerns prosaically an *enterprise*, an 'undertaking' deemed beautiful, or more gallantly *d'une belle qu'on entreprend*, 'a beauty towards whom one makes approaches', in which fashion and to what effect. In homage to the pointlessly approached beauties, one might even twin these two hamlets.

At the foot of Montfort flows the Huisne, a discreet fairly grassy river a few metres wide, crossed by two bridges; the most upstream, old enough to be called 'Roman', and which overlooks a ruined mill, is prettily arched, as though to compensate for the exiguousness of the river; the Romans wouldn't have gone to so much trouble for so little. This artificial length is itself overcompensated for by a narrowness preventing cars, and virtually pedestrians, from passing each other; hence a nowise Roman system of alternating lights. Yet, since the bridge's two extremities aren't in view of one another and reversing would be difficult there, you come to wonder how carts managed before the invention of this system. Which makes for many questions, quite apart from this one: why have the local town councillors scorned the plain and simple solution of having the two bridges as reciprocal one-way passages?

The Maine countryside is pleasant in any direction. To leave for a moment the sacred Paris–Angers route, I recall that one of my most powerful musical experiences was, one Sunday afternoon at the beginning of the sixties, listening to Mahler's *First Symphony*, courtesy of a small already 'high fidelity' although monophonic transistor, in a hired boat on lake Sillé-le-Guillaume, whose acoustics I can at least recommend. You can't miss it: it's on the road to Mayenne, north-east of Sainte-Suzanne (the San Gimignano of the Chouan bocage), as Loué is (pretty much) on the road to Laval. Loué, of course, was the village, nowadays well known for its poultry farming, where in the fifties or sixties François Reichenbach shot a short film entitled *The Sweetness of Village Life*. That was still the gentle France [la France tranquille].

Nativity. Before the manger, the shepherds and the Three Wise Men are waiting, blazing one cigarette after another. At last, Joseph emerges and announces: 'It's a girl!' Imagine the rest.

Noh. Even more than the Italian, the Japanese university has a hierarchical and even, it goes without saying, feudal structure. Apart from one or two sublime Zen parks and gardens in Kyoto, a few (the word is weak) Buddhist or Shintoist (I've never really been able to tell the difference) temples in Nara, a saké soirée with Maurice Pinguet in Tokyo, an instructive visit to the NHK studios, a Noh afternoon where I found myself for a moment the only still waking spectator, and a dinner in a traditional inn where I remained for three hours, seated upon my heels, wrestling with disingenuous chopsticks, my most remarkable memory from an academic visit, in November 1985, is the following: during a botanical and gravelly excursion, I was escorted by a student who'd apparently been instructed always to walk two steps behind the noble visitor. This student, I knew, spoke perfectly correct French, and I saw no reason to deprive myself of his conversation, and vice versa. I thus slowed down in order to be level with him. He, respectful at least of the instruction, slowed down just as much in order to maintain the requisite distance. I thus slowed down a little more, and he inevitably did the same. The walk immobilised little by little like, precisely, a stage crossing in a Noh performance, inevitably tending towards a standstill worthy (apologies for this new comparison far less imbued with local colour) of the track races at the pre-war Vel'd'Hiv'.[368] I eventually stopped completely, vaguely hoping to see him take off at full pelt to leave me stuck there and win the contest. He obviously did no such thing, certain that I'd have to resume my solemn march. So I attempted the decisive acceleration, but, as every track cyclist will confirm for you, it's virtually impossible to shake off, even on foot, an opponent following you, as Groucho Marx put it, from behind. I thus remained in the company, so to speak, of my follower, walking as quickly as I could, not to ditch him, but as far as possible to curtail this mutually gruelling pavane.

Noms de pays: le nom/Place-names: The Name. On the 3rd February, 1794, a member of the People's Society of *Grenoble* proposed to name this city Grelibre, 'Grefree'. A host of cities were then being rechristened in accordance with the spirit of the times,

---

[368] 'Le Vélodrome d'hiver', colloquially known as the Vel'd'Hiv, was formerly an indoor bicycle racing track in the 15th arrondissement of Paris.

among others: Lyon: *Emancipated-City*; Toulon: *Port-The-Mountain*
(you can see which one[369]); Marseille, punished for I can't recall
what counterrevolutionary crime: *Commune-Without-Name*. But
Grelibre is, to my knowledge, the only example of such a proposal
based upon a fanciful etymology (you can also see which one); a
reason, perhaps, for it being rejected or, at least, never applied: the
Terror wasn't fond of puns, especially when they were good. But
Stendhal claims that Louis XVIII, precisely, affected still to use,
in private, this stillborn, and apparently defamatory, appellation,
out of spite following a skirmish in 1816.

Nostalgia. Sterile regret for an imaginary past.

Nuits d'été/Summer nights. One (*Upon the Lagoons*) of the six poems
by Gautier upon which Berlioz based this 'cycle' of melodies speaks
of a dead woman who was the fictive speaker's 'beautiful friend', and
four others (*Villanelle, The Spectre of the Rose, Absence, The Unknown
Island*) are addressed to a woman, hence the plausible hypothesis
of a masculine speaker. Only *To the Cemetery* has no connotation
of gender, but it incurs the pressure of the context, and the hardly
avoidable identification of the 'lyrical I' with the poet himself, even
with the composer. It is known that Berlioz envisaged or accepted
different voices according to the melodies, which allows certain
conductors, like the very Berliozian Colin Davis, and after him John
Eliot Gardiner, to divide them between masculine and feminine
voices (soprano, mezzo, tenor, baritone). Even if none really calls
for a man's voice, logical plausibility and coherence might suggest
entrusting the whole series to a male singer, tenor or baritone, by
means of the necessary transpositions, a common method for many
other interpretations – for example Schubert's or Schumann's *Lieder*.
In fact, I know of no recorded instance of such a distribution, and
the majority of the known and/or recorded interpretations are by
female singers, sopranos like Jessye Norman or mezzos like Janet
Baker. Most Berlioz fanatics consider to be matchless that of Régine
Crespin, whose range, if it may be so described, embraces these two
tessituras: as a soprano, she has sung Sieglinde, Brünnhilde, Elsa,
the Marschallin, and she may perhaps be most correctly considered a

[369] *La Montagne* was a political group during the French Revolution.

soprano endowed with a fine deep register – but for these melodies, the discographies generally describe her as a mezzo. So here we are with an ensemble of poems that we naturally take to be uttered by a man, sometimes addressed to, sometimes about a woman, but sung by a woman – and, in the present case, someone who couldn't be any more of a woman, and by no means utilised as a classic *travesti*. Intended or not by the composer, this ambiguity contributes greatly to the charm of the work. Listen to Crespin saying *'Ma belle amie est morte ...'*, 'My beautiful friend has died ...', or *'Reviens, reviens, ma bien-aimée ...'*, 'Come back, come back, my beloved ...', and tell me how you're affected by this vocal brushing of two femininities, one of which, in sum, is speaking for *you* (since the 'lyrical *I*' is also that of the listener). One always evokes the duets or trios of female voices in Mozart (*The Marriage, Cosi*) or in Strauss (*The Knight of the Rose*), and one quite rightly infers from this a congenital relation of one and the other composer to the *mundus muliebris*. We might well include Berlioz in this affective gynaeceum: listen again to Dido and Anna's duet in *The Trojans*, or that of Ursula and Hero in *Beatrice and Benedict*. In both cases, as somewhat in the *Marriage* between the Countess and Suzanne, or in *Cosi* between Fiordiligi and Dorabella, one of the two women is the heroine, and the other the confidante. This more typically feminine relationship doesn't escape the imagination of a true musician; we can obviously include Racine here: *'Songe, songe, Céphise ...'*, 'Think, think, Céphise ...', *'De cette nuit, Phénice ...'*, 'Of that night, Phénice ...', *'Est-ce toi, chère Élise'*, 'Is it you, dear Élise?'; and let it not be said that these spoken duets merely await their musician: he's there already.

More recently, Pierre Boulez (who certainly doesn't portray himself as an unconditional Berliozophile) entrusted the *Nights* to three different voices 'in order, he said to the *Monde de la musique* [*World of Music*], to preserve the original tonalities. These pieces, composed independently, weren't originally a cycle for just one type of voice. With a single performer, you must either transpose the pieces too low for a high voice, or transpose the pieces too high for a low voice ... . Convention is a heavy burden! Like everyone else, I harbour my share of conventions. I'm so used to hearing a woman's voice singing *The Spectre of the Rose* that it still surprises me to hear it with a man's voice!' It surprises me too, and it's a surprise I really struggle to welcome. But I don't think it's only through attachment to 'convention' – if at least Boulez means thereby what is more commonly called tradition.

Obstacle. Gaston Bachelard proposed, now over half a century ago, the notion of the 'epistemological obstacle', parodied a little later as the 'epistemological cut'. The cut has gone out of fashion, the obstacle is still there, or rather the obstacles, of which Bachelard identified a few. The lesson of *The Formation of the Scientific Mind* remains to be pondered, but I find a salutary synthesis thereof in the historian Daniel Boorstin: 'The greatest obstacle to discovery isn't ignorance, but the illusion of knowledge.' But the crassest [la plus crasse] ignorance needing to be scoured away [à décrasser] consists precisely of the illusion of knowledge generated by naive obviousness: the course of the sun, the fall of bodies proportionate to their mass, the natural horror of the void, the variable oscillation of the pendulum, the heredity of acquired characteristics ... Since I've begun with serious quotations, here's another, from Gérald Bronner, to hang upon your wall in homage to Galileo, Darwin, Einstein: 'The authority of science is never so contested as when its conclusions run contrary to the natural slope of our mind, and yet it is always there that it is the most useful.' I'd only here wish to amend the overly hasty word: 'conclusions'. The worst of obstacles, at any rate, is the slope.

Oedipus. Camus wanted to imagine a happy Sisyphus. For Oedipus, there's nothing to imagine: one indeed suspects that he was so, and more than once, just as others, apparently, have 'unconsciously' wished to be, before and after him. The rest of his story was merely just reparation for this favour of destiny. Someone with a positive, but perhaps optimistic, mindset assures me: 'Nowadays, that wouldn't occur, thanks to DNA sampling.'

Olivette. In the spring of 1955, recovering from a recurrence of hepatitis, I had to spend three months at La Ciotat, in a convalescent home for students, owned by the historian–patron Daniel Guérin; I can't recall by what tortuous circuit a still Stalinist student could wind up in an institution run, albeit from a distance, by a wealthy but notoriously (among other things) leftist intellectual. The home was prettily called *Rustique Olivette*, and I wonder if it still exists, and for what purpose. The conditions there were somewhat spartan, and I shared my bedroom with a young American, a student at what was then called *Idhec*,[370] and who was also recovering from a severe infection. This chance roommate was called Noël Burch, now known for his work as a theorist of the cinema – I describe him thus because his essay *Theory of Film Practice*, published in 1969, bore on its wrap-around band the typically theoretical slogan 'Against All Theory'. Since *Rustique Olivette* had no canteen, we ate our more or less prescribed meals upon the checked oilcloth of a little 'workmen's' restaurant, as they were then called, in this town where shipbuilding was still active. Our twice-daily return trips were spent conversing about film-making (the region lent itself to this because of its station[371]), occasionally about literature, but alas most often about politics. Burch was dismayed by my Marxist 'commitment', and for three months subjected it to ferocious criticism. Naturally, I resisted as firmly as I felt I had to, but deep down I felt my defences gradually weaken. In fact, this commitment was to collapse a year and a half later – beneath other blows it is true, ones no longer of the order of theoretical argumentation, but of historical self-evidence. It seems to me nonetheless that our harbourside discussions had, in subterranean fashion, somewhat contributed to my deprogramming. But for me the most interesting thing was that, one day, a few years later, having in the meantime lost contact with Noël Burch, I learned that he had himself joined the (French) Communist Party. I've often wondered whether, in our exchanges, I'd pushed him as much in the one direction as he'd pulled me in the other. I'd be saddened for him and ashamed of myself, but I shall doubtless never know, and it is quite possible that he has since followed, with a time lag, the path he'd helped me to take. I have, in fact, happened to lose certain other friends by virtue of this process: firstly, I find them apolitical or (for us, the nuance was negligible) 'reactionary'; secondly, I 'make them join'; thirdly, I leave the Party; fourthly (and finally?), each of us

---

[370] L'Institut des hautes études cinématographiques, the 'Institute of Advanced Cinematographic Studies'.

[371] An allusion to the short documentary film directed and produced by Auguste and Louis Lumière, *L'Arrivée d'un train en gare de La Ciotat* (*The Arrival of a Train at La Ciotat Station*) (1895).

'condemns' the other, they me as a turncoat, and I them as an incurable Stalinist.

These comical to-and-fros have at least allowed me, subsequently, to accept certain spectacular reversals in the *Search* ..., which are often deemed, quite wrongly, implausible. The opposing pathways of contagion and conversion are as unpredictable as they are reciprocal. I've known examples of this in other domains, including the following, in a more frivolous register: at the beginning of the sixties, I'd made the acquaintance (of the leading kernel) of the *Tel Quel* group, whose praises I quite naively sang before Roland Barthes. The latter objected that these young people appeared to him to be rather 'menofletters [gensdelettres]', and that one shouldn't get too attached to them. We know the rest.

Ondénia. The lift at 72, Rue de Rennes, a Haussmanian building with a confectionery undertone [de nuance pâtissière] where I occupied, between 1956 and 1959, a maid's room on the top floor (it was then called 'a seventh in the sixth'), broke down every other time. On the other occasion, fitted haphazardly within a stairwell that hadn't wished for so much, it only allowed for one male or female passenger, which severely staggered any visits, not to mention the gnawing anxiety about an unforeseen halt between two floors. The room itself, roughly six square mansard-roofed metres, could barely take any more, and comprised no water point, even a cold one. On the other hand, a disused fireplace accommodated by way of mantel a square panel of plywood equipped with three unenclosed loud speakers whose rearward sound would be lost in the skies over Saint-Germain-des-Près. It was M. Caillon, the magician of the Ondénia workshop, then located in the shopping arcade of the old Montparnasse station, who had calibrated it to the nth degree above a tuner and a valve amp bereft of any pointless cover. He called this system an 'infinite speaker', and assured me that I could dream of nothing better for sound quality. So I dreamed of nothing better, and this acoustic infinity boundlessly expanded my living space. A skylight overlooked, due north, Rue du Vieux-Colombier, but without seeing it, since the peculiarity of this kind of opening is to allow you to contemplate only the sky. By contrast, I could very well hear the firemen's siren as they, at night, burst out of their nearby station, apparently like me enjoying an infinite speaker beneath the stars.

Until its disappearance in the eighties, I maintained my patronage of Ondénia – which in the meantime, because of said station's transfer and the construction of the homonymous tower, had withdrawn, provisionally and forever, into a miniscule shop on the irksome Boulevard Edgar-Quinet. Hence the disparate equipment I long had at home, for Ondénia had nothing but contempt for the regular stacks of major brand 'systems'. Dear Caillon had a salesman-cum-handyman named Lucien, and our three-way conversations, technical or otherwise (Caillon, as his name somewhat indicates, was a native of Sougères, a small town in Puisaye, on the border with Forterre), dragged on interminably, for want of a throng, business having gradually shrunk to the repair of small 'transistors' for regulars from the new neighbourhood. Caillon felt this decline even more keenly in that he had never really approved of, nor therefore kept pace with, the abandoning of valve amps (you had to say 'tube' amps), which were considerably more musical to his ears: 'It's far more linear', he'd explain to me without fear of refutation: I never really understood the nature of this apparently decisive superiority.

The sole element of my 'system' [Le seul maillon de ma 'chaîne'[372]] not fashioned at Ondénia was the turntable, which M. Caillon forbore to make himself, because this accessory had, in his view, a primarily mechanical function – but he had his preferences regarding cells and diamonds. My record 'collection', survivor of a few migrations, was moreover most limited, which elicited an ambiguous compliment from Noël Burch: 'I've never seen a collection containing so few bad records.' I presently say 'ambiguous' because I've since 'realised' that a record collection containing few records necessarily contains few bad ones, even if all those it does contain are bad. Maybe that's what Noël meant, but I rather think that his opinion was sincere, and that in his way he was merely commending the absence of Tchaikovsky, as Mark Twain once commended that of Jane Austen in an empty library. I'm not sure what may have lain next to this praiseworthy abstention, apart from some Bach directed, in Stuttgart, by Karl Münchinger, a little jazz, my fondness for which, after a few years of latency at Rue d'Ulm, had returned with a vengeance, somewhat via *cool* jazz, greatly via the Jazz Messengers *hard-bop*, and above all by way of a ten-inch vinyl by the Clifford Brown-Max Roach quintet,

---

[372] 'The sole link in my 'chain'; in French a 'chaîne hi-fi' is a 'hi-fi system'.

which included *Jordu, I Can't Get Started, I Get a Kick Out of You* and *Parisian Thoroughfare*. Another certain memory, the *Kindertotenlieder* by Kathleen Ferrier and Bruno Walter. Like many others at the time and in France, I discovered Mahler through this cycle of melodies, and I was pretty much unaware that he'd composed anything else, even the adagietto of the *Fifth Symphony*, which Visconti had yet to reveal to the masses.

I understood very recently what had for so long endeared me to the maison Ondénia, and which I rediscovered in a certain store selling and repairing age-old computers and other obsolete satellites: it's the unabashed application of a wholly artisanal practice – handiwork – to equipment elsewhere considered (I mean by me) to pertain to the mysteries of 'high technology'. On Rue Pascal, below Boulevard de Port-Royal, amid a jumble of keyboards, on a pile of lopsidedly heaped monitors, the cover of your computer in distress is raised like the lid of a shoe box, the thing is connected to a cable that just happens to be lying around, a random screen and a makeshift keyboard are added, its hard disc, processor, motherboard and other organs heretofore unknown to you are inconsiderately patted, and the faulty element is replaced just as did the cobbler of your childhood a worn-through sole, or the 'bicycle seller' a breathless air chamber, and off you go again. It'll be some time before you catch the train of digital progress.

Opaline. At Launay, the daily purchases were ordered from the kitchen and performed in town by the mistress of the house, accompanied by her most devoted white knight. Once over the Cessard bridge and across Place de la Bilange, between the theatre and the Budan hotel, around which strutted the officers of the *Cadre Noir*,[373] in matching uniforms and kepis, short in stature, bowlegged, leaner than their riding crops, we'd turn our backs upon the overly vast cavalry quarter, with its rectilinear limestone blinded in the sunlight, forever on standby for the next equestrian display, and head left along Rue Saint-Jean to enter into the old Saumur, squeezed between the Loire and the château, and even

---

[373] A corps of instructors at the French military riding academy (École Nationale d'Équitation) at Saumur, in western France.

gloomier than in Father Grandet's days.[374] On account of an ever-recalcitrant 'arrow', the old 402 with its cross-eyed headlights behind its crested radiator grille parked without warning on a pavement, as close as possible to the charming Place Saint-Pierre, to a store selling early produce too soon past its best, and to a spruce 'ironmonger [marchand de couleurs]', as were then called the small provincial bric-a-bric-cum-hardware stores, where you could find virtually everything required for a household's upkeep: washing powder, soft soap, encaustic, walnut stain, linseed oil, candles for the evenings when the mains failed and whose half light we'd beguile with readings aloud – for instance of the *Notebooks of Malte* (we'd never pronounce the rest of title), and I can remember too a session entirely devoted to *The Abbess of Castro*, just to verify or belie those imprudent words: 'Stendhal is never boring.'

But the most enjoyable visit was the one to an antique dealer-cum-second-hand shop where Jacqueline would seldom forego haggling over some old thing from an indeterminate era, a naive view of the Bay of Naples with a plumed Vesuvius, an umpteenth opaline vase in a spectrum stretching from lavender to turquoise, but also a Rouen blue with a cracked white background, always chipped Delftware tiles or a green and yellow Moustier, for which room would be found beneath the château's tarnished wainscots – since the townhouse had already had its fill, to the point that one knew not where to stand a vase or place a lamp. The purchase of furniture was inevitably rarer, but it was nonetheless on such occasions that I learned to distinguish oak from walnut, elm from cherry wood, a dresser from a buffet deux corps – or again, in a different register, never to say *'Enchanté'*, 'Pleased to meet you', nor *'Messieurs-dames'*, 'Ladies and gentlemen', nor *'Au plaisir'*, 'See you again!', never to 'clink glasses', nor to offer one's hand to an older woman or man, to reserve *'Mes hommages'*, 'My respects' solely for well- or poorly married women, to kiss hands only in a thoroughly allusive manner: a whole civilisation nowadays, I presume, submerged, even in these anachronistic provinces.

At Launay as in Angers, styles and periods cohabited with a nonchalance betokening a fine sureness of choice. Eclecticism was the only standard of taste, secondarily defined by a most chic,

---

[374] Félix Grandet, in Balzac's *Eugénie Grandet* (1833), set in Saumur.

though quite natural, contempt for costly luxury and the Empire style, left for the solicitors and the doctors, and a clear preference for rickety Louis XVI wing or armchairs, with wood painted in largely flaking blue and white, perhaps left as they were on the premises along with the walls, and the compliments of the previous owners. From this aesthetic *Bildungsroman* has abided with me a poorly assuaged fondness for second-hand shops, at least as long as one might find there something other than what to them now passes for 'old', and which scarcely goes beyond the interwar years: I always expect to find there the Doumergue[375]-style 'dining room' of my childhood. I can still picture quite clearly some of these stores, perhaps all of them now vanished, and which I should like to cite in honour of the profession: those of Trudelle, near Le Mans, of Luce Vergé in Saint-Chéron, of Jourde in Toucy, of Pierre Deux in New York, on the corner of Bleecker Street and 10th Street, and, in an unfindable village in Forterre, that of a quite distinguished woman, who sold only admirable things 'in their original state [dans son jus[376]]', whose exotic name always escaped us, and whom we called, for the sake of simplicity, Kiri Te Kanawa. This nickname by default really suited her kind of beauty.

Optimist. 'A happy imbecile' (Bernanos, they say).

Oracles. One day, the great Hegel was taken to the foot of the Alps. His commentary, perforce philosophical, was keenly awaited. After a few minutes of contemplation, the author of the *Phenomenology of Spirit* uttered these four definitive words: 'The Alps are there.' A century and a half later, in the course of a very academic dinner in a New York restaurant, a famous French analyst heard, from the mouth of an ordinarily more buttoned-up host, various highly Oedipal childhood memories, visibly destined to call upon (if not to test) his interpretative competence. At the end of the meal, Oedipus made off for some practical reason, and everyone turned towards Tiresias, expecting a sophisticated commentary, and if possible in the form of a laborious pun. The oracle fell, for once limpid and moreover judicious, but somewhat disappointing for his devotees:

---

[375] Gaston Doumergue was the president of France between 1924 and 1931.
[376] 'in its juice'.

'Funny guy!' An eagle, as is known, can fly as low as a hen, and it isn't always what it does the worst.

Oratory. In March, 1992, I attended Greimas's funeral, which I expected to be a purely civil affair. The ceremony was held in I know not which frigid premises on Boulevard de Ménilmontant, at the foot of my native hill. By dint of homages paid in the name of a host of learned and other societies, it lasted several hours, a duration fit to extinguish any kind of emotion. Once again, Greimas was giving the floor to others – but this time, alas, without the privilege of the final word that the ritual of his seminar had so long afforded him. This funeral has remained for me the perfect emblem of institutional verbal intemperance. The share of religious (Catholic) discourse was considerable, and even more unexpectedly for me in that I had never really caught sight of this aspect of his personality: I'd merely found, occasionally, that he'd compromise himself rather too often with various associations that I supposed to be para-Jesuitical or crypto-Dominican. I'd imagined that this was for purely intellectual, or pragmatic, reasons: these societies of thought must have been interested, among others, in the Greimasian method, which offered them a new hermeneutic tool, and he himself must have felt disinclined to reject such favourably disposed audiences, ever ready as he was to improvise a new application of the semiotic square. I thus discovered, naively astounded, a confessional belonging that had always escaped my notice. Yet my greatest surprise related to the very fact of this astonishment, and the error it retrospectively implied on my behalf: for want of the factual information of which chance had deprived me, I'd always considered it obvious that a man of intellectual pursuits of Greimas's calibre could logically adhere to no religion. While discreetly slipping away, for fear of pneumonia, well before the final funeral oration, I was caught between two explanations: either the adherence to Christianity revealed a flaw in Greimasian thought, or my difficulty in admitting it revealed another flaw, my own. I suspect that these two hypotheses aren't quite mutually exclusive, but I can see that the coexistence of rational processes and religious belief remains inconceivable to me. I know that a nineteenth-century scientist claimed to pass from his oratory to his laboratory simply by closing one door and opening another, but, not having inherited this type of arrangement, I struggle to think what I would do with it, and even to understand what others might do with it.

Oxymoron. Contradiction, they say, in terms: learned ignorance, dark light (Corneille), forgetful memory (Supervielle), dreamy bourgeoisie (Drieu), military music, military (to say nothing of civil) justice, European union, Palestinian authority, realistic utopia, socialist realism, collective individualism (Tocqueville), direct democracy, liberal stranglehold (or straitjacket) (Marie-George Buffet), parallel convergences (Aldo Moro), relativist dictatorship (Josef Ratzinger), popular bank, moderate Islamism, reality TV, nice surprise, proven lie [mensonge avéré], etc. I (vaguely) knew a chaste spouse who considered a certain 'conjugal duty', as it was still called, to be a *pleasant chore*.

Pacifism. It was the most consistent of my father's political opinions, one whose origin wasn't too much of a mystery. I still have, in his hand, a kind of journal where he'd begun, in August 1914 and in the grip of enthusiasm, to recopy, in careful schoolboy handwriting, the official communiqués of the High Command. The ensuing events spared him this Pecuchetian activity, by way of a more first-hand experience: drafted in January 1916, a few months learning what he would later call his 'killer's trade', embarked in 1917 upon the calamitous Chemin des Dames offensive, wounded *in extremis* (September 1918) in the Ardennes, treated in a hospital near Oloron-Sainte-Marie (despite the imminent victory, the wounded were apparently expedited as far as possible from the theatre of operations), there would abide with him a sense of violent shame concerning his past naivety, and in 1930, that's to say more than ten years of reflection following his demobilisation at the end of 1919, he added to this volume, as pointless as it was aborted, a vengeful but disillusioned codicil on the chances of an enduring peace. He drew his doubts from the manifest absurdity of the Versailles Treaty, and from the contradictions of internal and external post-war politics, despite his approval of the attempts by Wilson and Aristide Briant – his other great man, after Jaurès and before Blum, at least for his postwar internationalism and his (fruitless) efforts in favour of a European Union. His pacifism was typically 'left-wing', he judged in hindsight that the combined action of European 'workers' might have averted this massacre, but he augured nothing good for what was to come. On the 24th September, 1938 (that is, five days before the Munich Agreement), a post-scriptum to this post-scriptum: there was a new 'mobilisation-but-not-the-war', and, as we know, this final reprieve would last a year, but my father was already convinced that the war had again become inevitable, and was mentally preparing his kit, his mess tin, his gas mask and his quarter-litre tinplate flask. I faithfully recopy, spelling included, its final paragraph almost effaced by the years: 'I do not know at the present time if war can be avoided; I do not believe so, for when drafting is underway, I reckon it is too late. In any event, as for me, I shall try to remain myself. I do not know if I will have[377] the courage to resist the torrent towards which the others would like to drag me. I will do, in any event, whatever I can to restore peace at the earliest and by every means, if I do not have the courage or the luck to die straight away.' In these lines as in everything preceding them, the Giono-esque accent is discernible, and for good reason: *Refusal to Obey* had appeared in January 1937, and I can still see this slim volume, beneath its white cover and bright red title, which moved around our house from room to room, like a tract or a profession of faith. I assume that Munich brought him, as to Giono and a few others, some swiftly deceived relief: Daladier, alighting his plane, had said *sotto voce* everything one ought to think of those applauding him upon his return from Bavaria. But of that, no commentary from my father's hand. His cup, presumably, was truly full, knowing already that this cowards' peace was the preparation of war by other means.

His most powerful argument against the existence of God stemmed from his memory of patriotic butchery. In the same private memoir, I find the following fairly clear paragraph (written in 1930): 'What was sad to note at that time, as still nowadays, is that the men who believed the most in God, and, consequently, those who ought to have done the most to spare us the criminal enterprise called war, showed themselves to be the most bent upon launching humanity into this adventure. We could cite the greatest patriots of 1914 and the greatest generals such as Déroulède, Barrès, De Castelnau, Joffre, Foch, Pétain, Gouraud, etc., and we would

---

[377] Genette's father here writes 'si j'aurais', 'I would have', rather than the probably intended 'j'aurai'.

see that they are all great Catholic believers [it can be seen that he carefully excepted the Protestants]. And, paradoxically, still today, after four years of war, it is the free thinkers and the disbelievers who are the most pacifist and the most human. A whole chapter would be required to deal with the relations between religion and war. But what must one think of God's so-called representatives who accept a war with good grace; and what can be said about the all-powerful, just and good God, who allows such crimes to be carried out, other than that the negation of his existence emerges from the least resoning [résonnement[378]] on this subject.' I don't know if my pious mother was aware of this diatribe, but she'd heard him muttering often enough, after others, that God's only excuse is that He does not exist, and for my part I've never been able to prove this 'resoning' wrong.

In fact, he no longer had to demonstrate fortune or courage: redrafted into the engineers in September 1939, he meandered, with or without his useless equipment, from Dieuze (Moselle) to Véretz (Indre-et-Loire), then doubtless a little further down, like everyone else, in the direction of Bordeaux, our eternal strategic haven, without seeing a German uniform from near or afar. I was then also myself on the roads of this civilian and military exodus, and we weren't to meet again until after the new armistice. Subsequently, said uniforms were not lacking in our landscape, and he had a few more years to ponder the good and the bad aspects of what he in any event refused, rightly or wrongly, to call *passivism* [*passifisme*].

Pantalon/Trousers. Towards the end of the fifties, at the bottom of Rue de Rennes, a workshop–boutique supplied trousers for all sexes, and nothing else, but always made-to-measure and entirely hand-stitched, like the famous French tailor at the White House. The vigorous woman who ran this boutique was also keen on the exclusive title of '*pantalonnière*'. She left coats, jackets and waistcoats for others, but never justified this abstention. With her, it wasn't particularly advisable to confuse hessian, cloth, serge, flannel, gabardine, Tergal (*vade retro*), jersey and velvet

---

[378] 'raisonnement' would be the correct spelling; 'résonnement' in French means 'ringing', 'sounding' or 'echo'.

– but I'd been forever immune from these philistine-catchers. In a few decades of practice and theory, she had elaborated a whole philosophy of her trade and clientele, which she'd gladly expound, always orally, like Socrates: fabrics, linings, measurements, styles, fittings, alterations, with or without gusset, with or without pleat, with or without turn-ups, with or without darts, crotch worn to the right or the left (for the gentlemen, I mean), button or zip-fly, button or clip-on braces, with or without belt loops – contrary to Henry Fonda in *Once Upon a Time in the West*, she didn't condemn the simultaneous contribution of these two modes of suspension, as long as their effect was the right kind of 'fall'. All of this came after an attentive examination of the item to be replaced (the client would wait, in vaudevillian dress, in the fitting room): wear and deformation patterns reflecting, through buffing and/or transparency, a type of usage, thus a specific type of profession, and more broadly a way of life. 'You can see the whole man in his trousers', she'd invariably conclude and without the least intended ambiguity in this formulation where metaphor, however, verged upon metonymy. From this sociocultural confessional, you emerged thoroughly exposed and pricked to the bone,[379] and the Flore's scruffy thinkers and Lipp's[380] potbellied politicians could go eat their hearts out.[381] Roughly upon this site a 'large-scale distribution' store is today being 'raised'.

Panthéon. The Liberation meant among other things, for me, the discovery of something that was pretty much absent from my universe during the Occupation years: the Press – which was scarcely called 'written', for want of a media counterpart, and despite the already active role of the radio. To tell the truth, I especially remember two weeklies: *Les Lettres françaises* [*French Letters*] and *La Rue* [*The Street*]. The second was a vaguely anarcho-Trotskyist publication, basically very literary and 'Saint-Germain-des-Prés', edited, if memory serves, by Léo Sauvage. Its first (or final?) edition presented itself as an 'edition for the custody of the title',

---

[379] 'percé à jour et piqué au sang', 'seen right through and pricked to the blood'.
[380] The 'Café de Flore' and the 'Brasserie Lipp' are both on the nearby Boulevard Saint-Germain, in the 6th arrondissement of Paris.
[381] 'pouvaient aller se rhabiller', 'could go and get dressed again'.

an expression that was obscure to me, and all the more fascinating; but said custody was nevertheless short-lived. The other, as we are only too aware, was officially literary and, under Aragon, displayed a rather sociable Stalinism adorned with a few hand-picked 'useful idiots' carefully preserved from any formal membership, as such more valuable on the outside. In my head, all of this settled more or less well, before it settled only too well, then really badly.

On certain mornings, then, I'd walk down to a newspaper vendor situated at the end of Quai de Seine, and I'd climb back up my hill reading a few titles. One January day in 1945, doubtless in said *Lettres françaises*, I discovered the following in poster-sized letters: 'Romain Rolland in the Panthéon!'[382] Surprised by this maximalist slogan, in regard to a writer whose 'disappearance' (as they say nowadays) had utterly eluded me, it took me a few minutes to comprehend that there was no hyperbole here, and that the author of *Jean-Christophe* had been, since the 30th December, well and truly in a condition to justify this demand. In a physical condition, I mean, and to my knowledge the consecration thus called for was never granted; but all things considered and as far as hills go, Vézelay seems to me somewhat better advised than Sainte-Geneviève.[383] However, Rolland doesn't lie there either, but a few paces away, closer to his native Clamecy. The places where the spirit blows perhaps aren't the best chosen for the body's rest.

There remains that the idea – my own, in sum, albeit via a misunderstanding – of a pre-death 'Pantheonisation', in cases of exceptional merit, had nothing absurd about it: it would suffice every now and then to bring, to the happy surviving chosen ones, the means of subsistence necessary for them still to benefit a little from their glory, as was done for centuries for Egyptian mummies; a few names today spring to mind for so many anticipated, but cryingly urgent, transfers. The *Académie*,[384] in compensation, would be reserved for those proven to be deceased, upon the

---

[382] Interment in the crypt of the Panthéon is highly restricted, authorised only by a parliamentary act for 'National Heroes'.
[383] Romain Rolland died in Vézelay, in Bourgogne-Franche-Comté; the Panthéon sits at the top of the 'Montagne Sainte-Geneviève' in the 5th arrondissement of Paris.
[384] The 'Académie Française', a prestigious French council for matters relating to the French language; it comprises 40 members, known as the 'Immortals'.

mere presentation of a right to inter. As for the Nobel – which Rolland, precisely, had obtained in 1916 – Borges lambasted the jury's supposed injustice towards him with the ferocious indulgence he knew how to wield: 'They probably think they've already given it to me.' I'm not sure if Marie Curie, who effectively did receive it twice, initially objected to the second: 'You're perhaps unaware that I already have it.' Nor if one must wait to have obtained it in order to refuse it, like Jean-Paul Sartre (and Julien Gracq with the Goncourt[385]). Nor which inadvertently Pantheonised person might one day object: 'Sorry, I'm already there.'

That the Nobel should be (sometimes barely, and often at the least belatedly, like Einstein's, awarded 16 years after the exploit of 1905) always anthumous and the Panthéon always posthumous entails for the second no privilege of perennity, on the contrary: if I'm not mistaken, there has never been any question of withdrawing from anyone a Nobel prize deemed to be definitively legitimate; on the other hand, since Mirabeau, it is easier, if not more frequent – through a change of political wind, a family retrieval, or other incidental causes – to exit the Panthéon than to enter it. This precariousness appears judicious to me, the things of glory being what they are, but it's enough to disquiet some 'great man' when the time comes to apply for it. All things considered, Rolland made the right choice, and Aragon, who thought he was urging him there, will not have had the opportunity to meet him there.

Pape/Pope. One morning in 1957, one of my good teachers, who, himself now an inspector general, had had me appointed to the *lycée* in Le Mans, came, as was then the done thing, to inspect me in my own little class. By way of report, he invited me to the Brasserie du Théâtre, Place des Jacobins, at the foot of the cathedral, and, before a copious cabbage hotpot which he, as a true man from Lorraine, 'lightened' with a few potatoes, he discussed my pedagogical performance without dwelling more than was appropriate on this overly professional subject for a dinner between friends, advising me only: 'Don't be too far above your pupils' level: one lesson ahead should suffice to inspire them.'

---

[385] The 'Prix Goncourt' is a prize in French literature, awarded annually by the 'Académie Goncourt'.

Bardadrac

I found, for my own part, this recommendation to be rather optimistic, but he'd already proceeded to comment upon my recent exit from the CP, an exit that interested him more and of which he approved, but not without evoking my years of militancy at Lakanal with a hint of nostalgia: 'In *khâgne*, you really were the pope', he concluded. As an ex-protestant [parpaillot] (which after all I was just as much as henceforth an ex-communist), I deemed this retrospective statement to be somewhat damning, and unfortunately justified in its worst aspects. I would doubtless have preferred to receive, like Julien[386] in his seminary, the nickname 'Martin Luther' – which I deserved, in a sense, during these first years in Le Mans, where I found myself ostracised, by the local cell, as a dangerous apostate. At any event, having moved from one *khâgne* to another and from the role of student to that of teacher, I was no longer in danger of receiving the mitre that looks so much like a dunce's cap.

I have again, since then, been described as a pope of this and sometimes of that, and on each occasion I'm taken aback by the ridiculousness of this election without a conclave, and whose field is generally sketched without any great pertinence: 'of literary structuralism', 'of formalism', 'of poetics', even, more recently, and most inaptly: 'of *la Nouvelle Critique*'. Media orthodoxy consumes great amounts of hackneyed novelties and apocryphal papacies.

Paradox. We often go to great lengths to correct a principle or a system without realising that it would be far simpler and more correct to abandon it: this was the case, for centuries, with Ptolemaic cosmology. Or else we expend great effort seeking how to do something we have simply no reason to do. Or again we seek 'the reason for that which is not': see the Silesian child born with a golden tooth, about which there were 'so many fine works' which 'lacked nothing, save that it were true that the tooth was made of gold'. Fontenelle, who relates this story, derived from it a precept as judicious as it is little-followed: 'Let us assure ourselves of the fact, before concerning ourselves with the cause.' Bayle,[387]

[386] Julien Sorel, in Stendhal's *Le Rouge et le noir*.
[387] Pierre Bayle (1647–1706), French philosopher and lexicographer.

for his part, cited a remark encountered in *The Art of Thinking* (Port-Royal Logic) regarding an equally uncertain 'fact': to the question 'Why do the foals that have been chased by wolves become better runners than the others', Plutarch allegedly replied 'that it is perhaps because it isn't true'. Since it's always better to return to the sources, Bayle read and reread 'the Original of the 8th chapter of the 2nd book of the *Table-Talk*, in which this question is examined', and there found no trace of this reply. Fine example of a circular illustration: why did Plutarch, who isn't considered a humourist, produce so witty – and profound – a reply? Perhaps because it wasn't him. It's true that *The Art of Thinking* refers not at all to the *Table-Talk*, and that said reply may perhaps be found in another of Plutarch's works, perhaps now lost, and where the question wouldn't even be examined. The matter, as ever, grows in obscurity as soon as one is concerned to illuminate it, and Fontenelle wasn't too wrong to plagiarise Bayle without quoting him, which averts many a difficulty.

But, above all, we are often alarmed at supposed paradoxes that in fact stem merely from the supposition of an erroneous premise, of the kind: 'How can so and so, who is so intelligent, do (or say) such stupid things?' Simply suppress the relative clause, the scales fall from your eyes and the question all by itself, for in human affairs, foolishness explains many things. 'How can socialism, which is so generous an idea, have caused millions of deaths and even more to become destitute?' (that one, I admit, is somewhat outmoded, I evoke it for merely historical reasons). 'How can God, who is infinitely good and all-powerful, allow the existence of evil?' Here, the erroneous premise resides not only in the predicates but in the subject itself. It is often said that the answer lies in the question; one ought more often to realise that the right answer is to refuse an idiotic question. And modern orthodoxy, which constantly valorises questions, held in principle to be fertile, against answers, held to be sterile, somewhat forgets that one question out of two (at least) proposes merely false enigmas, and is only an answer in disguise. In all these cases, popular wisdom expresses it well, in three words: 'Spot the mistake.'

Paranoid. Even a paranoiac, said Henry Kissinger, can have enemies; in any event, nothing prevents them from making some, they fail not to do so, and therefore want not for them.[388] Likewise, a mythomaniac can tell the truth, if only by omission, even a Bélise[389] can attract suitors, even a hypochondriac can fall ill (in fact, they already are), a misanthropist can love a coquette, and an imbecile change their mind. What Kissinger omitted to add, and which isn't unimportant, is that even a paranoiac can have friends: it suffices that they believe to have, or make, the same enemies. Nothing brings people closer together.

Paris. It's my favourite city. Unfortunately, since I've lived there, I never go there.

Party. In the fifties, membership of the Communist Party (or, more modestly, of one of its metastases, transmission belts that were called 'mass organisations') comprised two on the whole fairly distinct aspects. The first was that of *militancy*, which was practised on the 'ground', and within the framework of local and workplace cells, in the direction of an external world that it was a matter of transforming and/or converting; the 'cell meetings', whose function was purely practical, occupied this side of things (who is posting *L'Huma[nité]* this week, who is 'speaking' in the factory or the lecture hall, who is organising a delegation at the Assembly, etc.). The ritual marches, on the 1st May (République, Bastille, Nation, in variable order) or (nowadays, I fear, become obsolete) for the anniversary of the 'Bloody Week', up to the Communards' Wall,[390] and the grand propaganda meetings, at the 'Mutu[alité]' or the 'Vel' d'Hiv',[391] which were addressed to the whole population, were also the concern of these militant overtures. The high point of this was for us all, in March 1953, a kind of funeral service in honour of Stalin, with a deluge of appropriate orations ('the man we loved the most') and the *Pathetic Symphony* in its ponderously unabridged version. Collective emotion and memberships guaranteed within the hour: all fervour is contagious. I recall that Maurice Thorez

---

[388] '… il n'y manque pas, et du coup il n'en manque pas'.
[389] A character in Molière's *Les Femmes savantes* (*The Learned Ladies*) (1672).
[390] See note 11.
[391] La Maison de la Mutualité, 5th arrondissement of Paris, a symbolic location of left-wing militantism since the 1930s; for the 'Vélodrome d'hiver', see note 368.

was, until 1964 for the most hooked, 'the man we love the most *in France*'; the specification was restrictive: our devotion was pyramidal – I mean hierarchical.

The other aspect was that of *membership* properly speaking, which was practised in the form of meetings reserved for activists alone, but where each could feel the extent and strength of the Party as a whole, embodied by the presence of surely prestigious leaders placed higher up in the organisational chart. These gatherings without external purpose (scarcely any practical decisions were taken there) served primarily to bind militants together around the latest slogans fallen from on high and to rekindle their enthusiasm, their devotion to the Party and their allegiance to its 'line', then highly variable on account of struggles for influence among 'Maurice's' presumptive inheritors, but invariably 'just'. These profane masses were held alternatively in three fairly vast rooms, whose property status was uncertain, but typically located in what is now called the Parisian East: Rue Jean-Pierre-Trimbaud ('Maison des Métallos'[392]), in the 11th arrondissement, Rue de la Grange-aux-Belles, in the 10th, and Avenue Mathurin-Moreau, in the 19th. We thus went en masse, once or twice a year, to 'Timbaud', to the 'Grange' or to 'Moreau', places of which I'm unaware what remains today, and which merge for me in the same drab and disciplined memory.

Yet one mustn't imagine that, of these two aspects, the second was in the service of the first, as ordinarily the organ – here: the *apparatus* – is said to be in the service of its function. For its leaders and their manipulative subordinates, this was obviously the case, but for the innocent militants, it was rather the converse; besides, the function makes the organ, and here the function's function is ceaselessly to create and recreate the organ: we weren't so much in the Party in order to be activists, rather we were activists in order to justify and restimulate our belonging to the Party. The reason for this is simple: it isn't militancy, but childish adherence that ties militants to their heads, whose true function consists less in acting upon the world than in *maintaining* an apparatus from which they derived a power they pretty much only exercised, circularly, upon it itself. As for the mere members [adhérents], they found in the

---

[392] Once the site of the offices of the French union of metalworkers.

Party the warmth of a family and the foreshadowing of a society in accordance with their wishes. I'm not sure that these features are peculiar to Communism: every political party is in large part an autotelic machine, whose cardinal function is to keep itself going, by internal combustion.

Before his ignominious exclusion in May 1952, André Marty, one-time mutineer of the Black Sea and, for us, hero of the International Brigades, was, among the leaders, one of the most popular with the communist students owing to an unpredictable brio far more flavoursome than the rigid jargon [langue de béton[393]] practised by his fellows from the political bureau. Drunk on an empty stomach, in confidential meetings he'd ramble on at length without notes, or rather with, before him, an enormous bundle of index cards that he'd consult perfectly at random. I recall one session, in an obscure back room in the Jussieu neighbourhood, where he rounded on Georges Bidault,[394] then minister of Foreign Affairs; the tirade concluded with the following sketch: 'Comrades, Bidault went to Pisa.' Pause. 'And, comrades, what did Bidault see, in Pisa?' Pause; the answer was obvious, but you didn't interrupt this type of effect. 'He saw the tower, did Bidault, comrades.' Pause. 'And comrades, do you know how Bidault saw the tower?' Pause. 'He saw the tower straight, did Bidault, comrades.' Pause. 'And what does that prove, comrades?' Pause; at which point, we silently threw in the towel. 'It proves that Bidault is twisted, comrades! It proves that he's twisted!' We were in heaven, and I believe in fact that the eviction of this truculent orator, motivated by the most obscure grievances, would for certain among us be one of the first snags in the seamless tunic of our Faith.

The register of Jacques Duclos was rather less seasoned, and was sometimes frankly indigestible. We'd enliven the liturgical duration by listening out for a few obligatory clauses, among which linger in my memory: 'Incorrigible reactionary' (applicable to any politician of the right or centre); 'The bourgeoisie in newspaper form' (*Le Monde*, of course); 'The admission is of some size' (after every opportune quotation from a 'class enemy' – but we never

---

[393] 'language of concrete'.
[394] French politician (1899–1983) allied to the Christian-Democratic Mouvement républicain populaire (Popular Republican Movement) (1944–1967).

knew *which* size); and the ritual invocation of the *US News and World Report*, a likely organ of 'American imperialism', but whose function was pretty much limited to this purely formal mention, which an accent fallen headlong from the *gaves*[395] would turn into a formidable elocutionary exercise, as gruelling for the ears as for the tongue: Demosthenes, we said, but *with* the stones.

The person 'responsible for intellectuals' was then Laurent Casanova, Thorez's former personal secretary, and as such assumed to be a man of high culture. With a slightly starchy bonhomie, his emphatic discourse was, for its part, adorned with an elocution perhaps attributable to a *pied-noir*[396] substrate, but cultivated to the point of artifice, and which was for a few years the most faithfully imitated in the lower ranked hierarchy, at least on the left bank and in the southern suburbs. It involved effects of intonation impossible to render in writing, but I can still hear this 'Laurent' exclaiming, before the sanctimonious stalls of the Maison de la pensée française: 'Ah! so much rot has been said about Stendhal!' The rot in question consisted of the idea that Stendhal had been, like all bourgeois writers, an 'incorrigible reactionary', and this idea, suddenly deemed 'sectarian', was refuted by the orator himself, with Aragon's approval, he who had already, in 1948 and in writing, defended the *Charterhouse* against a few overhasty comrades. There passed through the room a faint shiver of defied authority: much assurance and authority were always needed to attack a 'workerist' deviation in a party purporting to be that of the proletariat. The trick, effective but delicate to handle, consisted in denouncing the 'leftist', to be slain as an opportunist disguised as a sectarian. I don't know to which cunning, of this kind or another, was owed a few years later the exclusion, in turn, of the fabulous Laurent, an episode that surprised everyone and astonished no one. Aragon himself, always slaloming between two agonising revisions, passed unscathed through all the purges, as in those scenes of slapstick comedy where a single character miraculously evades the custard pies flying all around him.

Between 1951 and 1955 there'd formed at the Rue d'Ulm

---

[395] A generic name referring to the torrential rivers on the western side of the French Pyrenees.
[396] See note 331.

a little band that its detractors of all persuasions described as the 'groupe folklorique'.[397] Its charismatic heart, somewhat our Dargelos,[398] was without contest Jean-Claude Passeron, around whom gravitated, in diverse orbits, a few party members from the same intake (literary, 1950), such as Jean Molino and François Jodelet, from the one preceding it, such as Maurice Pinguet, and from the one following it, such as Paul Veyne, Christian Metz and myself. Occasionally approaching the fringes of this nebula were a few former students, like Michel Foucault, whose reasons for still living more or less at the School weren't always very well defined. In addition to the love of cinema, and of music, or more exactly of *Don Giovanni*, our common trait was a well-displayed propensity to waste a not so precious time in long rambling conversations around a radiator in the 'aquarium'.[399] This activity, if it may be so called, doubtless betrayed an unstable aggregate of immaturities, disorders and existential malaises that what lay ahead would vanquish to a greater or lesser extent. Some, indeed, hid away nightly to work even so.

After Stalin's death and the (fleeting) signs of 'liberalisation' that promptly followed it, casting a retrospective doubt upon the validity of what had preceded them, our conviction tended to slacken, and the weekly cell meetings, in the back room of the local bistrot, became a purely formal ritual. Those still compelled to undergo them sought to add a little spice to this chore with stupid wagers. It would for instance be a question of uttering in the course of the discussion a word taken by chance from a dictionary, and which could have but little relation to the day's topic. The first to succeed in using it had won, I don't know what but probably from the same place. The only performance of which I have any memory is that of Jean Molino who, landed with the word *gauge*, placed it very swiftly, and as though perfectly naturally, declaring: 'The success of this demonstration will be the gauge of the Party's influence.' This pre-Oulipian hapax scarcely raised an eyebrow among the participants not privy to the game, since of these there yet remained a few. On another occasion, one of them

---

[397] 'folk group', but with a suggestion of 'weird bunch'.

[398] A character in Jean Cocteau's novel *Les Enfants terribles* (*The Holy Terrors*) (1929).

[399] 'Normalien' term for the entrance hall of the ENS.

began an intervention with a prudent: 'Perhaps I'm about to spout rubbish ... '. One of us, the day's minute-taker, carefully noted this oratory precaution, and summarised the rest as follows: 'He did as he said'; the opportunities for this were not wanting. From these crepuscular entertainments there has abided with me a holy horror of the thing called 'meeting' and of the neurosis called 'meetingitis [réunionnite]', whatever its nature, motive, pretext and agenda might be.

Passer/Appear on. In the austere seventies, a Rodier advertisement showed a perplexed young woman: 'I'd gladly write a book, but I don't know what to wear for my appearance on Pivot.'[400] Nowadays, the right question is rather: 'I'm not sure what to remove in order to appear on the telly.' If in doubt, remove everything, and above all don't feel that you have to write a book: it won't really be about that.

Pay. When she considered me too inclined to hyperbole, my mother used invariably to say: 'You're not from Marseilles!' Like everyone else, she held Marseilles to be the folk capital of the tall story, and to express it she used the figure, for its part typically Lyonnais, of antiphrasis. My father, I think I've mentioned this elsewhere, remarked rather, in his perfectly pragmatic way: 'We can see that you're not the one paying.' And when I asked too many questions: 'Now really, you want to know everything and pay nothing.' His rhetoric was wont to have an economic inspiration: for him, ever attentive to financial penalties, everything was paid for one day or another, one way or another, and 'paye [pay]' was evidently his (period- and class-relative, presumably) word for what is nowadays called 'salary', or more fiscally 'income'. *Paye* was also a unity of time: an interval, of course, between two pay days, then a month for skilled workers (including him), a fortnight, even a week for ordinary proletarians – not to mention the day labourers paid (or not) as their name indicates. Curiously, the shorter the lapse of time, the longer it seemed, and 'Ça fait une paye!' wasn't far from 'It's been an eternity!', even where the joke *'Amen* ta semaine avec la mienne, ça fera une bonne quinzaine [*Amen*, your week with mine will make for a fortnight fine]' was still all the rage. 'Pay day' was

---

[400] See note 325.

no longer as festive as at the time, not so distant, when the 'end of the month' would begin around the 15th and the end of the week on Wednesday evenings.

Be that as it may, those who were paid for the time worked – even 'per hour', which all the same didn't mean 'at the end of each hour' – were in some sense privileged compared to those, then more numerous, who were paid 'à la pièce', which didn't mean 'in small change',[401] but according to the number of pieces manufactured, that's to say according to the quantity of work supplied, hence the need to go as quickly as possible. They actually rather used to say 'aux pièces', a simplistic form of merit pay. From there derives, of course, the expression 'On n'est pas aux pièces [We aren't doing piecework]' (for 'There's no rush'), whose impending disappearance fills me with dismay.

Péniches/Barges. In those days, the rivers of the Île-de-France were still frequentable for whoever didn't look too closely. The chlorohydric and reglementary entity called a swimming pool was unknown to us, we only had 'bathing spots', with wooden duckboards and cork markers casually moored to the riverbank, in the very course of the river. There were two of them for our enjoyment, on the right bank of the Oise: one at Pontoise, precisely a sheer drop down from the municipal college, and another at Maurecourt, a few strokes away from the confluence, and thus directly opposite our Fin d'Oise neighbourhood. Leaving the lake for beginners, swimming properly so called took place in the open water, from one bank to the other of this very human-scale river where they used also to stage, on town festival days, water polo matches, diving competitions, sometimes clownish (in frock coat and top hat), from the top of the bridge, and even water jousting contests. Despite its feminine name, which kept us from regarding it as *un fleuve*[402] (besides, the language of the boatmen, or bargemen, which also governs, by contagion, the vocabulary of 'those ashore', does not know, in the English manner, of the latter term: for us, any watercourse was *une rivière*[403]), the Seine

---

[401] 'Pièces' might also mean coins.
[402] A river flowing directly into the sea.
[403] Strictly speaking, a river flowing into another river or a lake.

intimidated us somewhat more owing to its breadth, and above all to its more industrial role: the 'trains' of barges apparently coursing straight ahead, albeit from bend to bend, between Paris and Rouen seemed to permit no recreational use. On the Oise, in contrast, other trains, drifting at reduced speed between meadow and orchard, in the fleeting shade of the poplars, passed within reach of arms and legs. It must be added that most of the boat traffic then went by way not, as is the case today, of 'barges' pushed from the rear, but of wooden scows, sometimes self-guiding, more often pulled in lines of five or six by tugboats with a touching silhouette, with their overly tall funnel that would fold in when passing beneath certain bridges. So only the tugboat was equipped with a scabrous propeller, and the barges, connected by cables, were for us, especially when fully laden, their rails just above the water, perfectly inoffensive and welcoming. Moreover each of them, or at least the last one, was followed, like a word by its comma, by a little boat you had to call a '*bachot* [wherry]', and onto which you might catch a hold and let yourself be towed along, or hoist yourself for the price of a simple pull-up.

I've never known which rule this boarding practice contravened; I rather think that there was here an amiable legal vacuum, and in my memory the bargemen, if not their dogs, almost always welcomed us with a cordiality reeking of schnapps, the Chtimi accent and caulk tar. The game, since a game it was, comprised three varieties. The first, practised especially on the very closed loop at Neuville, consisted in going against the current by barge, or on the barge's boat, as far as Cergy, and then returning on foot as close as possible to the river bend, which is scarcely more than a kilometre long. The second, a little longer but hardly more athletic, since in the direction of said current: in swimming the return, or more often afloat on our backs. The third, more unpredictably: in returning with the next downstream train, which sometimes kept us waiting – but we had the time. All the while possibly passing from one barge to another, either by swimming or suspended from the hawser. None of this was dull, especially in a mixed group, and you can understand why we gladly forwent 'holidays' at the seaside. I personally had little choice, but I have retained from those summers a preference for river swimming, between two grassy and shaded banks.

A stupid but inevitable challenge consisted, then, in using these means to get to school in Pontoise. I can't quite recall if I happen to have met it one day, but I do remember very well having boasted thereof, along with a few others. The boast involved arriving a little late in class, your hair soaked under the playground tap, and excusing yourself with an 'I missed my barge' that fooled no one, apart perhaps from the odd teacher, who'd somewhat feign naivety and dispatch the latecomer to the 'monitor' with the harsh note: 'Has missed his barge again.' Glory was at this price.

Conflans was then the 'capital' of inland water transport (it still is, but it's the kingdom that is languishing) and was home to two symbols of this function: on land, a boarding school, known as the Boatmen's School, for the children of boatmen, and a chapel-barge, christened *I Serve*, moored at the base of this school, along Quai de la République, which threaded its way between the two. I had once walked along this quay twice a week, with my mother, to reach the market whose trestles would be arranged beneath the lime trees, upon a bank lined with several rows of barges awaiting hire – the defunct bargemen's 'turn-taking'. A third symbol consisted, on days of strike action for the profession, of a Seine that was totally barricaded, from one bank to the other, by two or three lines of scows moored cheek by jowl: the river version of the picket line, perfectly impregnable save for a naval battle. For fun and with the union's permission, you could thus cross the river without getting your feet wet. Whenever the strike ended, the barges would part every which way like sheets of breaking ice.

To these signs of more or less active sovereignty there has for a few decades been added (or substituted) another, more retrospective in kind: it's the Inland Water Transport Museum, which occupies a few rooms of the preposterous Second Empire building called 'old château Gévelot', at the entrance to the Parc du Prieuré, behind the Saint-Maclou church. An instructive visit: I recently there learned everything I ought always to have known about the techniques of an industry whose heyday made for my own, and in particular about the method, which in truth had already disappeared before my birth, and which was therefore spoken about, in the thirties, only in the past tense: *towing*. It involved, if I've understood it correctly, driving the barge forward by fastening it to a submerged chain, meaning, in short, by having it pull along the riverbed. After all, this is how we all move forwards, on two, four or a thousand feet. So little boats then had legs. I long believed that the cable cars in San Francisco operated in the same way, but I have since understood that it's rather the opposite, inasmuch as it is the cable itself, drawn by goodness knows what pulleys, which moves forward in order to haul the cars, a bit like the 'ficelle [thread][404]' in Lyon, but in a more complicated fashion owing to the changes in direction.

But scows die too. They called, precisely, 'Bras-Mort [Dead-Arm[405]]' a kind of stagnant backwater, abandoned by the current and the fish to the frogs and the toads, which stretched, opposite the quays at Conflans, between a desert island and the left bank of the Seine. It was a quiet berthing site, somewhat a place of retreat for barges in their death throes, and my father, who rather knew what he was talking about, claimed to see in the expression 's'ennuyer comme un rat mort [to be as bored as a dead rat[406]]' an ignorant malapropism for 's'ennuyer comme un bras mort [to be as bored as an oxbow lake]'. The walk there was a tad melancholic. It was pitilessly drained, a few years ago, for the benefit of the market gardens where I'd gathered potatoes at the time of the 'restrictions'. In a film that owes it its title, shot in 1951 by Marcello Pagliero,[407] you would find at least a few images evoking this nowadays twice dead arm.

Periods. Arthur Danto writes somewhere, evidently apropos of contemporary art: 'We are not only living in a new period, but in a new type of period.' This clearly assumes that the other periods of art all belonged to the same type, at least if we compare them to the one we are living in, and one can see quite well in what way contemporary art calls for this diagnosis of absolute difference, which is perhaps merely a hyperbolic, but fairly ingenious way of stating its radical novelty: each period differed from the one preceding it, but the latest differs from all of them in a way that differs from all their ways of differing among themselves. Lévi-Strauss, already cited, said that it is the differences that resemble each other; on the contrary, the difference proper to contemporary art would therefore differ from all those (other) differences. I wonder if this diagnosis

---

[404] A nickname for the funicular railway in Lyon.
[405] 'Oxbow Lake'.
[406] 'to be bored to death'.
[407] *Les Amants de bras-mort* (*The Lovers of Bras-Mort*).

wouldn't apply equally well, beyond its practice of art, to the whole of our epoch. So we wouldn't have entered a new century, but a new type of century.

These speculations run the risk of merely falling prey to a new type of historical blunder, which could be branded the *prospective illusion*. The only certain way for our century to be of a truly new type would be for it to be the last – and by the same token, of course, the first so to be.

Perpète/Life. I'm unaware of how there came about the shift in meaning affording this colloquial abbreviation[408] the sense of *far away*: 'I'd like to return home, but I live *à perpète*, "a lifetime away".' Perhaps by confusing it with *Pétaouchnoque*, or *Pétaouchnerque*, which means in slang (as a consequence of what other shift?) any supposedly distant country. But I find in *à perpète*, evidently by virtue of its penal connotation, a more fittingly dolorous sense of the distance to be crossed.

Person. In my day, the master's dissertation was (more modestly?) called a 'diploma in higher studies [diplôme d'études supérieures]'. I wished to devote mine to the study of 'The Individual in Diderot's Novelistic Work'. The choice of supervisor, concerning this author and at that time, left little room for hesitation. I thus proposed my subject to the only then recognised specialist in *Rameau's Nephew*, who deemed the word 'individual' too dry, and proposed in turn 'The Person … '. This concept, with its whiff of bourgeois humanism, hardly suited the entirely Hegelo-Marxist idea I had in mind, and which bore on the relation of conflict, or liberation, between the hero, or heroine, and society. I dug in my heels, and this other conflict culminated in the synthetic motion: 'The Individual *and The Person*, etc.' I didn't find much meaning in this miry doublet, and a few months later I presented a hundred or so pages where, beyond the obligatory title, the word 'person' featured no more than did the notion to which it must have referred in my supervisor's mind. This absence didn't go unnoticed, and my mark suffered its effects. I've since

---

[408] 'À perpète' abbreviates 'à perpétuité', meaning 'life imprisonment', but also colloquially 'forever'.

remained on pretty poor terms with usage of 'the person', and, in the plural, with its depressing employment in expressions such as 'elderly persons', 'handicapped persons' or 'homosexual persons'. This euphemising prefix generally augurs nothing good, as though one really had to specify that the individuals belonging to these species are nevertheless human persons.

Pessimist. 'Unhappy imbecile' (Bernanos, once again).

Philopena. As far as I can remember, we called 'playing philopena [faire philippine]' the fact of finding, intertwined like twin foetuses in their shared nest, two almonds, then known as 'philopena almonds', in the same shell; or rather, the ensuing two-person ritual, which consisted in saying 'Good morning, Philopena!', in I can't recall which circumstances, and to win I'm not sure what – a kiss, perhaps. The most mysterious thing was obviously the relation between the thing and the word, concerning which I learned very much later that it simply derived, by way of a false etymology, from the German *Vielliebchen* (sweetheart). Which explains nothing, moreover.

Photocopy. Still at the beginning of the sixties, I only used (and doubtless only knew of) carbon paper, and the machine for duplicating by means of the thin sheets of waxed paper called *stencils* – as a result, the far broader use of this word in English, though perfectly logical, still somewhat baffles me. The hand-cranked Roneo,[409] which we inevitably called a Juliette, was the mother of all militancy. Its extinction, along with that of the industrial proletariat, thwarted our revolutionary hopes. Its replacement, called the photocopier, was bereft of any aura, but not entirely of sex appeal. The first one I saw, in the course of a 'mission' in a more advanced country, purred away in the office of a joyful apparatchik who sang its praises (but didn't demonstrate it) in the following terms: 'Sit your favourite student on it, and you won't regret your investment.' The influence of French culture was guaranteed. No longer works with the ink-jet printer. Always prefer the original.

---

[409] The trade name for this kind of duplicating machine.

Piano. Often aqueous. See Liszt, *Beside a Spring, Water Games at Villa d'Este*, Ravel, *Playing Water*, Debussy, *Reflections in the Water, Gardens in the Rain, Goldfish*. An excellent French pianist felt this affinity, when, weary of touring, he one day dispatched his instrument to the bottom of the lake, then, having apparently fished it out, gave a recital on a raft, in the middle of the bay of Talloires.[410]

One November evening in 1983, in the basement of the *Village Gate*, the first to have arrived, I'd positioned myself as close as possible to the piano for a clear view of the excellent Kirk Lightsey, recently freed from the Dexter Gordon quartet, and who was performing there as a soloist. Kirk appeared, sat down, wiped his head glistening like an Ivorian forward's, played a few notes, grimaced, and noticed my presence: '*Are you the tuner? – No, I'm the audience.*' He guffawed kindly – without realising what a linguistic feat this improvisation represented for me. I thought for a few seconds about the story, well known to jazz lovers, about George Shearing (blind like Art Tatum) hearing Monk play and asking: 'When will he have finished tuning his piano?' But no one would have asked this question apropos of Lightsey, far more 'virtuoso', and, when so minded, with an ultralight touch.

I have always enjoyed watching a pianist play from close to: in Sceaux, I had often, and at length, attended the practice sessions of my cure companion Jean-François Basset, a marvellous amateur who conveyed to me his passion for the greats of the German tradition: Schnabel, Fischer, Backhaus, Gieseking, Kempff, and whom I believe I can still hear in Fauré's sixth *Nocturne*, which to my ears he played better than anyone. I also followed, on two or three occasions, Laurent de Wilde, then debuting in New York, and who played, in the afternoon and somewhat just for the practice, in a deserted café in Chelsea. Close enough, once again, to miss nothing of the play of his hands. The fascinating thing was the tiny moment of hesitation which often preceded the beginning or the continuation of a phrase, an irrefutable sign of the endlessly aleatory character of this form of art. I obviously never heard, beneath his fingers, the continuation he chose 'finally' not to pursue, but I almost saw it, in the form of a barely sketched movement. I'm not sure that such waverings are very compatible

---

[410] On Lake Annecy.

with collective performance, nor that their *possibility* resists the automatisms of the inevitable professional routine, but the truth of jazz inhabits this imperceptible trial and error. One can see something analogous in films such as Clouzot's *The Picasso Mystery*, or Hans Namuth's *Pollock*, which show these painters at work. But the painter's hesitation can't be negotiated in the same way as the musician's, since they can always (more or less) correct (or spoil) one brush stroke with another; similarly the writer, as is evidenced, by way of traces, in rough drafts, or as would be shown directly in a film (such a thing exists, perhaps) where they could be seen in the act of deletion. The improvising musician, for their part, can delete nothing: every instant, after each fraction of a second of doubt, it's already game on.

Since my tête-à-tête with Lightsey, the *Gate* has more or less closed down, as has, no doubt for good, *Bradley's*, on University Place, which had for ages been, in alternation with its competitor across the way the *Knickerbocker*, the absolute sanctuary for piano–double bass duets. It was a tiny lengthwise room, with a bar on the right just past the entrance, whose shadows seemed to be lit only by the bottles aligned behind the barman and the glasses hung by their feet over the counter, then five or six tables for dining and, in a corner on the left, just enough space for an acoustic double bass and a black baby grand – they said respectfully: 'Paul Desmond's old piano', which may sound strange insofar as Desmond was the alto saxophonist in the Dave Brubeck quartet, but after all an alto saxophonist has the right also to play the piano, and one day to bequeath his own to his favourite club. On good days, the duet sounded marvellously fine, despite the inevitable noise of glasses, plates and conversations, also despite, every now and then, the impatient *shush!* of purists wishing to hear the music better, and whose protestations would inevitably drown the whole thing out. A kind of decadence seemed to me to herald the end when Bradley, perhaps to attract more hard of hearing music lovers, managed to add to the duet a drum kit which, in such a space, was sometimes in danger of spoiling everything.

At Bradley's, the coasters made from the thick blotting paper consisted of a circle roughly ten centimetres across, bearing, in black on a grey-beige background, the circular inscription *Bradley's – New York City*, and, in the middle, the sketch of a bearded pianist bent over the keyboard of an upright piano, which then isn't yet Paul

Desmond's, or which is its minimalist representation, a stylised sketch whose original, on a larger scale and neatly framed, held sway in the corner reserved for musicians. Without realising how melancholic it would become (the place was to close a few weeks later), one day in the autumn of 1996 I took away one of these relics, which now never leaves the shelf above my desk. I wonder how many copies are still lying around in the world at large, but you can discern the layout, and a few other images of the place – including also the sign in the window indicating the days and times of the sets, the musicians' names and the cover charge: $8 min (which mercifully doesn't mean, as I had initially feared, '8 dollars per minute') – on the sleeve of the first record (there's now a second) *Kenny Barron Trio Live at Bradley's*, recorded there on the 3rd and 4th April of that fateful year, plate noises included. So a trio, with Ray Drummond, bass, and Ben Riley, drums. It was one of the rare commercial recordings made at 70 University Place, maybe the only one, and probably the last. It isn't unworthy of the spirit of a place of which Kenny Barron had for years been one of the subtlest incarnations.

Pierres/Stones. In April, 1970, the bossa nova was no longer really in fashion, wasn't yet timeless, and the *garota* sung by Jobim and Moraes had long since abandoned her way to school. On the narrow twisting road that climbed from Rio to Petrópolis – it was no doubt before the construction of a more rapid and less dangerous motorway – the tropical roots, it was said, could in a single night raise the asphalt to the point of immobilising cars, or at least of ruining their shock absorbers. This didn't occur either on the way there or the way back, and in between the coolness of a hanging garden contrasted with the suffocating humidity of the bay. In fact, the difference is palpable from the first slopes, and the poor in certain favelas, and also the privileged classes of the Santa Teresa district, a chic favela, already enjoy a better climate – and a finer view, despite the cute fashion for g-strings – than the suntanned folk on the beaches or streets with swaying scenery of Copacabana, Ipanema and Leblon. Around a blossoming tree whose name I have forgotten, a flock of hummingbirds perpetuated their immobile flight. I envy Stefan Zweig for having elected this sublime balcony to have done with all the rest.

I had begun a supposed teaching stay in Belo Horizonte, interspersed with a few excursions beneath the immense Minas sky – a colonial pilgrimage to Ouro Preto and Congonhas, a minute of reverence in the modern church at Pampulha. The not so incongruous proximity of Aleijadinho's baroque sculptures and Oscar Niemeyer's modernist volumes was for me a source of elation. I've since learned that certain town councillors had proposed replacing the latter's church with a copy of a church by the former, and that they'd had to fight hard to prevent this reduction of the binomial to a single term. It's true that the great Niemeyer, Kubitschek's favourite architect, had become a *persona non grata* under the military dictatorship. Two journalists from the local press asked me what I thought, not alas about urbanism, but about Brazilian literature. I replied naively that I only knew one or two novels by Jorge Amado – my reading of which dated back to my years of militant education. At that date and in this place, it was rather like mentioning Brecht in Berlin under Hitler or Pasternak in Moscow under Stalin; the embarrassed look exchanged by my interlocutors confirmed this for me, and the interview came to an appropriately sudden end.

For which I was soon punished with a bout of renal colic that interrupted my classes between two sessions, deprived me of a detour to Brasilia, and consigned me for a few days, on a drip, to a local hospital, whence I was sent as swiftly as possible back to the international airport at Galião, where I was to catch the next flight to Paris, in a state that led to my awaiting the departure time in a lounge reserved for the flight crews. From my chair, I enjoyed the privilege of hearing all of my future pilots' and hostesses' conversation, as they debated, with utterly professional *sang-froid*, an apparently trivial question: would the plane, scarcely any healthier than I was, after some makeshift repair, withstand the diagonal crossing of the Atlantic, or would it be preferable to wait for the hypothetical next available plane? The prospect of these long impatient hours tortured me in my chair, and I was preparing selfishly to advocate for the most expeditious solution, when I realised that no one had asked for my opinion. It was followed even so, and at the end of an almost bearable delay the failure was declared benign, and the patched-up galley, its crew, my stone and I sailed forth. The plane wasn't overly full, which allowed me to spend 15 or so hours in a horizontal position, which moreover by no means soothed my torment. All of a sudden, the pain completely ceased, replaced, miracle of contrast, by a feeling of ineffable well-being, and at the same moment I heard the captain's voice announcing that we were flying over the French coast. I hadn't known myself to be so sentimental, but it was perhaps only my stone that had sensed what I dare not call the barn. The subsequent x-rays showed that it was neither a Minas topaz stone, nor even a mere Citrine stone, nor even less the famous 'soapstone' in which the brilliant cripple of Congonhas[411] carved his Prophets.

Pinceaux/Brushes. I always find it bizarre that one should speak of the 'style' of a writer based on 'the idea of it given' (as they say on the literary programmes) by a first-person fictional text: a novel in the form a (retrospective) autobiography, like *Adolphe*,[412] of a diary, like *Nausea*,[413] of an oral monologue, like *The Fall*,[414] or of an interior monologue, like *The Laurels are Cut*,[415] not to mention indeterminate forms like that of *The Stranger*,[416] where nothing indicates along which path the narrative has reached us. It would seem to me more correct, or more prudent, to credit this style to the narrator supposedly holding the pen, addressing themself to a listener or to themself, or expressing themself through one or another of these channels. I therefore understand James Cain's irritation, in his preface to *Three of a Kind*: 'Commentaries about my style always astonish me, for I try above all to write as my character would write.'

I accept that this clause of prudence, or of presumption of what Malraux called the characters' stylistic 'autonomy', may appear excessive – particularly in a case like that of *In Search*, a narrative just as ambiguous, although in a different way, as *The Stranger*, since Proust hasn't clearly chosen between a fictional status, whereby 'Marcel' would be an autonomous and fictional character, and a factual autobiographical status whereby the author would be at one with his 'hero'. It can very well happen, and doubtless often does happen, that an author doesn't make the effort demanded by Cain to singularise the style of his hero (or witness) narrator. Especially

---

[411] The aforementioned Aleijadinho (1738–1814).
[412] By Benjamin Constant (1816).
[413] *La Nausée*, by Jean-Paul Sartre (1938).
[414] *La Chute*, by Albert Camus (1956).
[415] *Les Lauriers sont coupés*, by Édouard Dujardin (1887).
[416] *L'Étranger*, by Albert Camus (1942).

in a classical regime: I do not think that Marivaux thought of distinguishing those of Marianne and of Jacob, he whose every character always speaks the so readily recognisable and, in its time, so criticised idiom that was his own. And no more do I believe that Proust, in the constitutive undecidedness of his autofictional aim, ever felt such a necessity apropos of a hero–narrator with whom he has so many reasons to identify – whereas he never fails to individualise to the point of caricature the speech of his (other) characters. Yet one ought at least to reckon more carefully with these effects of characterisation, when a writer troubles to contrive them: it's clear that Clamence doesn't 'speak' like Meursault,[417] and I'm not sure that the Ferdinand (tout court) of *Death on Credit*[418] expresses himself quite like the one (Bardamu) in *Journey to the End of the Night*.[419] Carl Dreyer, to whom a critic pointed out, apparently in bad part, the diversity of his styles, replied that that was precisely what he had sought to do: 'To find a style that is valid only for a single film, for *this* milieu, *this* action, *this* character, *this* subject.' Which was, perhaps unwittingly, to paraphrase Beaumarchais, whom 'a man of much wit, but who is rather too sparing therewith', asked one evening why, in *The Marriage of Figaro*, one finds 'so many careless sentences, which are not in your style', and who replied: 'In my style, monsieur? If by some misfortune I were to have one, I should strive to forget it while writing a comedy, knowing nothing so insipid in the theatre as those monochromes where all is blue, all is pink, all is the author, whosoever he may be.' Ingres, on a similar occasion, replied more curtly: 'Monsieur, I have several brushes.'

Pitta. I'm probably muddling my memories of two trips to Israel, in the spring times of 1975 and 1985 – both of them, then, during the almost peaceful interval between the Six-Day War and the first Intifada. Of the province of Galilee – the only charming one in a land more often arid, like the stony knolls of Judea, between Jerusalem and the Dead Sea – I have retained two images: the little town of Safed, perched like a Provençal village, where several

[417] Clamence is the narrator of *The Fall*, Meursault that of *The Stranger*.
[418] *Mort à crédit*, by Louis-Ferdinand Céline (1936).
[419] *Voyage au bout de la nuit*, idem (1932).

synagogues have been shamelessly, it seems, established in old abandoned mosques, we know how. One of them, crowned with a kind of minaret, affirms its Jewishness with a light sky blue whitewash around its door; but I'm perhaps here conflating two or three of them. The other image is that, evangelical *par excellence*, of Capernaum, at the foot of the Golan and on the shores of Lake Tiberias, with its cypresses, its eucalyptus woods and its Greco-Roman ruins, of which one is, however, that, still or already, of a synagogue. This is the dream location for the miraculous draught of fishes and the walking on water, even if the rational 'explanation' of the latter episode would rather suppose the briny basin of the Dead Sea, where the miracle consists instead in being able to sink; but Mark and John are categorical: it is indeed upon the 'Sea of Galilee' that Jesus surfed barefoot. The contrast between Judea and Galilee, of which Renan made so much, obtrudes without fail in this land forever destined to double-being. When you've spent your childhood upon these idyllic banks, you need a truly cruel vocation to make off and die on a cross in Jerusalem.

The Old City, within its ramparts, was perhaps, despite its Western Wall and its Church of the Holy Sepulchre, the most captivating of the Arab medinas, and in a sense the safest, thanks obviously to the tutelage we know about. I remained for long minutes awaiting the fall of the *pitta*, the unleavened dough the local bakers throw sharply against the vertical oven wall, which drops therefrom the moment it is perfectly cooked, and which they catch unerringly before it touches the ground, like the marshmallow vendor in *Monsieur Hulot*. You doubtless had to overlook some of the current circumstances, just as much indulgence was required in matters of religion to appreciate the vesperal charm of the orthodox quarter at Mea She'arim – where, however, excessively overt miscreant tourists ran a high risk of execution by stoning. I was accommodated for a few days at the Hebrew University, perched on Mount Scopus, a few kilometres to the north-east, where one evening I saw a horse cast, another *pitta*, its black silhouette upon a stone wall reddened by the setting sun. I made one or two daytime round trips on foot between this citadel-campus and Temple Mount, along a winding road, memorable since the battles of 1948, but, one night, I had to take a taxi to return from dinner in West Jerusalem. For a reason unknown to me – another urgent mission, the influence of alcohol, a desire to exhibit his mastery – the driver, at the wheel of his powerful Bavarian saloon car, covered this distance at the wildest of speeds, Monaco Grand Prix style. I don't believe, though, that we took the narrow Via Dolorosa, famous since Jarry for another uphill race.[420]

Placard/Cupboard/Nick. It is to civil society what the desert is to the political class, and 'purgatory' to the literary sub-class. But there are a few differences. The first is that you may *cross* a desert, not a *placard* (except in certain vaudevilles), where you may only obediently wait to leave, making the least possible noise, and with no guarantee of release. The second is that you can immediately (upon entering) recognise the nick, on account of its physical and moral darkness, but you can only recognise a desert once it's been crossed: if you remain there, it's no longer a desert, but a pile of bleached bones. As for purgatory, a mixture of desert and nick, it generally comes after the cemetery, and you never know, and with good reason, if you must hope one day to exit it, for the heaven of a finally definitive glory, or fear to exit it one (other) day, for the hell of nothingness.

Planche/Board/Plank. On mine I have a little bread remaining, and probably a greater amount of soap.[421] 'The world's greatest philosopher, wrote Pascal (after Montaigne), upon a plank that is wider than need be, if there is a precipice below, although his reason may convince him of his safety, his imagination will prevail.' Leaving aside the anacoluthon, this observation seems to me to ascribe to the imagination that which appertains to the entirely physical phenomenon of vertigo; yet, if we accept this analysis, I think it could be symbolically extended to situations where neither the one nor the other intervene, and which instead attest to the error of reasoning that makes the assessment of a fact depend upon the gravity of another related, but independent, fact. The most frequent example of this is the determination of good people, when the justice system holds a mere suspect, to turn horror at

---

[420] An allusion to Alfred Jarry's article 'La Passion considérée comme course de côte [The Passion Considered as an Uphill Bicycle Race]' (1903).
[421] Genette is alluding to the expression 'savonner la planche à quelqu'un', 'to soap someone's board', meaning 'to sabotage, lay a trap, pull the rug out (from under someone)'.

a crime into certainty regarding the criminal's identity: 'It's so monstrous that it must be him.' Should the jury give way to this paralogism, judicial error is just around the dock. The scapegoat's sacrifice derives from the same irrepressible need to 'punish' at any cost, albeit a manifestly innocent person and without consideration of the risk of mistaken identity, or of the relation of cause and effect. Returning to Pascal's plank, the philosopher's error might be described in analogous terms: the probably fatal outcome of an improbable fall causes one to deem probable this very fall. I hope there exist simple equations to correct this type of intellectual parallax.

Planet. I can't recall who said: 'Ah, I shall remember this planet!' But I fear that it should now be this planet that has a few reasons to remember our disastrous passage.

Let's dream a little. In one or two centuries, the now habitable surface of Earth will unfortunately be but a vast sterile desert; fortunately, this desert will itself be covered by an immense ocean; unfortunately, its water will be too polluted to drink; fortunately, there'll be nobody left to drink it.

Pleonasms. There has existed for a few years an Association for research at the École des hautes études en sciences sociales;[422] this, in my view, functionally redundant structure *en abyme* has always delighted me, a little as though one were to name, I'll say at random, a director of music at *France Musique*, someone in charge of culture at *France Culture*, of books at Gallimard, of cars at Ford, of spirits at Pernod-Ricard, of power at EDF, of oil slicks at Total, a Commission for Laws at the National Assembly, a chair of therapeutics at the Faculty of Medicine, a Minister appointed to Government Action. But I'm wrong to speculate: I'm assured that most of these roles do indeed exist, titles included, and I discover in the overly polished 'masthead' of an evening newspaper people in charge, concurrently, of *publication*, of *editing*, of *writing* and even, who'd believe it, of *news*. For the press as for the book, the motto could be: fewer and fewer readers, more and more editors, writers, informers, publishers and

[422] See note 251.

published products, everything inevitably falling within the ambit of the aforementioned Caillon's law.

The truth is, no doubt, that every institution inevitably engenders organs necessary for its internal functioning, whose inflation risks compromising its end to the benefit of its means: this sterilising proliferation is obviously called bureaucracy, or, a more colourful and already-mentioned appellation, a 'Mexican army'. Hence the need periodically to revive a more or less torpid primary vocation, with the only instrument at an institution's disposal: a new institution at the heart of, or next to, the old one, as Tocqueville saw constantly occurring under the Ancien Régime. They'll probably have, one day, to instil an association for research at the heart of the association for research. By 'instil [instiller]', I of course mean 'establish [installer]': having participated in two or three of these organisms whereby a minister pretends to enlighten himself, I know that the key moment in their bustling activity is the one where his Excellence in quest of light proceeds to undertake this establishment. A few months thereafter it results in a report, personally handed over by the president of the aforesaid. Thus with his own hands and beneath the flashes (here is the awaited light), the minister then affects to weigh, even greedily browse the copious document, always already ephemeral and henceforth promised to the gnawing attention of the termites.

Pneumatic. At a time when there existed neither fax, nor e-mail, nor SMS, and when the telephone, perforce landline, was an inaccessible luxury, this means of tubular, intra-urban, perhaps only Parisian and nowadays abandoned communication (commonly called 'pneu') was a crucial accessory in any romantic relationship, able to convey more developed, or more complex, texts than the overly laconic telegram. I've never really understood the principle of its functioning – for instance, what pump supplied compressed air to the innumerable pipes along which travelled the cylindrical cases, like those of Havana cigars, where you rolled up the addressed paper, and how their branching valves opened and closed from one quarter to another – nor if it could (surely not) reach any kind of residence, and if not, how it reached its fortunate or unfortunate recipient. What I can still see is the envelope still crumpled from its underground journey occasionally awaiting me at the entrance lodge of the École, carelessly pinned to the corkboard, and whose sheets of paper, once opened and smoothed out with the palm of your hand, still bore, on every page, the tiny stigma of this mode of display, not to mention the sharp touch, often more painful still, of the text itself. The supposed urgency of these messages apparently forbade entrusting them like the others to the negligence of the communal lockers occupying one of the walls of the entrance hall. What was thus gained in visibility was often lost in discretion, since it wasn't long before the 'pneu' in question began circulating across courtyards and corridors, in officious pursuit of its victim. I'm not sure what part was played by this postal practice, evidently reserved for the most personal messages, in the distinction, derived from the Greek, between the *pneumatic* (peculiar to the Spirit) and the *grammatic* (peculiar to the Letter), which we applied to all things and people: it wasn't good to have oneself labelled a grammatic, since, according to the Gospel, it is the letter that kills and the spirit that gives life. Yet I do have a memory of a pneumatic that killed, but after all it was only a letter.

Poétique. The most intense part of the editorship, at first tricephalous then, quite swiftly, bicephalous, of the journal – initially published, according to one of the ironies with which history was not ungenerous in those years, 'with the cooperation of the Publications Service of Paris-Sorbonne' – and of the derived collection, consisted in a purely telephonic 'editorial board' meeting between Tzvetan and myself, where we expedited current affairs, striving to grant the verb *expedite* and the adjective *current* [*courantes*[423]] their strongest sense. This duo endured, for the journal, until November 1978, when we left the keys, the lock, the door and the threshold [le seuil[424]] to Michel Charles, and for the collection until March 1987, when Tzvetan decided, for reasons he has elsewhere given, to relinquish his half of the editorship. It (the board) exercised above all on Sundays, late in the afternoon, just after the 'Record Critics' Panel' on *France Musique*, and began with a few considerations, which no emergency could expel, regarding the day's programme. The 'Panel's' memorable trio (Panigel-Goléa-Bourgeois) had in

[423] The adjective can also signify 'running', from 'courir'.
[424] The journal and collection in question are published by *Les Éditions du Seuil*.

the meanwhile abandoned us, which may explain part of this disenchantment: what to talk about after this absence of preamble? But I can remember one Sunday when we had a rather hard time continuing in prose after listening to the *Arietta* from opus 111.[425]

In the first months, we had decided to round up as far as was possible the barons and vassals of what among ourselves we respectfully called the 'old structuralists', or 'pre-structuralists' of literary theory: in no particular order, Propp, Jakobson, Tynianov, the Russian formalists in general, the American *New Critics* and their English 'precursors' (Richards, Empson), Auerbach, Jolles, Curtius, Benveniste, Wellek, Wimsatt, Zumthor, Spitzer, Greimas, Riffaterre and, of course, Roland Barthes. This virtual gathering obscured various 'Tabouret' quarrels[426] within what, to our mind, formed an almost homogeneous clan. It was perhaps a way of anointing ourselves 'young structuralists', or 'structuralists' tout court and sans hyphen. From one generation to the next, the baton was lost pretty quickly, and 'post-structuralism', whatever that may have been (nobody ever knew), came along to efface it all – *neo*-structuralism having today been adjourned for a fortnight.

We were bizarrely complementary. Tzvetan has described the relationship with the statement 'I was the one who found the texts, and Genette the one who refused them' – somewhat forgetting that the converse also occurred. I'm not sure who nicknamed us 'Starsky and Hutch'. I have never known whether this allusion was intended to be gratifying, nor how, between us, was apportioned the double moniker which may truly be said to belong to its time.

Ponts/Bridges. For those who take an interest in this marvel of human ingenuity, and very early on I had several opportunities to do so, at least three varieties deserve respect – and three kinds of respect. The first, the oldest and most aesthetically admirable, is that of stone arch(es) bridges, such as the Romans taught us to build; there's no shortage of them here, even if some were blown up during the several wars that the 'old Europe' has known. I've

[425] Beethoven's Piano Sonata No. 32 in C minor.
[426] An allusion to the practice in the French Court under Louis XIV permitting certain duchesses or princesses to sit next to the queen on 'tabourets [stools]'; the custom occasioned much nobiliary infighting, known as the 'Querelle des Tabourets'.

already paid tribute to the humpback bridge over the Huisne in Montfort-le-Gesnois, but see the more ambitious one in Beaugency over the Loire, or the one in Bordeaux over the Garonne. The second, more recent, variety is that of suspension bridges, which in one leap span the course of a *rivière*,[427] or even of its entire valley (that of the Tarn near Millau), of a *fleuve*[428] (the Hudson beneath the George Washington Bridge, between Manhattan and New Jersey), of an estuary (the Normandy bridge), the head of a bay (Chesapeake Bay Bridge) or its entrance: the Golden Gate between San Francisco and Sausalito, the Verrazzano between Brooklyn and Staten Island. But I confess a particular soft spot, which isn't of an aesthetic order, for the third sort, one apparently better suited to American habits, which consists of a roadway, or railway, borne almost at water level by a series of low columns, often, I think, without any regard for perhaps inexistent river traffic, in one of those waterways of which there is no shortage between the two oceans, broad but without depth and strewn with large pebbles like stepping stones, which in Westerns herds of animals ford, or swim across, when impelled to do so. This is, I believe, the case of the Susquehanna which descends without haste from the north of the state of New York all the way to the aforementioned Chesapeake Bay, which provides it with a disproportionate estuary. Unless I'm mistaken, the Amtrak rails between New York and Baltimore traverse it in this manner and, during the overly short crossing, you may behold, a little further to the west (upstream, then), another bridge, doubtless a roadway, which well illustrates my description, if it is one, and which never failed to enthral me upon each passing. 'Overly short' applies only to this particular moment, for otherwise speed is not this line's strongpoint, nor of any other in this land wrongly reputed for its velocity. The United States is in many respects a country of slowness (bureaucratic, in particular: *red tape*), and certain of their rivers break records in this regard, thanks to a sometimes derisory slope: as I've recently learned, the Mississippi itself has a total vertical drop of merely 185 metres over a length of 3,780 kilometres; I have this from a reliable source; discount a few rapids at the beginning, and see what's left in the plain; besides, without the Missouri come from

---

[427] See note 403.
[428] See note 402.

the Rockies, it would arrive bone-dry at its delta, which would therefore be no such thing.

The Susquehanna, then, if only for its name, evidently Indian like the other two, deserves this brief nod, but likewise does the more often sung Shenandoah, which follows, just as lazily, the Blue Ridge mountain range along its western flank, and which you think you can see from somewhat high up while following the Skyline Drive, a pure marvel for tourists in the autumn, and even in the spring. This is the crest road you have to follow, from Baltimore to Washington, at least until Charlottesville, in homage to Jefferson and the revolutionary saga of the Virginian *gentlemen*. I find that the *Mayflower* Puritans, future persecutors of the witches, are in comparison a little over celebrated: they may well have founded New England's first colonies, but the American Republic was so rather by somewhat less bigoted (sometimes even atheist, like Thomas Paine) men of the Enlightenment: Jefferson, Franklin, Madison, the authors of the great texts of 1776 and 1787. These are the true *Founding Fathers*, and this is the America such as it was loved, for its ideas, for its works and for its style. When we, rightly, extol our 'spirit of 1789', we rather too easily forget these two years of precedence.

My apologies for these meanderings. A fourth variety has moreover just rather belatedly occurred to me, one doubtless tending to disappear: that of lift bridges, as in Saint Petersburg, which open vertically when boats pass by. They are definitely the most fascinating to behold in action: you just have to wait a little for the opportunity. I can't recall which north–south street still has one in working order, above the Chicago River, so narrow between the glistening buildings towering above it. This piously preserved archaic detail is one of the charms of this so rigorously modern city. Let us pity those with no waterway to cross.

A fifth and final one, but not 'for the road': the 'canal bridge', which allows one (artificial, of course) river to straddle another. The most remarkable over here, thanks to Gustave Eiffel, is probably that, so graceful with its Belle Époque lampposts, of Briare, which allows the canal of the same name to rejoin, above the river, the sidearm of the Loire, and whose old towpath is now pretty much only used by walkers, but the real pleasure is no doubt reserved for the (small) narrowboats and other pleasure crafts that still use it, and which can (rarely) see others passing beneath them. The

same canal's other masterstroke was, a little further to the east
and nowadays fallen into disuse, the Rogny Seven Rise Lock, by
which one rose from the Loing (thus the Seine) basin to that of
the Loire. I recognise that appending (even a septuple) lock to a
repertoire of bridges is somewhat cavalier, but I once sufficiently
frequented the one and the other kind to marry them today
without further ado. A third kind, furthermore, somewhat takes
after the first two, crossing the river like a bridge and requiring
a lock to offset the difference in level: it's the river dam, whose
eddies exhaled downstream a rather powerful poorly definable
odour which prompted us to say, quite simply: 'It smells of water!'

Poppy. Like all names of flowers, especially when passing from one
language to another, this one is a pleasant semantic conundrum.
It is translated as *pavot* or *coquelicot*, it being understood that
according to good taxonomical practice the second is considered
a variety of the first: wild *pavot*, which is inevitably bright red,
whereas the *pavot* that is cultivated, or at least sown by human
hand, as we did in our garden with no more than aesthetic
intentions, may display various colours, among which I recall a
very pale, and even very dull, pink. In other words the English
language here eschews, as it does between *fleuve* and *rivière*, a
distinction our own is compelled to make. I assume that the
botanists' universal Latin confirms it, but that's not my point. The
California poppy, rightly this state's official flower (*state flower*), is
less emblematically named *golden poppy*, even though its manifest
colour is the orange-red (a little more orange than our red
coquelicot) I saw on a few specimens encountered between my
roadside and the course of the Russian River. But in California,
ever since January 1948, one doesn't skimp on the *golden*, so much
so that the official depictions of this flower surreptitiously draw
the colour towards golden yellow. I'm quite willing to accept that
yellow-orange nuggets were found in the *foothills*, in the good
times, and methinks that a reddish metal, like gold mixed with
copper, used to be called 'American gold', but it was probably only
really an alloy, even if, as Hugo in defiance of etymology would
say, 'in *orange*, there is *or [gold]*'. The Californian poppy, which
for me thus evokes more the *coquelicot* than the *pavot* (both) of
my childhood, just as high upon its stem and similarly stirred by
the slightest wind, reveals to the touch, a huge tactile surprise,

leaves that are far less crumpled, in fact rather thick, smooth and pulpy like those of a tulip. I know you can attempt to sow this *pavot*-tulip in France. Yet, incompetence on my part or ill-will of the Puisaye climate, I've never succeeding in doing so, and I swiftly gave up, in the name of the self-evident fact that a wild flower blossoms only where it pleases it to blossom.

Port. Sailors are traditionally alleged to have a woman in every port. The truth would rather be that all men, sailors or no, seek a port in every woman.

Portrait chinois/Chinese Portrait. Bernard Pivot simply asked: 'What's your favourite word? And the one you hate the most?' But the majority of the guests replied, not based on words, but on the things to which they refer (of which Pivot neither disapproved nor was perhaps aware), of the kind: 'The word I like most is *generosity*, the one I hate is *meanness*.' Besides the unbearable display of fine sentiments, it's somewhat the same category error as when, playing the Chinese portrait game, instead of replying with a metaphor, you reply with a metonymy, for instance: 'If he were a pastry? – He'd be a little madeleine. – A flower? – A cattleya.' After the portrait *tout court*, a game with an entirely taxonomic principle, based on successive exclusions, Chinese portrait was our favourite game at Launay, not only for its peculiar charm, but also for the selection it would instantly effect between the *vulgum pecus* scarcely capable of a hackneyed quotation and the *happy few* able to express a perfectly subjective, though (closely) shared analogy. We assumed that Proust himself would have immediately understood what it was all about, and it seems to me moreover that he proved as much. I'd really like to say which analogical answers I would give, in his case, to the two aforementioned questions, but after so many years *the game is over*.

Posterity. A few years ago, in the corridor of some learned institution, an old professor dedicated to another discipline took me aside and whispered: 'My son tells me that you're a famous person.' I savoured for a moment this confidential notoriety which might, if it leaked out, cause me unduly to be supposed illustrious. But after all, as Daniel Boorstin said, *a celebrity is a person well known for being well known*. More simply, but with a different accent, Colette: 'If I were famous, people would know about it [Si j'étais célèbre, ça se saurrait].'

Fame is to be well-known [reconnu]; true glory is to be little-known [méconnu], nay notoriously little-known, or even, if possible and as Vialatte said apropos of Richardson, *justly* little-known. To achieve posterity, that retrospective glory, I can see two fairly reliable recipes: die quite young, like Mozart or Rimbaud (I know), or live to be quite old, like Hugo or Verdi; if you've already missed out on the first, try the second. The real hard cheese is to die on the same day as someone whose more noteworthy disappearance eclipses your own: see Cocteau under Piaf or Prokofiev under Stalin. I'd like to cite some other examples, but I realise that this case only applies to the deceased who are already somewhat known: dying at the same time as an illustrious person is within the reach of any John Doe, and doesn't suffice to confer upon you any silent glory: it will just be a reference point for your heirs. In fact, at whichever age, on whichever date, in whichever way it arises, death procures the expected bonus only on the basis of a certain threshold of prior notoriety: famous deaths [morts célèbres], including John Lennon's, are nearly always dead celebrities [célébrités mortes]. As for me, I wish humbly, like Stendhal, to be read in 1930.

Pourquoi/Why. They can't understand why nobody loves them. That is precisely the reason, and it's an oblique illustration of the formula according to which the answer lies in the question – or more accurately, here, in the fact of posing it.

Pourtant/Yet. I find somewhat underappreciated the virtue of this concessive adverb, which, if I see it clearly, pertains to the fact that it can better than any other (give it a try) emphasise the paradoxical opposition, even contradiction, between a supposed cause and a supposed consequence, *just as well in one direction as in the other*: 'It hasn't rained, and yet the pavement is soaked'; 'The pavement is soaked, and yet it hasn't rained'. You could of course say 'The pavement is soaked *even though* it hasn't rained', but more clumsily 'It hasn't rained *even though* the pavement is soaked'. Or, to push the physical difficulty a little further, 'It has rained, and yet the pavement isn't soaked'; 'The pavement isn't soaked, and yet it has rained'. Or, to enter into the supposed psychological paradox expressed by Swann: 'She wasn't my type, and yet I loved her'; 'I loved her, and yet she wasn't my type'. I say here 'supposed paradox', because, as Proust more or less said himself, in this domain (that of feelings), *yets* are unrecognised *preciselys*. In psychology, and it is what makes this 'science' so endearing, there are no paradoxes, or nothing but paradoxes, which are thus no such thing.

Pramousquier. For some peculiar reason, this village, situated on the Côte des Maures, somewhere between Cavalière and Le Rayol, is never mentioned – not even on the occasion of a so-called 'natural' catastrophe of the (inevitably) forest fire kind. It was, in the summer of 1937, the destination of a family trip in my uncle André and aunt Marthe's little Rosengart – my first car journey, and all in all for a long while the last. With my parents, there were necessarily altogether five of us in this pre-war ancestor of the future 4-CV, or rather five and half, including my cousin Annie, to be born in November. I have moreover few memories of this stay, hence fewer than of another, a year earlier, by virtue of the first 'paid holidays', at Erquy (Côtes-du-Nord), perhaps thanks to a photo I still have of my mother biting into a chicken wing on the terrace of a seaside restaurant. Of Pramousquier, curiously, no photo, but a landscape painted by André, the artist in the family, trained at the Boulle school, later to become an art teacher, architect–decorator in his spare time and a rather better than amateur painter. This painting, in a pre-post-Impressionist style, which he gave to my parents and which I have miraculously conserved despite so many vicissitudes, represents the garden entrance of a cottage, which was thought to belong to the grocer Félix Potin.[429] It was perhaps merely his caretaker's dwelling, yet, in the way it is depicted, it isn't lacking in grace, and I wouldn't like to learn that it has been destroyed to make room for a luxury residence. Passing along these shores 20 odd years later, I attempted a verification, with no result, maybe due to my inability precisely to situate the place, in Pramousquier or its environs. Anyway, nearly two other 20 odd years have elapsed since this fruitless attempt, and in the meanwhile, as I said, the very name of Pramousquier

---

[429] Félix Potin (1820–1871) founded France's first grocery store chain, and is considered to be a pioneer of modern mass distribution.

has pretty much disappeared from the news, if ever it did feature there. I shall soon be, as Chateaubriand said about everything, the last to remember it. It's a pretty toponym nevertheless, which I surely wouldn't have made up.

My only direct recollections of this trip are, on the way back along one of Napoleon's roads, a chilly halt at Puget-Théniers, where the Roudoule coos [où roucoule la Roudoule], and the vision, somewhere between Digne and Grenoble, of a coach fallen into a ravine, whence were climbing blood-soaked survivors asking for help, and something to drink.

Predictions. There exist only two kinds worthy of logical interest: those that in English are described as *self-fulfilling prophecies* (which contribute, like the Oedipal Oracle, to their own realisation), and those it describes as *self-negating*, or maybe as *self-defeating*, which contribute to preventing it; for instance, Le Pen in 2012: if his score had been correctly predicted, he would never have managed it. It might be objected that the latter was *not* prevented, but this is merely due to its lack of having been conceived; this objection is therefore something akin to a confirmation *a contrario*. Those concerning road safety, on the other hand, do sometimes achieve their goal, which is to see themselves fortunately refuted: this is what is then called the *Bison Futé*[430] effect. The refutation can also be unfortunate: 'Everyone will leave in the morning, so leave in the evening'; as a result, everyone, forewarned, sets off in the evening; it is a more perverse version, if that is conceivable, of the Delphic Oracle. For an obvious, yet profound, reason, this possibility does not affect weather forecasts.

Principles. Logic knew at least three of them: the principles of identity ('What is is, what is not is not'), of contradiction or contrariety ('The contrary of the true is false'), and of excluded middle ('Of two contradictory propositions, one is necessarily true and the other false'). Psychoanalysis has identified two others: of pleasure and reality, society has recently imposed upon us a sixth, the precautionary principle, and quantum physics a seventh, the principle of uncertainty, for which I'd happily under any

[430] See note 212.

circumstances abandon the other six, given my respect for an eighth, the principle of economy, otherwise known as 'Occam's razor', which I rewrite as follows: 'Let us not multiply principles beyond what is necessary.'

Printemps/Spring. Around 1954 or 1955, Michel Foucault occupied, Rue d'Ulm, the post of 'qualified psychology tutor [agrégé-répétiteur de psychologie]'. One day he invited us to visit an unheard-of innovation, his 'laboratory'. Slightly intimidated, we followed him into an extremely gloomy cubbyhole, from which he extracted what was evidently a shoe box. Within this box there fidgeted a white mouse which appeared to have undergone a highly traumatising experiment. 'What you can see there, commented Foucault with his sibilant and overarticulated diction, is the embryo of the Laboratory of Experimental Psycholozy [psycholozie] of the École Normale Supérieure.' The embryo, you understand, was not the mouse, but indeed the box, which has been, I hope, piously conserved.

Emerging occasionally from this exiguous laboratory, Foucault gave at the École a kind of seminar, always on psycholozy, including one, very militant, session, which I failed not to attend, about Pavlov – yes, Ivan Petrovitch, the man with the dog. It should be noted that this commendable experimenter (I'm speaking neither of Foucault nor of the dog) then found himself retrospectively anointed herald of 'proletarian science', like Michurin and Lyssenko. I'm unaware whether anyone, in this field, still claims to follow him, but for a few months, the key to all anthropology was for us his theory of the 'second signal system'. This mysterious system formed part of our articles of faith, along with the opposition between bourgeois science and proletarian science, the inheritance of acquired characteristics, the absolute pauperisation of the working class, the tendency of the rate of profit to fall, and constant recourse to the formula 'It is not by chance if … ', a password for all the purposes of a passably paranoiac pan-determinism. Foucault applied to all of this, as to everything else, a somewhat frantic acuity, which utterly prevented us from disentangling with him the part of sincere commitment from that of iconoclastic sarcasm. The supreme Leader was already dead and embalmed, the 'thaw' foreshadowed a major debacle, mental reservation was already exerting its devastating effects upon the neophytes, and the 'philosophy of 1968' was yet to exhume the putrid corpse of Marxism–Leninism.

In the meantime, the psycholozy teacher [caïman[431]] entertained himself by inventing amusing dissertation subjects for the philosophy *agrégation*; I can unfortunately call to mind just one of them: 'If a swallow does not a spring make, which one?' We did not, indeed, know which one, yet, still in the meantime, the spring made itself all alone, I mean, alas, without us.

Prizes. Every year, the Goncourt is regularly awarded ... *au restaurant Drouant*.[432] No writer can boast of such a performance, since this prize can only be obtained once (save, of course, for double identities: a ruse Elsa Triolet had been the first, in 1948, to envisage then abandon for her *Inspector of Ruins*, and which eventually brought success to Romain Gary under the name of Émile Ajar), whereas you can receive, as at least Marie Curie did, the Nobel Prize twice – not for literature, it's true (and not for the same science: physics, 1903, chemistry, 1911): the well-known reason is that the scientific Nobel Prizes crown a singular discovery, while the Nobel Prize for literature crowns an author for the 'the whole of his work', whatever may become of it afterwards. I don't believe that provision is made for its withdrawal if what does come after turns out, as is often the case, to be disappointing; they simply contrive to award it sufficiently late for this risk to be negligible.

Exceptions notwithstanding, the Goncourt, for its part, honours almost always and by dint of its very establishment, not a literary work in general, but a *novel* – a single one, and thus with no hope of any recidivism. The latter clause is a wise precaution. My favourite aesthetic object isn't always a work of art, my favourite arts aren't the 'representative' arts, my favourite representative art isn't necessarily literature, my favourite literature isn't necessarily fiction, and my favourite fictional genre, as I've perhaps already said, isn't the novel – this admirable genre to which we owe *The Odyssey* (yes, *The Odyssey*), *Don Quixote*, *Lost Illusions* or *War and Peace*, but whose growing hegemony, within a hair's breadth of

---

[431] See note 65.
[432] Meaning both 'to' and 'at' the Drouant restaurant. The Parisian restaurant has received the jury for the French prose literature prize the 'Prix Goncourt' since 1914.

a monopoly, rather gets on my nerves. I read in a periodical: 'At once an essayist and a writer ... '; little matter from which pen, and apropos of whom, this powerful dichotomy obliges one to conclude that an essayist can be enthroned as a writer only in the name of a different type of performance – we can see which one – than that of his essays, doubtless in the name of an unwarranted interpretation of the Barthesian distinction (itself most fragile) between *écrivains* and *écrivants*,[433] and of the utopia, strictly rejected by Barthes himself, of 'intransitive' writing. Similarly, I heard the presenter of an excellent literary programme say, more or less, as a probably unwitting disciple of Käte Hamburger (outside narrative fiction there is no salvation): 'Your books are divided into literature – that's to say the novel – and essays ... .' Silly Montaigne, Pascal, La Bruyère, Saint-Simon and a few others, including, incidentally, all poets and dramatists: farewell Racine, farewell Shakespeare. Valéry, Breton, Borges have written a good deal of what needs to be said about this, and yet they weren't really familiar with that flower of the beginning of the literary season [la rentrée littéraire] nowadays known as the 'first novel'. Since prizes there are, and several of them can be awarded, in France alone, on the same day and thus many more than 365 (or six) per year, I dream of establishing another, in homage to the late Guillaume Dustan,[434] which would be the prize for the final novel. The conditions of its conferral would be very strict, or rather they'd boil down to just one, as indicated fairly clearly by its virtual wording. It would obviously be withdrawn in case of relapse, like a common-or-garden Miss France title, with a retroactive financial sanction. A less hard-line, but already salutary, version would be the prize for the Second Novel [Second Roman], with the same conditions, that's to say taking the adjective in its strict sense,[435]

---

[433] See Barthes's essay 'Écrivains et écrivants' (1960), translated as 'Writers and Authors': an *écrivant*, or 'author', uses language transitively, as a means to a communicative end; an *écrivain*, or 'writer', is engaged with language intransitively, as an end in itself.

[434] The novelist Guillaume Dustan died in 2005, aged thirty-nine; *Bardadrac* was first published in 2006.

[435] 'Second' in French (vs. 'deuxième') can have the sense of 'second and final'.

as did Radiguet in his day.[436] Candidates in a hurry could always start with the second.

François Weyergans[437] relates that the day following his Goncourt Prize, his newspaper vendor said to him: 'I knew you were a writer, but not to that extent!' There are degrees to everything.

Professeurs/Teachers. From the rather haphazard education I received at school in Pontoise, I have retained two or three things that have served me in life. In the lower sixth form [En première], a teacher reminded us in each Latin class that one mustn't translate *legatus* by *legate*, on the legitimate grounds that 'only the pope has legates'. Another, in year 11 [en seconde], imparted to us in compensation the Latin phrase *Cæsarem legato alacrem eorum* [*Caesar, animatedly, [replies] to their ambassador/ César aime les gâteaux à la crème et au rhum/Caesar likes cream cakes with rum*]; and the Greek *Ouk élabon polin, elpis, éphé kaka, ousa, alla gar apasi* [*They did not capture the city, since they didn't have a hope of taking it/Où qu'est la bonne, Pauline? Elle pisse, et fait caca, où ça, à la gare à Passy/Where's the maid, Pauline? She's weeing and pooing, whereabouts, at Passy station*]. A third, in year 10 [en troisième], commented upon Lamartine's *The Lake* 'in the manner of Sainte-Beuve and Lanson', meaning by seeking 'biographical information' therein. Thus, from the line *Sur ses pieds adorés*, '*Upon her beloved feet*', he inferred that at any rate Elvire 'had feet', and from *Où tu la vis s'asseoir*, '*Where you saw her sitting*', that she had 'something to sit on'. I don't know what this satire owed to reading Proust – nothing, probably. A fourth, in year 9 [en quatrième], by grace of shortages, taught us at once (I mean alternatively) Greek and gymnastics; I've never known on which side lay for him the vicarious function, but he seemed to us more inclined to make mention, and use, of his undeniable physical strength in Greek classes than of his Hellenic competence in gym classes. I've conserved from this strange combination a somewhat blurred knowledge of verbs in *mi* and, regarding Greek civilisation, an essentially athletic idea that is not unfounded. To a fifth, in year

---

[436] Raymond Radiguet (1903–1923) was the author of two novels, *Le Diable au corps* (*The Devil in the Flesh*) (1923) and *Le Bal du Comte d'Orgel* (*The Ball of Count Orgel*) (1924).

[437] Belgian writer and film director (1941–2019).

8 [en cinquième], we ascribed gaffes he'd probably never produced, and which doubtless belong to the universal schoolkid's repertoire, like the following abiding cento: 'I can see some who aren't here. Do you like having fun? Well I don't. There's only one idiot here, and it's me. The first I catch leaving last, I'll take ten at random and give you all a detention. It's just too much: as soon as I open my mouth, some imbecile starts talking!' A sixth, in year 7 [en sixième] had failed the English *agrégation* because he couldn't translate *tolet* into the language of Shakespeare. Inevitably, this fatal word had subsequently been etched into his memory, and consequently into my own: as everyone knows, it is *thole*, and even *tholepin*. To those unaware of the meaning of the French word, I dedicate, cheating a little, this definition found in a dictionary: 'Wooden or metal holder set in the *toletière* [thole board]' (don't look up *toletière*). To the same we attributed this infallible recipe: 'The language of Shakespeare isn't difficult: for *cheval* say *horse*, and so forth.' I can't recall in which class officiated a, slightly maimed, seventh, who, at the start of each school year, would challenge his pupils in the following terms: 'You've got five minutes to laugh at my disability.'

Professional. To be so in one's life, nothing could be more ordinary. To be so even in one's death, even though one doesn't practise a 'high-risk' occupation, is more meritorious. The Classical age has bequeathed to us a few illustrious examples: Vatel for a belated tide,[438] Molière at his third *Juro*,[439] and, unjustly less celebrated, Lully, who beat time with his stick and with such force that he injured his foot, and died of a subsequent infection. I'm not sure whether we should add to them John Locke, who (they say) found in death the means to curtail his controversy with Leibniz: that

[438] Majordomo under Louis XIV, François Vatel (1631–1671) (according to a letter by Madame de Sévigné) was so distraught about the lateness of a seafood delivery, ordered for an extravagant banquet for 2,000 people, that he committed suicide by running himself through with a sword.
[439] In the fourth performance of his play *Le Malade imaginaire* (*The Hypochondriac*), Molière, interpreting the role of Argan, became fatally ill uttering the word 'Juro [I swear]'; managing to conceal his state from the audience, he subsequently died in his dressing room.

would be to turn the refusal of dialogue into a philosophically indecent virtue, though one that is quite tempting.

Profondeur/Depth. I don't like false depth, said Valéry pretty much – and even less the genuine variety (I'll add that nothing is more irritating than bad faith, save, sometimes, for its good version, and that nothing is more irksome than a bad mood, save, often, for a good one). The same added, as everyone knows: 'What's deepest about man is his skin.' One may forgive Andy Warhol many things for having once declared: 'I am deeply superficial' – which makes for a fine lifestyle, but which requires great means. Justice must also be done to him for never having made, at least to my knowledge, a silk screen transfer of the excessively famous photograph of Ernesto Guevara, taken in 1960 by Alberto Gutiérrez.

Public. 'If all my admirers bought my books, said Jules Renard, I should have fewer of them.' This reasoning is rather tricky (I'm disregarding a crude interpretation, which, playing on the *of them*, would say: 'If all my admirers bought my books, there would remain fewer of them for me to sell'): it implies on the face of it that having to buy Renard's books would dissuade his admirers from (persisting in) admiring him, and on a more ironic level that said admirers, at the moment, admire him without having bought his books, but not necessarily without having read them. Renard purports to be complaining that he is admired without being read, but in fact he is complaining that he is read without being bought, which isn't very generous for a man of the left. The meritorious (humble, disinterested, disillusioned) utterance would thus be rather: 'If all my admirers *read* my books, I'd have even fewer of them.'

Puisaye-Forterre. As Colette already knew, there is an indefinable relationship between these two little regions of west Burgundy, which makes the second at once a part of the first, and its antithesis. Farthest westward, Puisaye is a clayey, damp land, destined to grazing pastures, prickly hedgerows, cider apples, coppiced woodlands, grassy rivulets and ponds teeming with fish: '*ma Bourrgogne pauvrre*, "my poorr Bourrgogne"', Colette used to say. On its eastern flank, heralding the undulations of Auxerre,

Forterre, as its name might indicate,[440] is limestone country, a shadowless and almost waterless land for wheat, of which only the 'summits' of the hills bear a few clumps of trees, home to Sunday's game. The physical border between these two lands leaps out at the least geographically minded of walkers. Nothing in common, in sum – no more than between the Guermantes way and that of Méséglise, which present the same contrast – except that here inclusion functions just as powerfully as exclusion: *here*, it's Forterre, *while there* [*que là*] (on the other side of a little winding road), it's Puisaye, one cannot be mistaken; but *at the same time*, Forterre, none would contend otherwise, is *in* Puisaye. Profound philosophers have labelled this logical mystery with the term *inclusive disjunction*. We get around it (poorly) by calling *Puisaye-Forterre* this ensemble as indissociable as it is unassimilable. But you can also get to Guermantes *via Méséglise*: it's the prettiest way.

Que là: I'm fond of this colloquial conjunction, with a rather adversative function, perhaps an abridged form of '*tandis que*, 'whereas', or of '*alors que*, 'while', where *là*, '*there*', signals a reckoning with present, and generally disappointing, reality: 'We were expecting a good harvest, *que là*, "while there", everything is toast!'

Punta del Este. Arriving on the 26th February, 1985 for a brief teaching visit, our plane's descent at Montevideo was delayed for half an hour by an event that deserved indeed to be greeted in this way, or another: the arrival, for his official accession to power, of Julio Maria Sanguinetti, the first democratically elected president after the years of terrorism and ferocious repression evoked quite well in Costa-Gavras's film, *State of Siege*. It was perhaps merely the disembarkation of some foreign delegation, but I'm certain about the historical circumstance. For this reason among others, the stay was most enjoyable. During some pedagogical interval, Lisa and Isaac Behar took me for two or three days to this rather elegant seaside resort, where they'd reserved rooms in a hotel fitted out in an old water tower, one room per floor, and which reminded me of a certain restaurant housed in a tower-bastion in Veere, in the Netherlands. It was at Punta del Este that I became suddenly aware

---

[440] 'Forte-terre', 'Strong-earth'.

of the distinctive feature, even in cities, of the old buildings of Latin America – from the Cape Horn to the Rio Grande, and even a little beyond, to Texas or New Mexico – namely of comprising just one storey, and sometimes just a ground floor. Curiously, there's nothing miserly about such low buildings; on the contrary, a form of nobility, or maybe prodigality, through abstention: 'We have too much space stupidly to build upwards.' I hope certain suburbs – sometimes peaceful, sometimes dangerous – celebrated by Borges still display this characteristic, if only to contrast with the oh so Haussmannian centre of Buenos Aires, which isn't lacking in another kind of charm, for once very urban.

Pupitre/Desk. Among the domestic occupations that, at least in the countryside, distracted him from his work, RB notes: 'I make for myself a desk, a pigeonhole, an index card box.' It's what you might call paradoxical equipment, whereby the means divert you from the end. However, it is quite clear that this investment can be, in the long term, highly productive. I don't have too much of an opinion about pigeon holes or index card boxes – none at all if the pigeon hole serves to stow the index card box – but few arrangements foster intellectual work more than the presence, around the table, of one, two or three oblique desks that expand the usable surface without exacerbating the horizontal cluttering. And I'm not talking about the pedestal lectern upon which you can write standing up, like Hugo or Hemingway. Besides, the computer screen, which RB, I believe, did not use, is in its way a kind of luminous desk – and, of course, a pigeonhole and index card box with virtually infinite capacity. Distraction [Divertissement] (in the Pascalian sense) intervenes therefore only when you begin to 'make for yourself' boxes and desks beyond what is necessary. As for index cards, I recall those, no doubt blank (occasionally a notebook), that he used discreetly to remove from his pocket, in a restaurant, to jot down on the fly an idea, a word, which doubtless wasn't often related to the conversation of the moment. You pretended to have noticed nothing.

Quatre-chevaux. I had to spend the summer of 1952 in Conflans, with a few comrades of both genders, at my virtually native home put up for sale after three or four years of temporary letting. The transaction took several weeks, during which I lived for the last time around the places of my childhood, but the passions of the times caught up with us in a landscape that had hardly been designed for them. One evening, equipped with brushes and white paint, we set off to write, at the expense of I'm not sure what acrobatics, on the deck of the road bridge spanning the Seine, this monumental inscription, with or without exclamation mark: 'PEACE IN VIETNAM' – a militant masterstroke followed on the spot by some perhaps already unhealthy, and politically unwise, bathing. Yet no one felt obliged or able to remove it, and maybe it served, a few years later, to protest against another 'dirty war', which concerned us a little less directly. I have seen it since, and it might well still be there, just somewhat dulled by time, rendered obsolete by History and preserved for it, while the bridge itself, doubled by a more substantial viaduct, is nowadays no more than a passage for pedestrians and, presumably, cyclists.

With the proceeds from this sale, in the meantime equipped with the 'coveted pink card [carton rose[441]]', the following winter I bought a grey-green Renault Quatre-Chevaux with a sliding roof, which was perhaps the first student's car to park in the courtyard of the École, and which quite ironically made me look like a rich kid. But in those days batteries were skittish, and that winter, and those following it, were harsh. I thus spent a few early mornings in the snow turning an ineffective crank handle beneath the very window of Louis Althusser, who, ever kindly, never reproached me for it.

My first trip, just a few days after this acquisition, took me, in one absurd go, the engine barely run in, without any real experience of driving and at a time when the *Autoroute du Sud* was still, at best, in the boxes of the *Ponts et Chaussées*,[442] all the way to Menton, where I was not expected – and, to be more honest, where I'd been strongly advised against going, but to advise against is not to dissuade. The welcome was somewhat less cold than I deserved, and my everlasting passion of the moment, her father and myself spent one or two days in that very pre-war Riviera hotel, joined at dinner by a prominent apparatchik, who was doubtless there to organise affairs more political than my

---

[441] A colloquial name for the French driving licence.

[442] The *Corps des ponts et chaussées* (*Corps of Bridges and Roads*) is a French civil service organisation devoted to the construction and maintenance of roads.

own. The evening was a little unreal, but the strangest thing was that no one made me feel the incongruousness of a presence that was doubtless embarrassing for everyone. I suppose the two politicians were rather refreshed by this clumsy romance whose meaning was as obscure to them as it has become for me. The relationship between public life and private life occasionally had such licence, in a milieu that was only proletarian in its ideological point of honour. I eventually left the place all the same, returning via the Alpine road without having guessed with which important militant decision I had mingled my affective quandaries, and without having received an answer to questions I had in fact forgotten along the way.

The same car afterwards served for more politically correct purposes: for example, the placing of a wreath at the foot of Tom Paine's statue, in front of the Cité Universitaire, the day before a violently anti-American demonstration; as far as I can reconstitute these reasons, the gesture intended to signify that the 'anti-imperialist struggle' wasn't targeting, quite the contrary, the American people in what was, or had once been, 'progressive' about it. Another kind of, rather more scabrous, transport was, the following year, that, towards some suburban hideout and under the vigilant watch of François Furet, of an important Vietnamese militant then sought by the police, whose name (evidently 'de guerre') I've forgotten, and who must have since, in his own country, become at least a minister, and finally a victim of some purge. The risk was real, if not considerable as far as we were concerned, but our awareness of it hardly compensated for the remorse, common to our whole generation, of having missed out, by two or three years, on the opportunity for heroism that the Resistance had presented, and the still more mortifying uncertainty about the manner in which we would have borne this opportunity. The emboldening formula, in this type of case, was: 'The Party will ask more difficult things of you.' It certainly often asked more stupid things of us. The demonstration on the 28th May, 1952, against 'Ridgway-the-plague', where the bullets, on Rue de la Banque, rather whistled past our ears and where Jacques Duclos was nicked with, in his boot, pigeons presumed to be spies, had fairly well honoured, at once, both of these criteria.

Still in the same car (mine), my first trip to Italy, with

François Jodelet and Jean-Claude Passeron, in the summer of 1954, must have been quite long, and certainly too expeditious, since we got to *know* [*connûmes*], to speak like Flaubert, the two Ligurian Riviera, Florence, Sienna, Rome, Naples, Capri, the Amalfi Coast and, on our way back, Orvieto, Arezzo (and even Borgo San Sepolcro), Assisi, Perugia, Padua, followed by a week's stay in Venice, and a return via Verona, no doubt one or two lakes and I'm not sure which Alpine pass. Long and gruelling between the different stopovers, given the vehicle's dimensions and its whimsical handling. But everything is relative, since it exceeded in length and breadth the smaller Italian models, and one evening, in a narrow street in the Oltrarno, a kid in the process of peeing against a wall turned round as we passed by and, all the while soaking my bodywork, exclaimed, awestruck, with the 'Arabic' (dixit Stendhal) pronunciation peculiar to Tuscany: '*Ma! Une mahina amerihana!*'

Quies. In 1952, Antoine Pinay, then president of the Council and minister of Finance, decreed a cut in prices, of 5% I think, that we, enlightened avant-garde of the proletariat, considered a scandalous machination of the imperialist bourgeoisie. One of my comrades, already a brilliant Latinist and at the time a great consumer of 'boules Quies' [earplugs] (I can't recall if he used them to protect his sleep, or his work, or both, or if he'd selected this brand for its Latin name), purchased at the chemist's closest to the École, namely on Rue Gay-Lussac, one box per week, whose price he knew by heart, and he'd prepare the exact amount to save time, for Tacitus waits not. He entered the chemist's, asked, with his sonorous Provençal timbre: 'A box of boules Quies, if you would be so kind', received his weekly acoustic preservative, left the habitual sum on the counter, and headed towards the exit. The door already open, he heard the scrupulous apothecary reminding him: 'Monsieur, your change!' Stopped in his tracks and furious about the delay, he went back towards her believing he was thinking to himself: 'Ah, you bitch, you're applying the Pinay cut!' From her look of astonishment, he at once understood that he'd thought out loud. He got away with a change of dispensary (all applied said cut, of course, but he was now sufficiently informed by the event no longer to risk the same blunder, and to prepare the new amount), which henceforth took him triple the time each week, a victim at once of Pinay, of Tacitus, and of his overly resonant convictions.

I who suffer, as I've already mentioned, from hyperacusis, regret being so unable to bear this kind of anti-hearing aid, which adds to the noise outside an internal humming quite unfit to drown it out. I thus do without, even on the night of the *Fête de la Musique*.[443]

Quillet. As soon as I'd mastered the practice of reading, I made excessive use of the only dictionary present in the house, which was called the Illustrated Larousse in two volumes. I thereby learned at least half of what I've since forgotten. But a neighbour [une voisine] owned another one, called something like the *Encyclopédie Quillet*, whose title seemed to me more promising, the illustrations more colourful, and the content more instructive. I had access to it by special favour, but exclusively for on-site consultations. These peculiar conditions increased my interest tenfold, and I do believe I spent whole days flat on my stomach upon this amiable person's carpet, where I learned the other half of this ephemeral knowledge.

Radio Days. Like everyone born in 1930 or thereabouts, I belong to the 'radio generation' – the only one of its kind, since the only one, on either side of the Atlantic, to have grown up under the exclusive influence of that medium: before us, it barely existed, and was in poor shape; after us came the television generations, of which nothing announces the decline, except the arrival of the Web generations, and others. To this presence of the radio and absence of television I can only compare, in a quite different domain, the decade favoured, in the sixties of the same century, by the presence of the pill and the absence of AIDS. On the radio of the thirties, then, on short or long wave, amid the fading and the 'crackling', I remember among other things certain boxing matches, right hook, left jab, uppercut, clinch, the referee breaks it up, second round, left hook, etc. all the way to the throwing in of the towel and the final ring of the bell. My father would then get up, immediately turn off the set in the interests of economy, and comment like a connoisseur: 'Great match.'

---

[443] The 'Fête de la Musique (Festival of Music)' takes place in France every 21st June.

The Tour de France, still on the radio of course, was another matter. In those days, the mountain stages were still held on scarcely passable roads, and the Aubisque, the Tourmalet, the Galibet and especially the Izoard were truly the hell of the South, just as the cobblestones of Paris-Roubaix have remained the hell of the North. The greats of the era were called Antonin Magne, the two Maes (Romain and Sylvère), who weren't brothers, and of whom the first held the yellow jersey from end to end in 1935 (as had already Bottechia in 1925 and Frantz in 1928), little Archambaud, the heroic and hapless Vietto, who was inevitably called 'King René', the immense Bartali, who 'knocked the Tour for six' in '38 on the Izoard, and Speicher, who won the downhill stages 'at breakneck speed', a feat for me superior to all the others, with the exception of, as an enthusiastic journalist more recently said apropos of Marco Pantani, winning the Giro and La Grande Boucle[444] 'at the same time' (he no doubt simply meant 'in the same year', a more frequent exploit, at least since Coppi in 1949). But the breakaways within a single stage impressed me too, at least when they were 'solo [solitaires]' – an adjective whose power seemed to me without limit. It's true that their knowledge by hear-say, in these pre-TV days, rendered them paradoxically far more spectacular: one learned that, during a mountain stage, a given rider had 'gone off' alone, and, a few hours later, without too much intermediary information, that he had arrived half an hour – time enough for a good shower – ahead of his pursuers. One was thus apprised without ever having been able to 'witness', as we do nowadays on the small screen, of a ride that somewhat resembled a rise to heaven without a witness – the word 'ascent [ascension]' was fitting. I didn't for that matter really understand how several riders could break away together: the rigorous discipline of the relay technique escaped me, precisely – to my father's great despair, who occasionally endeavoured to impart it to me on the ground; yet, only ever cycling in tandem, we could certainly roll turns, but not 'attack' together an absence of peloton. I failed to understand, also, why a good rider couldn't win *all* of the stages – which no one, evidently, has either done nor dreamed of doing, except perhaps Faber in 1909 (six stages of which five consecutively), but I wasn't around, and Merckx: eight in 1970, but

---

[444] 'The Big Loop', another name for the Tour de France.

he was no longer around. Incidentally, and as far as I can remember, the idea would never have occurred to him that a rider might have been 'doped'. Assuming that he'd have grasped the meaning of this word, it would have made him fall from his saddle.

Certain races known as 'classics' took place not far from us, including, I believe, 'The Loops of the Seine', and especially the 'Polymultipliée', whose theatre was, unless I'm mistaken, the hill at Chanteloup – which wasn't yet called 'Chanteloup-les-Vignes', just as one never said 'Mantes-la-Jolie': these names doubtless came a bit later, when Chanteloup had lost its vines [vignes], and Mantes its prettiness [joliesse]; names bear to things, and especially to places, an often distant relationship, and serve as compensation. Be that as it may, and in spite (or because) of the flesh and blood spectacle they afforded the early birds, these classics rather wanted for prestige in my eyes, since you could, and for good reason, neither win *a* 'stage' that wasn't the *only one*, nor progress to an 'overall ranking' that merged with the one and only finishing order. I've never known whether the 'Polymultipliée' derived its name from a mysterious peculiarity of the gear ratios used, or from the fact that, ridden as a circuit, the Chanteloup hill was climbed several times. Another never elucidated mystery was that the circuit, apparently, comprised so to speak no downhill section, at least none worthy of the title breakneck.[445] Its key perhaps pertains to the well-known fact that all of l'Hautil's inclines, apart from the ascent from Chanteloup, are gently sloping.

Récit/Narrative. The way this term has been used for some time rather baffles me. I can see that one is thereby frequently opposing *narrative* to *novel*, apparently in the sense of 'nonfictional narrative'. My bafflement stems from the fact that I was raised with the age-old idea that the novel itself *is* a narrative – in principle fictional – and that this far vaster category encompasses several genres, fictional (novel, novella, epic, tale, myth, etc.) or not (history, reportage, biography, autobiography, etc.). Consequently, to oppose *narrative* to *novel* seems as incongruous to me as to oppose *animal* to *horse*. It occurs to me though that the volume of Gide's fictional works, published in the Pléiade in 1958, is

---

[445] 'tombeau ouvert', 'open tomb'.

entitled *Novels, Narratives and Farces, Lyrical Works*, and that this posthumous distribution refers back to another, published before his death (Gallimard, 1948) and thus doubtless authorised: *Narratives, Novels, Farces*. It is well known that Gide described at least *The Vatican Cellars* as a 'farce', as a fiction with a fairly fanciful, ironic, even burlesque tone, and that he laid claim to the status of 'novel' only for *The Counterfeiters*, which ascribes by default the label 'narrative' to all those of his works of fiction that were neither *The Counterfeiters*, the only novel, nor the *Cellars*, and other eventual farces. The justification for this choice may be found at least in 'Plan for a Preface for *Isabelle*', written in 1910, and often quoted: 'Why was I careful to call this little book a "narrative"? Simply because it doesn't respond to the idea I have of the novel; no more than do *Strait is the Gate* or *The Immoralist*; and because I wouldn't wish for one to be mistaken. The novel, such as I recognise or imagine it, comprises a diversity of points of view, subject to the diversity of the characters it portrays; it is for me a disconcerted work.' *Isabelle* appeared in 1911 without a preface, but with, as subtitle, the generic mention 'narrative', which thus applies retroactively to *The Immoralist* and *Strait is the Gate*, and implicitly I assume, subsequently, to *The Pastoral Symphony*, to *The School for Wives*, to *Robert*, to *Geneviève*, and perhaps to *Theseus*, to designate a work of fiction that is shorter (but doubtless not short enough to be described as a 'novella'), and above all less 'polyphonic', as one will later say – but that's perhaps how the surprising 'disconcerted' should be heard – than those to which Gide accords, in good or bad part, the status of novels. Works of monophonic fiction, with one character or with a very restricted cast, and above all with just one 'point of view', of which we may assume that Gide found (I don't know whether he mentioned this) precedents in Constant (*Adolphe*) or in Fromentin (*Dominique*), in the tradition of what has been called the 'personal novel'. We could therefore say that the abuse, through a restriction of meaning, of the term *narrative* finds there its letters of nobility, if modesty is any such thing, or this rather haughty way of declining (as already with Balzac) a somewhat suspect generic favour. Yet, as we can see, it isn't the same abuse: contrary to 'ours', Gide's, in the absence of an available and adequate third term, is clearly declared, and at least merits consideration. If criticism – especially in the media – had at its disposal a modicum of cultural memory, this precedent would be enough to cause embarrassment, since the choice 'novel or narrative' would refer it to two discordant alternatives: fiction or nonfiction, polyphonic or monologic fiction. But the condition has apparently not been met.

Refutation. After half a century, I struggle to put any order into the memories and traces remaining with me from the two years, chaotic in every respect, that elapsed between the summer of 1954 and the autumn of 1956. The competitive examination once passed, I was entitled to a so-called 'research' year from which I derived little benefit for the advancement of a phantasmal project, for I do believe that I devoted this murky period, interspersed with stays in the infirmary, to various intellectual endeavours that didn't have very much to do with it. For a reason that is scarcely mysterious to me today, the slow work of ideological recasting that before long would be named 'de-Stalinisation' began for me with some initial thoughts (so to speak) about the cinema. I remember having already had, in March 1954, upon the release in France of *La Strada*, a rather lively discussion with Georges Sadoul, to whom I'd occasionally go and say hello, Rue de Bretonvilliers, in his vast office adorned, on its rear wall, with a huge planisphere, its colours muted by a few years of daylight. This passing controversy evidently had political implications (what didn't in those days?), but the funny thing is that I cannot today recall which of us defended the film, and which condemned it – the one and the other, to be sure, in the name of a sound Marxist interpretation of this ideologically unclassifiable work. I'm not certain of having seen him since then, and in any event I could only with difficulty reconstitute my state of mind at the time. Perhaps it would suffice for me to find Sadoul's review in the right edition of the *Lettres françaises* in order to infer *a contrario* what my 'judgement' was, but I'm not sufficiently concerned by it to impose this investigation upon myself. The fact remains that my first disagreement with an orthodoxy already shaken by the death of the Supreme Leader and its immediate aftermath was expressed in relation to a film. I believe that I also, during the same spring, sketched for my part a defence and illustration of *Lola Montès*, Max Ophuls' baroque-esque masterpiece which didn't receive a good press on the left. This sketch was abandoned in a drawer, but not a diatribe entitled 'The French Neo-Scouts', which was published in November 1956 by the then monthly journal

Les Lettres nouvelles. The attack was aimed at two films equally representative of the era's left-wing self-righteousness: *If All the Guys in the World*, by Christian-Jaque, and *The Best Part*, by Yves Allégret. Beneath the display of fine sentiments that communist criticism had hailed as progressive, I sought to denounce a petit-bourgeois and (therefore) fundamentally reactionary ideology. It was a new way for me to oppose a cultural orthodoxy that, now no longer daring to vaunt the 'socialist realism' of the Zhdanov years, endorsed, more half-heartedly, its sugar coated by-products. I said this article had appeared in the *Lettres nouvelles*, but in fact, and quite wisely, Maurice Nadeau only published the first half – the most insignificant.

Things had in the meantime shifted onto a vaster terrain: I find on yellowed paper several drafts of what I wasn't afraid to call a 'general theory of ideology', where I strove to align an increasingly residual Marxism with a progressive awareness of the (shared?) autonomy of science and art. I forsake wading through this hodgepodge, it too paved with good intentions, but somewhere within it I fall upon the question, formulated literally in these terms: 'When is there art?' and followed by a resolutely relativist answer to this altogether premonitory question, and which might convince me of a kind of continuity of thought, if I believed in that sort of thing. I can see too that this effort to open up Marxism relied upon Stalin's well-known 'works' on linguistic theory, and more precisely upon his condemnation of Marr's ultra-Marxist theory, which had claimed to see a superstructure in language: 'Who, wisely objected the author of *Concerning Marxism in Linguistics*, who would have an interest in water no longer being called water?' (It wasn't Marr, meanwhile vanished into the vast dustbin of history, but indeed Raymond Queneau, who would reply one day: 'Me').

All of this was evidently brewing in several minds, and would culminate in, among other things, the book published in January 1956 by Pierre Hervé, *The Revolution and Fetishes*, a searing critique of what he called 'ideological extremism', or more brutally 'fetishism'. This book, doubtless rejected by the official publishers even though it too opened the umbrella of Stalinian moderation, was published by La Table Ronde, which gave the orthodoxy's guardians a supplementary argument for its emphatic condemnation – among which guardians was Jean-Paul Sartre, who then wasn't loath to play, as

Edgar Morin has said somewhere, at back-seat driving. The matter would very soon lead to its author's exclusion, who thereby found himself, and without having quite wanted or deserved it, the first to leave the party on account of a premature, paradoxical and all the more pernicious de-Stalinisation. It wouldn't be long before I followed him beyond the walls, for the same reasons but of my own free will, and I shall say thanks to which equally paradoxical helping hand.

In the autumn of 1956, the Russian tanks' entry into Budapest put paid to a few vague hopes of any internal opposition. Yet I had retained from my years at the École the habit of taking counsel on various subjects from the one who embodied for us, within the limits of our shared unreason, the voice of wisdom: Louis Althusser, whom we nicknamed, with an affectionate pleonasm, 'Old Alt'. In the fifties, consulting Althusser was, for every turmoil or case of conscience, political or otherwise, an exercise comparable to that of the Catholic confession, with, ultimately, not absolution, but the resolution of conflicts and, as we certainly did not say, the peace of the soul.

One finds in the 'Gallery of bastards [salauds]' in *Nausea* a character, Rémy Parrotin, with a similar role, in the service of a different (though no worse) cause, and whose method consists, faced with whatever rebellion is confided to him, in declaring that he understands it, that in a sense, perhaps, he shares it, even that he could take it a bit further, much further – so far in fact that seeing him, at the end of his reply, recover from it himself so clearly fortified in his faith, the humble rebel comes to doubt his doubt and returns to the fold. 'He was loved because he understood everything; you could tell him anything.' In the politically opposed register that was our own, Althusser, too, understood everything, but his understanding, I'm sure, was not feigned, his benevolence was sincere, and he was quite the opposite of a 'bastard'. In any case, in agreement or disagreement, you could but love him. From the then soothing twilight of his office on the ground floor, you always emerged miraculously reconciled with yourself and, more importantly, with the Line – though a little surprised by the efficacy of the session, acknowledging with as much admiration as chagrin: 'I've been Althussered again' (of this figure of speech at least, I am not the last surviving witness). So I went along once again to be Althussered on the mysteries of de-Stalinisation and subsequent re-Stalinisation. Dear Alt listened to me, as usual, with a full understanding of the case (mine, I mean), then, instead of refuting my remarks point by point, he decided to outflank it with the patent enormity of its logical consequence: 'What you are saying cannot be true, he pretty much told me, and with a rueful gentleness, for if it were true, it would mean that one should have to leave the Party.' Apparently, in those years and for many years yet, this formula constituted in regard to all of this the ultimate basis of his thinking, whose every reasoning culminated in the conclusion, obviously anterior to its premises: remain in the Party, which is only ever mistaken to good effect. For me, this refutation by the absurd was a ray of light. Once again, Althusser had resolved a crisis, but, on this occasion, against the grain of what he was seeking. I thanked him with a profusion whose irony he was doubtless too sincere to discern, along the lines of: 'Thank you for everything, it's because of you that I can see what remains to be done.' I've never known whether the practical consequences of this conversation had surprised him, or upset him, but anyway my departure didn't long remain isolated enough to merit any particular attention. I publicly tore up a 'card' I really ought rather to have kept for the purposes of salutary mortification.

Remparts/Ramparts. In *khâgne*, we had three ways of skipping incognito the lessons that to us seemed pointless. The simplest consisted in not going, but one still had to know where to be during this time: for example, follow *another* lesson, in another classroom. The sneakiest consisted in placing at the front of one's table a row of books high enough to hide from the teacher, shielded at regular intervals by falsely attentive facial expressions, a substitute activity: reading or writing relative to some other subject, occasionally to the same one. The teacher generally refrained from seeking to look more closely at what was afoot behind what was very officially called a 'rampart', and of course, each rampart sheltered different, strictly private, work, protected out of respect for the way each of us was supposed to be 'preparing for the competitive exam [concours]'. But the most effective consisted in burying oneself at the back of the classroom, where we'd placed a kind of wardrobe affording a more discreet refuge, for it offered no way of being observed from the teacher's rostrum. Since this refuge afforded only one or two places, accessing it entailed conforming to a strictly regulated taking of turns. There was nothing secret about its existence in itself, and there were occasions when a teacher, keen for some exceptional reason to address one of us missing from his seat, would yell from the height of his rostrum: 'So and so, I know that you are behind the wardrobe, I have something to say to you that is useful for the exam. Exit your refuge, so and so, appear, appear!' Only, it so happened that, through a window equally well hidden by the wardrobe, said refuge directly overlooked the park – since the Lycée Lakanal benefited from a private park quite tempting on fine days. 'So and so' thus hadn't always remained behind the wardrobe: occasionally he'd jumped out of the window, was frolicking in the leafy shade, and was no longer in a position to appear. In the best of cases, he'd return just before the end of the lesson. One way or another, we'd make it known to him that he had in the meantime been called. He finally appeared, and apologised, so to speak: 'Forgive me, Master [the formal respect due to our teachers demanded the use of this title], I had fallen asleep. – Ah I see, replied the Master, I nearly awoke you, it is for me to apologise to you!' Thus went, liberal and cosy, a 'competitive exam preparation' whose results statistics were a harsh illustration of the method.

Rendez-Vous. They were due to meet very late in the afternoon, on the square, between the Théâtre-Français and Avenue de l'Opéra, which was yet to bear the name of André Malraux, at the stop of the bus that descends Rue de Richelieu in the direction of the Guichets du Louvre. The scene of the missed rendez-vous was familiar to him, and he obscurely anticipated its repetition. The light was fading, the street lights were coming on. After 30 or 45 minutes of impatience, he was ready to call it a day, when he saw the arrival, immobile behind the lighted window of a bus that was slowing down, of the no longer hoped-for face. He was pleased he'd waited until this moment: had he left one minute earlier, the meeting would have been missed through his fault, and with it many things, perhaps forever. The 48, then, stopped before him, a few passengers got off, others got on. The familiar profile remained frozen behind its window, without a glance to the left, and the vehicle resumed its journey towards Saint-Germain-des-Près. It was like a death. There remained for him only to assess, on this familiar theme, an unprecedented and all in all quite subtle variation: he couldn't exactly say that she hadn't come to the rendez-vous, and nothing even proved that she hadn't missed the stop inadvertently, and that she would not, confused and repentant, alight pointlessly at the next stop. He believed no such thing, but the following days he abstained from asking any questions, and things continued along their way until their terminus, and even a little beyond.

After six years of rollercoaster ordeals comprised of captures, abandonments, resumptions [de prises, de déprises, de reprises], surges, lapses, revivals, relapses, let downs [faux bonds], rebounds [rebonds], evasions, unexpected delays, pinned-up pneumatics, impromptu phone calls, fulfilled or disappointed expectations, variably enduring reprieves, he received one day a long sorry letter which called for no reply. As things then stood, the statement of their break-up wasn't exactly a revelation, it ought to have been a relief, and perhaps it was, despite his wish, where there entered a certain dose of perverse curiosity, to let the experience run all the way to its end. He put the letter in his pocket and made his way to a film showing, on the Champs-Élysées, where he knew he would find its sender: it was the first projection of a film by Robert Bresson. Upon leaving, he accompanied her home. The walk was long, and in the deepening night her fine Modigliani-esque face faded with every step. They spoke without really knowing what about, but he was careful not to mention the letter he continued to crumple between his fingers, and he felt his companion gradually convince herself that he was yet to receive it. He wondered whether she would let this final meeting remain there, without evoking the crux of the matter out loud. That would perhaps have been the simplest thing: he'd 'receive' the letter the following day, and the rest would be a finally wordless history. But it was he who saw it thus: she, as he was later to assume, dreaded it otherwise, on account of the misunderstanding. She eventually took the initiative, as though to confirm her decision to herself: 'I sent you a letter … .' He interrupted, as casually as possible: 'Yes, I received it – and I've read it', and, while – to speak like James – his last vessel blazed away on the horizon, he improvised a flippant diversion supposed to bring things back to their proper proportions, reciting to himself *a parte* the classic formula for a mortifying farewell: 'To think that I wasted, etc.'[446] For

---

[446] A reference to Charles Swann's well-known interior monologue at the

want of a more complete reading, he was unaware that a being of flight knows no point of no return, and that the only law of destiny is for it ever to reserve for you yet one more surprise.

Rentrée/Back to school. At the beginning of the fifties, I had to escort by car, with his mother, a boy of around 12 for whom what we now call 'schooling' wasn't easy, all the way to a religious boarding school in Redon. Not only religious, but perfectly Catholic, perhaps even run by Jesuits. I wouldn't be able to recall why this officially Protestant family had resorted to so extreme a measure – probably because no lay (even less Huguenot) institution offered, within relative proximity to Angers, such a guarantee of strictness in its discipline. It was the dreariest '1st October' you could imagine. The college in question was a construction from another century, with dark corridors, gloomy classrooms, sinister dormitories. The entry procedures were more in keeping with a prison register than with a fatherly welcome. Paralyzed by these trappings, the boy withdrew into an ominous silence. For fear of increasing his despair with the spectacle of our compassion, we felt compelled to disappear as swiftly as possible, and leave him alone in the hands of his future guardians. Our way back was doubly crepuscular, and very unusually silent. This risky attempt would result fairly soon in a predictable failure, and the rest, I believe, wasn't much more successful. For me this memory was once and for all associated with the already less than joyful idea of the 'start of the school year', and, very unjustly, with my image of the fine town of Redon, which perhaps isn't, despite the grey water of its canal, the 'Venice of the West', but, more modest and slumbrous, something like an Armorican Delft – without faience, I presume, and without Vermeer.

Repertoires. Drawn from I know not what sources, my parents' literary culture was complemented by a kind of musical culture whose origin was more patent: my maternal grandfather, a Huguenot typographer, descended from the Camisards,[447] having

conclusion of Marcel Proust's 'Un Amour de Swann [Swann in Love]', the second section of *Du côté de chez Swann* (*Swann's Way*) (1913).
[447] Southern French–Protestant insurgents who rebelled against the

moved from Nîmes up to La Croix-Rousse,[448] was a member of an association there called 'Les Enfants du Gard [The Children of the Gard]', which also served as a choir, and he sang a little in the choruses of the Lyon Opera. Passed on to his two daughters, his repertoire thus formed the primary basis of our own, the second evidently being the radio. There resulted a predominantly nineteenth-century hotchpotch (and, when sung, always in its French version) of Gounod, Massenet, Lalo ('Aubade', from *The King of Ys*), Bizet (*Carmen*, *The Pearl Fishers*), Dukas (*The Sorcerer's Apprentice*), Mussorgsky (*A Night on Bald Mountain*), Delibes, Saint-Saëns (*Danse macabre*), Chabrier (for *España*), Grieg (*Peer Gynt*), Sibelius (*Sad Waltz*), Charpentier (Gustave, for the 'great aria' from *Louise*, which I can never hear without a shiver), Rossini, the overture to *William Tell* and *The Barber of Seville*, at least for 'the calumny aria' ('And the miserable one … '), Verdi (*Rigoletto*: 'As feathers in the wind...'), Puccini (*Tosca*: 'The stars were brightly shining … ', *La Bohème*: 'What a cold little hand … '), a few pieces by Liszt (*Dream of Love*) and by Chopin ('*Sadness*'), Mozart for 'Cherubino's Aria' ('My heart sighs … '), Tchaikovsky (*Nutcracker*, alas), Borodin for *In the Steppes of Central Asia*, Strauss (Johann) for *The Blue Danube*, Franz Lehár for one or two operettas, Reynaldo Hahn for *Ciboulette*, Granados for one of the *Spanish Dances*, Schubert for the *Unfinished Symphony*, a few *Lieder* (which we didn't call thus) among which a liquefying *Serenade*, Weber (two or three overtures, and the *Invitation to the Dance*), Mendelssohn for a wedding march, Wagner for a few overtures or preludes, Ravel of course for *Bolero*, but also for the *Pavane for a Dead Princess*, whose title at least my mother liked, Toselli for his *Serenade*, and, my word, I'm not sure who for a *Romance of Master Pathelin*: 'I think of you when I awake … '. Two other romances linger in my memory, of which one (*Romance of the Sage*) came to us from the *The Juggler of Notre-Dame*, and the other, again anonymous through amnesia, 'There was once a king of Thule, to whom his faithful wife … '. As regards the religious, or what was taken as such: the air from the *Suite in D Major* by Johann Sebastian,

persecutions that followed Louis XIV's Revocation of the Edict of Nantes (1598), making Protestantism illegal.
[448] In Lyon.

more familiarly called 'Bach's air', the aria from Handel's *Serse* (*'Ombra mai fù'*), called more absolutely 'Handel's largo' – since that from *Rinaldo* (*'Lascia ch'io pianga'*) had become in Huguenot country the canticle: 'Lord, guide and sanctify … ', which was sung in particular at first communions, which wasn't to prevent me from dodging my own. And again, in a lighter register, André Messager (*Ciboulette*), Rudolf Friml (*Rose-Marie*, an American-Viennese operetta), Maurice Yvain, responsible along with Albert Willemetz for Mistinguett's best songs, Christiné, whose *Phi-Phi* was our suburban *Belle Hélène*, a few of Paul Delmet's melodies then sung by Vanni Marcoux, and that sublime refrain whispered by Lucienne Boyer, and whose author I have forgotten: *Parlez-moi d'amour* [*Speak to Me of Love*]. Every Sunday morning, my parents would bicker over which of them was 'clashing' and which 'was singing out of tune'; the nuance eluded me, but my father put a stop to the competition by crediting himself with (he did indeed have) 'a fine voice for writing'. His active repertoire, taken from the tenor Georges Thil, included among other things two arias from *Werther*, the 'Invocation to Nature' ('Oh nature, queen of time and space… ') and 'Why awake me, oh breath of springtime?' and the cavatina 'Ah! rise, sun!' from *Roméo et Juliette*, three pieces that continue to merge in my memory.

With respect to films, the palette was inevitably narrower. Outings were few and far between, the only cinema, also known as the village hall, in Conflans, a long shed in the shape of a stranded whale, at the other end of town, wasn't much of a resource, leisure trips to Paris were a rare luxury. However, my parents weren't unaware of the good French popular cinema of the thirties (*Under the Roofs of Paris, Freedom for Us, They Were Five, Port of Shadows, Daybreak, Stormy Waters, Grand Illusion, The Human Beast*), nor of a certain American cinema: some Westerns (at least *Stagecoach*), but especially comedies ('American comedy' then sounded like a generic pleonasm) such as *The Awful Truth, It Happened One Night, Mr. Deeds Goes to Town, You Can't Take It with You, Mr. Smith Goes to Washington* or *Bringing Up Baby*. But less heed was paid to directors (Clair, Duvivier, Renoir, Carné, Ford, McCarey, Capra, Hawks: it's me naming and renaming them today) than to actors, and Albert Préjean, Gabin, Michèle Morgan, Clark Gable, Claudette Colbert, Cary Grant, Irene Dunne, Katharine Hepburn, James Stewart and Gary Cooper were at their zenith, along with the imponderable dancing duo formed by Ginger Rogers and Fred Astaire. My family evidently didn't have exclusive rights to this repertoire. Cultural baggage of the time, but also of their class, it belonged, more generally and as I was later to realise, to what was then called the 'working class elite'.

Just after the war, I briefly frequented a film club located in Poissy, roughly ten kilometres from home. I'd obviously travel there by bike, since the hall where the screenings took place had a well-guarded shelter. I'm at least certain of having then seen a John Ford film that is scarcely mentioned any more, and which I've never had the opportunity to see again, *The Long Voyage Home*, adapted in 1940 from a play by Eugene O'Neill. It was a story of sailors lost on the South Sea, of stopovers with wahines, and of a disillusioned return to the port of Cardiff. One could behold, among others, Thomas Mitchell, Ward Bond, Barry Fitzgerald, and a few of Ford's other 'favourite actors'. I was captivated by the climate, the slow pace, the chiaroscuro, the tropical eroticism. My own nocturnal return was as zigzagging as a tipsy seaman's jig on a wharf agleam with drizzle and rotgut. Then, in the Parisian cinemas, I discovered at least *Citizen Kane* and *Double Indemnity*, and no doubt *Gone with the Wind*. It was the happy time when the Hollywood catalogue of the wartime years was being belatedly unearthed, and where one didn't yet really quite see, in the velvet glove of the 'Blum-Byrnes agreements', the iron fist of American imperialism.

Resquille/Chiselling. Thrifty with almost everything else, he uniquely refused to restrict his consumption of bread. Before the war, he'd never return from work without glancing anxiously at what served us as a bread bin, invariably protesting, *à la* Queneau, 'Yaxadpain? [Il n'y a que ça de pain?/Is that all the bread there is?]'. Throughout the long years of 'restrictions', whenever possible he'd take charge of this morning purchase, for which he had devised a clever procedure, consisting in asking the baker for: 'One kilo *five hundred*', pronouncing the final two words more loudly, which the baker–cashier, at the other end of the counter, would hear in isolation; she would therefore clip the tickets for 500 grammes without checking the actual purchase, and made him, consequently, pay a third of its price. The latter point somewhat ruffled his moral conscience; for him, to 'chisel' with tickets wasn't to steal, but he couldn't see, in this instance, how to separate these two activities, and still less how to avoid the one without revealing the other. He eventually resigned himself to this internal conflict, promising himself to make amends after the war. Unfortunately, said restrictions somewhat survived the Occupation, and even, unless I'm mistaken, the chiseller himself, who had to take his venial sin away with him.

Restriction mentale/Mental reservation. Apparently clumsy wording can in fact pertain to a verbal strategy, for example, to exonerate oneself from a proven offence without lying: a brute accused of regularly beating his wife replies: 'Your Honour, I have only beaten her once [,] without meaning to' – this doesn't work in writing, where you must choose between the exonerating comma and its damning absence. Or, to confirm an insult while pretending to retract it: 'I said you were a crook, it's true; I apologise to you: I'm wrong'. Or, like a certain critic, to mock under the cover of a compliment: 'All of your ideas are interesting: some because they are correct, others because they are original.'

Retro-Cratylism. 'It is the most Parisian of cities, therefore they called it Paris' (Vialatte). 'You, Victor Hugo, so worthy of that glorious name … ' (Esprit Bellemère, chemist, model, they say, of M. Homais,[449] receiving the poet in his fine town of Veules). I can't recall which metaphysician, quoted by Jean Paulhan, said, but in verse, that the orange truly deserves its name, for it has thereof the appearance, the shape and the colour, and even the flavour. No treatise of logic or rhetoric mentions this farcical variety of paralogism, retro-Cratylian in sum, which motivates the thing by its word.

Réverbère/Street light. We are really unfair with the drunken man who, having lost his key in the street, looked for it beneath a street light, not because he thought he'd dropped it there, but because it was the only place with enough light for him to search for it. The majority of our actions, individual or collective, are undertaken not where they should be, but where, for us, they can be. To paraphrase Pascal, being unable to make what is necessary possible, we make what is possible necessary.

---

[449] An apothecary in Gustave Flaubert's *Madame Bovary* (1856).

Rustine/Repair patch. *Ô nymphes, regonflons des souvenirs divers,* 'O nymphs, let's rise again with many memories'.[450] One said with bitterness, in those ill-equipped years, *'Partir, c'est crever un pneu',*[451] 'To leave is to burst a tyre'. Great use was then made of a rubber-based, odorous and doubtless somewhat psychotropic adhesive substance named 'Dissolution', which served to repair inner tubes punctured by some generally unfindable 'sharp object', except when it was a matter of a drawing pin clearly owed to malice. In principle, a simple self-adhesive repair patch [rustine] ought to have sufficed, but I'm not sure what mistrust with regard to this overly recent invention long made us favour the old method, which went as follows: upend the bicycle [bicyclette] (or bike [vélo]), place it upside-down, balanced on its saddle or its handlebars (from which inconveniently protruded a bell, preferably called a *'timbre'*), loosen the axle nuts with a spanner, or better, its butterfly nuts by hand, remove the wheel, take the tyre off its rim using two or three 'tyre-removing irons' (without pinching the inner tube, which would risk causing a new and worse puncture), unscrew the valve's retainer nut, extract the inner tube, unscrew the valve cap, hold this cap between your lips while refraining from swallowing it, so as to keep both hands free, reinflate the tube, spit out the valve cap, screw it back on, plunge the tube into a water basin in order to locate the site of the hole thanks to the air bubbles emerging therefrom, re-deflate the inner tube, dry it, scratch it around the hole using an *ad hoc* small metallic rasp, or simply some sandpaper, cut out a roundlet of rubber the size of a hundred-*sous* coin, open the tube of 'Dissolution', if at least its cap hasn't once and for all stuck to the tube since it was last used, spread this rubber in a viscous state around the puncture hole, wait while it dried a bit, but not too much, or blow on it, but not too much either, so as to hasten, neither too much nor too little, its return to an (almost) solid state, apply the piece of rubber to the relevant area, keep the whole thing firmly squeezed for an appropriate number of seconds, reinflate it a little, plunge it again into the basin to check that air was no longer escaping (otherwise this meant the failure of

---

[450] From Stéphane Mallarmé's 'L'Après-midi d'un faune [The Afternoon of a Faun]' (1876); 'regonflons' can also mean 'replenish' or 'reinflate'.
[451] A transformation of the proverb 'partir, c'est mourir un peu', 'to leave is to die a little'; 'crever' also signifies 'to perish'.

the entire, practically unrepeatable, operation), dry it again very carefully, leave it slightly reinflated and coat it with a very thin layer of magnesium silicate (*vulgo*: with talc), replace it on the wheel rim, with the valve properly inserted into the orifice specially placed in said rim, find the valve nut, screw it back on, check that no other malicious sharp object may be found on the underside of the tyre, replace the tyre again using the tyre-removing irons become in the meanwhile tyre-replacing irons, pat the whole thing to ensure a good fit, unscrew the valve cap, reinflate the inner tube inside its tyre to the maximum (but no more), check the valve's proper functioning by applying light and brief pressure to its hypersensitive retractile button, screw the valve cap back on, put the wheel back in place in its calliper while ensuring its equilibrium between the brake pads, spin it while still ensuring said equilibrium, static and dynamic, tighten the axle's nuts or butterfly nuts (enough so there's no danger of them becoming undone, but not to the point of jamming them irreversibly), continue until there's a perfect rotation, nuts or butterfly nuts tightened, replace the bicycle, or the bike, right side up, perform a few laps of the garden as a final check, and patiently await the next puncture.

As you'll have understood, I have described (while simplifying, since I'm not taking into account the additional operations peculiar to the repair of a rear wheel inner tube, with disengagement and re-engagement of the chain on the sprocket) the operation in its most domestic version – at home, then, or more precisely in the basement, a space conducive to this type of activity. The ambulatory version involved a bag appended to the saddle and furnished with all the small utensils mentioned above, with the exception of the water basin. A river, a stream, a pond, a puddle, a gutter, occasionally a fountain, if any were to be found nearby, could serve the same purpose. In the event of absolute drought, the most effective way was to listen to the suitably inflated inner tube upon an embankment, in the silence of the countryside, or to make it pass within a few millimetres of your lips, the part of the (masculine) body reputedly the most sensitive to this type of effect, until the source of the light breath of air has been identified. In case of doubt, you could, once returned safely home, repeat the operation in its most canonical forms. The most scrupulous saw fit to apply the old method (Dissolution) to the new material (repair patches [rustines]), and (more or less) quickly understood that two precautions are often worth less than one, in other words that the best is the enemy of the good, and *le trop ennemi du pneu*, 'the too much the enemy of the tyre (or the little [peu])'.

The extent of the damage occasionally made the operation so difficult that you had as a matter of urgency to push your bicycle (or bike) to the shadowy workshop of the 'bicycle seller', who, in the best of cases, would postpone you till the next day but one: 'Have you seen all the people waiting? My apprentice is sick, and I haven't got six arms!' On said next day but one, you learned that the inner tube, and sometimes the ty-er ['peneu'] itself had had to be changed: 'See for yourself the state it was in: you must have been riding with a flat!' *Riding with a flat*, or *on the wheel rim*, or, in the worst case, *with the tyre off its rim*, was a mortal sin, which it was better not to commit, or at the very least never to confess. As for the name *rustine*, whose object would one day prevail over these archaic practices, I have never known whether this fairly well-coined word originated or not from a registered trademark, and whether or not it referred, via its etymology, to its rural usage.

Saga. From two stays, which were yet very far apart, and which I conflate somewhat: the freshly coloured wooden gabled houses at the port of Bergen, the snow-covered mountains seen from the plane on the way back from Oslo, the Munch of the National Gallery, learning to pronounce it 'Mounk', a trip across the fjord with a couple of friends, in a motorboat, one chilly Sunday morning, a ski-jump, the longships of the Viking Museum, a long walk down to the university, skirting the Royal Palace along the way, unsuccessfully championing European membership for a country that already saw in this not the slightest advantage, roast reindeer with cranberry, or maybe blueberry, sauce, Nordic light and hospitality, the sudden feeling of being closer to my origins here than in the warmth of the 'south', the unforgettable fact that my hotel was called *Saga*.

Samaras. I wonder what nowadays remains of certain recreational habits from my childhood, such as: catching a maybug, attaching to it a spit ball at the end of some thread and watching it play at helicopters across the classroom; cramming your pockets full of horse chestnuts because each of them was more beautiful than the last; crumpling up a mint leaf the better to smell it; cutting off a branch of nettles to check that the leaves, thus deprived of their source of venom, no longer sting; sticking a card in a bicycle fork so that the noise of its rubbing against the spokes should imitate that of a motorbike; cracking with the blow of a hammer little powder tablets wrapped in paper, placed on a stone or cement floor, tiny bangers that we called 'fuses'; smoking dried stems of mugwort or elderberry; putting ears of beard grass up your sleeve so they might crawl all the way to your shoulder; biting into a ripe quince hoping that this one will be less bitter than the others; gathering, to press them over the bridge of your nose, ash or elm samaras which, as Leonardo da Vinci had observed, twist and twirl like propellers as they fall.

Sana/Sanatorium. The treatment centre at Aire-sur-l'Adour, a magic mountain[452] with neither mountain nor magic, where I spent the summer of 1950, was rather mild of regime and climate. The more seriously ill haunted other, more bracing islets of the archipelago known as the 'French Students' Sanatorium' foundation, like Saint-Hilaire-du-Touvet, on a slope of the Chartreuse. Myself infected with a common-or-garden pleurisy, it was through hear-say that I learned about the properly pulmonary afflictions – shadows, nodules, caverns – periodically revealed by radioscopy sessions, streptomycin treatments, various surgical interventions, all intended to deactivate the lung in order to assist its healing: the straightforward pneumothorax (no less periodically reinflated, like a common inner tube, via 'flange section' sessions and 'insufflations' of gas into the pleura), the more severely debilitating extra pleural pneumothorax and thoracoplasty (a 'thoraco' to those in the know), with removal of a few ribs: Roland Barthes subsequently immortalised at least one of them. I was only entitled, for my part, to the regular administering of a painful gastric intubation in pursuit of Koch's bacillus (KB for the initiated), under the supervision of the doctor–director and by those among us whom two or three years of medical studies had thrust into the position of 'intern'. Yet, by dint of the promiscuousness peculiar to the sanatorium universe, from the head doctor down to the

---

[452] An allusion to Thomas Mann's novel *The Magic Mountain* (1924).

humblest pleuritic, we all considered ourselves to be amateur phtisiologists.

At Aire, then, the treatment suffered a few infringements. The centre's door closed quite poorly, and, downstream from the bridge, the riverbank offered its idyllic decor – elegant houses, flowery gardens – to more or less illicit walks, but which could be said, in a sense, to be in aid of our health. I'm not sure whether you might also so describe the jars of *foie gras* and the bottles of Monbazillac, of Jurançon, and occasionally of a Pacherenc come down the river, all of it very lukewarm, with which our young girl friends from the local business secretly gratified us. By way of thanks, we had formed a 'Negro Spiritual' group which performed at a festival whose date and pretext I have forgotten: '*Swing low, sweet chariot*'. Between the boarders at the centre and the external population, relations were cordial and, curiously, without any health-related mistrust or principles of precaution. I remember too having attended one or two corridas, at Dax, Mont-de-Marsan or Vic-Fezensac, and also the explosive conflagration of a *toro de fuego* at a festival in Bayonne. Once past the Adour, you entered another *département*, another province, nowadays one would say region, via the suburbs of Barcelonne-du-Gers, whose name, with its two *n*s, was doubly the stuff of dreams. A local chain of food stores was called (is still called) *Guyenne et Gascogne*: a whole swathe of history and geography.

I hope I'm not overly romanticising my memory of this medicalised parenthesis in the light of the South West. Besides, the cold war had had one of its wafts of warmth that summer, and we, communist patients, spent our afternoon 'silence cures' eloquently convincing, and unfortunately not without success, our roommates that South Korea had attacked the North on behalf of American imperialism. The morning 'treatments' were more peacefully reserved for tuning in, on what perhaps wasn't yet called France Musique, to a long-running broadcast by Jean Witold, he of the repetitive and occasionally stumbling elocution, devoted to Mozart's piano concertos. The principal militant activity consisted, at Aire as in the rest of the Foundation, in infiltrating, as far as was possible, the sort of union, affiliated to the UNEF,[453] that was the 'Association générale

---

[453] 'Union Nationale des Étudiants de France', 'The National Union of

des étudiants en sanatorium [General Association of Students in Sanatoriums]' (AGES). The manoeuvres required by this takeover kept us pretty busy, with many a so-called general assembly and corridor machination: it was an *in vitro* traineeship in the manipulation of 'mass organisations'. At the start of the school year, officially cured (of my pleurisy, but not alas of the rest), I was dispatched, for a year of convalescence, to a home closer to Paris.

The Foundation owned two or three 'aftercare' establishments in this vicinity, which welcomed invalids apparently sufficiently out of danger to resume their studies while also following a consolidatory, or simply confirmatory, therapy. One such establishment was situated in Paris, Rue de Quatrefages, between Arènes and Mosquée, and thus on the edge of the Latin Quarter; the overall head doctor of the Foundation (Dr Douady, father to all of us) then resided there, if I'm not mistaken, and François Furet, a survivor from Saint-Hilaire, was already there wielding a faintly condescending charisma. Another (mine), in Sceaux, Avenue Franklin-Roosevelt, faced one of the entrances to the park. As far as I can remember, it consisted of two buildings: the most withdrawn, at the end of a lawned garden, housed the majority of the (individual) bedrooms, including my own; the other directly overlooked the avenue, and comprised, in addition to a few other bedrooms, the administrative offices and the medical equipment, a dining room, and a kind of shared, rather cramped and very bustling (I think you had to cross it to reach the exit) lounge for the boarders' use, where could be found a radio set and a record player whose stack of records didn't rise very high, even if they were still thick wax discs, which we thought we were treating kindly, at 78 rpm, by using needles made of wood. We listened on repeat, for want of a vaster selection, to selections by Dinu Lipatti (the *Partita in B-flat Major* and three *Chorales* by Bach, Schumann's *Piano Concerto*, Ravel's *Alborada del gracioso*), a Victoria motet performed by the 'Agrupación Coral de Cámara de Pamplona' (I don't particularly suspect my memory of inventing the name of this choir, and I'm sure that the record began with the spoken utterance: *O vos omnes de Victoria*), some Monteverdi Madrigals by the Nadia Boulanger Ensemble, wherein perhaps already featured the exquisite Hugues Cuenod, an Ella Fitzgerald

Students of France'.

compilation in frenzied scat style (*Lady Be Good, How High the Moon, Mr. Paganini, Flying Home*), a few songs by Atahualpa Yupanqui: *Duerme negrito, Basta ya, Preguntitas sobre dios* – and a kind of *kaddish* in memory of the victims of what wasn't yet called the Shoah (nor the Holocaust, nor even less the genocide) where you could hear intoned the list of the extermination camps in Poland: in those years of deafening silence on the subject, this heart-rending chant ought to have sufficed to revive its memory. Of the radio in this place, I have no recollection beyond a long evening of legislative election results, results that were dismaying for 'us', but which we could at least attribute to the scandalous artifice of 'grouped electoral lists [apparentement]', the technical details of which I have forgotten. The sandy path that led from one building to the other also served as a pétanque area. At a time when this game was yet to become a national sport, the only ones to shine were a few native southerners, who had from the cradle mastered the art of pointing and shooting, and regarded as a hopeless amateur anyone who'd seen the light of day north of the Loire – even, in my case, north of the Seine.

But the Seine, in those days, could also be understood as a *département*, and Sceaux fell within its bounds, Paris being in sum merely its administrative centre. The very notion of 'Hauts-de-Seine', geographically obscure (I assume it pays homage to the hills at Clamart and Meudon), evidently had no currency. Even Versailles reigned over a different world: that of Seine-et-Oise, which was yet to be carved up into Yvelines, Essonne, Val-de-Marne and Val-d'Oise. Linked to the Luxembourg gardens by the metro line owing it its name, Sceaux was like a provincial appendix to the Latin Quarter, a noble suburb by virtue of its vast park, its Neoclassical château, and above all of the older and most charming 'Petit Château', also known as 'Château des enfants de la duchesse du Main [The Château of the Duchess of Main's Children]', which then housed the municipal library. The Lycée Lakanal was only 200 or 300 metres away. This proximity allowed me sporadically to follow a final year of *khâgne*, swapping residency at the *lycée*, in truth already hardly austere (preparatory class students benefited there from individual bedrooms) for that, even more liberal and above all more cordial, of the aftercare centre. My supposedly fragile condition entitled me to a reduced scholarly regimen; that is, I'd only attend certain classes (I've forgotten which ones), and was exempt from the majority of compulsory exercises. Each of the two establishments acted as an alibi for the other and vice versa, without excessive monitoring from either side, and to the great benefit of the neighbouring countryside. It was in short a year of free study, whose happy outcome doubtless owed much to some destiny-repairing justice. I would yet prolong, at Rue d'Ulm, this privilege of extraterritoriality by escaping the first-year students' shared dormitories in favour of a bedroom in the small infirmary building, Pasteur's ex-laboratory. Its narrow first-floor corridor afforded opportunities to brush furtively against the mistress of the house, and to inhale her perfume, whose name for once eludes me.

The continuation (and end) of my 'schooling' was spent for the most part in another individual bedroom whose window overlooked the old 'Ernests'' courtyard.[454] I think I spent the whole summer of 1955 'in hiding' (despite its name, this status wasn't entirely illicit, and even less was it exceptional), pending an army call-up that did not occur, because at the final moment a wise doctor advised me to declare, with supporting radiographs, my pleuritic past before what was called a 'Reform Commission'. The x-rays worked wonders, and I found myself forever exempt from military service, in a year when the other branch of destiny was beginning to be called, for 27 months, the Algerian War, a curriculum to be avoided – and by the same token unexpectedly returned to the 'Éducation nationale', which assigned me to the lycée in Amiens. Here ends the list of the benefits I owe the famous bacillus.

Scorpion. In France, the left is useless, the right is almost worse, and doubtless vice versa; fortunately, there is no centre. To find one's way around, one can never read too much Machiavelli, Hobbes, Locke, Montesquieu, Rousseau, Kant, Tocqueville, Marx, Weber, Aron, but most of all one should reread or see again *The*

---

[454] The 'Cour aux Ernests' is a 'Normalien' nickname for the main courtyard at the ENS, Rue d'Ulm: the 'Ernests' actually refer to the goldfish in the central fishpond, so named after the director Ernest Bersot, who is said to have first placed them there.

Godfather, Le Sapeur Camember,[455] *Gribouille,*[456] *Les Pieds-Nickelés,*[457] *L'Arroseur arrosé,*[458] chapter VIII of the *Fourth Book,*[459] not forgetting a few fables by La Fontaine, among which at least *The Frogs Who Desired a King*. Apropos of frogs, here's another opportunity to recall the story of the scorpion who asks one to take him upon its back in order to cross a river. 'Don't take me for an imbecile,' replies the frog, I know full well that once we're in the middle, you'll sting me to death! – Don't take me for an imbecile either: if I stung you to death, we'd both drown!' The frog yields to this reasoning, and embarks the scorpion. In the middle of the river, the scorpion stings it. Before sinking together, the frog berates him for his stupidity. 'I know, says the scorpion, but what can I say, *'Tis my character!'*

Scotland Yard. If I'm reading the guide books aright, the headquarters of the British police force was initially established at Great Scotland Yard, between Whitehall and the Thames, and was soon informally called 'Scotland Yard', as were its services, through a simple place-name metonymy. Transferred at the end of the nineteenth century to New Scotland Yard, a little further south, it retained without difficulty its first nickname, become, as they say, mythical. Retransferred, even further south, to the corner of Broadway and Victoria Street, it was, this time, very officially rechristened 'New Scotland Yard', without regard for its new location. I hope one day to see the residence of the British prime minister dispatched to the other side of the Thames and rechristened 'New Downing Street'. After all, the Labour Party has indeed become 'New Labour', with or without relocation. We perhaps ought to have imitated this onomastic wisdom by naming 'New Rue de Rivoli' the Bercy headquarters of the Ministry of

---

[455] 'Sapper Camember' is a character in the cartoon strip series *Les Facéties du Sapeur Camember* (*The Pranks of Sapper Camember*) (1890–1896) by Marie-Louis-Georges Colomb (1856–1945), French botanist, populariser of science and pioneer of French comics under the pseudonym 'Christophe'.
[456] A credulous and simple-minded French folk character.
[457] 'Nickel-Plated Feet', a long-running French comic series, originally created by Louis Forton (1908).
[458] *The Sprinkler Sprinkled*, silent comedy by Louis Lumière (1895).
[459] By François Rabelais (1552).

Finance, 'New Rue de Lille' that of the UMP[460] on Rue La Boétie, and 'New Old House[461]' that of the Socialist Party, Rue de Solférino. But in New York, Madison Square Garden has left Madison Square to join Pennsylvania Station, between Seventh and Eighth Avenue, without even feeling compelled to call itself New Madison Square Garden, a vexing transfer for whoever might seek it in its erstwhile place, pending further promised shifts. The unforgettable *Cotton Club* moved, in 1936, from Harlem to Times Square, without for all that becoming *New Cotton Club*, and *Birdland*, more recently, from 55nd Street to 44th, without becoming *New Birdland*. I don't think our *New Morning* succeeded an *Old Morning*, nor even a *Morning tout court*, and I'm not too afraid that it should one day become *New New Morning*, nor that my favourite clothes shop *Old England* should become *New England*, which would entail a slight change of style. It's true that, in New York, buildings also, and without shifting, chop and change their names, at the whim of the market's fluctuations. It doesn't overly bother me that the insipid Gulf &Western should have become the 'Trump International Hotel', nor that Philip Johnson's ridiculous Chippendale-style ATT the 'Sony Plaza', but I have great difficulty in calling 'General Electric' the ever young RCA, figurehead of the Rockefeller Center, or 'MetLife' old Gropius's Pan Am. Let us hope at least that Mies's masterpiece, luminescent at dusk over Park Avenue, remains forever the 'Seagram' it still is.

Scruples. Roland Barthes would often say that he couldn't abide the telephone, which hardly encouraged you to call him, but, aware of this effect, he'd immediately forestall it by assuring that he only hated calling himself, and that he was on the contrary delighted to *receive* a phone call. This nuance seemed to me paradoxical, but I know not what accent of truth made it credible, and after all, if an unforeseen call may disturb you, having to call someone, without knowing in which disposition you may find them, can also occasion anxiety, as can, moreover, *having to do* anything whatsoever: nothing is more distressing than the contemplation of

[460] 'Union pour un mouvement populaire [Union for a Popular Movement]', a centre-right political party (2002–2015).
[461] The 'Vieille Maison [Old House]' is a traditional nickname for the French Socialist Party.

a diary, from which the best means of escape is to do everything before you had to.

It is against this background that I recall a circumstance where he took a step that could only have cost him dearly: one day in October 1977, he told me on the phone about his mother's passing, adding simply: 'I should not have wished for you to have learned of it in the newspapers.' I happen to have known her little, having only met her once, and in that respect at least I was anything but a close friend. I have therefore to assume that there were several of us who learned of and shared his mourning in this fashion, several whom he wished to spare learning of it 'in the newspapers'. I know of no more moving mark of what is called, a little awkwardly, sensitivity [la délicatesse]. For this type of concern for others, his own word was rather: *scruple*.

In February 1980, when I heard on the radio about the accident he'd suffered on Rue des Écoles, not for one moment did I believe it was serious. Then I learned that he was in intensive care at the Salpêtrière, bristling with tubes; I thought he wouldn't like to be seen in this state, and I decided, before going to visit him, to await an improvement that surely couldn't fail to occur. I continued whole-heartedly to believe in his imminent recovery, and the news of his death, one month later, surprised me just as much as if nothing had ever let it be feared. I'm still astonished by this sudden bout of optimism, and I wonder in vain about its reasons, excluding in principle (through cowardice, maybe) cowardice. The same *wishful thinking* convinced me, in June 2004, of Jacques Derrida's recovery, he whom I saw, after several years, at New York University's Parisian dinner. His treatment had been reduced, I saw and heard him to be vigorous, almost cheerful, and I naively believed him, as did others perhaps, to be on the road to recovery. We parted with a confident 'See you soon'. We know the rest, concerning which I'll never know if he himself sensed it and was putting up a front, or if he shared our illusions.

For Roland Barthes, the truth is perhaps that I had *already* seen what I didn't wish to see. It was on a plane taking us to New York, in November 1978, him for a lecture and me for a more protracted stay. We weren't in the same cabin, and at some point I went over to speak to him. He was fast asleep, head leaning back, mouth open, and, for an instant, I saw him as dead as the mummy in *Plain-Chant*,[462] sans its golden mask. I made sure of the contrary without waking him, and returned to my seat. A limousine chartered by the university, awaiting to lead him safely onwards, took us, with me as an extra, to the Village. I've a fairly distinct memory of the lecture ('For a long time I went to bed early') that he delivered in a large room of the Law School overlooking Washington Square, and of the seminar that was held around him, the following day or the day after, with the cream of the local intelligentsia. I found most imprudent the way he'd announce *urbi et orbi* the writing of a novel to come, and I believe I said to him at the time: 'You really aren't superstitious!' It wasn't a particularly kind remark, but instead of taking offence at it, he replied simply: 'I'm confident', which was tantamount to a confirmation. Indeed, I always heard him speak without anxiety about his book projects, with the notable exception of *Fragments of a Lover's Discourse*, which he long deemed 'unpublishable' – we know what came to pass – but it wasn't at all the same anxiety, and it probably wasn't even anxiety: merely a doubtful evaluation in the form of an editorial forecast, erroneous as almost all of them are. He was thus ordinarily 'confident', and wasn't afraid to devise projects in public: he would continue to do so during his two final years of seminars at the Collège de France, where he reduced to an object of study a truly asymptotic project, destined to be accomplished only in its own 'preparation'.[463]

Since we were in a vein of indiscretion, someone (else, I hope, but I'm not too sure) quizzed him about his dreams. The couch wasn't far away, and there was no dearth of unpaid analysts in the room. He replied, a little more coolly, that he hated dreaming, and that he protected himself from nightmares, moreover more irritating than terrifying ('vague questions of conscience, tiny scruples', he clarified, if you can describe that as a 'clarification'), by taking a 'very light sleeping tablet' every evening. I drew the conclusion that boredom [ennui], more than anything else his *bête noire*, harassed him even in his sleep. There was obviously no further mention of this between us, but I do still wonder if his

---

[462] A poem by Jean Cocteau (1923).
[463] An allusion to Barthes's final seminar (1978–1980) *La Préparation du roman* (*The Preparation of the Novel*).

final nights in the hospital were as devoid of dreams as he had constantly wished. Dying of boredom, that occasionally abused hyperbole, might well be the very worst of deaths.

Secretary. A charming old lady, on the telephone, asked whether she might speak to 'Gérard Genette's secretary'. If I'd replied 'This is he', I would only have elicited another question. If I'd avowed the truth – that 'Gérard Genette' did not have a secretary – I would doubtless have horribly disappointed the old lady. I thus (quite needlessly) disguised my voice to reply – presumably as an undersecretary or a zealous manservant, that I would go and see if the official secretary were available. After about a minute, and in my real voice, I introduced myself as 'Gérard Genette' himself, apologising for the regrettable absence of his assistant (a more socially correct term, as we know, which I presumed her capable of translating into her class idiom). The old lady's embarrassment was worse than that which I had wished to spare her: she was so sorry to disturb me in person for a perfectly minor matter. It was about knowing whether it would be possible to send me a manuscript at the address corresponding to the telephone number found in the directory, and which obviously couldn't have been my *personal* address, assumed to be safely ex-directory.

Sector. It took me ages to understand why this term was applied to the power supply that illuminated us in my childhood (it wasn't used for much else, for want of 'household appliances') by way of the meter and its 'fuses' (then merely slack lead wires taken from a coil if necessary), then I did understand it, then forgot, and I continue to find strange this at once technical, informal and nowadays I fear outmoded designation. English expresses it quite well as the *mains*, which refers to the network, but considered in its totality rather than divided into 'sectors'. And it carefully differentiates the pinned male connector (*plug*) from the encased female connector (*outlet, socket*) – for which (when wall-mounted) the most current word, so to speak, is quite simply *the wall*, as though the electricity were supplied by the wall itself, which will probably be the case one day, since the Internet can already come to us via the good old 'sector', pending the same for the water supply or the rubbery 'city' gas pipe. I was moved to learn, from the mouth of his Admiral son, that I share with Charles de Gaulle the displeasure he felt upon changing a fuse [un fusible] – at least when this term didn't refer to a prime minister.[464] But in his case and at La Boisserie,[465] it was because he hated wasting his time. In mine, it's because I never know how to distinguish, as they are sold today, a new from a faulty fuse, and I'm always afraid, should I make a wrong move, of blowing the meter, or indeed the sector.

Semaine/Week. The disingenuous *Intelligent Design* had yet to be invoked. My father was against it before the term existed, without his knowing so, and in his own way: 'God perhaps created the world in a week, but it wasn't the best thing He has done', thus blaming, at least so I supposed, as much the method (shoddy work) as the result: a bungled job. Concerning the method, there has moreover been controversy from the outset, since Genesis tells us in the same verse (2:2): 'And on the seventh day God ended His work which He had made; and He rested on the seventh day from all His work which He had made.' So the first Sunday was at once a working and a rest day, unless we should suppose it initially a working, then a rest day; but what time was the break? It's all a bit muddle-headed, and the product, indeed, is still suffering the effects. In my youth, we called an 'English week' (the word *week-end* had no currency with us) a week when work ended on Friday evening, or, more often, on Saturday at midday. That of Creation perhaps anticipates this half-measure with a vaguely trade-unionist connotation. When he was asked what God had done best (versus creating the world), he feigned to seek an answer, then eventually replied: 'Perhaps resting on the seventh day; unfortunately too late: the damage had already been done. He ought to have begun that way.'

Seminars. In the sixties, that of Algirdas Julien Greimas, under the auspices of the École des hautes études, was held, however – courtesy of Claude Lévi-Strauss's patronage –, in a little room at the Collège de France. There was something stimulating about his rather muddled magisterium, even if I was disconcerted by the slightly dogmatic complexion of his method, the sectarian attitudes

---

[464] 'le fusible' can also signify 'the fall guy' or 'the scapegoat'.
[465] De Gaulle's family home in Colombey-les-Deux-Églises, in the Haute-Marne department in north-eastern France.

(scissions included) of his school, his light almost transparent eyes, and the way his forearms, on account of short or rolled-up sleeves, emerged, white and bare, from those of his jacket. In accordance with one of the accepted definitions of the genre, the sessions were regularly and entirely outsourced to colleagues from the most diverse disciplines, with the exception of the final five minutes, when the Master would confirm the relevance, for the discipline evoked on that day, of a semiotic interpretation. The wealth of his address book and the availability of his successive invitees confounded me, but after all the possible refusals remained unknown to us.

That of Roland Barthes, in the countless ever provisional rooms hired by the École des hautes études, was most often a soliloquy without any discussion – a session was sometimes delegated to a deserving or promising student, but almost never to an external colleague: interdisciplinarity, one day renamed, to make it seem novel, 'transdisciplinarity', remained for him a concept unsullied by any application – I can only recall, in the early years, some kind of lecture by Marthe Robert, which occasioned quite a thrill among the least well informed, who imagined it to betoken a love affair. In its years of great attendance, around May '68 – until, exasperated by this crowd on the verge of hysteria, he finally 'closed' it for the use of the *happy few*, as was Nadia Boulanger's class at Fontainebleau[466] – this seminar was held in the lecture hall of the current 'Société d'encouragement à l'industrie nationale [Society for the Development of National Industry]', on Place Saint-Germain-des-Prés, beneath a pediment itself topped with some sort of Orpheus as androgynous as the hero of *S/Z*,[467] then in a former theatre (or maybe cinema) on Avenue Rapp. It was somewhat 'the subway at rush hour [le métro à six heures]': this whole little world was, had been, would be or claim to be Barthesian, before scattering into the most heterogeneous, and sometimes absurd, movements. Only one person in this studious throng sought not to be Barthesian – needless to say, Barthes himself, who moreover, when he couldn't avoid this adjective, curiously abridged it by

[466] Juliette Nadia Boulanger (1887–1979), renowned French music teacher and conductor.
[467] Published in 1970, this is Roland Barthes's structural analysis of Honoré de Balzac's novella *Sarrasine* (1830), in which the narrator recounts the story of the eponymous character's love for the castrato opera star La Zambinella.

saying *barthien*. I have no direct knowledge of what became of this audience, for alas too little time, at the Collège de France, for the sessions were held on Saturday mornings, an unmissable market day at Roussainville-le-Pin.

For my part, I only escaped the most often monologic aspect, even in intimate settings, of this type of teaching in the United States, where students – who pay to attend – suffer from no inhibitions, and naturally intervene with a question, a comment, an objection, without it ever being necessary to invite them to do so. At NYU, the department of French literature's so-called 'seminar' hall, a small windowless room in the middle of the sixth floor of the building on the corner of University Place and 8th Street, opens via two doors onto corridors leading to the professors' and assistants' offices, the photocopier, and other facilities. The session was held very late in the afternoon; the students would arrive, a little wearied by a day of mercenary work outside, and settle around the large oval table, which served primarily to accommodate their cups of white coffee, occasionally a partly eaten fruit or the remains of a hamburger. If they did take any notes, it was most readily done on clipboards, placed upon their knees, whose clips held a pad of ruled lemon-yellow paper, for me two inseparable mainstays of American *écrivance*.[468] At the end of the two hours, the lift was privy to more personal remarks, but always branded with that curious mixture of deference and familiarity denoted by the address 'Professor So and So' – never 'Sir'. Anyway, I was just passing, *visiting*, never very far from the plane that brought me over, nor from the one, the same perhaps, that would take me back, and this transitory status never let itself be forgotten. At the foot of the building, the American night dispersed us to the four cardinal points, without inviting one really to loiter.

Sexes. I find (in translation) from the pen of Adolfo Bioy Casares the dreadful pun 'gynaecological tree'. If he'd been acquainted with it, my father would have doubtless gladly applied it to the tireless inventorying of respective ages and kinships, the unpaid

---

[468] Genette here borrows Barthes's term denoting 'utilitarian' or 'transitive' writing; see note 433 for the distinction *écrivain/écrivant*.

civil registry service practised by the feminine side of the family, ensuring at every turn that cousin X, born in … , really was the daughter of uncle Y, who died in … . But the anthropologists, I believe, take it as a given fact that, at least in our culture, mnemonic ability is unequally distributed between the sexes, spatial memory (locations, itineraries, etc.) being more active in men, and its temporal variety (dates of events, and particularly of family events) more so in women. At the well-known risk of explaining that which is not, they refer this supposed distribution to an ancestral datum: in the happy prehistoric days, men, responsible for hunting, fishing and gathering, had to develop a memory for places, routes, waterways and cardinal points, whereas women, held back in the cave by household chores, stoked the group's hereditary consciousness in what Balzac no less maliciously called the 'great female confabulation'.

To have done with the old war of the sexes, I thus propose a simple, practical and equitable division: attribute all of time to women, to men all of space (they'll be better off in the long run: time passes, space remains). I'll add, in an attempt to rehabilitate this politically incorrect entry, that I know of nothing more stupid, and obscurely phallacious [phallacieux], than the *topos* 'Men are more this, women are more that', which always amounts to observing that women are more feminine than men, and sexiprocally [sexiproquement]. There would perhaps be greater pertinence in inventorying and questioning, for each period and each culture, the list of secondary sexual characteristics invented, presumably, by civilisation. The most incomprehensible, for me, remains the reversed direction for the buttoning of clothes: button to the right, buttonhole to the left for men, and vice versa for women (with no regard for left-handers of either sex). Now what fanatic of small differences could have dreamed that one up?

Sibling. Among the obligatory choices that make a language constraining, I'd readily count, peculiar to French compared with English, the lack of a less determined term corresponding to the *sibling* that serves to designate, without any gender distinction, a brother *or* a sister, without for all that depriving them, if otherwise necessary, of the potential choice between *sister* and *brother*. I should like to be able to speak of an entity born of the same parents as me, but not to (have to) specify its sex by saying 'my brother' or 'my sister', and thus to be able to embrace both entities within a single concept. It so happens that I have *neither a brother nor a sister*, and that I cannot say so without placing these two lacunae end-to-end. In English, I might regret having no *siblings*, which would allow me to save a little time. Inversely, I pity the English person for having always to choose between *time* and *weather*[469] – but I envy them for being able to decide between these two 'prestigious' positions: *chairman* and *president.*[470]

Signal/Know. A young man whom I asked why he'd fled his family home replied: 'Because every sentence my father said to me began with: *Je te signale que ...* , *'I'll have you know that ...* '. You'd run away for less than that.

Sistine. One must of course visit the famous chapel, for what remains, at the bottom of the walls, of the exquisite frescoes by Botticelli, Perugino, Ghirlandaio, etc. Unfortunately, outside of the times when a conclave is afoot, the place is always packed with gawkers, their necks straining towards the ceiling by dint of a mysterious epidemic of torticollis. More unfortunately still, this ceiling's guilty party also engulfed two such frescoes, on the west wall, in a huge and scarcely equitable *Last Judgement.* This loss is, I fear, irreparable. But I learn that the author of *Rome*[471] considered those who shared this opinion to be 'delicate minds', in the evidently pejorative sense of the expression, a sense that surely takes aim at some sort of ironic snobbery – the only valid kind. I can live with this one, which I believe to share with my country neighbour Charles Swann, and I'd gladly campaign for the extolling of little masters and the minor arts, if the very fact of campaigning were not seriously contrary to the correctly understood interests of said snobbery. Convincing the many to share your tastes is the surest way of finding yourself hampered by them, or even forbidden any contemplation at all. I do not, therefore, wish for the admirers of Michelangelo's frescoes to convert to those of Ghirlandaio: I only regret that historical happenstance should have placed the

---

[469] In French, 'le temps' signifies both time and the weather.
[470] In French, 'le président' would be used for both English terms.
[471] Stendhal (*Rome, Naples and Florence* (1817)).

ones and the others in the same room. Fortunately, most objects of admiration are better separated in space: the crowd thronging before the *Mona Lisa* is a blessing for the picture rails they desert.

Socialism. Capitalism, we still know, is the exploitation of man by man. Socialism, as we now know, is the converse. Gorbachev, who was asked when the failure of 'real socialism' began, replied soberly: 'October 1917'.

Sophistry. Since a married woman was countering him with what was then called fierce resistance, he resorted war-wearily to the following specious argument: 'If you continue to refuse, you'll end up like Emma Bovary, or like Anna Karenina.' He obtained from this paradox complete success, which he was no longer expecting: one always underestimates the persuasive power of sophistry.

Souvenances/Remembrances. In question here is something completely different, of course, from Proustian reminiscence, the involuntary memory of an object long buried in forgetfulness, and revived by a sensation shared by the moment present and the moment past: it has to do with objects (things, events, images, words, people, etc.) whose memory has indeed been conserved, and which can be found by exploring just a little, through conscious and organised anamnesis, the more or less hard drive of one's memory. In 1978, Perec produced a well-known list of them (479 'to be continued'), whose title and style are, as he himself indicates, borrowed from Joe Brainard's *I Remember*. Daniel Percheron has since (1983), under the same title, proposed a further 365, which have perhaps remained unpublished, but many other more or less analogous collections have appeared, to be taken or left at face value, ironically, or any which way. This means that it is now *a genre*, as such open to any and everyone. My reason for paying it particular, although limited, attention in a context rather more broadly devoted, among other things, to the evocation of memories is, first of all, that here they most often appertain to a (minor) historical past, and one that 'evokes its time [fait époque]'; next, that the henceforth ritual formula (and which be must reiterated upon each occurrence), 'I remember', refers less to an object than to the fact of remembering it. Its specific aim is the individual memory of this collective past. To say, like

Perec, 'I remember Dario Moreno [Je me souviens de Dario Moreno]', is not to recall that a few decades ago there existed a singer with this name, but rather to *register* [*constater*] that you can still remember him. In this genre alone, and in homage to its reinventor, we may allow ourselves the gauche '*Je me souviens que* ... [I remember that ...]'.[472] You can also occasionally register that you do not remember someone or something: this is an 'I have forgotten', which entertains a somewhat oblique relation to memory: forgetting is a hollow memory.

I remember automobiles by Delage, Delahaye, Talbot, Rossengart, Hotchkiss, Voisin, Salmson, De Dion-Bouton, Panhard & Levassor, Chenard & Walcker, Hispano-Suiza.

*

I remember the three-year field system.

*

I remember the radio stations called 'Sottens', 'Beromünster' and 'Monte Ceneri', whose names you could read on the dials of the old vacuum tube radios.

*

I remember buses with open platforms at the rear, where you would board once the belt enclosing it had been unhooked by the conductor, who would then punch, introducing it into a kind of horizontal food mill with a rattling crank handle, one or several tickets depending on the number of 'zones' you'd be travelling through, tickets that you had yourself torn off, along the perforated line, from a little roll whose remainder was kept on your person for other journeys to come. Once the operation had been successfully performed, the conductor would allow the driver to set off again by pulling upon the handle of a chain quite akin to those of the period's toilet flushes.

*

I remember 'Oi you, your dad isn't a glazier!' which meant: 'You are blocking my view.'

*

I remember the way arrogance and presumptuousness would be castigated:

[472] Instead of the more usual 'Je me rappelle que'.

'He thinks it's already happened'; you didn't know what, and it wasn't necessary to.

*

I remember that one franc *was worth 20* sous,[473] *and that they'd say: 'He's always short of 20* sous *to make a* franc.' *And also that a road, somewhere between Versailles and Saint-Germain, was called the '40* sous *road'; but I cannot recall why.*

*

I remember suburban train tickets known as 'round-trips', consisting of a small card of which you had carefully to retain a third, separated from the other two by a perforated line, for the return journey; and that it often got lost.

*

I remember the Mille Miglia motor race, which took place on small Italian roads, at full tilt.

*

I remember the time when Le Point[474] *was a literary and artistic journal, which devoted an issue to Mallarmé.*

*

I remember the 'painters' orchestra', supposed to bring together (in a variety of roles): on violin: Ingres; on trumpet: Géricault; and on tambourine: Rembrandt.

*

I've forgotten the name of the Minister for the Status of Women, who declared: 'I am for the equality of the sexes, and I am myself prepared to take the necessary steps.'

*

I remember two Lyon specialities, in fact very generic: (pike) quenelles, which you had to pronounce qu'nelles *(as one says G'neva), and* bugnes, *which are, in sum, empty doughnuts, doughnuts with nothing, but sprinkled with sugar, and which you were meant by rights to favour over all the others: there's nothing like a slice of apple to spoil a doughnut.*

---

[473] Equivalent to the British 'shilling'.
[474] French weekly news magazine, founded in 1972.

*

I remember Yvette Guilbert[475] *in* Madame Arthur, *in* Le Fiacre [The Carriage] *and in* Verligodin *(or just about).*

*

I remember the first petrol pumps, which the attendant actioned with his arm, and whose five litre tanks, positioned high above, glowed in the sun like translucent lanterns.

*

I remember In a Persian Market, by Ketèlbey.[476]

*

I remember Mireille,[477] *Jean Sablon,*[478] *Germaine Sablon,*[479] *Jean Nohain,*[480] *Franc-Nohain*[481] *who wrote* L'Heure espagnole[482] [Spanish Time], *but I lose my way in their family connections.*

*

I remember Marie Dubas,[483] *Damia,*[484] *Fréhel,*[485] *Renée Lebas,*[486]

[475] French cabaret singer and Belle Époque actress (1865–1944).
[476] Albert William Ketèlbey, English composer, conductor and pianist (1875–1959).
[477] Mireille Berl (1906–1996), French singer and songwriter; collaborated with Jean Sablon, Germaine Sablon and Jean Nohain.
[478] French singer, songwriter, composer and actor, one of the first French singers to adopt a jazz idiom (1906–1994).
[479] French singer, film actress and WWII resistance fighter (1899–1985); sister of Jean Sablon.
[480] French playwright, lyricist and screenwriter, also a noted television producer and presenter (1900–1981).
[481] Pseudonym of Maurice Étienne Legrand (1872–1934), French librettist and poet; father of Jean Nohain.
[482] By Maurice Ravel.
[483] French music-hall singer, diseuse and comedian (1894–1972).
[484] Stage name of Marie-Louise Damien (1889–1978), French singer and actress.
[485] Stage name of Marguerite Boulc'h (1891–1951), French singer and actress.
[486] French singer and producer (1917–2009).

Georgette Plana,[487] *Berthe Silva,*[488] *Lys Gauty,*[489] *Lucienne Delyle,*[490] *Lucienne Boyer*[491] *and Lina Margy*[492] *in* Le Petit vin blanc [The Little White Wine].

*

I remember Jean Rochefort[493] *and Jean-Pierre Marielle*[494] *as a duet in* Paris jadis [Paris Long Ago], *lyrics by Jean-Roger Caussimon, music by Philippe Sarde: 'Dans l'Paris des républiques, l'accordéon nostalgique ... ', 'In the Paris of the republics/The nostalgic accordion ... '.*

*

I remember mixed metaphors: 'This sabre is the happiest day of my life',[495] *'Harvests nipped in the egg',*[496] *'A virgin forest where the hand of man has never set foot', 'The ship of State is navigating upon a volcano',*[497] *'This budding star who already sings with a master's hand', 'It's the drop of water that sets off the powder keg',*[498] *'Life is a web of dagger blows that one must swallow drop by drop',*[499] *'The slow-down of growth is accelerating', 'The ravages of time, which have already dried so many tears, will allow grass to grow upon the wounds', 'A ferment of discord*

---

[487] French singer and actress (1917–2013).
[488] Pseudonym of Berthe Francine Ernestine Faquet, French singer (1885–1941).
[489] French cabaret singer and actress (1900–1944).
[490] French singer (1913–1962).
[491] French diseuse and singer (1901–1983).
[492] Pseudonym of Marguerite Verdier, French singer (1909–1973).
[493] French actor (1930–2017).
[494] French actor (1932–2019).
[495] From draughtsman, lithographer, actor and writer Henry Monnier's (1799–1877) fictional character Monsieur Joseph Prudhomme, who, along with Madame Prudhomme, was a caricature of the conformist and sententious Parisian bourgeoisie; the character was notoriously prone to unintentionally absurd turns of phrase.
[496] 'coupées dans l'œuf', 'cut in the egg', derived from the expression 'étouffer dans l'œuf', 'choke in the egg', 'to nip in the bud'.
[497] Another quotation from Monsieur Joseph Prudhomme.
[498] Derived from 'la goutte d'eau qui fait déborder le vase', 'the drop of water that causes the vase to overflow', 'the straw that breaks the camel's back'.
[499] From Christophe's *Les facéties du sapeur Sapeur Camember (The Pranks of Sapper Camember)* – see note 455.

has been cast among us, and, if we don't cut it at its root, it will quickly become a wildfire capable of drowning the land'.

*

I remember the time when Raymond Kopa[500] began playing for the SCO, meaning, presumably, for the Sporting-Club de l'Ouest,[501] and when the conductor, Pierre Dervaux I believe, stopped a concert (maybe just a rehearsal) with the Orchestra of Angers to announce triumphantly: 'The SCO is leading 1–0!'

*

I remember that at the beginning of the sixties the Fnac[502] was written FNAC, an acronym for 'Fédération nationale d'achat des cadres [National Purchasing Federation for Executives]', and managed a modest store on Boulevard de Sébastopol, on the pavement to your right as you came from Châtelet, and where only reasonably priced cameras were sold.

*

I remember ration cards where adolescents were listed as 'J 3',[503] a designation that survived for a few years during the period of 'restrictions', finally (finally?) making way for the 'ados', 'teenagers' of today.

*

In the Lascaux Cave, which you could still actually see for yourself at the end of the fifties, I remember a menacing mastiff visiting it with its owners, and a terrorised little girl yelling so as to reassure herself: 'A pas peur, chien!', 'Don't be afraid, doggy!'

*

I can't recall who said: 'Experience is a school where the lessons are costly, but it's the only one where even imbeciles can learn something.'

*

I remember 'Polop!', which pretty much meant 'Pas de ça Lisette!', 'No way, José', or maybe 'Arrête ton char!',[504] 'Come off it!'

---

[500] French footballer (1931–2017).
[501] Angers SCO, a football club based in western France.
[502] A large French retail chain selling electronic and cultural products; founded in 1954.
[503] I.e. 'Jeunesse 3', 'Youth 3'.
[504] 'Stop your chariot!'

*

I remember 'La Douleur [Sorrow]', *an all-purpose vocative like* 'You there' *or* 'What's-your-name', *in remarks like* 'Hey, La Douleur, *are you going forwards or backwards?*'

*

I remember the following three titles from 'Le Poulpe [The Octopus]' *collection:*[505] Stop the Tiling, Parkinson The Death-Knell, *and* Ouarzazate and Die.

*

I remember Patrice Lumumba,[506] *Joseph Kasavubu*[507] *and Moïse Tschombe,*[508] *in 1960, in what was no longer called the Belgian Congo, not yet Zaire, and not yet once again the Congo.*

*

I remember The Poet and the Peasant, *by Franz von Suppé.*[509]

*

I remember 'Chapeau bas devant la casquette, à genoux devant l'ouvrier', 'Hats off before the caps, on bended knee before the worker'. *But I also remember that right-wingers called the workers of the Popular Front* 'Salopards à casquettes', 'bastards with cloth caps'; *I believe they even said, to compound the insult,* 'salopards en casquette', 'cloth-capped bastards'.

*

I remember ordinary Caporal tobacco and Superior Scaferlati.

*

I remember Charpini[510] *and Brancato,*[511] *among other things in* 'Push,

---

[505] A series of French detective novels, launched in 1995.

[506] Congolese politician and independence leader (1925–1961), first prime minister of the Democratic Republic of Congo in 1960.

[507] Congolese politician (1915–1969), first president of the Democratic Republic of Congo from 1960 to 1965.

[508] Congolese businessman and politician (1919–1969), prime minister of the Democratic Republic of Congo from 1964 to 1965.

[509] Austrian composer of light operas and theatre music (1819–1895).

[510] Jean Émile Charpine (1901–1987), French variety artist.

[511] Antoine Brancato (1900–1991), French variety artist.

push the swing' from Véronique,[512] *in 'Tell me about my mother' from* Carmen, *in 'We've been on a beautiful journey' from* Ciboulette,[513] *in 'Yes, it is she! It is the goddess' from* The Pearl Fishers,[514] *in the turkey air from* The Mascot,[515] *all duets which they sang rather better (in terms of expression) than many more prestigious mixed couples.*

*

I remember that Tristan Bernard,[516] when someone wished to help him put on his overcoat, would grumble: 'It's already plenty annoying to do it by oneself.'

*

I remember the Belle Époque song Fascination: 'Je t'ai rencontré simplement/Et tu n'as rien fait pour chercher à me plaire', 'I simply met you/And you did nothing to seek to please me ... '.

*

I remember Rossini's Cat Duet *performed by Elisabeth Schwarzkopf and Victoria de Los Angeles.*

*

I remember Conchita Supervia, among other things in the Musetta aria from La Bohème, sung in French: 'D'un pas léger ... ', 'With a light step ... '.

*

I remember that Debussy said of the Right of Spring: 'It's primitive music with all modern conveniences.'

*

---

[512] Opéra comique (1898), music by André Messager, libretto by Georges Duval and Albert Vanloo.
[513] Operetta (1923), music by Reynaldo Hahn, libretto by Robert de Flers and Francis de Croisset.
[514] Opera (1863), music by Georges Bizet, libretto by Eugène Cormon and Michel Carré.
[515] Opéra comique (1880), music by Edmond Audran, libretto by Alfred Duru and Henri Chivot.
[516] French playwright, novelist, journalist and lawyer (1866–1947).

I remember Lily Pons,[517] *Mado Robin,*[518] *Ninon Vallin*[519] *and Germaine Lubin.*[520]

*

I remember Geneviève Tabouis,[521] *who would always tell us: 'Attendez-vous à savoir', 'Be prepared to know ... '.*

*

I've forgotten the name of the president of the United States who discovered one day that most *of their imports come from abroad, and who pitied the French for having no word to translate the English* entrepreneur.

*

I remember 'Ne fermez pas la porte, le Blount s'en chargera', 'Do not close the door, the Blount will take care of it.[522]

*

I remember Over the Rainbow, *by Harold Arlen, as it was recorded in October 1955 by Sarah Vaughan, far better than by its creator Judy Garland.*

*

I remember the children's comic strip by Alain Saint-Ogan,[523] *the father of Zig and Puce, which was called something like* Mitou and Toti Through the Ages.

*

I remember this remark by Jean Gabin in Daybreak, *before the drama unfolded*: 'Your place is nice: it isn't very big, but it's really small even so.'

---

[517] Pseudonym of Alice Joséphine Pons (1898–1976), French–American operatic soprano and actress.
[518] Madeleine Marie Robin (1918–1960), French coloratura soprano.
[519] Eugénie 'Ninon' Vallin (1886–1961), French soprano.
[520] French dramatic soprano (1890–1979).
[521] French historian and journalist (1892–1985).
[522] A sign seen on early twentieth-century doors in France: the 'Blount' is the name of the door closing mechanism, named after its American inventor Eugene Blount.
[523] French comics author and artist (1895–1974).

*

I remember that La Rose Rouge[524] *was owned by Nico Papatakis,*[525] *and* La Fontaine des quatre saisons[526] *by Pierre Prévert,*[527] *or perhaps even the other way round.*

*

I remember the appearance of Angie Dickinson in John Wayne's doorway, in the 16th minute of Rio Bravo.

*

I remember the time when the typical Himalayan summit was called Gaurishankar, and when the only frequently mentioned dinosaur was the diplodocus.

*

I remember that Christopher Colombus's three caravels were the Santa Maria, *the* Pinta *and the* Niña, *and that La Pérouse's*[528] *two frigates were* La Boussole *and* L'Astrolabe. *That the first died in misery, and the second, 'massacred by savages', on the island of Vanikoro.*

*

I can't recall who said: 'If I is an other [Si je est un autre[529]*], then there aren't many people.'*

*

I remember that Elisabeth Schwarzkopf was often called 'Schwarzkopf', but Gundula Janowitz always 'Gundula'. And Maria Callas's true fans never called her 'Callas', even less 'la Callas', but simply 'Maria'. And that no one would have dreamed of calling Dietrich Fischer-Dieskau 'Dietrich', nor Glenn Gould 'Glenn', nor for that matter Charlie Parker 'Charlie', nor Stan Getz 'Stan' – but on the other hand always 'Ella', 'Billie', 'Dizzy', 'Miles', 'Dexter', and sometimes even, pure snobbery, 'Thelonius'.

---

[524] Brasserie on Rue de la Fayette in the 10th arrondissement of Paris.
[525] Ethiopian-born Greek–French filmmaker (1918–2010).
[526] Erstwhile cabaret on Rue de Grenelle in the 7th arrondissement of Paris.
[527] French film director, screenwriter and actor (1906–1988), brother of the poet Jacques Prévert (1900–1977).
[528] Jean François de Galaup, comte de la Pérouse (1741–1788), French naval officer and explorer.
[529] A famous quotation from Arthur Rimbaud's correspondence; the more standard translation in English is 'I is another'.

*

I remember The Corruption of Adoré Floupette.[530]

*

I remember Georges Van Parys,[531] *to whom is owed among other things the music from* French Cancan *and from* The Grand Manoeuvres.

*

I remember the canuts[532] *protest song:* 'Pour chanter Veni Creator *il faut avoir chasuble d'or* ... *',* 'To sing Veni Creator *you need a golden chasuble* ... *'*.

*

I remember cameras with 'coupled rangefinders', the last word in progress in the thirties and forties; I suppose the expression has vanished simply because all cameras now of necessity comprise a coupled (with what?) rangefinder, or what advantageously relieves them of it.

*

I remember that Dexter Gordon, at the end of his set at the Village Vanguard, *raised his tenor saxophone, like a Holy Sacrament, to the heavens.*

*

I remember this poem: Je hais les tours de Saint-Sulpice/Et quand je les rencontre/Je pisse/Contre, 'I hate the towers of Saint Sulpice/ And when I encounter them/I piss/Against them', *but I've forgotten who its author is.*

*

I remember Michel Debré,[533] *who sang* La Marseillaise *so off key that you could distinctly hear* The Internationale.

*

---

[530] Adoré Floupette is the collective pseudonym of French authors Henri Beauclair and Gabriel Vicaire; the *Déliquescences d'Adoré Floupette* (1885) is a literary spoof satirising French symbolism and the Decadent movement.
[531] French composer of film music and operettas (1902–1971).
[532] Lyonnais silk workers in the nineteenth century, who staged many worker uprisings: their revolt in 1831 is thought to be one of the first of its kind.
[533] First prime minister of the French Fifth Republic.

I remember As Time Goes By: '*You must remember this...*', *which you hear (not enough) in* Casablanca.

*

I remember 'Passe-moi le sel, Marcel', 'Pass me the salt, Marcel'', 'Fonce, Alphonse', 'Hurry up, Alphonse', 'À la tienne, Étienne', 'Cheers, Étienne', 'Relaxe, Max', 'Relax, Max', 'Fais-moi la bise, Denise', 'Kiss me on the cheek, Denise', 'Bonne fête, Paulette', 'Happy Birthday, Paulette', 'Ça roule, ma poule', 'How's it going, babe?', and also 'En route, mauvaise troupe', 'Okay you lot, let's be off', which rhymed more vaguely, and also 'En voiture, Simone', 'Let's get a move on', which no longer rhymed at all, and even 'Monte là-dessus, et tu verras Montmartre', 'Climb up there, and you'll see Montmartre',[534] *which is completely unrelated.*

*

I remember the days when Ralph Lauren sold only 'Polo' shirts with a matching logo upon a very classy absence of left breast pocket, and Banana Republic pseudo-Saharan 'sports' clothes, the tropical equivalent of the Nordic-sporty style of Abercrombie & Fitch, so convenient for fly fishing in the Western torrents.

*

I remember Julie Christie in John McCabe, *Robert Altman's masterpiece.*

*

I remember Antoine Pinay,[535] *who had the look of a voter and a loan name,*[536] *and Giscard d'Estaing,*[537] *who also had a loan name,*[538] *doubly so, but certainly not the look of a voter.*

---

[534] Title of a song by Lucienne Boyer (1922); the expression signifies an ironic refusal.

[535] Conservative politician (1891–1994), served as French prime minister from 1952 to 1953.

[536] 'et un nom d'emprunt': 'un nom d'emprunt' usually denotes an 'assumed name' or 'alias', but here Genette is alluding to the National Loan launched by Pinay's government in 1952, which became known as the 'emprunt Pinay', the 'Pinay loan'.

[537] Valéry Giscard d'Estaing (1926–2020), liberal-conservative statesman, also known as 'Giscard' or 'VGE', minister of the Economy and Finance from 1969 to 1974, president of France from 1974 to 1981.

[538] See preceding footnote. The bond issued by the French state in 1973

*

I remember the 'trusts' and the '200 families', ancestors of the 'liberal straitjacket [carcan libéral]', but not in detail. And I can't recall who pointed out that social inequalities are greatly exaggerated: after all, the 200 richest families only ever amount to 200.

*

I remember Félix Leclerc,[539] *Gilles Vigneault*[540] *and Robert Charlebois*[541] *singing 'When Men Will Live for Love' at a festival on the Île d'Orléans, in Montreal.*

*

I remember the MP Coudé du Foresto,[542] *whose name gradually became a term of disparagement.*

*

I remember Edgar Faure[543] *who had no hair and spoke with a lisp,*[544] *who invented for Morocco the oxymoronic concept of independence within interdependency, and for French universities that of bestowed autonomy, who saw Mme. Coty as 'a model for Olida',*[545] *who asserted immodestly, but not implausibly: 'Only two men could have prevented*

on Giscard d'Estaing's initiative was known as the 'emprunt Giscard', the 'Giscard loan'.

[539] French–Canadian singer–songwriter, poet, writer, actor and Québecois political activist (1914–1988).

[540] Canadian poet, singer–songwriter and Québecois nationalist (1928–).

[541] Québecois author, composer, musician, performer and actor (1944–).

[542] Yvon Coudé du Foresto, Corsican politician (1961–1977), French minister of Agriculture from 1947 to 1948.

[543] French politician, lawyer, essayist, historian and memoirist; served as prime minister in 1952 and again in 1955, was appointed minister of Education in 1968.

[544] 'qui n'avait qu'un cheveu, mais sur la langue', literally 'who had only one hair, but on his tongue': 'avoir un cheveu sur la langue' is to speak with a lisp.

[545] Germain Coty was the wife of René Coty, president of France from 1954 to 1959. Olida was a well-known French commercial meat company and sales outlet (1855–1993): the expression 'mannequin chez Olida' was formerly used to refer unkindly to women deemed to be overweight.

Bardadrac

the French Revolution: Turgot,[546] *but he was dead; and me, but I wasn't yet born [mais ze n'était pas né]', and who, not having prevented May '68, succeeded in making it return to its lecture halls, by (momentarily) abolishing the lecture halls.*

*

I remember the minister of Food Supplies, after the war, whom we called 'High Commissioner the Belt'.

*

I remember 'gas bag' cars, during the Occupation, which drove around with large bottles laid upon their roofs, but I've never really known what these bottles contained.

*

I remember the (thrice) President of the Council Henri Queuille,[547] *who wisely asserted 'I know of no difficulty that a little negligence won't manage to resolve', and of whom it was said with admiration: 'He is immobilism in action, nothing will stop him.'*

*

I remember Signé Furax, a series by Pierre Dac[548] *and Francis Blanche*[549] *on Europe 1, where the baddies gave themselves away by always saying 'indibutably'; and the ensuing trend.*

*

I remember that RATP, Régie autonome des transports parisiens [Independent Public Company for Parisian Transport], was formerly, more pertinently, called TCRP: Transports en commun de la région parisienne [Public Transport Company for the Parisian Region]. I remember the CPDE, but I can't recall if these initials referred to the supply of water [eau], or of electricity.

*

I remember Simon and Garfunkel, who sang Mrs. Robinson *in* The Graduate. *I also remember Peter, Paul and Mary.*

---

[546] Anne Robert Jacques Turgot (1727–1781), French economist and statesman, physiocrat, advocate of economic liberalism.
[547] French politician (1884–1970).
[548] French humorist (1893–1975).
[549] French actor, singer, humorist and author (1921–1974).

*

I remember the jazz manouche guitarist who, in my adolescence and through oral tradition, we believed was called 'Jean Goréna'.[550]

*

I remember the Chicago style, binary jazz, free jazz and modal jazz.

*

I remember Michèle Barzach.[551]

*

I remember 'kif kif bourricot', 'it's all the same, stupid'.[552]

*

I remember Fachleitner, a racing cyclist in the fifties, a native or inhabitant of Manosque, who owed his participation in the Tour de France in 1952 to Jean Giono's personal intervention with Jacques Goddet.[553]

*

I remember the Ye Waverley Inn, *somewhere in the West Village, where you might have thought you were in the depths of the oldest New England.*

*

I remember Savignac's[554] *posters, including the mauve Monsavon cow and Maggi the half-ox.*

*

I remember the weightlifter Charles Rigoulot, whom they called 'the world's strongest man'.

*

I remember Jean Taris, champion swimmer, whom I saw, from the Quai

---

[550] Phonetically similar to a French pronunciation of 'Django Reinhardt'.

[551] French gynaecologist, psychoanalyst and politician (1943–); served as minister of Health in Jacques Chirac's second government (1986–1988); president of UNICEF France from 2012 to 2015.

[552] The expression allegedly derives from the Arabic expression 'kïf kïf', meaning 'exactly the same', and 'bourricot', 'donkey'.

[553] Director of the Tour de France from 1936 to 1986.

[554] Raymond Savignac, French graphic artist famous for his commercial posters (1907–2002).

de la République, win a long-distance race on the Seine back when the state of its water was still fit for this type of competition. I also remember that the Traversée de Paris [Crossing of Paris], which the same Taris must have won, was the showpiece event of this now forsaken sport.

*

I remember the song En douce [Quietly], *by Albert Willemetz and Maurice Yvain, sung by Mistinguett:*[555] *'J'ai fait ça en dou-ce/Sans fair'tant de complications/En pleine cambrous-se/Derrièr'les fortifications … , 'I did it qui-etly/Without causing such a fuss/In the middle of no-where/Behin' the fortifications … '.*

*

I remember Marianne Oswald,[556] *Agnès Capri,*[557] *Fabien Loris,*[558] *who were the first (and best) interpreters of Prévert and Kosma.*

*

I remember Catherine Sauvage[559] *in* Surabaya Johnny *and* The Bilbao Song, *by Kurt Weill.*

*

I remember the gas masks that were distributed at the beginning of the 'phoney war', in the autumn of 1939, which smelled strongly of bad rubber, and whose grey and cylindrical tins working-class households ended up recycling for various more pacific purposes.

*

I remember the battle of the Voracious and the Tenacious.[560]

*

I remember 'Quand mon verre est plein, je le vide; quand il est vide, je me plains', 'When my glass is full, I empty it; when it is empty, I complain.'

[555] Stage name of Jeanne Florentine Bourgeois (1873–1956), French actress and singer.
[556] Stage name of Sarah Alice Bloch (1901–1985), French singer and actress.
[557] French actress and writer (1907–1976).
[558] French actor (1906–1979).
[559] French singer and actress (1929–1998).
[560] From Alfred Jarry's *Ubu roi* (*Ubu the King*) (1888), a parody of the battle of the Horatii and the Curiattii (in French 'les Horaces et les Curiaces'), via Livy and Pierre Corneille's *Horace* (1640).

*

I remember Donald Byrd's hard-bop *quintet, somewhat derived from the Jazz Messengers, sometime in the sixties, at the* Chat-qui-pêche, *which must have been located on the homonymous, and even no doubt eponymous, and moreover tiny, street, between Rue de la Huchette and the Quai Saint-Michel; and a similarly tiny restaurant, two steps – perhaps just one – away, which was called 'Papille', and whose window bore the notice: 'Papille goes to sleep at 11pm.'*

*

I remember the mille-feuilles from the Mercure Galant, *nowadays vanished, on Rue des Petits-Champs.*

*

I remember the Galerie 55, *Rue de Seine, where Pierre Doris,*[561] *Jacques Dufilho,*[562] *Hubert Deschamps*[563] *used to drop by. Jean-Pierre Darras*[564] *and Philippe Noiret,*[565] *nocturnal escapees from the TNP,*[566] *would play Racine and Louis XIV in sketches by Yves Jamiaque. And* L'Écluse *(the first, Quai des Grands-Augustins), where Cora Vaucaire*[567] *and Barbara*[568] *would sing.*

*

I remember the Caméléon, *where you'd hear good jazz in the sixties. It was on Rue Saint-André-des-Arts, but I still see it clearly on Rue de Buci.*

*

I remember La Villa, *where you could hear Kenny Barron in the nineties, and which was located just next to the entrance of the Éditions du Seuil, another of whose locations overlooked the* Whisky à Gogo, *and now* L'Alcazar.

---

[561] French actor and humorist (1919–2009).
[562] French actor (1914–2005).
[563] French actor (1923–1988).
[564] French actor (1927–1999).
[565] French actor (1930–2006).
[566] 'Théâtre national populaire', 'People's National Theatre', founded in 1920, originally located at the Palais de Chaillot in Paris.
[567] French singer (1918–2011).
[568] Stage name of Monique Andrée Serf (1930–1997), French singer.

*

I remember the Capoulade, *which, in the fifties, was on the corner of Boulevard Saint-Michel and Rue Soufflot, with a* self-service restaurant *upstairs, where, if you ordered a steak accompanied with steamed potatoes, the order would be relayed by the waiter as a 'steamed steak!'*

*

I remember Bing Crosby, Dean Martin, Nat King Cole. I've forgotten Frank Sinatra.

*

I remember the 'Cafés Biard', which were always taken, and often mistakenly, to be 'cafés-billards [billiards-cafés]'.[569]

*

I remember the time when, not having checked the 'oil level', you always ran the risk of 'throwing a rod [couler une bielle]', and of having to reach the next garage 'on three legs'. I assume that six or eight (or more) cylinder engines better withstood this damage, but I've never had the opportunity to verify it. I remember that the expression 'couler une bielle' had a figurative meaning, which I have forgotten.

*

I remember that car cylinders were forever getting sooted up, whence a risk of self-ignition; to tell the truth, I'm not quite sure about this causal connection, but self-ignition in itself was a scary phenomenon, for you always feared not being able to stop the engine, at least until the tank was empty.

*

I remember that good drivers could be distinguished by their practice of 'double-clutching': a well measured step on the accelerator when in neutral between two ratios, in order to push the engine to the desired speed before changing down.

*

I remember that you had occasionally to give the engine 'a breather', clean the spark plugs, adjust the distributor, grind the valves, of which there were then just two per cylinder, activated by a camshaft whose ne plus

---

[569] 'Biard' and 'billard' are homophonous in French.

ultra was to be positioned 'overhead [en tête]', but I've never exactly known over which head [en tête de quoi].

*

I remember that it didn't take much for the steering to 'drift to the right', or, more seriously, 'drift to the left'. For example, poorly balanced tyre pressure or an asymmetrical wearing of the tyres, which you had periodically to swap in order to offset this defect.

*

I remember the record store La Boîte à Musique [The Music Box], *which could be found on Boulevard Raspail, and another record store called* Chantecler, *Boulevard Saint-Michel, where you could listen to music on headphones for a coin. I remember that a shop where records [des disques] were sold was called a 'record store [disquaire]'.*

*

I remember Audrey Hepburn in Robin and Marian.

*

I remember Victor Boucher[570] in the drunkard's monologue in Our Lord's Vineyard:[571] *'Physically, I prefer Gisèle ... '.*

*

I remember that the premiere of Phi-Phi,[572] *planned for the 11th November, 1918, was postponed, said a banner placed across the poster, 'on account of victory'.*

*

I remember that Vladivostok isn't the capital of Kamchatka.

*

I remember the plumber who wasn't sure whether to embark his son on long-term studies, fearing that upon finishing 'his job prospects would be blocked'.

*

I remember George & Ira Gershwin, Irving Berlin, Cole Porter, Jerome

[570] French actor (1877–1942).
[571] French comedy (1932), directed by René Hervil.
[572] Operetta (1918), music by Henri Christiné with a libretto by Albert Willemetz and Fabien Solar.

Kern & Oscar Hammerstein, Hoagy Carmichael, Vernon Duke, Richard Rodgers & Lorenz Hart, Harold Arlen, Leonard Bernstein of course, and Stephen Sondheim.

*

I remember Karl Münchinger and the Stuttgart Chamber Orchestra in the Brandenburg Concertos *and the* Four Seasons, *pretty much the first long-playing high-fidelity phonograph recordings,* called ffrr,[573] *no doubt released by Decca.*

*

I remember the shoes, under the Occupation, whose soles were made from wood that was 'jointed', that's to say split into staggered rows, if you see what I mean, so as to match the suppleness of leather or rubber soles. We were also familiar, but probably slightly earlier or slightly later, with what was called 'chrome plated' leather, meaning, it seems, 'tanned with chrome alum'. I have already recalled the scientific definition of alum, which is self-evident anyway ('hydrated double sulphate of potassium and aluminium'), but none of that really tells us how you obtain chrome *alum.*

*

I remember Yma Sumac,[574] whose fleeting glory was due to the extravagant breadth of her vocal range.

*

I remember the very popular Spinoza *café in Pest, the borscht served in an old inn, on the Buda hill, whose name I have forgotten, and the Opera that performed* Nabucco *in its original version, helpfully subtitled in Magyar. This obscure Babylonian affair didn't emerge particularly clearly therefrom.*

*

I remember the Parlophone *label, offspring of the old* Okeh, *which released 78 rpm jazz records available in France just after the war; I'm not too sure about its catalogue, but it seems to me that it included at least Louis Armstrong.*

*

[573] Full frequency range recording.
[574] Peruvian soprano (1922–2008).

I remember Paul Reynaud[575] *for 'The two-Sunday week is over', for 'The iron route has been cut off',*[576] *and for 'We shall triumph because we are the strongest'.*

*

I remember the Hôtel des Roches Blanches [White Rocks Hotel], in Treboul, which overlooked from its cliff the Baie de Douarnenez.

*

I remember topo, 'spiel', *which referred to any kind of explanatory discourse, and also* même topo, 'same old story', *which spared its repetition, and again* Tu vois le topo, 'You get the picture', *which rid one of it altogether.*

*

I've forgotten the name of the birdman, 'modern Icarus', who crashed on his first successful attempt.

*

I remember the property developer who averred not without reason: 'After all, concrete is grey matter too.'

*

I remember empirio-criticism, a theory of knowledge professed at the end of the nineteenth century by Richard Avenarius and Ernst Mach (moreover discoverer of the speed of sound, and one of Einstein's supposed precursors), a theory excoriated, and thereby popularised, in 1909, by Lenin in his pamphlet Materialism and Empirio-criticism.

*

I remember the cartoonist Colomb, whose pen name was Christophe;[577] *the sapper Camember, who dug a second hole wherein to place the earth from the first, and so on; Cosinus the scientist*[578] *who assured that: 'No sooner will you have reached the Pont-Neuf than I'll have caught up with*

---

[575] French politician (1878–1966), holder of various ministerial posts between 1932 and 1950, prime minister in 1940, deputy prime minister in 1953–1954.
[576] A reference to the alleged allied control of Narvik (Norway) in April 1940, stopping the supply of Swedish iron to the German war industry; German forces had in fact already taken Narvik.
[577] See note 455.
[578] The main character in Christophe's comic strip *L'Idée fixe du savant Cosinus* (*Cosinus the Scientist's Idée Fixe*) (1893).

you *[Vous ne serez pas arrivés au Pont-Neuf que je vous aurai rattrapés]'*; and the Fenouillard family,[579] which, having left Saint-Remy-sur-Deule to visit the Antwerp museum in Brussels, accidentally went all around the world, its head, father of Artemis and Cunégonde, having 'successively' lost several hats, but kept hold of his umbrella.

*

I remember a few art house cinemas, at a time when they were perhaps not yet so called: Les Agriculteurs, *somewhere between Saint-Lazare and Batignolles, whose seats were comfortable club armchairs; the* Studio 28, *Rue Tholozé, on the western flank of the Butte;*[580] *the* Studio 43, *Rue du Faubourg-Montmartre, for its part very east-facing (*Cossacks of the Kuban, *etc.); the* Studio Parnasse, *Rue Jules-Chaplain, north of the Vavin crossroads; the* Studio Raspail, *Boulevard Raspail, south of the same crossroads; the* Studio Bertrand, *Rue Bertrand, the* Pagode, *Rue de Babylone*; Le Ranelagh, *on the street of the same name;* Les Ursulines, *on the eponymous road;* Le Panthéon, *Rue Victor-Cousin. They aren't all the same age (I think the two first-mentioned were the oldest), they haven't all vanished or renounced their vocation, but their heart isn't really in it.* Le Champollion *is still there, but I don't know if it has retained its rear projection mirror.*

*

I've forgotten who said, and about whom: 'Beware of this guy, he believes everything he says.'

*

I remember Jules Verne's novels, and especially Mathias Sandorf.

*

I remember Jean Racine, who used no more words than someone with a baccalaureate today, but not the same ones, and which he arranged more artfully; I wonder at the critics who on the one hand note his lexical parsimony, and on the other his poetic genius, without seeing that the latter is largely due to the former: that was his thing.

*

[579] *La Famille Fenouillard* (*The Fenouillard Family*) (1889–1893), another of Christophe's comic strips.
[580] La Butte Montmartre, 18th arrondissement of Paris; a 'butte' is a small hill or hillock.

I remember Pierre Corneille, beloved of schoolboys for Je suis Romaine, hélas! puisque mon époux l'est,[581] 'I am Roman, alas! since my husband is so', *for* Le désir s'accroît quand l'effet se recule,[582] 'Desire increases when fulfillment is postponed', *for* Prends un siège, Cinna, et assieds-toi par terre/Et si tu veux parler, commence par te taire,[583] 'Now take a seat, Cinna, and sit upon the floor/And if you wish to speak, start by holding your peace', *and for* Fuis la mauvaise science, et cours après la bonne,[584] 'Flee from the wrong science, and pursue the right one'.

*

I remember that, in the early days of television news, Pierre Dumayet[585] would let a whole news story unfold without further commentary save for the closing remark: 'Ben mon vieux!', 'Well I never!'

*

I remember the beginning of the French lyrics adapted to the melody of Whispering: *'Ah, if I had three francs 50!', but I've forgotten what this modest sum was to be used for.*

*

I've forgotten, if I ever knew it, the scientific name for the 'dove tree'.

*

I remember that the no. 12 metro line (Porte de la Chapelle–Mairie d'Issy) was formerly called the 'North–South', a title and status that might as legitimately, or more legitimately (albeit in the other direction) have been claimed by the no. 4 line, Orléans–Clignancourt.

*

[581] 'Mon époux l'est' can also be roughly heard in French as 'mon poulet', 'my chicken': Corneille subsequently rewrote the line (from *Horace* (1640)): 'Je suis romaine hélas, puisqu'Horace est romain'.
[582] 'l'effet se recule' can also be heard in French as 'les fesses reculent', 'the buttocks recede': from *Polyeucte* (1642).
[583] These lines are from a parody of Corneille's *Cinna* (1643) by Raymond Rua (1970).
[584] 'Cours après la bonne' can also mean 'chase after the maid': this line is from Corneille's translation (1656) of Thomas à Kempis' *The Imitation of Jesus Christ* (1418–1427).
[585] Writer, producer and journalist (1923–2011).

I remember the cellar of the Lorientais, *Rue des Carmes, where Claude Luter's orchestra used to play, but I've forgotten the name of the little room, a little further up the same road become in the meanwhile Rue Valette, on the other side of the street and on the ground floor, where the same orchestra sought refuge when the* Lorientais *closed down.*

*

I remember this popular jibe, which greeted any less-than-credible remark: 'Me fais pas rire, j'ai les lèvres gercées!', 'Don't make me laugh, my lips are chapped!'

*

I remember the buildings where you couldn't access the upper floors without having asked the caretaker for the 'cord' ('Cord, please! [Cordon, siouplait]'), which (in hindsight) presupposes the presence of a door between the vestibule and the stairwell, or perhaps the lift. Entry codes and other intercoms with drop-down menus have abolished this function, which the caretaker would perform at night, presumably, in his 'first sleep', by pulling upon a cord placed by the headboard, and which opened said door with a delicate click.

*

I've forgotten to what referred the expression 'the last 15 minutes', which can evidently be applied to many 15 minutes, but not necessarily to the one, 'of fame', promised everybody by Andy Warhol.

*

I remember Enrico Fermi,[586] who said: 'A successful experiment is only ever just another experiment; an experiment that fails is a discovery.' This quip is valid in all domains, public or private.

*

I remember Ambre Solaire, which is, besides, making a comeback following a lengthy eclipse, and an advertisement for this product consisting of the wooden effigy of a woman, which we'd pretend to embrace then send the photo to our friends. In the fifties, when you arrived at the Côte d'Azur in the late morning on the train weaving between the beaches and the final slopes of the Esterel, a sweet perfume would waft through the carriages. It came not from the sea, since the

---

[586] Italian physicist (1901–1954).

Mediterranean has no more odour than it does tides, but indeed from this product, as heady as it was ineffective.

*

I remember this definition of the École Polytechnique[587] *student: 'He knows everything, but nothing else.' And the ENA*[588] *graduate who complimented a lower-Alpine shepherd (Gaston Dominici,*[589] *I imagine): 'You've a very fine sheep there' – You, replies Gaston, you must be from the ENA. – How did you guess? – Easy: it isn't a sheep, it's my dog.'*

*

I remember Second Empire[590] *humour: 'There isn't only la bouteille de Leyde [the Leyden jar], there's also Madame de ***',*[591] *'The leopard is dappled by nature, M. de *** by the Emperor, and the Emperor by the window', and 'France has 40 million subjects, not to mention the subjects of discontent' (Rochefort*[592]*). I remember* Italia fara da se [Italy will make herself, by herself],[593] Fate ma fate presto [Do it, but be quick about it], Vittorio Emmanuele Re d'Italia [Victor Emmanuel King of Italy] (VERDI),[594] Not a single gaiter button is missing,[595]

[587] The École Polytechnique is a prestigious and highly selective 'Grande École', specialising in the sciences and technology.

[588] See note 137.

[589] Convicted in 1957 of murdering three Britons; Roland Barthes discusses the case in *Mythologies* (1957).

[590] The Second French Empire, under Napoleon III (1852–1870).

[591] Presumably a play on the homophony 'de Leyde' and 'laide', 'ugly': 'There's also Madame (who is) Ugly'.

[592] French politician and writer of *vaudevilles* (1831–1913).

[593] Well-known saying by Charles Albert, king of Sardinia from 1831 to 1849, in the context of prospective Italian unity and independence.

[594] A reference to Vittore Emmanuele II (1820–1878), king of Sardinia then of a unified Italy in 1861 – the slogan 'Viva VERDI' spread throughout Italy in the 1860s.

[595] Marshal Edmond Le Bœuf (1809–1888) thus expressed his confidence in the French forces' alleged preparedness ahead of war with Prussia in 1870.

The chassepots would go off by themselves,[596] *and* The chassepots worked wonders.[597]

*

I remember 'Frederick II of Prussia and Catherine of Russia together put pressure on the Divan, and the Sublime Porte eventually half-opened', a sentence whose historical (I mean chronological) plausibility I've never been able to verify.

*

I remember 'Maurice Thorez, France's first party'

*

I remember Édouard Depreux,[598] SFIO[599] MP, mayor of Sceaux, once or twice minister of National Education (or Public Instruction?) under the Fourth Republic, at least once minister of the Interior, for this reason dubbed 'Doudou the Truncheon', and who declared one day: 'The communists aren't on the left, they're in the East.' This saying is therefore wrongly attributed to Guy Mollet,[600] who only invented Molletism, or who rather gave a name to the recipe as old as the Republic: get elected on the left, govern on the right, and, when fall one must, fall again to the left, and so forth. Depreux was subsequently one of the founders of the PSU,[601] precisely... .

*

[596] Marshal MacMahon (1808–1893), then chief of state of France, retorted thus, in 1873, to the legitimists' wish to replace the Revolutionary tricolour with the Royal white flag. The 'chassepot', a bolt action breech-loading rifle, became famous for having been the French forces' principal weapon in the Franco-Prussian war (1870–1871).

[597] A telegram from Marshal Adolphe Niel (1802–1869) following victory against Garibaldi's forces at Mentana in November 1867.

[598] French socialist, journalist, essayist and politician (1898–1981).

[599] 'Section française de l'internationale ouvrière [The French Section of the Worker's International]', founded in 1905 and succeeded in 1969 by the Socialist Party (*Parti socialiste*).

[600] French politician (1905–1975), led the SFIO from 1946 to 1959 and was prime minister from 1956 to 1957.

[601] 'Parti socialiste unifié [Unified Socialist Party]' (1960–1990), situated politically between the SFIO and the French Communist Party (*Parti communiste français*).

I remember the young friend of Paul Fort,[602] *somewhat illiterate, but whom he cultivated for this single and fine reason: when she was asked to read out loud the name 'Shakespeare', she distinctly pronounced* Schopenhauer; *and another, closer to us and even to me, who thought she knew that films begin with a* panegyric.[603]

*

I remember the 'gueules cassées [broken faces]',[604] *and the lottery tickets supposed to help indemnify them.*

*

I remember the cabarets in Montmartre where, ever since Bruant, late-coming spectators would be greeted with the charitable refrain: 'Ah, c'te gueule, c'te gueule, c'te gueule ... ', 'Ah, that face, that face, that face ... '.

*

I remember Robinson, *a children's magazine from the fifties, wherein featured among others 'Mandrake the Magician' and 'The Pronto Family'.*

*

I remember the sociological survey where the polled participants were divided into 'Men/Women/No Opinion'.

*

I remember André Marie,[605] *minister of Public Instruction (or of National Education), additionally mayor of Barentin, in the Lower-Seine region, where he'd assembled a large number of modern sculptures, including Rodin's* The Walking Man *(but not Giacometti's).*

*

I remember Grove Court, in Greenwich Village, the little courtyard with such a provincial, colonial, already almost Southern charm that you dream on each visit of inhabiting one of the two or three very old houses huddled there. I remember Saint Luke's Garden, a small curate's garden

---

[602] A French poet associated with the symbolist movement (1872–1960).

[603] Rather than with a 'générique', 'opening credits'.

[604] An expression used in the wake of World War One to refer to war veterans with disfigured faces.

[605] French 'Radical Party' politician (1897–1974, briefly prime minister in 1948.

surrounding Saint Luke's Chapel, in the West Village. The church dates
from the beginning of the nineteenth century, and the garden is apparently
maintained by the community of parishioners. Maintained here means
nursed, so fragile does it seem in the tarmac and concrete vicinity of Hudson
Street, on the western fringes of Greenwich Village. You cautiously explore
it on paved pathways, minding not to touch any of the plants.

*

I remember Olympe de Gouges[606] *and Théroigne de Méricourt,*[607] *stars*
of the Revolution, whom I always confuse.

*

I remember the Lent sermons by R.P. Riquet,[608] *broadcast after the war,*
and which made him seem like the new Massillon, but who remembers
Massillon?[609]

*

I remember an advertisement for the US News and World Report
magazine, which posed (but to whom?) this pertinent question, but one
that is difficult to translate without loss: 'Do you sometimes feel you
know more than you need to know about more than you need to
know about and not enough about what you know you ought to
know more about?'

*

I remember the spinach ravioli served by father Milo (or Millo?) on
the terrace of his inn, at the entrance to the village of Peillon, in the
Nice countryside, the most hilltop of all hilltop villages, which one of
its faithful has justly described as a 'vessel petrified by a mysterious
mythological embargo'. I also remember the Hôtel du Pic d'Anie,
in Lescun, where you had to go outside to find the toilets, situated a little
further down the (same) street. And its exhilarating view of said peak.

*

[606] French playwright and political activist (1748–1793), advocate for women's
rights and abolitionism; executed during the Reign of Terror for attacking
the Revolutionary government.
[607] Belgian singer, orator and organiser in the French Revolution (1762–1817).
[608] Jesuit priest, theologian and former Resistance fighter, the most popular
preacher in postwar Paris (1898–1993).
[609] Jean-Baptiste Massillon (1663–1742), French Catholic bishop and preacher.

I remember Georges Bidault,[610] *who, with a contemptuous wave of his arms, pushed aside the enthusiastic crowd during de Gaulle's descent of the Champs-Elysées at the liberation of Paris, and who, a little later, snatched a vote from the Assemblée [Nationale] thanks to this well-turned aphorism: 'It's better to brush your teeth in a stemmed glass [verre à pied] than to wash your feet [pieds] in a tooth glass.'*

*

I've forgotten the name of the Communist MP who, when asked to shorten his speech, gave this thunderous reply: 'Monsieur the President, the proletariat never shortens anything!'

*

I remember Hedy Lamarr[611] *in* Ecstasy *by Machatý. And you?*

*

I remember that 'Mistinguett' was in fact called Jeanne Bourgeois, 'Jean Gabin' Jean Alexis Moncorgé, 'Bourvil'[612] *André Raimbourg, but 'Joséphine Baker' Joséphine Baker, and 'Maurice Chevalier' Maurice Chevalier.*

*

I remember Albert Préjean[613] *in* Under the Roofs of Paris, *Roland Toutain*[614] *in* The Rules of the Game, *Raymond Aimos*[615] *in* They Were Five, *René Lefèvre*[616] *in* The Crime of Monsieur Lange.

*

I remember the 'small lacunars of Pierre-Marie Foy',[617] *but I've forgotten of what their lacunae consisted; of this, perhaps.*

---

[610] See note 394.
[611] American film actress (1914–2000).
[612] French comic actor and singer (1917–1970).
[613] French actor (1894–1979).
[614] French actor, songwriter and stuntman (1905–1977).
[615] French actor (1891–1944).
[616] French actor and writer (1898–1991).
[617] This appears to be a reference to the 'Marie-Foix syndrome', or 'lateral pontine syndrome', first described by the French neurologists Pierre Marie (1853–1940), Charles Foix (1882–1927) and Théophile Alajouanine (1890–1980).

Bardadrac

*

I too remember the Vase of Soissons.[618]

*

I shall remember to die: I have tied a knot in my handkerchief.

Spitzbergen. I had one day unearthed somewhere or another an adventure novel published in a series that couldn't be more commercial, and by a then unknown author who is now forgotten, at least by me. It was entitled *The Seagull of Spitzbergen*, which wasn't inept as an incitement to geographical reverie. Of this two-bit story, only the name of a probably secondary and certainly Basco-Béarnais character (he lived exclusively on garbure[619]) has remained with me: Spridon Purif Harmorigaray, and the explanation of his middle name by the vagaries of the calendar: its bearer was born on the 2nd February, the immutable Feast of the Purification of the Virgin Mary, a highly pleonastic ceremony which coincides moreover, God must know why, with the Presentation of Jesus at the Temple. This feast, which is more commonly called Candlemas, which is greeted by an orgy of crêpes whose relation to these two sacred events likewise eludes me, which calendars nowadays register more readily as Presentation, was so then, apparently, by the abbreviation 'Purif', like the famous 'Fêtnat'[620] of the Africans once blessed by the cares of our ancestors the Gauls with pale blue eyes [par nos soins d'ancêtres gaulois à l'œil bleu-blanc[621]]. The subsequent

[618] According to Gregory of Tours (AD 538–594), the legendary Vase of Soissons was stolen from a cathedral by King Clovis I in the wake of the Battle of Soissons (AD 486); Clovis subsequently agreed to return the vase, but a recalcitrant soldier smashed it with his axe, the vase then being given back in its broken state. A year later, Clovis slayed this soldier with his own axe, commenting 'Just as you did to the vase at Soissons!', an utterance popularised in the schoolbooks of the French Third Republic (1875–1940) as 'Souviens-toi du vase de Soissons!', 'Remember the vase of Soissons!'
[619] A thick meat, bean and vegetable stew typical of the south-west of France.
[620] 'Fêtnat' is the calendar abbreviation for 'Fête nationale', i.e. Bastille Day, 14 July; in certain French colonies it was customary to give children the first name of the particular saint on whose day the birth occurred; this practice led to 'Fêtnat' being used for children born the 14th July.
[621] Genette is here alluding to the beginning of Arthur Rimbaud's 'Mauvais sang [Bad Blood]' in *Une Saison en enfer* [A Season in Hell] (1873): 'J'ai de

question was: what would have become of his civil status if he'd been born on Epiphany Day?

Stanhope. In the spring of 1969, during the 'Easter' holidays at Yale, I took Babette along with me to discover New York, which I didn't know much better than she did. The train journey was rather bleak: it was from there that I had my first glimpse of Bridgeport, whose reputation is apparently well earned. Once out of Central Station, goodness knows what inspiration, or recommendation, led us to the Tudor Hotel – from the name, presumably, of the enormous Tudor City, which overwhelms the eastern extremity of 42nd Street, within sight of the UN buildings on the East River. The comfort of this hotel almost matched that of my hovel in New Haven, and we thought it best, wishing anyhow to visit the Village, to decamp first thing in the morning towards the Fifth Avenue Hotel, just to the north of Washington Square. It wasn't much better, and we decided, for the end of our stay, to head back to the Stanhope, still on Fifth, but opposite the Metropolitan Museum, that's to say distinctly higher up in every respect, if only for the breakfast brought to you on a rolling table. Like Cocteau's *enfants terribles*,[622] we pretended always to have lived amid this Fitzgeraldian luxury. Just a few steps away from there, in the suite of Baroness Nica de Koenigswarter, Charlie Parker had died 14 years earlier, collapsed in front of a television set, transfixed by one will never know which idiotic programme.

Statistics. On the jury of a thesis defence, a great French historian from the last century, beset by insomnia, was discreetly cutting the pages of the thesis of which he was the adjudicator – in those days, theses had necessarily to be printed before their defence, and these volumes appeared with their pages still uncut. All of a sudden, he stopped dead, and, in his emotion, exclaimed without realising what this intervention revealed about the state of his reading: 'But what do I see? Statistics? Ah, Monsieur, my congratulations, this is History as it ought to be done!'

mes ancêtres les gaulois l'oeil bleu blanc', 'From my ancestors the Gauls I have pale blue eyes'.
[622] *Les Enfants terribles (The Holy Terrors)* (1929).

I quite like, however, the oft-invoked principle that claims, sometimes quite rightly, to combat supposedly dominant prejudices by putting this supposed sociological measuring tool in its place. I call it the Principle of Statistical Equality. It posits that there are no more (nor fewer) x in a given class y than in all the others: for instance, that there are no more suicides in cities than in the countryside, no more cuckolds in the French navy than in the others, nor more diabetics in volume 2 of the telephone directory than in volume 1, etc.

I read moreover somewhere: 'The majority of people are more stupid than the average.' I think I understand that this apparently absurd (though rather tempting) statement isn't quite so from a mathematical point of view: it doubtless suffices that the level of intelligence of the minority should offset its smaller number. But this optimistic explanation remains to be verified, and is anyway contradicted by Malraux's salutary opinion, which should obviously be pushed to its logical conclusion: 'In every minority, there yet remains a majority of imbeciles.' But I have even more faith in the Chinese proverb, which is valid in all circumstances, and even in the West: 'You think yourself original, and you're in the statistics.'

Stop/Hitch-hiking. Towards the end of the forties, Youth Hostels were furiously divided between secular and *more* secular federations, with a sometimes Trostskist, sometimes Trotskyist impregnation, hence the acronyms UFAJ, CLAJ,[623] etc., which I would no longer be able to tell apart. Mine, in any case, had its Parisian headquarters on Rue Jean-Dolent, in the tutelary shadows of the La Santé Prison. The connection between them was the almost exclusive love of Prévert's then unpublished poems, which circulated through oral or duplicated tradition. To my affiliation to one of them, I owed several 'descents' towards *le Midi* (it wasn't yet called the 'South', and I still baulk at this misleading loanword) or the Alps, by means of hitch-hiking [en auto-stop], or more precisely of lorry-hiking [en camion-stop]: I can't recall what youth-hostelling point of honour kept us from stopping private

[623] Respectively: 'Union Française des Auberges de Jeunesse [French Union of Youth Hostels]' and 'Centre Laïc des Auberges de Jeunesse [Secular Centre of Youth Hostels]'.

cars. The lorries most readily welcoming us were especially those, in the summertime, transporting fruit, descending empty and heading back from Cavaillon bursting with crates of peaches and melons. On the outward journey, they could be chartered, if that's the right word, on their way from les Halles (Baltard's, needless to say[624]), or else we'd await them a few kilometres from Paris (at Rungis, for example), on the *nationale* 6, or on the 7, which branches off it at Fontainebleau then to rejoin it at Lyon via Nevers and Moulins. The share of unforeseen events was pretty much equal in both cases, but misfortune could occasionally compel you to sleep in the great or not so great outdoors[625] somewhere between Corbeil and Fontainebleau. The empty lorries sped along at a better rate, but would shake you more vigorously beneath their tarpaulin, especially during the whirling descent around the glazed tiles of La Rochepot. The way back was slower, but more cushioned, and more flavoursome. I can't recall aboard which one I rallied, in the summer of 1946, a few better equipped comrades, for a refreshing descent of the Arve by canoe, from Sallanche to Annemasse, with bivouacs on the banks for the evening stopovers, and for sole daily meal a dense gruel made from chocolate-flavoured flour, where your spoon would stand up straight when it managed to enter it at all, and which we aptly enough called 'concrete'.

Stroboscope. A subtle philosopher, seductive to the very tips of his fingernails, once wrote, apropos of a writer friend of ours, that his work called for a 'stroboscopic' reading. I have always wondered whether this term could mean anything more than turning the pages sufficiently quickly (*flip book*) for them to merge in a semblance of movement, as is done to 'animate' certain illustrations. Even understood in this way, the recommendation might be applied to many others, or rather to them all: it wouldn't be ill-advised to stroboscope, once it has been digitised, the whole of universal literature, which would thereby doubtless receive, like the particles in a cyclotron, some additional quantum of energy, and maybe of

[624] Victor Baltard (1805–1874) was the architect of Paris's fresh food market 'Les Halles', demolished in 1971 to be replaced by the current shopping mall 'le Forum des Halles'.
[625] 'une première nuit à la belle ou moins belle étoile': 'a first night under the beautiful or less beautiful stars'.

meaning. It isn't without reason that the same philosopher also devoted himself to thinking about the cinema. All of his thought was somehow stroboscopic, which moreover showed itself even better in oral improvisations – of which we have some fine traces. During thesis defences, he stunned the candidate, perforce anxious about what he was going to have to 'answer', with the whirlwind statement of what he had 'found' in the thesis ('What you're telling us, in sum, is that ... '), and of what else might have been found there. For the other members of the jury, save for postprandial torpor or an urgent meeting, this controlled delirium was a veritable enchantment.

Subjects. 'All men are born subjects.' Bossuet,[626] to whom we owe this politically no longer correct, but philosophically still interesting (though occasionally contested) thought, doesn't tell us how they die, but it can be inferred. He ought besides to have taken better account of the following reservation, later well known in Versailles: 'The king is not a subject.' All men, then, except one. But there are subjects and subjects. I see too in Littré that he whom we more poetically call the Eagle of Meaux was branded, in the back alleys, a 'Mauléoniste', 'because of his liaison with Mlle. de Mauléon, with whom strange rumours claim he had been united through a secret marriage'. I had no idea, they hide everything from you at school. Even if he writes less well than Bossuet, one never rereads Littré enough.

Sûr (c'est)/Certainly. A rural and purely phatic expression, which thus attests merely to the reception of the message. Heard for instance in my village: 'I have a toothache – Ah well, *c'est sûr.*' 'Young' city-dwellers today prefer: 'C'est clair [It's clear]' – but it's already less certain [moins sûr].

Susceptibilité/Touchiness. The most unpleasant form of self-love. One reads (almost) in Giraudoux: 'You were already ugly, stupid and mean,[627] and now with age you're becoming touchy.' Exists for men.

---

[626] Jacques-Bénigne Bossuet (1627–1704), French bishop and theologian, renowned as a brilliant orator and French stylist.
[627] 'laide, bête et méchante': the speaker is here referring to a woman.

Talent. 'You can shake my hand, talent isn't contagious' (Louis Jouvet). In the fifties, weak in the Classics and thus campaigning for the creation of a modern literature *agrégation*, we'd adopted this intentionally arrogant slogan, which proved effective: 'You who have no talent, think of those who do.'

Temps de rivière/River weather. In the Launay dialect, this expression referred to a spring-like day, with an alternation of blue sky and moderately rapid-moving light clouds, rather chilly and suitable for excursions along the banks of the Loire or the Vienne – without regard, as usual, for the gender difference between *rivière* and *fleuve*.[628] The saying, which has remained in a few family repertoires, is unknown to the meteorologists, who are in no danger of adopting it, for the thing hardly exists any more on this continent, whose climate remains temperate, if at all, merely by dint of the statistical average.

From Angers to Launay (or back), we had in principle a choice between two routes along the right bank of the Loire. The quickest, I suppose, crossed the Val d'Anjou, via Beaufort-en-Vallée and Longué. For a reason unknown to me, Jacqueline, at the wheel of the antique family 402 with rear-facing folding seats, systematically avoided it. Still on the right bank, you could rejoin the river upstream of the Ponts-de-Cé, then drive alongside it on the levee road, which you left between La Croix-Verte and Villebernier in order to reach, once passed over or beneath the 'Lyon–Nantes' road, one of the two entrances, courtyard side or park side. This route didn't particularly enjoy her favour either, perhaps because the levee road, charted, as its name indicates, upon a dangerous overhang, isn't always charitable to distracted or, as she didn't like you to say, 'whimsical' drivers.

The preferred itinerary followed, illogically, the left bank of the river – which we had therefore to cross twice, once at the Ponts-de-Cé, then at Saumur – by way of Gennes and Trèves-Cunault. Here there is no longer exactly a levee, but a riverbank road just above the water, at the foot of already troglodyte hillsides, narrow, winding, but pleasant and shady, at least as far as the area

---

[628] The Loire is *un fleuve*, i.e. flows directly to the sea, whereas the Vienne, an affluent of the Loire, is *une rivière*.

around Saint-Hilaire-Saint-Florent, where there'd mingle, in a good wind, the aromas of sparkling white, of button mushrooms, and of the thoroughbred dung that a connoisseur has said to be 'the very perfume of Saumur'. But the main reason for this choice was Cunault's Romanesque church, with the buried nave (nine steps leading you down to the west portal), and the low-built steeple, almost hidden in the roof of the aisle, and whose rustic elegance is (almost) without equal. The disadvantage of this itinerary was to deprive us of the view of Glanfeuil Abbey, with, on fine days, the mirage effect evoked by Michelet: 'If you gaze from the shore, the other bank appears suspended in mid-air, so faithfully does the water reflect the sky.' Hence this other variant, not much quirkier than the others: right-bank levee road between Angers and Les Rosiers, cross the bridge that links Les Rosiers to Gennes, and continue as aforesaid. A final one headed a little further inland south of the river, through Brissac and Doué-la-Fontaine. Her declared intention was to approach the Mauges countryside, which its mysterious name and the memory of the Wars in the Vendée[629] adorned, between Angers and Cholet, with a certain historical prestige.

As soon as I had my own car, I set about 'collecting' rivers – meaning swimming in the greatest possible number of them, at the rate of at least once in each. My collection was never as copious as I had wished, but the intention guided some of my trips, at least in France. Just as certain mountaineers nowadays attempt one summit after another, I strove to experience one river after the next in the shortest time possible. My record, hardly commendable because geography-assisted, was the sequence Mayenne–Sarthe–Loire, which meet a little north of Angers to form the Maine, making four, and finally flow into the Loire at Bouchemaine, making five. Confluences are obviously propitious spots, and I thought I could in fact discern, from one water to another, differences of flow, of content, of colour, of taste and of transparency, and ascertain their mode of fusion: the Seine and the Oise at Conflans, of course (I'd known it from birth or pretty much, and had often gazed upon it from the place justly called the 'Pointil', which is our Bec

---

[629] A counter-revolution between 1793 and 1796 in the Vendée region of western France.

d'Ambès[630]), the Seine and the Yonne at Montereau, and, near Candes, the Loire and the Vienne. But it was also necessary, to do things properly, to test each river up- and downstream of each of its affluents: the Seine at Andrésy isn't the Seine at Herblay, and the Loire at Montsoreau isn't at all the Loire at Chouzé.

None of this is any longer seasonable, but from it has abided with me a certain disdain for sea beaches, with their overly salty water, overly repetitive waves and overly flat, and as though overly abstract, horizon. Bachelard is indeed right to assert the 'supremacy of terrestrial over marine water', and that 'natural reverie will always give preference to freshwater, water that refreshes, water that quenches'. So one can be a tad thalassophobic without being in the least hydrophobic, but I'm just afraid that one day soon there should be no river fit to quench anybody at all.

Terminal. I'm unaware who, nowadays, runs the TWA terminal at JFK airport. With its roof of outstretched wings, it is one of Saarinen's masterpieces, and the interior by no means disappointed. I thus avoided choosing any other company as far as possible, especially on the way back, where a somewhat neurotic safety margin allowed me ample time to explore the site. In the other direction, the Kafkaesque formalities of the landing, the prohibited crossing of the invisible yellow line, the order to write afresh a form poorly filled out on the plane (the day's number placed inopportunely before that of the month), the obsessive fear of missing baggage, rather spoiled for me the arrival upon this land of liberty, even if the final stamp on my passport was supposed to guarantee my rights as an *exchange visitor*. I wasn't really over with the preliminary procedures: the queue at the consulate, the written confirmation of (henceforth) non-belonging to the PCF,[631] the sworn pledge to having no relative on US soil, not to impinge in any way upon the health of the president or to be smuggling any continental living being or organism (animal, vegetal, bacterial or other), the final meeting with an in every respect deterrent lady consul, the fear of a postal strike on the day of finally receiving the

---

[630] The point of confluence of the Garonne and the Dordogne, in the Gironde estuary in south-west France.
[631] French Communist Party.

irreplaceable *J-1* visa, and I could go on. On the way back, then, no problem, except that a well-intentioned friend had convinced me, during my first stay, that I needed proof of an obscurely fiscal authorisation to return, prettily named (ever since the *Mayflower*, presumably) a *sailing permit*, hence an anxious half a day spent on the benches of goodness knows which official office of the State of Connecticut, for a document that nobody would ask me for at the boarding gate. As a result, I thought I could subsequently dispense with this permission to cast off, but not without a touch of uncertainty. For if it is unfortunate not to be able to enter the United States when you are expected there, it must be even more so not to be able to leave when you're expected elsewhere.

Terre/Land. Long ago I read a short story by Tolstoy, whose sentiment I find instructive, and which I shall brazenly summarise here. It's a kind of prose fable. Its title is 'How Much Land Does a Man Need?' An apparently generous, in fact highly perverse, nobleman grants a poor muzhik the ownership of the entire area of good land that he'll be able to circumscribe by walking around it for as long as possible. Overjoyed with the godsend, the muzhik naively sets off, broadening as much as he can the circle of his domain, ever roaming, despite his growing tiredness, an extra verst when he might reasonably have come full circle. In the end, exhausted, he collapses to the ground and breathes his last. Immediately, those accompanying him dig a precisely measured grave where he has fallen, and cover him up for evermore. That is exactly, concludes the narrator, 'how much land a man needs'.

Timing. You can say what you like, but this boy had one hell of a sense of timing. See the series of coincidences that clearly owe nothing to chance: he's born on Christmas night, dies on Good Friday, is resurrected on Easter Sunday, and ascends to heaven – you couldn't make it up – on Ascension Day. I can see nothing like it, in our National History, save for the entirely profane mischievousness with which the people of Paris chose, to take the Bastille, precisely the 14th of July.

Titre/Headline. My most bitterly entertaining journalistic memory concerns a headline; it must be remembered that, far more even than the radio or television, the written press – even or especially the most allegedly 'cultural' kind – makes great use of headlines, and that it often unnecessarily complicates matters,[632] with many a catch-all formula and, even for me, dismaying pun. It seems furthermore that the eminent dignity of the 'headline editors' protects them from the checks of the editor-in-chief, and even of the sub-editors: nowadays it is in headlines that the most handsome quantity of misusages, misprints and other contributions to the medialect may be found. The principle of this paradox is obviously that of the famous 'purloined letter': the more visible something is, the less is it seen. I had 'given', as they say, to one of these pages an account of a very serious work on modern American painting, and my review vied, for dullness, with the work reviewed. Fortunately, the newspaper in question benefited from (and perhaps still does) the collaboration of a highly waggish 'headline editor', who knew how to lighten things up. The author generally has no control over this final intervention, which will, however, inevitably be imputed to him by its readers, if by any chance there are any. My account was published, then, headlined as follows: '*L'Amérique en tient une couche*[633] [America as Thick as Two Short Planks].' Painting, layer [couche]: I'll leave you to think about it for a moment.

Today. The (linguistic) illusion of travellers consists, as Jean Paulhan noted, in taking the most hackneyed stereotypes literally. I remember my perplexity the first time I heard, addressed to me, the American expression: *How are you today?*, which is distinguished from our '*Comment allez-vous?*' only by this perfectly expletive, and moreover optional, temporal specification. It so happened that the ritual question was asked by the cashier in a supermarket where I'd never previously set foot. The *today* thus made me think, stupidly, that we had already met each other elsewhere, and that she was solicitously seeking information about the evolution, in between times, of the state of my health. I remained speechless, myself

---

[632] 'qu'elle y cherche souvent midi à quatorze heures': 'that it often there seeks noon at 2pm'.

[633] The French expression derives from the nineteenth-century peasant practice of positing layers ('couches') of manure within which e.g. mushrooms may be fertilised; by analogy, saying that someone accustomed to such tasks 'en tient une couche [has got a layer of it]' was to suggest that this person's grey matter itself resembled a layer of manure.

pondering the matter, while my cashier [caissière], who evidently couldn't have cared either way [qui n'en avait évidemment rien à encaisser[634]], moved on to the following customer: *Next!* This uncertainty, and my inability, at any rate, to respond idiomatically to what I took to be a genuine question, paradoxically made me adopt the correct attitude, which is to give *no* answer. I subsequently learned that, in more personal relationships, the right answer was something like *Oh, fine!*, or *Great!*, whatever your actual state [état] might be, which it would be frankly unseemly, precisely, to mention [de faire, justement, état]. Anyhow, over there, everyone is always doing well *today*, and will always find you, even at death's door, to be in superb form. A habit to get into, like, among other things, that of length measurements in inches, feet, yards and miles, shirt sizes (collar and sleeves) to match, the refrain *before* the verse in songs, whose jazz versions moreover retain as theme only the *chorus*, thermometers in degrees Fahrenheit, the virtually de rigueur *middle name* initial, the sacrosanct comma between the family name and the eventual mention *Jr.*, and between the second-to-last item on a list and the *and* which precedes the last (*Dad, Mom, and Myself*), bound *hardback* books with titles printed on their spine from top to bottom, 110 volts power supplies, electric sockets with parallel slits, lightbulbs, for instance in closets, whose power switch consists of a little chain which you pull like the toilet flushes from your childhood, the use of balconies as dumping grounds, the 7 without a line through it, yellow ruled paper, 216 × 281 sized writing paper, professional envelopes closed with a piece of string wound around a cardboard eyelet, scrambled eggs with bacon for breakfast (a pure marvel), queues before the usher's desk in restaurants, the jingling ring of the old telephones, floors counted from a first which is our ground floor, sash windows, doors that always open (*watch your step*) outwards, times divided into AM/PM, weeks beginning on Sunday, dates where the month appears before the day, the calculation of fuel consumption, not in litres per 100 kilometres, but in *miles per gallon*, in other words in kilometres per litre, traffic lights suspended in the middle of the street, swaying in the slightest gust of wind and taking off with the first cyclone, the full stop as a comma, the comma as a full stop in figures, weeklies dated from

---

[634] 'who evidently had no cash to take for it'.

the day, not of publication, but of expiry, whence costly misunder-standings, officially sponsored (*endowed*) university chairs, which make Professor So and So the 'John D. Rockefeller, Jr. Professor So and So', shop or restaurant signs in the French style, with a name generally as un-idiomatic as can be, till the favour is returned: I saw a hundred times in Greenwich village a little clothes store sporting a supposedly enticing *Comme ça des Halles*.[635]

Toujours/Always. 'It is truly rare that a woman should understand that being prepared to love her *always* is not to be prepared to love her *all of the time*' (Ghazal, quoted by Vialatte). It isn't necessary to endorse this condescending alleged observation – but which one might well apply to the other sex – in order to appreciate the fine temporal nuance implied by it, and which is too often overlooked.

Tourists. Tourist's nightmare.

Tournage/Filming. One fine day in 1956, a fortuitous interlinking of various acquaintances led me to the studio where *A Man Escaped* was being filmed. The first assistant was the very young Louis Malle, and the lead actor a still almost anonymous non-professional. It wasn't exactly the set of *Hellzapoppin*: the afternoon (and no doubt again the following day) was devoted to a few dozen takes of a single shot where the hero had to utter, as soberly as possible, a snippet of a sentence where, I can't recall why, it was a question of dollars. Certain directors, like Jean Renoir, know how to balance their demands with clauses as contradictory as they are reassuring, like the classic 'It's perfect; while we're about, let's do it again, just for fun!' Robert Bresson scorned this type of precaution. The moment a scene was cut, it went without saying that it should be reprised *da capo*, without any other explanation than, occasionally, a 'Too expressive!' suggested with an implacable gentleness: his 'Jansenist' aesthetic (a period cliché), as ever, made extravagant use of limited means, with no fear of wasting whatever film remained. The tormented actor set about flattening his tone of voice to the point of aphonia, but it was always still too expressive, and the truth is that it inevitably expressed an exhaustion that could scarcely be imputed to the character: this was the director's unavowed,

[635] *'Like that from the Halles'.*

but unconcealed, aim. The visitors' hope of being present at the final take evaporated, while the suspicion grew that the master of this doubly carceral ordeal would eventually, as often happens, return to the first. I left the set without knowing for sure, and of course the screening of the film, a few months later, provided me with no answer, other than the, if you like, reassuring observation that the shot in question, no more contentious than any other, hadn't been cut during the edit. I thereby forever fell out with any quest for perfection in art. As for the condemned man, he apparently drew from this experience the conviction that it was better to be placed on the right side of the camera. He became Louis Malle's assistant, at the foot of another gallows,[636] then, escaping once and for all, the fully-fledged director of *A King Without Distraction*,[637] and later of an admirable (thanks among others to Jacques Dufilho) TV film inspired by Paul Morand's masterpiece: *Milady*.[638]

Tout (ou rien)/All (or Nothing). In an episode from the *Columbo* series, entitled something like *Fatal Exercise*, the illustrious lieutenant, more poorly attired than ever, having already had to leave his extinguished cigarillo in the ashtray (no smoking here), directs himself to the reception desk of I'm not sure which *high tech* firm in order to obtain the telephone number of a former employee of this enterprise. The receptionist, tall, young, beautiful and condescending, types the name of the ex-employee on the keyboard of a period computer, that's to say, I believe, driven by spools of magnetic tape. The machine starts up, gets to work, then begins to spew out doubtless largely obsolete data on the perforated-margin paper of a rackety old-style printer. Columbo frets, writhes before the desk, grows impatient, recalls that he just needs a telephone number, asks two or three times if it will take long. The receptionist, increasingly contemptuous, makes it known to him by way of silence that it will take, no more nor less, the time it needs to take. Columbo resigns himself, flags, the minutes pass. The clatter of the printer eventually falls silent. Columbo points this out to the receptionist, who coldly acquiesces: 'Indeed',

[636] An allusion to *Ascenseur pour l'échafaud* (*Elevator to the Gallows*) (1958).
[637] By François Leterrier (1963).
[638] Morand's novella was published in 1936; the TV film in question was made in 1977.

removes the sheet, tears it along some dotted line, holds it out to him, covered with useless information. Columbo gazes at the sheet and repeats one last time that he'd only requested a simple phone number. The receptionist, now almost friendly, finally explains to him: 'The computer can only give all or nothing.' Columbo notes the lesson, memorises the number, drops the sheet, enters the lift, exits immediately to retrieve his cigarette end from the ashtray: a tiny revenge, *à la* Chaplin, of the human over bureaucratic rigidity, and over the inflexibility of technical hardware. All of this, of course, in the very olden days, in the protohistory of the computer age, but anyway, *zero-one*, it's surely still, and forever more, the horribly binary logic of the 'all or nothing'.

Trace. In the spring of 1973, Roland Barthes spent the Easter holidays with his family in the 'light of the South West',[639] in the house, at the entry to the village, whose blue shutters shaded into the irises flowering at the foot of the wall. Behind the house, an orchard garden extended as far as a vista of the Adour – which I'm perhaps today dreaming through retrofiction. In the basement room, Henriette Barthes silently nurtured a log fire which Roland was eager to explain was not 'in the farmhouse style', but that it really did serve to heat the house: the small farmhouse was already, or still, an overly socially connoted object for it to be associated with this unpretentious domestic hearth. The author of *The Empire of Signs* devoted his time, in those days, to tracing on paper – I'm no longer sure whether he used ink, gouache or watercolours ('Watercolours are diabolical') – generally non-figurative quasi-forms, somewhere between writing, drawing and painting, which somewhat evoked Masson, somewhat Michaux, somewhat Twombly of course, sometimes rather the miniature sketch of a Pollock *drip painting*, if such a thing were possible; but his own mark, always light and as though trembling, was identifiable from the outset. This aspect of his work, we know, had suddenly appeared in 1971, but I think I really discovered it on that day, as he turned for us the pages of one of his portfolios – since one really must call 'pages' these more than modest sheets

---

[639] This is the title of an essay by Barthes about his home region ('La Lumière du Sud-Ouest') (1977).

of paper that seldom exceeded our A4 format, and where he would deploy what he elsewhere calls 'script without purpose', or the 'signifier without signified'. To appropriate for this private craft the very support of professional writing – sometimes with the involuntarily ironic letterhead of the École des hautes études – was a way of uniting, if not of merging with one gesture these two activities, and perhaps of transferring onto the first the quasi-ludic lightness of the second, which he liked to think of as, like playing the piano, an activity for amateurs. For him, no art – any more, I think, than literature – could really withstand the constraints of a profession.

He gifted us one of these pages – drawn with a 'marker' pen, it seems – with the dedication I now have before my eyes: 'For Babette, this little 'text', Roland Barthes, 14 Sept [sept] 72.' *Sept*, although followed by no full stop, evidently doesn't stand for the number 7 [sept] (July), but indeed for *September*. And since I'm quite certain of the date of our visit, the 20th April 1973, I must infer that the inscribed date is not that of the dedication, but rather of the production of the work, that the author had had this piece of paper at his disposal for a few months, that he had dated (and perhaps signed) it on the day of its composition, and that he had simply inscribed the dedication properly speaking at the time of our visit, between 'text' and signature. However, nothing, either in the handwriting, or in the hue of the ink, attests to any kind of temporal gap between the inscription of the dedication, that of the signature and that of the date, whereas most of his (other) papers aren't signed at all (his name being, most often, simply borne on the rear side), and are only dated in pencil; neither is there ever a title – not even 'untitled' – that might, too indiscreetly, lay claim to the status of a work. A historical investigation would perhaps illuminate this enigma, but none will say why it is only today that I have noticed it, 30 years later, upon my return from a kind of pilgrimage to the Adour, descending, this time, from Aire to Urt – where, moored beneath the only bridge, there dozed the last *galupe*, before the homonymous country inn which might well be considered the country inn *par excellence*.[640]

---

[640] A 'galupe' is a typically Gascon flat-bottomed boat, commonly used for the transportation of goods until the beginning of the twentieth century; Genette is here referring to a riverside restaurant in Urt (still) called 'La Galupe'.

Yet if the 'text', on pale blue paper, consists of that subtle interlacing of commas 'without signified' (and what signified could there be for an interlacing of commas?), coming to a halt, as almost all of them do, a few centimetres from both sides so as to respect its own margin of silence, I find myself even more touched by the final presence, in the dedication, date and signature, of the author's *writing*. I say 'signature' by convention, but I don't believe that RB ever *signed* anything at all other than by inscribing his name, abbreviated or not – *Roland Barthes*, *R Barthes*, RB, sometimes, more intimately (yet still without a full stop), *Roland B* -, in the same handwriting as the text it served to authenticate, in defiance of the supposedly inimitable flourishes with which we generally adorn our initials. Sufficed to identify him, without any possible counterfeit, a way of writing so full and so fluid, loyal through thick and thin to fountain pen and blue ink, viscerally (for once, but as often in his case, this adverb is required) hostile to the uniformly spun tracings of the ball-point: his harshest stylistic judgement was, scarcely metaphorically: 'bic writing'. The notorious degree zero, which has sometimes been reflected back to him as a minimalist slogan, was for him not that puritanical or nonchalant indifference to the medium, one that aims for a purely ideal denotation by means of a connotation-free and transparent form. The 'illness' about which he feigned to complain, or be astonished by, was on the contrary, as we know, to 'see language'. Language or drawing, in all these little 'texts' he was inviting us (better) *to see writing*.

A counterproof, perhaps: in these same 1970s, at the close of a rather lengthy thesis defence, before rising and leaving the room, he tore up a sheet of paper whose debris he, in the absence of a paper basket, left on the jury's table. Since I hadn't yet left, a student asked me whether she could gather up the precious handwriting. I replied that I certainly had no permission to give or refuse, but that she could always act as though I were not there. She pieced together the torn up sheet, and together we saw that it was – absolute degree zero – unsullied by any inscription. The fetishist student nevertheless took away these fragments, which will perhaps be found again one day in some truly exhaustive exhibition. A little later, I asked RB for the key to this mystery. 'It's quite simple, he replied: I didn't want anyone to see that I'd found nothing to note down during the session. But it would probably have been better to take this blank page away with me.'

Which goes to show that the absence of trace is still a trace.

Transition. After 1956, that's to say in the aftermath of the Shakespearian episode of the 'Report attributed to ... '[641] – a palinode as appalling for its theoretical poverty as it was astonishing for its purported historical 'revelations', moreover swiftly buried by the leadership of the French PC and nearly as swiftly annulled by the repression (which one had indeed to 'attribute' to the very same) of the Hungarian uprising – the political exit from Stalinism was brought about along the most diverse pathways. Some embarked upon an illusory course of 'internal opposition', others sought their salvation in external groupuscules whose purpose was moreover the same: to tinker with the incurable. I can't recall what sequence of particular coincidences guided me momentarily towards the only one, perhaps, whose strategy was altogether autonomous and intellectually commendable: *Socialisme ou Barbarie* [*Socialism or Barbarism*]. The group, more familiarly known as 'S or B', led (under various pseudonyms: 'Chaulieu', 'Cardan', etc.) by Cornélius Castoriadis, Claude Lefort and a few others, owed its name to the journal that it published, and of which I read a few editions, then, retroactively, the whole collection, with a comprehensible excitement: the critique of totalitarianism was there apparently radical and formulated from a 'revolutionary' point of view, on the basis of a Trotskyist-inspired neo-Bolshevism reassessed to be itself tainted with bureaucratic degeneration; it thus went back from Stalin to Lenin, and somewhat from Lenin to Marx, quite rightly shunning the exotic ersatz of the period: Titoism, Maoism, Castroism, third-worldism in general. Considered within the vaster perspective of the non-Marxist political thought on the subject (Arendt, Aron ...), this aim was no doubt less original than I then believed, yet, coming from where I was coming, it afforded me a good transitional object, and something like a drunk tank. Once admitted that Kautsky was further to the left

---

[641] A reference to Nikita Khrushchev's (1894–1971) so-called 'Secret Speech' ('On the Cult of Personality and its Consequences') made to the twentieth congress of the Communist Party of the Soviet Union on 25 February 1956, in which Krushchev denounced the 'cult of personality' fostered by Joseph Stalin and notably criticised the political purges enacted between 1936 and 1938 under his rule.

than Bernstein, Lenin further to the left then Kautsky, Trotsky further to the left than Lenin and 'S or B' further to the left than Trotsky, you could, transiting that way, eventually find yourself, in all good revolutionary conscience, a little to the right of Kautsky, somewhere alongside Bernstein, Léon Blum and finally (but too late) Mendès France.[642] That was at least how it worked for me, up to the moment I realised that the best of answers can do nothing for a bad question.

In March 1957 I'd given *S or B* an article on the 'communist opposition in France' (concerning the aforementioned attempts at internal opposition, from which I had quickly recovered, seeing them mired in an oxbow of the Rubicon), then in *Arguments*[643] (in September), upon Edgar Morin's invitation, a sort of exposé of 'S or B''s ideas, a rather scholarly but not too unfaithful synthesis, insofar as one could synthesise a thought in fact less homogeneous and more shifting than my presentation supposed. I took this mission most seriously: popularising 'S or B' in *Arguments* was rather to trumpet the semi-clandestine in the semi-confidential, but one was working for History's archives. Displaying a neutrality hardly congruent with the habits of one or the other journal, this article was balanced (corrected?) by a text from Morin himself, sharply critical with regard to 'S or B', and deftly entitled 'Solecism or Barbarism', to which he proposed that I should reply in turn. I toyed for a few minutes with the idea of raising the stakes in this register with a 'Solipsism or Borborygmus', then it struck me first that in view of this title the identity of its target wouldn't be readily apparent to the hypothetical readership, then and above all that I had nothing to place beneath this tortuous flourish, and

---

[642] Kark Kautsky (1854–1938), Czech–Austrian philosopher and Marxist theorist; Eduard Bernstein (1850–1932), German social democratic Marxist theorist and politician; Léon Blum (1872–1950), French socialist politician and three-time prime minister; Pierre Mendès France (1907–1982), French politician, prime minister of France from 1954 to 1955, represented the (then) social-liberal 'Parti républicain, radical et radical-socialiste' ('The Radical-Socialist and Radical Republican Party'), or 'Parti Radical' ('Radical Party').
[643] Founded in 1956 by Edgar Morin, Roland Barthes, Jean Duvignaud and Colette Audry, published by the Éditions de Minuit until 1962; sustained a 'revisionist' Marxist line informed by heterodox Marxists and the social sciences.

it was Lefort who was tasked with closing the 'debate'. I then understood that the little I had written had for me exhausted the subject; I had arrived, on this matter, at the stage of detachment: after the disinfection, the disaffection. It must be said that the few nocturnal and smoke-filled meetings in which I'd participated had left me perplexed: beyond the split between a neo-libertarian and a neo-Leninist wing, the logic of internal confrontation and reciprocal excommunication, the polemical erethism, the process of indefinite division peculiar to ultra-minoritarian groupuscules, were there in full swing, way beneath the theoretical level evidenced by the journal. I remember an evening where one of the two masterminds, at a loss for arguments, having eventually said '*Merde* [Screw you]' to the other, the latter replied with an irrefutable '*Merde à toi* [Screw you too]'. Between these great minds, such an exchange must really, in hindsight, betoken a slight ideological migraine.

A third philosopher was then also active (if it can be called 'activity'), somewhat clandestinely, in the group – a manifestly very intellectual group, but fortunately endowed, like long ago the provisional government of 1848, with *a*, moreover very educated, worker. Jean-François Lyotard was teaching philosophy at the Prytanée military school (hence the clandestinity) at La Flèche, and I was at the *lycée* in Le Mans. At that time, it was still quite rare for disillusioned ex-Stalinians to pass through 'S or B', which rather aimed at the intermediary category of ex-orthodox Trotskyists, even if that particular orthodoxy already presented its own range of nuances and diverse dissidences. My case thus elicited a definite interest, and my circumspect attitude called for some additional information. Notified of the fact by the central body, Lyotard thus invited me, in a brasserie on the Place de la République (in Le Mans), to a kind of job interview, or assessment test. On the fatigued moleskin, I recounted something of my previous life and its recent episodes. He listened to me with interest, up to the moment when, going back a little further than my adhesion to the famous Concept, I mentioned to him that before this fatal leap I had myself been rather tempted by Trotskyism – that's to say, more precisely, that around 16 years of age I must have recited Prévert during the evenings in Youth Hostels, read excitedly one or two editions of *La Vérité* [*The Truth*],[644] found that the labels 'Fourth

---

[644] French Trotskyist newspaper and journal, founded in 1929.

International' and 'International Communist Party' weren't lacking in appeal within the post-war political landscape, and reckoned to be as brilliant as Columbus's egg the simplistic watchword, then brandished by the extreme left, of the 'sliding scale of prices and wages'.

This analepsis was suddenly more than my examiner's benevolence could bear. Directing upon me an eye turned frankly severe, he concluded more or less: 'In short, if I understand correctly, you were *first* Trotskyist, *then* Stalinian?' There was apparently something inconceivable and, for that matter, reprehensible about this order of succession; in effect, my case, certainly not unique, had been like that of a Huguenot embracing Catholicism *after* St Bartholomew's Day, without Le Béarnais's[645] cynical excuse. Yet this implicit rebuke shocked me in turn. I gladly accept that one should criticise my follies, but not particularly that I be told in which order I ought to have committed them, and besides I'm not always certain that Trotskyism should really be credited with a huge superiority over Stalinism, the number of victims left aside. The doubtful performance of the brilliant Leon during his assumption of power by no means guarantees that he would have evinced more moderation than his unfortunate rival if things had turned to his advantage, and neither do the political manoeuvrings of his French disciples merit a diploma in democracy. All things considered, I sometimes think that the ex-Stalinians have often turned out rather less badly, as though one exited better (on condition, certainly, that exit one does) from a severe 'flu than from a bad cold, or rather, because French communism, however infected with intellectual inanity and sectarianism it might have been, constituted a 'mass' party contending with the world outside, and, therefore, in its (bad) way, an apprenticeship in realism and relative political rationality. I also believe that as a good working-class son I took all forms of leftism to be the posturings of 'rich kids' and back-seat drivers

---

[645] An allusion to King Henri IV (1553–1610; born in Pau, in the traditional province of Béarn), who converted to Catholicism on 25 July 1593 in order to retain control of his kingdom in the face of opposition from the Catholic League contesting his right to reign over France as a Protestant (hence the utterance: 'Paris vaut bien une messe', 'Paris is well worth a mass').

Bardadrac

– with no one at the wheel.[646] Later on, May '68 didn't really help to sway me from this doubtless expeditious appraisal.

I replied, therefore, that I hadn't escaped the catechism of a great Church in order to hear the sermons of a little chapel, however friendly it may be. We left each other mutually disappointed, and my flirtation with 'S or B' pretty much ended there. I'm still grateful to Jean-François Lyotard for having shortened this transition – but a transition towards what, I was yet to know. I thought to have successively understood, thanks to Lenin, that leftism was an infantile disorder of communism, then, against Lenin, that communism was an acute infection of socialism; it was left for me to understand of what socialism is itself a symptom, then finally to admit that neither the diagnosis nor the choice of treatment were any longer my concern. This was a matter for a few months, after which, definitively freed from any militant obligations, I affected *urbi et orbi* an indifference to this type of question which led to my being nicknamed, by a benevolent but mocking friend [amie], 'the apostle of indifference'. There remained only for me to unravel this oxymoron by forsaking apostolates of any kind.

When, many years later, the one and the other having come such a very long way, I recalled this scene to he who had for his part become the apostle of the postmodern, he replied amicably, as though to efface an outmoded differend,[647] that I must have lived it in a dream. I believe no such thing, but, in effect, it was a pretty long nightmare that had taken, from one transition to another, a little time to dispel, just as when, in anticipation of waking up, you dream that you are already awake. What remains still, or perhaps increasingly, incomprehensible to me is that I should one day have committed myself to a path (political militancy, militancy in general) so contrary to my natural inclination, assuming I have one.

Trépied/Tripod. It took me a few years to admit that three-legged furniture – a pedestal table, for instance – might be (was even certainly) more stable than four-legged furniture. Once I'd absorbed this physical paradox, I thought it possible to extrapolate

[646] 'mouches du coche – sans coche': 'the coach's flies – with no coach'.
[647] An allusion to Jean-François Lyotard's *Le Différend* (*The Differend: Phrases in Dispute*) (1983).

from it that two-legged furniture would be even more stable. Disappointed with the outcome, I returned to my pedestal table, and observed that stability doesn't guarantee horizontality: it is its necessary but non-sufficient condition. Now, one expects a table (for example, barring cheating, a billiard table, and more often a dining room table) to possess these two qualities at once, and permanently. In a restaurant, a four-legged table evasively described as 'wobbly' may be intermittently horizontal, which is even more troublesome than if this were never the case, like the imagination for Pascal, a power all the more deceptive for not always being so. A small wedge may prove salutary. A good waiter always keeps a few in reserve in his waistcoat pocket.

Tribulum. One August afternoon in 1958, in a car between Madrid and Zaragoza, risen I can't recall why upon a kind of plateau close to Medinaceli, we witnessed a practice that has nowadays, I imagine, vanished: upon a large threshing floor covered with ears of corn, the peasants' horses were being made to pull some sort of slightly curved sledge whose scraping along the ground served to separate the grain from the straw. These yokes turned back and forth on the floor in an apparently improvised ballet, but one doubtless regulated by centuries of habit, and which entailed no collisions, despite the cloud of dust it raised and which surrounded it. This sledge is the Romans' famous *tribulum*, whose Spanish name I have forgotten. I can still see the peasants each standing upright upon his sleigh and gripping the reins like a Ben Hur without wheels; I'm assured that this memory is a pure invention, and that the peasants merely run alongside their horses. A few years later, in I can't remember which antique shop, I found an example of a *tribulum*, which would have made a handsome object to hang upon the wall. I can't remember what reason, probably financial, deterred me from its purchase, and I cannot get over it.

Trivium. In 1965, junior lecturer, for yet two more years, in French literature at the Sorbonne, I had to respond in the same week to two professional offers: a '*caïman*'[648] post at the Rue d'Ulm, in the same discipline, or that of head of the French Institute in London.

[648] See note 65.

I could pretty much handle the first, and it presented the advantage of extricating me from strictly university teaching, which hardly filled me with enthusiasm, with its obligatory curricula and its hierarchical subjections. The second was presented to me as being 'prestigious', a stepping stone towards a diplomatic–cultural career. My inability to decide between these two moderately tempting paths threw me onto a third. As often at this time, and without being overly concerned by the discomfort this type of step might cause him, I consulted my mentor-in-spite-of-himself, who had told me, on our first meeting: 'You don't have the look of a *normalien*', which I'd taken as a compliment. He didn't have a high opinion of the *caïman*'s role, retained a lukewarm memory of his own years in the service of Cultural Relations, and, all evenly poised attention and benevolent neutrality, readily abstained from any indiscreet advice. He thus made a subtly evasive speech, up to the moment when, while listening to him, I became aware of the real reason for this pointless consultation: neither the Rue d'Ulm nor the Institute in London appealed to me as much as the École (then called *pratique*) des hautes études where for three years I had seen him, for his own part, teaching apparently happily. I don't know where I found the composure to ask him if I might reasonably apply for a post of assistant professor there. His response became even more hesitant, although not discouragingly so: in the best-case scenario, and even with his endorsement (he was more wont to do favours than to give advice), whose effectiveness he underestimated, the matter would necessarily take a little time. I decided at once that I'd wait as long as required, but that I had at all costs to hitch my wagon to that star. Thinking back, I suppose I might have tolerated, although joylessly, the tasks of a *caïmanat*, but a career as a cultural apparatchik in the chanceries of the Republic would have led me quite swiftly to the darkest distress. I'm just astonished that I'd been able to consider it, albeit only for a minute, and every day I bless the little touch of fate that protected me from it.

Trois/Three. 'When there are three of you, it is better to be one of the two.' I don't know to what political situation Bismarck applied this maxim, but it seems to me to have validity in all domains.

Trotte/Long Way. Unit of spatial measure, stylistic twin of the temporal unit *paye*.[649] Hence this period dialogue: '*Ça fait une paye qu'on ne vous a vus*, "We haven't seen you for ages" – It's because, from our place, *ça fait une trotte*, "It's a bit of a trek".' Don't conclude, it would be too simple, that you need a *paye* to cover a *trotte*.

Tuesday. In the eighties and nineties, the Phil Woods quintet performed quite frequently at the *Fat Tuesday*, a basement club on Third Avenue, slightly to the north of Astor Place if I'm not mistaken. The music, typically *bop revival*, was energy itself, in the image of its exuberant alto saxophonist, in every way Charlie Parker's heir, and who was never without the blue-black sailor's cap from my childhood. The pianist was the excellent Hal Galper, and the trumpet player Tom Harrell, whom a slightly delicate mental state inclined towards almost perfect immobility, save for his agile fingers upon the valves. During the break between sets, he remained in his place on the podium, imperturbable, without moving a muscle or looking at anyone in the little smoke-filled room, while his companions would be knocking one or two back at the bar. You wondered if he'd leave his inner dream on time, but at the resumption he reprised his part as though nothing were the matter, just a little more sparing with notes than his leader, with a more restrained line and tone, even when he didn't abandon his trumpet for a flugelhorn. This impression probably owed much to the nature of his presence, but I haven't heard enough of his recordings to be able to decide. In any event, the symbolically silent presence, somewhat in the background, of an ever *inward* partner and the contrast and complementarity of the two styles, made these evenings, as they say, magical, and at any rate unforgettable – here's the proof. On other, rarer evenings, Joe Henderson – who isn't celebrated as much as he deserves – demonstrated on tenor saxophone the most sovereign elegance of style, confirmed *de visu* by his willowy figure, delicate features, and short salt and pepper beard.

Tunnel. I'm starting to glimpse it, at the end of the light.

---

[649] See the entry 'Paye', above.

Turenne.[650] Upon his death, the Sun King, for once well enlightened, promoted, by way of posthumous homage, a generous batch of new marshals, who were prettily called 'Turenne's small change': nothing less was required to match his worth. This collective promotion in turn duly passed away and sank into oblivion, but of the victor of Turckheim[651] there remains in Paris a long shirtmaker's street [rue chemisière],[652] and a curiously anachronic effigy. At the top of this street, upon a small triangular square, one may see a charming statue, the work of Lucien-Benoît Hercule (1846–1913, the pedestal advises). It represents a life-sized young boy in imagined military dress, his left foot proudly placed on the stock of a cannon. The little pedestal declares: 'Turenne as a child'. This representation, less farcical than the famous 'death mask of Mozart as a child', certainly has a historical reason that I'm unaware of, and which is known by the historians, if not of the art of war, then at least of sculpture. I shan't seek to know more about it, but one thing seems certain to me: this statue cannot have been 'taken' (as is said of photos) from life, the future great captain posing on his future cannon; first, because this adolescent probably didn't already deserve that one should consider dedicating a statue to him, next because at this hypothetical date (1620 or a bit later) his future sculptor was very much yet to be born. The representation is therefore highly conjectural. I don't know how many great men, throughout the world, have qualified for this kind of retrospectively premonitory homage, but I find this one to be most welcome where it stands, and, though far less frequented, as delightful for the Marais district as the Beaumarchais which, a few pedal turns further down and for a more transparent historical reason, overlooks another triangular square, at the corner of Rue Saint-Antoine and Rue des Tournelles. From the latter to the former, the diagonal relationship is moreover well founded: the child marshal is the spitting image of Chérubin bound for the military glory promised him by Figaro.[653]

---

[650] Henri de La Tour d'Auvergne, viscount of Turenne (1611–1675), a French general and marshal general of France.
[651] The Battle of Turckheim (1675) saw forces led by Turenne, having taken the village of Turckheim (north-eastern France), defeat the armies of Austria and Brandenburg.
[652] Rue de Turenne, in the Marais district of Paris, 3rd and 4th arrondissements.
[653] In Beaumarchais' *The Marriage of Figaro* (1784).

Ulm. Another Parisian, one-way, street, which, as we know, begins at *Normale-Sup* and ends at the Panthéon. François Mauriac[654] said of this school that it is undoubtedly difficult to enter but almost impossible to exit. I assume he was referring to the annoying habit possessed by certain alumni[655] of mentioning at every turn a supposedly prestigious schooling. He might have added, though, that it isn't too difficult to exit when you have never entered therein.

If I'm to believe Vialatte quoting perhaps Léon Bopp[656] (his text isn't too clear on this point), the École normale supérieure was, in his day, called '*le monde où Lanson*[657] *nuit* [the world where Lanson does harm/*le monde où l'on s'ennuie*/the world where one gets bored]'. I admire Péguy[658] for having disdained this mean metathesis.

Ultima. You can find a great number of such last words collected in the book that Claude Aveline devoted to them; but I shall rely upon the selection made by the same Vialatte, and I'll make my own 'top choice': nothing beats, for care shown to others, the policeman 'who hanged himself, leaving this little note on the kitchen table: "There's some soup left in the cupboard, don't throw it away, it's still good"'; nor, for the sense of *timing*, Lope de Vega's sally: 'Now I can actually admit it: Dante has always bored me.' You'd happily die for less than that. Soon, I shall be able to admit that I've never been able to finish *The Man Without Qualities*; Musil neither, for that matter. It's said that Chekhov, perhaps to spare his loved ones the utterance in their own language, murmured as he passed away, but in German: *Ich sterbe*. In my village, and maybe elsewhere, you don't say, when leaving your hosts: 'I'm going', but rather, with a sense of anticipation whose nonchalance I appreciate: 'I've left' (an even more nonchalant variant is the leave-taking recently heard in the same place: 'May the Lord keep you: as for me, I don't have the time!'). I

---

[654] French novelist, dramatist, critic, poet and journalist (1885–1970).

[655] 'Archicubes', in 'Rue d'Ulm' jargon.

[656] Swiss writer and philosopher (1896–1977).

[657] Gustave Lanson (1857–1934), French historian and literary critic, taught at the Sorbonne and the École Normale Supérieure, Rue d'Ulm, also visiting professor at Columbia University in New York City; championed a deterministic and 'scientific' approach to literary history.

[658] Charles Pierre Péguy (1873–1914), poet and essayist. A former student of Lanson at the ENS, Péguy later vehemently opposed Lanson and his method.

Bardadrac

don't know if this phrase has ever been used as an *ultima verba*, but I shall endeavour to think of it when the moment comes. My father-in-law, who was bored on his deathbed just as he was everywhere else apart from in his garden, said simply: '*C'est exagéré*', 'This is just too much.' It was roughly Immanuel Kant's *Sufficit!*

A more brutal sub-genre is the word uttered or the gesture performed beneath the guillotine, or at least upon the scaffold. Everybody knows Danton's ('Show my head to the people, etc.'), Louis XVI's ('Do we have any news of M. de La Pérouse?'[659]), and that, ascribed to more than one, of the condemned man slipping on the final step, in God knows what sort of puddle, and exclaiming: 'Not a good start!' But Michelet, visibly fascinated (who wouldn't be?) by this situation, relates a few others, more discreet in kind. That of the 'poor little Nicole', dragged away with the Saint-Amaranthe family, who carefully smartened herself up on the plank and, in a sweet little voice, asked the executioner: 'Monsieur, do I look okay like this?'; that of the scrupulous fellow who, before lying down, set his watch; or that of the book lover, who continued reading from the cell to the cart, from the cart to the blade, and who, at the very last moment, placed his bookmark at the right page. You'd search in vain for a finer mark of respect for the written word.

Venices. Every cardinal point, every province has its Venice or its Venices, of which its advertising pamphlets boast. You just need a lagoon, one or two canals, or a conveniently ramified river. I shall certainly forget a few, but Bruges is the Venice of the North, and Saint Petersburg too, and Copenhagen, and Amsterdam, Strasbourg is the Venice of the East, Redon the Venice of the West, and Quimperlé too, Annecy the Savoyard Venice, Ornans the Franche-Comté Venice, Sète the Languedoc Venice, Martigues is, as the song says,[660] the Provençal Venice, Bayonne the Basque Venice, Bamberg the Venice of Franconia, Miami the Venice of Florida, Venice, as its name indicates, claims to be the Californian Venice, Pont-Audemer is the Norman Venice, La Ferté-Bernard the Perche Venice, Montargis the Gâtinais Venice, Saint-Fargeau the Venice of Puisaye, Vendôme the Venice ... of the Vendômois,

---

[659] See note 528.
[660] *Adieu, Venise provençale* (1934), sung by Henri Alibert.

the Saint-Martin canal quarter is Paris's Little Venice, Amiens, by virtue of its floating gardens, is the Picardy Venice, the Poitevin marshes the green Venice, Bangkok the Asian Venice, Recife the Brazilian Venice, Mexico still contains a little of what was once (without knowing it) the Aztec Venice, the Tofinou's lagoon, in Benin, is the African Venice, Venezuela, as its name indicates and courtesy of the Orinoco's bends, is in its entirety the Little Venice of South America, and New Orleans has had enough of being the Venice of Louisiana, itself in its entirety the green Venice of the Old South. In sum, only Venice is the Venice of nothing, or anyone, else.

Vérité/Truth. It will always be lacking, says Vialatte more or less, the allure of the lie; this lack constitutes perhaps its most unerring *index sui*.

Verre d'eau/Glass of Water. At the 'heroic' outset of the October revolution, a theory, which was attributed to Vladimir in person, and which was called the 'theory of the glass of water', stated that making love is in no way more important than drinking a glass of water when you're thirsty. Today gone out of fashion, one might see in it a tell-tale sign of machismo-Leninism. They nowadays also call 'theory of the glass of water' the (more correct) idea that a glass of water dispersed in time can extinguish a fire that, an hour later, would resist the intervention of a whole barracks of firemen. The relation between these two principles is crystal clear. Let's not throw the theory out with the glass of water [Ne jetons pas la théorie avec l'eau du verre[661]].

Village. An occasional seminar teacher at New York University, I'd always stay, during these periods, in Greenwich Village, and never very far from the capriciously diagonal thoroughfare that is Bleecker Street. In this disparate but throughout flavoursome quarter, the Italian restaurants (*Porto Bello, Ponte Vecchio, Grand Ticino* ...), concentrated within the central quadrilateral demarcated by 3rd Street, LaGuardia Place, Houston Street and Sixth Avenue, have

---

[661] 'Let's not throw out the theory with the water from the glass', derived from the saying: 'Ne jetons pas le bébé avec l'eau du bain', 'Let's not throw the baby out with the bathwater'.

been there, presumably, since the days when the Village was a fragment of Little Italy, and they haven't broken with this tradition; I can't recall which one was distinguished by the way the prepared dry parmesan was grated directly above your plate of *pasta*, as is elsewhere done for you with a pepper mill. In the West Village, somewhere towards Seventh Avenue, there opened one day an *Alfredo* as cramped as it was acclaimed, where you were required to show your credentials, even on the telephone. It was a marvel, yet, for some reason, by my next stay it had already vanished.

The fish and seafood restaurants, among which the very welcoming *Jane Street Seafood* (glasses of cold water and bowl of *coleslaw* placed as a matter of course upon the dark wooden table), also gradually (and temporarily?) died out at the end of the eighties. To find clams and sea bass worthy of their names, you had therefore to leave the Village, either by heading up to the *Grand Central Oyster Bar*, or by heading down to Fulton Street market (now transferred to the Bronx) or, even further down, towards *Fraunces Tavern* on Pearl Street, as Georgian as you could wish for, where you could also contemplate, upstairs, a purportedly authentic copy of the Declaration of Independence, unless this memory be itself apocryphal. Or better, to the place of memory, today unforgivably no more, that was the rather too vast but very old-style *Gage & Tollner*, still on Fulton Street, but well beyond the East River, where I discovered, late in the day, the flavour of lukewarm and very lightly cooked oysters. To the west of Washington Square, on Waverley Place, could be found a most elegant restaurant named *The Coach House*, dedicated to Southern cuisine, with black *de rigueur* styled waiters, which was a must for any really grand occasion, on a par with the *Russian Tea Room*, which has yet to leave the foot of Carnegie Hall.

Upmarket grocery stores were divided between *Balducci*, once again on Sixth Avenue, and *Dean & DeLuca*, a little further down on Broadway, in the Cast Iron District, where you could order those enormous lamb chops whose equivalent cannot be found in France as regards either the size, the cut, or the flavour. But you could always count, 24 hours a day and 365 days per year, upon the Korean on the corner of Broadway and 3rd Street, at least for a pack of beer and a crab and celery stalk salad.

The jazz clubs, apart from the miniscule *Bradley's* on University Place, which I've already celebrated elsewhere, have more or less held firm in the shadow of the (I hope) indestructible *Village Vanguard* on Seventh Avenue and, more recently, of the *Blue Note* on 3rd Street. The New York jazz scene has often relocated, since the Harlem of the thirties and the 52nd Street of the *bop* era, but for a few decades now it has burned brighter here than elsewhere, all styles combined. For home listening, the preferred recourse was a specialist radio station, whose name and frequency I have forgotten, unless it was *Jazz 88*, which, in the eighties and nineties, broadcast from Newark under the auspices of the Rutgers University jazz department, and which we received quite well on the other side of the Hudson. It aired ten or so titles in succession, but only announced their details at the end of the series. With a little memory and attention, you could then verify or correct your hypotheses. And then the *Towers* store, heading back up Broadway a little, for, upstairs, its jazz and classical music records (vinyl, then compact discs); you just had to traverse the pop *chaophony* [cacopharnaüm[662]] on the ground floor (rhythm and blues, rock and roll, hard rock, punk, techno, country, electronica, techno house, IDM, and I'm forgetting the ones I've never known) in order to reach the staircase. The conjoined side-lining of classical and jazz has, since then, become a kind of international commercial norm. It's hard to tell whether it preludes their complete eviction, or whether technical progress will not on the contrary, let's dream a little, eliminate to their advantage the sale of all the rest, which may for what it's worth be downloaded from what is no longer even called the Internet.

Ever since my first stay, I've been able to recognise the Village, with my eyes closed, by its heady odour, a mixture of fried food, incense, vanilla and encaustic; vanilla and incense were predominant, I don't know why, in a bazaar whose name I have forgotten, and which was located on 3rd Street, a few steps away from the *Blue Note*, where we'd spend hours in search of we knew not what, before buying something else. I can still recognise it by its characteristic noises: the strident sirens of ambulances and police cars, the deep throb, like liners entering the harbour, of the enormous fire engines, the planes turning back and forth, awaiting a runway,

---

[662] A 'chimera-word' combining 'cacophonie' (cacophony) and 'capharnaüm' ('shambles', 'mess').

over Manhattan; the latter in particular, I suppose, is nowadays less joyous than in my day, when, for passengers ready to grab their luggage and correcting for one last time their customs and police declarations, this low-altitude flight over the skyscrapers made for a fine first act. Of all these noises, the most unmistakable is the dull unrelenting rumble of large bore engines, just punctuated by somewhat discreet, as though muffled, wholly unaggressive horns: nothing like the Parisian racket of yesteryear. Deeper still, the fire engines' foghorns, from which at no hour did you escape. What remains once and for all in my ears, for having been subjected to it for a good couple of months, housed at 2, Washington Square Village, on the corner of 3rd Street and Mercer Street, is the *beep-beep-beep* of the *road construction* contraptions (since over there one doesn't just *construct* buildings, but also roads and streets, and often with the same concrete) on Mercer, which began in the small hours of the morning (small at least according to my internal clock) to cease just as abruptly quite early in the afternoon: the American worker returns to his suburb in time for a shower upstairs, the family dinner and the *access prime time* serial. Scraped down to its bare bones, Mercer Street was apparently reconcreted to a good depth and, I hope for my successors, for a few centuries yet. The first *beep*, though emitted without notice, didn't awaken us with a start, filtered as it was by the remains of sleep, by a semi-conscious expectation, and often even joined the final scraps of dream. By virtue of a well-known paradox that, despite its universality, I'd gladly call the *Mercer effect*, the sudden silence attending the final *beep* was far more perceptible, and even, sometimes, slightly painful, as though one's tormented eardrum had succumbed at once to an incurable deafness. It's the literal meaning of the cliché 'deafening silence'.

Vitesses/Speeds. He distinguished, like everyone else, that of light, that of sound, that of a galloping horse in the bay of Mont-Saint-Michel, and that, already proverbial, of a fart (which as a veteran of the trenches he'd call 'news from behind the lines') on an oilskin.[663] But his favourite unit of measure, without much changing the

---

[663] The expression 'comme un pet sur une toile cirée' would translate more idiomatically as 'like a bat out of hell'.

frame of reference, was that of a kick up the backside, which he also called *'vitesse grand V'*, 'speed with a big S', and which he claimed, on bad mood days, but without yet speaking of 'real time', to be superior to the c of $E = mc^2$. I did my best to dodge the control experiment.

Volupté/Delight. *'Jouissance,*[664] writes RB, isn't that which *responds* to desire (satisfies it), but that which surprises it, exceeds it, reroutes it, diverts it.' I think I understand this definition, where the *other* of *jouissance* is obviously *pleasure*, but I can imagine another – certainly less subtle – version of this couple, where *jouissance* would simply be a non-expected pleasure, one not preceded by desire, in sum: not desired. This kind of pleasure manifestly exists: just as there are unsatiated desires, so are there unforeseen pleasures, which one might well name *jouissances*. This, quite arbitrary, act of naming is obviously contrary to common, nay vulgar, usage (where *jouissance* simply designates the final orgasm), but the most troublesome thing about this binary paradigm is that it excludes, or at the least overlooks, a third, more classical (and romantic, and even typically Beylist[665]) term: *volupté*, *'delight'*, whose fall into disuse perhaps gauges the impoverishment of our aesthetic consciousness – in a broad sense. It would be good to be able to evade the forced choice, through excluded middle, between pleasure and *jouissance* by way of delight, whatever we wish to understand thereby. But thereby the difficulty today would perhaps be to make oneself heard without misunderstanding [de se faire entendre sans malentendu[666]].

Waterzooi. Zarzuela from Ghent (after all, Charles V,[667] like my paternal grandfather, was a native of Ghent).

Weekend. *Otium* of the people.

Wright. I suppose my earliest physical contact with his work dates back to our first visit to the Guggenheim Museum in New York, in the spring of 1969, and the latest to a tour of a few 'Prairie' style

[664] 'Jouissance' can signify 'enjoyment', 'bliss', or 'orgasm'.
[665] Marie-Henri Beyle (1783–1842), a.k.a. 'Stendhal'.
[666] 'Entendre' in French can signify both 'to hear' and 'to understand'.
[667] This dish is said to have been a favourite of Charles V (1500–1588).

houses in Chicago – at least of the imposing Robie House, on the
very campus of the university – in the spring of 1986. In 1974,
during a stay in Madison, I'd been able to visit Taliesin, for long the
master's home and studio, nowadays a museum, and two or three
country houses, among which the humble and very low Second
Jacobs House, with its semi-circular concave façade, where you enter
on the tips of your toes so as not to disturb its current occupants,
moreover more sensitive to the (legendary) discomfort than to the
historical prestige of their abode, and the more spectacular Pew
House, which overlooks Lake Mendota. In 1976, I had to hunch
my shoulders to pass, via Route 101, beneath a lowered arch of the
aqueduct-shaped building otherwise known as the Marin County
Civic Center, in San Rafael (California), and I cannot recall what
indeed I may have bought or not bought, on Maiden Lane, in San
Francisco, in the Morris Gift Shop, since become an art gallery,
whose virtually windowless brick façade opens (barely) by way
of a cleverly asymmetrical semi-circular door, and whose interior
comprises a spiral ramp, an obvious allusion – or perhaps anticipation: the two works are pretty much contemporary – to that
of the Guggenheim. For a while I toyed with the intention, no
doubt realised by others, of exploring *de visu* all that remains of
Wright's work, at least upon the soil of what Jean Prévost, after
Samuel Butler, called *Usonia*, in an unduly forgotten book (*Sketch of
American Civilisation*) where he mentions, precisely, this artist – who
for his part called *Usonian houses* the individual houses with which
he peppered his native Wisconsin during the Depression period. I
regret by the way that the name Usonia, such a good fit, should not
have been adopted from the outset by the United States: it would
spare us many a geopolitical muddle. I'm not aware of him having
built anything in Europe, and I have never even had the opportunity
to admire other than on plans and from photos the ultra-famous
Kaufmann House of Bear Run, over its forest waterfall. Such
remains today my overly lacunary personal relationship to he whom
I consider, as everyone ought, to be one of the two or three greatest
creators of the twentieth century – even if a non-negligible portion
of his work dates from the nineteenth. Despite his connection with
Sullivan, who was one of its pioneers, he didn't really pursue the
skyscraper genre. His own genius inclined him less to the harsh
geometry of tall buildings than to the whimsical fancy of private
houses, and was stirred by an, often cantilevered, horizontality – a

dimension that doesn't struggle as much as one thinks to express itself upon American soil: the space isn't wanting, and *Prairie* isn't an idle word [un mot en l'air[668]].

Harsh geometry is, conversely, the feat of Mies Van der Rohe. The parallel between these two geniuses is a *pons asinorum* of art history, and I don't wish to venture into it here. The theme of this antithesis is not, at least, an opposition between the horizontal and the vertical: Mies built (or planned) too many single-storey low buildings, of matchless purity – from the German Pavilion in Barcelona to the Crown Hall of the IIT in Chicago – to allow one to reduce him to a single dimension. Like Wright, he was able to conquer the horizon of the great plains and, despite the exception of the miraculous Seagram, his work is, similarly, far more Chicagoan than New York-based. This is the rationalist modernity that Wright's 'organic' architecture unceremoniously bestrode to join one to the other *fin-de-(19th)-siècle* Art Nouveau and a postmodern Baroque which, with Gehry, Koolhaas and a few others, is still thriving in the twenty-first. In this sense, of course, the oldest of the two is today the most contemporary, but there is nothing irrevocable, by definition, about this advantage. I would definitely not like to have to choose between the classicism of the ones and the romanticism of the others; fortunately, no one is asking me to, and a few, like Aalto, Saarinen, Le Corbusier or Niemeyer, have occasionally achieved their synthesis, or alternation, and ultimately I find a kind of aesthetic pleasure in this prolonged wavering between Apollo and Dionysus, which perhaps defines architecture itself, as the music of space.

Xanthippe. It is said that western philosophy owes everything to this sourpuss, whose crabbiness obliged her husband permanently to abandon the marital home, hence the walks along the Ilissos, the daemon, irony, maieutics, Diotima, and everything that ensued right up to the hemlock. Another version claims that Socrates had married the shrew in full knowledge of the facts, with the sole purpose evidently not of taming her but indeed of practising patience, which shows him to be already a philosopher, but a Stoic, before the wedding. This version is doubtful, since for the

[668] 'a word in the air'.

practice in question, he ought on the contrary to have forced himself to remain at home, close to his domestic tyrant. Yet the two hypotheses aren't incompatible: Socrates marries a virago for the purposes of mortification, but soon can't take it anymore, relinquishes the ordeal, and, as a result of his bad conscience, spends the rest of his existence, philosophical in a different way, leading his disciples astray.

Yeux/Eyes. Certain authors seem hard put to determine the colour of their heroines' eyes. See Emma Bovary: 'What was beautiful about her was her eyes; although they were brown, they appeared black because of their lashes'; the nuance is in truth quite weak, and I doubt that so-called 'black' eyes are ever anything but dark brown, but anyway Flaubert is apparently keen on this distinction. See also Gilberte Swann (but, of course, it's at once more complicated): 'Her dark eyes gleamed and since I did not know then, nor have I learned since, to reduce a strong impression into its objective elements, since I didn't have, as one says, enough "power of observation" to isolate the notion of their colour, for a long time afterwards, whenever I thought of her, the memory of their radiance instantly presented itself to me as that of a vivid azur, since she was blonde: so that perhaps, if she had not had such dark eyes – which struck one so the first time you saw her – I would not have been, as I was, most particularly in love with her blue eyes.' Emma's brown eyes seemed black, Gilberte's dark eyes turn blue in a memory rationalised after the event (one remembers them *because* they were dark, but one pictures them to oneself as blue *since* she was blonde). Cécile's, in Aragon's *The Communists*, are dark in the first version, blue in the second. Lotte's, in *Werther*, were dark without nuance nor repentance: 'While she spoke, I drowned in her dark eyes.' Only it so happens, if the historians are to be believed, that those of her 'model', Charlotte Buff, were blue (which is to say, I think, more suitable for drowning in). Goethe thus felt the need to change their colour, and Thomas Mann, in *Lotte in Weimar*, suggested that this modification might constitute 'poetic licence' – which doesn't necessarily imply, I imagine, that black is more poetic than blue; the person in question [l'intéressée] humbly assures us that 'the dark eyes come from elsewhere' – but from where (from whom)? As for Chimène's, Corneille took no chances:[669] they're forever spoken of (not by him, moreover), but their colour is never seen. It is often said that women match the colour of their eyes to that of their dress, but it is also known that eye-witness accounts have never been able to agree upon that (those) of Napoleon, who yet did not have this excuse, nor any other. Perhaps Morand is the one to provide the key to these mysteries: 'Remedios' eyes are dark, or grey, or blue. How can you tell? All eyes have every colour.'

Ygrec/Y. I've never known how this word is written (it might just as well be *Igrec*, even if it's evidently the Greek *upsilon*), nor for that matter if there is any question of writing it: apart from *esse* and *té*, to refer to S- or T-shaped objects, the names of letters are for us a blind (but not mute) spot of language. The fact remains that this one, at Launay, was used, in the form of a casual interjection, to dismiss an unresolved problem, an unanswered or uninteresting question: we said 'Oh, *Ygrec!*' (or *Igrec*), and the page, whatever it might have been, turned, as they elsewhere say: 'Peu importe [No matter]', 'Basta', 'Laisse tomber [Forget it]', *Never mind, Whatever, Nitchevo*, or, in Egypt and whenever possible: *Maalesh*. I'm also unaware of the reason for this choice, which has stuck with me, but I can imagine none other more apt. The end of the story is sadder: a few years later, since we couldn't happen to agree upon the name (supposed, by reason of pedigree, to begin with a Y) to give to a grey-blue-coloured Burmese kitten (I mean Burmese grey-blue, not to be confused with the common Chartreux grey-blue; but there also exist, more rarely, dark hazel-coloured Burmese), one of us, wearily, proffered '*Ygrec!*', and this refusal to seek further served as his baptism. A discreet and degenerate town cat, who only ever communicated by means of the pseudo-mathematical formula '*Moins-un* [minus one]' (the Burmese version of the traditional 'miaow', pronounced without liaison: '*moin-un*'), whom the car trip to the countryside terrorised, and who, in order to see nothing of it, would curl up as low down as possible, preferably beneath the

---

[669] A reference to Pierre Corneille's *Le Cid* (1636): in the play, Chimène is in love with Rodrigue but duty must prevail over her feelings after he slays her father. The expression 'avoir les yeux de Chimène', 'to have Chimène's eyes', has come to mean to look amorously but furtively at someone, 'to make sheep's eyes' or 'to look dreamily'.

brake pedal, he never really adapted to the Puisaye climate, even in memory of Colette, and ended up beneath the wheels of another car, 30 steps away from his favourite bench. The eponymous saying almost passed away with him. It gradually returned to use, but the insouciance of yore had gone.

Yosemite. The heart of the Yosemite National Park is the course of the Merced river, which flows calmly amid very green prairies, at least in the springtime. The whole spectacle is secured by the immense granite rock faces, like those of the Capitan or the Half Dome, which soar above the glacial trough-shaped valley, and by the waterfalls tumbling down from them. The pleasure I felt there doubtless stems from a preference for feeling myself physically towered over (but protected) by a landscape contemplated from below, rather than overlooking it myself from the height of a 'panoramic' viewpoint, which, inevitably, squashes and flattens it, be it the Grand Canyon in person. The fondness for elevated places that Proust attributes to Stendhal's heroes has been alien to me since my childhood, and a certain proclivity to vertigo helps not to free me from this weakness, if it is one. Concerning Yosemite, at any rate, I take solace in seeing that Amsel Adams,[670] who knew a bit about the area and his profession, appears to have shared this fondness for low-angle shots. The Earth seen from the sky can give rise to superb, preferably abstract, tableaux, but a landscape isn't a painting: Amiel said it well, it is a 'state of the soul'; it is also a state of the body. It isn't there just to be seen, but to be *experienced.*

Zabriskie. From the shadeless palm trees of Los Angeles to the one-armed bandits of Las Vegas, a sideways jaunt through Death Valley isn't exactly a shortcut, just an offer you can't refuse. In February, there's hardly any danger of perishing there from thirst or the heat, but your anxiety, kindled in advance by the place name, bears primarily upon the sound of the engine and the needles on your dashboard: the sole misadventure awaiting you here is a mechanical breakdown. With this doubt, the solitary tourist often refrains from turning off the ignition at the (very well demarcated) places where they believe it necessary to stop in order to enjoy the

---

[670] Amsel Easton Adams (1902–1984), American photographer.

view and confide it to film, for fear of a failure upon restarting. So they thus hardly dare to move away from the bonnet, for a non-one-armed bandit might be lurking behind the least rock. Your glance is furtive, your aim circumspect, the trip finally rushed, especially if you are expected. You can always say (and even prove) that you have traversed the Valley of Death.

Zarzuela. It is the well-known name of a country house close to Madrid, where resides my favourite queen, but also of an ever-savoury brand of typically Hispanic operetta or opéra bouffe, which has survived and will survive perhaps a few centuries of fashions and counter-fashions, and furthermore of a theatre in Madrid more or less exclusively devoted to this genre. Concerning the linking of these various senses, historians' opinions diverge. One might at least hazard a guess that the oldest meaning of the word, whence all the others might derive, is a 'kind of *bouillabaisse*', an Iberian *waterzooi*, a culinary *bardadrac* (in colloquial English: *clean up the kitchen*), as typically Spanish as the inn so called,[671] where you find only what you bring along. Someone proposed that the latter definition could apply to reading. It isn't here that this opinion will be contested.

Zut/Drat. This might be my last word.

---

[671] 'Une auberge espagnole' literally means a 'Spanish inn', figuratively a 'potluck dinner'.

Bonus

Never neglect the little things in life

(Vladimir to Estragon)

I shall, then, take advantage of this new edition[672] first of all to beat my breast about a mix-up, p. 422, which it would be dangerous to perpetuate, between *throwing a rod* and a *spark plug failure*: it is the second kind of damage that causes you simply to ride 'on three legs'; the first, far more serious, ultimately bursts the cylinder jacket, even the engine block itself. It is imperative, I'm also reminded, to unscrew the valve cap, p. 387, *before* extracting the inner tube from its rim: don't even try it. P. 251, I attributed to Coluche a (bad) joke about the pope that should perhaps be credited to André Santini. The aquarium gag, p. 144, is quite simply, how could I have forgotten it, in *Monsieur Hulot's Holiday*, and the story about the scorpion, p. 395, is quoted by Orson Welles in *Mr. Arkadin*. The poet who sprinkles (at the same time?) the twin towers of Saint-Sulpice, p. 415, is Raoul Ponchon. The false (very false) ladybird, p. 1, is called scientifically a *pyrrhocoris*, and more informally a '*gendarme* [policeman]'. The dove tree, p. 427, is a *davidia involucrata*. Page 26, a man of letters successful in all genres lived from 1757 to 1811 under the name of Louis-Abel Beffroy; I wonder what indeed might have prompted the municipality of Conflans-Sainte-Honorine to give his name to a street opened, I imagine, at the beginning of the twentieth century, but I shall stick with this (moderately) flattering hypothesis.

---

[672] Originally published by the Éditions du Seuil in 2006, *Bardadrac* was republished in Seuil's 'Point Essais' series in 2012.

For all of this belated information, I shall permit myself no *name-dropping* under the cover of gratitude, but it is at times like these that you appreciate having competent and/or well-connected friends.